ACTIVATING HUMAN AND FUNDAMENTAL RIGHTS BEFORE THE EUROPEAN COURTS

This open access book adds a new dimension to the longstanding research on the co-existence of the European Court of Human Rights and the Court of Justice of the EU, and their inter-related action and explicit interaction.

As the two Courts are increasingly called upon to interpret corresponding rights, particularly owing to the ever-growing importance of fundamental rights in the EU legal order, the stakes intensify. Prior studies have mostly focused on the constitutional and substantive issues connected to this interaction. This book focuses on another dimension: the lesser-told yet fascinating tale of two – increasingly substantively overlapping – European-level judicial systems with their own procedures and institutional idiosyncrasies, their own terminology, their own epistemic communities of practitioners and scholars, and their own relationship to national law.

In this collection a team of experts – academics and practitioners – from both systems bridges the gap between these two worlds of fundamental and human rights protection, investigating their commonalities and differences. They address the questions 'who can go where?', 'on what procedural roads?', 'at what speed?' and 'to what final destination?'.

This book is an essential resource for anyone working or studying the protection of fundamental and human rights in Europe.

Volume 141 in the Series Modern Studies in European Law

Modern Studies in European Law
Recent titles in this series:

Judging Composite Decision-Making:
The Transformation of European Administrative Law
Filipe Brito Bastos

EU Diplomacy in Multilateral Fora
Edited by Christine Kaddous and Frank Hoffmeister

The Market Citizenship Illusion:
Free Movement Rights for Atypical Workers
Alice Welsh

Actors and Roles in EU Disability Law
Edited by Delia Ferri and Eva S Krolla

The Impact of War (in Ukraine) on the EU
Edited by Inge Govaere, Sacha Garben and Eleanor Spaventa

The European Judiciary: A Community of Law and a Community of Judges
Edited by Alejandro Saiz Arnaiz and Joan Solanes Mullor

Dissensus over Liberal Democracy: Insights from European Judges
Edited by Ramona Coman, Viktor Kazai, Leonardo Puleo and Andrew Bradley

Structural Principles of EU Law
Marcus Klamert

Environmental NGOs and Access to Justice before the CJEU
Mario Pagano

Dealing with Rule of Law Crises in the European Union:
Challenges from a Comparative Federalism Perspective
Niels F Kirst

EU Citizenship and Responsibility:
The Evolving Roles of the Union, the Individual, and the Member States
Maria Haag

EU Cities Facilitating the Commons:
Building Blocks of European Constitutional Law for Local Democracy
Chiara Salati

EU Competence and Power
Hannah Bogaert

Activating Human and Fundamental Rights Before the European Courts
Edited by Elise Muir, Sacha Garben and Inge Govaere

For the complete list of titles in this series
see www.bloomsbury.com/uk/series/modern-studies-in-european-law/

Activating Human and Fundamental Rights Before the European Courts

Edited by
Elise Muir
Sacha Garben
and
Inge Govaere

• HART •
OXFORD • LONDON • NEW YORK • NEW DELHI • SYDNEY

HART PUBLISHING

Bloomsbury Publishing Plc

Kemp House, Chawley Park, Cumnor Hill, Oxford, OX2 9PH, UK

1385 Broadway, New York, NY 10018, USA

Bloomsbury Publishing Ireland Limited, 29 Earlsfort Terrace, Dublin 2, D02 AY28, Ireland

HART PUBLISHING, the Hart/Stag logo, BLOOMSBURY and the Diana logo are trademarks of Bloomsbury Publishing Plc

First published in Great Britain 2026

A catalogue record for this book is available from the British Library.

A catalogue record for this book is available from the Library of Congress.

Library of Congress Control Number: 2026935140

ISBN: HB: 978-1-50998-769-6
ePDF: 978-1-50998-771-9
ePub: 978-1-50998-770-2

Typeset by Compuscript Ltd, Shannon

For product safety related questions contact productsafety@bloomsbury.com

To find out more about our authors and books visit www.hartpublishing.co.uk. Here you will find extracts, author information, details of forthcoming events and the option to sign up for our newsletters.

ACKNOWLEDGEMENTS

We would like to thank the speakers and participants of the conference on 'Activating the Protection of Fundamental and Human Rights at European Level' on which this book is based. The conference took place in Bruges on 7–8 March 2024, and was co-organised by the Law Department of the College of Europe and the Institute for European Law of KU Leuven.

We are very grateful to the researchers of the RESHUFFLE project Victor Davio, Cecilia Rizcallah, Orlando Scarcello and Lucia van der Meulen with whom the idea of this conference was born. Lucia and Victor, in particular, have provided invaluable input to flesh out the programme of the conference and thus table of contents of this book.

Saskia Willems, Alexandros Lympikis and the assistants of the Law Department of the College of Europe have given much support to the organisation of the event in Bruges. Giulio Dipietro has done a wonderful work assisting the copy-editing of the book.

This collective project has received the invaluable financial support of the College of Europe as well as of the RESHUFFLE research project hosted by the Institute for European Law of KU Leuven and supported by the European Research Council (European Union's Horizon 2020 research and innovation programme, grant agreement No 851621).

CONTENTS

PART VI
FINAL DESTINATION REACHED? COMPLIANCE AND NON-COMPLIANCE

PART VII
CONCLUSION

LIST OF CONTRIBUTORS

Laurence Burgorgue-Larsen, Professor of Law at the Sorbonne Law School (Paris 1 – IREDIES) and member of the International Commission of Jurists

Joyce De Coninck, FWO Postdoctoral Fellow at the University of Ghent and EUI Max Weber Fellow at the European University Institute

Kanstantsin Dzehtsiarou, Professor in Human Rights Law and Associate Dean for Global Engagement at the University of Liverpool

Elif Erken, Postdoctoral Candidate at the Montaigne Centre for Rule of Law and Administration of Justice at Utrecht University

Sacha Garben, Professor of EU Law at the College of Europe (Bruges)

Janneke Gerards, State Councillor at the Advisory Division of the Council of State of the Netherlands and Professor of European Fundamental Rights Law at Utrecht University

Inge Govaere, Professor of European Law and Director of the Ghent European Law Institute (GELI) at the University of Ghent, Director of the European Legal Studies Department at the College of Europe (Bruges)

José A. Gutierrez-Fons, Référendaire in the Chambers of the President of the Court of Justice of the EU

Kathleen Gutman, Référendaire at the Court of Justice of the EU

Joni Heliskoski, Justice at the Supreme Administrative Court of Finland

Sara Iglesias Sanchez, Professor of EU Law and Administrative Law at the Universidad Complutense of Madrid and Attachée at the chambers of the Registrar of the CJEU

Alexander Kornezov, Judge at the Court of Justice of the EU

Frédéric Krenc, Judge at the European Court of Human Rights

Jasper Krommendijk, Professor of Human Rights Law and Director of the Research Centre for State and Law at Radboud Universiteit (Nijmegen)

Philip Leach, Professor of Human Rights Law at Middlesex University (London) and member of Matrix Chambers

David Milner, Head of the Human Rights Intergovernmental Co-operation Division and Secretary to the Steering Committee for Human Rights, Council of Europe

Elise Muir, Professor of European Law and Head of the Institute for European Law of KU Leuven, Visiting Professor at the College of Europe (Bruges)

Síofra O'Leary, Hauser/Remarque Fellow at New York University and Former President of the European Court for Human Rights, Vitising Professor at the College of Europe (Bruges)

Virginia Passalacqua, Assistant Professor, University of Turin and Research Affiliate, Collegio Carlo Alberto

Ellen Penninckx, Lawyer at the Registry of the European Court of Human Rights

Luca Prete, Référendaire at the Court of Justice of the European Union

Felix Ronkes Agerbeek, Member of the Legal Service of the European Commission

Allan Rosas, Former Judge at the Court of Justice of the EU, Visiting Professor at the College of Europe (Bruges)

Takis Tridimas, Professor of European Law and Director Luxembourg Centre for European Law (LCEL) at the University of Luxembourg, Visiting Professor at the College of Europe (Bruges), Distinguished Visiting Professor, Florida State University

PART I

Setting the Scene

1

Exploring the Judicial Systems of the ECtHR and the CJEU Side by Side: On the Necessity to Bridge the Systems and Close the Gaps

ELISE MUIR,[1] SACHA GARBEN AND INGE GOVAERE

1. Introduction

The co-existence of the European Court of Human Rights (ECtHR) and the Court of Justice of the European Union (CJEU), and their inter-related action and explicit interaction, has fascinated legal scholars for some time.[2] As these two courts are increasingly called upon to interpret corresponding rights,[3] particularly owing to the ever-growing importance of fundamental rights in the EU legal order, the stakes intensify. The study of this evolving relationship between the two European courts has mostly focused on the (plethora of) constitutional and substantive issues that arise in the interaction between these two legal systems. There is, however, a somewhat overlooked but equally significant dimension to the relationship: the lesser-told tale of two – increasingly substantively overlapping – European-level judicial systems with their own procedures and institutional idiosyncrasies, their own terminology (human rights versus fundamental rights), and with their own epistemic communities of practitioners and scholars, and their own relationship to national law.

[1] This contribution is part of the RESHUFFLE research project hosted by KU Leuven and supported by the European Research Council (European Union's Horizon 2020 research and innovation programme, grant agreement No 851621).

[2] Recently A Petti, C Hillion, T Bekkedal, Special Issue on 'Fundamental Rights Protection in Europe: Shedding Light on a System of Interrelated Regimes' (2025) 32(2) *Maastricht Journal for European and Comparative Law*.

[3] This was anticipated by Article 52(3) CFREU, according to which '[i]n so far as this Charter contains rights which correspond to rights guaranteed by the [ECHR], the meaning and scope of those rights shall be the same as those laid down by the said Convention. This provision shall not prevent Union law providing more extensive protection.'

1.1. Two Procedural Worlds

The two courts perform different functions, and this is reflected in important procedural differences too. The ECtHR is a human rights' court, external review of human rights compliance by its Member States being its exclusive focus. As such, it interprets the European Convention on Human Rights (ECHR), which it understands as 'a "constitutional instrument of European public order" in the field of human rights'.[4] It operates at supranational level, acts as a subsidiary organ, and can only be seized after exhaustion of national judicial remedies.[5] The CJEU instead performs a function that is closer to that of a 'supreme court'[6] in a legal system that it identifies as a 'common legal order',[7] with a constitutional overtone.[8] Fundamental rights protection is thus primarily an internal feature of the functioning of the Union.[9] The CJEU can review the compatibility of acts of EU organs, as well as that of the Member States in the fields covered by EU law, against EU fundamental rights.[10] Importantly, the Court can, or must,[11] also be called to answer questions on the interpretation of EU (fundamental rights) law from national courts or tribunals seized of any disputes in the fields covered by EU law. In that context, the CJEU thus regularly interpret EU fundamental rights law relevant in litigation which may involve either public or private parties before any national court or tribunal. Importantly, that can only occur within the fields covered by EU law.[12]

Against this background, the two legal systems feature different procedural mechanisms that allow for the activation of fundamental rights protection by each of these two Courts.[13] It is this lesser-told tale, about which surprisingly little has been written, that is the focus of this book. *What are the respective strengths and weaknesses of the web of procedural rules that allows to activate protection by each of these two Courts?* This is the key question that this book seeks to answer by turning the spotlight on the

[4] ECtHR, App no 45036/98 *Bosphorus Hava Yollari Turizm ve Ticaret Anonim şirketi v Ireland* ECLI:CE:ECHR:2005:0630JUD004503698 (ECHR, 30 June 2005) para 156.

[5] ECHR, Section II.

[6] See T Tridimas, 'Sharing Uniformity: A New Era Beckons' in *Yearbook on Procedural Law of the Court of Justice of the European Union* 5th edn (2023) *LCEL Research Paper Series 1/2024* 2, 22.

[7] CJEU, Case C-156/21 *Hungary v Parliament and Council* ECLI:EU:C:2022:97, para 127.

[8] See, eg, CJEU, Opinion 2/13 *Accession of the EU to the ECHR* ECLI:EU:C:2014:2454, para 158: 'The fact that the EU has a new kind of legal order, the nature of which is peculiar to the EU, its own constitutional framework and founding principles, a particularly sophisticated institutional structure and a full set of legal rules to ensure its operation, has consequences as regards the procedure for and conditions of accession to the ECHR.'

[9] On the different functions of the two courts, see also S O'Leary, ch 2.

[10] This is best exemplified by the joint reading of Article 19 TEU, and Article 51 CFREU.

[11] Article 267, para 3, TFEU.

[12] Article 51(1) CFREU; CJEU, Case C-617/10 *Åklagaren v Hans Åkerberg Fransson* ECLI:EU:C:2013:105, para 21.

[13] On the procedural dimension of the ECHR, see for instance J Gerards, AC Buyse and M Andenas (eds), Special Issue on 'Heads and Tails. Admissibility and Remedies at the European Court of Human Rights' (2024) 5 *European Convention of Human Rights Law Review* 291; on EU procedural law see generally K Lenaerts, I Maselis and K Gutman, *EU Procedural Law* (Oxford, Oxford University Press, 2014) and R Barents, 'EU Procedural Law and Effective Legal Protection' (2014) 51 *Common Market Law Review* 1437; and on fundamental rights specifically see, eg, D Krotov and F Kupsch, 'Poking the Bear or Waking the Sleeping Beauty? The Potential of Fundamental Rights Complaint Procedures Before the CJEU' in A Heger, M Malkmus (eds), *On the Relation between the EU Charter of Fundamental Rights and National Fundamental Rights* (Springer, 2024).

specifics of each judicial system. This is particularly important and timely as the technicalities for litigating and enforcing European human and fundamental rights have been developing quickly in recent years. As is illustrated throughout the book, the two Courts are both being asked to respond to multiple, pressing challenges, such as the need to protect vulnerable groups (eg, migrants) or against systemic threats (eg, to judicial independence), owing to speedy procedures and measures (eg, interim measures, expedited or urgent procedures), the necessity to address repetitive infringements (eg, pilot-judgments before the ECtHR), the protection of the integrity of judicial processes and the authority of rulings (eg, financial sanctions and penalty payments), or the increasingly integrated European judicial architecture (eg, advisory opinions before the ECtHR co-existing with the possibility of preliminary rulings before the CJEU). The central argument underlying this project is that, in acknowledging both the important systemic differences between the two Courts, and the potential for judicial protection of fundamental rights also through EU law, the two systems could better complement each other than is currently already (to some extent) the case.

1.2. A Bridging Exercise

In practice, legal scholars all too often focus either on the Convention system, or on the EU legal order, or they examine their cross-over through a lens coloured by one of the systems. This book uniquely brings together in dialogue the two sources of expertise, that of European human rights lawyers on the one hand, and that of European Union lawyers on the other hand, and this both from academia and legal practice alike. Such an exercise fills a gap, by addressing the needs of litigants and their advisors who may be wondering which forum will best meet their needs. Importantly, it will also assist national courts which have to navigate a particularly complex web of norms and procedures.[14] Indeed, since 2018, some national top courts have the possibility of approaching both the ECtHR and the CJEU to ask for guidance on the interpretation of European human or fundamental rights.[15] Furthermore, the same cases may also be brought at different stages before each of the two Courts.[16] Last but not least,

[14] As evidenced by L van der Meulen, *National Courts as EU Fundamental Rights Courts: An analysis of Dutch, German and Belgian adjudication on fundamental rights exceptions to transfer decisions under the European Arrest Warrant and Dublin Regulation* (Asser Press, forthcoming in open access).

[15] Article 267 TFEU requires from courts or tribunals against whose decisions there is no judicial remedy under national law to ask questions on the interpretation of EU law to the CJEU. Since 2018, for the States which have signed and ratified it, Protocol No 16 to the ECHR, allows the highest courts and tribunals of a State Party to request the ECtHR to give advisory opinions on questions of principle relating to the interpretation or application of the rights and freedoms defined in the Convention or the protocols thereto.

[16] This is well illustrated with reference to *Jehovah's Witnesses v Finland*, on the collection of data by Jehovah Witnesses during door-to-door preaching, and *Executief van de Moslims van België and others v Belgium*, on the slaughtering of animals and religious freedom and non-discrimination, to provide but two recent examples. ECtHR, App no 31172/19 *Jehovah's Witnesses v Finland* ECLI:CE:ECHR:2023:0509JUD003117219; CJEU, Case C-25/17, *Jehovan todistajat* ECLI:EU:C:2018:551; see, eg, cross-references by the ECtHR to the case law of the CJEU at paras 85–87. ECtHR, App nos 16760/22 and 10 others *Executief van de Moslims van België and others v Belgium* ECLI:CE:ECHR:2024:0213JUD001676022CJEU; CJEU, Case C-336/19 *Centraal Israëlitisch Consistorie van België et autres* ECLI:EU:C:2020:1031; see for instance cross-references by the ECtHR to the case law of the CJEU at paras 115 ff.

establishing connections between expert communities that have developed largely independently from each other, contributes to a sharper understanding and contextual analysis of the respective roles and powers of each of the two Courts.[17]

This bridging exercise in the first place calls for *distinguishing* between the systems, all the more so since their different features may be able to contribute to cross-fertilisation and to better understanding their respective limits. As such, it is not suggested that the CJEU should be confused for a human rights court, nor that the ECtHR has lost its *raison d'être* for EU Member States. The ECtHR aims to pursue 'the maintenance and further realization of Human Rights and Fundamental Freedoms',[18] making human rights its very *raison d'être*. To the contrary, it is fully acknowledged that the CJEU is not a human rights court, as it needs to balance fundamental rights protection with a multitude of other imperatives. It is also acknowledged that EU law must comply with the law of the ECHR, as well as in fact internal fundamental rights law.[19] If, and when, the respective functions of these Courts overlap and/or completement each other, one may look for potential cross-fertilisation. Conversely, when these diverge, it is important to be clear as to their respective limitations. This will prove all the more important upon the accession of the EU to the ECHR pursuant to Article 6(2) of the Treaty on European Union (TEU), as the intensity of interactions between the case law of the two Courts is bound to deepen. There is thus much need for exploring the respective strengths and weaknesses of the web of procedural rules that allows to activate protection by each of these two Courts, as well as to bridging the gap between the expertise of ECHR and EU lawyers.[20]

The bridge which we wish to consolidate between the two legal systems, is clearly pinpointed by **Síofra O'Leary** in chapter two. Recalling the different functions of the two Courts, while stressing how closely intertwined the EU and the ECHR systems have become, she strongly challenges the view by which the two Courts may be competing or significantly diverging. Instead, emphasis is placed on the long-standing human rights dialogue between the two courts through convergence and cross-referencing. It is deftly illustrated that it is difficult to find a Convention article (and related case law) in relation to EU Member States in which some cross-referencing does not occur, in one direction or the other. Where significant or long-lasting divergences do occur between the two Courts, this will often be explained by the different functions of the Courts and the distinct constraints that they each face. Síofra O'Leary calls on European courts to be clear and transparent on these matters, and calls on scholars and practitioners for bridging gaps in knowledge of and between the two systems. This important chapter thus paves the way, as from Part I of the book devoted to 'Setting the Scene', for the subsequent contributions to focus on the procedural specificities of each judicial system.

[17] As called for by careful observers of the interplay between them, see V Davio, *EU Fundamental Rights: A Source of Special Significance for the European Court of Human Rights* (Larcier Intersentia, forthcoming in open access).

[18] ibid, Preamble (3), original text, unchanged.

[19] See, eg, Article 6(3) TEU; Articles 52(3) and 53 CFREU.

[20] One could also have added the perspective of national courts, this however proved to be too much for one single publication. The national perspective has thus only be inserted where the EU and the national rules of procedures are so closely intertwined that they are best presented as a whole, as in the contribution by Gutman and Kornezov on interim measures.

2. Key questions

2.1. Who Can Go Where?

The first concrete question that this book explores, in Part II, is ***who*** can contribute to shaping human and fundamental rights before the two European courts? Rather than reiterating the basics of access to the ECtHR and CJEU (which can be found in handbooks on ECHR and EU law respectively), the underlying idea is to reflect on those actors or mechanisms that play a particularly important role in the protection of human and fundamental rights. The focus is put on collective enforcement and third-party interventions, each examined in turn by emphasising the respective strengths and weaknesses of each of the two systems. These tools may not only help compensating for the vulnerability and isolation of victims of violations of rights when it comes to litigating, they also are essential contributions to the deliberative process taking place before courts to fill in essential gaps in protection.

The 'Collective enforcement of fundamental rights via the CJEU and the ECtHR' is explored by **Janneke Gerards and Elif Erken** in chapter three. It examines whether and to what extent the two courts leave room for individuals, or civil society groups, to seize a court in the public interest, with the aim of contributing to general justice, rather than or in addition to seeking purely individual justice. Such forms of collective action may indeed alleviate the burden on isolated litigants, as well as shed light on the implications of a case beyond the specific situation of an individual, thereby making a legal challenge resonate for other individuals, groups of persons or even systems. The authors show that avenues for the collective enforcement of fundamental and human rights remain very limited before the European top courts, while pointing at a developing trend in opening up new paths when environmental and climate cases are concerned, in EU as well as in ECHR law.

Precisely because the two European courts are rather difficult to access for civil society, **Virginia Passalacqua**'s chapter four then examines 'Third-party interventions before both the ECtHR and the CJEU'. Although not limited to non-governmental actors, such interventions are often understood as an alternative way for civil society to access courts. Contributing to addressing the lack of comparative study of third-party interventions between the two courts, the author complements her legal analysis with available empirical data on each judicial system. She notes that non-state actors participate much more in proceedings before the ECtHR, while Member States engage more in interventions before the CJEU, where they benefit from a special status. Recalling the important systemic differences between the two courts, the author also draws thoughtful parallels between them. She bitterly regrets the difficulty of accessing data on third-party interventions before both the ECtHR and the CJEU. She further calls for greater transparency on the criteria of admission of third-party interventions before the ECtHR, and for more awareness of the unbalance between state and non-state actors' interventions before the CJEU.

Joyce De Coninck in chapter five, 'Deliberative Discourse in Developing the EU's Human Rights Responsibility', in turn emphasises the importance of courts acting as a platform where a wide range of views on how to address essential protection gaps can be heard. To that effect, the author builds on the theory of human rights experimentalism developed by Gráinne De Búrca,[21] and critically reflects on the difficulty of challenging the liability of the EU's Border and Coast Guard Agency ('Frontex') for breaches of human and fundamental rights law before the CJEU. Stressing that the manner in which human rights have developed to ensure the liability of States under international human rights law may not be transposed as such to EU organs, the author interestingly calls for novel approaches to ensure the liability of EU organs under human and fundamental rights law. More specifically, she urges the CJEU to open its doors to direct actions in damages against EU organs such as Frontex, and to indeed thereafter act as a deliberative forum.

2.2. On What Procedural Roads?

Part III of the book explores key procedures specific to each of the two European courts, which are of particular interest to understanding the general dynamics of litigation of European human and fundamental rights law. The purpose is not to simply reiterate the basics of the procedural law of the ECtHR and the CJEU, but instead to disseminate knowledge and invite reflection on selected contemporary trends. The underlying objective is to highlight possible complementarities between the two judicial systems, by stressing either how these differ and might address each other's weaknesses, or the extent to which they may be similar and thus invite cross-fertilisation. For that purpose, two contributions devoted to the ECtHR discuss the pilot-judgment procedure and the advisory opinion. Two further contributions are devoted to the CJEU and focus on how the main procedures involving Member States before the CJEU, namely infringement proceedings and the preliminary ruling procedure, may be used to litigate fundamental rights. This part closes on a bridging contribution engaging with the relationship between the advisory opinion procedure before the ECtHR, and the preliminary ruling procedure before the CJEU.

The pilot-judgment procedure at the ECtHR is scrutinised by **Kanstantsin Dzehtsiarou** in chapter six. The procedure was developed internally by the ECtHR, and used for the first time in 2004, before being 'codified' in the Rules of Court. The procedure may be initiated by the Court where the facts of an application reveal 'the existence of a structural or systemic problem or other similar dysfunction which has given rise or may give rise to similar applications'.[22] The author recalls the rationale for the creation of the mechanism and further examines its actual use in case law of the ECtHR from the past decade. This allows to reassess the functions that the mechanism actually performs nowadays, shedding light on the challenge for the ECtHR to balance the advantages of the procedure with its inherent weaknesses. It is demonstrated that the procedure is most often used to address questions that have been dealt with by the Court already, and relate to remaining structural challenges. Overall, and unless

[21] G de Búrca, *Reframing Human Rights in a Turbulent Era* (Oxford, OUP, 2021); G de Búrca, 'Human Rights Experimentalism' (2017) 111 *American Journal of International Law* 277–316.

[22] ECtHR, Rules of the Court (28 March 2024), Rule 61.

the recent ruling in *Cannavacciuolo and Others v Italy*[23] opens a new era, the author observes that, instead of being a forward-looking instrument which it could be, the procedure is currently primarily used to 'reinforce the existing standards rather than to develop the new ones'. Hence the call for a greater use of the mechanism whilst cautioning that the weak enforcement of pilot-judgments may be particularly detrimental to the reputation of the court.

The implementation of Protocol 16, which since 2018 allows the highest courts and tribunals of 22 States Parties to request an advisory opinion from the ECtHR is explored by **Jasper Krommendijk** in chapter seven. Asking whether the mechanism is 'purposeless or promising?', the author analyses the opinions drafted by the ECtHR to date, as well as the way national courts used the procedure. For that purpose, empirical insights related to Protocol 16 as well as derived from interviews are relied on. Parallels are also drawn with the Article 267 of the Treaty on the Functioning of the European Union (TFEU) preliminary ruling procedure in EU law. The author observes that although the two mechanisms serve different purposes, they also share many similarities. For instance, some of the features of the preliminary ruling procedure before the CJEU may find an echo in the early practice of the ECtHR under Protocol 16 in relation to the assessment of the admissibility of questions. Interestingly, the ECtHR is found to have given greater clarity to national courts on how to use the procedure, as well as to have reached a subtle balance between providing abstract, yet useful, guidance to the national courts. To improve the system further, national courts are called upon to make greater use of the possibility to share their own views on the questions they submit to the ECtHR, so as to enhance the dialogical dimension of the mechanism.

Turning to EU law, **Luca Prete** in chapter eight examines the procedure that allows the European Commission (or a Member State) to seek a ruling from the CJEU finding that a(nother) Member State has infringed its obligations under EU law. The author focuses on situations where such infringement actions, which far exceed the rules recognised in classical international law to ensure that obligations of States are fulfilled, are specifically used for the protection of fundamental rights. The chapter sheds light on how the recent practice of the European Commission as well as that of the CJEU may be progressively transforming the procedure into a useful addition to the toolbox for the enforcement of EU fundamental rights law. It is highlighted that, although still overall limited in number, rulings by the CJEU in infringement actions can establish that a Member State has acted in breach of its EU law obligations in the field. Such procedures may also for instance be complemented by interim measures, may target general and persistent infringements of EU fundamental rights law, and/or ultimately lead to important financial sanctions. The author thus invites the European Commission to consider making more use of infringement procedures to indeed enhance the application of EU fundamental rights law.

In chapter nine, **Takis Tridimas** explores the second – and essential – prong of the EU judicial system, whereby the monitoring of compliance with EU (fundamental rights) is entrusted primarily to the vigilance of individuals. This chapter is indeed devoted to 'The preliminary ruling procedure and fundamental rights: a tale of judicial

[23] Apps nos 51567/14 and 3 others ECLI:CE:ECHR:2025:0130JUD005156714.

supremacy'. As the author shows, the preliminary ruling procedure, which allows national courts to obtain answers from the CJEU to questions on the interpretation or validity of EU law in the context of disputes pending before them, places national courts at the forefront of the protection of EU fundamental rights. By design, the procedure is close to citizens, facilitates the immediate invocation of EU (fundamental rights) law before national courts and allows its 'fusion' in national legal systems. The existence of the procedure has thus facilitated the development of a fundamental rights discourse in the EU. It is then perhaps only natural, as the author demonstrates, that the procedure is treated both by the CJEU and the ECtHR as pivotal in the EU judicial system and an integral part of the right to judicial protection. Is the procedure then an effective way to protect fundamental rights? The author's tentative answer is that the procedure overall 'fares reasonably well'. He argues that the preliminary ruling procedure is not actually difficult to use and is rather democratic, it also allows the CJEU to occasionally show leadership in fundamental rights cases, leaving essentially no discretion to the national court. Yet, Takis Tridimas also identifies avenues for improvement, in particular in so far as access to justice is concerned, and limitations inherent in the nature of the procedure as a form of inter-judicial dialogue.

As made clear in the previous chapter, the preliminary ruling procedure is central to the system of judicial protection in the EU, and particularly important for the protection of fundamental rights in EU Member States. Its relationship to the advisory opinion procedure provided for by Protocol 16 of the ECtHR thus warrants attention. Building on the contributions by Jasper Krommendijk and Takis Tridimas, chapter ten by **Felix Ronkes Agerbeek** reflects on 'Knowing whom to ask: judicial dialogue under Protocol No 16 ECHR and Article 267 TFEU considered in light of EU accession to the ECHR'. The contribution shows how the relationship between the advisory opinion before the ECtHR, and the preliminary ruling procedure before the CJEU, illustrates broader challenges of the process of EU accession to the ECHR. The author sheds light on the added value for courts of the Member States to make use of the preliminary ruling procedure in fundamental rights' cases, and explains how and why the new version of the draft accession agreement specifies that the advisory opinion mechanism does not extend to EU Member's states highest courts in matters of EU law.

2.3. The Need for Speed

The judicial systems of both the ECtHR and the CJEU are designed so as to ensure effective judicial protection of the rights protected in their respective system. Part IV of the book further explores how concrete problems related to the need for speed and efficiency in processing calls for protection of human and fundamental rights are tackled. Some of the features of the mechanisms discussed in the previous part of the book, devoted to specific procedures for the protection of human and fundamental rights, are also intended to contribute to addressing needs of speed and efficiency. The pilot-judgment procedure, for instance, can be understood as a mechanism to enhance the efficiency of the functioning of the ECtHR. Yet, in this fourth part of the book, rather than discussing key procedural avenues to bring or process claims for protection, we draw attention to tools that address in overall more specific and technical terms, the need for speedy and efficient responses to threat to human and fundamental rights. We have invited the authors to highlight key trends and contemporary challenges before each court. Also here, we start with two contributions on the ECtHR, delving into how to address repetitive claims and the need for interim protection, before turning to the CJEU and exploring speedy procedures and interim measures in an EU law context. The authors share their critical views on these various fronts, with many valuable suggestions for reforms.

David Milner in chapter eleven investigates 'Repetitive strain at the European Court of Human Rights: responding to the caseload caused by structural and systemic problems'. Complementing the chapter by Kanstantsin Dzehtsiarou focused on the pilot-procedure, David Milner takes the reader through the web of tools, such as the 'well-established case law procedure', envisaged and available to improve the functioning of the ECtHR and to better address repetitive threats to the Convention. For that purpose, the chapter spells out and assesses not only developments in the case law of the ECtHR, but also efforts at intergovernmental level to seek to address the workload of the Court in relation to repetitive cases. The author for instance draws attention to the importance of non-contentious approaches developed in recent years as a potentially effective means of resolving certain disputes. He concludes by arguing that the Court has, in particular in recent years, taken a number of initiatives that have significantly increased its capacity to process repetitive cases efficiently and effectively, and that the State parties have overall been cooperative.

This analysis of the ECtHR system is complemented by **Philip Leach** in chapter twelve, by looking at 'Injunctive relief at the European Court of Human Rights – progress and push-back'. This contribution provides critical insights on contemporary developments both in the case law and in the rules of procedure and practice of the ECtHR in relation to the Court's injunctive relief mechanism under Rule 39 of the Rules of Court. The mechanism originates in the 1970s and garnered ever-greater prominence, attracting much (political) attention, in recent years. The author explains how the scope of interim measures has extended well beyond expulsion cases to 'encompass a broad range of situations which create a serious risk of jeopardy to an individual's safety and security', as in the case of asylum seekers and migrants, thereby also calling for differentiation and greater prescriptiveness in the types of measures under use. After recalling that the main States have historically shown willingness to comply with interim measures, the author expresses considerable concern that the more recent rule of law backsliding in Europe has also encompassed some States' attitude towards urgent stipulations issued by the ECtHR. He concludes by welcoming the recent reform of Rule 39 and yet calls for more transparency on the use of interim measures and greater speed in decisions on merits.

Turning back to EU law, chapter thirteen by **Sara Iglesias Sanchez** explores how the CJEU addresses the need for speed in the context of preliminary ruling procedure which, as she stresses, is the main avenue to ensure the application of EU fundamental rights law in the Member States. She focuses on what ensuring speedy processing of preliminary questions from national courts may bring to the protection of fundamental rights in a contribution entitled 'Reasonable Time before EU Courts: What is at Stake? Expedited and Urgent Preliminary Rulings as a Vehicle for Fundamental Rights'. The chapter most helpfully contextualises the specifics of the expedited and urgent procedures, the latter having been created by the Treaty of Lisbon (2009) in the specific context of the Area of Freedom, Security and Justice (covering in particular EU migration, asylum and criminal law). The analysis identifies the features of each mechanism, also sketching the working of the 'priority treatment' of certain requests, and looks at how these tools have co-existed in the past 15 years. On this basis, the author calls into question the narrow scope of the urgent procedure and invites a more encompassing reflection on how the procedures under examination interact. More specifically, she emphasises the need for greater consistency in the relevant legal frameworks and its application when it comes to protecting fundamental rights.

This contribution on expedited and urgent preliminary rulings at the CJEU ought to be read alongside chapter fourteen on 'Interim Measures and Fundamental Rights in EU Law: Some Reflections and Possible Reforms' by **Kathleen Gutman** and **Alexander Kornezov**. The chapter revisits the case law on interim measures in EU law. For that purpose, the authors draw insightful parallels between different forms of interim measures at EU and national level under EU law, as well as between the EU and the ECHR systems for interim measures. The rules on interim measures under EU law – which may relate to preliminary ruling procedures, as well as to other actions before the Court – were drafted and conceptualised before EU law became as engaged with fundamental rights as it is nowadays. There is thus 'no time to waste' to reconsider the extent to which interim measures under EU law may contribute to the system of protection of fundamental rights in the EU. To that effect, the authors argue that the rules on interim measures have 'significant untapped potential' and are 'ripe for development on numerous fronts' to realise such potential. For instance, they invite reflection on the possibility of applying for interim measures before filing the main action, as well as for the law on interim measures before national courts to be revisited with a view to integrating the need to protect fundamental rights pending the outcome of the main action.

2.4. The Internal Workings of the Two Courts

The quest for the effective judicial protection of rights is not only to be found in rules of procedures on the processing of claims, it also has a strong imprint on the internal structure of courts. This is the subject matter of Part V. These structures, and the way they are used, evolve to address emerging trends, such as the ever-greater interplay between the law of the ECHR and that of the EU, as well as the increase of litigation in certain fields, as migration or armed conflicts. Understanding the specifics of the structure of each court helps to shed light on important differences between the judicial system. The functions of each of the two courts differ, as already noted; their workload, financial and human resources, as well as linguistic constraints. The two first chapters of this part of the book, on the ECtHR, examine the internal organisation of that Court and zoom into the process of deliberations and separate opinions that characterise its working. The next two chapters, on the CJEU, elaborate on the internal organisation of that other top Court, before inviting reflection on how the right to an effective judicial remedy provides interpretative guidance in the application of the Statute and the Rules of Procedure of the said Court.

In chapter fifteen on 'The organisation of the internal work of the ECtHR', **Ellen Penninckx** shows how the organisation of the ECtHR is adapting rapidly to ensure the adequate processing of individual applications lodged pursuant to Article 34 ECHR. The latter is understood as the 'cornerstone' of the Convention system. She starts with contrasting the considerable workload of the Court with its limited resources. Her contribution further recalls that the Grand Chamber (17 judges) is the 'supreme decision-making body' and illustrates the very important role of staff from the Registry in assisting the Judge Rapporteur for the purpose of producing the first draft of judgments or decisions. Unlike the CJEU, such case-lawyers are not attached to a special judge and work under the authority of the Registrar. A Jurisconsult confidentially advises the Court to enhance the quality and consistency of its case law. Experts within the services of the Registry and the Jurisconsult have in recent years developed specific expertise on EU law (among other important emerging fields), to provide internal peer-review within the Registry, and specific research reports from the services of the Jurisconsult.

Frédéric Krenc further develops on 'Deliberations and Separate Opinions at the European Court of Human Rights' in chapter sixteen. His contribution sheds light on how the Court's rulings are prepared and made. Before the ECtHR, and unlike at the CJEU, the identity of the Judge Rapporteur remains unknown, public hearings are rather uncommon, and deliberations take place in English as well as in French. The deliberations are secret, as before the CJEU, yet the Convention allows judges to deliver a separate, concurring or dissenting, opinion on judgments. A judge may thus decide (or not) to visibly distinguish his or her reasoning from that of the majority. Separate opinions may also be issued in relation to advisory opinions, although in this context, the Court overall seeks to speak 'with one voice'. The author observes that separate opinions have overall in recent years increasingly tended to focus on the degree of review exercised by the Court. There are no specific rules governing separate opinions, yet he recalls that basic judicial principles apply. There is for instance a duty of collegiality, which implies that issues raised in a separate opinion have been addressed during the deliberations. In this context, he invites reflection on whether separate opinions should be sent to the relevant composition of the court so as to be taken into account in drafting the judgment. The author concludes by highlighting the many valuable functions of separate opinions, in particular the incentive for judges to seek to convince each other with a view to achieving collegial decisions, without having to attach a dissenting opinion.

The theme of 'Fundamental Rights and the Internal Functioning of the CJEU' is addressed by **José Gutierrez Fons** in chapter seventeen. As there are no legal rules to deal specifically with fundamental rights before the CJEU, his contribution examines the impact of fundamental rights in the internal functioning of the Court of Justice as a matter of practice, from the initial stages of processing a case until the deliberations. The paper places special emphasis on what takes place 'even behind the scenes' and includes reflections on the 2024 reform of the Statute of the Court. First and foremost, the rules on the organisation and functioning of the Court ought to themselves be interpreted in light of EU fundamental rights, including the right to data protection. The author draws attention to the importance of the Registrar, the Research and Documentation Directorate (RDD), and the President of the Court in examining, informing and making key decisions in the early stages of the processing of a case. The RDD, for instance, provides specific expertise on the development of ECtHR case law. The President of the Court, for another example, plays a decisive role in drawing the Court's attention to whether preliminary questions falling within the scope of the 2024 reform for the purpose of being treated by the General Court, in fact raises 'independent questions' that warrant them being processed by the Court of Justice itself. In order to make such a determination, the author argues that 'the fundamental rights dimension of the case must have a certain *gravitas*' and illustrates how that may be done. He further stresses the importance of the Grand Chamber, mapping out the key features of the cases referred to it, and demonstrating that questions pertaining to the protection of fundamental rights often catch its attention.

Taking the invitation by José Gutierrez Fons to read the rules on the organisation of the CJEU in light of fundamental rights to the letter, chapter eighteen by **Joni Heliskoski** engages in 'A Survey on the Role of Article 47 of the Charter of Fundamental Rights in the Application of the Statute and the Rules of Procedure of the CJEU' ('Rules'). As the author notes, given the role of the Court of Justice in amending this Statute, and in the adoption of these Rules, it was perhaps to be expected that there are no cases from that same Court finding that these texts conflict with Article 47 of the Charter of Fundamental Rights of the European Union (CFREU). The contribution instead analyses the cases of the Court of Justice, as well as those of the General Court, on how the Statute and the Rules of both EU courts have been read in light of Article 47 CFREU. This evidences a 'clear recognition' of the role of Article 47 CFREU as an interpretative tool to shape the organisation of the proceedings of both courts, as illustrated in case law on the time limits to initiate proceedings. The author further observes that, unlike most other courts at domestic and international level, the CJEU cannot autonomously decide on its Statute and Rules. This is subject to the involvement of EU political institutions.[24] While this may be understandable in so far as these texts deal with more than the mere internal organisation of the EU courts, the author argues that the involvement of the EU's political institutions in the internal organisation of the Courts as such is problematic.

2.5. Final Destination Reached? Compliance and Non-compliance

The crucial issue of compliance, or lack thereof, with judgments of the two European Courts is the focus of Part VI of this book. This is naturally of utmost importance to the effective protection of rights, and perhaps where the need to shed light on the complementarities of the two systems under examination is the greatest. The authors paint very

[24] Indeed, Article 281, second paragraph, TFEU states that 'The European Parliament and the Council, acting in accordance with the ordinary legislative procedure, may amend the provisions of the Statute, with the exception of Title I and Article 64. The European Parliament and the Council shall act either at the request of the Court of Justice and after consultation of the Commission, or on a proposal from the Commission and after consultation of the Court of Justice'; Article 253, last paragraph, TFEU states that 'The Court of Justice shall establish its Rules of Procedure. Those Rules shall require the approval of the Council.'

contrasting pictures of the overall effectiveness of the systems of the ECtHR, and of that of the CJEU respectively.

Laurence Burgorgue-Larsen in chapter nineteen presents a sobering analysis of '(Non-)Compliance with the rulings of the ECtHR in the Age of illiberal and dictatorial turn'. The author comes back on the multiple initiatives taken by the political organs of the Council of Europe, such as the pilot-judgment procedure and the 'failure to fulfil obligations' procedure, to deal with growing workload and emerging challenges. She also welcomes initiatives taken by the Court itself, such as the priority policy including a new category for 'impact cases', and its new line of case law on judicial independence. Yet, she contrasts these positive developments with the scathing observation that the ECtHR system does not any more rely on a politically and socially homogeneous group of Member States. She bitterly denounces bad faith politics from States who remain in the system, although they 'have strictly no interest in complying with the Court's judgments'. Building on earlier work of ECHR political organs as well as on an own thorough analysis of selected cases of non-compliance provided in an annex, the author identifies, and critically examines, the approaches of a number of 'bad players' ranging from illiberal democracies to a complete state failure. She singles out three particularly sensitive areas of concern: the sharp rise in inter-state applications; calling for creative thinking to upgrade the ability of the ECtHR to address them; as well as threats to democracy and the rule of law through Article 18 ECHR (Limitation on use of restrictions on rights) violations and threats to judicial independence. Closing with a reflection on strategies of non-compliance, she shares her doubts that reforms of the ECtHR system may be effective to address the extreme bad faith of its illiberal and authoritarian members.

A less pessimistic reading on the current state of compliance with judgments in the EU is offered by **Allan Rosas** in chapter twenty on '(Non-)Compliance with the rulings of the CJEU'. As he notes, in the EU, the current state in terms of compliance is 'far from catastrophic'. It is in fact better than it was in the first 80 years of US constitutionalism and in the earlier years of European integration. The author observes that, given the uncertainties on the 'desired direction, forms and pace of European integration', compliance is rather counter-intuitively good overall. Compliance with preliminary rulings, which are identified as the key avenue to enhance compliance with EU (fundamental rights) law through the intermediary of national courts, are 'at least satisfactory'. As for infringement actions, most judgments finding a failure to comply with EU law appear to be executed. Yet, the author takes stock of the existence of a number of challenges to the authority of EU (case) law, which may take different forms and are highly important in constitutional terms. Although there exists 'no silver bullet and no quick fixes', the author explores complementary avenues for improvement, such as enhancing teaching and training on EU law. Echoing Luca Prete, he argues in favour of relying on infringement actions to tackle 'systemic failures' to comply with EU (fundamental rights) law, as well as on the basis of Article 2 TEU alone in cases of 'systemic and serious breaches of the values' listed therein. He also calls for higher financial sanctions in infringement rulings, and stresses the possibility of budgetary off-setting in cases of non-payment. The chapter concludes by recalling the existence of the mechanism of political responses to attacks on EU values under Article 7 TEU, and of financial conditionality.

3. Conclusion

The book closes, in Part VII, with concluding thoughts by **Elise Muir** on 'Exploring the judicial systems of the ECtHR and the CJEU side by side: Looking beyond differences'. Chapter twenty-one brings together the main findings teased out from the wealth of contributions introduced above. She highlights how both judicial systems are heavily dependent on access by individuals to national courts. This explains parallel trends in recent reforms to enhance quality, transparency and efficiency in internal rules and practices of both courts, as well as synergies in the case law of the two courts on the independence of national judges. Yet the importance of access by individuals to national courts also comes with shared challenges when it comes to the representation of public interests, or the interaction between the advisory opinion mechanism and the preliminary ruling procedure. The author further comes back on contemporary threats to the system(s) for the protection of human and fundamental rights in Europe. Acknowledging the concerns, she also highlights parallel patterns in the ability of courts and legal systems to develop new tools to seek to address threats. She concludes with an invitation to further look for complementarities between the ECtHR and the EU system, building on their respective differences and strengths to address their weaknesses.

2

Activating the Protection of Human Rights at European Level

College of Europe (Bruges), Belgium

Keynote Speech

7th March 2024

SÍOFRA O'LEARY
President of the European Court of Human Rights

1. Introduction

It is an honour to represent the European Court of Human Rights (the Court) at today's conference and to participate in a discussion on the procedural characteristics of European human rights law. It is also a pleasure to be back at the College of Europe. One of the reasons I particularly welcome this event is that it seeks to bridge a gap in European law, bringing together experts from Convention and EU law circles to contrast and compare questions of access to justice and court procedures.

After almost nine years as a Strasbourg judge, which followed almost two decades at the Luxembourg court, my impression remains that expertise in the two fields remains surprisingly fragmented. We see this in academia – although some brilliant exceptions are present at today's conference – and we see it at times in how cases are pleaded before the Court in Strasbourg (and perhaps also in Luxembourg). In many States, different ministries – Justice or Foreign Affairs – take charge of legal proceedings before the two European courts. In their pleadings, even in fields such as immigration and asylum, which for 27 Council of Europe States is now highly regulated at EU level, representatives may present the national law relevant to their complaint without explaining the broader EU law *system* of which that national law forms a part.[1] Thus, in areas of law heavily influenced or regulated by EU law in which human rights considerations play a significant role, one still sees, in 2024, respondent states omit any or a detailed reference to the relevant

[1] See the dissent in ECtHR, App no 56324/13 *AM v France* ECLI:CE:ECHR:2016:0712JUD005632413, para 4.

provisions of EU law which those states have in turn transposed and which their national courts, whose decisions are primarily under scrutiny in Strasbourg, have sought to apply.

The mechanics of EU law are often insufficiently explained by parties appearing in Strasbourg, as if they have not considered their possible contextual relevance for the Strasbourg bench. Just yesterday I presided over a Grand Chamber case concerning data, lawfully intercepted following judicial authorisation in the context of criminal proceedings, transmitted by the public prosecutor to a national competition authority for the purposes of a separate investigation verifying possible price fixing.[2] The case is pending and so I will make no comment on the legal issues which arise therein. However, since the respondent State is an EU Member State, one could have anticipated the complaints, which concern legal and not natural persons, being placed in any relevant EU law context. Strasbourg hearings are recorded and available on the website so I leave it to others to decide if that terrain was well explored or not.

Rather than eating into the procedural terrain which will be covered in detail by successive speakers and panels, I thought I would touch generally on the current articulation between the European Convention on Human Rights and EU law. How has the relationship between the two courts and the two legal orders evolved, what are the essential dynamics we observe today, and what might the future hold?

* * * * * * * * * * * * *

2. Early Milestones

When discussing the relationship between the two European Courts and their case law, one must not forget the key features that distinguish the two systems. The mission of the Strasbourg Court is to establish a minimum standard for human rights protection across the 46 heterogenous member states of the Council of Europe. The mission of the CJEU, on the other hand, is broader in that it seeks to ensure the uniform interpretation of EU law generally. To date, its jurisdiction in relation to fundamental rights has been limited by the scope of application of EU law and by the all-important principle of conferral. As the President of the CJEU often stresses:

> [T]he EU system of fundamental rights protection is an *internal* component of the rule of law within the EU.[3]

In contrast, the Strasbourg Court exercises an external and subsidiary review of whether Member States have complied with their Convention obligations, in a system which is based on shared responsibility. However, the Convention is also, in the words of the Strasbourg Court, 'a constitutional instrument of European public order in the field of human rights'.[4] The Strasbourg Court is a regional human rights court whose sole

[2] For the Chamber judgment, see ECtHR, App no 2799/16 *Ships Waste Oil Collector BV v the Netherlands* ECLI:CE:ECHR:2023:0516JUD000279916.

[3] K Lenaerts, 'The ECHR and the Court of Justice: Creating Synergies in the Field of Fundamental Rights Protection', Opening of the Judicial Year at the ECtHR, 26 January 2018.

[4] See ECtHR (GC), App no 45036/98 *Bosphorus Hava Yollari Turizim ve Ticaret AS v Ireland* ECLI:CE:ECHR:2005:0630JUD004503698, para 156, citing ECtHR, App no 15318/89 *Loizidou v Turkey* (preliminary objections) ECLI:CE:ECHR:1995:0323JUD001531889, para 75.

task is to interpret the Convention, such that the subsidiary nature of its review should not distract observers from the Convention's broader scope and depth. In addition, whatever the distinct nature of the EU system, the terms of EU law make the ECHR in some sense part of the EU's constitutional *acquis*.

As regards the early milestones in the developing relationship between EU law and the Convention, while 27 of the States Parties to the Convention are also EU Member States, as long as the EU is not a Party itself, the standards and measures adopted by its institutions cannot be challenged per se before the Court.[5] As per Article 6 § 3 TEU, human rights, as guaranteed by the ECHR and as they result from the constitutional traditions common to the Member States, constitute general principles of EU law. However, as the CJEU stated in *Kamberaj* and subsequent rulings, Article 6 § 3 TEU does not govern the relationship between the ECHR and the legal systems of EU Member States. Moreover, as the EU has not acceded to the ECHR, the latter does not constitute a legal instrument which has been formally incorporated into the legal order of the EU.[6]

Nevertheless, as you know, questions relating to EU law and to compliance with human rights by EU institutions and by EU Member States when acting within the scope of EU law have been raised regularly before the Strasbourg Court and the former European Commission of Human Rights. As early as 1958, the Strasbourg Commission held that:

> if a State contracts treaty obligations and subsequently concludes another international agreement which disables it from performing its obligations under the first treaty, it will be answerable for any resulting breach of its obligations under the earlier treaty.[7]

This formula, taken from the landmark case *X v Germany*, was a clear signal from the Strasbourg institutions that a transfer of powers from the member States to an international organisation could not lead to a gap in accountability for human rights violations. In relation to the EU and EU Member States, this theme – the need to avoid accountability gaps – has been recurrent ever since and lies at the heart of the question of accession.

In the following decades, and particularly from the 1980s onwards, the Strasbourg Court dealt with numerous applications raising questions regarding its competence to examine acts of the then European Communities.[8] Applications brought directly against the EC, and later the EU, were and are declared inadmissible as being incompatible *ratione personae* with the Convention.[9] Applications brought against EU Member States concerning their national implementation of EU law are a different story.[10] An old but

[5] ECmHR, App no 8030/77 *Confédération française démocratique du travail v the European Communities* (10 July 1978); ECmHR, App no 13258/87 *M & Co v the Federal Republic of Germany* (9 January 1990); ECtHR (GC), App no 24833/94 *Matthews v the United Kingdom* ECLI:CE:ECHR:1999:0218JUD002483394, para 32.

[6] CJEU, Case C-571/10 *Kamberaj v Istituto per l'Edilizia Sociale della Provincia autonoma di Bolzano (IPES) and Others* ECLI:EU:C:2012:233, paras 60 and 62, and CJEU (GC), Case C-617/10 *Åkerberg v Fransson* ECLI:EU:C:2013:105, para 44.

[7] ECmHR, App no 235/56 *X v Germany* (10 June 1958).

[8] Some early examples include, ECmHR, App no 8030/77 *CFDT v European Communities* (dec) (10 July 1978); ECmHR, App no 13539/88 *Dufay v European Communities* (dec) (19 January 1989).

[9] ECtHR, App no 13645/05 *Cooperatieve Producentenorganisatie van de Nederlandse Kokkelvisserij UA v the Netherlands* (dec) ECLI:CE:ECHR:2009:0120DEC001364505; ECtHR, App no 37937/07 *Lechouritou and Others v Germany and 26 other Member States of the European Union* (dec) ECLI:CE:ECHR:2012:0403DEC003793707.

[10] ECtHR (GC), App no 45036/98 *Bosphorus* (see n 4 above), para 137; ECtHR, App no 12323/11 *Michaud v France* ECLI:CE:ECHR:2012:1206JUD001232311, para 102; ECtHR (GC), App no 17502/07 *Avotiņš v Latvia* ECLI:CE:ECHR:2016:0523JUD001750207, para 101.

powerful example is *Matthews v the United Kingdom* in which the Court examined the organisation of European elections in Gibraltar. The UK had applied the relevant provisions of the Maastricht Treaty only within the UK, and thus not in Gibraltar. The Court considered that the UK should have amended its election legislation to secure the right to elections in the European Parliament in Gibraltar. As a Contracting Party it remained responsible under the Convention for the consequences flowing from its other Treaty obligations.[11] Looking back today at the *Matthews* judgment, which dates from 1999, in the designation of the European Parliament as a legislature within the meaning of Article 3 of Protocol no 1, we see the ECtHR endorsing the emerging components of the EU's developing constitutional architecture.

Of course, the major advancement concerning the articulation of the relationship between EU law and the Convention came in the early 2000s with the *Bosphorus* judgment and the Court's establishment of a legal test for the presumption of equivalent protection.[12] This presumption applies when a Member State has no discretion in the implementation of its EU obligations. It is rebuttable only if the standard of protection for ECHR rights is found to be manifestly deficient. As you know, it is based on two pillars – the substantive guarantees offered by the international organisation in question and the procedural mechanisms available for controlling their observance.

The EU is considered to benefit from the presumption because, on the one hand, it offers equivalent protection of substantive guarantees. This was demonstrated, according to the court in *Bosphorus*, by its then extensive references to the ECHR and ECtHR case law in relevant cases. Following the entry into force of the Lisbon Treaty, the substantive guarantees were further anchored in the Charter and the crucial 'pegging' clause in Article 52 § 3.[13] On the other hand, the supervisory mechanisms available under EU law – most notably the preliminary reference procedure – can be deployed when required to ensure substantive compliance.[14] On this latter point, the Court has attached considerable importance to the role and powers of the CJEU, despite the fact that individual access to that court is far more limited than access to the Strasbourg Court under Article 34 of the Convention.[15] The centrality

[11] ECtHR (GC), App no 24833/94 *Matthews* (see n 5 above), para 33.

[12] ECtHR (GC), App no 45036/98 *Bosphorus* (see n 4 above). See also, as regards the origin of this concept, ECmHR, App no 13258/87 *M & Co v the Federal Republic of Germany* (dec) (9 February 1990).

[13] See ECtHR (GC), App no 45036/98 *Bosphorus* (see n 4 above), para 159; relied on in ECtHR (GC), App no 17502/07 *Avotiņš* (see n 10 above), para 102.

[14] It is worth recalling, in this regard, the ECtHR's Art 6 case law in which it has enjoined national courts, where necessary, to provide reasons for a refusal to refer. See, eg, ECtHR, App nos 3989/07 and 38353/07, *Ullens De Schooten and Rezabek v Belgium* ECLI:CE:ECHR:2011:0920JUD000398907, where this requirement was developed and ECtHR, App no 17120/09 *Dhahbi v Italy* ECLI:CE:ECHR:2014:0408JUD001712009, where the ECtHR found a violation of art 6 due to a failure to give reasons. This case law has been both criticised (J Malenovsky, 'Le renvoi préjudiciel perçu par trois cours 'souveraines'' (2013) 21 *Journal de droit européen* 214) and welcomed (C Timmermans, 'The Relationship Between the ECJ and the ECtHR' in A Arnull et al (eds), *A Constitutional Order of States* (Oxford, Hart Publishing, 2011), 151 and 155, by members and former members of the CJEU. It is essential, in the view of the present author, not to lose sight of the underpinnings of the *Bosphorus* presumption when examining the justification for this limited Art 6 ECHR reasoning requirement; reasoning which, furthermore, supports the preliminary reference procedure as the EU's judicial keystone.

[15] ECtHR (GC), App no 45036/98 *Bosphorus* (see n 4 above), paras 160–65; ECtHR, App no 12323/11 *Michaud* (see n 10 above), paras 106–111; ECtHR (GC), App no 17502/07 *Avotiņš* (see n 10 above), para 104.

of the preliminary reference procedure to the EU's judicial architecture is fully understood and respected.[16]

The Convention does not prohibit Contracting Parties from transferring sovereign power to an international organisation to pursue cooperation in certain fields of activity. It is striking in *Avotins v Latvia*, for example, how the Court set out its stall in relation to the EU's mutual-recognition mechanisms for the construction of the area of freedom, security and justice, holding:

> The Court has repeatedly asserted its commitment to international and European cooperation (…). (…) it considers the creation of an area of freedom, security and justice in Europe, and the adoption of the means necessary to achieve it, to be wholly legitimate in principle from the standpoint of the Convention.[17]

However, the State Parties remain responsible under Article 1 of the Convention for all acts and omissions of their organs, including those stemming from the necessity to comply with international legal obligations, a point to which I will return.[18]

The presumption of equivalent protection safeguards two goals. Firstly, it ensures that a State Party is not faced with a dilemma when it is obliged to rely on the legal obligations incumbent on it as a result of its membership of an international organisation to which it has transferred part of its sovereignty, in order to justify its actions or omissions arising from such membership vis-à-vis the Convention. Secondly, it also serves to determine in which cases the Court may reduce the intensity of its supervisory role, as conferred on it by Article 19 of the Convention.

Since I'm spending some time looking back to the future, I think it is also worth mentioning the concern expressed in certain quarters after the Treaty of Lisbon entered into force, when the Luxembourg court began to find its stride in Charter cases. There was then talk of a risk of the 'autonomisation' of fundamental rights in the EU and of the CJEU going it alone.[19] Citing, in this respect, the increased references in the Luxembourg court's case law to the autonomy of EU law, certain authors pointed to a commensurate decline or indeed the absence of references in judgments dealing with human rights of relevant and sometimes extensive Strasbourg case law on the same or similar points.[20]

I have always considered that criticism of the decline in references to the ECHR and Strasbourg case law was somewhat overstated. It failed to take into account a natural institutional desire to bed in a new legal instrument such as the Charter.[21] Nevertheless,

[16] See, eg, ECtHR, App no 55385/14 *Baydar v Netherlands* ECLI:CE:ECHR:2018:0424JUD005538514 and ECtHR, App no 25137/16 *Sanofi Pasteur v France* ECLI:CE:ECHR:2020:0213JUD002513716.

[17] ECtHR (GC), App no 17502/07 *Avotiņš* (see n 10 above), para 113.

[18] ibid, para 153.

[19] See, eg, J Callewaert, 'To Accede or not to Accede: European Protection of Fundamental Rights at the Crossroads' (2014) 4 *Journal européen de droits de l'homme* 496; J Polakiewicz, 'EU Law and the ECHR: Will Accession to the ECHR Square the Circle? The Draft Accession Agreement of April 5, 2013' (2013) 6 *European Human Rights Law Review* 592, and the UN OHCHR, 'Report on the Importance, in the Interests of Universality, of the CJEU not Detaching Itself from the Wider Body of International Human Rights Law' (2015) *The European Union and International Human Rights Law*.

[20] G de Búrca, 'After the EU Charter of Fundamental Rights: The Court of Justice as a Human Rights Adjudicator?' (2013) 20 Maastricht Journal of European and Comparative Law 168.

[21] See S O'Leary, 'Courts, Charters and Conventions: Making Sense of Fundamental Rights in the EU' (2016) 56 *Irish Jurist* 4.

given the importance, the nature and the underpinnings of the *Bosphorus* presumption, it is relevant to consider how a Strasbourg judge, or indeed a national one, obliged to observe both EU and Convention law, is to understand CJEU case law if it is silent on relevant ECtHR case law or excessively selective when it does so refer, despite the explicit terms of Articles 52 § 3 and 53 of the Charter. The former Charter provision is, after all, a codification of the ECHR's special significance for the CJEU. It emphasises that the ECtHR is responsible for setting the minimum standard. But of course the ECtHR is also competent to raise that standard over time, in accordance with the Convention's vocation as a living instrument. This means that careful and considered analysis of relevant Strasbourg case law is and will remain essential.[22]

****

3. Current Articulation of ECHR and EU Law

Moving to the present day and the current articulation between the Convention and EU law, I think it is also worth contesting the thesis that the two European Courts are in competition or that their case law is repeatedly and significantly divergent.[23] This is simply not borne out by an overview of their output in recent years. Nor, given the origins of the Convention and EU law's underpinning values – namely common constitutional traditions – or the DNA of EU fundamental rights law as evidenced in the EU Charter, would this be possible, never mind desirable.

The human rights dialogue between Luxembourg and Strasbourg is long-standing. From the 1970s onwards, the CJEU has referred to the ECHR in its judgments, often at considerable length.[24] This relationship was of course formalised with the adoption of the Charter and the maintenance of the ECHR as a source of EU law in Article 6 § 3 TEU. The Strasbourg Court also frequently refers to EU law and to the case law of the CJEU.[25]

Where secondary EU legislation explicitly codifies human rights as contained in the Convention and interpreted by the Strasbourg Court, the flow is understandably more

[22] See also K Lenaerts, 'The Place of the Charter in the EU Constitutional Edifice' in K Lenaerts et al (eds), *The EU Charter of Fundamental Rights – A Commentary* (Oxford, Hart Publishing, 2014) 1581.

[23] See, eg, O'Leary, 'Courts, Charters and Conventions' (2016).

[24] The first reference to the ECHR was made in CJEU, Case C-36/75 *Rutili v The Minister for the Interior* ECLI: EU:C:1975:137. In the 1989 *Hoescht* case, the then ECJ stated that 'fundamental rights are an integral part of the general principles of law the observance of which the Court ensures, in accordance with constitutional traditions common to the Member States, and the international treaties on which the Member States have collaborated or of which they are signatories. The European Convention for the Protection of Human Rights and Fundamental Freedoms of 4 November 1950 is of *particular significance* in that regard' (CJEU, Joined Cases C-46/87 and C-227/88 *Hoescht AG v Commission of the European Communities* ECLI:EU:C:1989:337).

[25] See T Lock, 'The Influence of EU law on Strasbourg Doctrines' (2016) 41 *European Law Review* 804; S O'Leary, 'The EU Charter Ten Years On: A View from Strasbourg', in M Bobek and J Prassl (eds), *The EU Charter of Fundamental Rights in the Member States* (Oxford, Hart Publishing, 2020); J Callewaert, 'Convention Control Over the Application of Union Law by National Judges: The Case for a Wholistic Approach to Fundamental Rights' (2023) 8 *European Papers* 331, 337.

pronounced in one direction. This is well-illustrated by the judgments of the CJEU on EU directives on minimum guarantees in criminal procedure, which explicitly refer to the Convention and the Court's case law on Article 6 as the benchmark.[26] Conversely, there are domains which are strongly developed in EU law, while historically they have received less attention within the Convention framework. In these areas, the flow may predominantly stem from Luxembourg to Strasbourg. Equality law is a prime example of this as it is deeply ingrained in the EU project and has been extensively fleshed out in its primary and secondary law for decades.[27] In contrast, Article 14 ECHR has been described in the past as second-class or 'Cinderella',[28] although it has gained greater significance in the case law of the Strasbourg Court over the past two decades.[29]

In the realm of data protection, we see the impact of Article 8 case law on the early development of EU data protection law and the case law of the CJEU. Here one needs to distinguish between Convention 'articles' and Convention 'rights', the latter being broader than the former. This point seemed to have got somewhat lost in the closing paragraphs of the CJEU judgment in *Tele2 Sverige*, which emphasised the absence in the Convention of an *article* equivalent to Article 8 of the Charter.[30] The Strasbourg Court has a long record of cases dealing with data protection and continues to develop it, thereby responding to technological progress, institutional developments and present-day conditions in digitalised societies which have to deal with organised and cybercrime as well as the threat of terrorism. As such, it has laid down standards for lawful and

[26] See the recent judgments of the CJEU in CJEU, Case C-564/19 *IS* ECLI:EU:C:2021:949, para 101; CJEU, Case C-420/20 *HN* ECLI:EU:C:2022:679, para 55; CJEU, Case C-347/21 *DD* ECLI:EU:C:2022:692, § 31; CJEU, Case C-242/22 PPU *TL* ECLI:EU:C:2022:611, para 40 and CJEU, Case C-348/21 *HYA and Others* ECLI:EU:C:2022:965, paras 39–41, 53–58. For examples in the other direction, see the use made by the Strasbourg Grand Chamber of the more developed language of the EU directive on the right of access to a lawyer in ECtHR (GC), App no 50541/08 *Ibrahim and others v the United Kingdom* ECLI:CE:ECHR:2016:0913JUD005054108, paras 210 and 259. See further J Callewaert, 'The Recent Luxembourg Case-law on Procedural Rights in Criminal Proceedings: Towards Greater Convergence with Strasbourg' (*EU Law Live*, 4 May 2023) https://eulawlive.com/op-ed-the-recent-luxembourg-case-law-on-procedural-rights-in-criminal-proceedings-towards-greater-convergence-with-strasbourg-by-johan-callewaert/ accessed 30 May 2025 and N Daminova, 'European Court of Human Rights on the "Stockholm's Roadmap Directives": The Quest for a Coherent Application of "Due Process" Rights in Europe?' in I Gambardella, V Davio (eds) *EU Directives on Procedural Rights in Criminal Matters: 15 Years After the Roadmap, Where Do We Stand and Where Do We Go?* (*EU Law Live Weekend Edition*, 25 September 2023) https://eulawlive-com/weekend-edition/weekend-edition-no156/ accessed 30 May 2025.

[27] See, eg, as regards EU primary law, Articles 2, 8 and 10 TEU and Articles 19 and 157 TFEU, and, as regards EU secondary law, the Race Equality Directive (2000/43/EC) and the Equality General Framework Directive (2000/78/EC).

[28] R O'Connell, 'Cinderella Comes to the Ball: Art 14 and the Right to Non-discrimination in the ECHR' (2009) 29 *Legal Studies* 211.

[29] See J Gerards, 'The Discrimination Grounds of Article 14 of the European Convention on Human Rights' (2013) *Human Rights Law Review* 99, 100. See also N Bamforth, 'Prohibited Grounds of Discrimination under EU Law and the European Convention on Human Rights: Problems of Contrast and Overlap' (2006–2007) *Cambridge Yearbook of European Legal Studies* 1, 27, on increased synergies and differences between the two systems. Some fairly recent developments in Strasbourg have been overtly influenced by CJEU case law. Think, for example, of the recognition of notions such as indirect discrimination (ECtHR (GC), App no 57325/00 *DH and Others v the Czech Republic* ECLI:CE:ECHR:2007:1113JUD005732500) or discrimination by association (ECtHR, App no 23682/13 *Guberina v Croatia* ECLI:CE:ECHR:2016:0322JUD002368213) or EU Charter and Equality law references in cases like ECtHR (GC), App no 20452/14 *Molla Sali v Greece* ECLI:CE:ECHR:2018:1219JUD002045214.

[30] See CJEU, Joined Cases C-203/15 and C-698/15 *Tele2 Sverige AB v Post- och telestyrelsen and Secretary of State for the Home Department v Tom Watson and Others*ECLI:EU:C:2016:970, para 129.

human-rights compatible surveillance practices which have in turn influenced, at least in part, the CJEU.[31] For instance, the strict approach towards the legality requirement, as enshrined in Article 8 and adopted by the Court in *Huvig*[32] regarding the issue of telephone surveillance, was picked up by the CJEU, from *Digital Rights Ireland* onwards.[33] In certain regards of course the case law of the two courts on surveillance may differ, with the Strasbourg Court not looking at data protection rights in isolation and attributing more prominence than has the CJEU to the positive obligations of States under other Convention provisions, according them, in line with one of the basic tenets of the system, a wider margin of appreciation.

For a good recent example of how the two systems are interacting in this domain, look no further than the judgment of the Court in *Škoberne v Slovenia*, on Article 8 and traffic and location data accessed by law enforcement authorities.[34] The Strasbourg court referred extensively to CJEU case law on the same issue but also made clear, in conclusion, that the admissibility of evidence collected in violation of Article 8 falls to be determined with reference to the Court's *Bykov* line of case law on Article 6.[35] Another example of the articulation between EU and Convention law in this field is to be found in the recent judgment of the CJEU plenary in *La Quadrature du Net*.[36] Following a significant number of preliminary reference requests from Member State constitutional and supreme courts in relation to the consequences of the interpretation of EU law in the *Tele2 Sverige* line of case law, the CJEU appeared to pivot towards greater acceptance, in line with the Strasbourg Court's approach, of a hierarchy of seriousness when it comes to interferences in the data protection context and of the need for more careful balancing between the individual rights and general interests at stake.[37]

Convergence and cross-referencing are also evident in instances where the Luxembourg court had previously handed down preliminary rulings on analogous issues at the behest of parties who later come to Strasbourg. This was, for example, the

[31] See further S O'Leary, 'Balancing Rights in a Digital Age' (2018) *The Irish Jurist* 59 and G Malgieri and P De Hert 'European Human Rights, Criminal Surveillance, and Intelligence Surveillance: Towards "Good Enough" Oversight, Preferably but Not Necessarily by Judges' (2017) *Brussels Privacy Hub Working Paper* 1.

[32] ECtHR, App no 11105/84 *Huvig v France* ECLI:CE:ECHR:1990:0424JUD001110584.

[33] CJEU (GC), Joined Cases C-293/12 and C-594/12 *Digital Rights Ireland Ltd v Minister for Communications, Marine and Natural Resources and Others and Kärntner Landesregierung and Others* ECLI:EU:C:2014:238. The ECtHR has also referred extensively to CJEU case-law in the context of surveillance practices. See, eg, the extensive presentation of applicable EU law, notably the GDPR, and CJEU case law in ECtHR (GC), App no 35252/08 *Centrum för Rättvisa v Sweden* ECLI:CE:ECHR:2021:0525JUD003525208, paras 92–130 and ECtHR (GC), App no 58170/13 and others *Big Brother Watch and Others v the United Kingdom* ECLI:CE:ECHR:2021:0525JUD005817013, paras 202–41.

[34] ECtHR, App no 19920/20 *Škoberne v Slovenia* ECLI:CE:ECHR:2024:0215JUD001992020.

[35] ibid, para 146, referring to ECtHR (GC), App no 4378/02 *Bykov v Russia* ECLI:CE:ECHR:2009:0310JUD000437802, paras 89–91.

[36] CJEU, Case C-470/21 *La Quadrature du Net and Others v Premier ministre and Ministère de la Culture* ECLI:EU:C:2024:370.

[37] ibid, at para 116: 'In balancing the rights and interests at issue, those fundamental rights must yield on occasion to other fundamental rights or public-interest imperatives, such as the maintenance of public order and the prevention of crime or the protection of the rights and freedoms of others. This is, in particular, the case where the weight given to those primary considerations is such as to hinder the effectiveness of a criminal investigation, in particular by making it impossible or excessively difficult to identify effectively the perpetrator of a criminal offence and to impose a penalty on him or her …', citing ECtHR, App no 2872/02, *KU v Finland* ECLI:CE:ECHR:2008:1202JUD000287202, para 49.

case in *Satakunnan v Finland* on the mass publication of tax information,[38] or *Jehovah's Witnesses v Finland* on data collection.[39] These cases also demonstrate that preliminary rulings may be the start but are not always the end of national courts' and litigants' engagement with European human rights law.

Nowadays it is difficult to think of a Convention article and accompanying case law in relation to EU Member States in which some cross-referencing does not occur. In relation to Article 9, for example, whether as regards the wearing of religious symbols in the workplace or the slaughtering of animals, Luxembourg turns to Strasbourg for guidance,[40] but the reverse can occur too.[41]

In recent years, particularly effective symmetry and synergy can be found in case law pertaining to the rule of law and, in particular, to the safeguarding of judicial independence. The recent judgment in *Tuleya v Poland* provides a particularly good example.[42] The case concerned preliminary investigations in view of disciplinary proceedings against a Polish judge due to, amongst other things, a preliminary question referred by the applicant judge to the CJEU regarding the compatibility of the domestic disciplinary system with EU law. The Court relied on several rulings of the CJEU to conclude that the preliminary investigations relating to a request for a preliminary ruling were contrary to Article 8 ECHR.[43]

In this respect, what one could call virtuous and effective circles have formed on rule of law issues. Both Courts have been referring extensively to the case law of their European counterpart, and in doing so, have strengthened the effectiveness of the protection of the rule of law afforded by their respective jurisprudence. As another example, consider the opinion of the Advocate General in the case of *Simpson and HG* which strongly relied on the Court's chamber judgment in *Guðmundur Andri Ástráðsson v Iceland* to define the notion of 'tribunal established by law'.[44] The judicial dialogue did

[38] ECtHR (GC), App no 931/13 *Satakunnan Markkinaporsi OY and Satamedia OY v Finland* ECLI:CE:ECHR:2017:0627JUD000093113 which concerns the freedom to impart information in the context of an order restraining mass publication of tax information. See references to CJEU case law on data protection and freedom of expression in paras 55–79, 133, 149–51, 158–59, 188, 193, 197 and 212.

[39] See ECtHR, App no 31172/19 *Jehovah's Witnesses v Finland* ECLI:CE:ECHR:2023:0509JUD003117219 which relates to a decision prohibiting the Jehovah's Witnesses religious community from collecting and processing personal data during door-to-door preaching without the data subjects' consent. See references to CJEU case law on collection of personal data in door-to-door activities in paras 39–41, paras 85–87. It is of note that in both *Satakunnan v Finland* (ibid) and *Jehovah's Witness v Finland*, the Court underlined the significance of judicial dialogue between the CJEU and the national courts of EU Member States, in the form of preliminary references to the CJEU, for the protection of fundamental rights within the EU Union (*Satakunnan*, para 212; *Jehovah's Witnesses*, paras 85–87).

[40] See, eg, CJEU (GC), Case C-157/15 *Achbita* ECLI:EU:C:2017:203 and the follow up case law, and the reference to the ECtHR's ruling in *Eweida and others v the United Kingdom* in para 39 of *Achbita*. (ECtHR, App nos 48420/10, 59842/10, 51671/10 36516/10 *Eweida and others v the United Kingdom* ECLI:CE:ECHR:2013:0115JUD004842010).

[41] See, eg, ECtHR, App nos 16760/22 and 10 others *Executief van de Moslims van België and others v Belgium* ECLI:CE:ECHR:2024:0213JUD001676022 and its reference to CJEU case law (para 115).

[42] ECtHR, App nos 21181/19 and 51751/20 *Tuleya v Poland* ECLI:CE:ECHR:2023:0706JUD002118119.

[43] In particular, the ECtHR referred to relevant CJEU case law to determine that the interference in the form of a preliminary investigation regarding a request for a preliminary ruling was contrary to Article 267 of the TFEU. For this reason, the Court concluded that the interference with the applicant's right to respect for his private life was not 'prescribed by law' within the meaning of Article 8 of the Convention (ibid, paras 434–38).

[44] See ECtHR (GC), App no 26374/18 *Guðmundur Andri Ástráðsson v Iceland* ECLI:CE:ECHR:2020:1201JUD002637418, referred to in CJEU, Joined Cases C-542/18 RX-II and C-543/18 RX-II *Erik Simpson and HG*, Opinion of Advocate General Sharpston ECLI:EU:C:2019:977, paras 94–96, and subsequently in the judgment of the Grand Chamber of the CJEU, ECLI:EU:C:2020:232, para 74.

not end there but circled back to Strasbourg. In its Grand Chamber judgment concerning the same Icelandic case, following referral, the Court, in turn, extensively referred to the case law of the Luxembourg court – including the Grand Chamber judgment in *Simpson and HG* which had been handed down in the interim.[45]

As a result of this intensive indirect dialogue between the two European courts, a shared understanding of the requirement to have tribunals established by law has emerged. In this way, the European Courts have sought to construct a solid bulwark against threats to common values underpinning the Convention and the EU Treaties – common values which derive from Europe's common constitutional heritage.[46]

It is of course true that there were some areas in which the case law of the two European courts seemed to diverge or showed potential for doing so. Think, for example, of the potentially difficult conciliation of the principle of mutual trust with the protection of human rights of individuals or groups of individuals.[47] Here too, however, recent case law demonstrates signs of increased alignment. As mentioned previously, in *Avotiņš v Latvia* the Grand Chamber confirmed the legitimacy, in principle, of mutual trust mechanisms integral to the functioning of EU law.[48] However, it also emphasised that their application in practice should not endanger respect for human rights and recalled the requirement imposed by the Convention according to which the court in an executing State must at least be empowered to conduct a review commensurate with the gravity of any serious allegation of a violation of human rights in the issuing State.[49] Mutual recognition mechanisms must not leave gaps or give rise to particular situations which would render the protection of the human rights guaranteed by the Convention manifestly deficient.

The CJEU, in cases such as *Aranyosi and Căldăraru*,[50] *Dorobantu*,[51] *Openbaar Ministerie*[52] and *EDL*,[53] has further elaborated on the functioning of mutual trust mechanisms with reference to the primacy, effectiveness and unity of EU law. But, with time,

[45] See the extensive references to CJEU case law in ECtHR (GC), App no 26374/18 *Guðmundur Andri Ástráðsson*, (see n 44 above), paras 130–39 and 239.

[46] See, for an excellent illustration of this, the CJEU (GC), Joined Cases C-562/21 PPU and C-563/21 PPU *X and Y v Openbaar Ministerie* ECLI:EU:C:2022:100, paras 79–80, regarding the execution of an EAW issued by an EU Member State and the two-step assessment required under EU law: 'In the context of that assessment, the executing judicial authority may also take account of the case-law of the European Court of Human Rights, in which a breach of the requirement for a tribunal established by law in respect of the procedure for the appointment of judges has been established (…). For the sake of completeness, it should also be added that those relevant factors also include constitutional case-law of the issuing Member State, which challenges the primacy of EU law and the binding nature of the ECHR as well as the binding force of judgments of the Court of Justice and of the European Court of Human Rights relating to compliance with EU law and with that convention of rules of that Member State governing the organisation of its judicial system, in particular the appointment of judges.'

[47] Contrast especially the early case law of ECtHR in ECtHR (GC), App no 30696/09 *MSS v Belgium and Greece* ECLI:CE:ECHR:2011:0121JUD003069609 with that in CJEU (GC), Joined Cases C-411/10 and C-493/10 *NS v United Kingdom* ECLI:EU:C:2011:865.

[48] ECtHR (GC), App no 17502/07 *Avotiņš* (see n 10 above).

[49] ibid, para 114.

[50] CJEU (GC), Case C-404/15 *Aranyosi and Căldăraru v Generalstaatsanwaltschaft Bremen* ECLI:EU:C:2016:198.

[51] CJEU (GC), Case C-128/18 *Dorobantu* ECLI:EU:C:2019:857.

[52] CJEU, Joined Cases C-562/21 PPU and C-563/21 PPU *Openbaar Ministerie* (see n 46 above).

[53] CJEU (GC), Case C-699/21 *EDL* ECLI:EU:C:2023:295.

it seems to have nuanced some of the terms of Opinion 2/13,[54] emphasising the need to ensure *effective* protection of fundamental rights and explicitly referring to the long-standing role of the ECtHR and its case law. In turn, this has allowed national courts, exceptionally, but where required, to rebut the presumption of fundamental rights compliance in some cases involving the area of freedom, security and justice.

As I mentioned earlier, the Strasbourg Court assesses EU Member States' compliance with their Convention obligations in the light of the *Bosphorus* presumption of equivalent protection, where the conditions for its application are met.[55] *Bivolaru and Moldovan v France* concerned the surrender of an applicant to the Romanian authorities under a European arrest warrant (EAW).[56] The Strasbourg Court considered that the presumption could apply. The discretionary power on the part of the national judicial executing authority to assess the facts and circumstances and the legal consequences which they entailed had to be exercised within the framework strictly delineated by the CJEU's case law and in order to ensure the execution of a legal obligation in full compliance with EU law, namely Article 4 of the Charter. The latter guaranteed equivalent protection to that provided by Article 3 of the Convention. In those circumstances the executing judicial authority could not be said to enjoy an autonomous margin of manoeuvre in deciding whether or not to execute a European arrest warrant, such as to preclude application of the presumption of equivalent protection. Assessing whether a respondent State enjoys some sort of discretion under EU law, which is relevant to the operation of the presumption, is a delicate matter. The Strasbourg Court has to ensure that the conditions for the operation of the presumption are present without trespassing into an interpretation of EU law which it is not competent to make.[57]

In *Bivolaru and Moldovan*, for the first time, the Strasbourg court found that the presumption ceased to apply because the protection which had been afforded by the courts in the executing State was manifestly deficient.[58] Cogent information on the risk of Article 3 violations in the issuing State, given the centre where it was proposed that the applicant would be detained on execution of the EAW, had been ignored by the French authorities.

The Court also carefully takes into account the important enforcement interests that are at stake in the framework of, for example, the EAW. The judgment in *Romeo Castaño v Belgium* bears witness to this. In that case, the refusal by Belgium to execute a EAW issued by Spain was found to have violated the procedural limb of Article 2 of the Convention, the refusal not having been underpinned by a sufficient factual basis.[59]

In this context, let me reiterate that the Strasbourg court does not have the authority to assess the validity or the correct interpretation of EU law. It must refrain

[54] See CJEU, Opinion 2/13 *Opinion pursuant to Article 218(11) TFEU* ECLI:EU:C:2014:2454, paras 191–92.

[55] ECtHR (GC), App no 45036/98 *Bosphorus* (see n 4 above).

[56] ECtHR, App nos 40324/16 and 12623/17 *Bivolaru and Moldovan* ECLI:CE:ECHR:2021:0325JUD004032416.

[57] See ECtHR, App no 44460/16 *O'Sullivan McCarthy Mussel Development v Ireland* ECLI:CE:ECHR:2018:0607JUD004446016, para 112, where it left open a question regarding the effects of an infringement judgment.

[58] ECtHR, App nos 40324/16 and 12623/17 *Bivolaru and Moldovan v France* (see n 56 above).

[59] ECtHR, App no 8351/17 *Romeo Castaño v Belgium* ECLI:CE:ECHR:2019:0709JUD000835117.

from trespassing into the exclusive domain of the CJEU in this regard.[60] Its role is confined to ascertaining whether the effects of adjudication by national courts and authorities in EU Member States in an individual case are compatible with the Convention. Nevertheless, the Court may sanction the lack or incorrect application of EU law in light of the Convention, thereby contributing to its effective implementation.

Sometimes case law differences may appear to be significant and more long-lasting.[61] Most of the time, however, this results from the fact that the Strasbourg Court and the CJEU are faced with different legal constraints that are specific to their respective legal systems and carry out an examination whose nature is somewhat distinct. In such circumstances, it is the task of the European Courts to be clear and transparent that such divergence exists, and why, to facilitate the work of national courts. An illustrative case to consider is *Krombach v France*.[62] In this case, the Court made it clear that the fact that the principle of *ne bis in idem* has a transnational dimension in EU law has no bearing on the applicability of *ne bis in idem* in ECHR law which only applies *within* the national legal systems of the Member States. Let me emphasise here however, as the Strasbourg Court did in its ruling, that the Convention does not prevent the States parties from granting more extensive legal protection, be it through domestic law, other international treaties, or EU law.[63]

****

4. ECHR and EU Law Articulation in the Future

So what does the future hold and what does it require of us as European jurists and judges? I'll focus in my conclusions on questions relating to judicial dialogue, methodological alignment, Article 2 and accession.

In terms of judicial dialogue, that between the Strasbourg and Luxembourg courts has gone from strength to strength in recent years. Informal, bilateral meetings between the two courts take place and are open and constructive. Cross-referencing

[60] See, eg, ECtHR, (GC), App no 12738/10 *Jeunesse v the Netherlands* ECLI:CE:ECHR:2014:1003JUD001273810, para 110; ECtHR, App no 39061/11 *Thimothawes v Belgium* ECLI:CE:ECHR:2017:0404JUD003906111, para 71 or ECtHR, App nos 40324/16 and 12623/17 *Bivolaru and Moldovan v France* (see n 56 above), para 135. See, however, ECtHR, App no 27122/14 *Spasov v Romania* ECLI:CE:ECHR:2022:1206JUD002712214, on the thin line which may exist in some exceptional cases.

[61] The case law on mass surveillance, for instance, continues to show some differences as regards derogations and legal safeguards. Compare, for example, the CJEU's Grand Chamber judgments in CJEU (GC), Case C-293/12 and C-594/12 *Digital Rights Ireland* (see n 33 above) and CJEU, Joined Cases C-203/15 and C-698/15 *Tele2 Sverige AB v Post- och telestyrelsen and Secretary of State for the Home Department v Tom Watson and Others* ECLI:EU:C:2016:970 with the ECtHR's Grand Chamber judgments in ECtHR (GC), App no 35252/08 *Centrum För Rättvisa v Sweden*, ECLI:CE:ECHR:2021:0525JUD003525208, and App nos 58170/13, 62322/14 and 24960/15 *Big Brother Watch and others v the United Kingdom* (see n 33 above). See, however, the recent plenary judgment of the CJEU in Case C-470/21 *La Quadrature du Net* (see n 36 above), for some signs of adjustments on the CJEU's side.

[62] ECtHR, App no 67521/14 *Krombach v France* ECLI:CE:ECHR:2018:0220DEC006752114.

[63] ibid, paras 38–39.

continues apace. The *Bosphorus* presumption survived both the obligation to accede in Article 6 TEU and the indefinite postponement by Opinion 2/13 of the execution of that obligation. Mutual recognition, a potential sticking point of considerable importance, has, as I have explained, been the subject of important judgments on both sides. The development of EU legislative standards in domains such as whistleblowing,[64] domestic violence,[65] the digital environment,[66] and artificial intelligence[67] all point to the need for further fruitful judicial dialogue in future.

Article 52 § 3 of the EU Charter ensures that the EU must respect the Convention minimum standard as its floor. However, it is worth repeating that the living instrument doctrine means that the Convention standard may adapt and is adjusted over time,[68] such that the CJEU will have to keep track of such changes for Article 52 § 3 of the Charter to be respected. In addition, it is important to stress that dialogue in this field is not and can never be bilateral. National judges must remain key. If one looks at the use by national courts of the preliminary reference procedure since recognition in the Lisbon Treaty of the equal legal value of the Charter, national judges clearly see judicial dialogue in the field of human rights in trilateral terms. This is well demonstrated in questions referred to the CJEU which engage extensively with the ECHR.[69]

As regards methodological alignment, the assessment of fundamental rights in a democracy entails complex balancing exercises either between individual rights

[64] See, as regards EU law, Directive 2019/1937/EU of 23 October 2019 on the protection of persons who report breaches of Union law [2019] OJ L 305, which had to be transposed by the EU Member States by 17 December 2021. See also the recent ruling in ECtHR (GC), App no 21884/18 *Halet v Luxembourg* ECLI:CE:ECHR:2023:0214JUD002188418 on the protection of whistle-blowers and the references to EU law in paras 58, 99, 101, 106.

[65] See in particular the proposal for an EU Directive on combating violence against women and domestic violence COM/2022/105. The Commission has also repeatedly emphasised the need to align EU law with established international standards, notably those set out in the Istanbul Convention, which the EU has now ratified.

[66] As regards EU law, see the EU Digital Markets Act and Digital Services Act which have been adopted and which entered into force on 1 November 2022 and 16 November 2022 respectively. As regards the Court's case law, see, eg, ECtHR (GC), App no 64569/09 *Delfi AS v Estonia* ECLI:CE:ECHR:2015:0616JUD006456909, regarding the award of damages against an internet news portal for offensive comments posted on its site by anonymous third parties (see references to EU law, paras 50–57, 147) and ECtHR (GC), App no 45581/15 *Sanchez v France* ECLI:CE:ECHR:2023:0515JUD004558115 on a criminal fine imposed on a politician for failing to delete Islamophobic comments made by third parties from his Facebook 'wall' which he used for his election campaign (see references to EU law, paras 74–78). In relation to early examples of AI case law see ECtHR, App no 11519/20 *Glukhin v Russia* ECLI:CE:ECHR:2023:0704JUD001151920 on the use of facial recognition technology to sanction demonstrators.

[67] Note that, following the conference, the AI Act was adopted (see Regulation (EU) 2024/1689 of the European Parliament and of the Council of 13 June 2024 laying down harmonised rules on artificial intelligence [2024] OJ L, 2024/1689).

[68] See, eg, the clarification and consolidation of the general principles on whistle-blowing in ECtHR (GC), App no 21884/18 *Halet* (see n 64 above) or the development of the Court's case law on the recognition of same-sex couples as explained in ECtHR (GC), App nos 40792/10 and 2 others, *Fedotova and Others v Russia* ECLI:CE:ECHR:2023:0117JUD004079210, paras 167, 209.

[69] As regards preliminary references, see CJEU (GC), Case C-404/15 *Aranyosi and Caldararu* (see n 50 above), and CJEU (GC), Case C-216/18 PPU *LM* ECLI:EU:C:2018:586; or CJEU, Case C-128/18 *Dorobantu* (see n 51 above) on prison conditions in the context of execution of an EAW, where detailed questions translating, in reality, ECtHR case law on Art 3 ECHR and prison conditions were addressed to the Court of Justice by a German court. See also, more recently, the invocation of the ECHR in a reference on access of a minor to legal assistance in criminal proceedings in CJEU, Case C-603/22 *MS and others* ECLI:EU:C:2024:685, para 57.

(eg, privacy v expression) or between the rights of the individual and the collective interest (eg, privacy v national security or the fight against crime). The balance struck often reflects or has to take into consideration complex societal choices. The ECtHR has repeatedly stated that:

> [I]nherent in the whole of the Convention is a search for a fair balance between the demands of the general interest of the community and the requirements of the protection of the individual's fundamental rights.[70]

Balancing is the bread and butter of a human rights court. However, as per Opinion 2/13, EU fundamental rights, as recognised in particular by the Charter, have to be interpreted and applied within the EU in accordance with the special characteristics of the constitutional framework referred to in that opinion.[71]

As different and more complex human rights questions have arrived in Luxembourg, requiring the CJEU to engage in more and more difficult and sensitive balancing exercises, one can discern some methodological alignment with the Strasbourg Court in its approach in some cases or on some issues. Use of emblematic tools of Convention law – such as the living instrument doctrine or the margin of appreciation – can be seen in recent CJEU case law. The latter was used, for instance, to find a balance between animal welfare and freedom of religion in the context of ritual slaughtering,[72] or to adjust the CJEU's first preliminary rulings in relation to the wearing by employees of religious symbols.[73] Was some sort of EU living instrument doctrine not present at least in spirit in the Opinion of Advocate General Ćapeta in *KS and KD* on jurisdiction in relation to the CFSP matters and the protection of fundamental rights?[74]

As regards Article 2 TEU, one sees very clear symmetry between the values underpinning the Council of Europe and the Convention and the EU. And we see growing use of this values provision by the CJEU and its interlocutors, in particular the European Commission, in recent years. In its two conditionality judgments regarding Poland and

[70] ECtHR, App no 14038/88 *Soering v the United Kingdom* ECLI:CE:ECHR:1989:0707JUD001403888, para 89.

[71] CJEU, Opinion 2/13 (see n 54 above), paras 155–76.

[72] CJEU (GC), Case C-336/19 *Centraal Israëlitisch Consistorie van België and others* ECLI: EU:C:2020:1031, para 67 on the margin of appreciation and para 77 on the living instrument doctrine. On the subject of ritual slaughter, see also the judgment of the ECtHR in ECtHR, App nos 16760/22 and 10 others, *Executief van de Moslims van België and others* (see n 41 above).

[73] See, eg, CJEU (GC), Joined Cases C-804/18 and C-341/19 *IX v WABE eV and MH Müller Handels GmbH v MJ* ECLI:EU:C:2021:594, para 86 and para 88.

[74] CJEU, Joined Cases C-29/22 P and C-44/22 P *KS and KD v Council and Others* Opinion of Advocate General Ćapeta, ECLI:EU:C:2023:901, para 124: 'EU institutions and bodies are always bound by fundamental rights, and the choice to infringe those rights is not an available political or strategic choice, including in the area of the CFSP. If the purpose of the jurisdictional limitation in the CFSP is to prevent the EU Courts from intervening in political and strategic decisions in the area of the CFSP, such a purpose does not require the exclusion of jurisdiction to review alleged breaches of fundamental rights. There is a limit imposed on political and strategic decisions, as they can never be in breach of fundamental rights. Article 24(1) TEU and Article 275 TFEU must, therefore, be interpreted as not preventing the EU Courts from policing such constitutional limits by hearing actions for damages brought by individuals for alleged breaches of fundamental rights by CFSP measures.' See, subsequently, CJEU, Joined Cases C-29/22 P and C-44/22 P *KS and KD* ECLI:EU:C:2024:725, for the CJEU's reconciliation of its narrow jurisdiction in relation to the CFSP with Article 47 of the Charter and Articles 6 and 13 ECHR.

Hungary, for example, handed down in 2022, the CJEU held, in relation to Article 2 TEU values, that:

> [they] have been identified and are shared by the Member States. They define the very identity of the European Union as a common legal order. Thus, the European Union must be able to defend those values, within the limits of its powers as laid down by the Treaties.[75]

These are landmark judgments, which come at a critical time, and which built on previous judgments, such as *Associação Sindical dos Juizes Portgueses*,[76] in which the CJEU innovatively and to great effect combined Articles 2 and 19(1) TEU.[77] However, one of several questions which now arise in Europe's multi-level system for the protection of human rights is what future role Article 2 TEU is set to play. Must it be invoked in combination with another 'concretising' provision of EU law, or can it serve as a self-standing basis for the defence of the rights which the values listed in that provision seek to protect?[78]

The Treaty of Lisbon[79] and the recognition of the equal legal value of the Charter were premised on the explicit inclusion of the principle of conferral and general provisions setting out the limits to the scope and functioning of EU law. Those provisions sought, in essence, to channel and even to control the potentially centripetal force of the Charter and EU law more generally.[80] As previously evidenced in the case law of the

[75] CJEU, Case C-156/21 *Hungary v Parliament and Council* ECLI:EU:C:2022:97, para 127; reflected also in CJEU, Case C-157/21 *Poland v Parliament and Council* ECLI:EU:C:2022:98, para 145.

[76] CJEU (GC), Case C-64/16 *Associação Sindical dos Juízes Portugueses v Tribunal de Contas* ECLI:EU:C:2018:117.

[77] See LD Spieker, 'Breathing Life into the Union's Common Values: On the Judicial Application of Article 2 TEU in the EU Value Crisis' (2019) 20 German Law Journal 1182, who argues that the combination of Articles 19 (1) TEU and 2 TEU have a mutually-amplifying effect, with the former facilitating judicial enforcement of the value at stake due to its greater precision and Article 2 TEU providing an extension of scope beyond that of the EU Charter and EU law more generally.

[78] See, eg, LS Rossi, 'La valeur juridique des valeurs. L'article 2 TUE: relations avec d'autres dispositions de droit primaire de l'UE et remèdes juridictionnels' (2020) 56 *Revue trimestrielle de droit européen* 639; or LD Spieker, 'Breathing Life into the Union's Common Values' (2019). See also M Bonelli, 'Infringement Action 2.0: How to Protect EU Values before the Court of Justice' (2022) 18 European Constitutional Law Review 30.

[79] Treaty of Lisbon amending the Treaty on European Union and the Treaty establishing the European Community, signed at Lisbon, 13 December 2007 [2007] OJ C 306/1.

[80] See CJEU, Case C-235/17 *Commission v Hungary (Usufruct Over Agricultural Land)* Opinion of Advocate General Øe, ECLI:EU:C:2018:971, paras 68–69: 'It is important not to lose sight of the context in which that question [relating to when the Court of Justice of the European Union has jurisdiction to determine a failure to respect the rights guaranteed by the Charter on Fundamental Rights of the European Union] arises. In essence, the extent to which the Member States are bound, under EU law, by the requirements regarding the protection of fundamental rights is a constitutional issue, which is delicate and fundamental, concerning the division of powers in the EU. Requiring Member States, in their actions, to respect fundamental rights as provided for in EU law has the effect of limiting the regulatory and policy approaches available in those Member States, while the power of the EU to set the boundaries of what is possible increases correspondingly. … Moreover, institutionally, at issue is the extent to which the [Court of Justice of the European Union], as the highest court, has the jurisdiction to take the place of national constitutional courts and the European Court of Human Rights … in monitoring the legislation and actions of the Member States in the light of fundamental rights. Undoubtedly mindful of those issues, the drafters of the Charter took care expressly to limit the circumstances in which it applies to national legislation.' On the limits to CJEU jurisdiction following the Treaty of Lisbon see K Lenaerts, 'Exploring the Limits of the EU Charter of Fundamental Rights' (2012) 8 European Constitutional Law Review 375.

CJEU, where a situation was not covered by EU law, it was to national remedies and, if they failed, to Strasbourg and the ECHR that litigants were directed.[81]

For decades, the central core of human rights and freedoms underpinning our democracies have been safeguarded by national constitutional courts, subject to the external supervision of the ECtHR.[82] The latter not only renders justice in a given case, but also elucidates, safeguards, and develops the rules instituted in the ECHR, thereby contributing to the observance by Contracting Parties, including EU Member States, of the Convention engagements undertaken by them.[83] As the EU evolved into the integrated and comprehensive legal and political system that it is today, it was thus through the ECHR system that strength and concrete expression was given to the common European values now set out explicitly in Article 2 TEU.[84] Good illustrations of the importance of the ECHR system for the EU's value alignment and defence can be found in the Copenhagen accession criteria, in being a party to the ECHR as a sine qua non of EU membership or even post-membership,[85] in the terms of the TEU and the Charter itself, and in the importance accorded in the Commission's annual Rule of Law Reports to Member State execution of Strasbourg judgments. The latter are the expression of the ECtHR's specific mandate to sanction infringements of human rights committed by the Member States, on condition that domestic remedies have been exhausted and that subsidiarity and applicable margins are respected.

The future use to which Article 2 TEU is put, the expansion of EU competences, the accession of the EU to the ECHR provided for in Article 6 § 2 TEU, greater future alignment between EU and Council of Europe membership, given that eight members of the latter are in line to accede to the former, or the ongoing war on our European borders, to name but a few;[86] all these things will influence how a conference of European lawyers will discuss the same topics we will discuss today and tomorrow several years hence.

This brings me to my final considerations, which relate to EU accession to the Convention.[87] Since June 2020, the 46+1 group has held regular meetings in view of finding a new accession agreement. During these meetings, the group undertook to resolve all issues raised in Opinion 2/13. Their final meeting took place in March 2023

[81] See, eg, CJEU (GC), Case C-256/11 *Dereci and Others* ECLI:EU:C:2011:734, paras 70–73; or CJEU, Case C-235/17 *Commission v Hungary* Opinion of Advocate General Øe (see n 80 above), paras 108–09.

[82] See, eg, the extensive case law referenced in the ECtHR Factsheet on the right to vote www.echr.coe.int/documents/d/echr/FS_Vote_ENG accessed 30 May 2025.

[83] ECtHR (GC), App no 35589/08 *Nagmetov v Russia* ECLI:CE:ECHR:2017:0330JUD003558908, para 64.

[84] See, eg, ECtHR (GC), App no 23380/09 *Bouyid v Belgium* ECLI:CE:ECHR:2015:0928JUD002338009, para 89 (concerning the value of human dignity); ECtHR (GC), App no 24833/94 *Matthews* (see n 5 above), para 42 (concerning the concept of effective political democracy); ECtHR, App no 54711/15 *Jurčić v Croatia* ECLI:CE:ECHR:2021:0204JUD005471115, para 83 (concerning gender equality and non-discrimination); ECtHR (GC), App no 26374/18 *Guðmundur Andri Ástráðsson* (see n 44 above), para 211 (concerning the value of the rule of law); ECtHR (GC), App no 20452/14 *Molla Sali* (see n 29 above) (concerning the rights of minorities); and ECtHR (GC), App no 43835/11 *SAS v France* ECLI:CE:ECHR:2014:0701JUD004383511, para 128 (concerning pluralism, tolerance and broadmindedness are hallmarks of a democratic society).

[85] See, eg, CJEU, Case C-327/18 *Minister for Justice and Equality v* RO ECLI:EU:C:2018:733, para 61.

[86] Turkey, North Macedonia, Montenegro, Serbia, Albania, Moldova, Ukraine and Bosnia Herzegovina have all been recognised as candidates for EU membership.

[87] Article 59(2) of the ECHR states that 'the European Union may accede to this Convention.' Article 6(2) of the TEU provides that 'the Union shall accede to the European Convention for the Protection of Human Rights and Fundamental Freedoms'.

and the only outstanding issue concerns EU acts in the area of the Common Foreign and Security Policy, which the EU undertook to address internally. Therefore, the future of EU accession lies, for the time being, in the hands of the EU and its Member States. As President of the Strasbourg Court (and a former one by the time of publication), I do not consider it appropriate to comment on a draft agreement which is the subject of ongoing discussion and political negotiation. Such discussion is best left to others and, in the context of the conference, to the expert panel at the conference, representing both sides of the negotiating table. However, I can say that I find it striking how much has been written on Opinion 2/13, and yet how little consideration has been given to the concrete dynamics and consequences of EU accession were it to occur – the inclusion of a non-State actor into the Convention system, the question of the necessary autonomy of the ECtHR within the Council of Europe, given that it lacks its own budget and legal personality, the consequences for the *Bosphorus* presumption of equivalent protection, the funding, training and recruitment of suitable staff (which should occur well in advance of accession itself) or the type of applications which would be lodged against the EU before the Strasbourg Court. The latter will be radically different to those in which the Strasbourg Court currently looks indirectly, via Member State transposition and application, at EU law. Accession should not just be viewed and discussed as a politically desirable outcome. It should be prepared for in detail and in advance as a major constitutional departure for both the EU and Convention systems. Whatever final agreement is reached, it must ensure a bridge between those two systems which works well in practice.

****

In conclusion, while the two European systems analysed during the course of the conference may differ, the universality and indivisibility of the human rights and fundamental freedoms which they both seek to protect is clearly stated in both the TEU[88] and the EU Charter and is central to their effective protection within Europe's multi-level system for the protection of human rights. It is now over 30 years since the first major EU competence expansion in the Maastricht Treaty with implications for human rights protection and it will soon be 16 years since the EU Charter was recognised as having equal legal value to the EU Treaties. As the scope of EU law has expanded, jurisdiction over fundamental rights has grown accordingly, and the CJEU enters terrain previously occupied by national supreme and constitutional courts and, as a last resort, the ECtHR. Many of the dynamics which I have sought to explore in this keynote are due to this increasing overlap in matters which are brought before the two European courts. Navigating this multi-level system has been challenging and it will continue to be so. It falls to judges and jurists at national and European level to be rigorous and clear about the system and standards we want to uphold and to work together to contribute to harmonious and effective protection of human rights across Europe. Bridging gaps in knowledge of and between the two systems, as this event seeks to do, is a small but essential part of that endeavour.

[88] See Article 21(1) TEU and the reference in CJEU's judgment in Joined Cases C-29/22 P and C-44/22 P *KS and KD* (see n 74 above), para 66.

PART II

Who Can Go Where?

3

Collective Enforcement of Fundamental Rights via the CJEU and the ECtHR

JANNEKE GERARDS AND ELIF ERKEN

1. Introduction

In this chapter, we address the procedural possibilities of collective enforcement of fundamental rights through litigation by individuals and civil society organisations via the Court of Justice of the European Union (CJEU) and the European Court of Human Rights (ECtHR). Our point of departure is that, of course, having access to justice through individual court proceedings is essential. If individuals have become a victim of a violation of a fundamental right or if there is a concrete threat of being subjected to such a violation, they must be able to obtain redress by using an effective legal (preferably judicial) remedy. However, it has increasingly come to be recognised that individual litigation can, among other things, be highly burdensome and expensive for individuals. Moreover, many fundamental rights issues extend beyond the individual case and may be structural in nature. It might be difficult to address these through individual procedures that focus on the concrete circumstances of a specific case. To protect fundamental rights effectively, it therefore may be desirable to also make use of collective forms of enforcement.[1] By that notion, the present chapter refers to procedural avenues that allow individuals or civil society groups to seize a court in the public interest with the aim of contributing to general justice rather than (or on top of) purely individual justice.[2]

[1] See, eg, Ol De Schutter, 'Public Interest Litigation before the European Court of Human Rights' (2006), 13 *Maastricht Journal of European and Comparative Law* 9, 10–11. In addition, more focus is nowadays on forms of ex-ante-protection, such as fundamental rights impact assessments, especially in relation to algorithmic and AI-based decision-making. See, eg, H Janssen, M Seng Ah Lee and J Singh, 'Practical Fundamental Rights Impact Assessments' (2022) 30 *International Journal of Law and Information Technology* 200; A Montelero, 'Human Rights Impact Assessment and AI', in A Montelero (ed), *Beyond Data. Human Rights, Ethical and Social Impact Assessment* (The Hague, Springer, 2022); J Gerards, I Muis et al, *Fundamental Rights and Algorithms Impact Assessment – FRAIA* (Netherlands Ministry of the Interior, 2022) www.government.nl/documents/reports/2022/03/31/impact-assessment-fundamental-rights-and-algorithms accessed 7 May 2025.

[2] ibid. See also J Gerards and L Glas, 'Access to Justice in the European Convention on Human Rights System' (2017) 35 *Netherlands Quarterly of Human Rights* 11. Moreover, it has been argued that collective procedures may help to streamline litigation and thereby reduce the overall burden of the judiciary; *cf* S Bogojevic, 'Judicial Protection of Individual Applicants Revisited: Access to Justice through the Prism of Judicial Subsidiarity' (2015) 34 *Yearbook of European Law* 5, 8.

Civil society organisations, notably NGOs, play an increasingly important role in such collective enforcement actions.[3] In addition to their possibilities for intervening in court proceedings and in assisting in the implementation of judgments, which are explored elsewhere in this volume,[4] they can do so in different ways. Best known is their option to engage in strategic or public interest litigation, with NGOs representing a larger group of persons (eg, children or migrants) or an identifiable, relatively specifically defined general interest (eg, the interest of non-discrimination or protection of personal data). Less known, but perhaps equally important is that they can support individual litigants in bringing proceedings and can assist (or even formally represent) them throughout judicial procedures. Those proceedings are then individual in nature and are focussed on individual redress, but the assistance and support by NGOs may help highlight more general issues that go beyond the individual case and are relevant also to the position of others.

The current chapter aims to describe and analyse the various legal possibilities that individuals and civil society organisations currently have to engage in collective enforcement of fundamental rights via the CJEU and the ECtHR. Procedural rules on standing and their consequences for individuals' and civil society's ability to enforce fundamental rights are core to the subsequent sections. Section 2 discusses the procedural possibilities that individuals and civil society organisations have to enforce fundamental rights via the CJEU, whereas Section 3 focusses on the various rules on admissibility and representation at the ECtHR. Section 4 compares and integrates these findings to provide a general idea of the currently existing possibilities for collective enforcement of fundamental rights at the level of the European supranational courts. The paper concludes that on that level there is considerable potential, but there are still important limitations to the ability of individuals and civil society organisations to engage in collective enforcement of fundamental rights.

[3] The section on NGOs and the ECtHR draws on a previous publication by one of the authors of the current chapter; see E Erken, 'Scholarly and Empirical Consideration on Expanding Access for Non-governmental Organisations before the European Court of Human Rights' (2025) 6(2) *European Convention on Human Rights Law Review*. The contribution here presents a condensed version of the data and arguments presented therein, tailored specifically to the distinction between individual and general justice.

[4] See ch 4. See on third party interventions, eg, J Krommendijk and K van der Pas, 'To Intervene or Not to Intervene: Intervention Before the Court of Justice of the European Union in Environmental and Migration Law' (2022) 26 *The International Journal of Human Rights* 1394; C Loven, *Fundamental Rights Violations by Private Actors and the Procedure before the European Court of Human Rights* (Antwerp, Larcier/Intersentia, 2022); N Bürli, *Third-Party Interventions before the European Court of Human Rights* (Cambridge, Cambridge University Press, 2018). On the role to be played by NGOs and NHRIs in the execution of judgments, see eg, A Küçüksu, 'Enforcing Rights Beyond Litigation: Mapping NGO Strategies in Monitoring ECtHR Judgement Implementation' (2022) 22 *Human Rights Law Review* 1; E Erken, 'Non-Governmental Organisations and National Human Rights Institutions Monitoring the Execution of Strasbourg Judgments: An Empirical Perspective on Rule 9 Communications' (2021) 21 *Human Rights Law Review* 724; E Erken, 'The Participation of Non-Governmental Organisations and National Human Rights Institutions in the Execution of Judgments of the Strasbourg Court' (2020) 1 *European Convention on Human Rights Law Review* 248; S Dothan, 'A Virtual Wall of Shame: The New Way of Imposing Reputational Sanctions on Defiant States' (2017) 27 *Duke Journal of Comparative and International Law* 141; L Miara and V Prais, 'The Role of Civil Society in the Execution of Judgments of the European Court of Human Rights' (2012) *European Human Rights Law Review* 528; L McIntosh Sundstrom, 'Advocacy Beyond Litigation: Examining Russian NGO Efforts on Implementation of European Court of Human Rights Judgments' (2012) *Communist and Post-Communist Studies* 255.

2. Collective Enforcement of Fundamental Rights by Individuals and NGOs via the CJEU

2.1. Introduction

EU law offers a variety of procedural possibilities for EU fundamental rights to be further interpreted and enforced by the CJEU, as is also explained in other chapters in this volume. Of interest to the current chapter are the options for individuals and civil society organisations to contribute to the collective enforcement of fundamental rights, for instance through public interest litigation or representation of individuals in cases that might have a broader impact. As the present section shows, such options are limited. Direct standing rights for individuals and civil society organisations before the CJEU exist, but as explained in Section 2.2, it is very difficult for them to contest EU legislative and regulatory acts for incompatibility with the EU Charter. To a certain degree, as is set out in Section 2.3, this is different for the preliminary reference procedure of Article 267 of the Treaty on the Functioning of the European Union (TFEU). The indirect access to the CJEU that this procedure offers, allows individuals and civil society organisations to engage the CJEU in explaining and detailing the meaning of EU Charter provisions. However, it is shown that this procedure, too, is difficult to use by individuals and civil society organisations with the purpose of collective enforcement of fundamental rights.

2.2. Direct Collective Enforcement of EU Fundamental Rights: Article 263 TFEU

In cases brought under Article 263 TFEU, the CJEU may be asked to focus its attention on the compatibility of individual EU acts with the EU Charter of Fundamental Rights.[5] This provision provides an important procedural instrument to enforce EU fundamental rights in individual cases and offer individual justice. Successful individual annulment actions have been brought, for example, against sanctions that formed a breach of procedural and property rights, or in relation to breaches of privacy rights resulting from competition law enforcement actions.[6] This procedure clearly has some potential for collective enforcement of the EU Charter, in particular because of the broader

[5] On the level of EU civil servants, there are also possibilities to bring a case on a violation of a fundamental right, for instance when employment decisions have been made without taking due account of the civil servants' freedom of expression or when internal rules seem to be discriminatory. However, since the present paper focuses on access to court on the level of the Member States, these procedures are not further addressed.

[6] On sanctions mechanisms, see famously CJEU, Joined Cases C-584/10 P, C-593/10 P and C-595/10 P *European Commission and Others v Kadi* ECLI:EU:C:2013:518. On privacy breaches in competition law proceedings, see, eg, CJEU, Case C-583/13 P *Deutsche Bahn AG and Others v Commission* ECLI:EU:C:2015:404; see also, eg, J Wouters and M Ovádek, 'Fundamental Rights in EU Competition Enforcement', in J Wouters and M Ovádek (eds), *The European Union and Human Rights* (Oxford, Oxford University Press, 2021). De Schutter has shown that in some cases, NGOs or organisations can act on behalf of individuals in this respect (De Schutter, 'Public Interest Litigation' (2006) 20).

precedential relevance of the resulting judgments of the CJEU.[7] Moreover, although civil society organisations cannot lodge such complaints on behalf of an individual applicant,[8] they still can play a role in the background by assisting individual applicants in identifying legal arguments and procedural strategies.

Nevertheless, Article 263 TFEU procedures on individual EU acts infringing fundamental rights tend to focus on obtaining individual redress and usually concentrate on the concrete circumstances of the case. From a perspective of collective enforcement and public interest litigation, it could be more useful for individuals and civil society organisations to ask the CJEU to look more generally into the compatibility of EU legislation with fundamental rights. Indeed, Article 263(4) TFEU allows for procedures to be brought contesting the compatibility of EU legislative and regulatory acts with the Charter of Fundamental Rights of the European Union (CFREU or Charter). However, in order for 'non-privileged' actors (individuals, organisations) to have standing, they must be able to show that their complaint concerns an act which is of 'direct and individual concern to them', or a regulatory act 'which is of concern to them and does not entail implementing measures'.[9]

The CJEU has given a restrictive interpretation to the standing requirements of Article 263(4) TFEU.[10] The criteria applied by the Court in this respect are those laid down in its classic 1963 *Plaumann* judgment.[11] According to the Court,

> persons other than those to whom a decision is addressed may only claim to be individually concerned if that decision affects them by reason of certain attributes which are peculiar to them or by reason of circumstances in which they are differentiated from all other persons and by virtue of these factors distinguishes them individually just as in the case of the person addressed.

Even though Article 263(4) was reformulated slightly in the Lisbon Treaty with the aim of widening the standing rights, the *Plaumann* criteria continue to apply in defining if a party is sufficiently individually concerned.[12] This strict interpretation of the requirements of Article 263(4) TFEU by the CJEU makes it very difficult for individuals and civil society organisations to contest any form of legislation or regulatory acts. This is true also if a procedure concerns an alleged violation of fundamental rights issues and is of a rather more collective nature. This is illustrated by the judgment in *Sabo and Others*, where the CJEU held that:

> the claim that an act infringes fundamental rights is not sufficient in itself for it to be established that the action brought by an individual is admissible, without running the risk of

[7] This is witnessed clearly by the judgment in *Kadi* (see n 6 above), which also proved to be of relevance to many other cases concerning EU sanctions.

[8] Associations, such as NGOs and most other civil society organisations, can only bring annulment proceedings if they have standing themselves under Article 263(4) TFEU; see, eg, CJEU, Case C-565/19 P *Carvalho and Others v European Parliament and Council of the European Union* ECLI:EU:C:2021:252, paras 85–87.

[9] Article 263(4) TFEU. Until the Lisbon Treaty entered into force in 2009, the standing requirements were formulated in an even stricter manner, but the change has not had any effect on the CJEU's interpretation; see further, eg, M Rhimes, 'The EU Courts Stand Their Ground: Why Are the Standing Rules for Direct Actions Still So Restrictive? (2016) 9 *European Journal of Legal Studies* 104.

[10] See, eg, De Schutter, 'Public Interest Litigation' (n 1) (2006) 14–16.

[11] CJEU, Case C-25/62 *Plaumann & Co v Commission of the European Economic Community* ECLI:EU:C:1963:17. See also, eg, Rhimes, 'The EU Courts Stand Their Ground' (2016) 109.

[12] CJEU, Case C-583/11 P *Inuit Tapiriit Kanatami* ECLI:EU:C:2013:625, paras 50–61. See further, eg, Rhimes, 'The EU Courts Stand Their Ground' (n 9) (2016) 124–143 and 142.

> rendering the requirements of the fourth paragraph of Article 263 TFEU meaningless. Indeed, it is apparent from the settled case-law of the Court that the extent of the alleged adverse impact on the observance of the appellants' fundamental rights cannot give rise to non-application of the rules for admissibility expressly laid down by the fourth paragraph of Article 263 TFEU.[13]

Over time, many scholars have argued that the strict (interpretation of the) standing requirements should be mitigated in view of the obligations following from the right to access to justice.[14] The ECtHR, too, has expressed some criticism of the limited direct standing rights for individuals at the CJEU.[15] So far, however, such criticism has led to only limited change, which focusses on the obligations arising under the Aarhus Convention in the field of environmental law protection.[16] In that particular area, in response to a critical report by the Venice Commission and the supervisory committee for the Aarhus Treaty, an EU 'roadmap' was presented in 2018 to consider possibilities for broadening individuals' and legal persons' access to the justice.[17] This led the EU legislature to adopt a new regulation to allow for better public scrutiny of EU acts affecting the environment by NGOs and other members of the public.[18] Since 2023, not only environmental organisations, but also 'other members of the public' may ask for review when they can demonstrate an impairment of their rights and they are directly affected by such impairment in comparison with the public at large, or when they can demonstrate a sufficient public interest.[19] Specifically in environmental law cases, the

[13] CJEU, Case C-297/20 P *Sabo and Others* ECLI:EU:C:2021:24, para 29. See similarly CJEU, Case C-565/19 P *Carvalho and Others v European Parliament and Council of the European Union* ECLI:EU:C:2021:252, paras 48–49 and 77.

[14] See, eg, (with many further references) P-A Van Malleghem and N Baeten, 'Before the Law Stands a Gatekeeper – Or, What is a "Regulatory Act" in Article 263(4) TFEU? *Inuit Tapiriit Kanatami*' (2014) 51 *Common Market Law Review* 1187; G Winter, '*Plaumann* Withering: Standing before the EU General Court Underway from Distinctive to Substantial Concern' (2023) 15 *European Journal of Legal Studies* 85; L Bergkamp, 'Private Party Standing and EU Risk Regulation Expanded Standing Rights in the Public Interest' (2016) *European Journal of Risk Regulation* 557.

[15] See, eg, in ECtHR (GC), App no 17502/07 *Avotiņš v Latvia*, ECLI:CE:ECHR:2016:0523JUD001750207, the ECtHR remarked that 'the Court has recognised that the mechanism provided for by European Union law for supervising observance of fundamental rights, in so far as its full potential has been deployed, also affords protection comparable to that for which the Convention provides. On this point, the Court has attached considerable importance to the role and powers of the CJEU, despite the fact that individual access to that court is far more limited than access to this Court under Article 34 of the Convention …' (para 104). According to the ECtHR, moreover, if a national court erroneously decides not to refer a case to the CJEU for a preliminary ruling, this may mean that the level of procedural protection offered by EU law falls short of the level of 'equivalent protection' to the ECHR that it normally accepts; see ECtHR, App nos 40324/16 and 12623/17 *Bivolaru and Moldovan v France* ECLI:CE:ECHR:2021:0325JUD004032416, para 131.

[16] See, eg, J De Geyter, 'Revisiting the Standing Debate before the EFTA Court through the Lens of Post-Lisbon EU Developments Regarding Locus Standi' (2023) *Nordic Journal of European Law* 131. See also European Parliamentary Research Service, *Implementing the Aarhus Convention Access to Justice in Environmental Matters* (October 2017) 6.

[17] Ref Ares(2018)2432060 – 08/05/2018, available via https://unece.org/fileadmin/DAM/env/pp/compliance/Requests_from_the_MOP/ACCC-M-2017-3_European_Union/Correspondence_with_the_Party_concerned/frPartyM3_13.06.2018_att_Roadmap_access_to_justice.pdf.

[18] Regulation (EU) 2021/1767 of the European Parliament and of the Council of 6 October 2021 amending Regulation (EC) No 1367/2006 on the application of the provisions of the Aarhus Convention on Access to Information, Public Participation in Decision-making and Access to Justice in Environmental Matters to Community institutions and bodies [2021] OJ L 356/1.

[19] Article 1(3) of the Regulation, adding a new paragraph 1a to Article 11 of the Aarhus Regulation (Regulation (EC) No 1367/2006).

new regulation significantly widens the standing rights of individuals and civil society organisations. It potentially allows them to ask the CJEU to pronounce itself on the compatibility of EU law with the right to the environment (Article 37 CFREU) and related rights, such as the right to life (Article 2 CFREU), the right to private life (Article 7 CFREU), or property rights (Article 17(1) CFREU).

It will be clear, however, that by far the most fundamental rights cases are not concerned with environmental law matters. Consequently, the *Plaumann* test and the CJEU's strict interpretation of Article 263(4) TFEU continue to apply in the great majority of cases related to the Charter. EU procedural law thus offers only few direct possibilities for the enforcement of fundamental rights in collective complaints through procedures instituted by individuals (either or not backed by civil society organisations) at the CJEU.[20]

2.3. Indirect Collective Enforcement of EU Fundamental Rights: Article 267 TFEU

Regardless of the limited possibilities for individual standing at the CJEU, Cichowski has shown that the preliminary rulings procedure allows civil society actors and individuals to play a significant role in working policy and legislative change in the EU.[21] They can lodge a case at a national court and, if need be, this court can (or is even obliged to) ask the CJEU to interpret, specify and further develop the various provisions of the EU Charter of Fundamental Rights, thereby clarifying the obligations of both member state and private actors to respect and protect these rights (Article 267 CJEU).[22] Indeed, the CJEU can even be asked to decide on the compatibility of EU legislative or regulatory acts with the EU Charter. Thus, the procedure complements Article 263(4) TFEU and fills the legal protection gap left by that provision.[23]

To illustrate the collective action potential of the indirect route, it can be noted that Cichowski has found that it has made a difference to the enforcement of fundamental rights when there are significant standing rights on the national level for individuals and NGOs (as she shows was traditionally the case in equal treatment law), as compared to the situation where litigation is more difficult (as used to be the case in environmental law).[24] She demonstrates that, at least in earlier decades, many more preliminary questions related to social policy issues and equality were brought before the CJEU than questions related to environmental law matters. As a consequence, the CJEU was able to build a significant and strong case law on equal treatment matters, which has greatly

[20] See also A O'Neill, 'Strategic Litigation before the European Courts' (2016) 16 *ERA Forum* 495, 498.

[21] R Cichowski, *The European Court and Civil Society. Litigation, Mobilization and Governance* (Cambridge, Cambridge University Press, 2007); see also O'Neill, 'Strategic Litigation' (2016) 498.

[22] For a recent example, see CJEU, Case C-471/22 *Agentsia "Patna infrastruktura" (Financement européen d'infrastructures routières)* ECLI:EU:C:2024:99, paras 49–50. See further, eg, Van Malleghem and Baeten, 'Before the Law Stands a Gatekeeper' (2014); Winter '*Plaumann* Withering' (2023) 15; Rhimes 'The EU Courts Stand Their Ground' (2016) 147.

[23] For a recent example, see CJEU, Case C-623/22 *Belgian Association of Tax Lawyers and Others* ECLI:EU:C:2024:639.

[24] Cichowski, *The European Court and Civil Society* (2007) 246.

contributed to the general protection and enforcement of the non-discrimination principle. By contrast such a contribution initially could hardly be seen in environmental law cases.[25] Hence, if there are possibilities to bring collective or public interest claims before a national court and to incentivise that court to refer preliminary questions to the CJEU, fundamental rights can be protected through strategic litigation.[26] This indirect procedural route can thus facilitate collective enforcement of fundamental rights.

However, the effectiveness of such indirect enforcement of EU fundamental rights depends on several factors.[27] First, the willingness and capacity of national courts to refer questions to the CJEU may greatly differ between the Member States and even between national courts.[28] Indirect access to the CJEU, and therefore the possibility to ensure collective enforcement of fundamental rights, thus may be unevenly distributed between and within the Member States.

Second, since lower courts have no obligation to refer, individuals and civil society organisations may need to bring lengthy and complicated proceedings at the highest level before they can achieve their objective of authoritative, general clarification of how fundamental rights must be effectuated in a particular context.[29] This makes the indirect system into a time-consuming and expensive one, which will not be easy to use for individuals and civil society organisations (in particular smaller ones).

Third, even if a case is referred, it is not guaranteed that the national court frames the questions in the fundamental rights terms favoured by the individual or NGO and, moreover, the CJEU is free to reformulate them.[30] In Rhimes' words: 'The overall effect is that the party cannot meaningfully be said to be challenging the provision in question; it surrenders its case to national courts and the vagaries of the Art 267 procedure'.[31]

Finally, as Cichowski has emphasised, an important disadvantage of the focus on indirect enforcement through the preliminary reference procedure is that 'limiting … funding and formal EU access points available to civil society could discourage transnational mobilization'.[32] The potential for obtaining fundamental rights protection through Article 267 is strongly dependent on the availability of national procedural rules of standing for NGOs and similar civil society groups. If procedural options for public interest litigation exist, they offer an important gateway for civil society organisations to have access to the CJEU and for allowing that Court to engage in explanations of

[25] Considerable limitations in standing rights for environmental organisations still exist in many EU Member States; see eg European Parliamentary Research Service, *Implementing the Aarhus Convention Access to Justice in Environmental Matters* (October 2017) 4.

[26] See similarly, eg, Bogojevic, 'Judicial Protection of Individual Applicants Revisited' (2015) 6.

[27] See also, eg, Van Malleghem and Baeten (n 14) 1214.

[28] See, eg, J Krommendijk, *National Courts and Preliminary References to the Court of Justice* (Cheltenham, Edward Elgar, 2021); C Donnelly and T de la Mare, 'Preliminary Rulings and EU Legal Integration: Evolution and Continuity' in G De Búrca and P Craig (eds), *The Evolution of EU Law* 2nd edn (Oxford, Oxford University Press, 2021) 251ff.

[29] *cf* Van Malleghem and Baeten (n 14) 1215. Problematically, moreover, even courts that are obliged to refer preliminary questions do not always do so; see further, eg, J Krommendijk, '"Open Sesame!": Improving Access to the ECJ by Requiring National Courts to Reason their Refusals to Refer' (2017) 42 *European Law Review* 46.

[30] Rhimes 'The EU Courts Stand Their Ground' (2016) 159; Van Malleghem and Baeten (n 14) 1215.

[31] ibid.

[32] Cichowski (n 21) 254.

the Charter.[33] By contrast, as Donnelly and De la Mare have indicated, if national standing rules are not receptive to interest group or public interest litigation, there are much fewer opportunities for engaging the CJEU in collective fundamental rights cases.[34] In that situation, bringing a case on a fundamental rights issue and asking for preliminary questions depends on individual applicants who have suffered a breach of their fundamental rights by EU law.[35] Of course, civil society organisations then still may play a role by offering active support to such individuals and by helping them convince a national court to present a preliminary reference to the CJEU.[36] Nevertheless, these disadvantages show that collective enforcement of fundamental rights through engaging the CJEU by means of Article 267 is not self-evident or easy for any of the parties concerned.

2.4. Conclusion

The binding Charter of Fundamental Rights has grown to be an important instrument to protect fundamental rights. Many preliminary references are made to the CJEU each year, asking for clarification of the meaning of the EU fundamental rights or even requesting the Court to judge on the compatibility of EU legislative or regulatory acts with the Charter. The preliminary rulings procedure thus has clearly allowed the CJEU to contribute to the collective enforcement of fundamental rights. Moreover, Article 263(4) TFEU allows persons who have been directly affected in their fundamental rights by individual EU acts, such as decisions in the field of competition law or sanctions, to argue before the CJEU that the decision should be annulled because of its incompatibility with rights protected by the Charter. Due to their value as precedents, these cases may have an impact that transcends the individual case and allows for more general protection and enforcement of fundamental rights.

At the same time, this section has shown that these procedural avenues both have their own difficulties and limitations, and do not easily allow individuals and civil society organisations to make strategic use of the CJEU's capacity to further develop the Charter. It is very difficult for them to make use of the direct annulment procedure with an aim of collective enforcement of fundamental rights, with the recent exception of cases concerning environmental law. The preliminary rulings procedure offers more opportunity to engage the CJEU, but as an avenue for public interest litigation, it is inefficient, causes delays and additional costs, and creates inequality of treatment between member states.[37] Hence, overall, it seems that the current system of judicial remedies in the EU is not particularly responsive to the trend to collective protection of fundamental rights.

[33] Donnelly and de la Mare, 'Preliminary Rulings and EU Legal Integration' (2021) 231.

[34] ibid.

[35] As Donnelly and de la Mare argue, to obtain access to the CJEU, individuals sometimes even have to consciously break the rules, which is 'highly unsatisfactory' (Donnelly and de la Mare, 'Preliminary Rulings and EU Legal Integration' (2021) 255).

[36] However, empirical research would be necessary to find out whether and if so, how, such support and bundling of capacities is already offered in the various Member States.

[37] See, eg, Winter (n 14) 16.

3. Collective Enforcement of Fundamental Rights via the ECtHR

3.1. Individual and Collective or General Justice before the ECtHR

To explain the possibilities for collective enforcement of fundamental rights at the ECtHR, it is useful to highlight the special double role of this Court first. At its founding, the European Convention system – established with the horrors of the Second World War fresh in mind and the dangers of Communism present – was meant to sound the 'alarm' if European States would fall towards totalitarianism.[38] As such, protecting the rights of individuals was not the main purpose of the Convention system, but rather the safeguarding of a more general or collective form of justice.[39] Yet, over time, the status of individual applicants increased in prominence and with the adoption of Protocol No 11 in 1998, the system of individual petitioning became a mandatory part of the Strasbourg protection mechanism for the signatory States.[40] Over the years, this system of individual petitioning has come to be characterised as the European Convention on Human Rights (ECHR) system's 'crown jewel'.[41] The Court itself has specified that the right to individual application 'has … become of high importance and is now a key component of the protection mechanism'.[42] Still, the Court has never abandoned its initial, core mission and plays a 'crucial double role' in protecting fundamental rights.[43] This double role entails that it provides redress for individual victims, but also delivers general interpretations of Convention rights and 'determines issues on public-policy grounds in the common interest',[44] thus setting the general standard of human rights protection in the Contracting States.[45] In addition, in many cases, the Court does not limit itself to deciding purely in the concrete circumstances of the case, but reviews the compatibility of legislation or policies with the Convention in a more general fashion.[46] Hence the Court can be said to offer both individual and more collective or general justice.

In view of this double nature and function of the ECHR system, this section takes a closer look at the legal possibilities individuals and civil society organisations have

[38] E Bates, 'The Birth of the European Convention on Human Rights – and the European Court of Human Rights' in J Christoffersen and M Rask Madsen (eds), *The European Court of Human Rights between Law and Politics* (Oxford, Oxford University Press, 2011) 21.

[39] Gerards and Glas, 'Access to Justice' (2017) 17.

[40] Council of Europe, Protocol No 11 to the European Convention for the Protection of Human Rights and Fundamental Freedoms, Restructuring the Control Machinery Established Thereby, ETS 155, 11 May 1994.

[41] L Helfer, 'Redesigning the ECtHR: Embeddedness as a Deep Structural Principle of the ECHR Regime' (2008) 19 *European Journal of International Law* 125, 159.

[42] Gerards and Glas (n 2) 18, citing ECtHR, App nos 46827/99 and 46951/99 *Mamatkulov and Askarov v Turkey* ECLI:CE:ECHR:2005:0204JUD004682799, para 122.

[43] J Gerards, 'Abstract and Concrete Reasonableness Review by the European Court of Human Rights' (2020) 1 *European Convention on Human Rights Law Review* 218, 218.

[44] See, eg, ECtHR (GC), App no 30078/06 *Konstantin Markin v Russia* ECLI:CE:ECHR:2012:0322JUD003007806, para 89.

[45] Gerards, 'Abstract and Concrete Reasonableness Review' (2020); Gerards and Glas, (n 2) 18.

[46] Gerards (n 43).

to engage the ECtHR in collective enforcement of the Convention rights. Section 3.2 discusses how and to what extent individuals and NGOs can invite the ECtHR to look into a certain fundamental rights issue by lodging an individual application under Article 34 of the Convention. Subsequently, Section 3.3 addresses the question of how the standing rights in the ECHR system relate to the Court's general justice function and to what extent the right to petition can be used for collective enforcement of fundamental rights.

3.2. Standing Rights under Article 34 ECHR

Individuals and NGOs alike are empowered by Article 34 ECHR to bring cases to the Court. As stipulated by this Article, 'any person, non-governmental organisation or group of individuals claiming to be the victim of a violation by one of the High Contracting Parties of the rights set forth in the Convention or the Protocols thereto' can lodge an application. This provision thus clearly provides direct access (after the exhaustion of domestic remedies and satisfying other admissibility requirements) to the Court for (groups of) individuals as well as NGOs.

However, as further detailed by the Court, a fundamental criterion to fulfil in order to make out a claim under Article 34 is the so-called 'victim requirement'. This requirement entails that only those applicants who can demonstrate to have been directly affected by a violation of one or more Convention rights can bring a case before the Court. The Court has emphasised that the victim requirement is 'indispensable for putting the protection mechanism of the Convention into motion'.[47] In practice, the Court allows for some 'flexibility'[48] by accepting petitions by applicants who can show to be indirectly affected by a violation of a Convention right, or by those who convincingly argue that they are likely to be affected by such a violation.[49]

The Court has often emphasised that the victim requirement results in the inadmissibility of *actio popularis* complaints, that is, abstract complaints that are lodged without a direct victim.[50] Consequently, though subject to a number of exceptions, NGOs can only bring complaints when they themselves can claim to be a victim of a violation of fundamental rights.[51] They can do so, for example, if their registration as an NGO has been refused (arguably contrary to the freedom of association or expression as protected by Articles 10 and 11 ECHR) or if there are indications that their communications have

[47] ECtHR, App nos 47039/11 and 358/12 *Hristozov and Others v Bulgaria* ECLI:CE:ECHR:2012:1113JUD004703911, para 122.

[48] As noted by C Heri, 'Climate Cases as Public Interest Litigation before the European Court of Human Rights' in J Bendel and Y Suedi (eds), *Public Interest Litigation in International Law* (Oxon, New York, Routledge, 2024) 320.

[49] See, generally, J Gerards, *General Principles of the European Convention on Human Rights* (Cambridge, Cambridge University Press, 2023) for an overview of the ECtHR's case law on the victim requirement. The Court's *Practical Guide on Admissibility Criteria* (2023) is useful for such an overview as well, available at www.echr.coe.int/documents/d/echr/admissibility_guide_eng accessed 3 June 2025.

[50] See the Court's *Practical Guide on Admissibility Criteria* (2023). For an example of an *actio popularis* case see, ECtHR, App no 66274/09 *Ligue des Musulmans de Suisse and Others v Switzerland* ECLI:CE:ECHR:2011:0628DEC006627409.

[51] Notably, recent climate change jurisprudence, ECtHR (GC), App no 53600/20 *Verein KlimaSeniorinnen Schweiz and Others v Switzerland* ECLI:CE:ECHR:2024:0409JUD005360020.

been intercepted (potentially in violation of Article 8 ECHR). Collective enforcement of fundamental rights in cases that do not directly affect NGOs' own fundamental rights is much more difficult, as the exceptions to the victim requirement are very narrowly constructed by the ECtHR. A rare example of such an exception can be found in the case of *Valentin Câmpeanu*, and more recently, climate change cases have been added to the list of exceptions.[52] In the case of *Câmpeanu*, the death of a young, particularly vulnerable person led the Court to allow an NGO bringing a case on behalf of this applicant, among other things to ensure that the State would not escape accountability for the severe violations that had been suffered by the victim.[53]

Regardless of these formal limitations, it must be noted that civil society organisations can still play a role in lodging individual complaints. Most importantly, as several scholars have demonstrated, and as noted in the introduction of this chapter, NGOs may feature as direct representatives of applicants before the Court to aid them in securing some form of relief for the violations allegedly suffered by them.[54] It is difficult to fully map this type of engagement of NGOs before the ECtHR, as not all of their participation and assistance finds its way to public record. This notwithstanding, over the years, scholarly research has given insight into this type of NGO activity.[55] This shows that the Court has dealt with a wide variety of complaints initiated or supported by NGOs in order to aid individual victims find relief for their violations suffered. NGOs are reported, for instance, to have successfully litigated cases coming from former conflict-zones,[56] assisting victims to secure financial relief and giving an acknowledgement of their suffering.[57] However, such assistance has securing individual justice, more than general justice and collective enforcement of human rights, as its priority.[58]

3.3. Collective Enforcement and General Justice via the ECtHR

As noted in Section 3.1, in addition to delivering individual justice in cases brought to it under Article 34 of the Convention, the Court also provides a more general or constitutional form of justice. Indeed, the Court may issue judgments of principle, that is, a judgment that 'elucidates, safeguards and develops the rules instituted by the Convention' and thereby 'generate[s], maintain[s] and develop[s] ethical norms for

[52] ECtHR (GC), App no 47848/08, *Centre for Legal Resources on behalf of Valentin Câmpeanu v Romania* ECLI:CE:ECHR:2014:0717JUD004784808. For a more recent application of the principles developed in *Câmpeanu*, see ECtHR, App nos 27584/20 and 39768/20 *KJ and Others v Russia* ECLI:CE:ECHR:2024:0319JUD002758420. For climate change jurisprudence, see ECtHR (GC), App no 53600/20 *Verein KlimaSeniorinnen Schweiz and Others v Switzerland* ECLI:CE:ECHR:2024:0409JUD005360020.

[53] ECtHR, *Centre for Legal Resources on behalf of Valentin Câmpeanu v Romania* (ibid n 52 above), para 112.

[54] See, for instance, HN Haddad, *The Hidden Hands of Justice: NGOs, Human Rights, and International Courts* (Cambridge, Cambridge University Press, 2018); L Hodson, *NGOs and the Struggle for Human Rights in Europe* (Oxford, Hart Publishing, 2011).

[55] Most relevant, in this respect, are the works by Haddad, *The Hidden Hands of Justice* (2018) and Hodson, *NGOs and the Struggle for Human Rights* (2011). See also Erken (n 3).

[56] Haddad, *The Hidden Hands of Justice* (2018). For case studies NGO litigation strategies in the Russian context, see for instance L McIntosh Sundstrom, 'Russian NGOs and the European Court of Human Rights: A Spectrum of Approaches to Litigation' (2014) 36 *Human Rights Quarterly* 844.

[57] Erken (n 3).

[58] For examples of (practical) limitations to access to justice at the ECtHR, see Gerards and Glas (n 2) (2017).

the community to which it applies'.[59] The Court's use of the pilot-judgment procedure and its reliance on indicating 'general measures' to be taken to remedy a violation are said to be indicative of the Court's efforts to provide general justice.[60] Similarly, as was mentioned above, the Court may find national legislation *in abstracto* to be incompatible with the Convention.[61] These mechanisms show that at least in some cases, 'the Court's focus is on solving the underlying structural problem rather than on deciding individual cases'.[62]

Hence, Article 34 and the strict victim requirements notwithstanding, applicants and their representatives may choose to seek recourse to the Court 'with a purpose of advocacy, in the sense of using an individual case to obtain a change in the system …'.[63] While both private lawyers and civil society organisations may seek out the Court with such an aim in mind,[64] NGOs in particular are known for pursuing such objectives. As was explained in Section 3.2, they can do so, for instance, by attaching themselves to an individual (case) and thereby, through acting as direct representatives or as supporters of applicants behind the scenes, striving to effectuate certain changes.[65] In this respect, a recurring discussion seems to be held on whether the strict standing requirements maintained by the Court should be relaxed for NGOs in order for the Court to better pronounce judgments that focus on general rather than individual justice.[66] Among other things, it has been argued that the skills and expertise of NGOs would allow them to bring cases to the Court that represent larger, structural problems. This, as has been suggested, could help the Court effectively address such issues through a more limited number of quality cases.[67]

Although creating a rather more collective procedure at the ECtHR clearly has advantages from a perspective of enforcement of fundamental rights, such proposals have been met with scepticism, too. First and foremost, some hold that such type of interest litigation is anti-majoritarian and point out that it may provide a way to circumvent the democratic decision-making process.[68] In support of this perspective, critics argue that

[59] ECtHR, App no 40016/98, *Karner v Austria* ECLI:CE:ECHR:2003:0724JUD004001698, para 26; S Greer and L Wildhaber, 'Revisiting the Debate about 'Constitutionalising' the European Court of Human Rights' (2013) 12 *Human Rights Law Review* 655; L Wildhaber, 'Rethinking the European Court of Human Rights' in J Christoffersen and MR Madsen (eds), *The European Court of Human Rights between Law and Politics* (Oxford, Oxford University Press, 2011).

[60] Gerards and Glas (n 2) (2017).

[61] In more detail, with many examples, see Gerards, 'Abstract and Concrete Reasonableness Review' (2020).

[62] Gerards and Glas (n 2).

[63] V Costa Ramos, 'Lodging an Application with the ECtHR – The Attorney's Perspective' (2021) 12 *New Journal of European Criminal Law* 76.

[64] E Kindt, 'The Pilot Judgment Procedure at the European Court of Human Rights: An Evaluation in the Light of Procedural Efficiency and Access to Justice' (PhD thesis, University of Gent, 2018).

[65] Haddad, *The Hidden Hands of Justice* (2018). See, for instance, O'Neill (n 20), for a quick overview of a number of strategic litigation cases before the ECtHR.

[66] See, eg, S Dothan, *International Judicial Review: When Should International Courts Intervene?* (Cambridge, Cambridge University Press, 2020); Hodson, *NGOs and the Struggle for Human Rights* (2011); M Frigessi di Rattalma, 'NGOs before the European Court of Human Rights: Beyond *Amicus Curiae* Participation?' in T Treves, M Frigessi di Rattalma and A Tanzi (eds) *Civil Society, International Courts and Compliance Bodies* (The Hague, T.M.C. Asser Press, 2005).

[67] H Keller and V Gurash, 'Expanding NGOs' standing: climate justice through access to the European Court of Human Rights' (2023) 14 *Journal of Human Rights and the Environment* 194.

[68] See O'Neill (n 20) 496; Hodson, *NGOs and the Struggle for Human Rights* (2011) 149.

NGOs represent 'the will of organised interests …', and as such, lack the 'capability to carefully weigh different interests …', which has led some to 'fear that the participation of NGOs may give too much power to those with strong views, leading to insufficient attention to the public interest at large'.[69] In addition, while NGOs and public interest concerns are at times mentioned in the same breath, it is sometimes noted that NGOs are not necessarily general or public interest advocates; indeed, the various groups that litigate in the public interest may 'disagree fundamentally about what the public interest requires'.[70] This puts the finger on another concern, which relates to the question of who NGOs actually represent.[71]

Such issues have become particularly salient in light of recent developments at the Court. In its landmark judgment in the *KlimaSeniorinnen* case, the Court has expanded access for those NGOs that, among other things, can show to work 'for the protection of those rights against the threats arising from climate change'.[72] Among other requirements, in order to be granted standing, an NGO needs to be 'able to demonstrate that it can be regarded as genuinely qualified and representative to act on behalf of members or other affected individuals within the jurisdiction who are subject to specific threats or adverse effects of climate change on their lives, health or well-being as protected under the Convention'.[73] By choosing this route, the Court has given impetus to the assumption that by granting greater access for NGOs to lodge climate-related cases, they could, for instance, help individual litigants overcome their vulnerability, their lack of legal and environmental expertise as well as hurdles with respect to the victim requirement, causality and issues of future harm.[74] At the same time, account must be taken of some reservations that arise with this approach. Granting greater access to certain NGOs out of an incredibly large pool, based on the subject matter they advocate for, can lead to difficult questions for a system that deals with a multitude of (competing) individual rights complaints. Moreover, the Court requires the applicant NGO to be representative to act on behalf of those subject to adverse consequences of climate change. Yet, as illustrated in the previous paragraph, some have pointed out that NGOs more generally are unable to convey a 'common good'.[75] This tension is also revealed in the judgment, with the Court accepting that the KlimaSeniorinnen association could be said to 'represent a vehicle of collective recourse aimed at defending the rights and interests of individuals against the threats of climate change …', while at the same time, a popular vote in Switzerland had rejected the targets set and manner in which CO_2 would be reduced.[76]

[69] M Beijerman, 'Conceptual Confusions in Debating the Role of NGOs for the Democratic Legitimacy of International Law' (2018) 9 *Transnational Legal Theory* 147, 159. See also Erken (n 3).

[70] A Southworth, 'Conservative Lawyers and the Contest over the Meaning of "Public Interest Law"' (2005) 52 *UCLA Law Review* 1223, 1271.

[71] See, for instance, J Mertus, 'From Legal Transplants to Transformative Justice: Human Rights and the Promise of Transnational Civil Society' (1999) 14 *American University International Law Review* 1335; MS Polizzi and A Murdie, 'NGOs and Human Rights' in T Davies (ed), *Routledge Handbook of NGOs and International Relations* (Abingdon, Routledge, 2019). This argument, and works cited, also features in Erken (n 3).

[72] ECtHR, *Verein KlimaSeniorinnen Schweiz and Others v Switzerland* (see n 51 above), para 502.

[73] ibid.

[74] Keller and Gurash, 'Expanding NGOs' Standing' (2023) 215.

[75] See, eg, Mertus, 'From Legal Transplants to Transformative Justice' (1999) 1373.

[76] ECtHR, *Verein KlimaSeniorinnen Schweiz and Others v Switzerland* (see n 51 above), para 75.

Another standard that can be seen to be defined in the *KlimaSeniorinnen* judgment raises similar concerns as those existing in relation to standing in EU law. To have standing before the Court in climate cases, NGOs must show that they are 'lawfully established in the jurisdiction concerned or have standing to act there'.[77] The latter element suggests that the NGOs' standing at the ECtHR is dependent on the degree to which NGOs are granted standing rights on the national level. Consequently, if a State does not have any public or collective interest litigation instruments in place, or if standing rights for NGOs are limited, the NGOs based in such States will not have a possibility to have access to the ECtHR either. This may result in differences in access to justice in different European States and it may – in an uneven manner – restrict NGOs possibilities to engage in collective enforcement of climate justice rights.

3.4. Conclusion

This section has given insight into the role that individuals and civil society organisations, in particular NGOs, can play in collective enforcement of fundamental rights via the ECtHR. Individuals clearly may raise more general issues that transcend their individual case, just like NGOs in climate cases. The standing rights of NGOs are generally limited to situations where their own rights are directly affected – with a few exceptions, including climate cases as a result of the recent landmark judgment in the *KlimaSeniorinnen* case.

Nevertheless, the above has equally shown that NGOs can have an important indirect role to play as representatives or supporters of individual applicants. In these capacities they can assist individuals in obtaining individual justice, but they can also use their specific abilities and resources to contribute to a form of general justice and collective enforcement of fundamental rights. However, as also pointed out in this section, due regard must be paid to the drawbacks this could entail and to the potential of undue divergences between States that the newly defined criteria for NGOs standing in climate cases may create.

4. Conclusion

This chapter set out to give an insight into how and to what extent individuals and civil society organisations can contribute to collective enforcement of fundamental rights via the CJEU and the ECtHR. The analysis shows that in both systems, there is potential, but there are also limitations.

In the EU system, individuals can directly contest fundamental rights violations if they are caused by individual EU acts that directly concern them. Such direct actions of annulment under Article 263(4) TFEU can contribute to wider enforcement of fundamental rights through the precedential effect of the resulting judgments. Civil society organisations can play a role in such cases by assisting individuals and helping them seek procedural strategies that would lead to a broader, collective impact of the CJEU's rulings.

[77] ibid, para 502.

By contrast, when individuals have been affected by EU legislative or regulatory acts, or are mainly seeking further clarification of EU fundamental rights law, their procedural possibilities are more limited. There are few possibilities for individuals and civil societies to bring direct annulment proceedings regarding EU legislative or regulatory acts. Only in the field of environmental law (and therefore relevant to fundamental rights related to environmental issues), a new EU regulation allows for a wider range of direct applications to be made by individuals and civil society organisations.

Mostly, collective enforcement of fundamental rights in the EU system is effectuated through indirect means. Individuals and other private actors can bring proceedings at the national level and argue before the domestic court that a preliminary reference must be made to the CJEU. When these actors engage in public interest litigation, such preliminary references can result in general interpretations and findings by the CJEU, which have *erga omnes* effect and can work real legal change. At the same time, there are many indications that preliminary references are not always made and even if this is done, the issues might be reformulated in a way that does not fully reflect the litigants' perspectives. Moreover, the potential for raising matters of general justice is strongly related to the existence of national procedural laws allowing for public interest litigation or collective complaints. The result is an uneven distribution of opportunities of collective enforcement by individuals and non-governmental organisations in the various EU member states.

The potential of individuals and civil society organisations to contribute to collective enforcement of fundamental rights possibly might be increased by accession of the EU to the ECHR. After all, as a consequence of that accession, each individual, group of individuals, corporation or NGO could petition the ECtHR if they are harmed in their own interests, regardless of the type of act that has affected their rights, that is, regardless of whether the harm has been done by a national administrative act or legislation, or by individual or regulatory EU acts. It has been shown in the above that the ECHR system's possibilities for offering general justice and for public interest litigation are also relatively limited, especially now that civil society organisations have few procedural options to lodge collective complaints. Nevertheless, such organisations appear to play a role of importance in pursuing general justice by means of representing and supporting individual applicants. In addition, the recent *KlimaSeniorinnen* judgment of the ECtHR has formally widened NGOs' standing rights to allow them to present and defend interests related to fundamental rights in climate cases.

Hence, on the one hand, it can be concluded that the formal possibilities for public interest litigation are still relatively limited on the supranational level. Especially now that the EU does not form part of the Convention system as yet, it can be difficult for individuals and civil society organisations to actively use litigation strategies to tackle structural and systemic human rights problems. On the other hand, both in the EU and in the ECHR system, standing rights are on the rise, especially where environmental and climate cases are concerned. Indeed, it has been noted that the possibilities for NGOs to take part in the ECtHR's proceedings are so strong now that some drawbacks related to representativeness and power of NGOs may arise. However, if such issues are duly considered, the existence and development of procedural options for individuals and civil society organisations to play a role in enforcement of fundamental rights is valuable.

4

Third-party Interventions before Both the ECtHR and the CJEU

VIRGINIA PASSALACQUA*

Third parties' interventions are regulated differently before the European Court of Human Rights (ECtHR) and the Court of Justice of the European Union (CJEU). This chapter first summarises the different regimes that govern third parties' participation in each court in light of recent developments, noting significant differences. While civil society organisations increasingly file interventions before the ECtHR, the most critical procedure before the CJEU does not admit interventions by private parties but only by the Member States' governments and EU institutions. The chapter then reflects on whether the rules of the two Courts are appropriate to guarantee adequate access and representation of the diverse interests affected by the case. In the international and supranational context, we should pay particular attention to whether the regulatory frameworks governing third-party interventions can give voice to under-represented minorities, thus counteracting the risk of a pro-state or majoritarian bias.

1. Introduction: Third-party Interventions as an Alternative Way for Civil Society to Access the European Courts

The two most relevant regional courts in Europe are rather difficult to access for civil society. Both the ECtHR and the CJEU do not admit *actio popularis* or associational standing, which is the right of associations and groups to bring action in defence of their stated goals or the broader interests they represent. Before the ECtHR, associations and groups can bring an action only if they are the victim of a human rights violation (what Gerards and Erken call 'victim requirement').[1] In cases before the CJEU, associations can bring an action only as legal persons directly (and/or individually) affected by an

* I thank the editors for inviting me to contribute to this volume. I am grateful to Elise Muir for all her thoughtful comments and suggestions during the drafting process.

[1] The chapter by Gerards and Erken (ch 3) in this volume deals specifically with NGOs' access to justice in fundamental rights cases before the ECtHR and the CJEU and explains in detail the procedural limits that exist at these two Courts.

EU act;[2] this stringent requirement earned the CJEU the title of 'hostile to collective action'.[3] Given these restrictive standing rules, third-party interventions (hereinafter, TPIs), also called amicus curiae,[4] often assume a compensatory role before the ECtHR and the CJEU, as they give civil society an alternative way to access the Courts, have their say and participate in highly impactful proceedings which would otherwise be inaccessible.[5]

Although important, we should beware of this supposed compensatory role of TPIs. Arguably, TPIs cannot fully make up for the lack of associational standing. Through TPIs, groups cannot bring new cases to the attention of the courts or remedy accountability gaps; they can only intervene in already pending legal actions.[6] As De Schutter explains, one of the key arguments in favour of associational standing would be that they expand judicial review by bringing under the courts' scrutiny illegal acts that would otherwise be left unremedied because they affect diffuse or common interests.[7] TPIs cannot play this 'rule of law' function.

However, there is a second argument in favour of associational standing that De Schutter mentions, and this can be extended to TPIs. It is the 'adjudication-participation' argument that sees the judicial decision as 'legitimate to the extent that it is adequately informed and that it is the outcome of a truly deliberative process, in which all the relevant interests are represented and can bring before the judge their diverse perspectives'.[8] Accordingly, the participation of third actors, such as civil society, in the form of an intervention or an amicus curiae brief, could improve judges' deliberations by providing different views and context.

This chapter adds a third argument in support of associational standing and TPIs, which De Schutter does not mention. Expanding associations and third parties' presence in court may give voice to minorities, disenfranchised, or under-represented

[2] CJEU, Case C-25/62 *Plaumann v Commission* ECLI:EU:C:1963:17; A Albors-Llorens, 'Judicial Protection before the Court of Justice of the European Union' in C Barnard and S Peers (eds), *European Union Law* (Oxford, Oxford University Press, 2014) 255; M Pagano, 'Overcoming Plaumann in EU Environmental Litigation: An Analysis of NGOs Legal Arguments in Actions for Annulment' (2019) *Diritto e processo* 311; S Villani, 'L'accesso alla giustizia ambientale da parte delle ong nel quadro giuridico dell'unione europea alla luce della prassi recente' (2023) *Rivista Eurojus* 149.

[3] C Harlow and R Rawlings, *Pressure Through Law* (London, Taylor and Francis, 1992) 525.

[4] Even if some jurisdictions treat TPIs and amicus curiae differently, they are regulated alike before the two European courts. The notion of TPIs is broader, as it includes any non-party that participates in the proceedings, including subjects that defend their particular and personal interests. Instead, the term amicus curiae generally indicates actors who submit an expert opinion, thus bringing their expertise to the judge to improve the quality of the adjudication or influence the court.

[5] As De Schutter noted, TPI's compensatory role was already recognised by the Advocate General of the Court of Justice in *Confédération nationale des producteurs de fruits et légumes*, one of the seminal cases where the Court started restricting its legal standing. CJEU, Joined Cases 16/62 and 17/62 *Confédération nationale des producteurs de fruits et légumes and others v Council of the European Economic Community*, Opinion of AG Lagrange, ECLI:EU:C:1962:40. O De Schutter, 'Public Interest Litigation before the European Court of Justice' (2006) 13 *Maastricht Journal of European and Comparative Law* 9, 11.

[6] There is a growing literature on the EU's accountability gap in the human rights field. See J De Coninck, 'Effective Remedies for Human Rights Violations in EU CSDP Military Missions: Smoke and Mirrors in Human Rights Adjudication?' (2023) 24 *German Law Journal* 342; J De Coninck, *The EU's Human Rights Responsibility Gap. Deconstructing Human Rights Impunity of International Organisations* (Oxford, Hart Publishing, 2024); M Gkliati, 'Shaping the Joint Liability Landscape? The Broader Consequences of WS v Frontex for EU Law' (2024) 9 *European Papers* 69.

[7] De Schutter, 'Public Interest Litigation' (2006).

[8] ibid.

groups. These groups often have a hard time making their voices heard through the democratic legislative process, and they rely on courts to defend their rights and challenge majority-designed legislation. TPIs can serve to increase the visibility of these voiceless members of our communities and thus enhance 'participatory democracy', understood as 'the multiplication of opportunities for citizens' participation beyond elections'.[9]

At the same time, we shall not ignore the limits and possible downsides of TPIs. Even if it is true that TPIs, by definition, expand the number of voices and opinions that reach the courts, there is no guarantee that the result would be a more balanced proceedings, representative of all the relevant interests at stake. First of all, a varied set of actors can file TPIs: from small trade unions to big corporations, from fishermen associations to Member States' governments. There is no guarantee that these actors will defend minorities or under-represented groups; quite the opposite, because TPIs are filed upon the initiative of non-parties in the case, chances are that they are more used by resourceful actors, ending up amplifying the voice of subjects who already occupy a position of advantage in the case or in society.[10] In these instances, TPIs would not increase representation but rather risk empowering the already powerful. This chapter will show that this risk is neither hypothetical nor far from the practice of the two European courts, where, besides resources, procedural rules play a critical role in shaping the type of actors that access courts through TPIs.

Commentators also raised concerns that expanding legal standing and opportunities for TPIs may increase 'the likelihood of judicial involvement in public policymaking' and further the process of judicialisation of politics.[11] According to this view, opening the courts' doors would encourage political actors to use justice to achieve their goals, resulting in a greater involvement of courts in the definition of public policies. The increasing judicialisation of politics, in turn, could damage European courts' reputation and undermine the executive and legislature's prerogative to decide over critical political questions.[12] In response to this argument, we can recall the view of other scholars who noted that this critique often implies a narrow view of what is 'political' in the case law, and it seems to submit to an artificial distinction between the legal and the political spheres.[13] This view risks ignoring that the (European) courts' role is inherently political, regardless of who brings legal actions or files TPIs.

[9] A Alemanno, 'Beyond EU Law Heroes: Unleashing Strategic Litigation as a Form of Participation in the Union's Democratic Life' (2024) 25 *German Law Journal* 822, 828; C Krenn, *The Procedural and Organisational Law of the European Court of Justice: An Incomplete Transformation* (Cambridge, Cambridge University Press, 2022) 104.

[10] This trend has been noted in the literature on strategic litigation, where it was found that resourceful interest groups are more likely to use courts. A Hofmann and D Naurin, 'Explaining Interest Group Litigation in Europe: Evidence from the Comparative Interest Group Survey' (2020) *Governance* 4; A Hofmann, 'Who Does and Who Does Not Engage in Strategic Litigation in European Law?' (2024) 25 *German Law Journal* 856, 860.

[11] R Hirschl, 'The Judicialization of Politics' in Robert Goodin (ed), *The Oxford Handbook of Political Science* (Oxford, Oxford University Press, 2011) 265–266.

[12] ibid 262.

[13] A Bailleux, 'Beyond Judicial Activism: Europe's Judicial Narratives and the Polity-Cal Role of the Court of Justice' in M Dawson, B De Witte and E Muir (eds), *Revisiting Judicial Politics in the European Union* (Cheltenham, Edward Elgar, 2024) 51; A Vauchez, 'From Close-Ups to Long Shot: In Search of the "Political Role" of the Court of Justice of the European Union' in C Kilpatrick and J Scott (eds), *New Legal Approaches to Studying the Court of Justice: Revisiting Law in Context* (Oxford, Oxford University Press, 2020) 52.

The chapter starts by providing an overview of the rules that regulate TPIs before the CJEU and the ECtHR. The two courts regulate TPIs differently due to reasons linked to their different functions and histories.[14] Sections two and three explain how these procedural rules modulate the possibility of filing interventions, by both Member State governments and non-state actors. Section four, by relying on existing empirical research, shows how these rules affect interventions before the two courts in practice. It shows that civil society actors, helped by more expanding access rules, intervene more before the ECtHR, while Member States intervene more before the CJEU, where they have a privileged status. Section 5 shows some alternative avenues that civil society actors use to reach the CJEU and which partially compensate for the lack of access. Finally, the chapter concludes by reflecting on whether the rules on TPIs strike a good balance between majoritarian and minoritarian views.

2. Third-party Interventions before the European Court of Human Rights

Initially, the possibility to file TPIs was not provided by the judicial system of the European Convention for the Protection of Human Rights and Fundamental Freedoms (ECHR). The procedure to file TPIs was introduced by the ECtHR judges, who inserted it when writing the Court's rules of procedure in 1983. According to scholarly accounts, they probably did so because they felt some pressure to regulate this matter after receiving different requests to intervene from the UK government and a British NGO.[15] Still, interventions before the ECHR took a while to take off. In the first ten years, the ECtHR received only 30 interventions: ten from the UK; ten from Italy; and ten from international NGOs.[16] The numbers are very different today, as we shall see in the following sections. Suffice it to say here that 2022 was the year when the record of interventions was broken: 26 Member States asked for permission to intervene in the case of *Ukraine v Russia (X)*, an unprecedented number.[17]

Today third-party interventions before the Strasburg Court are regulated by Article 36 of the ECHR and by Rule 44 of the Court Procedure. Article 36(1) grants the 'right to submit written comments' to the Member State who is not the respondent in the case, but whose national filed an application against another Member State. Article 36(2) gives 'any person concerned' the possibility to file an observation upon

[14] J Krommendijk and K van der Pas, 'To Intervene or Not to Intervene: Intervention before the Court of Justice of the European Union in Environmental and Migration Law' (2022) 26 *The International Journal of Human Rights* 1394.

[15] A Dolidze, 'Anglo-Saxonizing Rights: Transnational Public Interest Litigation in Europe' (2011) 105 *ASIL Proceedings of the 105th Annual Meeting* 47, 49.

[16] ibid 50.

[17] J Batura and I Risini, 'Of Parties, Third Parties, and Treaty Interpretation: Ukraine v Russia (X) before the European Court of Human Rights' (*EJIL: Talk!*, 26 September 2022) www.ejiltalk.org/of-parties-third-parties-and-treaty-interpretation-ukraine-v-russia-x-before-the-european-court-of-human-rights/ accessed 19 February 2025; ECtHR, App no 11055/22, *Ukraine v Russia (X)* (case pending).

the President of the Court's invitation;[18] as specified in Rule 44, this means that any person, if not invited, may ask and be granted leave to intervene by the President.[19] Rule 44 further specifies the conditions for admissibility, such as the time limit and the language of the intervention. Notably, in 2023, Rule 44 was amended as the culmination of a reform process initiated in 2018 that aimed, among other things, at supporting third-party intervention.[20]

Unfortunately, the ECtHR does not publish information on the number of requests for intervention that it receives and rejects, so it is not easy to assess how strictly its admissibility criteria are applied in practice. However, during her period of work and research at the ECtHR, Nicole Bürli, the author of an extensive study on TPIs before the ECtHR, managed to obtain internal statistics from the Court, where it is reported that one-third of all the applications to intervene are rejected.[21] This is a relatively high number and calls for more transparency and clear admissibility criteria by the ECtHR.

In part, the 2023 Practice Directions published by the President of the Court shed some light on this issue. The document clarified that the TPI's 'chief purpose is to enable the Court to become acquainted with the views of States and other persons who are not parties to a case before it on the issues raised by that case, and be presented with information or arguments which are broader than or different from those put forward by the parties.' It is clear here that the Court sees TPIs as an instrument similar to amici curiae, as they should provide 'legal or factual points capable of assisting it in resolving the matters in dispute before it', 'as impartially and objectively as possible'.[22] In practice, however, TPIs are often filed in support of one of the parties in the case.

A clear example of this partiality comes from TPIs filed by States' governments. According to Bürli, Member States file TPIs to defend and/or reinforce their sovereignty:

> Analysis of all judgments that received at least one member-state intervention revealed that states contribute predominantly to elements of judicial restraint. This means first and foremost that TPIs by Member States argue for a wide margin of appreciation, subsidiarity, and a historical interpretation of the Convention.[23]

A similar conclusion was reached in a study by Dzehtsiarou. He analysed all the States' interventions before the Grand Chamber of the ECtHR and concluded that these are primarily concerned with 'self-interest', meaning protecting their own legal system

[18] Article 36: '1. In all cases before a Chamber or the Grand Chamber, a High Contracting Party one of whose nationals is an applicant shall have the right to submit written comments and to take part in hearings. 2. The President of the Court may, in the interest of the proper administration of justice, invite any High Contracting Party which is not a party to the proceedings or any person concerned who is not the applicant to submit written comments or take part in hearings.'

[19] ECHR Rules of Court, Rule 44.

[20] ECHR, 'European Court Clarifies Third-Party Intervention: Amendments to Rules of Court and New Guidelines' https://hudoc.echr.coe.int/app/conversion/pdf/?library=ECHR&id=003-7600935-10455264&filename=European%20Court%20clarifies%20third-party%20intervention%20.pdf, accessed 19 February 2025.

[21] N Bürli, *Third-Party Interventions before the European Court of Human Rights: Amicus Curiae, Member-State and Third-Party Interventions* (Cambridge, Intersentia, 2017) 186.

[22] Practice Directions. Third-party intervention under Article 36 § 2 of the Convention or under Article 3, second sentence, of Protocol No 16.

[23] Bürli, *Third-Party Interventions* (2017) 185.

and position vis à vis international obligations.[24] However, the ECtHR seems to be aware of this strategic purpose and thus accords to States' TPIs limited weight in its adjudications.[25]

3. Third-party Interventions before the Court of Justice of the European Union

There are important differences between the rules governing TPIs before the CJEU and the ECtHR. Contrary to the ECtHR, which expects TPIs to be impartial and more similar to an amicus curiae, the CJEU understands TPIs as intrinsically partial, as they must support one of the parties in the case.[26] Moreover, the CJEU's rules change depending on whether TPIs are filed by the Member State governments or by non-state actors. Thus, I will address them separately.

3.1. Governments as Third Parties: The Double-privileged Member States

According to Article 263 of the Treaty on the Functioning of the European Union (TFEU), which regulates the procedure for the annulment of an EU act, the Member States occupy a privileged position in Luxembourg.[27] But this is not true only for this procedure. According to Article 40 of the Statute of the Court, Member States can always intervene in cases before the CJEU to support one of the parties[28] and according to Article 23, Member States can file observations in the preliminary reference procedure too (Article 267 TFEU), which is the most important procedure of the EU legal order and allows national courts in any Member State to submit a question of interpretation or validity of an EU norm to the CJEU. The Member States share this privileged position together with the Commission and any EU institution that was involved in the adoption of the EU act at stake;[29] all these actors and institutions receive a notification every time a preliminary question is referred, and they have two months to file their submissions. Krenn critically wrote that these rules have created 'an inner circle of

[24] K Dzehtsiarou, 'Conversations with Friends: "Friends of the Court" Interventions of the State Parties to the European Convention on Human Rights' (2023) 43 *Legal Studies* 381, 400.

[25] ibid 400.

[26] Last line of Article 40 of the Statute of the Court of Justice of the European Union: 'An application to intervene shall be limited to supporting the form of order sought by one of the parties.'

[27] According to Article 263 of the Treaty on the Functioning of the European Union, Member States governments are 'privileged applicants' before the Court: they have always legal standing to bring an annulment action before the CJEU, regardless of whether the EU norm at issue concerns them directly or not. This is starkly different from private applicants, such as natural and legal persons, who are 'non-privileged' applicants. H Rasmussen, 'Why is Article 173 Interpreted against Private Plaintiffs?' (1980) 5 *European Law Review* 112.

[28] Article 40 of the Statute of the Court of Justice of the European Union. K Lenaerts, K Gutman and JT Nowak, *EU Procedural Law* (Oxford, Oxford University Press, 2023) 733.

[29] Statute of the Court of Justice of the European Union, Article 23.

participants, in particular the Commission and Member State governments, that have become repeat players in ECJ proceedings.'[30] Notably, in 2024 such an 'inner circle' was potentially expanded: the last amendment to the Statute of the Court gives the European Parliament, the Council, and the European Central Bank the right to be notified every time a preliminary question is referred and to intervene if they have a particular interest in the case.[31] We will see whether this will translate into a more active role for these EU institutions.

In the previous section, we said that before the ECtHR, Member States tend to intervene to defend their laws and sovereignty. In Luxembourg, things are a bit more complex: the governments' positions before the CJEU can take very different colours. The Member States' interests in a case can be of a legal or political nature, aiming at shaping the doctrinal interpretation of an EU norm or pushing for a preferred policy outcome.[32] For instance, depending on the matter at stake, governments can be pro or against further European integration.[33]

In recent years, we have seen the position of intervening Member States becoming stronger before the Court of Justice, in quantitative and qualitative terms. First, they have significantly increased their participation in the preliminary reference procedure.[34] Second, they have started coordinating their interventions before the Court:

> In 2002, an informal network of national agents before the CJEU was set up at the initiative of the Netherlands. […] Information on new cases before the CJEU, for example, is frequently shared via email to inform other agents of the importance of a specific case, or to inquire whether other Member States are considering intervening in a specific case. More substantive coordination as to the position adopted in specific cases takes place on a bilateral basis. For instance, in situations where a number of Member States have a shared interest, national agents may exchange views and align positions.[35]

By sharing information and coordinating their positions, Member States' agents can increase the likelihood of their intervention having an impact on the adjudication of the Court. Empirical research has shown that Member States' interventions have a substantive effect on the CJEU's decisions.[36] According to a study by Larsson and Naurin, the

[30] Krenn, *The Procedural and Organisational Law* (2022) 58; M Galanter, 'Why the "Haves" Come out Ahead: Speculations on the Limits of Legal Change' (1974) 9 *Law & Society Review* 95.

[31] Article 23 of the Statute of the Court of Justice of the European Union as amended by Regulation 2024/2019 of the European Parliament and of the Council of 11 April 2024. To be sure, the possibility for these EU institutions to intervene where they had a particular interest in the issues raised by the national court was already informal practice at the Court, which decided to formalise it with this amendment.

[32] J Dederke and D Naurin, 'Friends of the Court? Why EU Governments File Observations before the Court of Justice' (2018) 57 *European Journal of Political Research* 867.

[33] See for instance CJEU, Joined Cases C-29/22 P and C-44/22 P *KS and KD v Council and Others* ECLI:EU:C:2024:725, paras 102–112, where several Member States have intervened, some of them in favour and some of them against an expansion of the CJEU's judicial review power.

[34] MP F Granger, 'When Governments Go to Luxembourg … the Influence of Governments on the Court of Justice' (2004) 29 *European Law Review* 3, 8.

[35] M Bulterman and C Wissels, 'Strategies Developed by – and between – National Governments to Interact with the CJEU', in B de Witte, E Muir and M Dawson (eds), *Judicial Activism at the European Court of Justice* (Cambridge, Edward Elgar, 2013) 269.

[36] The question of whether the Member States' interventions have an impact on the CJEU was object of a heated debate among lawyers and political scientists. See: CJ Carrubba, M Gabel and C Hankla, 'Judicial Behavior under Political Constraints: Evidence from the European Court of Justice' (2008) 102 *The American*

effect is larger when Member States align and demonstrate 'unity' before the Court, and when they promote further legal integration.[37] The same authors argue that this effect is due to the CJEU's concern about the possibility that its judgments will be later overridden by a political majority in the Council, thus the Court uses the submissions to calculate the risk of override and adjust its ruling accordingly.

Beyond the risk of overrides, which hopefully affects only a minority of cases, the Member States' observations are an important source of information for the CJEU. Contrary to the ECtHR, which is called to rule on alleged violations of international human rights norms in individual disputes, the CJEU is asked to provide an authoritative interpretation of EU law that will shape harmonisation and guide the practice of national courts and public authorities. It is thus crucial for the Court to understand how EU law is applied in national contexts and the challenges that may arise to European integration. This is especially true when the intervention is filed by the government of the State from where the preliminary reference originates: the government's representative may provide insights into the functioning of a specific national law and practice or may give factual information that not even the referring judge possesses. This information is important to fill the gaps in the CJEU's knowledge of the case, to help it adjudicate on the legal and factual context, and even to challenge the referring court's account.[38]

3.2. Non-governmental Actors as Third Parties: A Road Uphill?

The procedural setting of the CJEU contributes to giving the general impression that, in comparison to courts where the NGOs' role is more prominent, such as the ECtHR, the CJEU is more unwelcoming for civil society. As mentioned in Section 1, for individuals and groups, it is extremely difficult to bring direct actions before the CJEU because of how the Court was procedurally designed.[39] For this reason, most fundamental rights cases discussed before the Court of Justice arrive at the Court via indirect action: the above-mentioned preliminary reference procedure.

When we talk about TPIs before the CJEU, it is important to distinguish between indirect and direct actions, because the rules are different. Legal and natural persons can file TPIs in direct actions, provided two conditions are met. First, these direct actions should not be 'cases between Member States, between institutions of the Union or between Member States and institutions of the Union';[40] this means that natural persons

Political Science Review 435; A Stone Sweet and TL Brunell, 'Constructing a Supranational Constitution: Dispute Resolution and Governance in the European Community' (1998) 92 *American Political Science Review* 63; A Stone Sweet and TL Brunell, 'The European Court of Justice, State Noncompliance, and the Politics of Override' (2012) 106 *The American Political Science Review* 204.

[37] O Larsson and D Naurin, 'Judicial Independence and Political Uncertainty: How the Risk of Override Affects the Court of Justice of the EU' (2016) 70 *International Organization* 377, 404–405.

[38] V Passalacqua and F Costamagna, 'The Law and Facts of the Preliminary Reference Procedure: A Critical Assessment of the EU Court of Justice's Source of Knowledge' (2023) 2 *European Law Open* 322.

[39] Article 263 TFEU and CJEU, Case C-25/62 *Plaumann v Commission* ECLI:EU:C:1963:17. Rasmussen, 'Why Is Article 173 Interpreted' (1980); M Pagano, *Environmental NGOs and Access to Justice before the CJEU* (Oxford, Hart Publishing, 2025).

[40] Statute of the Court of Justice of the European Union, Article 40.

and civil society associations cannot have their say in some of the most politically salient cases such as infringement proceedings, where the Commission asks the Court of Justice to assess whether a Member State has breached EU law.[41] The second condition is that legal or natural persons must 'establish an interest in the result of a case'. This has been interpreted strictly by the Court, and we can say that rather than be simply interested in the result of the case, the intervener seems required to prove that it is directly affected by the judgment.[42] As the Court clarified, the intervener should show 'a direct, existing interest in the ruling' and not just 'an interest in relation to the pleas in law or arguments put forward.'[43] Such interest in the case 'can be considered to be sufficiently direct only in so far as that result is capable of altering the legal position of the applicant'.[44] Thus, the interest in the result of the case must be read as referring to the final decision by the Court and not to any point of law touched upon by the judgment. The third party's interest in the case can be represented by an association, such as an organisation of undertakings; this, however, must have clearly stated in its object the mandate to defend its members' interests.[45]

With environmental organisations, the Court decided to adopt a more flexible criterion, in consideration of their goal of protecting the general interest and the consequent difficulty in proving that a judgment directly affects their legal or economic position.[46] The Court clarified that environmental organisations can intervene if they meet two criteria: first, there is a direct link between the case and the organisation's field of activity; second, 'the case raises questions of principle liable to affect the interests defended by the organization'.[47] This has not been always the case, at least in the past. In *Castelnou Energia*, the General Court granted permission to intervene to Greenpeace Spain in consideration that its activity is carried out in Spain, the Member State concerned by the judgment; instead, the Court rejected the request of two other environmental organisations because, despite having the same aim and object, they carry out their activities in the EU as a whole.[48] Arguably, this leaves some questions open regarding the level of involvement that the organisation must show in order to be admitted to intervene in the case.

[41] Lenaerts, Gutman and Nowak, *EU Procedural Law* (2023) 175.

[42] CJEU, Order of the President, Case C-104/16 P *Front Polisario v Council of the European Union* ECLI:EU:C:2016:443. Here the Court accepted the intervention of Comader, an association of farmers, because 'des questions de principe soulevées par le litige peuvent être considérées, ainsi que l'expose la Comader, comme étant de nature à affecter les conditions et les modalités d'exportation vers l'Union des produits relevant de cet accord et, par voie de conséquence, les intérêts des membres de la Comader' ['some of the questions of principle raised by the dispute may be considered, as explained by Comader, as being of a nature to affect the conditions and arrangements for exporting to the Union products covered by this agreement and, consequently, the interests of the members of Comader', translation by the author].

[43] CJEU, Order of the President, Case C-26/23 P *Minority SafePack – one million signatures for diversity in Europe v Commission* ECLI:EU:C:2023:618.

[44] ibid.

[45] Order of the CJEU, Case T-429/13 *Bayer CropScience AG v European Commission* ECLI:EU:T:2014:920, para 39.

[46] I Anrò, 'L'amicus Curiae Presso La Corte Di Giustizia Dell'Unione Europea: Qualche Riflessione per l'apertura Delle Porte Del Kirchberg' (2023) *Rivista del Contenzioso Europeo* 67.

[47] CJEU, Order of the President, Case C-499/18 P *Bayer CropScience AG and Others v European Commission* ECLI:EU:C:2019:107, para 6.

[48] Order of CJEU, Case T-57/11 *Castelnou Energía, SL v European Commission* ECLI:EU:T:2012:580, paras 18–21.

What has been said so far concerns direct actions, but the rules change for indirect actions, namely in the preliminary ruling procedure. Here, legal and natural persons cannot file third-party interventions unless they were already a party in the national proceedings that gave rise to the preliminary reference. This marks a stark difference with the position of the Member States and EU institutions, which can always intervene in the preliminary reference procedure by submitting observations and participating in the oral hearing.

The main reason behind the exclusion of non-State third parties from the right to intervene shall be found in the Court's case law, which qualified the preliminary reference procedure as 'non-contentious' and thus subject to different rules. Indeed, the overmentioned Article 40 of the Statute does not seem to make any distinction between direct and indirect actions, and could be read as applying to the preliminary reference procedure too.[49] However, the Court interpreted the scope of Article 40 restrictively in the famous case of *Costa v Enel*, where Edison, an Italian energy company, filed a request to intervene that was rejected.[50] The CJEU explained its refusal with an argument related to the nature of the proceedings: this is not a 'contentious procedure', designed to settle a dispute between two parties, thus it is governed by special rules. These special rules are enshrined in Article 23 of the Statute, mentioned in the previous sub-section, which gives only Member States, EU institutions and other selected EU bodies and third States the possibility to intervene.[51]

According to the CJEU's restrictive reading, third-party interveners are admitted only if they were already a party to the national proceedings, in line with Article 97 Rules of Procedure that establishes: 'The parties to the main proceedings are those who are determined as such by the referring court or tribunal in accordance with national rules of procedure.'[52]

An important consequence of Article 97 is to create a rather fragmented situation for what concerns the legal standing rules before the CJEU, to the point that it is fair to say that the CJEU, in the preliminary reference procedure, has as many TPI rules as the number of Member States.[53] This might not be a trivial issue as it means that individuals and legal persons residing in Member States with more relaxed rules for TPIs have better chances to intervene and bring their views before the CJEU. A case in point is the UK, which has rather generous rules regarding TPIs and the courts of which referred

[49] Article 40 generally states that 'Member States and institutions of the Union may intervene in cases before the Court of Justice. The same right shall be open to the bodies, offices and agencies of the Union and to any other person which can establish an interest in the result of a case submitted to the Court. Natural or legal persons shall not intervene in cases between Member States, between institutions of the Union or between Member States and institutions of the Union. Without prejudice to the second paragraph, the States, other than the Member States, which are parties to the Agreement on the European Economic Area, and also the EFTA Surveillance Authority referred to in that Agreement, may intervene in cases before the Court where one of the fields of application of that Agreement is concerned. An application to intervene shall be limited to supporting the form of order sought by one of the parties.'

[50] CJEU, Order of the President, Case 6/64 *Costa v Enel* ECLI:EU:C:1964:34.

[51] Statute of the Court of Justice of the European Union, Article 23.

[52] Rules of Procedure of the Court of Justice of the European Union, Article 97. See also CJEU, Order of the President, Case C-73/07 *Tietosuojavaltuutettu v Satakunnan Markkinapörssi Oy and Satamedia Oy* ECLI:EU:C:2007:507 where the Court denied the European Data Supervisor the possibility to intervene.

[53] To be precise, within the same Member State standing rules may vary depending on the procedure (whether administrative, criminal or civil procedure etc).

one of the most famous strategic litigation cases, with five intervening NGOs.[54] And it is not by chance that it is again from the UK the only case where the CJEU has refused the intervention of a party despite the fact that the referring national court had admitted it; in *Football Association Premier League*, the Court refused the intervention of five legal persons even if recognised as parties by the referring judge because 'the applications have been made only with a view to participating in the proceedings before the Court and that the applicants do not intend to play an active part in the proceedings before the national court after delivery of the judgment giving a preliminary ruling.'[55] The Court here applied similar reasoning to that of *Foglia v Novello*, where the division of labour between the national court and the CJEU can be somehow reconsidered if there is a risk of abusing the Article 267 TFEU procedure.[56]

Arguably, the CJEU's restrictive interpretation of the right to intervene in the preliminary reference procedure can have detrimental consequences on the Court's capacity to acquire relevant information on the case.[57] Third parties might greatly contribute to the CJEU's knowledge by providing information on the factual and legal background of the case, in line with De Schutter's 'participatory adjudicatory' argument outlined in the introduction.

4. Do Different Rules Affect the Number and the Actors Filing Third-party Interventions? A Comparison of the Two Courts

We have seen that the two Courts regulate TPIs very differently, and only the CJEU grants privileged status to some actors over others. Thus, it seems reasonable to expect that this regulatory framework conditions the practice of TPIs and has substantial influence over, first, the number of TPIs submitted to the two Courts; and, second, the type of actors that file interventions before the two courts.

In particular, the ECtHR regulates TPIs in a rather lay way, regardless of who files them. In this case, we may expect that Member States and other actors file interventions at a similar rate and possibly in similar cases, namely cases where the issue at stake is

[54] CJEU, Joined Cases C-411/10 and C-493/10 *N S and M E and Others* ECLI:EU:C:2011:865. On the role of civil society actors in migration litigation see S Carrera and B Petkova, 'The Potential of Civil Society and Human Rights Organizations through Third-Party Interventions before the European Courts: The EU's Area of Freedom, Security and Justice' in B De Witte, E Muir and M Dawson (eds), *Judicial Activism at the European Court of Justice* (Cambridge, Edward Elgar Publishing, 2013); V Passalacqua, 'Who Mobilizes the Court? Migrant Rights Defenders Before the Court of Justice of the EU' (2022) 15 *Law and Development Review* 381.

[55] CJEU, Order of the President, Joined Cases C-403/08 and C-429/08 *Football Association Premier League Ltd*, para 9, cited in R Schiano, 'La procedura del rinvio pregiudiziale' in C Iannone and F Ferraro (eds), *Il rinvio pregiudiziale* (Torino, Giappichelli, 2020) 181.

[56] CJEU, Case 244/80 *Foglia v Novello* ECLI:EU:C:1981:302; A Tizzano, 'Litiges Fictifs et Compétence Préjudicielle de La. Cour de Justice Européenne' (1981) 85 *Revue générale de droit international public*; Passalacqua and Costamagna, 'The Law and Facts' (2023) 276.

[57] Passalacqua and Costamagna, 'The Law and Facts' (2023); Krommendijk and van der Pas, 'To Intervene or Not to Intervene' (2022).

likely to be relevant beyond the specific applicant and can impact more States than only the respondent Member States.

The CJEU regulates TPIs differently depending on the actor who files them. When the intervener is a Member State, no restriction applies. On the contrary, the Court does not admit interventions by legal and natural persons in the preliminary ruling procedure and conditions interventions in other actions to the stringent criterion of showing that they are directly affected by the case's result.

Considering this, we expect that Member States file similar TPIs before the two Courts, as they are privileged actors before the CJEU and are not restrained by the ECtHR. At the same time, we can expect that NGOs file far more TPIs before the ECtHR than before the CJEU.

Interestingly, empirical research on the two courts only partially confirms such expectations. First, to my knowledge, we lack a comparative study of interventions before the two courts, so I had to rely on empirical works that focus either on one Court or on the other. To evaluate the ECtHR practice, I relied on two studies: one by Van den Eynde and the other by Nicole Bürli. Considering the different scopes of their inquiry, they yielded compatible results.[58]

As Van Den Eynde shows in her article, the number of TPIs filed by NGOs before the ECtHR steadily increased in recent years. While initially limited to only a few interventions annually, the number rose to over 40 per year after 2010.

Van den Eynde (2013) counted only the TPIs made by NGOs (defined as private, independent, not-for-profit organisations that defend human rights) up to 2012. She found that 'the final number at the time of writing is 294 [amicus curiae] briefs submitted in 237 cases.' Many of these TPIs were filed before the Grand Chamber: 'The Grand Chamber has delivered 307 judgments in total and saw NGOs' interventions in 65 of them – that is in 21 per cent of the cases.'

Nicole Bürli's study is more recent, from 2017, and it counted all the TPIs, submitted by any actor, filed from 1979, the year of the first intervention by the UK, to 2016.[59] According to her research, the ECtHR received 667 interventions, of which 518 qualify as amicus curiae by NGOs and 117 are from States, prominently by the UK. This research also reveals that, in the face of rather equal standing rules for TPIs, Article 36 is markedly more used by non-state actors.

For the Court of Justice, data on Member States' interventions is provided by political scientists' studies, while, to my knowledge, we have no comprehensive study of non-state TPIs. According to a database used in two studies by Dederke and Naurin and Larsson and Naurin, analysing 1599 preliminary rulings issued by the CJEU from 1997 to 2008, 62 per cent of the proceedings contained at least two Member State interventions, meaning at least one intervention beyond that of the Member State from where the preliminary reference originated (which is virtually always present).[60] The average

[58] L Van den Eynde, 'An Empirical Look at the Amicus Curiae Practice of Human Rights NGOs Before the European Court of Human Rights' (2013) 31 *Netherlands Quarterly of Human Rights* 271; Bürli (n 21).

[59] Bürli (n 21).

[60] Larsson and Naurin, 'Judicial Independence and Political Uncertainty' (2016) 392.

number of Member States' TPIs for each case is 3.6.[61] Interestingly, the UK was also the most active intervener before the CJEU.[62]

As I previously indicated, to my knowledge, there is no comprehensive empirical study of TPIs before the CJEU that considers both state and non-state actors. However, we can confidently say that the number of non-state actors who have managed to file a TPI before the CJEU is significantly lower than in the ECtHR. Even though, as we will see in the next section, this is partly changing due to some creative efforts by civil society actors.

We can conclude that the rules of the courts do not entirely account for the varying engagement with TPIs. While our expectations regarding NGOs and non-state actors are confirmed, as they participate significantly more in proceedings before the ECtHR, the Member States engage more in interventions before the CJEU. We can only make hypotheses as to the reason behind such disparity. This can partly be due to the different roles and jurisdictions of the two Courts: the CJEU has a broader mandate than the ECtHR, as its judgments affect more aspects of the national legal orders, such as trade, competition law, free movement of persons, etc. Moreover, the CJEU's judgments have a harmonising effect on the national legal order, providing for rules of interpretation that bind national authorities in the entire EU. In comparison, the ECtHR has a narrower task: adjudicating whether a State is responsible for a human rights violation in a concrete dispute. To be sure, the ECtHR's interpretation is binding on all the States that are members of the ECHR, but its rulings are likely to have a less direct impact on the national laws of the States that are not defendants in the case. For these reasons, it is reasonable to think that Member State governments perceive the CJEU as a more threatening Court that, with its judgments, can directly shape the direction of European integration and, thus, the degree of autonomy left to them.

5. Anomaly or Creativity? Shadow Interventions and Informal Amici Curiae

It should be mentioned that all the aforementioned empirical studies, both regarding the CJEU and ECtHR, suffer difficulties in accessing data on TPIs. Indeed, interventions are visible only insofar as they are mentioned somewhere in the Courts' judgments and are destined to be ignored in all the instances where the Court makes no mention of them. To give a concrete example, Bürli counted three cases where the United Nations High Commissioner for Refugees (UNHCR) intervened,[63] but the UNHCR itself stated on their website that it intervened in 54 cases.[64] This suggests that there is a vast number of interventions destined to remain under the radar.

[61] Dederke and Naurin, 'Friends of the Court?' (2018) 870.
[62] ibid 870; Larsson and Naurin (n 37) 392.
[63] Bürli (n 21) 8.
[64] The UNHCR regularly publishes the text of its interventions on its website: www.unhcr.org/publications/unhcr-interventions-european-court-human-rights accessed 19 February 2025.

The invisibility of TPIs can also be seen in the CJEU. For instance, in a recent case involving a clash between animal rights and religious freedom, a coalition of animal rights NGOs, the Eurogroup for Animals, published an online document addressing the Court of Justice that started in the following way:

> We take the liberty to submit this Amicus Curiae brief to your attention in a spirit of constructive collaboration. While we are well aware that – under the current Court's Statute and Rules of Procedure – this brief won't formally be admissible to the proceedings, we hope that it could inform your deliberation, given the nature erga omnes of your forthcoming preliminary judgment in such an important, consequential case.[65]

This animal rights NGO has used an online blog as a platform to reach the judges of the Court of Justice and circumvent the inadmissibility of amicus curiae briefs. Similar informal amici curiae have been submitted in the migration field; for instance, when the case of *Elgafaji*, the very first important case regarding the interpretation of the 1951 Refugee Convention, was referred to the Court of Justice, the UNHCR published a brief on its website advocating for a specific interpretation of the Geneva Convention on refugees.[66] The case of *Elgafaji* was not initiated as a test case, but we cannot rule out that the UNHCR opinion had an impact on the Advocate General and the Court's interpretation.

Since then, the UNHCR has issued informal amici curiae in 22 cases. While we do not know whether the CJEU reads these documents, we know that, at least in one instance, the Advocate General did. At the CJEU, the Advocate General is tasked with issuing a first opinion on the case to help the Court's adjudicating process; while the CJEU's decisions are written in a relatively sober style, the Advocate General can be less formalistic and often cites academic works and other sources. In one case, Advocate General Eleanor Sharpston explicitly acknowledged the UNHCR statement:

> The UNHCR occasionally makes statements which have persuasive, but not binding, force. His Office has published various statements which relate to the interpretation of Article 1D of the 1951 Convention: a commentary in its Handbook on procedures and criteria for determining refugee status under the 1951 Convention and the 1967 Protocol, a note published in 2002 (and revised in 2009) and a 2009 statement (also subsequently revised) which relates expressly to Ms Bolbol's case. I intend to treat this last as an unofficial amicus curiae brief.[67]

Publishing informal amici curiae online is just one technique that collective actors use to participate informally in preliminary ruling proceedings. Another creative technique used by the Vrij University Migration Law Clinic is to submit their expert opinions as an attachment to one of the parties' written observations, hoping that the EU judges will read them. This strategy allowed the Clinic to informally participate in several

[65] A Alemanno and NM de Sadeleer, 'Humanising Animal Slaughter Need Not Infringe Religious Freedom (Amicus Curiae Brief in C-336/19 Centraal Israëlitisch Consistorie Van België and Others)' (*Eurogroup for Animals*, 21 October 2020) www.eurogroupforanimals.org/news/amicus-curiae-cjeu-case accessed 19 February 2025.

[66] UN High Commissioner for Refugees, 'UNHCR Public Statement in Relation to Elgafaji v Staatssecretaris van Justitie before the Court of Justice of the European Union' (*Refworld*, January 2008) www.refworld.org/docid/479df7472.html accessed 20 January 2021.

[67] CJEU, Case C-31/09 *Bolbol v Bevándorlási és Állampolgársági Hivatal* Opinion of AG Sharpston, ECLI:EU:C:2010:119, para 16.

cases, although there was no guarantee of being heard.[68] In all these cases, the collective actors' names are not featured in any official document of the case, and the only way that academics have to trace their presence is through qualitative analysis; it is thus possible that, as it happens for the ECtHR, many interventions at the CJEU will also go under the radar.

6. Conclusion: Are TPI Rules Fit for Purpose? Some Reflection on the Need to Rebalance the Procedural Power Imbalance

This chapter has explored and contrasted the regulatory frameworks governing TPIs before the ECtHR and the CJEU. It has shown that the two courts adopt markedly different approaches: while the ECtHR, at least formally, applies the same rules to both state and non-state actors, the CJEU distinguishes sharply between them, granting Member States a privileged status that allows them to intervene in all its proceedings.

The chapter also highlights some challenges associated with TPIs before the CJEU and the ECtHR. Both courts offer different levels of accessibility and transparency for third-party involvement, raising questions about the inclusivity and legitimacy of their decision-making processes.

At the ECtHR, the rules governing third-party interventions have the merit of treating state and non-state actors equally. However, they are open to criticism due to their lack of transparency, particularly regarding admissibility criteria. As Bürli indicates, one-third of TPI requests are rejected by the President of the Court, but the grounds for such decisions remain largely opaque. This lack of transparency undermines the ECHR's commitment to fostering civil society's participation in the cases. Without clear criteria and reasoning for admitting or rejecting TPIs, less experienced NGOs and civil society actors can be discouraged from participating, and the ECtHR's proceedings may be seen as less open to a range of perspectives that could enrich its deliberations.

In contrast, the CJEU's procedural framework makes interventions in direct actions very difficult for non-state actors and completely denies them the possibility of filing a TPI in preliminary reference cases, which often involve interpreting fundamental rights within the EU. This issue is exacerbated by the fact that Member States, due to their privileged position, can always intervene and frequently utilise this mechanism to defend their national legislation. This scenario raises concerns about whether the CJEU's approach adequately accounts for the interests of parties who may be unable to participate formally. The Court's openness to Member States, paired with its simultaneous exclusion of other interested parties, indicates an imbalance in the deliberative process. This potentially amplifies the influence of governments and majoritarian positions while neglecting proper representation of minorities and public interest organisations.

[68] See the Vrij University Clinic website: https://migrationlawclinic.org/category/expert-opinions/ accessed 19 February 2025.

Paradoxically, TPIs at the CJEU risk being an instrument to defend majoritarian views rather than to give voice to the underrepresented.

Whether the current rules governing TPIs in both courts align with the ideal 'adjudication-participation' model remains an open question. If judicial legitimacy depends on a deliberative process inclusive of diverse perspectives, as many commentators suggest, then the European Courts' existing frameworks may fall short. The ECtHR's lack of transparency and the CJEU's closed stance toward TPIs could hinder a balanced representation of all the interests at stake, especially in cases where parties are unequal in resources or influence. Allowing broader third-party participation could help to address these disparities and enhance the legitimacy of judicial outcomes by ensuring that decisions are informed by the broadest possible array of perspectives.

In sum, while TPIs have the potential to contribute meaningfully to the courts' deliberative processes, reforms are needed to strengthen this practice in the judicial frameworks of the CJEU and ECtHR. Transparent criteria for admitting TPIs at the ECtHR and reconsideration of the closed approach to non-state parties at the CJEU would be steps toward fostering a more balanced and participatory adjudication model. Such changes could help ensure that judicial proceedings are not only legally sound but also perceived as equitable and legitimate by the wider public.

5

Deliberative Discourse in Developing the EU's Human Rights Responsibility

JOYCE DE CONINCK

1. Introduction

A crucial component in the activation of human rights, is enforcement through judicial mechanisms, ensuring rights are effective rather than merely theoretical or illusory. Courts fulfil several established key functions in the human rights space: they ensure that human rights instruments are applied in a dynamic and evolving manner[1] and address legal lacunae; they contribute to clarifying the scope of human rights protection offered to individuals, including its scope *ratione personae*; they mediate between majoritarian rule and minority perspectives and provide protection to vulnerable groups and minorities whose rights may otherwise be eroded. This is particularly relevant in contexts where (geo-)political shifts, such as the right-wing turn in Europe, threaten to diminish previously entrenched rights through legal innovations and the misappropriation of human rights.[2]

Courts additionally act as interlocutors by translating human rights *commitments* into actionable and justiciable human rights *obligations*. A distinction here is made between human rights *responsibility*, human rights *commitments* and human rights *obligations*. According to this distinction, legal responsibility for human rights violations typically only arises when the commitments found in various human rights sources (eg, in customary law, treaty law, domestic constitutions) have been translated into legally enforceable *obligations* that have not been respected.

In performing its functions, including its translation work, courts have at their disposal a wide array of sources referred to here as 'deliberative input' or 'deliberative discourse'. These sources range from the arguments advanced by litigating parties in legal proceedings which offer interpretations of international or constitutional law to NGO and civil society interventions, domestic legislation and advocacy, all of which

[1] P Alston (ed), *The Complexity of Human Rights – From Vernacularization to Quantification* (Oxford, Hart Publishing, 2024) 8.

[2] G de Búrca and K Young, 'The (Mis)Appropriation of Human Rights by the New Global Right: An Introduction to the Symposium' (2023) 21 *International Journal of Constitutional Law* 205.

offer deliberative input on how such rights are to be interpreted to remain effective and attuned to social reality.[3]

In a rule-based order, courts thus constitute a site to deliberate over and decide upon unresolved questions of human rights, by teasing out what it means to enjoy human rights effectively. Courts contribute to the clarification of what human rights mean for individuals (such as their scope of protection), who enjoys such rights mindful of jurisdictional limitations, as well as how such rights are to be modulated into actionable obligations for duty-holders. In turn, *access* to courts is a crucial component to ensuring effective enjoyment of one's rights, as courts can only fulfil their role in the human rights space when called upon in a dispute or cases of legal uncertainty. Access to courts becomes all the more relevant when novel questions of rights protection, with limited precedent and limited legislative guidance, are raised.

There is no question that the European Union, including its many institutions, bodies, offices and agencies – referred to here as EU entities – is also legally bound by human rights.[4] Despite this certitude, novel questions arise from the EU's commitment to human rights, including what the EU's powers as a non-state actor with state-like traits are in determining the scope of human rights protection;[5] who can rely on 'EU human rights'; whether identical jurisdictional limitations exist as with State responsibility;[6] what the limits are of human rights in light of the conferral of competence between the EU and its Members and how the EU's commitment to human rights (as per the Charter of Fundamental Rights (CFREU) and general principles of EU law) have translated into enforceable and justiciable human rights obligations, which bind EU entities.[7] As the role of courts has traditionally and overwhelmingly been limited to determining *State* responsibility for human rights harms and the Court of Justice of the European Union (CJEU) has only dealt with the what, the who and the how of the EU's human rights responsibility in a limited manner, there is a significant knowledge gap about how human rights may be activated, or made effective, by EU entities and within the EU legal framework.[8] This relative absence is exacerbated as there is also less deliberative input on how human rights should be activated by EU entities than there is concerning State responsibility both within and beyond the courts.

[3] Alston argues that in a first iteration of human rights, lawyers and judges downplayed the importance of various sources of deliberative input and focused primarily on legalistic sources. P Alston (ed), *The Complexity of Human Rights* (2024) 14.

[4] EU entities referred to in the present contribution encompass EU institutions, bodies, offices and agencies and are bound by the Charter of Fundamental Rights by virtue of Article 51 as well as by virtue of general principles of EU law.

[5] For instance: when or in what scenarios may the right to privacy and data protection be invoked vis-à-vis EU entities when they collaborate with EU Member States? See on this topic: J De Coninck and S Tas, 'Investigating Five Dimensions of the EU's Liability Regime: Marián Kočner' (2025) 62 *Common Market Law Review* 195. Differently, in what instances may human rights protection be demanded from EU entities in the realm of EU trade agreements? See on this topic: J De Coninck and P Van Elsuwege, 'Human Rights Respectful Trade' (2024) 42 *Berkeley Journal of International Law* 247.

[6] G Raimondo, *The European Integrated Border Management: Frontex, Human Rights, and International Responsibility* (Oxford, Hart Publishing, 2024) 165–172.

[7] J De Coninck, *The EU's Human Rights Responsibility Gap: Deconstructing Human Rights Impunity of International Organisations* (Oxford, Hart Publishing, 2024) 39–61.

[8] ibid. See also (adopting different terminology while expressing similar questions from a disciplinary angle): S Besson, 'The Bearers of Human Rights' Duties and Responsibilities for Human Rights: A Quiet (R)evolution?' (2015) 32 *Social Philosophy and Policy* 244.

Mindful of this relative absence, this contribution argues that access to Courts – and notably to the CJEU – constitutes an indispensable component of the development of EU human rights responsibility. Without the type of deliberative input facilitated through meaningful access to courts, EU human rights responsibility is at risk of being the design of a select few through legislative processes characterised by a democratic deficit. Limited access to the CJEU to litigate EU human rights responsibility may furthermore encourage Member States to disregard their own human rights obligations by transferring powers to EU entities, as the lack of comprehensive deliberative input may result in a shielding of EU entities from human rights responsibility before the CJEU.[9] After all, if human rights violative conduct by EU entities is directed at individuals that do not meaningfully participate in the EU's legislative or political processes and their access to the CJEU is notably limited, how then can EU entities effectively be challenged in court?

This is not to say that the deliberative input in determining EU human rights responsibility must per se be identical to that regarding States, including before courts. But precisely because deliberative input is significantly more limited on novel questions of EU human rights responsibility, meaningful access to the CJEU as a path for providing such deliberative input is all the more important for ensuring that rights protection remains effective within Europe. Access to the CJEU serves as an essential conduit for advancing counter-majoritarian arguments and addressing trends that, if left uncontested, could work to exclude rights-holders from rights-protection under EU-wide policies, legislation and operational conduct and work to erode human rights more generally.

With this in mind, the contribution begins by first clarifying the role of deliberative input in shaping human rights responsibility for States through the lens of the theory of 'human rights experimentalism' and how accordingly, deliberative input has contributed to ensuring the effectiveness of human rights. Second, the contribution argues that because States are different actors from EU entities, with distinct powers and capacities, the manner in which human rights have been interpreted, enacted and applied for States cannot simply be transplanted to EU entities, warranting novel approaches in answering the novel questions of EU human rights responsibility. Finally, turning to the limited deliberative input that exists in shaping EU human rights responsibility, this contribution argues that deliberative input must be safeguarded through meaningful direct access to the CJEU, as this provides a necessary site to grapple with and mould the novel approaches to EU human rights responsibility and, more specifically, determine the what, the who and the how of human rights protection: what the scope of this responsibility is, who enjoys EU human rights protection and how the EU's commitment to human rights should be translated into concrete human rights obligations.

[9] J De Coninck, 'Shielding Frontex: On the EU General Court's "WS and Others v Frontex"' (*Verfassungsblog*, 9 September 2023) https://verfassungsblog.de/shielding-frontex/ accessed 6 May 2025; J De Coninck, 'Shielding Frontex 2.0: The One with the Impossible Proof' (*Verfassungsblog*, 30 January 2024) https://verfassungsblog.de/shielding-frontex-2-0/ accessed 6 May 2025; L Hillary and B Schotel, 'The Implications of the 2023 Frontex Judgment on the EU Agencies and the Legal Credibility of the Court' (*European Law Blog*, February 2024) https://doi.org/10.21428/9885764c.75ef70e0 accessed 6 May 2025.

2. Deliberative Input and Human Rights Experimentalism

The determination of the scope of human rights protection, who enjoys it and how human rights commitments translate into enforceable human rights obligations for States, has been the subject of a wide range of explanatory accounts. These include the 'vernacularisation' of human rights,[10] the 'vascularisation' of the judicial process,[11] the legalisation of human rights[12] and the theory of discordant parity,[13] all of which can be explained through the lens of human rights experimentalism,[14] informing the European Court of Human Rights (ECtHR) consensus doctrine, and in turn, similar determinations by the CJEU.[15]

Seen through this lens, human rights commitments are understood and made actionable as a result of deliberative democratic legislative processes, through legal mobilisation, academic exchange, and advocacy, among others. Different actors and stakeholders, operating at different domestic, regional, and international levels before different fora and with different objectives in mind, deliberatively engage with each other, eventually giving rise to a consensus on how human rights commitments are to be understood. At least in theory, such consensus subsequently informs the reasoning and findings of the ECtHR and (explicitly and implicitly) the CJEU's rulings on the responsibility of Member States for human rights, as per Article 52(3) of the Charter and the EU Member States common constitutional traditions and ensuing practices.[16]

This deliberative discourse fosters dynamism in the way human rights bind States, ensuring that these rights are not merely 'theoretical or illusory' but instead 'practical and effective'.[17] It also reinforces the notion that the instruments embedding these rights function as 'living instruments'.[18] Thereby, these translation processes prevent human

[10] SE Merry, 'Transnational Human Rights and Local Activism: Mapping the Middle' (2006) 108 *American Anthropologist* 38; SE Merry and P Levitt, 'The Vernacularization of Women's Human Rights' in S Hopgood, J Snyder and L Vinjamuri (eds), *Human Rights Futures* (Cambridge, Cambridge University Press, 2017); DM Goldstein, 'Whose Vernacular? Translating Human Rights in Local Contexts' in M Goodale (ed), *Human Rights at the Crossroads* (Oxford, Oxford University Press, 2013).

[11] T Soave, *The Everyday Makers of International Law: From Great Halls to Back Rooms* (Cambridge, Cambridge University Press, 2022).

[12] BA Simmons, *Mobilizing for Human Rights: International Law in Domestic Politics* (Cambridge, Cambridge University Press, 2009).

[13] E Benvenisti and A Harel, 'Embracing the Tension Between National and International Human Rights Law: The Case for Discordant Parity' (2017) 15 *International Journal of Constitutional Law* 36.

[14] G de Búrca, *Reframing Human Rights in a Turbulent Era* (Oxford, Oxford University Press, 2021); G de Búrca, 'Human Rights Experimentalism' (2017) 111 *American Journal of International Law* 277.

[15] K Dzehtsiarou, *European Consensus and the Legitimacy of the European Court of Human Rights* (Cambridge, Cambridge University Press, 2015); P Kapotas and VP Tzevelekos, *Building Consensus on European Consensus – Judicial Interpretation of Human Rights in Europe and Beyond* (Cambridge, Cambridge University Press, 2019).

[16] Article 52(3) CFREU functions as a tool to coordinate the protection offered under the CFREU with the protection offered for corresponding rights found in the ECHR, holding that the latter functions as the minimum level of protection for the former.

[17] See ECtHR, App no 6289/73 *Airey v Ireland* ECLI:CE:ECHR:1979:1009JUD000628973.

[18] S Fredman, *Comparative Human Rights Law* (Oxford, Oxford University Press, 2018) 132; R Ita and D Hicks, 'Beyond Expansion or Restriction' Models of Interaction between the Living Instrument and Margin of Appreciation Doctrines and the Scope of the ECHR' (2021) 10 *International Human Rights Law Review* 40; G Letsas, 'The ECHR as a Living Instrument: Its Meaning and Legitimacy' in A Føllesdal, B Peters and G Ulfstein (eds), *Constituting Europe: The European Court of Human Rights in a National, European and Global Context* (Cambridge, Cambridge University Press, 2013).

rights from becoming ossified[19] in the pursuit of a particular form of deliberative and remedial justice.[20]

The concept of 'vernacularisation' of human rights points to the anthropological study that traces the process of translation of 'universalistic human rights into local understandings of social justice', offering insights 'into the transformation of meanings and practices within small social settings, highlighting aspects of its circulation and use that can be obscured by the focus on the state in international relations and legal scholarship'.[21] Similarly, this process can also be described in the opposite direction, by how 'local actors shape the global system, raising issues, generating public support, and constituting social movements that convert problems into human rights issues'.[22]

This process of vernacularisation is reminiscent also of the manner in which human rights issues were historically 'legalised' internationally, including through the tireless work of Raphael Lemkin, Eleanor Roosevelt, Charles Malik, and Max Sørenson who advocated for a Universal Declaration of Human Rights (UDHR) with legally binding characteristics.[23] Crucially, Simmons points out that 'a good deal of the momentum for making the principles of the UDHR legally binding came from individuals and groups that did not directly represent state interests'.[24] In turn, the UDHR was complemented with the development of the International Covenant for Civil and Political Rights and the International Covenant on Economic, Social and Cultural Rights. In parallel, regional human rights instruments developed, proliferated and were incorporated into domestic constitutions and legal orders, thus consolidating the legalisation of human rights through constitutional and (democratic) legislative processes across international, regional and domestic legal regimes.[25]

Turning to the transformation of human rights protections and commitments into concrete human rights obligations within *judicial* fora, Soave points to the 'vascularisation' of the judicial process in international law and before international courts and tribunals. He argues that, when placing this process under a microscope, the formal rules lose in importance against the practices and relationships paving the path for 'discursive normativity based on narratives, strategies of persuasion, expert vernaculars

[19] JHH Weiler, 'A Constitution for Europe? Some Hard Choices' (2002) 40 *Journal of Common Market Studies* 563.

[20] G Letsas, *A Theory of Interpretation of the European Convention on Human Rights* (Oxford, Oxford University Press, 2007).

[21] SE Merry and P Levitt, 'The Vernacularization of Women's Human Rights' in S Hopgood, J Snyder and L Vinjamuri (eds), *Human Rights Futures* (Cambridge, Cambridge University Press, 2017) 213–214; see generally SE Merry, *Human Rights and Gender Violence: Translating International Law into Local Justice* (Chicago, University of Chicago Press, 2006).

[22] ibid.

[23] BA Simmons, *Mobilizing for Human Rights: International Law in Domestic Politics* (Cambridge, Cambridge University Press, 2009) 352–353. See also with respect to non-Western women delegates who partook in the drafting of the UDHR: R Adami, *Women and the Universal Declaration of Human Rights* (New York, Taylor and Francis, 2018).

[24] ibid.

[25] S Meckled-Garcia and B Çali (eds), *The Legalization of Human Rights: Multidisciplinary Perspectives on Human Rights and Human Rights Law* (Oxon, Routledge, 2005). See more generally on the interaction of international (human rights) law with domestic legal orders: D Shelton (ed), *International Law and Domestic Legal Systems: Incorporation, Transformation and Persuasion* (Oxford, Oxford University Press, 2012).

and modes of world sense-making'.[26] Precisely these practices and relations allow for what he calls the vascularisation of the international legal order, allowing it, in other words, to breathe and develop.[27]

Different still, Benvenisti and Harel examine the 'discordant parity' between the different adjudicatory spheres of international and constitutional courts, highlighting that 'delineating the scope of human rights is a deliberative enterprise based on competing ideals'.[28] Building on this, the authors argue that the 'conflict between international and state norms respects human agency and therefore need not be resolved but in fact celebrated and even intensified'.[29] They continue by pointing out that 'at the same time, because interpreters must accept the relevancy and pertinence of equivalent norms of the parallel and complementary body of law, they must consult the parallel sources with the view to accommodate them unless serious considerations suggest otherwise'.[30]

De Búrca brings these explanatory accounts together by advancing a 'transnational experimentalist theory of human rights law and advocacy'.[31] She explains that experimentalist thinking

> proposes that social and political action and change can – and should – come about not by means of hierarchical direction or systems of control from above, but through an iterative system of contestation and learning from on-the-ground experience, in conjunction with ongoing collective reflection, reaction, and institutional response, and in the interaction over time between multiple actors and institutions at various levels.[32]

She highlights that 'the attraction of an experimentalist system lies precisely in its decentralized, participatory, and iterative character'.[33] Seen through this lens, the human rights regime is thus considered a participatory, iterative and most importantly, deliberative endeavour.[34]

These deliberations – through democratic legalising processes, judicial interventions, advocacy and practices – all directly and indirectly inform whether consensus has been achieved on particular human rights issues brought before European courts. Building on work by Morawa, Dzehtsiarou describes consensus as fulfilling a mediating role between a dynamic or purposive interpretation of European human rights instruments on the one hand and States' margin of appreciation on the other.[35] Accordingly, European consensus constitutes a tool of the ECtHR to interpret the European Convention on Human Rights (ECHR) on the basis of emerging common European approaches. Consensus is not synonymous with unanimity; rather, it is reminiscent of the CJEU's reliance on 'common

[26] T Soave, *The Everyday Makers of International Law: From Great Halls to Back Rooms* (Cambridge, Cambridge University Press, 2022) 18.

[27] ibid.

[28] E Benvenisti and A Harel, 'Embracing the Tension between National and International Human Rights Law: The Case for Discordant Parity' (2017) 15 *International Journal of Constitutional Law* 36, 57.

[29] ibid.

[30] ibid.

[31] G de Búrca, *Reframing Human Rights in a Turbulent Era* (Oxford, Oxford University Press, 2021) 38.

[32] ibid.

[33] ibid 39.

[34] ibid 41.

[35] K Dzehtsiarou, *European Consensus and the Legitimacy of the European Court of Human Rights* (Cambridge, Cambridge University Press, 2015) 23.

constitutional traditions' in understanding EU fundamental rights law when the ECtHR endeavours to establish a form of agreement or convergence (of rules, principles and/or practices) across State Parties on questions of human rights law.[36]

The foregoing suggests that to attain European consensus on the manner in which human rights are legalised, interpreted, transposed, and applied in Europe, there is a process of participatory deliberation that happens at a local, regional, and international level in an experimentalist manner and in no particular order. Such iterative exercises of participatory deliberation then infuse adjudicatory processes and aid the European courts – the CJEU and the ECtHR – in drawing conclusions on the state of human rights protections. The deliberative process informs the appraisal of consensus by the relevant courts in determining what the scope of human rights obligations of States is, who enjoys human rights protections, and how such human rights are made actionable to ensure that they remain practical and effective in continuously evolving societies.

More specifically, such deliberative processes have helped determine which legal issues are governed by human rights (eg, abortion, euthanasia, and the death penalty under the right to life; pushbacks on high seas or automated returns at land borders under the *non-refoulement* principle; governance of social media platforms and hate speech under the right to privacy).[37] Such deliberative practices have also helped refine and broaden the limits of territorial application of fundamental rights, giving rise to (exceptional) cases where human rights may be considered to apply extra-territorially (eg, situations of extraterritorial state-agent control, effective control and cases with special features).[38] Finally, such deliberative practices have guided the development of how commitments to human rights as embedded in human rights instruments, have been translated into concretised and actionable negative, positive, procedural and substantive obligations. For instance, such practices (eg, domestic and legislative developments, litigation, advocacy) have given rise to actionable, enforceable positive obligations on behalf of States to comply with the *non-refoulement* principle (eg, verify the conditions of return in the country of return, including whether the country of return has a functioning asylum system; individual investigations of requests for international protection even in the absence of a claim to that effect when confronted with irregular arrivals by sea).[39]

Importantly, this deliberative and experimentalist process is one that has taken place for human rights that bind *States* and how *States* incorporate, interpret, enact, and apply such rights. This same process has not yet occurred in a meaningful manner or to the same degree in determining how human rights apply to EU entities, which – despite showing state-like traits – is not a state.

[36] ibid 9, 11, 12.

[37] See, eg, WA Schabas, 'Right to Life/Droit à la Vie' in *The European Convention on Human Rights: A Commentary* (Oxford, Oxford University Press, 2015).

[38] ECtHR (GC), App no 4871/16 *Hanan v Germany* ECLI:CE:ECHR:2021:0216JUD000487116, paras 132–136; ECtHR (GC), App no 36925/07 *Güzelyurtlu and Others v Cyprus and Turkey* ECLI:CE:ECHR:2019:0129JUD003692507, paras 182–187.

[39] ECtHR, App no 39090/20, *MA and ZR v Cyprus* ECLI:CE:ECHR:2024:1008JUD003909020, para 83.

3. Distinguishing States and EU Entities

3.1. The EU's Functionally Limited Mandate and Dependent Enforcement Capacity

The discussion thus far prompts the question of whether the development of EU human rights responsibility should be subject to its own and separate experimentalist translation process, distinct to that of States, and why. This question brings to the fore three crucial characteristics that differentiate the EU from States within the realm of human rights governance.

First, the EU as a non-state entity with an explicit and functionally delineated mandate does not have the kind of unbridled regulatory power that States do, due to the principle of conferral.[40] In its mandate the EU as a supranational organisation is functionally limited to the powers conferred on it by its Member States, even if in practice it has vast regulatory powers that are not always explicitly articulated in EU primary law. According to the letter of the law, and unlike its Member States, the EU can thus only do what it has been legally mandated to do by EU primary law.[41] Closely connected to this, the EU does not have a general mandate to regulate human rights. Instead, it can only foresee in human rights protections insofar as such protections fall within the scope of its competences. It is thus functionally restrained and does not have the regulatory and legislative powers that Member States do in developing its respective human rights regime and practice.

Second, the EU does not have the kind of enforcement infrastructure that its Member States have to comply with human rights obligations. Whereas States will have enforcement structures such as police, military, and administrative agencies at their disposal, this is much less so for the EU. Instead, to enforce its policies, the EU is largely reliant upon its Member States. In turn, this means that EU entities can never be considered to be functioning fully independently. Consider for example, the border management work entrusted to Frontex (the European Border and Coast Guard Agency): while the agency now has its own standing corps, it consistently underscores that Frontex merely conducts itself in a supporting role and thus cannot be considered to act independently of the EU Member States.

Finally, there are notable connections between the EU's system of human rights protection and that of the Council of Europe. The ECHR has special significance for the EU legal order (Article 6 TEU), and Article 52(3) CFREU dictates that for corresponding rights – that is to say, rights found in the Charter that are also found in the ECHR – the latter will operate as the minimum level of protection for the EU.[42] However,

[40] See: J Klabbers, 'The EJIL Foreword: The Transformation of International Organizations Law' (2015) 26 *European Journal of International Law* 9. See also: J Klabbers, 'The Emergence of Functionalism in International Institutional Law: Colonial Inspirations' (2014) 25 *European Journal of International Law* 645. Functionalism understood through the work of Klabbers refers to the idea that international organisations have been set up with the objective of fulfilling a particular function.

[41] M Klamert, 'Article 5' in M Kellerbauer, M Klamert and J Tomkin (eds), *The EU Treaties and Charter of Fundamental Rights: A Commentary* 2nd edn (Oxford, Oxford University Press, 2024).

[42] This includes the case law which interprets the ECHR. See Comment to Article 52(3) in the Explanations to the Charter of Fundamental Rights: Explanations relating to the Charter of Fundamental Rights [2007] OJ C303/17.

there are also notable differences between both regimes of human rights protection. Following the principle of conferral, the Charter rights can only be invoked in relation to other areas of EU law. This means that the Charter provisions are not self-standing and must be invoked in tandem with provisions of EU law, as the EU was not granted general competences to regulate human rights (Article 51 CFREU). Next, the Charter makes explicit that its scope of application is not restricted to States, but applies in full and without territorial restraint to EU entities. Finally, the manner in which the rights may be limited in the Charter differs significantly compared to the ECHR: the equivalence in protection standard for corresponding rights as per Article 52(3) CFREU only applies insofar as the EU's autonomy, or the primacy, unity or effectiveness of EU law is not adversely affected.[43] This means that although the ECHR and ensuing case law function as the minimum level of protection for rights that are found both in the Charter and the ECHR, this level may be contested if providing the same level of protection would endanger the autonomy, unity, primacy, and effectiveness of EU law.

The argument made here is that if the EU's human rights commitments are to lead to effective human rights protection, this requires a nuanced understanding of how the EU's functional idiosyncrasies prompt a differentiated understanding of that protection. Notably, to what extent do these idiosyncrasies change the scope of human rights protection the EU can afford, who enjoys human rights protection by EU entities and how are EU human rights commitments translated into actionable, justiciable, and enforceable human rights obligations?

3.2. Novel Questions in the Realm of EU Human Rights Protection

Given that States and EU entities may be too distinct to warrant an automated transposition of the manner in which human rights have been translated into actionable claims for individuals vis-à-vis the State, a number of associated and unresolved questions surface regarding the what, the who and the how of EU human rights protection.

[43] See regarding Article 52(3) CFREU, see: Explanations relating to the Charter of Fundamental Rights [2007] OJ C303/17. See also S Peers and S Prechal, 'Article 52 – Scope and Interpretation of Rights and Principles' in S Peers, T Hervey, J Kenner and A Wards (eds), *The EU Charter of Fundamental Rights – A Commentary* (Oxford, Hart, 2021) para 52.115. Article 53 CFREU complements this provision by holding that the Charter cannot be invoked to interpret the rights therein in a manner that would restrict or adversely affect rights as recognised by EU and international law, including the ECHR. However, the CJEU's Grand Chamber recalled that pursuant to the principle of primacy, when national authorities implement EU law '*national authorities and courts remain free to apply national standards of protection of fundamental rights, provided that the level of protection provided for by the Charter, as interpreted by the Court, and the primacy, unity and effectiveness of EU law are not thereby compromised*' CJEU, Case C-399/11 *Melloni v Ministerio Fiscal* ECLI:EU:C:2013:107, para 60. For these Charter provisions to not be inherently contradicted by the Explanations thereto, Peers and Prechal argue that this means that only higher standards of protection may be precluded by the caveats of autonomy, primacy, effectiveness or unity of EU law. Any other reading would entail that EU human rights protection could fall below the minimum level of protection provided for by the ECHR and ECtHR for corresponding rights. See Peers and Prechal, 'Article 52' (2021) para 52.121.

3.2.1. What is the Substantive Scope of Protection?

As already mentioned, the EU's mandate is functionally limited because it can only act once it has been conferred the necessary powers to act by the EU Member States. This entails, in turn, that it currently has no general power to regulate human rights in the European Union. In addition, the manner in which the division of competences is implemented and exercised between the EU and its Member States is changeable. Where EU entities share powers with EU Member States, as is the case in border management and in police cooperation, the way in which those powers are shared can fluctuate, as determined by secondary legislation. This renders the scope of human rights protection, which the EU may afford, subject to a case-by-case assessment in the respective domains of EU competences. Within the context of the EU's Integrated Border Management for instance – a shared competence between EU entities and EU Member States – the powers afforded to the EU's Border and Coast Guard Agency (Frontex) have changed significantly over time.[44] Where initially this Agency had only a supporting role in relation to national borders and coastguards, it now has its own standing corps (to be expanded significantly), as well as vast executive powers. Within this vein, there is a clear evolution in the manner in which human rights clauses were and continue to be embedded in its legal framework. Similar developments are evident in a wide range of EU competences (such as common commercial policy,[45] the mining and extraction framework;[46] sanctions;[47] climate;[48] data-processing and police cooperation,[49] Artificial Intelligence,[50] platform governance[51]) and will continue to develop in line with the EU's dynamic competence division.

This is different from States whose competences are not functionally constrained in this way and are not subject to these types of legislative developments. Hence, as the EU's powers continue to evolve (in any direction), the scope of human rights protections it offers also continues to change, leading to questions about how such competence dynamism alters the scope of protection offered by the relevant EU entities.

[44] De Coninck, *The EU's Human Rights Responsibility Gap* (2024) 208–221.

[45] De Coninck and Van Elsuwege, 'Human Rights Respectful Trade' (2024).

[46] Regulation (EU) 2017/821 of the European Parliament and of the Council of 17 May 2017 laying down supply chain due diligence obligations for Union importers of tin, tantalum and tungsten, their ores, and gold originating from conflict-affected and high-risk areas (Conflict Minerals Regulation) [2017] OJ L130/1.

[47] T Ruys, 'The European Union Global Human Rights Sanctions Regime (EUGHRSR)' (2021) 60 *International Legal Materials* 298.

[48] Directive (EU) 2024/1760 of the European Parliament and of the Council of 13 June 2024 on corporate sustainability due diligence and amending Directive (EU) 2019/1937 and Regulation (EU) 2023/2859 (CSDDD) [2024] OJ L2024/1760.

[49] De Coninck and Tas, 'Investigating Five Dimensions' (2025).

[50] Regulation (EU) 2024/1689 of the European Parliament and of the Council of 13 June 2024 laying down harmonised rules on artificial intelligence and amending Regulations (EC) No 300/2008, (EU) No 167/2013, (EU) No 168/2013, (EU) 2018/858, (EU) 2018/1139 and (EU) 2019/2144 and Directives 2014/90/EU, (EU) 2016/797 and (EU) 2020/1828 (AI Act) [2024] OJ L2024/1689, Article 1.

[51] R Griffin, 'Rethinking Rights in Social Media Governance: Human Rights, Ideology and Inequality' (2023) 2 *European Law Open* 30.

3.2.2. Who is Protected and What is the Territorial Scope of Protection?

Generalist human rights instruments are typically restricted territorially. This means that States are typically held to protect, respect and fulfil human rights vis-à-vis individuals within their territories. Only in exceptional cases will States have human rights obligations abroad or beyond their respective territories. While the question of the extra-territorial reach of (Member) States' human rights obligations has been the topic of extensive litigation, such disputes typically revolve around whether the disputed conduct fell within a State's territorial jurisdiction or not.[52] In Europe, such adjudication is guided by the territorial jurisdiction limitations clause in the ECHR, which holds that the ECHR applies primarily territorially. Such a clause – found also in other international human rights instruments – ensures that States are not excessively or unreasonably burdened with obligations to protect, respect and fulfil human rights obligations extraterritorially.[53] Recognising that individual State policies may have extraterritorial effects, the state-centric human rights regime has captured such extra-territorial effects: when states conduct themselves abroad or their conduct has extraterritorial effects, they will only be obliged to protect, respect and fulfil human rights when they have established state-agent control over identifiable individuals abroad or when they have effective control over (identifiable) individuals or territories abroad.[54] In these exceptional instances States' human rights obligations will apply to varying degrees.

The rules on extraterritorial human rights obligations of EU entities exhibit two notable differences. First, for EU entities such a territorial limitations clause is missing in the text of the Charter. This suggests that according to the letter of the law, EU entities are bound to protect, respect and fulfil rights both within as well as beyond EU territory. Second, the extraterritorial effects of EU conduct and policies scale differently than the extraterritorial effects of single Member State conduct, with significant implications for legal review. Both points are dealt with briefly in turn below.

On this first point, Article 51 CFREU provides that the Charter human rights protections must be respected by EU entities, with no mention of territorial or extra-territorial limitations.[55] Some argue that the absence of a specific territorial limitations clause should prompt a restrictive reading of the CFREU's jurisdictional limitations (eg, EU entities are only obliged to respect, protect, fulfil human rights *within* the EU), others argue this absence means the Charter binds EU entities also beyond EU territory.[56]

[52] See generally: M Milanovic, *Extraterritorial Application of the Human Rights Treaties – Law, Principles, and Policy* (Oxford, Oxford University Press, 2011).

[53] The ECtHR has consistently repeated that the rights in the ECHR and obligations stemming therefrom are 'primarily territorial' as per Article 1 ECHR, with three notable and strictly interpreted exceptions giving rise to extra-territorial control (eg, state-agent control over an individual; effective control over a territory; situations exhibiting 'special features'). ECtHR, App no 20914/07 *Carter v Russia* ECLI:CE:ECHR:2021:0921JUD002091407, para 123.

[54] Exceptionally, the Strasbourg Court has held that extraterritorial application of the ECHR may arise in cases exhibiting 'special features'. See n 55 below.

[55] Raimondo, *The European Integrated Border Management* (2024). See also: M Milanovic, *Extraterritorial Application of the Human Rights Treaties – Law, Principles, and Policy* (Oxford, Oxford University Press, 2011) 227.

[56] ibid.

The latter interpretation could have significant consequences for EU entities inasmuch as this could mean that its human rights obligations are potentially boundless and not restricted by territorial borders.

This distinction becomes all the more relevant in light of the different scale at which EU policies and conduct operate. Consider, for example, the earlier question of making human rights more effective in EU free trade agreements: what does this mean, who is impacted by such free-trade agreements and whom or what entities does this protect?[57] Would such human rights protection provide enforceable rights for individuals abroad (beyond EU territory) and, if so, how would this be operationalised and before what judicial fora?[58] Consider also Bradford's 'Brussels Effect', which describes the EU's unilateral influence and impact as a global market power.[59] One of the consequences flowing from the EU's 'Brussels Effect' is that the impact of EU market policies – good or bad – extends not just to market players and stakeholders in the EU's territory, but also beyond and outside of the EU, to unidentifiable publics in infinite and granular ways. Consider finally, the EU's Integrated Border Management (Article 77 of the Treaty on the Functioning of the European Union (TFEU)) and the Common European Asylum System (Article 78 TFEU): the rules developed under these provisions apply to the EU as a whole, precisely to prevent individuals from lodging claims in other Member States where an original claim in one Member State has failed. This means that in the realm of borders, asylum, and migration the EU's policies and laws operate at a different territorial scale, with different consequences on third country nationals who come into contact with these rules. As the locus of power and ensuing governance shifts from individual Member States to the EU in various domains of EU law, a scaling effect emerges, amplifying and increasing the regulatory reach of these powers to entities and publics abroad.

Accordingly, while individual Member States also grapple with the extraterritorial reach of their conduct and policies, the reach of EU powers means that not only EU citizens in a direct (democratic) relationship with EU entities and identifiable individuals within and beyond EU territory are impacted by these policies individually; the impact of EU conduct and policies additionally extends to (inseparable) collectivities of third country nationals who do not have such direct (and democratic) relationships with EU transnational cooperative governance. This transnational regulatory expansion cannot be captured by the exceptional rules governing extraterritorial application of human rights for States, as these rules (eg, state-agent control, effective control and special features) hinge on being able to specifically identify the individuals and territories affected through extraterritorial state conduct.

Furthermore, when policies or conduct emanating from EU entities specifically, are at risk of violating human rights, only one avenue of legal review is available in contesting such conduct. However, such human rights review is subject to extremely strict admissibility and evidentiary thresholds. In other words, even though conduct and policies by EU entities may have a wider range of human rights implications, the avenues for legal review diminish exponentially both in access and in substance. When an individual State conducts itself in a human rights violative manner, individuals abroad will typically

[57] De Coninck and Van Elsuwege (n 5).
[58] ibid.
[59] A Bradford, *The Brussels Effect* (Oxford, Oxford University Press, 2020).

have a range of domestic procedures at their disposal that may be leveraged to obtain human rights review, complemented by regional and international avenues. Conversely, in seeking to challenge EU entities directly for their human rights conduct abroad, only direct procedures before the CJEU may be triggered. This paradox is exacerbated by the fact that the human rights review offered through the EU's legal regime – unlike that for State responsibility – will be counterbalanced continuously (because of the EU's functional mandate) with the integration objectives of the EU (eg, through reference to the autonomy, primacy, unity, and effectiveness of EU law). In short, this means that despite the exponentially scaled impact of conduct and policy by EU entities – with limited to no deliberative input of third country nationals who are frequently the primary recipients of such effects – there is a notable decrease in the possibility of legal review when such conduct gives rise to effects that violate human rights than when compared to extra-territorial human rights impacts by States.

It is precisely this shift towards policies that increasingly and more meaningfully impact the human rights of collectivities abroad, which prompts novel questions about EU human rights protections unaccounted for in the deliberative experimentalist developments characterising the crystallisation of such rules for States. Should this scaling effect be accounted for in considering who is governed by the EU's human rights protections? And if so, in what way?

3.2.3. *How are Commitments Translated into Obligations?*

Finally, what does it mean for the EU to be bound by human rights, including the fundamental rights embedded in the CFREU? Building on the premise that the EU is fundamentally different from its Member States, these differences raise the question of whether the EU even has the capacity to fulfil negative and positive, procedural and substantive human rights obligations in the same way and to the same extent as its Member States.

Consider, for example, the right to life, which imposes not only the negative obligation to refrain from arbitrarily taking life, but also a positive substantive obligation to prevent arbitrary loss of life when State authorities are reasonably aware of threats to life. Does an analogous positive obligation exist for the EU, which does not have its own standing corps of public enforcement officials akin to the law enforcement authorities of states? If not, how then can this concrete positive obligation be modulated for the EU, so that its commitment to the right to life is not devoid of practical significance, while ensuring that its human rights commitments are commensurate with its increased powers?

Slightly more complex, consider the right to environmental protection under Article 37 CFREU. The climate judgments by the ECtHR have only just begun to determine what concrete human rights obligations for States flow from the right to life, the prohibition of ill-treatment, and so forth.[60] Conversely, the CJEU has yet to rule on this right. In the absence of clear indicators as to how these obligations in the sphere of

[60] ECtHR (GC), App no 53600/20 *Verein Klimaseniorinnen and others v Switzerland* ECLI:CE:ECHR:2024:0409JUD005360020; ECtHR (GC), App no 7189/21 *Carême v France* ECLI:CE:ECHR:2024:0409DEC000718921; ECtHR (GC), App no 39371/20 *Duarte Agostinho and others v Portugal and 32 others* ECLI:CE:ECHR:2024:0409DEC003937120.

environmental protection are to be understood even for States, how should analogous obligations be modulated for the EU, which differs both in enforcement and legislative capacity from its Member States?

These questions are not merely of academic interest. In recent cases brought before the CJEU's Grand Chamber concerning Frontex's human rights responsibility, the distinct nature of Frontex and the EU generally was raised as an argument to prevent reading enforceable human rights obligations into the Frontex Regulation.[61] Specifically, the argument was made that the subsidiary and supporting roles offered by Frontex prevented enforceable obligations to comply with the *non-refoulement* principle and the prohibition of collective expulsion from applying to Frontex.[62]

3.2.4. A Maturing Human Rights Regime?

Many of the aforementioned questions are novel precisely because of the distinct nature of the EU as a non-state actor. At the same time, these questions were also at the very core of litigation and legal mobilisation, legislative developments, advocacy, and grassroots initiatives as human rights protections were being developed to govern State conduct. In that sense, it could very well be argued that the EU's human rights regime is simply a nascent regime, that it is in the process of maturing in the same manner as the traditional human rights regime matured for States and that it should undergo this same organic process. Indeed, the binding nature of the Charter vis-à-vis EU entities was only constitutionally consolidated by the Treaty of Lisbon in 2009 and questions of the human rights responsibility of EU entities are a relatively new phenomenon that have picked up momentum only recently in light of the increasing operational conduct of EU entities.

Yet, this assumption misses the nuance that the manner in which these novel questions may be decided cannot follow a similar method of deliberation as in the case of States because of the EU's legal design. The peculiar nature of the EU as a non-state entity prevents the equivalent – not identical – type of deliberative, iterative processes that characterised the crystallisation of human rights regulation for States.

4. Access to the CJEU as a Deliberative Safety-Valve to Effective EU Human Rights Protection

4.1. Deliberative Limitations in EU Human Rights Responsibility

If human rights experimentalism captures the deliberative, participatory, iterative processes shaping the state-centric human rights regime and is key to ensuring that rights remain practical and effective for all, to what extent do such processes exist in developing the EU's human rights regime? While empirical studies can offer more detailed insights, the design of the legal framework of the EU's human rights regime

[61] Case C-136/24 P *Hamoudi v Frontex* ECLI: EU:C:2025:977. CJEU, Case C-679/23 P *WS and Others v Frontex* ECLI:EU:C:2025:976.

[62] ibid. Throughout the hearings of the appeal in *Hamoudi v Frontex*, the Frontex representatives consistently recalled that Frontex is not a State and therefore cannot be held to that particular standard of protection.

allows for initial conclusions to be drawn about the level of deliberative input in its development compared to that of States.

4.1.1. The Legal Design of the EU Legislative Process

One of the first areas where the difference in deliberative input becomes apparent is in legislative developments. Democratic legislative processes have contributed and continue to contribute to the development of the state-centric human rights regime by limiting certain qualified rights, by carving out situations in which certain protections do not apply, and by identifying certain obligations that must be met to comply with certain human rights commitments. On the basis of existing laws in European States, the ECtHR or the CJEU respectively may subsequently conclude that a given consensus exists with respect to a particular human right. Importantly, such consensus will be derived with consideration of democratic legislative processes across a wide range of domestic proceedings. In turn, this consensus may lead to the crystallisation of a human rights rule (eg, regarding the scope, personal application, or obligations of human rights) in the case law of the ECtHR, or to supranational (EU) or even international legislative developments.

Conversely, due to competence conferral and division, *domestic* legislative processes cannot determine how human rights are made effective vis-à-vis EU entities as this remains a prerogative exclusive to the EU legislator. In other words, whereas at least 47 domestic legislative processes – including all the implicated and varied actors mobilising on such domestic levels – can feed into how human rights are understood within the state-centric human rights regime, there is only a single legislative procedure that can contribute to the development of the EU's human rights responsibility in specific domains of EU law. Practically speaking this means that even though 27 EU Member States *are* represented within the EU's legislative process, there is a notable difference in the sheer breadth and diversity of legislative negotiation (eg, one legislative procedure to determine human rights responsibilities of EU entities as opposed to 27 separate legislative procedures to determine human rights responsibilities of Member States), the implicated actors represented in this process, and thus the deliberative input that is engaged with in determining human rights protections by and responsibility for EU entities. This observation is furthermore supported by the scholarship attesting to the EU's democratic deficit,[63] as well as the work unveiling the lack of diversity in the EU institutions[64] and the distance between the development of EU law and the social realities and lived experiences of those impacted by EU law.[65]

[63] See for instance: P Magnette, 'Democracy in the European Union: Why and How to Combine Representation and Participation?' in S Smismans (ed), *Civil Society and Legitimate European Governance* (Cheltenham, Edward Elgar Publishing, 2006).

[64] I Solanke and N Dube, 'Re-imagining EU Law and Legal Institutions' (*European University Institute*, 28 February 2025) www.eui.eu/events?id=576548 accessed 6 May 2025. See also more generally on how diversity at international courts may be justified in pursuing deontological and consequentialist legitimacy. The deontological perspective acknowledges that diversity at international courts is required to ensure democratic legitimacy of the Court, whereas the consequentialist approach refers to enhanced legitimacy of international courts due to the impact that diverse voices may have on the outcome of judgments. See on this matter: F Baetens, 'Identity and Diversity on the International Bench: Who is the Judge?' in F Baetens (ed), *Identity and Diversity on the International Bench: Who Is the Judge?* (Oxford, Oxford University Press, 2021).

[65] L Azoulai, 'Reconnecting EU Legal Studies to European Societies' (*Verfassungsblog*, 19 March 2024) https://verfassungsblog.de/reconnecting-eu-legal-studies-to-european-societies/ accessed 6 May 2025.

Finally – and mindful of the scaling effect of EU policies previously mentioned – EU policies increasingly govern the human rights of individuals not situated within the European Union. Yet, despite the vast implications of such extra-territorial conduct (eg, through free trade agreements;[66] through acquisition of critical raw minerals;[67] through externalisation of border controls[68]), those largely governed and most impacted by these measures (individuals abroad) are presented with limited, to no, opportunity to provide input on the development of such policies, much less the design of human rights protections embedded in such policies. And with the far-reaching human rights implications of such policies applying to third country nationals, it becomes less likely that their interests will be represented or meaningfully accounted for in the EU legislative process, at risk of exhibiting and perpetuating signs of 'neocolonial imperialism'.[69]

4.1.2. The Legal Design of Judicial Review of EU Human Rights Responsibility

The scope of human rights protections – who enjoys them and how the EU's human rights commitments translate into enforceable obligations – risks becoming a purely theoretical inquiry if no mechanisms exist to uphold these rights when they are violated. To address this, the EU's legal framework includes rules ensuring that EU entities can be held legally accountable when they fail to respect, protect, or fulfil human rights obligations.

Zooming out briefly, three types of direct actions may be lodged against the EU, its entities, or its instruments. First, the annulment procedure (Article 263 TFEU) allows a claim to be brought before the CJEU against an EU legislative, regulatory, or individual act that lacks conformity with superior rules of EU law, including the Charter. Second, a claim may be filed before the CJEU against an EU entity for failure to act (Article 265 TFEU), provided that the entity was under an enforceable obligation to do so or to conduct itself in a particular manner. The third type of direct action is the action for damages (Article 268 *in juncto* Article 340 TFEU), which individuals may bring before the CJEU to seek compensation for harm caused by EU entities. Such harm may include damages resulting from unlawful human rights conduct, though it is not limited to this.

As the present inquiry concerns the EU's human rights responsibility for harm incurred to individuals – rather than the legality of an EU entity's legal or regulatory act, or a failure to act where it was obligated to do so – the focus will remain on the

[66] De Coninck and Van Elsuwege (n 5).

[67] D Alejo and M Ibero, 'The EU and Its Supply of Critical Raw Materials: Balancing Resource Needs with Human Rights and Environmental Due Diligence – A Paradox?' (*Curiae Virides*, 10 January 2024) www.curiaevirides.eu/post/the-eu-and-its-supply-of-critical-raw-materials-balancing-resource-needs-with-human-rights-and-envi accessed 6 May 2025; 'MEPs Want to Suspend EU-Rwanda Deal on Sustainable Value Chains for Critical Raw Materials' (*European Parliament Press Release*, 13 February 2025) www.europarl.europa.eu/news/en/press-room/20250206IPR26752/meps-want-to-suspend-eu-rwanda-deal-on-critical-raw-materials accessed 6 May 2025.

[68] V Moreno-Lax and M Lemberg-Pedersen, 'Externalizing EU Migration Control while Ignoring the Human Rights of Migrants: Is There Any Room for the International Responsibility of European States?' (2019) *Questions of International Law* 5.

[69] E Tendayi Achiume, 'Migration as Decolonization' (2019) 71 *Stanford Law Review* 1509, 1539–42.

action for damages. The CJEU's *Bergaderm*[70] ruling affirms the conditions under which an EU entity may bear legal responsibility for its actions. To successfully claim the EU's (human rights) responsibility, an individual must prove: (1) unlawful human rights conduct that constitutes a sufficiently serious breach of EU (human rights) law; (2) a direct causal link between the conduct and the harm; and (3) resulting damage suffered by the individual.

While each of these conditions has been refined and qualified in subsequent case law, it is important to note that for these conditions to be met, it must be clear ab initio what the concrete human rights obligations are by which the EU is bound, and how such responsibility is modulated in cases where the EU has collaborated with EU Member States or third parties, including non-state actors. For instance, it will be difficult to ascertain whether a human rights breach meets the condition of 'sufficiently serious' when it is unclear whether and how the EU bears any concrete (positive, negative, procedural and substantive) human rights obligations to ensure the right to liberty (see supra). Similarly, determining whether the qualified test of causality between conduct, breach, and damage is met will be challenging if attribution rules remain unclear, especially in cases where the EU has contributed to human rights harm arising from joint actions with Member States or third parties.[71]

The action for damages is thus preconditioned on and presupposes the prior existence of legally enforceable obligations to hold an EU entity to account. In other words, for the action for damages to be a viable form of recourse against EU entities for complicity in human rights harms, it will be inevitable to clarify how the EU's human rights *commitments* translate to human rights *obligations*.[72] And while the action for damages was not originally developed as an action to establish EU human rights responsibility, it appears to be the sole appropriate form of direct action against EU entities akin to human rights responsibility procedures against States for damages.[73]

In addition to the formal and strict conditions to establish legal responsibility under the EU action for damages, recent case law before the General Court of the EU has underscored the importance of rules concerning the burden, standard and method of proof in determining EU legal responsibility. These developing lines of case law are particularly prominent and questionable in cases where EU entities engage in 'operational conduct' (eg, deploying CFSP/CSDP missions;[74] joint Frontex operations;[75] Europol investigations[76]) and such conduct gives rise to human rights harms.[77] These

[70] CJEU, Case C-352/98 P *Bergaderm and Goupil v Commission* ECLI:EU:C:2000:361.

[71] De Coninck (n 7) 65–68.

[72] ibid.

[73] M Fink, C Rauchegger and J De Coninck, 'The Action for Damages as a Fundamental Rights Remedy' in M Fink (ed), *Redressing Fundamental Rights Violations by the EU: The Promise of the 'Complete System of Remedies'* (Cambridge, Cambridge University Press, 2024).

[74] CJEU, Joined Cases C-29/22 P and C-44/22 P *KS and KD v Council and Others* ECLI:EU:C:2024:725.

[75] CJEU, Case C-136/24 P *Hamoudi v Frontex* ECLI: EU:C:2025:977. CJEU, Case C-679/23 P *WS and Others v Frontex* ECLI:EU:C:2025:976; CJEU, Case C-679/23 P *WS and Others v Frontex* (case pending).

[76] CJEU, Case C-755/21 *Marián Kočner v European Union Agency for Law Enforcement Cooperation (Europol)* ECLI:EU:C:2024:202.

[77] CJEU, Case C-136/24 P *Hamoudi v Frontex* ECLI:EU:C:2025:977. CJEU, Case C-679/23 P *WS and Others v Frontex* ECLI:EU:C:2025:976. See for a comment on this case and related cases concerning joint Frontex operations: J De Coninck, 'The Binoculars at the Borders of Europe: On Evidentiary Rules and Human Rights Protection' (*Verfassungsblog*, 19 February 2025) https://verfassungsblog.de/binoculars-at-europes-borders/ accessed 6 May 2025. On Europol, see: De Coninck and Tas (n 5).

cases illustrate how the principle of unfettered production and assessment of evidence in actions for damages is applied in a way that places exceptionally strict evidentiary burdens on individuals, often already at the admissibility stage of proceedings. In *Hamoudi v Frontex*, the CJEU's Grand Chamber has now confirmed that such stringent evidentiary burdens limit access to substantive appraisal by the Court, impairing the right to an effective remedy, which arguably limits the deliberative input the Court receives on novel questions of EU responsiblity.

Finally, although EU primary law foresees and even requires EU accession to the ECHR, to date these negotiations have yet to come to fruition. The previous draft accession agreement was rejected by the CJEU for failing to respect the unique characteristics and autonomy of EU law, and the renewed negotiations have now been concluded.[78] While numerous analyses scrutinised the various reasons why the previous accession attempt failed, many converge on a common theme: the EU, and the CJEU in particular, appears reticent to submit to external legal scrutiny over its human rights conduct.[79] While this may very well be explained by the EU's reliance on the principle of autonomy, and the unique characteristics of the EU legal framework, the lack of external legal review entails again that – unlike States which *are* subject to external human rights review – there is notably less deliberative input feeding into adjudication of EU human rights responsibility. Consider for example, the external legal review that occurs when States' conduct is challenged before the UN Human Rights Committee on account of alleged violations of civil and political human rights protected under international human rights treaties, while also being challenged before regional courts (eg, ECtHR and the CJEU), in addition to internal domestic (constitutional) courts. The sheer multiplicity of the available legal fora, but also the accessibility differences before these legal fora, bring different actors and stakeholders to a dispute fostering more and different forms of deliberative input and discourse across and within different spatial legal regimes. Seen from this angle, any pronouncements on human rights responsibility of States will likely have been more meaningfully substantiated *and* accounted for the deliberative input of a larger number of stakeholders.

Conversely, the singular, insulated, and internal focus of the EU's human rights responsibility review – through the direct actions and the action for damages specifically, complemented by the high evidentiary thresholds in accessing the action for damages, in addition to the obstacles to participation noted by Passalacqua in this contribution[80] – meaningfully limits the deliberative input that may be formally obtained for the purpose of resolving these novel questions of EU human rights responsibility.

[78] J Krommendijk, 'One Step Closer after *KS* and *KD*: EU Accession to the ECHR' (*Review of European Administrative Law*, 1 October 2024) https://realaw.blog/2024/10/01/one-step-closer-after-ks-and-kd-eu-accession-to-the-echr-by-jasper-krommendijk/ accessed 6 May 2025. See on the need for external human rights scrutiny: T Isiksel, 'European Exceptionalism and the EU's Accession to the ECHR' (2016) 27 *European Journal of International Law* 565.

[79] D Halberstam, '"It's the Autonomy, Stupid!" A Modest Defense of Opinion 2/13 on EU Accession to the ECHR, and the Way Forward' (2015) 16 *German Law Journal* 105; T Streinz, 'Avoiding an Odyssey – The EU's Accession to the ECHR' (*Verfassungsblog*, 30 September 2013) https://verfassungsblog.de/avoiding-an-odyssey-the-eus-accession-to-the-echr/ accessed 6 May 2025.

[80] See contribution by Virginia Passalacqua at ch 4 in the present volume.

4.2. Alternative Methods of Deliberative Discourse and Access to the CJEU

In line with the theory of human rights experimentalism, the development of the state-centric human rights regime is not exclusively determined by the legislative process or subsequent judicial review procedures. This also holds true for the development of the EU's human rights responsibility regime. And although deliberative input is both formally and substantively more limited in the EU's legislative proceedings and actions for damages compared to that of States (where legislative developments and adjudication occur across multiple spatial regimes and involve a wider range of actors) a range of alternative forums exist which can provide deliberative input that can influence legislative and adjudicatory processes to determine EU human rights responsibility.

Indeed, different EU entities may very well conduct studies and pronounce themselves on EU human rights responsibility. In turn, such findings may very well be relied upon or substantiate EU legislative developments or substantiate judgments before the EU courts. Think, for example, of the value of findings by the EU Ombudsperson in relation to alleged human rights misconduct by Frontex, or similar findings of this kind by the EU's Anti-Fraud Office (OLAF), cited in recent cases before the CJEU.[81] Similarly, MEPs may commission studies from experts in particular domains of EU (human rights) law, which may subsequently be relied upon,[82] and different Directorate Generals in the European Commission may rely on expert interventions, which in turn may rely on input by relevant stakeholders in the development of legislative proposals.

Beyond the EU institutions, deliberative input may be derived from civil society, as well as from academics, advocacy groups, and any other stakeholders active in these domains. Alemanno, specifically, notes the practice and value of shadow *amicus curiae* briefs, while advocating for formal recognition of such interventions at the CJEU.[83] Similarly, deliberative input may be delivered through legal mobilisation, academic writings in the form of blogs, academic articles or books, as well as participation by relevant stakeholders in (academic) conferences on the topic of EU human rights responsibility, all of which feeds back into legislative and adjudicatory processes, and back again into the myriad conversations and sites of deliberative discourse in a circular manner.

Without undermining these modes of deliberative input – the value and necessity of which are beyond doubt – it is important to recognise that they represent only a fraction of the necessary input for the development of EU human rights law to be genuinely deliberative and reflective of the values the EU seeks to uphold.

In other words, for the CJEU to fulfil its role in upholding the rule of law and to function as a counter-majoritarian force – particularly in politically sensitive areas

[81] CJEU, Case C-136/24 P *Hamoudi v Frontex* ECLI:EU:C:2025:977. CJEU, Case C-679/23 P *WS and Others v Frontex* ECLI:EU:C:2025:976.

[82] De Coninck and Van Elsuwege (n 5); L Bartels, 'Assessment of the Implementation of the Human Rights Clause in International and Sectoral Agreements' (In-Depth Analysis, European Parliament, Policy Department for External Relations, Directorate General for External Policies of the Union, requested by the DROI Subcommittee) www.europarl.europa.eu/RegData/etudes/IDAN/2023/702586/EXPO_IDA(2023)702586_EN.pdf accessed 6 May 2025.

[83] A Alemanno, 'Public Participation before the Court of Justice of the EU: Enhancing Outside Party Judicial Participation via Amicus Curiae Briefs' (2025) *Erasmus Law Review* (*forthcoming*).

where human rights issues are currently being contested – the importance of direct access to the Court in actions for damages related to human rights violations cannot be underestimated.

Since the CJEU's deliberations are not accessible to the wider public, and despite our understanding of the extensive judicial infrastructure operating behind, in support of, and in collaboration with the judges who serve as the Court's outward representatives, it remains unclear to what extent, if at all, these various sources of deliberative input influence the Court's reasoning on EU human rights responsibility.

Conversely, direct access through amicus briefs (if formalised) or third-party interventions, or even direct challenges to EU conduct facilitated through more equitable and fair rules on the burden, standard, and method of proof would allow for deliberative input that directly helps shape the interpretation of EU human rights responsibility in concrete cases of contestation. This would ensure that judicial decision-making not only considers the deliberative input provided through majoritarian forces but also safeguards fundamental rights, particularly for voices that might otherwise be marginalised or drowned out.

PART III

On What Procedural Roads?

6

Pilot-Judgment Procedure at the European Court of Human Rights

KANSTANTSIN DZEHTSIAROU[1]

1. Introduction

The pilot judgment procedure was developed internally by the European Court of Human Rights (ECtHR or Court) and initially was not even reflected in its Rules of Court. For the first time it was used in 2004 in the Grand Chamber judgment in *Broniowski v Poland*.[2] Subsequently, the Court 'codified' this procedure and now its regulations are enshrined in Rule 61 of the Rules of Court. It is still not mentioned in the European Convention on Human Rights (ECHR or Convention) which is the only legally binding text for the ECtHR. That said, the Rules of Court are very authoritative as they are internally designed and followed by the Court. Obviously, they cannot contradict the Convention, but they are very helpful in determining the operations of the Court. The current version of Rule 61 states that:

> The Court may initiate a pilot-judgment procedure and adopt a pilot judgment where the facts of an application reveal in the Contracting Party concerned the existence of a structural or systemic problem or other similar dysfunction which has given rise or may give rise to similar applications.

In the recent pilot judge of the ECtHR in *Cannavacciuolo and Others v Italy*, the Court reminded what the rationale behind the pilot judgment procedure is:

> the pilot-judgment procedure was conceived as a response to the growth in the Court's caseload, caused by a series of cases deriving from the same structural or systemic dysfunction, and to ensure the long-term effectiveness of the Convention machinery. [The Court] reiterates that the dual purpose of the pilot-judgment procedure is on the one hand, to reduce the threat to the effective functioning of the Convention system and, on the other, to facilitate

[1] I am grateful to David Milner and the participants of the workshop in the College of Europe in Bruges for their comments. All errors are mine.

[2] ECtHR (GC), App no 31443/96 *Broniowski v Poland* ECLI:CE:ECHR:2004:0622JUD003144396.

> the speediest and most effective resolution of a dysfunction affecting the protection of the Convention rights in question in the national legal order.[3]

It seems that the Court's aim in using the pilot judgment procedure is twofold. First, it aims to shield itself from multiple repetitive applications and second it is used to protect human rights of multiple victims of repetitive human rights violations as the problem is typical and can be solved more quickly and effectively at the national level. Arguably, this procedure may prove effective, provided that the Court is willing to employ it and, perhaps more importantly, that the respondent states are prepared to invest substantial resources in addressing the underlying issue. In this chapter I examine whether this is in fact the case and whether the pilot judgment procedure can lead to the intended results.

The pilot judgment procedure received a mixed academic reception. Some commentators argued that it is damaging to human rights protection in certain cases;[4] while others called it 'the most creative tool the Court has developed in its first fifty years of its existence'.[5] As is often the case, the truth is somewhere between these two positions. The pilot judgment procedure can be damaging in some individual cases as usually the adjudication of such cases is adjourned pending the pilot case and can postpone the redress but if the procedure works as intended it can solve a much bigger human rights challenge.

In this chapter I try to touch upon a few interconnected questions. I begin by examining the broader implications of the pilot judgment procedure. My argument here is that although the twofold purpose of the pilot procedure is made quite explicitly by the ECtHR, there are other possible ambitions and as a result associated risks that the pilot judgment brings to the case law. The Court's ambition to rule outside the clear scope of an individual case and to set specific remedies shows its desire to act beyond the normal judicial function of adjudicator which is a risky business as it assumes a lot of support from the contracting parties. The subsequent section of this chapter demonstrates that this more ambitious approach was not really utilised by the Court in the last ten years, moreover, the states are not always willing to follow the Court's rulings. Finally, I critically discuss the most recent pilot judgment in *Cannavacciuolo and Others v Italy* and consider if this judgment is a beginning of a new 'era' of pilot judgments.

The overall message of the chapter is that the pilot judgment procedure was born to address the problem of repetitive applications which was suffocating the Court and causing a major number of cases to be pending for many years. However, the pilot judgments are risky for the Court as they demand the respondent state to adopt clearly identified measures, usually within a defined period of time and therefore non-execution of such judgments is even more obvious than in other cases. This can undermine the Court's

[3] ECtHR, App nos 51567/14 and 3 others *Cannavacciuolo and Others v Italy* ECLI:CE:ECHR:2025:0130JUD005156714, para 489. Similar statement can be found in ECtHR, App no 50849/21 *Walesa v Poland* ECLI:CE:ECHR:2023:1123JUD005084921, para 316.

[4] It was argued for example that pilot judgment procedure should not be applied 'where the underlying "systemic" problem is not a particular law or policy, but discriminatory state ideologies rooted in national history'. D Kurban, 'Forsaking Individual Justice: The Implications of the European Court of Human Rights' Pilot Judgment Procedure for Victims of Gross and Systematic Violations' (2016) 16 *Human Rights Law Review* 731, 733.

[5] A Buyse, 'The Pilot Judgment Procedure at the European Court of Human Rights: Possibilities and Challenges' (2013) 3 *Law of Ukraine: Legal Journal* 303, 303.

legitimacy. Arguably, as a consequence, the questionable implementation record of pilot judgments forces the ECtHR to use this instrument sparingly and in relation to very well-established standards and matters.

2. What Does the Court Wish to Achieve with the Pilot Judgment Procedure?

The chapter by David Milner in this edited volume eloquently explains the origins of the pilot judgment procedure, so I will not repeat it here. I would only emphasise that the pilot judgment procedure was a significant reform and was definitely more than merely a technical change in the Court's approach to its case processing. It was argued that

> The very fact that pilot judgments are focused on the identification of systematic malfunctioning of the domestic legal order and on the indication of appropriate general remedial measures normatively extends the binding effect of the Court's judgments and changes their legal nature, accentuating the Court's constitutional function.[6]

Symbolically, the pilot procedure shows that the Court's demands to change legislation or implement a specific remedy are no longer subtle and logical outcomes of a given judgment, but a clear request explicitly enshrined in the judgment. By developing the pilot procedure, the Court has institutionalised its role as a body that can contribute to European Public Order[7] by effectively demanding the rules governing this order to be changed. Every pilot judgment creates a general rule applicable beyond a particular case and can be used to the similar pending or even future potential application.

In general, the nature of judicial adjudication is predominantly backwards looking. The ECtHR deals with 'conflicts' which have already taken place. The Court has limited tools to impact the ongoing situations: the interim measures being one of very few.[8] The pilot judgment procedure is both backward and forward looking. It is backward looking because it is aiming to resolve a high number of pending applications of violations that took place before the pilot judgment. It is forward looking because the Court considers the number of potential applicants in deciding to apply this procedure and more importantly it demands the respondent state to deal with typical human rights violations using a particular remedy. Relatedly, it has been argued that the ECtHR performs two interconnected functions:[9] an adjudicatory function; and a meta-function. To fulfil the former, the Court must resolve the conflict in a particular case; the latter, however, goes further, as the Court creates or emphasises rules of application that extend beyond the confines of an individual case. When

[6] M Fyrnys, 'Expanding Competences by Judicial Lawmaking: The Pilot Judgment Procedure of the European Court of Human Rights' (2011) 12 *German Law Journal* 1231, 1233.

[7] See K Dzehtsiarou, *Can the European Court of Human Rights Shape European Public Order?* (Cambridge, Cambridge University Press, 2021).

[8] See K Dzehtsiarou and V Tzevelekos, 'Interim Measures: Are Some Opportunities Worth Missing?' (2021) 2 *European Convention on Human Rights Law Review* 1.

[9] K Dzehtsiarou, *Can the European Court* (2021) ch 4. F de Londras, 'Dual Functionality and the Persistent Frailty of the European Court of Human Rights' (2013) *European Human Rights Law Review* 38. S Greer, L Wildhaber, 'Revisiting the Debate about 'Constitutionalising' the European Court of Human Rights' (2012) *Human Rights Law Review* 655.

the Court initiates the pilot judgment procedure, it exceeds the scope of a single case and compels the respondent state to take measures that go beyond the immediate outcome for the applicant. Thus, the Court's decision on the matter at issue becomes the rule intended to alter the accepted standard in the respondent state. Another interesting feature of pilot judgments is that they are procedurally innovative but substantively conservative because in the majority of such judgments the substantive standard is already well established; pilot judgments do not create or develop these standards but emphasise the need for their effective implementation on the national level.

The pilot judgment procedure seeks to address the weakness of the enforcement mechanism for the Court's judgments. The Contracting Parties have broad discretion in how they implement the Court's judgments, and this discretion can distort the standards envisaged by the Court. In the mid-1990s, the Court shifted from issuing purely declaratory judgments to providing much clearer and more unambiguous remedies;[10] this shift has arguably culminated in the pilot judgment procedure. Here, the Court typically specifies the general measures that should be adopted by the Contracting Parties.

This approach is not without risks. The pilot judgment procedure in the prisoner voting saga[11] led to questionable results and the United Kingdom implemented the bare minimum of what the judgment required.[12] Another example when the Court's pilot judgment backfired is the group of cases that followed a pilot judgment in *Ivanov v Ukraine.*[13] In this case the Court ruled that non-execution of the final national judgments is a violation of Article 6 ECHR and that the delay in execution should be covered by an appropriate compensation.[14] This is a rule of general application. Comparable judgments were also delivered in cases against Russia[15] and Moldova.[16]

In *Ivanov v Ukraine*, the Court stated that

> the respondent State must grant adequate and sufficient redress, within one year from the date on which the present judgment becomes final … In the Court's view, such redress may be achieved through implementation proprio motu by the authorities of an effective domestic remedy in those cases … If, however, the respondent State fails to adopt such measures following a pilot judgment and continues to violate the Convention, the Court will have no choice but to resume the examination of all similar applications pending before it and to take them to judgment so as to ensure effective observance of the Convention.[17]

The Court, however, could not fulfil its promise and failed to ensure that the standard set in *Ivanov* can be effectuated on the national level. In 2017 the Court pronounced a judgment in *Burmych and others v Ukraine*, in which it stated that

[10] P Leach, 'No Longer Offering Fine Mantras to a Parched Child? The European Court's Developing Approach to Remedies' in A Føllesdal, B Peters and G Ulfstein (eds), *Constituting Europe: The European Court of Human Rights in a National, European and Global Context* (Cambridge, Cambridge University Press, 2013).

[11] See K Dzehtsiarou, 'Prisoner Voting Saga: Reasons for Challenges' in H Hardman and B Dickson (eds), *Electoral Rights in Europe* (London, Routledge, 2017).

[12] E Adams, 'Prisoners' Voting Rights: Case Closed?' (*UK Constitutional* Law Blog, 30 January 2019) https://ukconstitutionallaw.org/2019/01/30/elizabeth-adams-prisoners-voting-rights-case-closed/ accessed 6 May 2025.

[13] This case is also discussed by David Milner in ch 11.

[14] ECtHR, App no 40450/04 *Yuriy Nikolayevich Ivanov v Ukraine* ECLI:CE:ECHR:2009:1015JUD004045004.

[15] ECtHR, App no 33509/04 *Burdov v Russia (no 2)* ECLI:CE:ECHR:2009:0115JUD003350904.

[16] ECtHR, App nos 476/07 and 3 others *Olaru and Others v Moldova* ECLI:CE:ECHR:2009:0728JUD000047607.

[17] ECtHR, *Yuriy Nikolayevich Ivanov v Ukraine* (n 14), para 99.

> despite the significant lapse of time since the delivery of the Ivanov pilot judgment on 15 October 2009, the Ukrainian Government have so far failed to implement the requisite general measures capable of addressing the root causes of the systemic problem identified by the Court and to provide an effective remedy securing redress to all victims at national level.[18]

The Court has subtly identified that its meta-function is to set the standard in its judgment, and it is the state's obligation to apply this standard making sure that the ECtHR is not flooded by the similar repetitive applications. However, the case of *Burmych* shows that the Court also fails to fulfil its technical function in these cases. Here, the Court simply transferred around 12,000 'clone' cases to the Committee of Ministers without any decision.[19]

Every time the Court delivers a pilot judgment, it tests its own reputation, legitimacy and the extent of its authority. Non-execution of an ordinary judgment of the Court brings some damage to the Court's legitimacy but non-execution of a pilot judgment I would argue is much more damaging. In the latter judgments, the Court gives clear instructions, sets time limits – this is much more intrusive in the respondent state's sovereignty than an ordinary judgment and non-execution of the former is much more obvious. Since the cases of non-execution do happen, the Court cannot act as if it is the ultimate authority in Europe, it needs to bear in mind what is possible and realistic. Demanding unrealistic standards undermines the authority of the Court. In the following section I argue that the Court utilised the pilot judgment procedure very sparingly over the last ten years. One possible explanation for that can be that somewhat less than satisfactory results in some previous cases such as *Ivanaov* made the ECtHR overcautious in applying this tool. Also, the Court's thinking can be that the pilot judgment procedure is an exceptional tool and cannot be used commonly, not to lose its 'special status'.

In any event, the pilot judgment procedure represents the Court's attempt to enhance its influence at the meta-level. This aims to provide a quick and effective resolution of structural challenges by emphasising them and forwarding them back to the national authorities with some instructions as to how to fix them. So, in order to achieve tangible changes, the Court needs to use pilot judgments more often: every time there is a systemic problem in law and practice of the Contracting Parties. A restrictive use of the pilot judgment procedure exposes the ECtHR to criticism that it fails to do enough to address its backlog of repetitive cases.

3. What Does the Court Aim to Achieve in the Most Recent Pilot Judgments?

3.1. Methodology

For this section, I reviewed the last ten years of the Court's case law to identify any patterns in the use of the pilot judgment procedure and to assess the impact of these judgments. I measure this impact in a broad sense by considering how many of these cases have been

[18] ECtHR (GC), App nos 46852/13 et al *Burmych and Others v Ukraine* (strike-out), ECLI:CE:ECHR:2017:1012JUD004685213, para 146.

[19] ibid, para 221.

closed by the Committee of Ministers, although this is not a perfect indicator of effectiveness. In many pilot judgments, the ECtHR does not require the respondent state to implement a specific remedy but merely to submit a road map for implementation to the Committee of Ministers. Evidently, this requirement can be fulfilled without the case being closed by the Committee as it only happens when all relevant measures are effectuated by the respondent state. It means that if the pilot judgment sets a deadline for submitting a roadmap, the fact that the Committee of Ministers does not close the case within the time scale established by the Court is not surprising. The road map is perhaps one of a few initial steps on a long road of enforcement of such cases. That said, the closure of a case by the Committee of Ministers is not an insignificant factor, as it suggests that the underlying problem has been (at least for the time being) resolved.

It is not a very straightforward task to identify the pilot judgments in the case law of the Court. The ECtHR has not published an official list of such rulings; although the Court's press unit prepared the factsheet on pilot judgments,[20] its comprehensiveness was verified by conducting a thorough search of the Court's database. This section looks at the last ten years; this time period was not selected for any principled reason but to review the most recent developments of the pilot judgment procedure. Rule 61 of the Rules of Court summarises the legal regulations of the pilot judgment procedure, and therefore I have used the HUDOC database[21] to identify all cases in which Rule 61 was mentioned.[22] Between 1 January 2015 and 1 January 2025, there were 17 judgments that mentioned Rule 61 – of which 12 were decided by the Chamber and five by the Grand Chamber. Some of these judgments mention 'Rule 61' but not the 'Rule 61' this research is concerned with;[23] for instance, in one of such judgments the Court considered application of pilot judgment procedure but decided against it;[24] in other cases, it was perhaps mentioned by mistake;[25] and in some other judgments it was mentioned because the ECtHR dealt with the follow up of another pilot judgment[26] or 'Rule 61' was referred to in the separate opinion and not in the main judgment.[27] In few cases, the applicant requested the pilot judgment procedure to be initiated but the Court dismissed this claim and in this case, such judgments were not taken into account for the present research project. This was the case in *NH and others v France*, where the Court was satisfied with the legislative reforms that took place in France since the submission of this application and decided against applying the pilot judgment procedure.[28]

[20] Available at www.echr.coe.int/documents/d/echr/fs_pilot_judgments_eng accessed 6 May 2025.

[21] Available at https://hudoc.echr.coe.int/eng{%22documentcollectionid2%22:[%22GRANDCHAMBER%22,%22CHAMBER%22]} accessed 6 May 2025.

[22] I used 'Rule 61' in inverted commas as the keyword.

[23] See ECtHR (GC), App no 41418/04 *Khoroshenko v Russia* ECLI:CE:ECHR:2015:0630JUD004141804; ECtHR (GC), App no 35343/05 *Vasiliauskas v Lithuania* ECLI:CE:ECHR:2015:1020JUD003534305; ECtHR (GC), App no 8701/21 *Pinkas and Others v Bosnia and Herzegovina* ECLI:CE:ECHR:2022:1004JUD000870121; or ECtHR, App no 33351/20 *Milanković v Croatia* ECLI:CE:ECHR:2022:0120JUD003335120.

[24] ECtHR, App nos 42399/13 and 8 others *Igranov and Others v Russia* ECLI:CE:ECHR:2018:0320JUD004239913.

[25] ECtHR, App no 3963/18 *Matkava and Others v Russia* ECLI:CE:ECHR:2023:1219JUD000396318.

[26] ECtHR (GC), App nos 46852/13 et al *Burmych and Others v Ukraine* (strike-out), ECLI:CE:ECHR:2017:1012JUD004685213.

[27] ECtHR (GC), App nos 1828/06 and 2 others *GIEM Srl and Others v Italy* ECLI:CE:ECHR:2018:0628JUD000182806.

[28] ECtHR, App nos 28820/13 and 2 others *NH and Others v France* ECLI:CE:ECHR:2020:0702JUD002882013.

After excluding all judgments that were irrelevant for this project there were only seven Chamber judgments left. To ensure the comprehensiveness of the search, I then used the keyword 'pilot judgment' and the search returned 66 judgments of which ten were Grand Chamber cases. Of course, the phrase 'pilot judgment' used in the text of the judgment does not necessarily indicate that that judgment is in fact a pilot judgment as there are plenty of contexts in which it can be mentioned but they were checked anyway.

This verification revealed no new cases but some curious oddities. For example, in *Gábor Nagy v Hungary (no 2)* the Court stated that it considered application of pilot judgment procedure and that the parties were consulted about it[29] but then no resolution of this issue was presented in the text of the judgment, and it was clearly decided that a pilot judgment procedure should not be applied. In *Tunikova and Others v Russia* the Court only stated in the table in the beginning of the judgment that it is a pilot judgment but there is no justification for application of the pilot judgment procedure and even more so, there is not even mention that this judgment is indeed a pilot judgment anywhere else in the text of this judgment.[30] That said, at the end of this judgment the Court has identified the measures that the respondent state needs to adopt; one can suggest that at some stage the Court was considering the application of the pilot judgment procedure to this case but then decided against it; despite that the reference to the pilot judgment procedure in the beginning of the judgment remained by mistake. For the purposes of this research, I did not consider this judgment as a pilot judgment.

In another judgment the reference to the pilot judgment in *WD v Belgium* was made in a partially dissenting opinion, but the initial search failed to identify it as it does not mention 'Rule 61' and it is available only in French and therefore the keyword 'arrêt pilote' was added to the search rendering 27 hits. However, no new pilot judgments except for *WD v Belgium* were identified through this search.

After making all these checks the number of pilot judgments in the last ten years reached eight Chamber judgments. Within the same period the Chambers and Grand Chamber of the Court delivered around 4000 judgments. This means that pilot judgments constitute only around 0.2 per cent of all Chamber and Grand Chamber judgments.

3.2. Pilot Judgments Over the Last Ten Years

This section will now briefly outline the nature of the problems highlighted in all those judgments, examine whether there are any patterns in application of the pilot judgment procedure and then try to offer some preliminary conclusions.

In the judgment of *Neshkov and others v Bulgaria* (2015),[31] the Court agreed to apply the pilot judgment procedure in relation to poor conditions in Bulgarian detention facilities. Here the Court found a violation of Article 3 and Article 13 ECHR.

[29] ECtHR, App no 73999/14 *Gábor Nagy v Hungary (no 2)* ECLI:CE:ECHR:2017:0411JUD007399914, para 5.

[30] ECtHR, App nos 55974/16 and 3 others *Tunikova and Others v Russia* ECLI:CE:ECHR:2021:1214JUD005597416.

[31] ECtHR, App nos 36925/10 and 5 others *Neshkov and Others v Bulgaria* ECLI:CE:ECHR:2015:0127JUD003692510.

The Court identified that there were almost 40 pending meritorious applications regarding condition of detention and the Court ordered to set up preventive and compensatory remedies in this case while it adjourned consideration of all other applications. It gave the national authorities 18 months to come up with effective remedies to tackle this problem. The case was closed by the Committee of Ministers in 2024 which is almost ten years after the initial judgment. The Committee of Ministers stated that

> overcrowding has been almost entirely eradicated and that prison conditions continue to improve, which facilitates the functioning of the preventive remedy. It also noted that there is a relative increase of the amounts awarded under the compensatory remedy.[32]

In the judgment of *Varga and Others v Hungary* (2015) the Court applied the pilot judgment procedure to condition of detention in Hungarian detention facilities. There were 450 similar potentially meritorious similar cases. The Court found a violation of Articles 3 and 13 and ordered Hungary to establish effective remedies in this area. In this case the Court did not set a deadline to develop the remedy but rather

> within six months from the date on which this judgment becomes final, [the authorities had to develop] a time frame in which to make appropriate arrangements and to put in practice preventive and compensatory remedies in respect of alleged violations of Article 3 of the Convention on account of inhuman and degrading conditions of detention.[33]

Undoubtedly, this obligation is much less onerous than introduction of the whole new remedy as in *Neshkov and others v Bulgaria*. The government introduced a remedy as a follow up to this case, but the ECtHR has not yet tested its effectiveness.[34] This case was discussed on 12–14 March 2024 by the Committee of Ministers and the execution is still pending.

In *Rutkowski and Others v Poland* (2015), the Chamber of the Court addressed another familiar issue in pilot judgments: the excessive length of judicial proceedings and the inadequacy of the remedy intended to address this problem. The Court noted that 300 similar cases were pending before the Committee of Ministers, with at least 100 new applications related to the same issue. It found a violation of Article 6(1) and Article 13 ECHR. However, the Court was somewhat vague regarding the deadline for the enforcement of this judgment stating that 'the respondent State must, through appropriate legal or other measures, secure the national courts' compliance with the relevant principles under Article 6 (1) and Article 13 of the Convention'.[35] That said, the Court has adjourned consideration of similar cases for two years making this effectively a deadline for the state. The Polish authorities submitted unilateral declarations in many of such cases, accepting the violation and offering compensation. However, this did not mean that the Government managed to adopt general measures. In 2023, this case was considered by the Committee of Ministers, and the execution process has not yet been closed.

[32] Available at https://hudoc.exec.coe.int/?i=004-3945 accessed 6 May 2025.

[33] ECtHR, App nos 14097/12 and 5 others *Varga and Others v Hungary* ECLI:CE:ECHR:2015:0310JUD001409712.

[34] ECtHR, App no 5433/17 *Domján v Hungary* ECLI:CE:ECHR:2017:1114DEC000543317.

[35] ECtHR, App nos 72287/10 and 2 others *Rutkowski and Others v Poland* ECLI:CE:ECHR:2015:0707JUD007228710.

In *Gazsó v Hungary* the applicants complained about the length of civil proceedings in Hungary. Here, the ECtHR accepted that the pilot procedure is appropriate:

> given notably the recurrent and persistent nature of the underlying problems, the number of people affected by them in Hungary and the need to grant them speedy and appropriate redress at domestic level.[36]

The Court identified 400 applications that deal with the similar issue submitted against Hungary. The ECtHR establish that the remedy needs to be introduced within a year from the date of the judgment. A remedy was introduced in 2021, but its effectiveness has not yet been tested by the ECtHR. The judgment is still pending execution.

In *WD v Belgium* (2016) the Court applied pilot judgment proceedings to the structural problem of detention of people with mental disabilities in prison psychiatric wings without provision of appropriate treatment.[37] This resulted in a violation of Article 5(1) ECHR. The Court justified application of the pilot procedure by the fact that there were 50 similar pending applications against Belgium. The Court gave Belgium two years to introduce appropriate measures in these cases. At the time of writing, the execution of the case is still pending. The Committee of Ministers stated the following:

> The Court identified the structural problem in question twelve years ago, and the deadline set in the WD pilot-judgment for resolving it, expired six years ago. Despite the undeniable efforts made by the authorities, the constant increase since 2019 in the number of internees in prison, still without sufficient and adapted therapeutic support, does not allow to conclude that 'tangible progress' has been made in resolving the structural problem. In line with its previous decisions in this group of cases, the Committee may therefore wish to adopt an interim resolution.[38]

In *Rezmiveş and Others v Romania* (2017) the Court decided to apply pilot judgment procedure in relation to the systemic problem of conditions of detention in Romania. At the time of the judgment there were over 3000 potentially meritorious pending applications.[39] The Court gave the Romanian authorities six months to 'provide a precise timetable, in cooperation with the Committee of Ministers, for the implementation of the appropriate general measures to remedy the problem of prison overcrowding and poor detention conditions'.[40] The judgment is still pending execution although some remedies have been introduced as a result of it.

Sukachov v Ukraine (2020) is another case concerning conditions of detention. The Court identified 120 similar pending applications.[41] In this case, the Court ordered that state must 'within eighteen months from the date on which this judgment becomes final … make available a combination of effective domestic remedies in respect of conditions of detention that have both preventive and compensatory effects'. The judgment is still

[36] ECtHR, App no 48322/12 *Gazsó v Hungary* ECLI:CE:ECHR:2015:0716JUD004832212, para 31.
[37] ECtHR, App no 73548/13 *WD v Belgium* ECLI:CE:ECHR:2016:0906JUD007354813.
[38] Available at https://hudoc.exec.coe.int/eng?i=004-1213 accessed 6 May 2025.
[39] ECtHR, App nos 61467/12 and 3 others *Rezmiveş and Others v Romania* ECLI:CE:ECHR:2017:0425JUD006146712, para 109.
[40] ibid.
[41] ECtHR, App no 14057/17 *Sukachov v Ukraine* ECLI:CE:ECHR:2020:0130JUD001405717, para 138.

pending execution although in 2024 a law introducing remedies in the context of the case was adopted by the Ukrainian parliament.

In *Wałęsa v Poland* (2023) the Court applied the pilot judgment procedure to the situation in Poland in which the independence of judicial institutions was consistently undermined as a result of the judicial reforms being initiated by the authorities. The Court identified 492 pending cases concerning judicial reform in Poland. Here the Court ruled that Polish authorities 'must take appropriate legislative and other measures to secure in its domestic legal order compliance with the requirements of an "independent and impartial tribunal established by law" and the principle of legal certainty as guaranteed by this provision'.[42] Interestingly, in this case, the Court did not establish any time frame for adopting these legislative changes but the relevant cases were adjourned for 12 months. The execution of this case is still pending.

3.3. Analysis

This brief outline of the current state of affairs allows me to identify certain patterns in utilisation and effectiveness of the pilot judgment procedure. I can then offer some insights into what the Court aimed to achieve by resorting to this tool over the past ten years.

The first striking observation is that the procedure is used very sparingly. One might even argue that it is underutilised, given the nature of systemic problems in European states that have been identified through the pilot judgment procedure. As indicated, the procedure has been employed in only 0.2 per cent of Chamber and Grand Chamber cases. While this statistical data is not particularly surprising – since pilot judgments are not expected to be used frequently – it appears that the Court has been very restrictive in applying the procedure during the last ten years. Of course, each pilot judgment has hundreds of applications behind it. Delivering one pilot judgment might deal with a very high number of applicants, but one can very plausibly suggest that there were more than seven systemic human rights problems in Europe in the last decade.

As early as in 2010 the state representatives were encouraging the ECtHR to use this tool more frequently and utilise its full potential.[43] If Professor Antoine Buyse is right and the pilot judgment procedure is 'the most creative tool the Court has developed in its first fifty years of its existence'[44] then it should perhaps be used in more cases. This last statement needs to be clarified by the fact that the Court also delivered the so-called quasi-pilot judgments in which it can also indicate general measures that the respondent states need to introduce. It means that these numbers alone do not tell the full picture of the ECtHR's desire to impact the legislative changes in the respondent states. What they say is that the Court treats pilot judgment procedure as a very serious instrument which is appropriate when some strict legal and perhaps political conditions are met.

[42] ECtHR, App no 50849/21 *Wałęsa v Poland* ECLI:CE:ECHR:2023:1123JUD005084921.

[43] E Widmer-Schlumpf Conclusions, 30 https://rm.coe.int/reforming-the-european-convention-on-human-rights-interlaken-izmir-bri/1680695a9d accessed 6 May 2025.

[44] Buyse(n 5), 303.

The following observations relate to the circumstances in which the Court resorts to the pilot judgment procedure. On a number of occasions, the Court stated that the pilot judgment procedure should be used to tackle the systemic human rights problem which is demonstrated by the number of pending applications and also by the number of people affected as well as the number of potential further applications in the future. Another observation stems from the fact that the Court has very wide discretion as to the number of pending cases that can be deemed appropriate for the pilot judgment procedure. The number of pending applications relevant to the pilot judgment procedure generally ranges from 40 to 4,000. The ECtHR has deliberately refrained from specifying a precise numerical threshold, leaving the determination of when to apply the procedure open to discretionary assessment.

Another relevant observation is that none of the pilot judgments between 2015 and 2025 were delivered by the Grand Chamber of the ECtHR although this has happened in the past.[45] Even the very first reference to pilot judgment was made in the Grand Chamber case *Broniowski v Poland*.[46] However, if one would search the term 'pilot' in this judgment it cannot be found in the Grand Chamber meritorious judgment. It was subsequently mentioned in the friendly settlement judgment[47] related to the same case but not in the main one It is therefore noteworthy that the Grand Chamber has avoided applying the pilot judgment procedure to any of its judgments for the past ten years. One explanation of this might be that pilot judgments do not normally deal with new and unclear rules which is the main 'area of expertise' of the Grand Chamber. Pilot judgments are usually concerned with the well-established human rights standards which are not properly embedded into the national legal system. Pilot judgments are often the follow ups of the previous similar judgments that the respondent state failed to implement. It is therefore unsurprising that pilot judgments are not delivered by the Grand Chamber. Having said that the pilot judgment delivered by the Grand Chamber might increase the pressure on the respondent state even further. Perhaps in certain circumstances, this can be deemed appropriate.

Another observation concerns the subject matter of the pilot judgments. In most of them the ECtHR dealt with conditions of detention – either in general detention facilities or in specialised wings for inmates with mental disabilities – or with the length of judicial proceedings. These judgments reiterate the standards that have already been explored in major detail not only by the Court itself but also by other Council of Europe institutions such as European Committee for the Prevention of Torture and Inhuman or Degrading Treatment or Punishment (CPT).[48] The only pilot judgment that was not on these two issues was *Wałęsa v Poland* but even there the Court dealt with the Article 6 ECHR (right to a fair trial) violation. It is therefore safe to suggest that by resorting to pilot judgments, the ECtHR does not really push the boundaries of the substantive scope of European Public Order,[49] but instead encourages the respondent states to adopt

[45] ECtHR (GC), App no 60642/08 *Ališić and Others v Bosnia and Herzegovina, Croatia, Serbia, Slovenia and the former Yugoslav Republic of Macedonia* ECLI:CE:ECHR:2014:0716JUD006064208.
[46] ECtHR (GC), App no 31443/96 *Broniowski v Poland* (n 2).
[47] ECtHR (GC), App no 31443/96 *Broniowski v Poland* (friendly settlement), ECLI:CE:ECHR:2004:0622JUD003144396.
[48] In case of conditions of detention. See www.coe.int/en/web/cpt/standards accessed 6 May 2025.
[49] Dzehtsiarou (n 7).

reforms in the area which is clearly and consistently problematic from the perspective of the ECHR law.

The final two observations arising from the analysis of pilot judgments concern the reaction of the respondent states to the ECtHR's application of the pilot judgment procedure. In most cases, governments object to the introduction of the procedure, arguing either that the issue is not widespread or systemic or that they have already implemented appropriate general measures to address the problem. In nearly all cases, the Court has had to justify the necessity of applying the pilot judgment procedure. This suggests that states recognise the distinction between ordinary and pilot cases and actively seek to prevent the application of the pilot procedure by raising objections.

Even though the special nature of pilot judgments appears to be acknowledged by respondent states, this does not necessarily mean they are 'immediately' enforced. Of all the pilot judgments issued by the ECtHR in the past ten years, only one has been fully executed and closed by the Committee of Ministers. The deadlines set by the Court for implementing these judgments are largely symbolic, as they are either vaguely defined – requiring only the initiation of the implementation process – or are entirely ignored. Often, these deadlines merely indicate that the Court will adjourn all pending applications on the same issue until the specified date. The lack of timely enforcement is, once again, not entirely surprising. These cases can involve complex reforms that often demand substantial financial resources. That said, the failure to enforce pilot judgments in a timely manner may ultimately undermine the legitimacy of the whole pilot procedure. However, one needs to be fair and acknowledge that the governments in almost every pilot judgment try to introduce the new remedy: sometimes with delay, sometimes less effective than required but it seems that there were no pilot judgments in last ten years which were completely ignored.

To briefly conclude, over the past ten years, the pilot judgment procedure has been used rarely and only in relation to well-defined and relatively uncontroversial human rights standards, such as conditions of detention or length of judicial proceedings. This is one of the reasons why none of the pilot judgments were delivered by the Grand Chamber. Such pilot judgments do not establish new standards but serve as pressure points for states to implement standards that have already been developed in previous case law.

Therefore, the core purpose of the pilot judgment procedure is to reinforce the existing standards rather than to develop the new ones. However, this does not always lead to the expected results. Although states often seek to prevent the application of this procedure, its impact on shaping governmental policies has been rather delayed. Of the pilot judgments delivered in the past ten years, only one has been fully executed and closed by the Committee of Ministers. Often, states fail to comply with the time limits set by the Court for implementing specific measures and remedies.

4. The Most Recent Development: *Cannavacciuolo and Others v Italy*

I chose 1 January 2025 as the deadline for this research project. However, I could not omit examining a significant new pilot judgment in the case of *Cannavacciuolo v Italy* which was delivered on 30 January 2025.[50] This was especially so, since the ECtHR chose to develop its approach to pilot judgments in this case, therefore I decided to dedicate this short section to the analysis of this very recent case.

Although it introduces a few significant developments in the case law,[51] this was again a Chamber judgment. It focuses on the positive obligations of the respondent state to protect the lives of applicants affected by pollution resulting from the illegal dumping and burial of hazardous and urban waste. Despite multiple reports, investigations, plans and other actions this problem persisted over the years and was known by the authorities from as early as 1988. The judgment is significant for instance because it specified a noticeable innovation in relation to admissibility of claims brought by organisations by limiting the potential impact of the new approach to admissibility developed in the *KlimaSeniorinnen v Switzerland* judgment.[52] Curiously, *KlimaSeniorinnen v Switzerland* which was the first climate change judgment of the Court was not a pilot judgment, although a judgment like this can potentially affect a very high number of potential applicants.

For the purposes of this research, the judgment in *Cannavacciuolo v Italy* is significant because it is the first pilot judgment in environmental pollution cases. The Court identified 36 similar pending applications. Despite the fact that technically this number is lower than the lowest number of applications in any other pilot judgment over the last ten years, the ECtHR stressed the high number of potential applicants and the high number of cases pending on the national level. Another noticeable, although not unprecedented, difference with other previous pilot judgments is that this case is not strictly speaking a follow up of another judgment that did not have a desired effect. The Court's judgments in *Di Sarno v Italy*[53] and *Locascia v Italy*[54] are relevant here but the ECtHR itself clearly distinguished them with the judgment under review.[55] The ECtHR listed a number of measures that Italy is expected to adopt and set the deadline of two years for adoption of these measures. The ECtHR here decided to be more prescriptive, and rather than setting a deadline for presenting a timetable for adoption of measures as in some other judgments discussed above, it ordered implementation of the specific measures identified by the Court.

What does this judgment mean for the utilisation of the pilot judgment procedure by the ECtHR? It might be the case that the Court will start using the mechanism more often and in relation to challenges that are not 'usual suspects' for application of the pilot judgment procedure. The latter was the predominant mode of operation of the pilot judgment procedure in the last ten years. It seems that on a number of occasions

[50] ECtHR, App nos 51567/14 and 3 others *Cannavacciuolo and Others v Italy* ECLI:CE:ECHR:2025:0130JUD005156714.

[51] See J Sommardal, 'A Landmark Judgment: Three Crucial Aspects of Cannavacciuolo and Others v Italy' (*ECHR blog*, 4 February 2025) www.echrblog.com/2025/02/by-dr.html accessed 6 May 2025.

[52] ECtHR (GC), App no 53600/20 *Verein KlimaSeniorinnen Schweiz and Others v Switzerland* ECLI:CE:ECHR:2024:0409JUD005360020. For analysis see G Letsas, 'The European Court's Legitimacy After KlimaSeniorinnen' (2024) *European Convention on Human Rights Law Review* 444; K Dzehtsiarou, '"KlimaSeniorinnen Revolution": The New Approach to Standing' (2024) *European Convention on Human Rights Law Review* 423.

[53] ECtHR, App no 30765/08 *Di Sarno and Others v Italy* ECLI:CE:ECHR:2012:0110JUD003076508.

[54] ECtHR, App no 35648/10 *Locascia and Others v Italy* ECLI:CE:ECHR:2023:1019JUD003564810.

[55] ECtHR, *Cannavacciuolo and Others v Italy* (n 50), para 448.

the Court was encouraged to utilise the pilot procedure more broadly than it is currently used. Moreover, the fact that *Cannavacciuolo and Others v Italy* is not the follow-up of other similar judgments also suggests that the Court is prepared to go off the well-trodden path. In effect, the Court confirmed that it can predict the number of repetitive applications and use the pilot judgment pre-emptively, clearly forward looking.

Having said all this, the broader deployment of pilot judgments to new areas is not without risks and these risks are perhaps both significant and rather well-known to the Court. The cases that involve pilot judgment procedure are complex, delay individual justice and often require significant investments from the respondent state and these resources might not be easily available. Therefore, the risk of non-execution is high which undermines the Court's legitimacy and reputation and does not solve the problem of repetitive applications. The deadline set by the Court provides the state with a clear target but also gives the commentators a clear indication of whether the Court's rulings are complied with. Without reading too much into this judgment, I can suggest that this might symbolise the Court's attempt to depart from the very limited and conservative use of the pilot judgment procedure over the last ten years. However, if the approach in *Cannavacciuolo and Others v Italy* will not result in enforcement by Italy (plenty of internal attempts failed before), the ECtHR might be reassured that creative thinking about the pilot judgment procedure is not what states really wish for despite some declarations to the contrary.

5. Conclusion

The pilot judgment procedure stands at a crossroads: it serves to protect the ECtHR from an overload of applications while also promising enhanced individual justice. The ECtHR presents pilot judgments as an innovation but seeks to avoid substantive developments of its case law through them. This multifaceted nature is also reflected in how states respond: authorities frequently argue against the use of the procedure in cases concerning their own jurisdictions, yet they often delay its enforcement. It seems as though the ECtHR has acquired an IKEA-style piece of furniture called 'pilot judgment' – but without assembly instructions. As a result, the Court is using certain parts of this mechanism for limited purposes. The forward-looking pilot judgments do not really enhance European Public Order as they are currently used, although in principle they can do so; instead they galvanise clear and uncontroversial standards that are not yet enforced in a particular Contracting Party to the ECHR.

7

Purposeless or Promising? Advisory Opinions from the European Court of Human Rights

JASPER KROMMENDIJK

1. Introduction

Since October 2018, 58 national courts of 22 States Parties have been able to request an advisory opinion from the European Court of Human Rights (ECtHR). These national courts can request such an opinion on the basis of Protocol No 16 (P16).[1] However, most contracting parties to the European Convention on Human Rights (ECHR) have not yet signed or ratified P16, mainly because they are concerned that national sovereignty and judicial discretion are undermined.[2] Over the past six years ten requests have been filed by courts in eight Member States (see Table 1). Three of them were refused. This edited volume provides a timely opportunity to reflect on the functioning of P16.[3] One's assessment of the experience so far with P16 depends on subjective perspectives; the glass can be seen as either half-full or half-empty, depending on one's expectations and outlook. Nonetheless, despite the initial lukewarm support it received, the P16 has been ratified by a substantial number of contracting parties and has actually been employed.[4] Yet

[1] 'Chart of signatures and ratifications of Treaty 214' www.coe.int/en/web/conventions/full-list?module=signatures-by-treaty&treatynum=214 accessed 27 May 2025.

[2] E Albanesi, 'Judicial Dialogue Through the Advisory Opinion Mechanism under Protocol No 16. The Academic's Perspective' (Speech at the Conference on Protocol No 16, Strasbourg, 13 October 2023) <www.echr.coe.int/documents/d/echr/summary-20231013-albanesi-conference-p16-eng> accessed 27 May 2025; JH Gerards and CMS Loven, *Protocol 16 ECHR. Background, Meaning, Effects and Experiences* (Utrecht, Utrecht University, 2023) repository.wodc.nl/bitstream/handle/20.500.12832/3293/3388-protocol-16-EVRM-full-text.pdf?sequence=7&isAllowed=y accessed 27 May 2025, 34–35.

[3] This chapter was finalised before the publication of Steering Committee for Human Rights (CDDH), 'Draft Report Evaluating the First Effects of Protocol No 16 to the European Convention on Human Rights' (DH-SYSC-PRO(2024)07REV, 15 October 2024) https://rm.coe.int/drafting-group-on-the-evaluation-of-the-first-effects-of-protocols-no-/1680b20c01 accessed 27 May 2025, 35. The chapter makes – where appropriate – references to (dis)similar conclusions.

[4] There was, for example, initial reluctance of the ECtHR. When the idea was first floated in the 2006 report of the Group of Wise Persons this led to an unenthusiastic response. 'Opinion of the Court on the Wise Persons' Report' (Plenary Court, 2 April 2007) www.echr.coe.int/documents/d/echr/2007_Wise_Person_Opinion_ENG

those who may have expected the ECtHR to be overwhelmed by applications may be surprised that only ten requests have been filed. Those who cautioned against the excessive use of P16 should consider its limited use in reality to be a success, reflecting the intention to limit P16 to the highest courts and particular types of questions.

This chapter evaluates the experience with the advisory opinion procedure in P16 over the past six years, with a focus on both the requesting national courts and the ECtHR. With respect to the national courts, the question is what courts have requested and for which reasons. For this purpose, the types of questions posed by national courts as well as their (legal) considerations to request an opinion are examined.[5] In order to answer the why-question, this chapter relies on empirical insights related to P16 and draws from interviews conducted by Gerards and Loven[6] as well as interviews with judges, attorneys general (AGs) and law clerks of the four highest Dutch courts conducted in the context of research on national courts' engagement with ECtHR judgments.[7]

With respect to the ECtHR, the chapter examines how the ECtHR has handled the ten requests to date from both a substantive and especially procedural perspective. The chapter explores how the ECtHR has interpreted the admissibility conditions, notably the restrictions of 'questions of principle' and 'case pending'. The analysis of the ECtHR perspective primarily relies on the P16 case law of the ECtHR as well as speeches and extra-judicial writings of ECtHR (and national court) judges.

Before these questions in relation to the practice and experience of national courts and the ECtHR are answered, Section 2 provides, by way of introduction, an overview of the objectives and most important characteristics of P16. It will compare P16 with the EU preliminary ruling procedure in Article 267 of the Treaty on the Functioning of the European Union (TFEU). The latter procedure has, since the founding of the European Economic Communities, functioned as the 'keystone' of the European judicial system; it served as a model and source of inspiration for P16.[8] The purpose of this comprehensive ECHR–EU comparison is twofold. It clearly accentuates the most important aspects of P16 while it also fits well with the focus of this volume dedicated to

accessed 27 May 2025; T Eicke, 'Judicial Dialogue Through the Advisory Opinion Mechanism under Protocol No 1. The Court's Perspective. Intervention by Tim Eicke' (Speech at the Conference on Protocol No 16, Strasbourg, 13 October 2023) www.echr.coe.int/documents/d/echr/speech-20231013-eike-conference-p16-eng accessed 27 May 2025.

[5] See more extensively, LR Glas and J Krommendijk, 'A Strasbourg Story of Swords and Shields. National Courts' Motives to Request an Advisory Opinion from the ECtHR Under Protocol 16' (2022) 3 *European Convention on Human Rights Law Review* 311.

[6] Gerards and Loven, *Protocol 16 ECHR* (2023).

[7] This project focuses on whether, how and why national courts engage with decisions of international human rights courts and monitoring bodies. The focus was not so much on P16, but some interviewees reflected on P16 and considerations that played a role in decisions not to request. 19 interviews were conducted in the period May–June 2024. P16 was discussed in seven interviews (interview 4, 5, 10, 13, 14, 17, 18). For more information about the project, see 'Denial or Dutifulness: Dutch Courts and Decisions of International Human Rights Courts' www.ru.nl/en/research/research-projects/denial-or-dutifulness-dutch-courts-and-decisions-of-international-human-rights-courts accessed 27 May 2025.

[8] D Fairgrieve, 'Judge Siofra O'Leary, President of the European Court of Human Rights, Strasbourg, on Protocol 16 of the European Convention of Human Rights. Interview' (2022) 2 *Mass Claims* 5, 9; *cf* P Gragl '(Judicial) Love is Not a One-Way Street: The EU Preliminary Reference Procedure as a Model for ECtHR Advisory Opinions under Draft Protocol No 16' (2013) 2 *EL Rev* 229, 239; CJEU, Opinion 2/13 *EU accession to the ECHR* ECLI:EU:C:2014:2454, para 176.

the interrelationships between both European human rights systems. In doing so, this chapter complements the contribution of Ronkes Agerbeek focusing on the relationship between both procedures.[9]

The structure of this chapter is as follows. Section 2 discusses the most important aims and characteristics of P16 and touches upon the relationship between P16 and the preliminary ruling procedure in Article 267 TFEU. Section 3.1 focused on the types of questions asked, while Section 3.2 focuses on the procedural handling by the ECtHR. Section 3.3 focuses on the admissibility review by the ECtHR and connects the admissibility requirements with national court's considerations to request. This examination paves the way for the reflection in Section 3.4 on the handling of the requests by the ECtHR from a more substantive perspective, touching upon the division of tasks between the ECtHR and national courts and the difference between interpretation and application of ECHR law.

Table 1 Overview of the ten P16 requests to date (2018–2024)

Member State	Number	Date of request	Date of delivery	Outcome	Subject
France	P16-2018-001	12 October 2018	10 April 2019 (5.9 months)	Accepted	Surrogacy and the recognition of a legal parent-child relationship
Armenia	P16-2019-001	2 September 2019[10]	29 May 2020 (8.9 months)	Accepted	Definition of an offence and 'legislation by reference'
Slovakia	P16-2020-001	25 September 2020	14 December 2020 (2.6 months)	Refused	Impartial prosecution of officers of the police force
Lithuania	P16-2020-002	5 November 2020[11]	8 April 2022 (17.1 months)	Accepted	General prohibition on standing for election after impeachment
Armenia	P16-2021-001	11 March 2021[12]	26 April 2022 (13.5 months)	Accepted	Statutes of limitation in relation to acts of torture

(continued)

[9] Ronkes Agerbeek especially discusses this relationship in the light of Opinion 2/13. F Ronkes Agerbeek, 'Knowing Whom to Ask: Judicial Dialogue under Protocol No 16 ECHR and Article 267 TFEU', in ch 10 of the present volume.

[10] The request was filed on 2 August 2019. The ECtHR requested twice further materials and explanations and it considered that the request was formally lodged on the second date.

[11] The original request was filed on 17 September 2020, albeit in the Lithuanian language. The Court provided English translations on the request of the ECtHR.

[12] The original request was submitted on 1 February 2021.

Table 1 ***(Continued)***

Member State	Number	Date of request	Date of delivery	Outcome	Subject
France	P16-2021-002	15 April 2021	13 July 2022 (14.9 months)	Accepted	Difference in treatment as to hunting rights
Finland	P16-2022-001	3 October 2022	13 April 2023 (6.3 months)	Accepted	Rights of a biological parent in adult child adoption proceedings
Belgium	P16-2023-001	4 April 2023	14 December 2023 (9.3 months)	Accepted	Denial of authorisation to work as security guard
Estonia	P16-2023-002	28 November 2023	19 February 2024 (2.7 months)	Refused	Termination of pre-trial criminal proceedings
Romania	P16-2024-001	6 February 2024	28 June 2024 (4.7 months)	Refused	Asset-audit proceedings and confiscation

2. Protocol 16 in Relation to Article 267 TFEU

This section describes the three most important differences between P16 and Article 267 TFEU (Section 2.2). These differences can be attributed to distinct objectives, namely enhancing dialogue between national courts and Strasbourg versus uniformity of EU law (Section 2.1). Despite these differences, there is potential overlap between both procedures, and a risk exists that P16 might be used to circumvent the partially obligatory EU procedure (Section 2.3).

2.1. Objectives of P16

The primary aim of P16 is to improve the interaction between the ECtHR and national courts. States held in the Brighton Declaration of 2012 that 'the interaction between the Court and national authorities could be strengthened by the introduction into the Convention of a further power of the Court'.[13] The preamble to P16 mentions enhanced interaction as the primary or even exclusive aim, while also pointing to the likely consequences of reinforced implementation of the Convention in accordance with the principle of subsidiarity.[14] Former ECtHR President Spielmann spoke of a

[13] Brighton Declaration of the High Level Conference on the Future of the European Court of Human Rights (20 April 2012), para B(12)(D).

[14] Preamble of Protocol No 16 to the Convention on the Protection of Human Rights and Fundamental Freedoms; Explanatory Report to Protocol No 16 to the Convention on the Protection of Human Rights

'protocol of dialogue'.[15] The ECtHR pointed to a possible longer-term consequence of enhanced interaction, namely a reduction of the burden because more cases would be handled satisfactorily at the national level.[16] P16 could thus prevent violations and reduce the need for individual applications.[17] The two main aims of promoting dialogue and reducing workload are also the main justifications for states to ratify P16.[18]

By contrast, the most important objective of the preliminary ruling procedure is to ensure consistency and uniformity in the interpretation of EU law.[19] The CJEU has highlighted this point ever since its landmark judgment in *Van Gend & Loos*.[20] Divergences in the interpretation of EU law across Member States are considered 'one of the most severe sins'.[21] The importance of uniformity is illustrated by the strict *CILFIT* test imposed by the CJEU. National courts 'must be convinced that the matter is equally obvious to the courts of the other Member States and to the Court of Justice'.[22] In addition, the importance of uniformity and the coherence of the EU legal system explain why the CJEU has reserved the power to declare an EU act invalid to itself, requiring *all* courts to refer if they doubt the validity.[23]

2.2. Characteristics of Protocol No 16

The different aims of the two procedures partially explain the varying setups and characteristics of the procedures. There are three notable differences. Before discussing these characteristics, it is important to emphasise the distinctiveness of each system. While the Convention system primarily revolves around a single general and open-ended document, namely the ECHR, EU law is based instead on an intricate system that aligns with

and Fundamental Freedoms (ECtHR, 2013) https://70.coe.int/pdf/protocol_16_explanatory_report_eng.pdf accessed 27 May 2025, para 25; Reflection Paper on the Proposal to Extend the Courts Advisory Jurisdiction (ECtHR, 2012) <www.echr.coe.int/documents/d/echr/Courts_advisory_jurisdiction_ENG accessed 27 May 2025, paras 4 and 9; Brighton Declaration (see n 13 above) para 12d; ECtHR, Request no P16-2020-001, *Decision on a request for an advisory opinion under Protocol No 16 concerning the interpretation of Articles 2, 3 and 6 of the Convention* paras 11 and 13.

[15] D Spielmann, 'Opening Speech' (Dialogue between Judges, Strasbourg, 31 January 2014) 31.

[16] ECtHR, Request no P16-2020-001, *Decision on a request for an advisory opinion under Protocol No 16 concerning the interpretation of Articles 2, 3 and 6 of the Convention*, para 2; Reflection Paper (see n 14 above) para 6.

[17] Fairgrieve 'Judge Siofra O'Leary' (2022) 7; S O'Leary, 'Judicial Dialogue Through the Advisory Opinion Mechanism under Protocol No 16' (Speech at the Conference on Protocol No 16, Strasbourg, 13 October 2023) prd-echr.coe.int/documents/d/echr/speech-20231013-oleary-conference-p16-bil accessed 27 May 2025, 2.

[18] See, eg, Drafting Group on the Evaluation of the First Effects of Protocols No 15 and No 16 to the European Convention on Human Rights (DH-SYSC-PRO(2024)02REV) 4. See also specifically the reasons for the Netherlands on p 24.

[19] CJEU, Opinion 2/13 (see n 8 above), para 174; CJEU, Case C-399/11 *Stefano Melloni v Ministerio Fiscal* ECLI:EU:C:2013:107, para 63.

[20] CJEU, Case C-26-62 *Van Gend & Loos* ECLI:EU:C:1963:1.

[21] Quote from an interviewed Dutch Supreme Court judge in J Krommendijk, *National Courts and Preliminary References to the Court of Justice* (Northampton, Edward Elgar Publishing, 2021) 31.

[22] CJEU, Case C-283/81 *CILFIT and Lanificio di Gavardo SpA v Ministry of Health* ECLI:EU:C:1982:335, para 16.

[23] CJEU, Case C-314/85 *Foto-Frost v Hauptzollamt Lübeck-Ost* ECLI:EU:C:1987:452.

treaties, a Charter and an extensive body of detailed EU secondary law. This scenario provides both the ECtHR and national courts considerable 'interpretative space'.[24]

First, P16 is limited to the highest courts and tribunals only. The restriction reflects the centrality of the requirement of exhaustion of domestic remedies in the Convention system (Article 35(1) ECHR). It can also be attributed to a wish to avoid 'a proliferation of requests' and ensure that the dialogue between courts takes place at 'the appropriate level'.[25] By contrast, all courts can invoke the EU preliminary ruling procedures, even lower district courts in first instance, as long as they satisfy the six criteria of constituting a 'court or tribunal' in the sense of Article 267 TFEU.[26] Notably, some countries, including Belgium, opted for a system whereby the designated Supreme (Administrative) Court(s) must obtain permission from the Constitutional Court for a P16 request.[27] Such a priority rule is impossible in relation to the EU preliminary ruling procedure.[28] The contracting parties thus have greater control regarding the courts or tribunals that can make a P16 request. This has again resulted in differences among states, with some designating various higher courts and others being more restrictive.[29]

Second, a request under P16 is always optional. By contrast, the highest courts are obliged to refer to the Court of Justice of the European Union (CJEU) when 'a decision on the question is necessary to enable it to give judgment'.[30] This means that courts are not obliged to refer to the CJEU if they can decide the case on the basis of national law, or if the particular facts of the case are such that they do not require a reference. The CJEU formulated two exceptions to the obligation to refer in its famous *CILFIT* judgment of 1982. The highest courts are not obliged to refer where the ECJ has 'already dealt with the point of law in question' (*acte éclairé*), or where 'the correct application of [EU] law may be so obvious as to leave no scope for any reasonable doubt' (*acte clair*).[31]

[24] Fairgrieve (n 8) 9.

[25] ibid 7. P16 goes, however, further than the initial proposal of the Group of Wise Persons that limited requests to courts or tribunals against whose decisions there is no judicial remedy under national law. This reflects the terminology in Article 267 TFEU. The Netherlands made a statement at the moment of ratification that the designated courts or tribunals cannot make a request in cases in which there is still a judicial remedy. Gerards and Loven (n 2) 27.

[26] CJEU, Case C-210/06 *CARTESIO Oktató és Szolgáltató bt* ECLI:EU:C:2008:723, para 55.

[27] One Belgian judge of the Cassation Court addressed a future 'guerre des juges', because he noted that the Cassation Court might 'want to avoid any possibility that we could not address requests for an opinion to Strasbourg, that we would first have to refer the case to the Constitutional Court, and that they would then de facto be the only body that could address requests for an opinion to Strasbourg. R6 as quoted in M Kappé, 'Unveiling Reasons of Belgian Highest Court Judges and Law Clerks (not) to Refer Preliminary Questions to the Court of Justice of the European Union: A Nuanced Legalist Image' (2023) NYU Jean Monnet Working Paper 6/23 JMWP-06-Marleen-Kappe.pdf (jeanmonnetprogram.org) accessed 27 May 2025; Gerards and Loven (n 2) 37.

[28] A so-called 'question prioritaire de constitutionalité'. CJEU, Joined Cases C-188/10 and C-189/10 *Melki and Abdeli* ECLI:EU:C:2010:363.

[29] Romania, eg, designated 15 Courts of Appeal in addition to the High Court of Cassation and Justice and the Constitutional Court, while Estonia 'only' designated its Supreme Court. Fairgrieve (n 8).

[30] J Gerards, 'Advisory Opinions, Preliminary Rulings and the New Protocol No 16 to the European Convention of Human Rights: A Comparative and Critical Appraisal' (2014) 21 *Maastricht Journal of European and Comparative Law* 630, 640–45; Gragl, '(Judicial) Love' (2013).

[31] CJEU, *CILFIT* (see n 22 above), paras 14 and 16.

Third, unlike the CJEU judgments made after preliminary references, P16 advisory opinions are not binding (Article 5 of P16). Consequently, the requesting national court decides on the effects of the advisory opinion and whether and how it applies the ECtHR's interpretation to the facts of the case in the proceedings pending before it.[32] Hence, the court can decide not to follow the opinion, at least in theory.[33] By contrast, CJEU judgments are binding and even bind national courts other than the referring court.[34] However, the difference between the EU and ECHR procedure is in practice less stark. The de facto bindingness or *res interpretata* effect of P16 opinions has received ample attention in the literature.[35] The ECtHR made clear in its reflection paper that it considers opinions 'as valid case law which it would follow when ruling on potential subsequent individual applications'.[36] Consequently, opinions have 'undeniable legal effects' according to the ECtHR, similar to the effects and interpretative value of its judgments and decisions.[37] The case law of the ECtHR in the past six years reflects these postulations. The ECtHR has based its judgments in individual cases on its interpretations in opinions.[38] It relied on its first opinion following a French request on surrogacy in the case *Menneson v France*.[39] The ECtHR even did so in a Swiss case, despite the fact that Switzerland has not ratified P16.[40] This judgment thus confirms that opinions 'may have implicit *erga omnes* effects even for those Member States not parties to Protocol 16'.[41]

[32] Explanatory Report (see n 14 above) para 25.

[33] Reflection Paper (see n 14 above) para 7.

[34] Article 280 of the Consolidated Version of the Treaty on the Functioning of the European Union [2012] OJ C 326.

[35] See especially the distinction between 'vertical' non-binding effect' vis-à-vis requesting court and the undeniable horizontal' legal effects vis-à-vis all courts. E Albanesi, 'The European Court of Human Rights' Advisory Opinions Legally Affect Non-ratifying States: A Good Reason (From a Perspective of Constitutional Law) to Ratify Protocol No 16 to the ECHR' (2022) 28 *European Public Law* 1; Albanesi 'Judicial Dialogue Through the Advisory Opinion' (2023); Fairgrieve (n 8) 9; A Paprocka and M Ziólkowski, 'Advisory Opinions under Protocol No 16 to the European Convention on Human Rights' (2015) 11 *European Constitutional Law Review* 274, 284 and 291; Draft report (see n 3 above) para 76.

[36] Reflection Paper (see n 14 above) para 44; Explanatory Report (see n 14 above) para 27; C Giannopoulos, 'Considerations on Protocol No. 16: Can the New Advisory Competence of the European Court of Human Rights Breathe New Life into the European Convention on Human Rights?' (2015) 16 *German Law Journal* 337, 339–340 and 342; ECtHR, Request no P16-2018-001, *Advisory opinion concerning the recognition in domestic law of a legal parent-child relationship between a child born through a gestational surrogacy arrangement abroad and the intended mother*, para 26.

[37] Reflection Paper (see n 14 above) para 44; Explanatory Report (see n 14 above) 27; M Dicosola, C Fasone and I Spigno, 'The Prospective Role of Constitutional Courts in the Advisory Opinion Mechanism Before the European Court of Human Rights: A First Comparative Assessment with the European Union and the Inter-American System' (2015) 16 *German Law Journal* 1387, 1409; J Gerards, 'Advisory Opinion: European Court of Human Rights (ECtHR)' in H Ruiz Fabri, *Max Planck Encyclopedias of international Procedural Law* (Cambridge, Cambridge University Press, 2019), para 22; Eicke, 'Judicial Dialogue Through the Advisory Opinion' (2023) 4.

[38] CMS Loven, 'D.B. e.a. t. Zwitserland (EHRM, 58817/15 en 58252/15) – Over de bindende werking van Protocol 16-adviezen' (*European Human Rights Cases Updates*, 15 December 2022) www.ehrc-updates.nl/commentaar/212308#_ftn6; eg, ECtHR, no 47621/13, *Vavřička et al v Czechia*, ECLI:CE:ECHR:2021:0408JUD004762113; ECtHR, App no 2953/14 *Pantalon v Croatia* ECLI:CE:ECHR:2020:1119JUD000295314, para 45.

[39] ECtHR, App no 65192/11 *Menneson v France* ECLI:CE:ECHR:2014:0626JUD006519211.

[40] ECtHR, App nos 58817/15 and 58252/15 *DB et al v Switzerland* ECLI:CE:ECHR:2022:1122JUD005881715.

[41] A Nussberger, *The European Court of Human Rights* (Oxford, Oxford University Press, 2020); *cf* S O'Leary and T Eicke, 'Some Reflections on Protocol No 16' (2018) *European Human Rights Law Review* 220; Concurring opinion of Krenc in *D.B. et al v Switzerland* (n 40 above), para 17. For criticism see the partly dissenting opinion of Elósegui ibid.

Former President O'Leary argued that this broader jurisprudential authority stems from the Grand Chamber formation ('the most solemn judicial formation'), the principled nature of the questions as well as the interventions of states other than the state to which the requesting court pertains.[42] The legal effects of opinions also stem from the subsequent possibilities for individuals to lodge a complaint with the ECtHR on the basis of Article 34 ECHR if the requesting court ignores the opinion.[43] Nonetheless, the foregoing does not deprive the requesting court of any margin of manoeuvre, just like the EU preliminary ruling procedure.[44] Particularly because requests relate to principled (and often sensitive) matters, there is often a considerable margin of appreciation for the requesting national court when applying the rights as interpreted by the ECtHR in its opinion (see also Section 3.4).[45] The ECtHR, for instance, referred to a wide margin of appreciation in regulation of the procedure for adult adoption; this means that Article 8 ECHR does not require that a biological parent is granted the status of a party or the right to appeal the granting of the adoption.[46]

National court judges who made use of P16 have generally complied with the opinion, with a view to maintaining a good relationship with the ECtHR.[47] Interestingly, the non-binding character has discouraged some judges or courts from making a P16 request; they may have preferred instead the obligatory EU procedure, as discussed in the next subsection.[48]

2.3. Relationship between P16 and Article 267 TFEU

It is important, especially considering the focus of this edited volume, to examine how P16 relates to Article 267 TFEU. Neither P16, nor the explanatory report thereto, touch upon this relationship. The newly created possibility of advisory opinions was one of the reasons for the CJEU to declare the draft revised agreement on the accession of the EU to the ECHR incompatible with Article 6(2) TEU in its notorious Opinion 2/13 of December 2014. P16 was perceived to introduce the possibility that national courts could avoid their obligations to refer to Luxembourg by filing a non-committal request to Strasbourg 'only', which ultimately results in a non-binding opinion. The Full Court pointed to the risk that the preliminary ruling procedure 'might be circumvented'. This issue is especially problematic because that procedure is seen by the CJEU as 'the keystone of the judicial system established by the Treaties'.[49] The CJEU held that 'By failing to make any provision in respect of the relationship … the agreement envisaged is liable adversely to affect the autonomy and effectiveness of the preliminary reference

[42] Fairgrieve (n 8); O'Leary, 'Judicial Dialogue Through the Advisory Opinion' (2023) 3.

[43] This has, to date, not happened yet. Reflection Paper (see n 14 above) para 45; Fairgrieve (n 8) 9.

[44] J Krommendijk, 'Between Interpretation and Application. Case-specific CJEU Judgments in the Preliminary Ruling Procedure' (2023) 6 *Nordic Journal of European Law* 1.

[45] Albanesi (n 2); Gerards and Loven (n 2) 25–26.

[46] ECtHR, Request no P16-2022-001 *Advisory opinion concerning adoption of an adult*, para 62.

[47] Respondents note that they 'would have to be of very strong character to disregard an opinion.' Gerards and Loven (n 2) 50.

[48] Interview 13; Gerards and Loven (n 2) 7 and 44–45.

[49] CJEU, Opinion 2/13, (see n 8 above), para 198.

procedure.'[50] The recent Draft Accession Agreement (DAA) of March 2023 contains a legal solution to avoid this circumvention. It stipulates:

> Where a court or tribunal of a member State of the European Union that has ratified Protocol No 16 to the Convention, in the context of a case pending before it, encounters a question relating to the interpretation or application of the rights and freedoms defined in the Convention or the Protocols thereto, that court or tribunal shall not be considered as a highest court or tribunal of a High Contracting Party for the purposes of Article 1, paragraph 1, of Protocol No 16 to the Convention if the question falls within the field of application of European Union law.

Consequently, after the EU's accession to the ECHR, the ECtHR will not accept a request from a designated court if the question falls within the field of application of EU law for its failure to satisfy the first admissibility condition.[51] Another safety stop from an EU law perspective is the possibility for the European Commission to start an infringement procedure vis-à-vis the respective Member State for violating Article 267 TFEU, possibly in conjunction with Article 6(2) TEU and/or Article 344 TFEU.[52] On these bases, the Commission can sanction the circumvention of the EU procedure by national courts when these courts 'only' request an opinion from the ECtHR and fail to refer to the CJEU even though there is (also) a question of EU (fundamental) rights law. The foregoing, however, does not seem to deprive national courts of the possibility to request an opinion from the ECtHR about the remaining questions about ECHR law *after* they referred questions on EU law to the CJEU.[53]

A study of the P16 case law reveals that so far there has been no problematic situation as feared by the CJEU in Opinion 2/13. The issue, however, surfaced to a certain extent in the tenth Romanian request. This request relates to Law No 176/2010 on integrity in the performance of public duties and the holding of public office that constitutes a measure implementing EU law within the meaning of Article 51(1) of the Charter, as confirmed by the CJEU and also acknowledged by the ECtHR.[54] The ECtHR decided not to accept the request on other admissibility grounds, namely the lack of a question of principle (as discussed in Section 3.3). The ECtHR merely noted that the requesting High Court of Cassation had not explained why it used P16 instead of the preliminary ruling procedure.[55] Had the request satisfied the other admissibility conditions, it would seem logical that the ECtHR refused to answer the request on the basis of the fact that the national court should have referred to the CJEU instead, in line with Article 5 DAA.

[50] ibid, para 199.

[51] Article 51 of the Charter of Fundamental Rights of the European Union [2000] OJ C 364/1; CJEU, Case C-617/10 *Åkerberg Fransson* ECLI:EU:C:2013:105. See also Ronkes Agerbeek in ch 10 of this volume.

[52] This has so far happened twice. CJEU, Case C-516/22 *Commission/UK (Arrêt de la Cour suprême; Micula)* ECLI:EU:C:2024:231; CJEU, Case C-416/17 *Commission v France (Advance payment)* ECLI:EU:C:2018:811; O'Leary & Eicke (2018), 19.

[53] Compare this with the practice following the simultaneous reference of the Dutch Supreme Court to the CJEU and the Benelux Court of Justice dealing with intellectual property cases. The Benelux court awaited the answers from the CJEU. CJEU, Case C-337/95 *Dior v Evora* ECLI:EU:C:1997:517; Benelux Court of Justice 16 December 1998, *Dior/Evora*, case A 95/4.

[54] CJEU, Case C-40/21 *TAC v Agenția Națională de Integritate* ECLI:EU:C:2023:367, para 27; ECtHR, App no P16-2024-001 *Decision of the Court on the request received from the High Court of Cassation and Justice of Romania for an advisory opinion*, para 22.

[55] ECtHR, Request no P16-2024-001 *Decision of the Court on the request received from the High Court of Cassation and Justice of Romania for an advisory opinion*, para 49.

Empirical research reveals that national court judges sometimes juggle the two procedures. Nonetheless, there seems to be a preference among national courts for the EU procedure, particularly considering the obligatory EU framework (as discussed in Section 2.3).[56] A P16 opinion is only seriously contemplated when it is evident that there are no EU law aspects to the case.[57] This focus on Luxembourg also stems from the growing awareness and reliance of litigants on EU (fundamental rights) law and the Charter.[58] This point is further reinforced by the (recent) expansion of EU legislation affecting or involving fundamental rights, such as the GDPR, the AI Act and harmonisation in the criminal area.

3. Six Years of the Advisory Opinion Procedure

This section examines the experience with P16 over the past six years. It focuses on the types of questions requested (Section 3.1); the procedural handling of the requests by the ECtHR, including duration, intervention, reformulation and separate opinions (Section 3.2); and admissibility (Section 3.3). It ends with a discussion of the substantive handling of the requests and the level of abstract versus case-specific guidance (Section 3.4).

3.1. Substance: The Requests Submitted

Various observations can be made in relation to the types of requests. First, most requests have involved relatively easy – arguably *clair* – questions.[59] The requesting courts seemed interested mainly in obtaining external and authoritative support in politically sensitive matters.[60] This has also been the experience of some stakeholders involved. ECtHR judge Koskelo noted that most requests relate to societal or political sensitivities and controversial issues at the domestic level.[61] Judge Soulard of the French *Cour de cassation*, who was involved in the first French surrogacy request, explicitly stated that advisory opinions can be useful in terms of providing legitimacy to the judgment of the requesting court, especially if striking down a national law for violating the ECHR is an extremely delicate matter.[62] He held that the opinion of the ECtHR can

[56] Interview 10. AG Harteveld mentioned this overlap as a reason not to make a P16 request when the case falls within the scope of EU law, given that EU law offers at least the same level of protection as the ECHR and because national courts are obliged to refer to the CJEU. Dutch Supreme Court 29 October 2019, ECLI:NL:HR:2019:1635 (conclusion AG Harteveld), para 7.4.

[57] Gerards and Loven (n 2) 7 and 44–45.

[58] ibid 42.

[59] The CDDH likewise concluded that none of the requests raised systemic issues. Draft report (see n 3 above) 83.

[60] A so-called 'sword'. Glas and Krommendijk, 'A Strasbourg Story of Swords and Shields' (2022).

[61] The Finnish request is an exception because it is specific to a concrete case. P Koskelo, 'Concrete Lessons to be Learned from the First Proceedings under Protocol No 16 – The Court's Experience' (Speech at the Conference on Protocol No 16, Strasbourg, 13 October 2023) www.echr.coe.int/documents/d/echr/speech-20231013-koskelo-conference-p16-eng accessed 28 May 2025, 1–2; *cf* Gerards and Loven (n 2) 54.

[62] C Soulard, 'Le dialogue judiciaire par le biais du mécanisme d'avis consultatif en vertu du Protocole no 16. Les attentes de la juridiction nationale et le suivi au niveau national' (Speech at the Conference on Protocol No 16, Strasbourg, 13 October 2023) https://prd-echr.coe.int/documents/d/echr/speech-20231013-soulard-conference-p16-fra accessed 28 May 2025, 8.

bolster the authority of the national court, particularly in situations of an impasse.[63] Another example of a request with notable political dimensions is the (first) Armenian request in relation to the prosecution of the former President.[64] It is perhaps not surprising that the ECtHR subtly noted in the second Armenian case that it is primarily for national courts 'to resolve problems of interpretation of domestic legislation'.[65]

Relatedly, requests have also been filed in situations where – in the words of Judge Koskelo – there are 'conflicting findings or positions' at the domestic level.[66] This could involve cases in which there were tensions between courts and the legislature, or where various national courts have adopted different positions. Both ECtHR judge Koskelo and French judge Soulard mentioned the second French request on the regulation of hunting rights submitted by the French Council of State, whose case law was challenged by the legislature.[67] The question was whether there was a difference in the treatment of landowners' associations set up before and after the creation of an approved municipal hunters' association. Interestingly, after the request was filed in Strasbourg a different section of the Council of State raised a similar question on constitutionality to the Constitutional Council, who subsequently determined that there was no difference or treatment or disproportionate interference with the right to property. The ECtHR emphasised the wide margin of appreciation and recalled that it had found no violations in similar cases.

Second, three requests were made after the ECtHR determined violations of the ECHR.[68] This was a reason for the ECtHR not to answer one question in the Lithuanian request in relation to the impeachment of a member of parliament (Section 3.3.2).[69] Judge Soulard of the French Court of Cassation, for example, admitted that the question in the surrogacy case was more a question of execution of a previous ECtHR judgment than an unprecedented question of principle.[70] He pointed to the intense academic debate and lively public and parliamentary debates after the earlier conviction of France by the ECtHR. The discussions centred on the scope of the ruling in *Menneson v France*, especially the refusal to enter the birth certificate of a child born abroad in relation to the intended mother. Earlier determinations by the ECHR of violations also featured in the second Armenian request on statutes of limitation in relation to acts of torture.[71]

[63] ibid 1.

[64] ECtHR, Request no P16-2019-001 *Advisory opinion concerning the use of the 'blanket reference' or 'legislation by reference' technique in the definition of an offence and the standards of comparison between the criminal law in force at the time of the commission of the offence and the amended criminal law.*

[65] The ECtHR also 'reiterated' four times. ECtHR, Request no P16-2021-001 *Advisory opinion concerning the statute of limitations and torture*, para 70.

[66] Koskelo, 'Concrete Lessons to be Learned' (2023) 2. This reasoning is also reflected in the extra judicial writing of the SC President De Groot who expects that the Dutch SC will primarily use P16 in relation to 'nationally highly conflictive cases'. G de Groot, 'Beginselen van procesrecht en de hoogste rechter: mag, moet en gaat de Hoge Raad ooit in dialoog met het EHRM?' (2016) 4 *Tijdschrift voor Civiele Rechtspleging* 8, 11.

[67] ECtHR, Request no P16-2021-002 *Advisory opinion on the difference in the treatment of landowners' associations set up before and after the creation of an approved municipal hunters' association*, para 24; Koskelo, 'Concrete Lessons to be Learned' (2023) 2; Soulard, 'Le dialogue judiciaire' (2023) 7.

[68] Koskelo, 'Concrete Lessons to be Learned' (2023) 1-2; Soulard, 'Le dialogue judiciaire' (2023) 4.

[69] ECtHR, App no 34932/04 *Paksas v Lithuania* ECLI:CE:ECHR:2011:0106JUD003493204.

[70] ECtHR, App no 65192/11 *Mennesson v France* ECLI:CE:ECHR:2014:0626JUD006519211; Soulard, 'Le dialogue judiciaire' (2023) 4.

[71] ECtHR, App no 40094/05 *Virabyan v Armenia* ECLI:CE:ECHR:2012:1002JUD004009405; ECtHR, Request no P16-2021-001 *Advisory opinion concerning the statute of limitations and torture*, para 56.

3.2. Procedure: Handling by the ECtHR

3.2.1. *Length of Proceedings*

The Rules of Court stipulate that requests 'shall be processed as a matter of priority' (Article 93(2)).[72] The Guidelines even allow for expedited treatment of a request involving 'an urgent examination' and 'speedy ruling' in special circumstances.[73] So far, this not happened. There has been an awareness among ECtHR judges that the time should be kept to a minimum, especially with a view to making the new procedure work.[74] 'Time is of the essence' also applies to avoiding unnecessary delays in the pending cases before the requesting court.[75] According to Judge Koskelo, the ECtHR 'has made considerable efforts to design and improve its internal working methods', including a special track of prompt internal processing.[76] The ECtHR tries to process requests in a single round of deliberation by the Grand Chamber.[77] In addition, it tries to keep the opinions concise and considerably shorter than 'normal' Grand Chamber judgments.[78] The goal is to deliver the opinion within half a year.[79]

In most requests to date, the ECtHR has not achieved this self-imposed goal (see Table 1). Four requests took between 5.9 and 9.3 months to be decided, and three other requests took between 13.5 and 17.1 months to be decided. However, these periods are still shorter than the average time in Luxembourg, which is around 17 months.[80] The two 'inadmissible' requests were rejected in less than three months, and the most recent request was rejected in just under five months. The failure to meet the self-imposed goal can be attributed to reasons beyond the ECtHR's control, such as the COVID-19 pandemic. Another external reason is that the requesting court did not provide all the necessary information from the outset.[81] In other cases, the complexity of the case complicated the process and sometimes required more than one deliberation.[82] The second French request was suspended for almost three months after a question *prioritaire de constitutionalité* was submitted to the

[72] This policy is in line with the ECtHR's general priority policy, as part of which it grants priority to cases 'raising an important question of general interest'. The priority policy encompasses seven categories and is based on the 'importance and the urgency of the issues raised', see Rule 41 of the Rules of Court (ECtHR, 28 March 2024). Reflection Paper (see n 14 above) para 39.

[73] Guidelines on the implementation of the advisory-opinion procedure introduced by Protocol No 16 to the Convention (approved by the Plenary Court on 18 September 2017; update approved by the Plenary Court on 25 September 2023), www.echr.coe.int/documents/d/echr/guidelines_p16_eng accessed 28 May 2025, para 30.

[74] Fairgrieve (n 8) 8. 'within as short a time frame as possible'. ECtHR, Request no P16-2021-002 *Advisory opinion on the difference in the treatment of landowners' associations set up before and after the creation of an approved municipal hunters' association*, para 58.

[75] O'Leary, 'Judicial Dialogue Through the Advisory Opinion' (2023) 3; Koskelo, 'Concrete Lessons to be Learned' (2023) 3; Eicke, 'Judicial Dialogue Through the Advisory Opinion' (2023) 3.

[76] Koskelo, 'Concrete Lessons to be Learned (2023) 4.

[77] ibid.

[78] ibid.

[79] ibid.

[80] 17.3 in 2022 and 16.8 in 2023. 'Annual activity report for the financial year 2023' (CJEU, Luxembourg, 2024) curia.europa.eu/jcms/upload/docs/application/pdf/2024-06/en-rapport_gestion_2023.pdf 28 May 2025, 8.

[81] Fairgrieve (n 8) 8. The ECtHR, for instance, prolonged the time-limit for Lithuanian Government with one week. ECtHR, Request no P16-2020-002 *Advisory opinion concerning impeachment legislation*, para 5.

[82] The first Armenian request, for instance, required three deliberations. Koskelo (n 61) 4; Fairgrieve (n 8) 8.

Constitutional Council.[83] Overall, however, the ECtHR can be commended for its efficient handling of the requests. This is particularly noteworthy considering the Grand Chamber formation of no fewer than 17 judges and the limited resources of the ECtHR.[84] Advisory opinions absorb valuable time of the Grand Chamber whose case docket amounts to an average of ten to 15 judgments a year.[85]

Avoiding delays is a primary consideration for courts, which explains why few requests have been made, especially in criminal and asylum cases.[86] National judges noted that in addition to the time in Strasbourg, a request involves time (and costs) in terms of preparation and internal coordination[87] as well as translation of the request into English or French. The wish to limit delays also ties in with a concern among national judges regarding the workload of the ECtHR.[88]

3.2.2. Other Procedural Aspects: Intervention, Reformulation and Separate Opinions

Other procedural aspects worth noting include intervention, reformulation and separate opinions. These three aspects are discussed in turn here. With respect to intervention, Article 3 of P16 makes clear that the state to which the requesting court pertains has a right to submit written comments and participate in any hearing, as does the Commissioner for Human Rights. The President of the Court may, in the interest of the proper administration of justice, invite any other High Contracting Party or persons to submit written comments or take part in any hearing. To date, states other than the state from which the request originated have intervened in only one of the seven admissible requests: the UK, the Czech Republic and Ireland intervened in the first French request.[89] NGOs intervened in four of the seven cases.[90] The Commissioner for Human Rights has never made use of his right to submit written comments. The requesting

[83] ECtHR, Request no P16-2021-002 *Advisory opinion on the difference in the treatment of landowners' associations set up before and after the creation of an approved municipal hunters' association*, para 7; Koskelo (n 61) 4.

[84] National court judges were positive about the relative quickness of the ECtHR. Gerards and Loven (n 2) 49.

[85] Fairgrieve (n 8) 9; Draft report (see n 3 above) para 66.

[86] Interview 13, 14, 17; AGs before the Dutch Supreme Court mentioned urgency as a reason for not referring in *Urgenda*. Dutch Supreme Court 20 December 2019, ECLI:NL:HR:2019:2006 (conclusion AG Langemeijer and Wissink), paras 5.6.4, 6.15–16. *cf* Dutch Supreme Court 29 October 2019, ECLI:NL:HR:2019:1635 (conclusion AG Harteveld); Gerards and Loven (n 2) 54.

[87] The highest Dutch courts also agreed to coordinate a request. One interviewee sketched this as an additional hurdle in addition to the internal coordination within the respective court. Interview 5.

[88] De Groot, 'Beginselen van procesrecht en de hoogste rechter' (2016) 11.

[89] ECtHR, Request no P16-2018-001 *Advisory opinion concerning the recognition in domestic law of a legal parent-child relationship between a child through a gestational surrogacy arrangement abroad and the intended mother*. Note both the Finnish and Belgian government did not submit any (further) written information.

[90] ECtHR, Request no P16-2018-001 *Advisory opinion concerning the recognition in domestic law of a legal parent-child relationship between a child through a gestational surrogacy arrangement abroad and the intended mother*, para 6; ECtHR, Request no P16-2019-001 *Advisory opinion concerning the use of the 'blanket reference' or 'legislation by reference' technique in the definition of an offence and the standards of comparison between the criminal law in force at the time of the commission of the offence and the amended criminal law*, para 8; ECtHR, Request no P16-2021-001 *Advisory opinion concerning the statute of limitations of torture*, para 7; ECtHR, Request no P16-2021-002 *Advisory opinion on the difference in the treatment of landowners' associations set up before and after the creation of an approved municipal hunters' association*, para 4.

courts are encouraged to include their 'own views on the questions'.[91] To date, courts have largely refrained from doing so.[92]

The ECtHR can reformulate or combine certain questions,[93] but has so far largely refrained from doing so. This reluctance contrasts with the initial willingness of the CJEU to salvage otherwise inadmissible questions in the early decades.[94] The ECtHR, for example, refrained from reformulating the general questions asked by the Armenian Constitutional Court that lacked a link with the pending domestic proceedings (Section 3.3.1).[95] While the ECtHR has never reformulated questions substantively and/or fundamentally, it has complemented questions or changed the order of answering. The ECtHR juggled with the two questions in the first French request and changed the order in addressing particular elements.[96] In the second French request, on hunting rights, the Court explicitly mentioned that it needed to answer two preliminary questions before replying to the question posed, 'having regard to the need for a sincere and loyal dialogue between international and national courts and to the utility that this opinion is intended to have'.[97] Interestingly, the ECtHR uses a similar justification as that of the CJEU for reformulations, relying on the need for dialogue and cooperation.[98] In the Finnish case, the Court merely summarised the three-layered question with the formulation 'the Supreme Court essentially asks whether …'.[99] This formulation clearly mirrors the standard phrases used by the CJEU, without altering the meaning of the references as such.[100]

[91] Guidelines (see n 73 above) para 12(e); Dzehtsiarou likewise encourages requesting courts to use their 'Voice'. K Dzehtsiarou, 'Keep Me in the Loop: Feedback Exchange between the European Court of Human Rights and States' (2023) 22 *The Law & Practice of International Courts and Tribunals* 591, 608.

[92] Koskelo (n 61) 5; Draft report (see n 3 above) para 29. One reason is that courts do not want to prejudice the opinion of the ECtHR and ensure their impartiality and objectivity. Group on the Evaluation of the First Effects of Protocols No 15 and No 16 to the European Convention on Human Rights (DH-SYSC-PRO(2024)02REV), para 10.

[93] Koskelo (n 61) 3.

[94] J Krommendijk, 'Wide Open and Unguarded Stand our Gates: The CJEU and References for a Preliminary Ruling in Purely Internal Situations' (2017) 18 *German Law Journal* 1359.

[95] ECtHR, Request no P16-2019-001 *Advisory opinion concerning the use of the 'blanket reference' or 'legislation by reference' technique in the definition of an offence and the standards of comparison between the criminal law in force at the time of the commission of the offence and the amended criminal law*, para 56. Nor did the ECtHR reformulate the third and fourth questions, even though judge Sarvarian expressed to be in favour of doing so in his concurring opinion 'to improve their lucidity'. ibid, para 9.

[96] While the requesting court started its first question with the refusal to enter the birth certificate of a child born abroad as a result of a gestational surrogacy in birth registrations, the ECtHR reflected first on the legal-parent relationship with the intended mother. ECtHR, Request no P16-2018-001 *Advisory opinion concerning the recognition in domestic law of a legal parent-child relationship between a child through a gestational surrogacy arrangement abroad and the intended mother*, paras 32–33. Note that the ECtHR held later that it reformulated the questions. ECtHR, Request no P16-2019-001 *Advisory opinion concerning the use of the 'blanket reference' or 'legislation by reference' technique in the definition of an offence and the standards of comparison between the criminal law in force at the time of the commission of the offence and the amended criminal law*, para 45.

[97] ECtHR, Request no P16-2021-002 *Advisory opinion on the difference in the treatment of landowners' associations set up before and after the creation of an approved municipal hunters' association*, para 57.

[98] CJEU, Case C-144/16 *Município de Palmela* ECLI:EU:C:2017:76, para 20.

[99] ECtHR, Request no P16-2022-001 *Advisory opinion concerning the adoption of an adult*, para 47.

[100] eg, 'the referring court asks, in essence/essentially.' CJEU, Case C-32/14 *ERSTE Bank Hungary v Attila Sugár* ECLI:EU:C:2015:637. For a discussion of these stylistic reformulations, see U Šadl and A Wallerman, '"The Referring Court Asks, in Essence": Is Reformulation of Preliminary Questions by the Court of Justice a Decision Writing Fixture or a Decision-making Approach?' (2019) 25 *European Law Journal* 416.

While separate *dissenting* opinions are allowed, this has not happened yet.[101] Former President O'Leary noted that the ECtHR 'has sought to speak with one voice'.[102] Similarly, (oral) hearings can be held, as mentioned in Article 3 of P16. Former President O'Leary explained that this option has never been considered necessary and will likely remain an exception.[103] This is because the ECtHR prefers 'a speedy response' and has to manage its limited resources (see Section 3.2.1).[104]

3.3. Admissibility

A panel of the Grand Chamber consists of five judges, including the President and the 'national' judge, who has the nationality of the state from which the request originates. The panel decides whether the request should be accepted, after which the Grand Chamber decides on the merits. The Grand Chamber can subsequently declare particular questions inadmissible.[105] Article 2(1) of P16 requires the panel to give reasons for any refusal to accept the request. Such reasoning enhances the constructive dialogue with the requesting court, especially considering the sensitivity of rejecting requests.[106]

P16 is based on four admissibility[107] criteria. These criteria are reminiscent of the conditions used by the CJEU in relation to the preliminary ruling procedure in Article 267 TFEU, as will be made clear in this section. Article 1(1) of P16 stipulates that the request should, first, be made by a highest court or tribunal that has been mandated on the basis of Article 10 of P16. Second, a request can be made in relation to a question of principle about the interpretation or the *application* of the ECHR (Article 1(1) P16). Third, a request can only be made in a case pending before the requesting national court (Article 1(1) P16). Fourth and relatedly, the requesting court shall give reasons for its request and provide the relevant legal and factual background of the pending case (Article 1(3) P16).

The first and fourth admissibility conditions have so far not played a role in the P16 case law of the ECtHR.[108] By contrast, the CJEU has not shied away from dismissing poor references as inadmissible or lacking jurisdiction. The CJEU has, in recent decades, examined whether the order for reference satisfies the requirements for the

[101] The Armenian judges Sarvarian and Harutyunyan wrote a concurring opinion in both Armenian requests.

[102] Fairgrieve (n 8) 8.

[103] Fairgrieve (n 8) 8; Draft report (see n 3 above) para 31.

[104] Eicke, 'Judicial Dialogue Through the Advisory Opinion' (2023) 3.

[105] ECtHR, Request no P16-2019-001 *Advisory opinion concerning the use of the 'blanket reference' or 'legislation by reference' technique in the definition of an offence and the standards of comparison between the criminal law in force at the time of the commission of the offence and the amended criminal law*, paras 45–47; Koskelo (n 61) 3.

[106] Explanatory Report (see n 14 above) para 15; Fairgrieve (n 8) 9; Eicke, 'Judicial Dialogue Through the Advisory Opinion' (2023) 3.

[107] It is interesting to note that the ECtHR only used the notion of admissibility in its most recent refusal. ECtHR, Request no P16-2024-001 *Decision of the Court on the request received from the High Court of Cassation and Justice of Romania for an advisory opinion.*

[108] The ECtHR, however, noted in relation to the Romanian request that the request court had not provided an explanation in the legal background as to why it referred to the ECtHR instead of the CJEU. ECtHR, Request no P16-2024-001 *Decision of the Court on the request received from the High Court of Cassation and Justice of Romania for an advisory opinion*, para 49.

content of the order for reference as laid down in Article 94 of the Rules of Procedure.[109] Similarly, the CJEU has declared requests for a preliminary ruling inadmissible when submitted by courts that are no longer independent.[110] It is unclear whether P16 leaves room for the ECtHR to reject a request by a designated highest court because of a lack of independence. The rest of this section focuses on the two admissibility conditions that have played a role in the P16 case law of the ECtHR.

3.3.1. Case Pending

A request can only be made in an actual 'case pending'. The ECtHR has confined advisory opinions to 'points that are directly connected to the proceedings pending at the domestic level' and not abstract questions of ECHR law.[111] ECtHR judge Koskelo highlighted the rationale of this admissibility requirement by noting that an interruption of domestic proceedings can only be justified when there is 'a genuine need' and an answer is 'necessary for the adjudication of the case'.[112] Hence, the ECtHR rejected the request from the Slovakian Supreme Court in 2020 in relation to effective criminal investigations, based on this condition.[113] The Slovakian court referred mainly to Articles 2 and 3 ECHR, while the pending case dealt with Article 6 ECHR. Noteworthy is that the ECtHR still provided the request court with some guidance by referring to relevant case law.[114]

In the Armenian request of 2019, the ECtHR only partly answered the questions posed after the panel of five judges had accepted the request. The Grand Chamber decided not to answer two of the four 'broad and very general' questions posed in an Armenian case about non-retroactivity, for the same reason.[115] The reason was the preliminary nature of the request. It had originated from main (criminal) proceedings before a first-instance court that used a domestic procedure of review of constitutionality. The consequence was that the main proceedings were 'pending at a very early stage and the relevant facts have not yet been the subject of any judicial determination'. This point was itself not an unsurmountable obstacle, but the Court mentioned that it 'frames

[109] Article 53(2) of the Rules of Procedure; eg, CJEU, Case C-318/00 *Bacardi-Martini and Cellier des Dauphins* ECLI:EU:C:2003:41; Case C-190/02 *Viacom Outdoor Srl v Giotto Immobilier SARL* ECLI:EU:C:2002:569; Recommendations to national courts and tribunals in relation to the initiation of preliminary ruling proceedings [2019] OJ C 380/1, paras 15–16.

[110] See, eg, in relation to a reference from the Polish Supreme Court (Chamber of Extraordinary Control and Public Affairs), CJEU, Case C-718/21 *LG v Krajowa Rada Sądownictwa* ECLI:EU:C:2023:1015.

[111] ECtHR, Request no P16-2018-001 *Advisory opinion concerning the recognition in domestic law of a legal parent-child relationship between a child through a gestational surrogacy arrangement abroad and the intended mother*, para 26; ECtHR, Request no P16-2019-001 *Advisory opinion concerning the use of the 'blanket reference' or 'legislation by reference' technique in the definition of an offence and the standards of comparison between the criminal law in force at the time of the commission of the offence and the amended criminal law*, para 55; Guidelines (see n 73 above) para 6.

[112] Koskelo (n 61) 2–3.

[113] ECtHR, Request no P16-2020-001, *Decision on a request for an advisory opinion under Protocol No 16 concerning the interpretation of Articles 2,3 and 6 of the Convention.*

[114] ibid, paras 20–22.

[115] ECtHR, Request no P16-2019-001 *Advisory opinion concerning the use of the 'blanket reference' or 'legislation by reference' technique in the definition of an offence and the standards of comparison between the criminal law in force at the time of the commission of the offence and the amended criminal law*, para 41.

the Court's approach'.[116] The request also illustrates the importance for the requesting court to provide sufficient reasons in line with the fourth admissibility condition.[117] It is difficult for the ECtHR to examine whether the questions are truly linked to the case pending if it lacks 'information as to the precise factual circumstances underlying the legal questions'.[118]

The ECtHR's approach in relation to 'case pending' reflects the requirement in Article 267 TFEU that a 'decision on the question is necessary to enable [the national court] to give judgment'. The CJEU has clarified that there must be a genuine dispute at the national level and that its answers must contribute to the resolution of that dispute.[119] This requires that the questions must be related to the facts and laws that are applicable in the dispute. The CJEU unequivocally held that its duty 'is not that of delivering advisory opinions on general or hypothetical questions but of assisting in the administration of justice in the Member States'.[120]

National courts tend to carefully consider the above factor when deciding whether to request. Empirical research regarding both Article 267 TFEU and P16 has shown that particularly when there is no obligation to refer, courts consider that a reference should have added value and be decisive for the pending case.[121] When the case can be decided on other grounds, there is no reason for a reference.[122] In only one instance did the Administrative Jurisdiction Division of the Dutch Council of State contemplate making a request, and it eventually refrained from doing so because the cases could be decided in such a way that the open ECHR question did not need to be answered.[123] The AG of the Dutch Supreme Court advised against a request for similar reasons in another case dealing with the applicability of the *Salduz* case law on legal assistance in relation to administrative sanctions. The AG identified and formulated 'interesting' and unanswered abstract questions of principle that have not been dealt with by the ECtHR.[124] The AG subsequently proposed not making a P16 request, because the questions could turn out to be hypothetical, since important questions of facts first needed to be assessed by a court of appeal.

3.3.2. *Question of Principle*

The admissibility condition of 'question of principle' concerning the interpretation and application of ECHR rights is the greatest hurdle for requesting courts. This point

[116] ibid, para 49.
[117] Guidelines (see n 73 above) para 6.3.
[118] *cf* Guidelines (see n 73 above) para 10: 'Requesting an advisory opinion before central factual or legal issues have been assessed at national level may influence the admissibility of the request.'
[119] CJEU, Case C-83/91 *Meilicke v ADV/ORGA FA Meyer AG* ECLI:EU:C:1992:332.
[120] CJEU, Case C-244/80 *Foglia v Novello* ECLI:EU:C:1981:302, para 18.
[121] Gerards and Loven (n 2); Krommendijk, *National Courts and Preliminary References to the Court of Justice* (2021).
[122] The ECHR issue should constitute the 'core aspect of the case'. Gerards and Loven (n 2) 7 and 44.
[123] The key question in the cases was whether the Deputy Minister of Security and Justice had obtained adequate 'individual and sufficient assurances', as required by ECtHR, App no 41738/10 *Paposhvili v Belgium* ECLI:CE:ECHR:2016:1213JUD004173810, para 191; Drafting Group on the Evaluation of the First Effects of Protocols No 15 and No 16 to the European Convention on Human Rights (DH-SYSC-PRO(2024)02REV) 68 and para 11.
[124] Dutch Supreme Court, 6 September 2024, ECLI:NL:HR:2024:1135 (conclusion AG Wattel), paras 7.15–17.

is illustrated by the fact that two of the three rejected requests were dismissed on this basis. Before considering the approach of the ECtHR, it should be noted that this condition is less restrictive than earlier proposals that aimed to limit P16 to 'cases revealing potential systemic or structural problems'.[125] The ECtHR for the first time explicitly dismissed the request of the Estonian Supreme Court for not involving a question of principle. The Court reiterated its previous pronouncement that 'questions of principle' warrant guidance from the Court given 'their nature, degree of novelty and/or complexity'.[126] It subsequently provided a rather extensive overview of its case law, in relation to the specific question of the respective case concerning *ne bis in idem*, and concluded that the question was the subject of 'well-established case-law of the Court'.[127] By refusing the request, the Grand Chamber clarified that it saw no role for itself in relation to relatively easy questions that merely require a reiteration of its 'well-established case law'.

Less than five months later, the ECtHR refused to accept the request of the Romanian High Court of Cassation in relation to the applicability of Article 6 ECHR to asset-audit proceedings. The ECtHR pointed to the well-developed case law that was also partly 'judiciously cited' by the Romanian court.[128] The ECtHR provided an additional reason for not accepting the request, namely there was still a pending contentious case in Strasbourg that it would decide shortly.[129] There is a third case in which this condition played a role as well, although the ECtHR did not explicitly specify the applicable admissibility condition. The Grand Chamber refrained from engaging with the first question in the Lithuanian case about the impeachment of an MP because the question related to the execution of (prior) Strasbourg judgments.[130] In doing so, the ECtHR implicitly suggested that the question lacked the required principled character and was more about application than interpretation (as discussed in Section 3.4).

In the last two refusals, the ECtHR relied on the Guidelines on the implementation of P16 that were updated in September 2023 and provide useful guidance for the highest national courts.[131] The Guidelines stipulate that a request is primarily warranted when it involves 'a novel point of Convention law', when 'the facts of the case do not seem to lend themselves to a straightforward application of the Court's case-law' or in a case that

[125] eg, proposal of Dutch and Norwegian experts as referred to in Reflection Paper (see n 14 above) para 28; *cf* Eicke, 'Judicial Dialogue Through the Advisory Opinion' (2023).

[126] ECtHR, Request no P16-2023-002 *Decision on a request for an advisory opinion under Protocol No 16 Concerning Article 4 of Protocol No 7 to the Convention*, para 20.

[127] The ECtHR gives an overview of case law in paras 22–29 and subsequently concludes that there no need for 'any further elaboration'. ECtHR, Request no P16-2023-002 *Decision on a request for an advisory opinion under Protocol No 16 Concerning Article 4 of Protocol No 7 to the Convention*, para 30.

[128] ECtHR, Request no P16-2024-001 *Decision of the Court on the request of the High Court of Cassation and Justice of Romania for an advisory opinion*, para 30.

[129] ECtHR, App no 17985/18 *Păcurar v Romania* (communicated). It noted that such contentious cases 'serve not only to decide those specific cases brought before it but, more generally, to elucidate, safeguard and develop the rules instituted in the Convention'. ECtHR, Request no P16-2024-001 *Decision of the Court on the request of the High Court of Cassation and Justice of Romania for an advisory opinion*, para 47.

[130] The request was accepted and the second question was answered. ECtHR, Request no P16-2020-002 *Advisory opinion concerning impeachment legislation* (8 April 2022).

[131] ECtHR, Request no P16-2023-002 *Decision on a request for an advisory opinion under Protocol No 16 concerning the interpretation of Article 4 of Protocol No 7 to the Convention*, paras 18 and 20; ECtHR, Request no P16-2024-001 *Decision of the Court on the request received from the High Court of Cassation and Justice of Romania for an advisory opinion*, paras 28–29.

'appears to be an inconsistency in the case-law'. The Guidelines mention the request by the Finnish Supreme Court as an example of best practice, because the Finnish court clearly set out the ambiguities and missing standpoints of the respective case law.[132] The approach of the ECtHR aligns with calls in the literature to limit P16 to 'truly novel issues'.[133]

The ECtHR's approach is not vastly different from the CJEU's. The ECtHR's reasoning in relation to questions of principle and the notion of 'well-established case-law' reflects the *acte éclairé* doctrine: 'where the reply to such a question may be clearly deduced from existing case-law'.[134] However, the CJEU uses this doctrine – and the *acte clair* – as an exception to the obligation of the highest courts to refer a preliminary question, not as an admissibility criterion. The CJEU does not declare straightforward *éclairé* references inadmissible, but instead issues a reasoned order decision that appears superficially not to differ much from its 'normal' judgments. Yet, it does so much faster, without the Opinion of an AG and in a three-judge formation.[135] The ECtHR's approach is not very different from the reasoned orders used by the CJEU: so far, the ECtHR's decisions have contained nine (Estonia) and 13 (Romania) substantive paragraphs with quite extensive considerations.[136] Accordingly, the ECtHR still provided the requesting courts with a useful overview even as it set clear limits about the invocation of P16. In doing so, it sidestepped the need to reprimand the courts for asking questions they should have been able to answer independently.

Just as with the 'case pending' requirement, national courts have contemplated the level of guidance in the existing case law of the ECtHR when making the decisions about whether to refer. The presence of sufficient guidance from the ECtHR is often mentioned as a reason not to use P16.[137] One interviewee noted that it is good that national courts interpret the ECHR, and in doing so, take upon a role as constitutional courts themselves.[138] Another interviewee pointed to the risk that the ECtHR may refuse to answer the request, which 'would be a real loss of face'.[139] Hence, courts are relatively likely to request when the case law of the ECtHR is non-existent, inconsistent or contradictory, or when a particular new (legal) question has not been addressed.[140] Interviewed Dutch judges also emphasised that requests should be limited to new interpretative questions, rather than dealing with the mere application of the ECHR.[141]

[132] ECtHR, Request no P16-2022-001 *Advisory opinion concerning adoption of an adult.*

[133] Dzehtsiarou, 'Keep Me in the Loop' (2023) 608; *cf* Concurring Opinion of Judge Sarvarian in ECtHR, Request no P16-2019-001 *Advisory opinion concerning the use of the 'blanket reference' or 'legislation by reference' technique in the definition of an offence and the standards of comparison between the criminal law in force at the time of the commission of the offence and the amended criminal law*, para 8.

[134] Article 99 of the Rules of Procedure of the CJEU; see also J Krommendijk, 'CILFIT in Strasbourg' (*VerfBlog*, 14 March 2024) verfassungsblog.de/cilfit-in-strasbourg/ accessed 28 May 2025.

[135] See, eg, Order of the CJEU, Case C-278/23 *MM v Ministero della Difesa* ECLI:EU:C:2024:111.

[136] See, eg, ECtHR, Request no P16-2024-001 *Decision of the Court on the request received from the High Court of Cassation and Justice of Romania for an advisory opinion*, paras 31–39 and 41–44.

[137] See, eg, Dutch Supreme Court 26 March 2021, ECLI:NL:HR:2021:442; Dutch Supreme Court 25 September 2020, ECLI:NL:HR:2020:1526; Glas and Krommendijk, 'A Strasbourg Story of Swords and Shields' (2022).

[138] Interview 14; *cf* Gerards and Loven (n 2) 45 and 54.

[139] Interview 5.

[140] Gerards and Loven (n 2) 7 and 44.

[141] Interview 5 and 14.

It remains to be seen whether the ECtHR will also consider other possible dimensions related to the notion of question of principle. Two possibilities emerge here. The first is a requirement of 'general importance', which requires a request to have relevance beyond the specific case. Such a reading would reflect the criteria for referral to the Grand Chamber in Article 43(2), requiring a 'serious question affecting the interpretation or application of the Convention …, or a serious issue of general importance'.[142] ECtHR judge Koskelo, for example, highlighted the usefulness of P16 in relation to issues of 'precedential significance' when the question is relevant for a larger number of cases.[143] Limiting the ECtHR guidance to issues of wide importance aligns with the wish of the Group of Wise Persons to enhance the 'constitutional role' of the ECtHR.[144] Some national judges seem particularly eager to refer questions that have an impact beyond the pending case.[145] French Court of Cassation judge Soulard, for example, emphasised the importance of the first French request on surrogacy beyond France and its likely impact on all states.[146]

Second, the ECtHR might also decide to refuse to answer questions where the answer 'admits of no reasonable doubt'.[147] This reflects the *acte clair* doctrine accepted by the CJEU in *CILFIT*. This doctrine is more subjective in nature than the *acte éclairé*, and it has showed up in the P16 case law. The ECtHR noted that, in addition to the request's inadmissibility for not satisfying the 'case pending' requirement, the Slovakian court did not need guidance as it had already formulated 'indications as to the answer' in its request.[148] This case illustrates a dilemma for requesting courts. If they include their 'own views on the questions', as the Guidelines recommend, they run the risk of being told they do not need further guidance.[149]

3.4. Division between the ECtHR and National Courts: Between Application and Interpretation

In its refusals, the ECtHR has consistently cited a standard statement in justifying its decision not to accept the request. It is phrased as follows:

> The aim of the procedure provided for by Protocol No 16 is not to transfer the dispute to the Court, which has no jurisdiction either to assess the facts of a case or to evaluate the merits of

[142] Fairgrieve (n 8) 7. In its reflection paper, the ECtHR provides five examples of contentious cases that could have been the subject of a request for an advisory opinion. Three of the five concern Grand Chamber judgments. Reflection Paper (see n 14 above) paras 30–31; Dicosola, Fasone and Spigno, 'The Prospective Role of Constitutional Courts' (2015) 1407; Giannopoulos, 'Considerations on Protocol No 16' (2015) 339–40; Paprocka and Ziółkowski, 'Advisory opinions under Protocol No 16 (2015) 289.

[143] Koskelo (see n 61 above) 2.

[144] Report of the Group of Wise Persons to the Committee of Ministers (979bis meeting, CM(2006)203), para 81; Fairgrieve (n 8) 9.

[145] Interview 5 and 14; *cf* the 'radiance effect' on a larger number of cases. Gerards and Loven (n 2) 7, 44 and 54.

[146] Soulard, 'Le dialogue judiciaire' (2023) 4.

[147] Article 99 of the Rules of Procedure of the CJEU [2012] OJ L 265/1.

[148] ECtHR, Request no P16-2020-001 *Decision on a request for an advisory opinion under Protocol No 16 concerning the interpretation of Articles 2, 3 and 6 of the Convention*, paras 22–24.

[149] Guidelines (see n 73 above) para 12(e).

the parties' views on the interpretation of domestic law in the light of Convention law, or to rule on the outcome of the proceedings.[150]

The ECtHR noted in a similar fashion that

> [I]t is not for the Court to take a stance on whether the national court is in a position to apply the Convention in a pending case taking account of rules of a constitutional nature, by which all domestic courts are obliged to abide.[151]

Here, the ECtHR alludes to a division of tasks between itself and the national courts. The ECtHR clarifies that its task is focused on delivering an interpretation *in abstracto*, while the application *in concreto* is left to the requesting court. This clear division on paper, however, masks a tension inherent in the design of P16, especially between the second and third admissibility conditions, notably the principled nature and the case pending requirements. P16 requires courts not to raise a broad and general question in the abstract but instead pose concrete questions that would enable the court to dispose of the case.[152] P16 even enables courts to request principled questions about the *application* of the ECHR in Article 1(1) P16. The 'case pending' admissibility condition also forces the ECtHR to stay within the confines of the request and avoids drawing broader conclusions.[153] At the same time, the principled nature invites national courts to move beyond highly specific situations and instead opt for questions of 'general importance' (Section 3.3). Similarly, the involvement of the Grand Chamber signals that the ECtHR's answer goes beyond the individual case.[154] President O'Leary aptly observed that the challenge is for the ECtHR 'to provide quality guidance without on the one hand resolving the domestic dispute, while on the other providing opinions which are not excessively vague or abstract.'[155]

This tension reflects a discussion in EU law about the interpretation versus application of EU law in the context of the preliminary ruling.[156] The CJEU has employed a division of tasks similar to the ECtHR. The CJEU consistently emphasises that there

[150] ECtHR, Request no P16-2023-002 *Decision on a request for an advisory opinion under Protocol No 16 concerning the interpretation of Article 4 of Protocol No 7 to the Convention*, para 19; ECtHR, no P16-2024-001, *Decision of the Court on the request received from the High Court of Cassation and Justice of Romania for an advisory opinion*, para 46; ECtHR, Request no P16-2020-001 *Decision on a request for an advisory opinion under Protocol No 16 concerning the interpretation of Articles 2, 3 and 6 of the Convention*, para 18.

[151] ECtHR, Request no P16-2020-002 *Advisory opinion concerning impeachment legislation*, para 93.

[152] '[T]he advisory-opinion procedure is not intended to allow for an abstract review of legislation …; nor can the Court deal with questions of Convention law that are abstract and general in nature'. Explanatory Report (see n 14 above) para 10; ECtHR, Request no P16-2020-001 *Decision on a request for an advisory opinion under Protocol No 16 concerning the interpretation of Articles 2, 3 and 6 of the Convention*, para 18; Guidelines (see n 74 above) para 6.

[153] The ECtHR, for example, did not reflect on different kinds of surrogacy arrangements, but instead focused on the specific type of surrogacy arrangement at issue in France's first request. ECtHR, Request no P16-2018-001 *Advisory opinion concerning the recognition in domestic law of a legal parent-child relationship between a child through a gestational surrogacy arrangement abroad and the intended mother*, paras 25–30; O'Leary, 'Judicial Dialogue Through the Advisory Opinion' (2023) 3.

[154] *cf* Soulard, 'Le dialogue judiciaire' (2023) 7.

[155] Fairgrieve (n 8) 10.

[156] G Davies, 'Activism Relocated. The Self-Restraint of the European Court of Justice in its National Context' (2012) 19 *Journal of European Public Policy* 76, 78; G Davies, 'Abstractness and Concreteness in the Preliminary Reference Procedure: Implications for the Division of Powers and Effective Market Regulation' in NN Shuibne (ed), *Regulating the Internal Market* (Cheltenham, Edward Elgar Publishing, 2006).

is 'a clear separation of functions' and that it can only interpret EU law and not take cognisance of or assess the facts of a case.[157] The latter remains the 'exclusive jurisdiction' of national courts.[158] Despite this clear division, the CJEU has at times stepped into the domain of the national judges by not limiting itself to interpreting EU law but also applying the interpretation to the national legal or factual context in case-specific judgments.[159] Several AGs have criticised the CJEU for its willingness to go along with such wishes for 'factual jurisprudence' and have called for 'self-restraint' by national courts and the CJEU.[160] The CJEU partly responded to these criticisms by limiting the obligation to submit a request for a preliminary reference in *Consorzio Italian Management* to questions about the correct interpretation of EU law.[161] In that way, the CJEU affirmed its final authority to define the correct *interpretation* of EU law but not necessarily the correct domestic *application*.[162]

The tendency towards 'factual jurisprudence' is perhaps not surprising from the perspective of national courts, which prefer case-specific answers. They do not request merely in the hope of receiving a response that indicates they 'should figure out the Convention issues for themselves'.[163] Empirical research on the EU preliminary ruling procedure based on interviews with judges has shown that national courts prefer so-called 'outcome judgments' that give a highly specific answer, leaving the national court no margin for manoeuvre.[164] Interviews conducted by Gerards and Loven regarding the motives for courts to make a P16 request have similarly shown that courts appreciate highly specific guidance.[165] Interviewed Dutch judges likewise reflected on the utility of the possible answer from the ECtHR. One judge noted that their court had considered a request in which the ECtHR was confronted with conflicting lines of case law. The judge doubted whether the ECtHR would make a choice and hence also doubted whether the request would be worth the effort, considering the length.[166] Other judges likewise noted that an answer along the lines of 'these are the broad outlines, figure it out for yourself' is not particularly useful.[167] These empirical insights are relevant to the ten requests made to date. Most are quite case-specific and are primarily

[157] CJEU, Case C-409/06 *Winner Wetten GmbH v Bürgemeisterin Bergheim* ECLI:EU:C:2010:503, para 49; CJEU, Case C-6/64 *Costa v ENEL* ECLI:EU:C:1964:66.

[158] CJEU, Case C-13/68 *SpA Salgoil v Italian Ministry of Foreign Trade* ECLI:EU:C:1968:54; CJEU, Joined Cases C-175/98 and C-177/98 *Lirussi v Bizzaro* ECLI:EU:C:1999:486, para 38.

[159] Krommendijk, 'Between Interpretation and Application' (2023).

[160] M Bobek, 'National Courts and the Enforcement of EU Law. Institutional Report' in MR Botman and J Langer (eds), *The XXIX FIDE Congress in The Hague, 2020 Congress Publications*, Vol 1 (The Hague, Eleven International Publishing, 2020); CJEU, Case C-338/95 *Wiener SI GmbH v Hauptzollamt Emmerich* ECLI:EU:C:1997:552, Opinion of AG Jacobs.

[161] CJEU, Case C-561/19 *Consorzio Italian Management and Catania Multiservizi SpA v Rete Ferroviaria Italiana SpA* ECLI:EU:C:2021:799.

[162] This change also aligns with the wording of Article 267 TFEU stipulating that references can be made in relation to the interpretation of the Treaties and the validity and interpretation of secondary EU law. It is interesting that Article 1(1) P16 explicitly refers to questions about the application of ECHR.

[163] T Moonen and L Lavrysen, 'Abstract but Concrete, or Concrete but Abstract? A Guide to the Nature of Advisory Opinions under Protocol No 16 to the ECHR' (2021) 21 *Human Rights Law Review* 752.

[164] Krommendijk, *National Courts and Preliminary References to the Court of Justice* (2021) 128.

[165] Gerards and Loven (n 2).

[166] Interview 13.

[167] Interview 17 and 18. Interviewee 18 noted that courts tend to interpret the ECHR themselves when they have more or less an idea of the possible answer of the ECtHR.

questions of *application* of the ECHR and the well-established case law of the ECtHR (Section 3.1). In other words, most of the P16 requests have involved relatively easy – arguably *clair* – questions.

Despite this natural tendency towards case-specificity, the ECtHR has so far seemed reluctant to fall into the same 'trap' as Luxembourg.[168] It has resisted the temptation to overly pander to national courts, using the rather elegant approach of repeatedly emphasising the division of tasks and clarifying that it does not have the jurisdiction to assess the facts of a case or the merits of the positions of parties.[169] The ECtHR, for example, pointed to the principle of subsidiarity and the national courts' primary responsibility for giving full effect to the ECHR in its recent refusal following the Romanian request. Hence, the ECtHR noted that the requesting court can 'settle the dispute appropriately' in the light of 'sufficient relevant material in its case-law'.[170] Indeed, the success of the ECtHR in avoiding being overly case-specific is actually evidenced by recurring criticism in the literature that the court is too abstract.[171] ECtHR judge Koskelo mentioned the 'very high' level of abstraction in the opinion in the French surrogacy case and noted that it 'did not contain more than a nutshell summary of the well-established general principles'.[172] A French judge involved also noted that the opinion lacked a concrete analysis of the situation at hand and hence did not answer all the questions of the French court.[173] The alleged difference between the ECtHR and CJEU can perhaps be attributed to the subsidiary nature of the Convention system as well as the generally wide margin of appreciation afforded to national courts.[174] By contrast, the CJEU might be inclined to restrict the room for manoeuvre of national courts, considering the uniformity and effectiveness of EU law (Section 2.1).

Nonetheless, the ECtHR has not shied away from providing tentative case-specific reflections. In its response to the Finnish request on adoption, the ECtHR held that 'it appears that the right claimed by the biological mother does not exist, even on arguable grounds, in domestic law. … It is, however, for the requesting court to determine whether … that is the case.'[175] The seemingly useful ECtHR answers can be partly attributed to the discursive and elaborate request by the Finnish court. Hence, it seems that a well-reasoned request that gives sufficient regard to the factual and legislative

[168] *cf* Koskelo (n 61) 4: 'The opinion should remain as strictly focused on the questions raised as possible.' *cf* Eicke noted that the ECtHR 'seeks to limit itself to giving the requesting court guidance'. Eicke, 'Judicial dialogue through the advisory opinion' (2023) 3.

[169] ECtHR, Request no P16-2024-001 *Decision of the Court on the request received from the High Court of Cassation and Justice of Romania for an advisory opinion*, para 40.

[170] It also emphasised that 'it is for the requesting court to determine, on the basis of that existing case-law and with reference to the relevant domestic law and the facts of the case pending before it, whether the proceedings in issue fall under the "civil" or "criminal" limb of Article 6 of the Convention'. ibid, para 45.

[171] Moonen and Lavrysen, 'Abstract but Concrete' (2021) 31. *cf* in relation to the abstract character of ECtHR, Request no P16-2019-001 *Advisory opinion concerning the use of the 'blanket reference' or 'legislation by reference' technique in the definition of an offence and the standards of comparison between the criminal law in force at the time of the commission of the offence and the amended criminal law* and ECtHR, Request no P16-2021-002 *Advisory opinion on the difference in the treatment of landowners' associations set up before and after the creation of an approved municipal hunters' association*; Gerards and Loven (n 2) 25.

[172] Koskelo (n 61) 4.

[173] Soulard, 'Le dialogue judiciaire' (2023) 6.

[174] *cf* Fairgrieve (n 8) 9.

[175] ECtHR, Request no P16-2022-001 *Advisory opinion concerning the adoption of an adult*, para 66; cf Draft report (see n 3 above) para 52.

context can enable – or even invite – the ECtHR to provide *in concreto* reflections. The requesting courts can thus steer the ECtHR towards a case-tailored answer by formulating their questions in a particular way or carefully describing the national legal and factual context.[176] By contrast, the ECtHR stays on an abstract level when the request does not include such information. An example of the latter is the opinion of the ECtHR in response to a Belgian request about the possibilities for refusing to authorise an individual to work as a security guard if the individual belongs to a religious movement that allegedly represents a threat to the state. The answer of the ECtHR remained quite abstract, giving a long list of reflections on the justification of the measure in light of the principles of necessity and proportionality.[177] This response can partly be attributed to the abstract formulation of the question, as well as the fact that the ECtHR 'has not been apprised of the material in the classified file compiled by the Belgian State Service'.[178]

4. Conclusion

How should one reflect on the six years of practice in relation to P16? As mentioned in the introduction, this depends on one's prior expectations and preferences regarding the seemingly conflicting objectives of P16 – namely the desire for both enhanced dialogue and a reduction in the workload of the ECtHR. If these two objectives are considered as essential parameters, the six years' practice leads to a rather bleak conclusion. Gerards and Loven rightly concluded that P16 has certainly not lived up to the efficiency expectation regarding a reduced workload.[179]

It is tempting to simply agree with Gerards and Loven that it is too soon to tell whether P16 contributes to better implementation of the ECHR and an enhanced dialogue.[180] Time will indeed tell. Yet, some reflections can be provided, also with a view of countering all too pessimistic portrayals of P16 as purposeless. One Dutch interviewee, for example, held that P16 has not been a success: 'you can hardly do anything with it'.[181] With respect to the dialogical function it is worthwhile to reflect on the extent to which the current functioning of P16 reflects a cooperative, heterarchical or horizontal logic that requires both national courts and the ECtHR to act in good faith in the spirit of dialogue and cooperation.[182] Such an 'it takes two to tango'[183] logic as a

[176] *cf* Krommendijk in relation to national courts and the CJEU. Krommendijk, 'Between Interpretation and Application' (2023).

[177] For a relatively positive review of this opinion, see J Sommardale, 'Maintaining Resilience in Human Rights Interpretation: The ECtHR's Approach to National Security in the Religious Movement Advisory Opinion' (*VerfBlog*, 31 October 2024) https://verfassungsblog.de/maintaining-resilience-in-human-rights-interpretation/ accessed 28 May 2025.

[178] ECtHR, Request no P16-2023-001 *Advisory opinion as to whether an individual may be denied authorization to work as a security guard or officer on account of being close to or belonging to a religious movement.*

[179] Gerards and Loven (n 2) 54; *cf* Draft report (see n 3 above) 81.

[180] Gerards and Loven (n 2) 54.

[181] Interview 4.

[182] See in relation to the CJEU J Hoevenaars and J Krommendijk, 'Black Box in Luxembourg: The Bewildering Experience of National Court Judges and Lawyers in the Context of the Preliminary Ruling Procedure' (2021) 46 *European Law Review* 61.

[183] Krommendijk, *National Courts and Preliminary References to the Court of Justice* (2021).

precondition was also relied on by ECtHR judge Koskelo: 'The key parameters of a meaningful and productive judicial dialogue through the advisory process lie both in the quality of the questions and the quality of the answers. Both are closely interlinked.'[184] From this perspective, one could criticise some of the requests by national courts. National courts have primarily used P16 to raise easy *clair* questions with a view of obtaining external and authoritative support in politically sensitive matters with conflicting findings or positions at the national level. Various requests also related to earlier ECtHR judgments determining violations of the ECHR. In addition, national courts largely refrained from including their 'own views on the questions'. The latter is especially lamentable from a dialogical perspective. It is to be hoped that future P16 requests are comparable to the well-reasoned request of the Finnish Supreme Court that is also mentioned as an example of best practice in the ECtHR Guidelines. The Finnish court clearly set out the ambiguities and missing points in the ECtHR case law.

One could, at the same time, be slightly more positive about the ECtHR. The ECtHR has by and large kept a close eye on its subsidiary role and the national courts' primary responsibility, as also reflected in the division of tasks in the context of P16. The ECtHR has so far resisted the temptation to provide national courts with case-specific and highly factual answers and opted for rather abstract answers instead. The ECtHR also used the requests to date to accentuate the boundaries of P16 by providing more clarity as to the admissibility criteria, most notably the condition of 'question of principle' concerning the interpretation and application of ECHR rights. This condition is the greatest hurdle for requesting courts and restricts P16 to novel issues instead of a reiteration of 'well-established case-law of the Court'. The ECtHR has thus threaded a fine line between being too strict and rude on the one hand versus providing courts with guidance relatively quickly on the other hand. The ECtHR has avoided showing outright disapproval when national courts have submitted legally 'easy' questions that they could have answered themselves. It has provided the requesting courts with useful abstract guidance anyway.[185] However, the ECtHR has set clear limits in its two most recent inadmissibility decisions and stated that it saw no role for itself in reiterating its well-established case law. These two reasoned refusals, as well as the updated Guidelines, provide much-needed clarity for national courts regarding how they should navigate P16. These clear admissibility criteria hopefully lead to discursive P16 requests on novel points of ECHR law and provisional answers from the requesting court. Such requests truly invite the ECtHR to enter into a dialogue.

[184] Koskelo (n 61) 2 and 4; *cf* Dzehtsiarou, 'Keep Me in the Loop' (2023) 609.

[185] The CDDH likewise concluded: 'The Court has progressively developed its methodological approach to delivering opinions on the questions raised by the requesting courts. In its earlier advisory opinions, the Court provided summaries of principles emerging from its case law that it considered as relevant to resolving the question submitted by the requesting court.' The CCDH also noted that the requesting courts have been largely positive about the usefulness of the ECtHR opinions on the basis of questionnaires. Draft report (see n 3 above) paras 57 and 67–69.

8

Infringement Actions for the Protection of Fundamental Rights

LUCA PRETE[1]

1. Introduction

The case law of the Court of Justice of the European Union (CJEU) shows that, in the last two decades, it has increasingly been asked to adjudicate on alleged threats to fundamental rights, including in the context of infringement proceedings. The progressive emergence of fundamental rights issues within those proceedings constitutes a relative novelty in the EU litigation landscape. Indeed, despite those rights having being declared to be part of the general principle of (then) Community law in the early 1970s, and the Commission having made frequent use of infringement proceedings as from the late 1970s, the two very rarely crossed paths before the Treaty of Lisbon entered into force.

At the outset, it may be worth recalling that infringement proceedings constitute a form of action set out in Articles 258 to 260 of the Treaty on the Functioning of the European Union (TFEU), which permits the Court of Justice (the Court) to rule on whether a Member State has, because of its conduct, failed to fulfil an obligation under the EU Treaties. The purpose of such proceedings is to determine whether the conduct complained of infringes EU law so that the Member State in question is required to terminate that conduct and remove the effects flowing therefrom.[2] A Court decision that finds, under Articles 258 and 259 TFEU, a Member State to be in breach of EU law has, however, a purely declaratory nature. Indeed, the Court does not have the power to annul, declare void or inapplicable a national measure. Nor can the Court order the Member State in question to take some specific action to remedy the infringement. It is for that Member State to take all the necessary measures to comply with an adverse ruling, as provided for in Article 260(1) TFEU.[3] Nevertheless, Article 260(2) and (3) enable the Court to

[1] Référendaire at the Court of Justice of the European Union. Views expressed in this article are the author's own and made in a purely personal capacity. The author would like to thank the editors of the present volume for insightful comments. This article reflects the state of the law on 31 December 2024.

[2] See, eg, CJEU, Case C-247/98 *Greece v Commission* ECLI:EU:C:2001:4, para 13; and CJEU, Case C-364/10 *Hungary v Slovakia* ECLI:EU:C:2012:630, para 68.

[3] See, inter alia, CJEU, Case C-6/60-IMM *Humblet v Belgian State* ECLI:EU:C:1960:48, paras 568–69; and CJEU, Case C-48/71 *Commission v Italy* ECLI:EU:C:1972:65, para 7.

impose financial penalties (a one-off lump sum and/or recurring penalty payments) in two circumstances. First, penalties may be imposed when the Court finds, following a new set of proceedings commenced by the Commission, that a Member State has not complied with a previous judgment handed down under Article 258 or 259 TFEU. Second, the Court may also impose penalties in the context of the first proceedings started under Article 258 TFEU, where the breach complained of consists in a failure 'to notify measures transposing a directive adopted under a legislative procedure'.

Infringement proceedings are a form of judicial procedure specific to the EU legal order. As the Court stated in one of its first cases, 'it is a procedure far exceeding the rules heretofore recognized in classical international law to ensure that obligations of States are fulfilled'.[4] The jurisdiction of the Court in cases of EU law infringements by Member States is compulsory and constitutes a corollary to membership in the European Union. In addition, the task of investigating and 'prosecuting' infringements is not left only to other Member States, for example those whose interests may be harmed by the alleged infringements. Although a Member State-to-Member State procedure is possible (Article 259 TFEU), the main responsibility to act against Treaty breaches lies with an independent institution that acts as 'Guardian of the Treaties':[5] the European Commission (Articles 258 and 260 TFEU). Indeed, in the context of infringement proceedings, the Commission does not act to protect its own rights but in the general interest of the Union, in accordance with Article 17(1) TFEU.[6] In fact, the Commission does not need to show that it has a specific interest in bringing proceedings, or that the contested national measure has an adverse effect on the Union, other Member States, or citizens and businesses. Nor is it required to prove some form of fault or guilt on the part of the authorities responsible for the alleged breaches. The specific aim pursued by the national measure presumed to be in breach of EU law is also immaterial. Infringement proceedings are 'objective' in nature: the Court only rules on whether or not the conduct complained of is consistent with EU law.[7]

Infringement proceedings are composed of two successive stages: a first administrative stage before the Commission, and a judicial stage before the Court. Those two formal stages of the procedure are, however, often preceded by an informal stage (typically, via the EU Pilot mechanism), in which the Commission services may get in contact with the authorities of the Member State concerned (and, if necessary, the complainant), in order to gather more information and, where appropriate, check whether the problem may be easily resolved by those authorities. The administrative stage of the procedure pursues a three-fold objective: to allow the Member State to put an end to any infringement, enable it to exercise its rights of the defence, and define the subject matter of the dispute with a view to bringing an action before the Court. In this stage, the Commission is first to send the Member State concerned a 'letter of formal notice', in which it draws the national authorities' attention to some measure which appears to

[4] CJEU, Case C-25/59 *Netherlands v High Authority* ECLI:EU:C:1960:34.

[5] See, among many, CJEU, Case C-471/98 *Commission v Belgium* ECLI:EU:C:2002:628, para 39.

[6] See, eg, CJEU, Case C-431/92 *Commission v Germany* ECLI:EU:C:1995:260, para 21.

[7] See, inter alia, CJEU, Case C-404/99 *Commission v France* ECLI:EU:C:2001:192, para 49; CJEU, Case C-226/09 *Commission v Ireland* ECLI:EU:C:2010:697, para 64; and CJEU, Case C-61/05 *Commission v Portugal* ECLI:EU:C:2006:467, para 32.

infringe EU law and asks those authorities to submit their observations within a given time limit. In the event that there is no response to that letter, or when the reply is found unpersuasive, the Commission may send the Member State concerned a 'reasoned opinion'. In the reasoned opinion the Commission is to specify precisely the grounds of complaint which it has already raised more generally in the letter of formal notice, and the allegations made against the Member State concerned, having considered any observations submitted by that Member State. The reasoned opinion also sets a date for the Member State to submit any further information and to take all necessary measures to comply. Should the Commission remain unconvinced by the Member State's observations, it may start judicial proceedings by submitting an application before the Court.[8] In that regard, it should be pointed out that, in the light of the wording of the Treaty provisions, the Commission enjoys broad discretion in deciding whether to bring proceedings under Articles 258 and 260 TFEU, when to bring them, and in respect of which Member States. The Court will normally not question the manner in which that discretion is exercised.[9]

The scope of infringement proceedings, in terms of both the forms of conduct which may be challenged and the rules whose breach may be raised, is very broad. On the one hand, those proceedings may concern *any* Member State's conduct, by means of a positive act or by omission, which is in breach of EU law. The alleged breaches may stem, in particular, from measures taken by the legislative, administrative and judicial organs of the State, including at regional and local level, and regardless of the degree of independence or autonomy those organs might enjoy from the central government.[10] Furthermore, Member States may be held liable for breaches which are the result of actions taken by entities established and/or operating under private law in certain circumstances (inter alia, because of public ownership or control, exercise of public powers or functions).[11] On the other hand, *any* breach of an EU rule on the part of a national authority can be the object of such proceedings. The jurisdiction of the Court in infringement proceedings is not limited or excluded, except in a few specific areas.[12] Indeed, although Articles 258 and 259 TFEU refer to Member States' 'obligation[s] under the Treaties', it is clear that these obligations are not only those which appear in the founding Treaties or in other acts of primary law. Those obligations may, in fact,

[8] Generally on the procedure, with references to the case law, see L Prete, *Infringement Proceedings in EU Law*, (The Hague, Kluwer Law International, 2017); T Materne, *La procédure en manquement d'Etat – Guide Pratique* 2nd edn (Brussels, Larcier, 2023); and K Lenaerts, K Gutman, J Nowak, *EU Procedural Law* 2nd edn (Oxford, Oxford University Press, 2023) ch 5.

[9] See, inter alia, CJEU, Case C-472/98 *Commission v Luxembourg* ECLI:EU:C:2002:629, paras 34–38; CJEU, Case C-255/05 *Commission v Italy* ECLI:EU:C:2007:406, para 38; and CJEU, Case C-323/13 *Commission v Italy* ECLI:EU:C:2014:2290, para 43. For critical views, see, C Hillion, 'The EU External Action as Mandate to Uphold the Rule of Law Outside and Inside the Union' (2023) *Columbia* 29 *Journal of European Law* 228, 277–80; and C Burelli, *La discrezionalità della Commissione europea nelle procedure di infrazione* (Turin, Giappichelli, 2024).

[10] See, eg, CJEU, Case 77/69 *Commission v Belgium* ECLI:EU:C:1970:34, para 15; CJEU, Case C-129/00 *Commission v Italy* ECLI:EU:C:2003:656, para 29; and CJEU, Case C-516/22 *Commission v United Kingdom* ECLI:EU:C:2024:231, para 54.

[11] See, eg, judgments in CJEU, Case 249/81 *Commission v Ireland* ECLI:EU:C:1982:402; and CJEU, Case C-173/94 *Commission v Belgium* ECLI:EU:C:1996:264.

[12] The main being, under Articles 24(1) TEU and 275 TFEU, the common foreign and security policy (CFSP). But see below Section 7 of this chapter.

also follow from general principles of EU law, or result from secondary legislation and, more generally, from any other act adopted by the Union, whatever its name and form, provided that it produces binding legal effects.

Consistently with these principles, and in the light of the wording of Article 6(1) and (3) of the Treaty on European Union (TEU), infringement proceedings may also be brought – by the Commission or any Member State – against alleged violations of *EU fundamental rights* committed by national authorities. The purpose of the present contribution is to give an overview of the proceedings started under Articles 258–60 TFEU on that matter, and to critically assess the contribution given by such proceedings to the protection of fundamental rights in the European Union. In essence, it will be shown that, since 2010, the Commission has started a number of cases concerned with presumed breaches of EU fundamental rights on the part of national authorities, including in some politically sensitive and/or legally complex cases. Most of those actions were eventually successful. That notwithstanding, the number of infringement cases raising fundamental rights issues brought before the Court has, to date, remained relatively limited. Whether it could or should be any different is outside the scope of the present chapter, being not a legal question but a policy one. That being said, I shall conclude by explaining why, in my view, there may be good grounds to take the view that, if the Commission is truly determined to strengthen the application of the Charter, including vis-à-vis the Member States when they implement EU law, it may need to consider stepping up its actions under Article 258–60 TFEU in that field.

2. The Pre-Charter Period

It is well known that the Court of Justice did not give any formal status to fundamental rights within the then EEC legal order until the late 1960s/early 1970s. It was at that moment that, in a number of judgments delivered in the framework of the preliminary rulings procedure, the Court stated that respect for fundamental rights formed an integral part of the general principles of law which the Court of Justice had to protect. The protection of such rights was inspired – the Court explained – by the constitutional traditions common to the Member States and the guidelines supplied by international treaties on which the Member States had collaborated or of which they were signatories.[13] As the Court made clear, those principles were also binding upon, and thus enforceable vis-à-vis, the Member States, when they acted within the scope of EU law, in particular when implementing EU law and when availing themselves of derogations therefrom.[14]

[13] See, especially, CJEU, Case 29/69 *Stauder v City of Ulm – Sozialamt* ECLI:EU:C:1969:57, para 7; CJEU, Case 11/70 *Internationale Handelsgesellschaft* ECLI:EU:C:1970:114, paras 3–4; and CJEU, Case 4/73 *Nold, Kohlen- und Baustoffgroßhandlung v Commission* ECLI:EU:C:1974:51, para 13.

[14] See, in particular, CJEU, Case 5/88, *Wachauf* ECLI:EU:C:1989:321, paras 17–19; CJEU, Case C-260/89 *ERT* ECLI:EU:C:1991:254, paras 42–45; and CJEU, Case C-368/95 *Familiapress* ECLI:EU:C:1997:325, para 24.

Despite those important statements of principle, fundamental rights played virtually no role in the context of infringement proceedings for a significant period of time. That is hardly surprising as far as the 1970s are concerned: until the Commission presided by Roy Jenkins took office in 1977, the Commission made rather prudent use of its enforcement powers under then Article 169 EEC, bringing only few proceedings which, moreover, turned mostly on technical issues.[15] Nevertheless, even after a change of policy in this field, and despite the relatively high number of cases initiated in the following years, there is no trace of the Commission raising problems concerning Member States' compliance with fundamental rights. For example, no reference to such rights can be found in the Court's case law before a judgment of 1983. Even in that case, however, it was the defendant Member State (Germany) that invoked a possible infringement of the fundamental right to property as a defence, in order to dispute the interpretation of the provisions allegedly breached, as suggested by the Commission. The Court gave short shrift to the argument.[16]

The situation did not significantly change in the following two decades, even when the Treaties were reformed and the first references to fundamental rights were introduced in some of their provisions. The case law shows that most of the arguments based on possible infringements of fundamental rights were not put forward by the Commission but – just as in the case mentioned above – by the Member States in default, in order to justify the contested national measures.[17] In fact, before the entry into force of the Treaty of Lisbon, the Commission had never brought an infringement action before the Court based mainly, let alone solely, on an alleged breach of a fundamental right. In the rare cases in which the Commission did raise such an issue, it generally appeared as a mere add-on to the main claims which were, in essence, of a sectorial nature. In those proceedings, the Commission usually contested breaches of provisions of EU primary or secondary law, read 'in conjunction with'/'in combination with'/'in the light of' some fundamental right(s). Tellingly, the combined reading of the provisions was not always reflected in the form of order sought by the Commission since, in the majority of the cases, the fundamental right aspect of the dispute was only referred to in the arguments put forward in support of the claims.[18] In order to flesh out the fundamental rights in question, the Commission usually relied on the relevant provisions of the European Convention on Human Rights

[15] See, especially, HAH Audretsch, *Supervision in European Community Law* 2nd edn (Amsterdam, North-Holland, 1986).

[16] CJEU, Case 113/82 *Commission v Germany* ECLI:EU:C:1983:99, paras 24–25.

[17] See, inter alia, CJEU, Case 249/86 *Commission v Germany* ECLI:EU:C:1989:204, para 21; CJEU, Case C-52/00 *Commission v France* ECLI:EU:C:2002:252, para 27; and CJEU, Case C-154/00 *Commission v Greece* ECLI:EU:C:2002:2540, para 27. For a more recent case, see CJEU, Case C-552/15 *Commission v Ireland* ECLI:EU:C:2017:698, para 23.

[18] See, inter alia, CJEU, Case 249/86 *Commission v Germany* ECLI:EU:C:1989:204, para 10; CJEU, Case C-424/99 *Commission v Austria* ECLI:EU:C:2001:642, paras 39–47; CJEU, Case C-441/02 *Commission v Germany* ECLI:EU:C:2006:253, paras 1 and 103–06; and CJEU, Case C-518/07 *Commission v Germany* ECLI:EU:C:2010:125, paras 22–24 and 33. See also CJEU, Case C-58/02 *Commission v Spain* Opinion of AG Geelhoed, ECLI:EU:C:2003:407, paras 39–40. For some reference to fundamental rights in one of the (very few) actions lodged before 2009 by a Member State under Article 259 TFEU, see CJEU, Case C-145/04 *Spain v United Kingdom* ECLI:EU:C:2006:543.

(ECHR) and, after its solemn proclamation in December 2000, of the Charter of Fundamental Rights of the European Union (CFREU).

3. The Commission's Post-Charter Policy

Following the entry into force of the Treaty of Lisbon – which made the CFREU legally binding, giving it primary law status – the Commission soon announced that it was ready to start cases with a fundamental rights focus. In particular, in its 2010 Communication 'Strategy for the effective implementation of the Charter of Fundamental Rights by the European Union', the Commission stated that, if a Member State were not to respect fundamental rights when implementing EU law, the Commission would, if necessary, bring proceedings under Article 258 TFEU before the Court. Priority would be given to the cases 'which raise[d] issues of principle or which ha[d] particularly far-reaching negative impact for citizens'. That said, the Commission pointed out that it was only entitled to intervene if the situation in question related to EU law, and that the factor connecting it with EU law depended on the actual situation in question.[19]

Admittedly, the meaning and scope of Article 51(1) CFREU (entitled 'field of application'), according to which the provisions of the Charter 'are addressed to the Member States only when they are implementing EU law', was a rather controversial issue at that time. That had an obvious and direct impact on the Commission's latitude to begin infringement proceedings for presumed infringements of EU fundamental rights.[20]

However, it was not long before the Court delivered its first rulings on this matter. In that regard, the Court emphasised, first of all, that the fundamental rights guaranteed in the EU legal order are applicable in all situations governed by EU law, but not outside such situations. More specifically, the Court stated that the concept of implementation of EU law, within the meaning of Article 51(1) CFREU, presupposes a degree of connection between an act of EU law and the national measure at issue, above and beyond the matters covered being closely related or one of those matters having an indirect impact on the other. For that purpose, it is necessary to determine, inter alia, whether that national legislation is intended to implement a provision of EU law; the nature of the legislation at issue and whether it pursues objectives other than those covered by EU law, even if it is capable of indirectly affecting EU law; and also whether there are specific rules of EU law on the matter or rules which are capable of affecting it. In extreme simplicity, the provisions of the Charter are applicable each time another rule of EU law is also applicable, which imposes some obligation of *facere* or *non-facere* upon the national authorities.[21]

[19] COM(2010)573, paras 10–12.

[20] For some views at the time, see A Łazowski, 'Decoding a Legal Enigma: the Charter of Fundamental Rights of the European Union and Infringement Proceedings' (2013) *ERA Forum 573*; and F Hoffmeister, 'Enforcing the EU Charter of Fundamental Rights in Member States: How Far are Rome, Budapest and Bucharest from Brussels?' in von Bogdandy, Sonnevend (eds), *Constitutional Crisis in the European Constitutional Area. Theory, Law and Politics in Hungary and Romania* (Oxford, Hart Publishing, 2015) 199.

[21] See, in particular, CJEU, Case C-617/10 *Åkerberg Fransson* ECLI:EU:C:2013:105; CJEU, Case C-399/11 *Melloni* ECLI:EU:C:2013:107; CJEU, Case C-265/13 *Torralbo Marcos* ECLI:EU:C:2014:187, and CJEU, Case C-206/13 *Siragusa* ECLI:EU:C:2014:126 ('*the Åkerberg Fransson case law*').

In fact, in the aftermath of its 2010 Communication, the Commission investigated under Article 258 TFEU a number of national measures which it presumed to have given rise to fundamental rights violations. That was the case, for example, of the expulsion measures against EU citizens of Roma-origin from France, the Hungarian media law, the deficiencies of the Greek asylum system, as well as the Lithuanian law banning circulation of information promoting homosexual relations. Most of those cases – some of which received significant media attention – were, however, settled during the pre-litigation stage of the procedure and, thus, did not reach the Court.[22] The Commission's strategy was, often, to tackle the fundamental right violation indirectly, by relying on a breach of some provisions of the Treaties or of sectorial legislation which embodied the fundamental right at issue.[23] The paradigmatic example of that approach is the case brought by the Commission against Hungary in 2012 for the compulsory retirement of judges, prosecutors and notaries.[24]

The more pro-active stance of the Commission in that regard may have received further impetus by the increased awareness by EU citizens of the possibility for that institution to take action under Article 258 TFEU against these types of infringements. Indeed, the Commission's Annual Reports on monitoring the application of EU law show that, especially from the mid-2010s onwards, the Commission started to receive more petitions and complaints concerning possible breaches of fundamental rights by national authorities.[25] In addition, the European Parliament too has, throughout that period, repeatedly called on the Commission to make more significant use of its powers under Articles 258 and 260 TFEU against possible infringements of fundamental rights.[26]

4. The Post-Charter Case Law: The Hungarian Trilogy

A turning point on this matter came some ten years after the entry into force of the Treaty of Lisbon, when the Commission sought to clarify *how far* it could go, in the context of an infringement procedure, in challenging Member States' conduct for alleged breaches of fundamental rights. Three cases brought against Hungary, decided by the Court (sitting as the Grand Chamber) in 2020 and 2021, are particularly relevant in that regard.

[22] See C Ladenburger, 'Protection of Fundamental Rights Post-Lisbon – The Interaction Between the Charter of Fundamental Rights, the European Convention of Human Rights and National Constitutions', Institutional Report, FIDE 2012, 12, with references to the cases.

[23] See, eg, M Dawson, E Muir, 'Hungary and the Indirect Protection of EU Fundamental Rights and the Rule of Law' (2013) *German Law Journal* 1959.

[24] Judgment in CJEU, Case C-286/12 *Commission v Hungary* ECLI:EU:C:2012:687.

[25] *cf* the data provided in the 2014 Annual Report (Part I, p 91) with the 2009 Annual Report (Section 2.3) and the 2010 Annual Report (Section 2.3).

[26] See, inter alia, the European Parliament's Resolutions of 25 October 2016 with recommendations to the Commission on the establishment of an EU mechanism on democracy, the rule of law and fundamental rights (Article 10), and of 4 June 2018 on monitoring the application of EU law 2016 (point 21). More recently, see also the Parliament's Resolution of 23 November 2023 on monitoring the application of European Union Law in 2020, 2021 and 2022 (point 13), and Report of 28 February 2024 on the Commission's 2023 Rule of Law report (points 76–79).

In the *Usufruct over Agricultural Land* case, the Commission explored the possibility to put forward claims based *solely* on an infringement of the CFREU. Indeed, in its application before the Court, the Commission included two distinct claims: one relying on Articles 49 and 63 TFEU (right of establishment and free movement of capital) and one on Article 17 CFREU (right to property). In his Opinion, Advocate General (AG) Saumsgaard Øe took the view that, with regard to alleged breaches of fundamental rights, two situations must be distinguished: those where the Member States implement EU rules (thus making those rules operational), and those where the Member States derogate from EU law (thus invoking a justification to defend the contested measure). Only in the former situation could the Commission – in his view – validly ask the Court to review the national measures against the provisions of the Charter alone. Indeed, that situation is entirely governed by EU law. By contrast, where a Member State is derogating from EU law, it is merely implementing national policy within an area that is subject to its competence. In such a case, the CFREU cannot be used – the Advocate General argued – as a gateway to bring into the scope of the Charter issues of fundamental rights that are unrelated to the (main) EU provisions at issue. Against that backdrop, he suggested that the Court dismiss the Commission's pleas based solely on the Charter.[27] Nevertheless, in its judgment, the Court dodged that question, ruling that, by cancelling the rights of usufruct over agricultural land which are held by nationals of other Member States, Hungary had breached Article 63 TFEU in conjunction with Article 17 CFREU. The Court probably considered that it did not need to enter into that issue to settle the case, since the incompatibility of the contested measure with EU law appeared obvious based on existing case law.[28]

In the subsequent *Higher Education* case, the Court did rule on some claims based solely on an infringement of the provisions of the CFREU. In its application, the Commission challenged two measures adopted by Hungary which made: (1) the exercise of teaching activities leading to a qualification by higher education institutions situated outside the European Economic Area (EEA) subject to the existence of an international treaty between Hungary and the third country in which the institution concerned has its seat; and (2) the exercise of the activities of foreign higher education institutions, including institutions having their seat in another Member State of the EEA, subject to the condition that they offer higher education in the country in which they have their seat. The Commission put forward three sets of claims '*en cascade*',[29] arguing that those measures breached an international agreement binding the Union (namely, the GATS), the rules on free movement (namely, Directive 2006/123 and Articles 49 and 56 TFEU) and – last but not least – the provisions of the CFREU relating to academic freedom (Article 13), the freedom to found higher education institutions (Article 14(3)) and the freedom to conduct a business (Article 16). In the judgment, the Court upheld all the Commission's arguments, in line with the Opinion of AG Kokott. Interestingly, in its

[27] CJEU, Case C-235/17 *Commission v Hungary* Opinion of AG Øe, ECLI:EU:C:2018:971.

[28] CJEU, Case C-235/17 *Commission v Hungary* ECLI:EU:C:2019:432. Para 66 thereof appears to suggest, however, a certain scepticism with regard to the AG's approach.

[29] I consider claims '*en cascade*' to be 'stand-alone' claims since whether each of them is admissible and well-founded requires an assessment that, in principle, does not depend on whether the other claims put forward in the same application are admissible and/or well-founded. That is not true with regard to claims based on two or more provisions read in conjunction.

analysis, the Court followed the scheme and order of claims set out in the application and, having assessed each of those claims separately, it also included three distinct statements in the operative part of the judgment.[30]

Finally, in the *Transparency of Associations* case, the Court held, again in agreement with the Advocate General, that, by imposing obligations of registration, declaration, and publication on certain categories of civil society organisations directly or indirectly receiving support from abroad exceeding a certain threshold, and providing for the possibility of applying penalties to organisations that do not comply with those obligations, Hungary had introduced discriminatory and unjustified restrictions. Those restrictions were considered contrary to the rules on the free movement of capital (Article 63 TFEU) *and* the fundamental right to respect for private and family life, the right to the protection of personal data, and the freedom of association (Articles 7, 8 and 12 CFREU). The Court examined the two complaints separately, although it then 'bundled' them in the operative part of the judgment.[31] Interestingly, in his Opinion, AG Campos Sánchez-Bordona had proposed to the Court a slightly different wording in that regard: to rule that Hungary had 'failed to fulfil the obligations incumbent on it under Article 63 TFEU *by infringing* Articles 7, 8 and 12 of the [Charter]'. He had in fact argued that, when the applicant alleges breaches the Treaty provisions on the four freedoms and the corresponding rights laid down in the CFREU, the Court had to find 'a way which enables the integration of both in a single set of review criteria'.[32]

In this trilogy of disputes, the focus of the Commission's case against the defendant clearly centres, for the first time, on violations of EU fundamental rights. In its judgments, the Court confirms – quite obviously, dare I say – that its jurisdiction under Articles 258–60 TFEU with regard to Member States' compliance with the CFREU is, save exceptions set out in the Treaties, a direct function of the scope of the Charter vis-à-vis the Member States. In other words, the principles stemming from the *Åkerberg Fransson* case law may be used to draw the outer limits within which a Member State may be sued before the Court by the Commission or other Member States for alleged violations of fundamental rights. Provided the situation is governed by EU law, the applicant's claims can naturally concern an infringement of the CFREU.[33]

The more restrictive position taken by AG Øe in the *Usufruct over Agricultural Land* case appears motivated by a (laudable) desire to respect the allocation of competences between the Union and the Member States, and provide an easy rule of thumb in that respect. Nevertheless, the Court seems to have disregarded that view altogether. In fact, as I have already observed elsewhere, the distinction proposed in that Opinion may appear somewhat formalistic, the crucial issue being more one of connection

[30] CJEU, Case C-66/18 *Commission v Hungary* ECLI:EU:C:2020:79266/18, and the Opinion of AG Kokott in the same case, ECLI:EU:C:2020:172.

[31] CJEU, Case C-78/18 *Commission v Hungary* ECLI:EU:C:2020:476.

[32] CJEU, Case C-78/18 *Commission v Hungary* Opinion of AG Campos Sánchez-Bordona, ECLI:EU:C:2020:1. Emphasis added.

[33] For some comments on these cases, see also M Bonelli, 'The "NGOs case": on how to use the Charter of Fundamental Rights in infringement actions' (2021) *European Law Review* 258; and V Kosta, D Piqani, 'Where Trade and Academic Freedom Meet: Commission v Hungary (LEX CEU)' (2022) *Common Market Law Review* 751. But see also A von Bogdandy, LD Spieker, 'Transformative Constitutionalism in Luxembourg: How the Court Can Support Democratic Transitions' (2023) *Columbia Journal of European Law* 65, 80.

or proximity between the two (sets of) provisions.[34] Although the provisions of the CFREU may be used to re-modulate or expand the reach of other provisions of EU law, there may well be situations in which the national measure being challenged is manifestly in breach of both non-CFREU provisions and CFREU provisions, with each of those breaches being capable of standing on its own two feet. Indeed, even if related, those breaches may concern different aspects or effects of the challenged measure. That may be so regardless of the 'label' affixed to the situation, as long as the CFREU provisions relied on can, in the specific circumstances of the case, be observed 'in the shadow' projected by the other applicable EU law provisions.

In particular, two situations come to mind. First, when the CFREU provision could play a gap-filling role: a situation is governed by a body of EU rules, but none of those rules covers specifically the problematic aspect or effect of the national measure. That phenomenon can be observed in relation to other general principles of EU law. The most remarkable example in point is the *PFOS* case against Sweden, in which the Commission claimed – and the Court accepted – that the defendant Member State had breached the duty of sincere cooperation (enshrined in current Article 4(3) TEU) by acting alone in an international forum, in an area of shared competences, without that action being in clear contradiction of any decision of the Council on the matter.[35] Second, the alleged infringement of the CFREU may constitute a significant 'aggravating factor', meaning that the seriousness of the infringement goes much further than that stemming from the mere breach of the non-CFREU provision(s). Let us think of the (entirely hypothetical) case in which a Member State were to give a tax exemption to certain groups or categories of traders and, moreover, only to those of a given race or religious faith. One could very well imagine that, in such a case, the applicant before the Court would seek a declaration from the Court that the measure in question is not only contrary to the rules on free movement and/or State aid, but also that such a measure infringes certain fundamental rights enshrined in the CFREU: first and foremost, equality before the law (Article 20) and non-discrimination (Article 21).

Similarly, the Court has not endorsed the 'integrated approach' proposed by AG Campos with regard to the national measures which allegedly restrict the Treaty-based freedoms of movement and, at the same time, the Charter-based economic freedoms. In essence, this confirms that the Court has recognised that the Commission enjoys wide discretion in how it wishes to formulate and structure its claims and form of order in its applications to the Court. One may suppose that the technique chosen (combined reading of the provisions, *en cascade*, in sequence, etc) will normally depend on the specific legal and factual circumstances of the case as well as, arguably, the 'spin' which the Commission wants to give to it. It cannot be ruled out, however, that such a choice might have some consequences. For instance, the assessment as to whether a Member State has adopted the measures necessary to comply with the first judgment of the Court, if and

[34] L Prete, B Smulders, 'The Age of Maturity of Infringement Proceedings' (2012) *Common Market Law Review* 285, 290–91.

[35] CJEU, Case C-246/07 *Commission v Sweden* ECLI:EU:C:2010:203. For a comment, see PJ Kuijper, 'Union Loyalty in Mixed External Relations and the Weight of Informal Preparatory Acts: *Commission v Sweden (PFOS)*' in Butler, Wessel (eds), *EU External Relations Law – The Cases in Context* (Oxford, Hart Publishing, 2022) 619. For another case, see CJEU, Case C-132/06 *Commission v Italy* ECLI:EU:C:2008:412.

when the Commission were to bring a second set of proceedings under Article 260(2) TFEU, could be different.[36] Another consequence might flow from a supposedly greater gravity of an independent breach of the CFREU (which, what is more, comes on top of a breach of other EU provisions): for example, an increase in the amount of the financial penalties imposed by the Court under Article 260(2) TFEU, or of the damages awarded by national courts to individuals acting for State liability.[37]

5. The Post-Charter Case Law (II): The *Bialowiecka Forest* Interim Measures

Although not directly related to a procedure which concerned fundamental rights, the *Białowiecka Forest* case appears relevant in this context. In that case, the Court had, among others, to rule on whether the interim measures provided for in Article 279 TFEU may include, as ancillary measures, periodic penalty payments against defendants that fail to comply with the main interim measures ordered. The issue arose in the context of an infringement action started by the Commission for possible breaches of the Habitats and Birds Directives by the Polish authorities, due to the increase of active forest management operations at a protected Natura2000 site. On the same day, the Commission had also lodged an application for interim measures, asking the Court to order the national authorities to halt those operations, pending the judgment in the main action, except where there was a threat to public safety. The requested measures were first granted *inaudita altera parte* in July 2017. In the following weeks, however, the Commission took the view that the Polish authorities had deliberately ignored the Court's order (when not openly contested it), as the logging operations continued unaffected. Thus, the question arose as to whether there were, within the EU legal system, any means of enforcing compliance with an order issued under Article 279 TFEU.

In its order of 20 November 2017, the Court answered that question in the affirmative. It emphasised that Article 279 TFEU confers on the CJEU the power to prescribe 'any interim measures' that it deems necessary. Although it is for the applicant to request such measures as it considers appropriate, the EU courts must satisfy themselves that the measures which they intend to order are sufficiently effective to achieve their aim. The EU courts enjoy broad discretion in that respect. Therefore, if it is deemed appropriate, they may also adopt, where necessary *ex officio*, any ancillary measure intended to ensure that its order is complied with. Such a measure may include – according to the Court – the imposition of periodic penalty payments, intended to encourage the

[36] Indeed, the formulation of the claims in the application affects directly the manner in which the Court formulates the operative part of the judgment. The operative part of the judgment given under Article 258 TFEU is, obviously, the starting point of the analysis which it carries out in proceedings started under Article 260(2) TFEU. See, eg, CJEU, Case C-95/12 *Commission v Germany* ECLI:EU:C:2013:676, paras 37–48 and the Opinion of AG Wahl in the same case, ECLI:EU:C:2013:333, paras 26–54.

[37] See S Prechal, 'Fundamental Rights and Treaty Freedoms: The "Derogation Situation" and Infringement Proceedings' in Prassl et al (eds), *The Internal Market Ideal* (Oxford, Oxford University Press, 2024) 151, 161. For an interesting comparative study on the subject, see E Baginska (ed), *Damages for Violations of Human Rights – A Comparative Study of Domestic Legal Systems* (Heidelberg, Springer, 2016).

relevant Member State to comply with the order. In the case at hand, the Court found it unnecessary to establish whether the first order had been complied with or not. There was enough evidence in the case file to cast doubt on whether Poland had complied or, at any rate, intended to comply with the new order. In such circumstances, the Court considered it necessary to 'enhance the effectiveness' of the interim measures ordered by providing for penalties to be imposed if Poland failed to comply with them immediately and fully. Poland was thus requested to send to the Commission, within 15 days, details of all measures adopted in order to comply. If the Commission were of the view that Poland had failed to comply with the order, it could request that proceedings be resumed. The Court would then give a decision by way of a new order. If the Court found an infringement, it would order Poland to pay 'a periodic penalty payment of at least EUR 100 000 per day', from the date of notification of the new order until compliance was achieved, or until the judgment in the main proceedings was delivered.[38] The case was not further pursued by the Commission since the national authorities accepted to comply with the first interim measures adopted by the Court. However, in two subsequent cases (both against Poland, one brought by the Commission and one by the Czech Republic[39]), the Court has in fact imposed the penalty payments requested by the applicants.

There is little doubt that the Court's decision in the *Białowieża Forest* case is nothing less than ground-breaking, and filled what was widely regarded as a gap in the Treaties, a fortiori when account is taken of the necessary length of the procedure before it can be brought before the Court.[40] In particularly serious and urgent situations – as may often be the case when fundamental rights are being breached – there is now a very effective and rapid tool that may coerce Member States to comply without delay with suspension injunctions and other similar measures adopted by the Court under Article 279 TFEU in the context of infringement proceedings.[41]

6. The Most Recent Policy and Case Law

The growing attention that the Commission gives to potential infringements of the CFREU provisions in the context of Articles 258 and 260 TFEU proceedings is witnessed by the progressively greater emphasis that it placed on such breaches in its latest communications in this field.

[38] Orders of the CJEU in Case C-441/17 R *Commission v Poland* ECLI:EU:C:2017:622 and ECLI:EU:C:2017:877.

[39] Orders of the CJEU in Case C-121/21 R *Czech Republic v Poland (Turów Mine)* ECLI:EU:C:2021:752; and Case C-204/21 R *Commission v Poland (Private life of judges)* ECLI:EU:C:2021:878 and ECLI:EU:C:2023:334.

[40] *cf* M Dawson, E Muir, 'Individual, Institutional and Collective Vigilance in Protecting Fundamental Rights in the EU: Lessons from the Roma' (2011) *Common Market Law Review* 751, 761–63.

[41] For a more detailed analysis, see L Coutron, 'La Cour de justice au secours de la forêt de Bialowieska' (2018) *Rechtswissenschaftliche Zeitschrift für die Deutsche und Europäische* 321; T Martin, 'Le large pouvoir d'appréciation du juge des référés au service de l'efficacité du droit de l'Union européenne' (2018) *Cahiers de Droit Europeen* 495–511; P Wenneras, 'Saving a Forest and the Rule of Law: Commission v Poland' (2019) *Common Market Law Review* 541; and L Prete, 'Can't See the Forest for the Trees? Penalties Under Article 279 TFEU' in Sarmiento et al (eds), *Yearbook on Procedural Law of the Court of Justice of the European Union* 1st edn (MPILux Research Paper 2020) 157.

For example, in its 2017 Communication, entitled 'EU law: Better results through better application',[42] the Commission (then led by JC Juncker) wrote that it intended to make a more strategic use of its discretionary power in starting proceedings, by prioritising its enforcement efforts 'on the most important breaches of EU law affecting the interests of its citizens and business'. Infringements of the CFREU provisions did not feature, as such, in the list of priorities given by the Commission (with the exception of 'infringements which affect the capacity of national judicial systems to contribute to the effective enforcement of EU law, as provided for in Article 19 TEU and Article 47 of the Charter'). However, the Commission also stressed that, in selecting the cases to pursue, it 'attache[d] importance to ensuring that national legislation complies with EU law since incorrect national legislation systematically undermines citizens' ability to assert their rights including their *fundamental rights*, and to draw fully the benefits from EU legislation'. The Commission also stated that it would 'also pay particular attention to cases showing a persistent failure by a Member State to apply EU law correctly'.[43]

Similarly, in its 2020 Communication on a new 'Strategy to strengthen the application of the Charter of Fundamental Rights in the EU', the Commission (Presided by U von der Leyen)[44] first recalled that 'as guardian of the Treaties it ensures that national legislation complies with EU law so that people can assert their rights, including their *fundamental rights*, and fully benefit from EU legislation'. It then 'reaffirm[ed] its commitment to monitor the application of the *Charter* and related EU laws, strengthen its dialogue with Member States and launch infringements as appropriate where there is a breach of EU law'. In that respect, it stated that it would 'continue to closely monitor cases where a Member State is showing a systemic failure in applying the *Charter* when implementing EU law'.[45]

More recently, in its 2022 Communication 'Enforcing EU law for a Europe that delivers', the Commission declared its commitment 'to stepping up its work to promote and uphold people's rights, fundamental freedoms and the rule of law'. To that end, the Commission underlined that 'key work streams such as the annual Rule of Law reports, the European democracy action plan and the renewed strategy for the implementation of the [Charter] combine in a major intensification of work to strengthen the EU's legal and democratic foundations'. The need to ensure a prompt and effective enforcement of EU law when the protection of fundamental rights is at stake is emphasised at several points throughout the communication.[46]

In fact, in the last five years, the Commission relied on various CFREU provisions to challenge Member States' compliance with EU law in numerous disputes brought under Articles 258 and 260 TFEU, including in some high-profile cases that were heard by the Grand Chamber of the Court. Yet again, in most of those cases the fundamental right aspect of the dispute did not lie at the centre of the legal questions that the Court had to deal with. The most interesting cases in that regard are probably

[42] As regards the Juncker Commission's policy on infringement proceedings, see K Banks, G von Rintelen, 'Infringement Procedures and the Juncker Commission' (2020) *European Law Review* 619.

[43] C/2016/8600. Section 3. Emphasis added.

[44] As regards the von der Leyen Commission's policy on infringement proceedings, see L Prete, B Smulders 'The Age of Maturity' (2012) 285, 296–300.

[45] COM/2020/711 final. Sections 1.1 and 3.1. Emphasis added.

[46] COM(2022) 518 final. See in particular, pp 1, 3–5, and 28.

the infringement actions started by the Commission against Poland to safeguard the independence of the judiciary, given the strong links existing between the principle of the Rule of Law (one of the values on which the Union is founded, under Article 2 TEU), the Member States' obligation to 'provide remedies sufficient to ensure effective legal protection in the fields covered by Union law' (set out in Article 19(1) TEU), and the fundamental right 'to an effective remedy and to a fair trial' (enshrined in Article 47 CFREU).[47] In one of those cases, however, apart from raising again an issue under Article 47 CFREU, the Commission also argued – and the Court agreed – that, by enacting certain legal provisions regulating judicial activities, Poland had infringed the right to respect for private life and the right to protection of personal data (guaranteed by Article 7 and Article 8(1) CFREU).[48] That said, issues under Article 47 CFREU were also raised in other cases which were not Rule of Law-related and concerned less sensitive areas of law.[49] Quite interesting are also three procedures brought by the Commission under Article 258 TFEU which concerned Hungarian legislation on international protection. Although those cases were mainly framed in terms of breaches of the relevant EU legislation, the Commission also relied on various provisions of the CFREU, in particular Article 18 ('right to asylum') and Article 47 thereof.[50] Finally, as it may be expected, certain cases involved some discussion of Member States' compliance with the internal market rules and, by way of a consequence, with the economic rights and freedoms guaranteed by the CFREU – the freedom to choose an occupation and right to engage in work (Article 15), the freedom to conduct a business (Article 16), and the right to property (Article 17).[51]

Moreover, in other cases the Commission has referred to the provisions of the CFREU in its legal arguments, without that being reflected in the form of order sought from the Court. For instance, the two actions started against Hungary and Poland against their respective legislation which, in essence, failed to grant the right to be a member of a political party to EU citizens who are not their own nationals but who reside in their territory, with the result that those citizens have less chance of being elected at municipal elections or elections to the European Parliament than their own nationals, are rather interesting. In both cases, the Czech Republic (defendant in one procedure and intervenient in the other) argued that the Commission's action was inadmissible in so far as, despite being formally based on Article 22 TFEU alone, it also relied on an alleged infringement of Article 12(1) CFREU (freedom of assembly and of association). The Czech Government took the view

[47] CJEU, Case C-192/18 *Commission v Poland (Independence of ordinary courts)* ECLI:EU:C:2019:924; CJEU, Case C-619/18 *Commission v Poland (Independence of the Supreme Court)* ECLI:EU:C:2019:531; and CJEU, Case C-791/19 *Commission v Poland (Disciplinary regime for judges)* ECLI:EU:C:2021:596.

[48] CJEU, Case C-204/21 *Commission v Poland (Independence and private life of judges)* ECLI:EU:C:2023:442. For another recent case in which Article 8 of the Charter was mentioned, see CJEU, Case C-658/19 *Commission v Spain (Personal Data Directive – Criminal law)* ECLI:EU:C:2021:138.

[49] CJEU, Case C-771/18 *Commission v Hungary (Charges for access to electricity and natural gas transmission networks)* ECLI:EU:C:2020:584; and CJEU, Case C-432/21 *Commission v Poland (Forest management and good practice)* ECLI:EU:C:2023:139.

[50] CJEU, Case C-808/18 *Commission v Hungary (Reception of applicants for international protection)* ECLI:EU:C:2020:1029; Case C-821/19 *Commission v Hungary (Criminalisation of assistance to asylum seekers)* ECLI:EU:C:2021:930; and Case C-823/21 *Commission v Hungary (Declaration of intent prior to an asylum application)* ECLI:EU:C:2023:504.

[51] CJEU, Case C-718/18 *Commission v Germany (Transposition of Directives 2009/72 and 2009/73)* ECLI:EU:C:2021:662.

that such a mismatch rendered the scope of the Commission's action unclear, thereby exposing the Court to the risk of ruling *ultra petita*. In his two Opinions, AG Richard de La Tour suggested that the Court dismiss the pleas of inadmissibility because 'it [was] apparent from the grounds of the application, unambiguously and in line with the reasoned opinion, that Article 22 TFEU, on which it is based, must be interpreted by putting it into context and by taking into consideration the links to the Charter and, in particular, Article 12(1) thereof'. Consequently, he came to the conclusion that, in its applications, the Commission had not alleged an infringement of Article 12(1) CFREU.[52] In its judgments of November 2024, the Court agreed with the Advocate General, and rejected the pleas of inadmissibility stating that 'as for Article 12 of the Charter, it is … clear from the application that the Commission submits that Article 22 TFEU must be interpreted in the light of that provision of the Charter, without pleading a standalone infringement of it'.[53] Accordingly, the Court went on to determine the scope of Article 22 TFEU by, inter alia, looking at the other relevant provisions of primary law, including Article 12 of the Charter.[54] On that basis, the Court upheld the Commission's actions.

Currently, there appear to be only three cases pending before the Court in which the Commission has challenged some State legislation under Article 258 TFEU and in which some provisions of the CFREU are expressly referred to in the form of order sought from the Court. The first case, brought in December 2022, concerns the 2021 Hungarian law adopting stricter measures against persons convicted of paedophilia and amending certain laws for the protection of children. The Commission takes the view that such law infringes a number of provisions of the EU Treaties and of EU legislation, as well as Articles 1 (human dignity), 7 (respect for private and family life), 8 (protection of personal data), 11 (freedom of expression and information) and 21 (non-discrimination) CFREU.[55] The second case too, lodged in February 2023, concerns Hungary. In its application, the Commission asks the Court to rule that, by adopting certain measures and by failing to adopt other measures concerning radio frequencies and spectrum, that Member State has failed to fulfil its obligations flowing from certain EU directives, some general principles of EU law and, last but not least, Article 11 CFREU.[56] Also the third case, lodged in December 2024, concerns Hungary. The Commission challenges Hungary's 2023 law on the protection of national sovereignty which, inter alia, established a Sovereignty Protection Office in Hungary, endowed with extensive powers of investigation. The activities of that office are – the Commission argues – largely excluded from judicial review and, based on a binary distinction between Hungarian and non-Hungarian activities and interests, it is empowered to operate in such a way that it need not take account of Hungary's membership of the European Union or Hungary's obligations under the EU Treaties. The Commission takes the view such a measure infringes a number of provisions of EU primary and secondary law, including Articles 7, 8, 11, 12, 47 and 48 CFREU.[57]

[52] Opinions of the AGs in Case C-808/21 *Commission v Czech Republic* ECLI:EU:C:2024:12, paras 44, 45 and 48; and Case C-814/21 *Commission v Poland* ECLI:EU:C:2024:15, paras 28–38.

[53] CJEU, Case C-808/21 *Commission v Czech Republic* ECLI:EU:C:2024:962, para 48, and (similarly) CJEU, Case C-814/21 *Commission v Poland* ECLI:EU:C:2024:963, para 64.

[54] ibid, paras 107–27, and 106–25, respectively.

[55] Action brought in Case C-769/22, [2023] OJ C 54/19.

[56] Action brought in Case C-92/23, [2023] OJ C 189/18.

[57] Action brought in Case C-829/24, [2025] OJ C/2025/124.

Since submissions in ongoing judicial proceedings are confidential, whether there are also pending cases in which the Commission (or the applicant Member State) has referred to the provisions of the CFREU in its legal arguments, without that being reflected in the form of order sought from the Court, cannot be ascertained.[58] Nevertheless, one may suppose that issues of fundamental rights might arise, for example, in those cases where the Commission has started proceedings for Member States' failure to correctly transpose directives – such as the Directive on the right of access to a lawyer in criminal proceedings and in European arrest warrant proceedings[59] – that aim at strengthening the protection of certain fundamental rights, and which largely codify the relevant case law of the Court and the ECtHR.[60]

It is, likewise, hard to obtain precise aggregate information about the cases concerned, directly or indirectly, with alleged violations of fundamental rights which have recently been closed, or are still being handled, by the Commission in the context of the administrative stage of the procedure. In its latest Annual Report on Monitoring the application of European Union (year 2023), the Commission refers to various procedures in which it has raised issues of compliance with the CFREU with the Member States in question. The precise number of those cases is, nonetheless, not available since the overall figures provided in the report are broken down by sector concerned, and not by the type of provisions allegedly breached. However, some detail on those cases may often be found by using the 'European Commission at work' search engine, which provides a link to the relevant press releases issued by the Commission. A number of rather interesting cases are shown in that database as being 'active' at the end of year 2024. For example, in January 2023, the Commission decided to send letters of formal notice to 22 Member States for failing to comply with certain obligations from the Regulation on the dissemination of terrorist content online. Those cases may, perhaps, raise issues under a number of provisions of the CFREU (Articles 8, 10 and 11 are the first that spring to mind).[61] In addition, in June 2023, the Commission has decided to open an infringement procedure against Poland for the new law on the State Committee for the Examination of Russian influence on the internal security of Poland. The Commission considers that law to breach, inter alia, Articles 8, 47 and 49 CFREU.[62]

7. Looking into the Near Future: 2024 and Beyond

Finally, four (actual or possible) developments in the case law should be mentioned since they have, at least at first sight, the potential to provide the Commission

[58] Save, of course, where the information may be revealed by other sources (such as Commission's press releases, or AG's Opinions).

[59] Directive 2013/48/EU of the European Parliament and of the Council of 22 October 2013 on the right of access to a lawyer in criminal proceedings and in European arrest warrant proceedings, and on the right to have a third party informed upon deprivation of liberty and to communicate with third persons and with consular authorities while deprived of liberty [2013] OJ L 294/1.

[60] See, eg, actions in Case C-660/24 *Commission v Hungary* [2024] OJ C/2024/7310, and Case C-681/24 *Commission v Czech Republic* [2024] OJ C, C/2024/7158.

[61] See Press Release IP/23/132 of 26 January 2023.

[62] See Press Release IP/23/3134 of 8 June 2023.

(or, for that matter, the Member States) with greater ability and interest to bring proceedings under Articles 258–260 TFEU for alleged breaches of fundamental rights.

First, as mentioned above,[63] by virtue of Articles 24(1) TEU and 275 TFEU, the CJEU does not have jurisdiction with respect to the Treaties provisions relating to the CFSP nor with respect to acts adopted on the basis of those provisions ('the CFSP derogation'), with two exceptions.[64] This means that infringement proceedings for alleged failures by Member States to comply with obligations stemming from the Treaty provisions on the CFSP, or from EU acts adopted solely on the basis of those provisions, is in principle excluded. Nevertheless, in recent years, the Court has progressively broadened the scope of its jurisdiction in this field by, on the one hand, interpreting the CFSP derogation narrowly and, on the other hand, interpreting the two exceptions to the derogation extensively. This process has culminated – at least for the time being – in two judgments which the Court delivered on 10 September 2024: *KS and KD* and *Neves 77*.[65]

In those judgments, the Court (in Grand Chamber format) went further than in its previous rulings in re-framing its jurisdiction in CFSP matters. In essence, the Court found that, in the light of the circumstances of the two cases, it did have the power to interpret a Council decision adopted on the basis of some CFSP provisions (*Neves 77 Solutions*), and to hear an action for compensation of harm allegedly suffered by two individuals as a result of various acts and omissions by the Council, the Commission and the European External Action Service, in the implementation of a Council Joint Action (*KS and KD*). More specifically, in the latter case, the Court first rejected the appellants' argument according to which the mere fact that a party claims an infringement of his or her fundamental rights would be, in itself, sufficient to declare that it has jurisdiction to hear and determine that action, even in the field of the CFSP. Nor could the CJEU's jurisdiction on this matter derive from the need to ensure the effectiveness of Article 47 of the Charter, the Union's obligation to accede to the ECHR under Article 6(2) TEU, or the monopoly which the CJEU has been conferred by Articles 268 and 340 TFEU over actions for non-contractual liability against the Union. Second, the Court turned to the scope of the CFSP derogation. In that regard, it stated that, under Articles 24(1) TEU and 275 TFEU, 'the [CJEU] does not have jurisdiction to assess the legality of, or interpret, acts or omissions directly related to the conduct, definition or implementation of the CFSP, and especially the CSDP, that is to say, in particular the identification of the European Union's strategic interests and the definition of both the actions to be taken and the positions to be adopted by the European Union as well as of the general guidelines of the CFSP, within the meaning of Articles 24 to 26, 28, 29, 37, 38, 42 and 43 TEU'. By contrast, those provisions do not detract from its jurisdiction with regard to acts and omissions which 'are not directly related to the political or strategic choices made by the

[63] See n 12 above.

[64] Namely, the 'border patrol' review under Article 40(1) TEU, and actions for annulment brought by individuals against decisions providing for restrictive measures against natural or legal persons adopted by the Council and based on CFSP provisions.

[65] CJEU, Joined Cases C-29/22 P and C-44/22 P *KS and KD v Council and Others and Commission v KS and KD* ECLI:EU:C:2024:725; and Case C-351/22 *Neves 77 Solutions* ECLI:EU:C:2024:723.

institutions, bodies, offices and agencies of the Union in the context of the CFSP, and in particular the CSDP'. Accordingly, the Court held that the General Court had erred in declaring the actions for damages brought by the appellants, based inter alia on grounds of alleged breaches of their fundamental rights, to be inadmissible for lack of jurisdiction. The importance of these rulings should not be underestimated. Given the horizontal nature and general wording of Articles 24(1) TEU and 275 TFEU, one could reasonably consider that, in those areas of CFSP activity which the Court held to fall outside the CFSP derogation, infringement proceedings should also be possible. If that is so, the CFSP should, probably, no longer be considered an area of *lex imperfecta*, as AG Wahl argued in *H v Council and Commission*, on the ground that 'no judicial procedure for enforcement and penalties in case of breaches is expressly provided for in the Treaties', and 'only limited remedies are available to individuals whose rights may be breached by acts adopted in the framework of the CFSP'.[66] Maybe in a not-so-distant future there will be infringement procedures against Member States for their failure to respect the fundamental rights enshrined in the CFREU when implementing (or for having failed to implement) some CFSP act.

Second, it is well-established case law that, under Article 258 TFEU, the Commission can bring proceedings against a Member State not only for specific infringements of EU law, but also for 'general and persistent' infringements thereof.[67] The latter concept appears to relate to systemic failures in the Member States which are demonstrated by widespread or repeated breaches of some specific legal obligation laid down in EU law.[68] This case law arguably implies that the Commission has the power to start a second procedure under Article 260(2) TFEU, and ask for the imposition of financial penalties, where the Member State in question has not remedied the systemic failure, regardless of whether or not it has remedied the specific instances of non-compliance which the Commission used, in the first procedure, to prove the systemic failure. Moreover, as the Court has consistently stated, 'the fact that proceedings [under article 260(2) TFEU] concern a failure to comply with a judgment relating to a general and persistent practice has the effect of rendering the failure to fulfil obligations in question more serious'.[69] If that is so, one could wonder whether an action under Article 258 TFEU based on an general and persistent infringement of one or more provisions of the CFREU (in combination or alongside an infringement of other EU provisions) could not be particularly effective where a Member State has shown its reluctance to protect those rights in some specific field. No such action has, so far, been brought before the Court. However, there is a case currently pending before the Court, where the Commission alleges a systemic

[66] Case C-455/14 P *H v Council and Commission*, Opinion of AG Wahl ECLI:EU:C:2016:212, paras 38–40.

[67] See, among many, CJEU, Case C-494/01 *Commission v Ireland* ECLI:EU:C:2005:250; CJEU, Case C-573/19 *Commission v Italy (Limit values – NO2)* ECLI:EU:C:2022:380; and CJEU, Case C-286/21, *Commission v France (Limit values – PM10)* ECLI:EU:C:2022:319.

[68] On that concept, see recently Case C-47/23 *Commission v Germany* Opinion of AG Emiliou, ECLI:EU:C:2024:708, paras 32–36 and 48–50. In scholarship, see P Wennerås, 'A New Dawn for Commission Enforcement under Articles 226 and 228 EC: General and Persistent (GAP) Infringements, Lump Sums and Penalty Payments' (2006) *Common Market Law Review* 31, 33–50; and L Prete, 'The Systemic Criterion in the Use of Infringement Proceedings' (2023) *German Law Journal* 1011.

[69] See, eg, CJEU, Case C-123/22 *Commission v Hungary (Reception of applicants for international protection II)* ECLI:EU:C:2024:493, para 112 and the case law cited.

and persistent infringement of certain provisions of EU law and, despite its claims not explicitly referring to any possible violation of a fundamental right, the legal analysis that the Court will have to carry out might possibly involve the interpretation of one or more provisions of the Charter. Indeed, the case concerns Slovak measures that allegedly discriminate Roma children at school.[70] Could that case provide a first blueprint for future actions against systemic infringements of the CFREU provisions by the Member States?

Third, the already mentioned case brought by the Commission against Hungary concerning its law adopting stricter measures against persons convicted of paedophilia and amending certain laws for the protection of children[71] has a particularly interesting aspect. Indeed, one of the Commission's claims is that, by adopting that legislation, Hungary has infringed Article 2 TEU. This is the first time the Commission has put forward such a claim before the Court. Whether Member States' disregard of the values enshrined in Article 2 TEU may be raised as an independent ground in the context of infringement proceedings is, in fact, an open question on which views in legal scholarship diverge.[72] The answer to that question is not unimportant in the present context: respect for human rights is not only one of the values expressly listed in that provision, but it is also generally considered one of the main components of the Rule of Law principle,[73] in respect of which there is a particularly well-developed case law of the Court. If the Commission's approach were to be endorsed by the Court, its ability to enforce Article 2 TEU – not as a provision giving context to other EU provisions, but on a stand-alone basis – through infringement proceedings would probably constitute an additional means to tackle particularly serious or systemic violations of EU fundamental rights by national authorities.

Fourth, in its recent judgment in *Commission v Hungary (Reception of applicants for international protection II)* – a case brought pursuant to Article 2690(2) TFEU – the Court considered the defendant's failure to comply with the first judgment of the Court to be 'exceptionally serious',[74] inter alia, because of the importance of the provisions which were the subject of the failure ascertained in that first judgment. Although those provisions consisted only in rules of secondary law, those provisions largely embodied, and were thus necessary to ensure compliance with, the fundamental rights enshrined in Articles 18, 19 and 47 CFREU.[75] As such, that failure warranted, the Court decided,

[70] Action in Case C-799/23 [2024] OJ C 2024/1402. See also Commission, Press Release IP/23/2249 of 19 April 2023.

[71] See n 55 above.

[72] See, among the many contributions on this topic, and with further references to scholarship, M Bonelli and M Clas, 'Crossing the Rubicon? The Commission's Use of Article 2 TEU in the Infringement Action on LGBTIQ+ Rights in Hungary' (2023) *Maastricht Journal of European & Comparative Law* 3; M Bonelli, 'Infringement Actions 2.0: How to Protect EU Values before the Court of Justice' (2022) *European Constitutional Law Review* 30; KL Scheppele, D Kochenov, B Grabowska-Moroz, 'EU Values Are Law, After All: Enforcing EU Values Through Systemic Infringement Actions by the European Commission and the Member States of the European Union' (2020) *Yearbook of European Law* 3; and M Schmidt, P Bogdanowicz, 'The Infringement Procedure in the Rule of Law Crisis: How to Make Effective Use of Article 258 TFEU' (2018) *Common Market Law Review* 1061.

[73] See, eg, Council of Europe, European Commission for Democracy Through Law (Venice Commission), Report on the Rule of Law, adopted on the 25–26 March 2011.

[74] Case C-123/22 ECLI:EU:C:2024:493, paras 96 ff.

[75] ibid, paras 105 and 108–10.

the imposition of particularly hefty financial penalties, including a lump sum of EUR 200 million (the highest ever imposed in similar proceedings), which largely exceeded those requested by the Commission.

8. Conclusions

It follows from the above that, after several decades in which the protection of fundamental rights played scarcely any role in the enforcement actions started by the Commission under Articles 258 and 260 TFEU, the situation has slowly and gradually changed after the entry into force of the Treaty of Lisbon. A number of elements encouraged the Commission to become more active in that regard: first and foremost, the legally-binding status given to the CFREU and some relatively favourable case law from the Court, both on the applicability of the Charter to the Member States and on the Commission's ability to enforce the Charter through infringement proceedings. Those elements fuelled, in turn, growing awareness in the public, which triggered more complaints and petitions in this field, and repeated calls by the European Parliament for bolder action from the Commission.

Since 2010, the Commission has in fact opened a number of investigations which turned mainly on presumed breaches of EU fundamental rights, including in some politically sensitive and/or legally complex cases. In many of those, the Commission managed to close the file during the pre-contentious stage of the procedure, having considered the Member State's remedial action to be satisfactory. In other cases, the Commission decided to refer the Member States in question to the Court and its claims were mostly successful. Moreover, in some of those cases, the Court gave important clarifications on the scope of the relevant CFREU provisions. That was so, inter alia, in the *Higher Education* and *Transparency of Associations* cases, which required the Court to interpret, in particular, Articles 7, 12, 13 and 14 CFREU, legal provisions which had not been invoked in many cases before.

Notwithstanding, it cannot be ignored that, on the whole, the number of cases raising fundamental rights issues brought before the Court under Articles 258–60 TFEU has been, to date, relatively limited. In the last few years, the Commission has started infringement proceedings, on average, in some 50 cases per year. A rough estimate suggests that CFREU provisions are referred to, by the parties and/or by the Court, in far less than 10 per cent of those cases. In the light of what the Commission indicated in its Annual Reports, it is also reasonable to presume that the *fundamental rights-* vs *non fundamental rights-* related cases ratio may not be substantially different with regard to the procedures that are closed during the administrative stage thereof.

The question of whether it could or should be any different is entirely legitimate, but not one to which a lawyer could easily answer. Indeed, whether it would be appropriate for the Commission to further increase its enforcement action in this field is mostly a *policy* issue.[76] And the Commission is indeed a political body.

[76] On this topic, see O De Schutter, Infringement Proceedings as a Tool for the Enforcement of Fundamental Rights in the European Union, Report for the Open Society European Policy Institute, 2017; and K Scheppele, 'The Treaties Without A Guardian: The European Commission and the Rule of Law' (2023) *Columbia Journal of European Law* 93. See also, more generally, RD Kelemen, T Pavone, 'Where Have the Guardians Gone? Law Enforcement and the Politics of Supranational Forbearance in the European Union' (2023) *World Politics* 779.

The Commission's task of acting as 'guardian of the Treaties' is only one of the tasks attributed to it by Article 17(1) TEU. Its enforcement activities must, therefore, not only co-exist, but possibly also be coordinated and run in tune, with its other activities, for example those of preparing and proposing legislation. Moreover, given the limited resources available to the Commission, and the laborious nature of investigations under Articles 258 and 260 TFEU, it is unrealistic to expect the Commission to police all possible infringements of which it may become aware – including those involving fundamental rights violations.

The same considerations apply, *mutatis mutandis*, to the Court of Justice, whose mission is, pursuant to Article 19(1) TEU, to 'ensure that in the interpretation and application of the Treaties the law is observed'. The protection of fundamental rights is certainly part and parcel of that mission which, however, remains broader in scope. In addition, even after the recent reform of the EU judicial architecture and the new distribution of jurisdiction within the CJEU, it is not obvious that the Court would be capable of handling, with the required swiftness and depth of the analysis, a significant increase in the number of infringement actions. After all, unlike the ECtHR and the (now defunct) European Commission for Human Rights, neither the CJEU nor the European Commission are human rights institutions. As a senior Commission official wrote in 2012 in his Institutional Report for the 2012 FIDE Conference, '[i]t cannot be in the interest of the EU's institutions to vindicate a power – and a corresponding responsibility – of human rights scrutiny for vast areas of Member State action … [which would also] risk exceeding the absorption capabilities of the Commission and the Court'.[77] For many observers, those considerations remain largely valid to date.

Accordingly, if the Commission's policy of selection and prioritisation of cases is not only reasonable but also inevitable, it may be worth considering whether possible breaches of fundamental rights should not have a higher rank in the list of priorities, or at the very least be explicitly mentioned in that list. Naturally, I am not referring to breaches in individual cases, of a limited scope, or having occurred in a very specific set of circumstances, since the national authorities themselves (national courts, ombudsmen, independent agencies etc) should be able to deal with them adequately. It may, however, be different where a national measure has the capacity to affect the rights of an indeterminate, or at any rate significant, number of individuals, especially where the national administrative and judicial authorities may (for legal or political reasons) be unable or unwilling to intervene. Those situations – provided the Member State's conduct falls within the scope of EU law[78] – may, arguably, be considered paradigmatic examples of the cases in which the Commission should carefully consider starting a procedure and, where serious and irreparable harm to individuals' rights may occur, also seek appropriate interim measures (suspensive injunctions coupled, as the case may be, with the threat of financial penalties) to prevent further damage. Moreover, this article has shown that some very recent cases (freshly decided or still pending before

[77] C Ladenburger, 'Protection of Fundamental Rights Post-Lisbon' (2012).

[78] A Richard, *Procédure en manquement d'état et protection des droits fondamentaux dans l'Union européene* (Brussels, Bruylant, 2021) argued that the scope of infringement proceedings should be extended in order to also cover breaches of fundamental rights that are unconnected with EU law. However, as the law stands, this suggestion appears to conflict with a number of constitutional principles of the EU legal order, *in primis* the principle of conferral.

the Court) may have the potential to provide the Commission with greater ability and interest to bring proceedings under Articles 258–60 TFEU for alleged breaches of fundamental rights.

It should not be overlooked that infringement proceedings have some specificities which makes them particularly apt and effective to tackle certain types of fundamental rights violations. In particular, they constitute the *only* judicial procedure in which the Court of Justice is directly called upon to determine whether a Member State's measure is consistent with the relevant provisions of EU law,[79] and the verdict of the Court in that regard is clear-cut, explicit and definitive. An adverse ruling by the Court under Article 258 TFEU compels the Member States in question to resolve the problem once and for all. As the Court has recently stated, 'the authorities of the Member State concerned participating in the exercise of legislative power are under a duty to amend national legislative provisions which have been the subject of a judgment establishing a failure to fulfil obligations so as to make them conform with the requirements of EU law'.[80]

The preliminary rulings procedure can also be used – and is indeed often used by litigants and national courts – to check whether national laws comply with EU law.[81] To that end, the two procedures are thus complementary. However, due to its structural limits, the preliminary ruling procedure cannot be considered a *perfect* substitute for infringement proceedings. In many cases, the Court has (or prefers to) leave the final assessment of the situation to the referring court, and cannot (or will not) rule directly on whether a given measure has actually infringed a fundamental right.[82] In addition, a ruling given under Article 267 TFEU may not have the (more extensive) consequences flowing from one given under Article 258 or 259 TFEU, since the main proceedings only concern the situation of the individuals who have brought those proceedings.[83] Furthermore, it is generally more difficult (and sometimes even impossible) for citizens and undertakings to challenge before domestic courts breaches of EU rules which do not confer subjective rights on individuals.[84] Last but not least, no judicial procedure enables the Court to impose financial penalties

[79] Similarly, K Lenaerts, 'The Rule of Law and the Coherence of the Judicial System of the European Union' (2007) *Common Market Law Review* 1625, 1636.

[80] CJEU, Case C-123/22 *Commission v Hungary (Reception of applicants for international protection II)* ECLI:EU:C:2024:493, para 57 and the case law cited.

[81] According to settled case law, although the Court does not, in a reference for a preliminary ruling, have jurisdiction to give a ruling on the compatibility of a national measure with EU law, it does have jurisdiction to supply the national court with a ruling on the interpretation of EU law so as to enable that court to determine whether such compatibility exists in order to decide the case before it. In practice, this means that, where a national court refers a question as to the validity of national legislation, the Court will rarely withhold its jurisdiction, and will typically reformulate the question to focus on the interpretation of EU law. This allows the Court simultaneously to assist the referring court in applying EU rules, while at the same time respect the formal allocation of jurisdiction between them. See, eg, CJEU, Joined Cases C-204/12 to C-208/12 *Essent Belgium* ECLI:EU:C:2014:2192, para 51 and the case law cited.

[82] See, eg, CJEU, Case C-633/22 *Real Madrid Club de Fútbol* ECLI:EU:C:2024:843.

[83] *cf* CJEU, Case C-178/97 *Banks and Others* Opinion of AG Ruiz-Jarabo Colomer, ECLI:EU:C:1998:571, paras 16–19.

[84] J Söderman, 'Le citoyen, l'administration et le droit communautaire' (1998) *Revue du Marché Unique Européen* 19, 35.

on Member States that do not comply with the consequences flowing from a judgment given by the Court under Article 267 TFEU.

Consequently, there appear to be good grounds to take the view that, if the Commission is truly determined to strengthen the application of the CFREU, including vis-à-vis the Member States when they implement EU law, it may need to consider stepping up its actions under Articles 258–60 TFEU in that field.

9

The Preliminary Ruling Procedure and Fundamental Rights: A Tale of Jurisdictional Supremacy

TAKIS TRIDIMAS

1. Introduction

This chapter engages with selective aspects of the relationship between fundamental rights and the preliminary reference procedure. What is the role of that procedure in fundamental rights cases? How do the two interact? Does Article 267 TFEU (Treaty on the Functioning of the European Union) lend itself to the vindication of rights, in particular, fundamental rights? The analysis proceeds as follows. It first explains the qualities of the reference procedure as a force of rights generation and the way it has facilitated the development of fundamental rights discourse. It then assesses the way it is perceived by the Court of Justice of the European Union (CJEU)[1] and the European Court of Human Rights (ECtHR). It continues by offering a tentative methodology for assessing whether preliminary references are an effective way of asserting fundamental rights. It finally provides some concluding remarks.

2. The Preliminary Reference Procedure as a Force of Rights Generation

By design, EU law is supported by a decentralised system of justice in which the courts of the Member States are the main fora for the assertion of EU rights. In this system, the preliminary reference procedure plays a pivotal role. It is the main gateway through which individuals may reach the CJEU. It is the only way in which they can assert

[1] Technically, under Article 19(1) TEU, the term 'Court of Justice of the European Union' includes both the Court of Justice and the General Court (GC). However, given that the GC is a newcomer to the preliminary reference jurisdiction, the term CJEU is used in this chapter with a narrower meaning to refer only to the European Court of Justice, the highest EU court.

rights against Member States or other individuals before the CJEU; and, owing to the restrictive standing under Article 263, fourth paragraph, TFEU, it is the main mechanism by which they can challenge the validity of EU acts. In historical perspective, the importance of the reference procedure can hardly be overestimated. It has been the main jurisdictional vehicle through which the constitutionalisation of EU law has been achieved. Its importance can be manifested in a threefold way: most foundational judgments, ie those that have defined the distinct qualities and the general principles of EU law, have been delivered in preliminary reference proceedings;[2] the procedure has served as the main jurisdictional platform for the development of EU fundamental rights; and, since the Treaty of Lisbon, it has enabled the building of a rich jurisprudence on the Charter. The above provide testament to the forces that have shaped EU law. The latter has been the result of litigation initiated by private parties much more than it has been the outcome of disputes involving sovereign or institutional actors. Article 267 TFEU and its predecessors are the key that unlocks the integration door.

Article 267 TFEU and its predecessors have been instrumental in building the corpus of EU fundamental rights. Starting with *Internationale Handelsgesellschaft*,[3] the case law progressively expanded the reach of EU fundamental rights to encompass not only EU measures but also national measures which implement or fall within the scope of EU law.[4] By positing that a national restriction on the fundamental freedoms cannot be justified unless it meets fundamental rights standards, the case law linked economic integration with the rule of law. The internal market is not just a free trade area but an economic system that adheres to liberal constitutional values. To start with, free movement ideals and fundamental rights protection were converging forces. EU fundamental rights placed the citizen at the heart of the internal market project and operated as a legitimating force. They also increased the scope of EU law. Since the justification analysis includes a fundamental standards inquiry, the broader the scope of the four freedoms, the greater the number of national measures that are subject to EU fundamental rights control. This strand of the case law reached its apex in the controversial *Carpenter* case.[5] However, since the CJEU recognised that fundamental rights play such an important role in EU law, it was a matter of time before they would come into a trajectory of conflict with free movement. *Schmidberger*[6] elevated fundamental rights to the apex of primary law norms. Since they emanate from

[2] See, eg, the principles of direct effect and primacy: CJEU, Case 26/62 *Van Gend en Loos* ECLI:EU:C:1963:1 and Case 6/64 *Costa v ENEL* ECLI:EU:C:1964:66.

[3] CJEU, Case 11/70 *Internationale Handelsgesellschaft* ECLI:EU:C:1970:114. In that case, the CJEU held that, despite the lack of a catalogue of EU fundamental rights, the EU is bound to respect fundamental rights as they emerge from the constitutional traditions common to the Member States, and therefore EU acts must comply with those rights.

[4] CJEU, Casec 5/88 *Wachauf v Bundesamt für Ernährung und Forstwirtschaft* ECLI:EU:C:1989:321; CJEU, Case C-260/89 *ERT* ECLI:EU:C:1991:254.

[5] CJEU, Case C-60/00 *Carpenter v Secretary of State for the Home Department* ECLI:EU:C:2002:434. In that case, the CJEU held that the deportation of a third country national who was the spouse of a British citizen on grounds of breach of UK immigration law was an unjustified restriction on the citizen's free movement rights since she was instrumental in enabling him to provide services to other EU States and breached his right to family life.

[6] CJEU, Case C-112/00 *Schmidberger, Internationale Transporte und Planzüge v Republik Österreich* ECLI:EU:C:2003:333: the CJEU held that the free movement of goods and the freedom of assembly and association are both fundamental rights under EU law and a balance must be drawn between the two. In the circumstances, it found the restriction imposed on the former to guarantee the latter to be proportionate and thus compatible with the EU Treaties.

the Treaties themselves they have, as a general rule, the same ranking with free movement rights and a balance has to be drawn between the two. *Schmidberger* and *Omega*[7] are key cases in many respects. The CJEU embraces national constitutional traditions; it projects itself as a one-stop shop for the protection of both inter-state economic rights and civil liberties; and, by so doing, it pre-empts Strasbourg. In parallel, the case law increased the range of fundamental rights protected by EU law and intensified the remedies available in case of violation.

All these developments occurred, first and foremost, via the judicial conversation facilitated by the preliminary reference procedure. This is not to say that the CJEU's rights jurisprudence has been built exclusively on Article 267 TFEU. The *Kadi*[8] litigation manifests the importance of the action for annulment for fundamental rights claims but does not question the centrality of the reference procedure as the main jurisdictional avenue for rights discourse, both in qualitative and quantitative terms. It is no accident that the overwhelming majority of the most important judgments on EU free movement rights, civil liberties, social rights, and general principles of EU law have been the result of preliminary references. By contrast, the jurisdictional prompt for some systemic principles of EU law, such as autonomy and institutional balance, has been direct actions.[9] This is because they pertain directly to governance, inter-institutional relations, and the interaction between the Union and the Member States. Where systemic principles affect rights, the preliminary reference procedure becomes the main playground for their development. Testament to this is provided by the rich case law on mutual trust and mutual recognition in the field of freedom, security and justice.

As a jurisdictional mechanism, the preliminary reference procedure is substance agnostic. It enables the elevation of a dispute to the CJEU both by private and state actors and does not commit to a specific interpretation of the law. It presents however some distinct elements which make it particularly suitable to rights-generation.

First, the dispute arises in a concrete situation where it is claimed that the legal position of a private party is affected. The *lis* is defined by individuals and national courts. These actors are in a much better position (and much more willing) to provide the raw material for rights-generation than political institutions, ie the Member States and the EU bodies. National agencies have little incentive to create more EU rights against themselves and the Commission could only attempt to do so as a proxy. This entails serious limitations: it is subject to resource constraints; it has discretion which rights to fight for, which it exercises on the basis of many considerations; and, most importantly, it lacks information. Proxy litigation cannot be a substitute for the initiation of disputes by those who can claim a right and show injustice on specific facts.

Second, the reference procedure vests EU law with jurisdictional proximity to the citizen. One of the most persuasive reasons given by the CJEU in *Van Gend en Loos*

[7] CJEU, Case C-36/02 *Omega Spielhallen- und Automatenaufstellungs-GmbH v Oberbürgermeisterin der Bundesstadt Bonn* ECLI:EU:C:2004:614. In that case, the CJEU found that German law which prohibited laser games simulating homicide entailed a restriction on the freedom to provide services but was justifed by the need to respect human dignity as understood in the German Basic Law.

[8] CJEU, Joined Cases C-402/05 P and C-415/05 P *Kadi & Al Barakaat International Foundation v Council and Commission* ECLI:EU:C:2008:461; and on appeal Joined Cases C-584/10 P, C-593/10 P and C-595/10 P *Commission v Kadi* ECLI:EU:C:2013:518.

[9] The same could perhaps be said about the emerging principle of solidarity.

in support of direct effect was Article 177 EEC (now Article 267 TFEU). In the words of the Court,[10]

> … the task assigned to the Court of Justice under Article 177, the object of which is to secure uniform interpretation of the Treaty by national courts and tribunals, confirms that the states have acknowledged that Community law has an authority which can be invoked by their nationals before those courts and tribunals.

It is in fact somewhat strange that the Court saw the preliminary reference only as an additional argument in support of direct effect. It is one of the most potent ones. Even though a reference can be made on the interpretation or validity of rules which are not directly effective, the existence of the procedure assumes the possibility of invocation of EU law before a national court. By elevating every national court into an EU court, it grants to EU law an immediacy that is normally reserved to national law. It is, in itself, a process geared towards the creation of rights.

Third, the preliminary reference jurisdiction has a propagating effect enabling EU law to be diffused within the national legal systems. By making every national court a court of EU law, it weaves Union law into the national legal system. It can be applied by any court having jurisdiction and it is assimilated into the system of national norms that make the applicable law in the dispute.

Article 267 has in-built faculties that give it a bias in favour of rights-generation: These are jurisdictional proximity to the citizen, immediacy in the invocation of EU law, and facilitation of fusion of EU rules in the national legal system. By enabling the invocation of EU provisions by private actors before judicial fora which are proximate to them, it makes it much more likely that EU law will be invoked and encourages resolution of disputes pertaining to EU law through the legal and not just the political process. Adjudication means that uncertainties about the meaning and scope of the Treaties are to be resolved in cases initiated by citizens through a rational process of argumentation and not only by politicians at the negotiating table. Seen in that perspective, it is no surprise that the reference procedure has been so pivotal to the establishment of fundamental rights and in legitimising the integration process.

In short, the preliminary reference has been the most precious piece of EU law hardware. Had the application of EU law been left only to the forms of direct action envisaged in the Treaties, its development would have been the result of a conversation among the Member States and the EU institutions, ie political actors representing different forms of public power.

3. The Perception of the CJEU

The CJEU treats the preliminary reference procedure as the crown jewel of the judicial protection system. By viewing it as an integral part of the right to judicial protection, it elevates it to a principle that subsists almost above the text of the founding treaties. The procedure has some distinct features.

[10] CJEU, Case 26/62 *Van Gend en Loos* (see n 2 above), para 12.

It is defined overwhelmingly in functional terms, its purpose being to ensure the uniform interpretation of EU law. The CJEU will accept jurisdiction to answer the question referred if it considers that failing to do so might prejudice the uniform interpretation of EU law. This functionalist approach makes for a very wide jurisdictional remit.[11] A striking example is provided by *Komstroy* discussed below. The preliminary reference jurisdiction is omni-present: it cannot be excluded by treaty silence; it is available even where the Treaties appear to exclude it; and it has a foreclosure effect in that dispute resolution mechanisms which threaten it cannot be accepted in the EU law universe.

In *Busseni*,[12] the CJEU held that, even though, in contrast to Article 177 EEC (now Article 267 TFEU), Article 41 European Coal and Steel Community Treaty (ECSC) only granted the Court jurisdiction to give preliminary rulings on validity and not on interpretation, the Court also has jurisdiction to give rulings on the interpretation of the ECSC Treaty. Otherwise, the objectives and the coherence of the Treaties would suffer.[13]

In Opinion 1/09,[14] foreclosure of the preliminary reference procedure rendered a draft agreement creating a unified pan-European patent litigation system incompatible with EU law. The draft agreement established a patents court which was bound to apply EU law and had the power and, in certain cases, the obligation to make references to the CJEU. The Court held that the draft agreement breached the integrity of the preliminary reference procedure and thus the autonomy of EU law because, within the limits of the jurisdiction, the patents court would be the only court capable of conversing with the CJEU to the exclusion of the ordinary courts of the Member States. The CJEU held that national courts are closely involved in the protection of individual rights conferred by EU law and their role within the preliminary reference system is 'indispensable to the preservation of the very nature of the law established by the Treaties'.[15] Opinion 1/09 suggests that the preliminary reference dialogue has an intimacy where there is little space for other interlocutors and, arguably, adopts a broader concept of autonomy than any other ruling. In contrast to other cases where the CJEU objected to dispute resolution mechanisms provided by international treaties,[16] in Opinion 1/09 the concern was not any direct curtailment to the jurisdiction of the CJEU but rather the jurisdiction of the national courts as the ordinary courts of EU law.

Building on Opinion 2/13,[17] *Achmea*[18] held that investor-state arbitration clauses in intra-EU Bilateral Investment Treaties (BITs) are incompatible with EU law. First, it held that arbitration tribunals set up by a BIT are not part of the judicial system of

[11] See, eg, CJEU, Case C-221/88 *ECSC v Busseni* ECLI:EU:C:1990:84; CJEU, Case C-741/19 *Republic of Moldova v Komstroy LLC* ECLI:EU:C:2021:655; both discussed below.

[12] CJEU, Case C-221/88 *ECSC v Busseni* (see n 11 above).

[13] ibid, para 16.

[14] CJEU, *Opinion 1/09 on the draft Agreement establishing a European and Community Patents Court* ECLI:EU:C:2011:123.

[15] ibid, para 84.

[16] See, eg, CJEU, *Opinion 1/91 on the draft EEA Agreement* ECLI:EU:C:1991:490.

[17] CJEU, *Opinion 2/13 on the Accession of the European Union to the ECHR* ECLI:EU:C:2014:2454. In its controversial ruling, the CJEU found the draft agreement on the accession of the EU to the Council of Europe to be incompatible with the EU Treaties because the role of the ECtHR under the draft agreement breached the autonomy of EU law and the exclusivity of the jurisdiction of the CJEU under Article 344 TFEU. This provision commits Member States not to submit a dispute concerning the interpretation or application of the EU Treaties to any method of settlement other than those provided for therein.

[18] CJEU, Case C-284/16 *Slovak Republic v Achmea* ECLI:EU:C:2018:158.

the contracting Member States and therefore cannot make a preliminary reference. Second, it found that there were not sufficient mechanisms to ensure that an arbitral award delivered by the investment arbitration tribunal would be subject to review by a Member State court so that questions of EU could be referred. The CJEU concluded that the possibility of submitting disputes pertaining to the interpretation of EU law to a body which is not part of the judicial system of the EU called into question not only the principle of mutual trust between the Member States but also the preservation of the particular nature of the law which is ensured by the preliminary ruling procedure. It was therefore incompatible with the principle of sincere cooperation.[19]

The activist use of Article 267 TFEU reached its apex in *Rosneft*.[20] Under Article 24(1) of the Treaty on European Union (TEU) and Article 275 TFEU, the CJEU does not have jurisdiction with respect to provisions on the Common Foreign and Security Policy (CFSP) of the EU or acts adopted on their basis, subject to two exceptions. It can monitor compliance with Article 40 TEU; and it can also rule on proceedings 'brought in accordance with the conditions laid down in the fourth paragraph of Article 263' TFEU, reviewing the legality of Council decisions imposing restrictive measures on individuals (Article 275 TFEU, second paragraph). Even though the above proviso appears to limit the Court's jurisdiction to direct actions only, in *Rosneft* the CJEU held that it has jurisdiction to examine the validity of restrictive measures in cases brought before it by a reference for a preliminary ruling.

The CJEU reasoned that direct actions and preliminary references establish a bifurcated model of jurisdiction intended to provide a complete system of legal remedies and procedures. The availability of the preliminary reference procedure as a means of review is 'an essential characteristic' of the EU system for judicial protection which extends to the review of legality of economic sanctions.[21] The Court held that neither the TEU nor the TFEU indicates that an action for annulment under Article 263 TFEU is the sole means for reviewing the legality of decisions providing for restrictive measures against individuals to the exclusion of a preliminary reference.[22] In the Court's reasoning, the reference in Article 24(1) TEU to the second paragraph of Article 275 TFEU serves to determine not the type of procedure under which the Court may review the legality of certain decisions, but rather the type of decisions whose legality may be reviewed, within any procedure that has as its aim such a review of legality.[23] This however pays lip service to the express language of Article 275 TFEU and finds only limited support, if any, in the text of Article 24(1) TEU.

The CJEU invoked an argument based on normative hierarchy. Referring to the values clause of Article 2 TEU, it stated that the very existence of effective judicial review is of the essence of the rule of law.[24] While Article 47 of the Charter cannot confer jurisdiction where the Treaties exclude it, the principle of effective judicial protection

[19] ibid, para 58.
[20] CJEU, Case C-72/15 *The Queen, on the application of PJSC Rosneft Oil Company v Her Majesty's Treasury* ECLI:EU:C:2017:236.
[21] ibid, para 69.
[22] ibid, para 70.
[23] ibid.
[24] ibid, para 73.

requires an asphyxiatingly narrow interpretation of the exclusion of the Court's jurisdiction in the field of the CFSP.[25]

Rosneft appears to draw a hierarchy between the preliminary reference procedure and direct actions. Whilst access to the Court via direct action can be limited, as is the case in relation to non-privileged applicants under Article 263TFEU, paragraph 4, indirect access via the preliminary reference procedure cannot be curtailed even in the presence of alternative routes to the Court. It is essentially a ruling of constitutional design which projects a certain conception of the EU system of judicial protection.

Rosneft is limited to the procedural plane. The CJEU does not extend its powers over new fields of Union law since a preliminary ruling is possible only where the Court has jurisdiction *ratione materiae* to rule on the validity of EU acts under Article 24(1) TEU and Article 275, second paragraph, TFEU. In other words, the ruling does not grant the Court jurisdiction over acts other than those submitted to it under the Treaties but expands the way they can be challenged.[26] It may be said that expanding the means of challenge interferes less with the powers of the other branches of government than expanding the acts that can be challenged, as was the case in *les Verts*[27] and *Kadi*,[28] or broadening the class of persons who can mount a challenge, as was the case in *Chernobyl*.[29] However, questions concerning what can be reviewed, how it can be reviewed, and who can initiate review are all questions of constitutional design which set up a system of checks and balances and can affect substantive outcomes. In any event, activism is not limited to process. In *KS and KD v Council*,[30] the CJEU held that, in CFSP, it has jurisdiction not only in situations that fall within one of the two exceptions provided for in Article 24(1) TEU, second subparagraph, and Article 275 TFEU but also in relation to the acts and omissions which 'are not directly related to the political or strategic choices' made by the institutions, and bodies in the context of the CFSP.[31]

In a nutshell, the CJEU has not only empirically built a formidable fundamental rights case law on the basis of its preliminary reference jurisdiction but it has empowered that jurisdiction. It views the procedure itself as an integral part of the right to judicial protection elevating it to the very top of the normative hierarchy of the Treaties.

4. The Strasbourg Court: An Uninvited but Welcome Guest

The Strasbourg Court has interjected as an important interlocutor in the preliminary reference procedure seeking to advance its effectiveness. Failure to make a reference is relevant in two respects. It may be a breach of Article 6(1) of the Convention for the

[25] ibid, para 74.

[26] Thus the Court only held the question referred admissible insofar as they related to the validity of restrictive measures against individuals. By contrast, it rejected as inadmissible questions pertaining to the validity of measures of general application.

[27] CJEU, Case 294/83 *Partie Ecologiste "Les Verts" v European Parliament* ECLI:EU:C:1986:166.

[28] ibid.

[29] CJEU, Case C-70/88 *Parliament v Council (Chernobyl case)* ECLI:EU:C:1990:217.

[30] CJEU, Joined Cases C-29/22 P and C-44/22 P *KS and KD v Council* ECLI:EU:C:2024:725.

[31] ibid, paras 116–17.

Protection of Human Rights and Fundamental Freedoms (ECHR) and it may dislodge the *Bosphorus* presumption.[32]

4.1. Article 6(1) ECHR

Compliance with Article 6(1) ECHR requires a national court to provide reasons for its judgment. In *Ullens de Schooten et Rezabek v Belgium*[33] and *Vergauwen and Others v Belgium*,[34] the ECtHR held that, as part of that requirement, a national court against whose decisions there is no judicial remedy has an obligation to justify its refusal to make a preliminary reference.[35] It must state the reasons why it considers that the question is not relevant, or that the provision of EU law in question has already been interpreted by the CJEU, or that the correct application of EU law is so obvious that it leaves no room for reasonable doubt.[36] This opens the door for the engagement of the ECtHR with the *CILFIT* criteria[37] although such engagement can be expected to be light touch. The ECtHR sees as its task to verify thoroughly whether reasons for refusal have been given but not to examine any errors that might have been committed by the domestic court in interpreting and applying the law.[38] In *Ullens de Schooten*, it was content to accept that the national courts had considered the points of EU law raised and did not engage with the applicants' arguments trying to show that their interpretation of EU law was erroneous.[39] What Strasbourg requires is reassurance that the national court has engaged with, and not ignored, EU law. Still, the decision between giving no reasons and giving bad ones may, in extreme cases, be difficult to make.

The importance of the preliminary reference procedure for the protection of fundamental rights is aptly demonstrated by *Georgiou v Greece*.[40] The president of the Greek Statistical Authority (ELSTAT) has been convicted for breach of duty for transmitting data concerning the state deficit to Eurostat without receiving the consent of ELSTAT as required by Greek law. In challenging his conviction, he had requested the Court of Cassation to make a preliminary reference but the court rejected his appeal without

[32] ECtHR, App no 45036/98 *Bosphorus Hava Yollari Turizm VE Ticaret Anonim Şirketi v Ireland* ECLI:CE:ECHR:2005:0630JUD004503698.

[33] ECtHR, App nos 3989/07 and 38353/07 *Ullens de Schooten et Rezabek v Belgium* ECLI:CE:ECHR:2011:0920JUD000398907.

[34] ECtHR, App no 4832/04 *Vergauwen and Others v Belgium* ECLI:CE:ECHR:2012:0410DEC000483204.

[35] It is not impossible that the refusal to make a reference by a lower national court may also be in breach of the Convention: see ECtHR, App nos 3989/07 and 38353/07 *Ullens de Schooten et Rezabek* (see n 33 above), para 59.

[36] ibid, para 62; ECtHR, App no 4832/04 *Vergaugen* (see n 34 above), para 90.

[37] CJEU, Case 283/81 *Srl. CILFIT and Lanificio di Gavardo Spa v Ministry of Health* ECLI:EU:C:1982:335.

[38] ECtHR, App nos 3989/07 and 38353/07 *Ullens de Schooten et Rezabek* (see n 33 above), para 61; ECtHR, App no 4832/04 *Vergaugen* (see n 34 above), para 89.

[39] ibid, para 66.

[40] ECtHR, App no 57378/18 *Georgiou v Greece* ECLI:CE:ECHR:2023:0314JUD005737818. For comments, see, among others, S Lindroos-Hovinheimo, 'ECtHR finds violation of the right to fair trial when national court does not seek preliminary ruling from the CJEU' (*European Law Blog*, 28 March 2023) www.europeanlawblog.eu/pub/ecthr-finds-violation-of-the-right-to-fair-trial-when-national-court-does-not-seek-preliminary-ruling-from-the-cjeu/release/1 accessed 3 September 2025.

making a reference and without giving any reasons for refusing to do so. The ECtHR found that the Court of Cassation's failure to provide any reasons why it considered that the question raised by him did not merit reference to the CJEU was a violation of Article 6(1) ECHR.[41] It could not be established from the content and reasoning of its judgment 'whether the question was considered irrelevant, whether it was viewed as relating to a provision that was clear or had already been interpreted by the CJEU, or whether it was simply ignored'.[42]

The most striking aspect of *Georgiou* is that the ECtHR was prescriptive in relation to remedies transitioning from guidance to command. In *Ullens de Schooten* and in *Vergauwen* the Court had found that reasons for refusal to refer had been given. In *Dhahbi*[43] it had recorded a violation of Article 6(1) ECHR by the Italian Court of Cassation for failure to give reasons and also of Article 14 ECHR and proceeded to award damages for the latter. It did not pronounce on remedy for breach of Article 6(1) ECHR. In *Georgiou*, the applicant had not claimed damages but asked for the domestic proceedings to be reopened. The ECtHR obliged stating that although, in principle, it is not its task to prescribe exactly how a State should put an end to a breach,

> restoration of 'the closest possible situation to that which would have existed if the breach in question had not occurred' … would consist, in the present case, in taking measures to ensure that the domestic proceedings are reopened, if requested, so that the request for a preliminary reference is examined by the Court of Cassation.[44]

This prescriptive, but in the circumstances entirely fair, position opens the road for upending the finality of final supreme court judgments. Judicial pronouncements that manifestly ignore EU process are compromised and at risk. *Georgiou* also has implications for EU remedies. It strengthens the view that, as a matter of EU law, the failure of a national court covered by the third paragraph of Article 267 TFEU to give any reasons for refusing to make a reference is a manifest breach which could potentially give rise to liability under *Köbler*.[45] Second, it means that the unreasoned refusal to make a reference is a breach of Article 47 of the Charter. This in turn places the Member State in question under an obligation to provide an effective remedy for the breach. It is for the national authorities to do so but such remedy must meet the requirements of equivalence and effectiveness.[46] *Georgiou* suggests that, in certain cases, the requirement of effectiveness may impose on the Member States the duty to reopen judicial proceedings. In this respect, it also lends a supporting hand to CJEU case law which, under certain

[41] ECtHR, App no 57378/18 *Georgiou* (see n 40 above), para 25.

[42] ibid, para 25.

[43] ECtHR, App no 17120/09 *Dhahbi v Italy* ECLI:CE:ECHR:2014:0408JUD001712009.

[44] ECtHR, App no 57378/18 *Georgiou v Greece* ECLI:CE:ECHR:2023:0314JUD005737818, para 33.

[45] CJEU, Case C-224/01 *Köbler v Austria* ECLI:EU:C:2003:513.

[46] According to the case law, where there are no specific EU rules, the protection of EU rights is subject to the national rules of procedure and remedies provided that those rules treat EU rights no less favourably than equivalent national rights (principle of equivalence) and, in any event, do not make their invocation excessively difficult or virtually impossible (principle of effectiveness): see CJEU, Case 33/76 *Rewe v Landwirtschaftskammer für das Saarland* ECLI:EU:C:1976:188; CJEU, Case 45/76 *Comet v Productschap voor Siergewassen* ECLI:EU:C:1976:191.

circumstances, requires national authorities to revisit final decisions if they have been taken in breach of EU law.[47]

The ECtHR has also been helpful in other ways. The making of a reference adds to the duration of the proceedings and there is at least anecdotal evidence to suggest that some national judges consider this to be a material factor in deciding whether to make a reference.[48] In *Pafitis v Greece*,[49] the ECtHR gave the CJEU the benefit of the doubt. In assessing whether the length of civil proceedings before the Greek courts was contrary to Article 6(1) ECHR, it did not take into account the time during which the proceedings were stayed pending a preliminary reference. As a result of it, the proceedings were prolonged by two years and seven months.[50] The ECtHR stated that, even though that period 'may at first sight appear relatively long, to take it into account would adversely affect the system instituted by Article 177 EEC [now Article 234 TFEU] and work against the aim pursued in substance in that Article.'[51]

It may not go unnoticed that both cases where the ECtHR found a violation of Article 6(1) ECHR for complete failure to consider the possibility of a reference (*Dhahbi* and *Georgiou*) involved national courts of cassation which traditionally are less familiar and less inclined to engage with EU law than administrative court. Also, in both cases, the litigants concerned had requested a reference to be made. Failure by a litigant to request a reference would make it more difficult for Strasbourg to find a violation but would not necessarily exclude it.

4.2. The Bosphorus Presumption

The ECtHR has also had the opportunity to consider their preliminary reference procedure in the context of the application of the *Bosphorus*[52] presumption. This posits that, since the EU offers equivalent protection of fundamental rights to that provided by the Convention, the ECtHR will only exceptionally intervene if, in the circumstances of a specific case, the protection of Convention rights is 'manifestly deficient'. The application of the presumption rests on two conditions, namely, 'the absence of any margin of manoeuvre on the part of the domestic authorities and the deployment of the full potential of the supervisory mechanism provided for by European Union law.'[53] The second condition means that, for the presumption to apply, the EU judicial control mechanisms must be 'fully brought into play'.[54] Thus,

[47] See, CJEU, Case C-453/00 *Kühne & Heitz NV v Productschap voor Pluimvee en Eieren* ECLI:EU:C:2004:17, and its progeny.

[48] This is a point repeatedly made extrajudicially by senior national judges from various Member States. See also T Tridimas, 'Knocking on Heaven's Door: Fragmentation, Efficiency and Defiance in the Preliminary Reference Procedure' (2003) 40 *Common Market Law Review* 9, 17 from which the points made here are taken.

[49] ECtHR, App no 20323/92 *Pafitis v Greece* ECLI:CE:ECHR:1998:0226JUD002032392.

[50] CJEU, Case C-441/93 *Pafitis v Trapeza Kentrikis Ellados AE* ECLI:EU:C:1996:92. The decision to make a reference was taken on 3 August 1993 and the ECJ delivered its judgment on 12 March 1996.

[51] Ibid, para 95.

[52] ECtHR, App no 45036/98 *Bosphorus* (see n 32 above).

[53] ECtHR, App no 17502/07 *Avotiņš v Latvia*, ECLI:CE:ECHR:2016:0523JUD001750207, para 105; ECtHR, App no 12323/11 *Michaud v France* ECLI:CE:ECHR:2012:1206JUD001232311, para 113–15.

[54] ibid, para 114.

the ECtHR will examine whether the national court which heard the applicant's claim utilised the preliminary reference procedure. In *Michaud*,[55] the failure of the French *Conseil d'Etat* to make a reference led the ECtHR to dislodge the presumption and proceed to a full examination of whether the requirements of Article 8 ECHR had been met by France.

There are a number of noteworthy aspects. In the eyes of Strasbourg, the use of the preliminary reference procedure carries important weight. Nonetheless, failure to make a reference does not necessarily lead to the presumption being dislodged. The ECtHR rejects 'excessive formalism': there is no need for a reference where 'no genuine and serious issue arises with regard to the protection of fundamental rights by EU law, or those in which the CJEU has already stated precisely how the applicable provisions of EU law should be interpreted in a manner compatible with fundamental rights'.[56] The ECtHR therefore gives itself a good margin of discretion to intervene and may enter into a determination of EU law matters, including whether there is a genuine and serious human rights issue under EU law, and what exactly has or has not been decided by the CJEU in earlier cases.

In *Avotiņš*, the ECtHR stated that its review of the use of preliminary reference procedure for the purposes of deciding whether Article 6(1) ECHR has been violated is different from its review for the purposes of deciding whether the *Bosphorus* presumption applies. In the first case, it determines whether the refusal to make a reference is in itself a violation of Article 6(1) ECHR and, in so doing, it takes into account the approach already established by the case law of the CJEU.[57] In the second case, it examines the decision not to request a preliminary ruling as part of its overall assessment of the degree of protection of fundamental rights afforded by EU law.[58] Whilst this explains the different purposes of each review, it does not tell us much as to how the review differs in substance. In *Avotiņš*, it stated that, whether the failure of the national court to make a reference is such as to preclude the application of the presumption 'should be assessed in the light of the specific circumstances of each case'.[59] But this is unhelpful. Clearly, the same applies in determining whether the refusal to make a reference is unreasoned and therefore amounts to a violation of Article 6(1) ECHR. That must also be determined in the light of the specific circumstances of each case. It appears that what the ECtHR meant is that the review carried out in the context of the *Bosphorus* presumption should be more intrusive. The few cases decided suggest that the ECtHR wishes to make sure that the presumption is limited to EU action and thus that the State took the steps to comply with EU law by utilising the preliminary reference procedure. In *Avotiņš* the ECtHR noted that the applicant had not requested a preliminary reference to be made nor advanced any arguments pertaining to the compatibility of the EU rules applicable with EU law such as to warrant a finding that a reference should have been made.[60]

[55] ibid.
[56] ECtHR, App no 17502/07 *Avotiņš v Latvia* (see n 53 above), para 109.
[57] ibid, para 110.
[58] ibid.
[59] ibid, para 111.
[60] ibid.

There is no doubt that the ECtHR case law encourages the use of the preliminary reference procedure. This is particularly important in the area of freedom, security and justice in relation to which, rightly, the ECtHR has been critical of the use of the mutual recognition model. Under EU law, mutual trust means that, when implementing EU law, the Member States may be required to presume that fundamental rights have been observed by the other Member States, so that, save in exceptional cases, they may not check whether that other Member State has actually, in a specific case, observed them.[61] According to the ECtHR, such limitation may cross the line. It must verify that the mutual-recognition principle 'is not applied automatically and mechanically … to the detriment of fundamental rights'.[62]

This raises a potential conflict: a preliminary reference might not be enough to absolve the State from the obligation to comply with Convention standards.[63] Be this as it may, the Strasbourg jurisprudence has strengthened the CJEU's vision of the preliminary reference procedure as a fundamental right in itself.

5. Is the Preliminary Reference an Effective Way of Protecting Fundamental Rights?

The previous sections examined the distinct qualities of the preliminary reference procedure, its historical role as a facilitator of fundamental rights protection and its role in the system of judicial protection as perceived by the CJEU and the ECtHR. There is no doubt that, in an historical perspective, it has been pivotal in facilitating the development of EU fundamental rights and that both the CJEU and the ECtHR view it as an integral part of the right to judicial protection. But how effective is Article 267 TFEU as a procedural mechanism for the purposes of fundamental rights adjudication? Assessing its effectiveness is not an easy task. It first raises a number of methodological questions. What criteria should be used to make the assessment? When can the protection of fundamental rights be said to be effective? When is a jurisdictional rule suitable for the assertion of rights? What are the standards of comparison? This section engages selectively with some of these questions.

The following criteria, which are both procedural and substantive, offer a possible methodology for assessing whether the preliminary reference procedure is effective:

(1) access to justice;
(2) procedural fairness;
(3) jurisdictional remit;
(4) suitability to addressing issues of principle;

[61] CJEU, *Opinion 2/13 on the Accession of the European Union to the ECHR* (see n 17 above), para 192; CJEU, Case C-216/18 PPU *LM*, ECLI:EU:C:2018:586 para 37.

[62] ECtHR, App no 17502/07 *Avotiņš v Latvia* (see n 53 above), para 116.

[63] See also ECtHR, App no 21055/11 *Pirozzi v Belgium* ECLI:CE:ECHR:2018:0417JUD002105511. For a case where the ECtHR found that there existed a manifest deficiency in the protection of fundamental rights such as to rebut the presumption of equivalent protection and a national authority executing a EAW ought not to have relied solely on the statements made by the requesting State, see, ECtHR, App nos 40324/16 and 12623/17 *Bivolaru and Moldovan v France* ECLI:CE:ECHR:2021:0325JUD004032416, para 126.

(5) duration of proceedings;
(6) compliance and enforceability.

A number of disclaimers must be made. The above list is not exhaustive. Also, the above criteria go some way but do not capture the universe of effectiveness. The term effectiveness should be understood in functional terms, echoing the classic formula of the Strasbourg jurisprudence. It means that rights must be 'practical and effective, not theoretical and illusory'.[64] Therefore, whether Article 267 TFEU can guarantee effective protection of rights[65] cannot be determined solely by reference to the letter of the law and the way it has been interpreted by the CJEU but must also take into account its practical application by the Court (eg, the duration of proceedings), the way Article 267 TFEU is used by national courts, and the obstacles arising in its practical application across the EU. The above criteria capture some, but not all, of these aspects.

It should also be borne in mind that focusing only on fundamental rights eschews a wider enquiry, which is more appropriate. The judicial process must not only afford an effective opportunity to citizens to uphold their rights but also facilitate the representation of all interested parties, uphold the public interest, and respect the powers of public bodies. A balanced assessment therefore requires an evaluation of its impact on all countervailing interests involved. The question of whether Article 267 TFEU is an effective way of asserting rights has to be seen in the wider context of courts as guarantors of the rule of law.

In EU law, there is an added dimension. Which fundamental rights are we concerned with? Those protected by the EU or those protected by national laws? Whilst in most cases they align, the expansion of EU competence and the growth of EU legislation, coupled with the constraints imposed by the principle of primacy, have brought the two sets of rights into a trajectory of conflict. Cases such as *Melloni*,[66] *NS*,[67] and *Tarrico*[68] illustrate that the level of protection guaranteed by the EU may fall short of the level of protection demanded by national law; and it will be recalled that, in *Avotiņš*, the ECtHR rang a loud bell of caution warning national courts not to abjure fundamental rights control in the name of the principle of mutual recognition. Is the preliminary mechanism better placed to uphold EU rather than national rights? The answer is in the negative. The reference procedure, being substance-agnostic, provides a mechanism for airing such conflicts. By offering the opportunity to both institutional and private actors

[64] See, eg, ECtHR, App no 12625/17 *Shahzad v Hungary* ECLI:CE:ECHR:2021:0708JUD001262517, para 50 (in relation to the prohibition of collective expulsion, Article 4 of Protocol No 4); ECtHR, App no 14038/88 *Soering v United Kingdom* ECLI:CE:ECHR:1989:0707JUD001403888, para 87 (Article 3 ECHR).

[65] The criteria outlined above are relevant in assessing the efficacy of Article 267 TFEU in relation to the invocation of all rights whether they are perceived as fundamental or not. There are many 'lesser' rights which may not be considered to be fundamental in the sense that they are of lesser importance or in the sense that they are not guaranteed by rules of constitutional status and thus do not enjoy entrenched protection but which must also be safeguarded.

[66] CJEU, Case C-399/11 *Melloni* ECLI:EU:C:2013:107.

[67] CJEU, Joined Cases C-411/10 and C-493/10 *NS v Secretary of State for the Home Department* ECLI:EU:C:2011:865.

[68] CJEU, Case C-105/14 *Taricco* ECLI:EU:C:2015:555; cp its aftermath: CJEU, Case C-42/17, *MAS* ECLI:EU:C:2017:93, and now CJEU, Case C-107/23 PPU *Lin* ECLI:EU:C:2023:606.

to participate, it facilitates a dialectical process through which the CJEU pursues multidimensional balancing.[69]

A further dimension of effectiveness is the comparative one. What are possible alternative mechanisms to which we might compare the preliminary reference procedure? One could envisage various alternatives. They include direct proceedings, a system of subsidiary jurisdiction, such as that exercised by the ECtHR, a system under which the CJEU exercises appellate jurisdiction over national courts of final instance, or even a tribunal standing alongside the CJEU which could determine disputes between the CJEU and national supreme courts.[70] Suffice it to say here that there are established paths of dependency which, in practical terms, would make it next to impossible to introduce such alternative systems. Also, any attempt to determine in the abstract and on the basis of counter factual-scenarios the comparative advantages and disadvantages of the preliminary reference vis-à-vis alternatives would be subject to many pitfalls.

We will examine in brief each of the criteria stated above.

5.1. Access

Although access to the CJEU via Article 267 TFEU is indirect in that proceedings have to be initiated before a national court, it is not difficult. The constituency is broad in that the CJEU can converse with any court or tribunal, no matter how junior. In fact, one of the most empowering features of the procedure is that it is highly democratic. Any national court, no matter how low it stands in the national judicial system, can converse with the CJEU. This is arguably the most instrumental aspect of the procedure. Many seminal judgments, such as *Van Gend en Loos*,[71] *Costa v ENEL*,[72] *Carpenter*,[73] and *Zambrano*,[74] resulted from references made by tribunals standing at the bottom of the hierarchy. Along with being significant for the making of law, such empowerment entails a transfer of political power within the domestic judiciary: courts that stand low in the national hierarchy can challenge rulings of higher courts by making references. Sometimes, references manifest an underlying judicial competition even among senior national courts.[75] The ability of any court to make a reference also functions as a corrective mechanism. It limits the legal effects of the unjustified refusal of a national court of last instance to make a reference in circumstances where

[69] This refers to the fact that the EU judiciary has to engage in a composite conciliation exercise drawing a balance between two competing interests (eg, a fundamental right and a public interest) and also, at the same time, deciding whether that balance, or how much of it, has to be settled at EU level or be left to the discretion of national institutional actors. For a discussion, see T Tridimas, 'Wreaking the Wrongs: Balancing Rights and the Public Interest the EU Way' (2023) 29 *The Columbia Journal of European Law* 185.

[70] For a suggestion along those lines (although not as a substitute to preliminary references), see JHH Weiler and D Sarmiento, 'The EU Judiciary after Weiss – Proposing a New Mixed Chamber of the Court of Justice' (*EU Law Live*, 1 June 2020) https://eulawlive.com/app/uploads/j-h-h-weiler-and-daniel-sarmiento.pdf accessed 3 September 2025.

[71] Case 26/62 *Van Gend en Loos* ECLI:EU:C:1963:1.

[72] Case 6/64 *Costa v ENEL* ECLI:EU:C:1964:66.

[73] CJEU, Case C-60/00 *Carpenter v Secretary of State for the Home Department* ECLI:EU:C:2002:434.

[74] CJEU, Case C-34/09 *Zambrano* ECLI:EU:C:2011:124.

[75] Consider the juxtaposition between the *Conseil d'Etat* and the *Conseil Constitutionnel* in CJEU, Case C-188/10 *Melki* ECLI:EU:C:2010:363.

it is under an obligation to do so. The question that was not referred may reach the CJEU in a subsequent case via a reference made by a lower national court.[76]

The CJEU is a welcoming court also in other respects. It has understood its jurisdiction very widely in terms of the legal issues that may be the subject matter of a reference and the circumstances under which the question is asked. It is prepared to entertain a reference even where the EU provision whose interpretation is requested does not apply by virtue of EU law but by virtue of national law;[77] and it can accept the reference, if it so wishes, even if the litigation before the national court appears staged to procure a reference.[78]

The main limitations on access are the following: the decision on whether and what to refer are matters of the national court; whether a person has standing to initiate litigation depending on national law; and legal aid is a matter of national law. Although these may create real obstacles, the case law does its best to overcome them by specifying the expectations of the principle of primacy and by recourse to the principles of equivalence and effectiveness.[79] A key judgment for access to justice is the *Portuguese judges* case.[80] Its importance goes beyond the principle of judicial independence for which the case is well known. It establishes, more generally, that systemic barriers to invoking EU rights are incompatible with the rule of law as an EU value. Such barriers that would fall short of the obligations of Member States to ensure effective remedies for the protection of EU rights under Article 19TEU, paragraph 1, would include, for example, a national law that required high fees as a condition of bringing administrative proceedings or a civil action.

The establishment of locus standi before a national court to assert an EU right is a matter for national law to decide subject to the requirements of equivalence and effectiveness. There is, in fact, limited case law in this area but the fundamental message is that a private party must, in any event, have the opportunity to claim breach of its EU rights before a national court. In some cases, standing may be treated as an intrinsic attribute of the right itself[81] whilst, in others, individuals may be treated as integration agents through the recognition of implied rights of action.[82] The issue of legal aid has also received some attention.[83]

There are, however, some areas which require further attention. The first is interventions in cases pending before the CJEU. The capacity of private parties and representative associations to intervene is limited and out of line with the importance of the CJEU in shaping the constitutional outlook of the European Union. In preliminary references, whether a party may intervene depends on the rules of procedure of the referring court.[84] This, however, does not take account of the fact that

[76] See, for an example, CJEU, Case C-285/98 *Kreil* ECLI:EU:C:2000:2.

[77] See CJEU, Joined Cases C-297/88 and C-197/89 *Dzodzi v Belgian State* ECLI:EU:C:1990:360, and its progeny.

[78] CJEU, Case C-144/04 *Mangold* ECLI:EU:C:2005:709.

[79] See n 46 above.

[80] CJEU, Case C-64/16 *Associação Sindical dos Juízes Portugueses v Tribunal de Contas* ECLI:EU:C:2018:117.

[81] CJEU, Case C-83/14 *Chez* ECLI:EU:C:2015:480.

[82] CJEU, Case C-237/07 *Janecek v Freistaat Bayern* ECLI:EU:C:2008:447.

[83] CJEU, Case C-279/09 *DEB* ECLI:EU:C:2010:811.

[84] Interventions in direct actions are governed by the Statute of the Court of Justice, Article 40. Private parties may not intervene in EU inter-institutional disputes, disputes between Member States, and disputes between EU institutions and Member States. In other cases, they may intervene if they can establish an interest in the result of a case but the case law has not interpreted that condition generously.

representative associations and interested parties, especially in Member States other than the one from whose court the reference comes, may simply not know that an issue has been raised before the CJEU until it is too late. Notably, in *Premier League*,[85] the CJEU did not accept an order made by the referring court joining additional parties to the proceedings for the purposes of making written and oral submissions to the CJEU even though they had not made observations before the national court itself. Perhaps, this is too strict an approach.

The second issue relates to the right of representative associations to initiate EU claims before national courts.[86] The vindication of rights can be much facilitated by empowering representative associations to bring proceedings. EU measures may expressly grant rights to such associations. This is the case, inter alia, in the field of equality law,[87] consumer law,[88] and data protection.[89] Encouraging public interest litigation is an effective way of promoting the enforcement of key Union policies and can be part of a wider strategy in which EU law has a greater say in the field of enforcement.

Notably, in recent years, the CJEU has shown some willingness to facilitate representative actions at national level. This can be illustrated by reference to *Meta Platforms Ireland*,[90] and *Deutsche Umwelthilfe eV*.[91]

The first case illustrates the inter-relationship between data protection law and consumer law. The CJEU interpreted generously Article 80 of the General Data Protection Regulation[92] which grants to data subjects the right to mandate non-for-profit representative associations to exercise their rights on their behalf and also gives Member States the option to allow such associations to act independently of the data subject's mandate. The CJEU held that a consumer protection association is within the remit of Article 80(1) in that it pursues a public interest objective consisting in safeguarding the rights of data subjects in their capacity as consumers.[93] It also held that it suffices if the persons allegedly wronged are identifiable as a category without the need

[85] Order of the CJEU, Case C-403/08 *Premier League* ECLI:EU:C:2009:789.

[86] See T Tridimas, 'Rights, Remedies, and Access to Justice in Consumer-Related Litigation: Is Union Law Fit for Purpose?' (2023) 3 *European Journal of Consumer Law – Revue européenne de droit de la consommation* 513, from which the analysis in this section borrows.

[87] Council Directive 2000/78/EC establishing a general framework for equal treatment in employment and occupation [2000] OJ L 303/16, Article 9(2); Council Directive 2000/43/EC of 29 June 2000 implementing the principle of equal treatment between persons irrespective of racial or ethnic origin [2000] OJ L 180/22, Article 7(2); Directive 2006/54/EC on the implementation of the principle of equal opportunities and equal treatment of men and women in matters of employment and occupation [2006] OJ L 204/23, Article 17(2). The effectiveness of such rights, however, is disputed. See also now Directive (EU) 2024/1500 of the European Parliament and of the Council of 14 May 2024 on standards for equality bodies in the field of equal treatment and equal opportunities between women and men in matters of employment and occupation, and amending Directives 2006/54/EC and 2010/41/EU, OJ L, 2024/1500, 29.5.2024, Article 10.

[88] See the Consumer Rights Directive (Directive 2011/83 on consumer rights [2011] OJ L 304/64), Article 23(2).

[89] See Article 80 GDPR (Regulation (EU) 2016/679 on the protection of natural persons with regard to the processing of personal data and on the free movement of such data [2016] OJ L 119/1), discussed below.

[90] CJEU, Case C-319/20 *Meta Platforms Ireland Limited v Bundesverband der Verbraucherzentralen und Verbraucherverbände – Verbraucherzentrale Bundesverband eV* ECLI:EU:C:2022:322.

[91] CJEU, Case C-873/19 *Deutsche Umwelthilfe eV v Bundesrepublik Deutschland* ECLI:EU:C:2022:85.

[92] Regulation (EU) 2016/679 of the European Parliament and of the Council of 27 April 2016 on the protection of natural persons with regard to the processing of personal data and on the free movement of such data, and repealing Directive 95/46/EC (General Data Protection Regulation) (OJ 2016 L 119, p 1).

[93] CJEU, Case C-319/20 *Meta Platforms Ireland Limited* (see n 90 above), paras 64–65.

to identify specific consumers concerned by the allegedly illegal data processing[94] or to prove actual harm suffered by the data subject in a given situation.[95]

Deutsche Umwelthilfe eV[96] concerned the right of environmental associations to bring proceedings under the Aarhus Convention. Deutsche Umwelthilfe eV challenged a decision of the German authorities granting approval to certain diesel vehicles arguing that the software approved was in breach of EU emission standards. The problem was that German law allowed environmental associations to contest measures authorising projects affecting the environment but not to contest decisions approving products. The CJEU held, however, that Deutsche Umwelthilfe eV enjoyed standing directly under EU law.

The CJEU also held that, while Article 9(3) of the Aarhus Convention does not have direct effect, national law must be interpreted to the fullest extent possible in accordance with its requirements.[97] Where a consistent interpretation of national law cannot be procured, Article 9(3) of the Aarhus Convention, read in conjunction with Article 47 of the Charter, imposes on Member States an obligation to ensure effective judicial protection of EU rights.[98] Thus, if a consistent interpretation was not possible, the referring court had to disapply the provisions of national law precluding an environmental association from being able to challenge a decision granting approval in breach of EU requirements. *Deutsche Umwelthilfe eV* is a celebration of the principle of effectiveness.[99]

5.2. Procedural Fairness

Given that the Article 267 TFEU procedure is designed as a mechanism of inter-judicial dialogue, it is less adversarial and the parties are less in control of the litigation than they are in a direct action. The following limitations may be identified:

- In contrast to direct actions where there is a full exchange of pleadings, parties have only one chance to submit observations. They do so without having the opportunity to know the observations of the other parties. This may limit their ability to address them effectively, their only chance to do so being the oral hearing;[100]
- Governments may intervene in the oral hearing without having submitted observations.[101] This means that the parties to the main proceedings may not have prior knowledge of the intervening Member State's views and specific arguments;[102]

[94] ibid, para 68.
[95] ibid, paras 70, 72.
[96] CJEU, Case C-873/19 *Deutsche Umwelthilfe eV* (see n 91 above).
[97] ibid, para 65.
[98] ibid, para 66.
[99] ibid, para 67.
[100] In principle, an oral hearing will take place although the Court may decide not to hold one if it considers that the written pleadings provide sufficient information for it to give a ruling: Article 76(2) Rules of Procedure of the CJEU. *cf* Article 76(3).
[101] See Article 96(2) Rules of Procedure of the CJEU and Article 23 of the Statute of the Court of Justice. In accordance with those provisions, statements of case written observations may be submitted not only by the Member States but also the Commission and other Union institutions and, in some cases, non-Member States. In practice, however, it is unlikely for a Union institution to present oral submissions without having submitted a written statement.
[102] See, eg, CJEU, Case C-304/14 *Secretary of State for the Home Department v CS* ECLI:EU:C:2016:674.

- The oral hearing tends to be too short. The formality and short duration of the oral procedure may not provide an effective opportunity to ventilate all aspects of the case. This limitation is not specific to preliminary reference proceedings. It also applies to direct actions but, given that most EU private rights are vindicated via preliminary references, it does have an important effect on them.

The above reflections should not be taken to suggest that the procedure for hearing preliminary reference cases falls short of the requisite standards of procedural fairness. They highlight its distinct nature as a form of inter-judicial dialogue. It is correct that there is a pro-institutional actor bias: the EU institutions, the Member States, and other institutional actors have the right to submit observations[103] whilst, as discussed above, private actors do not unless they are part of the proceedings before the referring court. But this is a manifestation of a more general approach which gives certain privileges to state and institutional entities [104] recognising their special status as public interest actors and is by no means unique to the EU system.[105]

5.3. Jurisdictional Remit

In the first place, it is for the referring court to decide what questions to refer and the parties cannot invite the CJEU to rule on other points. The CJEU, however, has ample discretion to reformulate the questions referred. It may give a ruling on the interpretation of a Union act other than that to which the order of reference refers if, in the light of the factual and legal background, it considers that it is helpful for the national court in order to decide the case.[106] It may even rule on the validity of an EU measure even though the question referred asked only for its interpretation.[107] Judicial creativity is here at its apex. In *Komstroy*,[108] the CJEU provided a ruling on a point which had not been asked by the referring court, and which was not necessary to answer

[103] See Article 23 of the Statute and Article 96(2) Rules of Procedure of the CJEU.

[104] See, eg, Article 263 TFEU in relation to locus standi in actions for annulment.

[105] For example, in the United States, the rate of success of certiorari petitions to the Supreme Court is much higher for the federal government than it is for private litigants.

[106] CJEU, Case C-315/92 *Verband Sozialer Wettbewerb v Clinique Laboratories and Estée Lauder* ECLI:EU:C:1994:34; CJEU, Case C-383/97 *Van der Laan* ECLI:EU:C:1999:64. An interesting example is also provided by the difference in view between the Court and the Advocate General as to the EU provisions applicable in CJEU, Case C-367/89 *Richardt* ECLI:EU:C:1991:376.

[107] See, eg, CJEU, Case C-16/65 *Schwarze* ECLI:EU:C:1965:117; CJEU, Case C-62/14 *Gauweiler* ECLI:EU:C:2015:400; CJEU, Case C-212/19 *Ministre de l'Agriculture et de l'Alimentation v Compagnie des pêches de Saint-Malo* ECLI:EU:C:2020:726. The cases however are exceptional. As a general rule, the Court will not rule on the validity of a measure unless it has expressly been asked to do so. This is because it is mindful to ensure that the rights of defence are respected. See CJEU, Joined Cases 141 to 143/81 *Holdijk* ECLI:EU:C:1982:122, para 6. The information contained in the order for reference not only enables the Court to answer the questions posed but is also circulated to all Member States and to the Union institutions concerned by the litigation, who can decide on its basis whether to submit written observations to the Court: see Article 23 of the Statute of the ECJ. Thus, as a general rule the Court may only examine issues which expressly or by implication arise from the order for reference and on which interested parties have had the opportunity to submit their views. See CJEU, Joined Cases C-133, C-300 and C-362/93 *Crispoltoni II* Opinion of AG Jacobs, ECLI:EU:C:1994:208, paras 87 ff.

[108] CJEU, Case C-741/19 *Republic of Moldova v Komstroy LLC* ECLI:EU:C:2021:655.

the questions referred. The Court extended its ruling in *Achmea* to arbitration clauses included in multilateral investment treaties, holding that the investor state arbitration mechanism provided in the Energy Charter Treaty cannot apply to disputes between a Member State and an investor of another Member State concerning an investment made by the latter in the first Member State.[109] This however was not relevant to the main proceedings which concerned a Ukrainian investor in Moldova. In *Komstroy*, the Court delivered the longest obiter dictum in its history. Although exceptional, such cases illustrate that the preliminary reference procedure is not perceived as an adversarial mechanism but as the main instrument to transmit impulses with a view to shaping the EU legal order.

Nonetheless, the limited capacity of the parties to determine the scope of the adjudication operates neutrally. By design, it favours neither the party that asserts a right nor the party that denies it.

5.4. Suitability to Addressing Issues of Principle

By its nature, the preliminary reference procedure is designed to settle issues of principle and law and not to establish facts. The enquiry involves the interplay of three elements, the facts, national law, and EU law. The first two are for the referring court to do whilst the third is for the CJEU. Nonetheless, the distinction between interpretation and application is very porous and the Court enjoys significant discretion as regards the specificity of its ruling. It may be concrete and prescriptive or leave margin for input by the referring court. This aspect of its jurisdiction operates as a constitutional valve: it regulates the flow of judicial direction and determines whether review of national choices is carried out solely by the CJEU. The present author has distinguished three categories of cases depending on the specificity of the ruling.[110] The Court may give an answer so specific that it leaves the referring court no margin for manoeuvre and provides it with a ready-made solution to the dispute (*outcome cases*); it may, alternatively, provide the referring court with guidelines as to how to resolve the dispute (*guidance cases*); finally, it may answer the question in such general terms that, in effect, it defers to the national judiciary on the point in issue (*deference cases*). This tripartite distinction is not watertight. The difference between the guidance and the deference category is one of degree and their boundaries are not always clear. Nevertheless, the categories identified above essentially encapsulate the alternative approaches of the CJEU in engaging with the national judiciary. Guidance and deference may be seen as illustrations of judicial subsidiarity: the CJEU appoints national courts as its agents and asks them to fulfil their part of the bargain. The outcome approach may be seen as a sign of leadership although leadership and activism may also be pursued through deference. The distinction among the three approaches is particularly striking in relation to the

[109] ibid, para 66.

[110] See, T Tridimas, 'Constitutional Review of Member State Action: The Virtues and Vices of an Incomplete Jurisdiction' (2011) 9 *International Journal of Constitutional Law* 737.

principle of proportionality but present also in the application of other principles.[111] Notably, many of the key fundamental rights cases have been outcome cases. The CJEU provides leadership leaving essentially no discretion to the national court.[112]

5.5. Length of Proceedings

A recurrent issue has been the increase in the workload of the CJEU and its effect on the duration of proceedings. Recent years statistics do not point to an acute increase in the number of preliminary references. The information provided in the annual reports of the CJEU, as summarised in the table below, indicates that the number of preliminary references introduced per year has remained fairly stable since 2017 and has had fluctuations within the period observed; there has not been a great increase in the duration of proceedings; the ratio of new to completed cases is not on an upward trend nor is the number of pending cases. It would appear therefore that the CJEU has succeeded in managing its case load.

A major development on this front is the transfer of preliminary jurisdiction in some cases from the Court of Justice to the General Court (GC).[113] This makes for better use of resources. It can be expected to reduce further the workload of the CJEU and enable it to focus more on cases that raise issues of constitutional importance. From the point of view of rights adjudication, it is a welcome development.

In 2024, 573 references were made, which is the second highest number of preliminary references made in a year since the establishment of the Court.[114]

Table – Preliminary references

	2017	**2018**	**2019**	**2020**	**2021**	**2022**	**2023**	**2024**
New cases	553	568	641	557	567	546	518	573
Completed cases	447	520	601	534	547	564	532	580
Duration of proceedings in months	15.7	16	15.5	15.9	16.7	17.3	16.8	17.2
Pending cases	661	709	749	772	792	774	760	753

Mention should be made here of the urgent preliminary reference procedure (PPU). This plays a key role for the protection of fundamental rights. It was introduced in 2008 to enable the CJEU to deal expeditiously with preliminary references in the

[111] See, eg, for a case where it was for the national court to establish, subject to the guidelines given by the ECJ, whether the principle of non-discrimination was breached: CJEU, Case C-453/08 *Karanikolas v Ministry of Agriculture* ECLI:EU:C:2010:482.

[112] See, eg, CJEU, Case C-60/00 *Carpenter* ECLI:EU:C:2002:434; CJEU, Case C-112/00 *Schmidberger* ECLI:EU:C:2003:333; CJEU, Case C-36/02 *Omega* ECLI:EU:C:2004:614; CJEU, Case C-144/04 *Mangold* ECLI:EU:C:2005:709.

[113] See Regulation No 2024/2019 of 11 April 2024 amending Protocol No 3 on the Statute of the Court of Justice of the European Union, OJ 12.8.2024.

[114] See the 2024 Statistics concerning the judicial activity of the Court of Justice, p 29. The highest number of references was in 2019, when 641 references were made.

area of freedom, security and justice, where the rights of the individual may be at risk as a result of the length of the proceedings.[115] The procedure has specific features:[116] a specific chamber is designated to hear such cases; participation is restricted to fewer parties; and communications takes place electronically. In cases of extreme urgency, the written stage of the procedure may be omitted.[117] The need for an Advocate General opinion may be dispensed with and, where an opinion is delivered, it tends to be shorter.[118]

The number of requests for a case to be treated under the urgent procedure has increased, especially since 2017. Most requests relate to cooperation in criminal matters and matters pertaining to borders, asylum and immigration, those two categories accounting for two thirds of the requests made since 2020.[119]

In terms of the duration of the proceedings, the PPU has proved a success. According to the annual statistics of the CJEU, since the introduction of the PPU in 2008, the average duration of proceedings has recorded an upwards trend but in no year has it exceeded 4.5 months. In fact, only in two years (2021 and 2022) did the average length of PPU proceedings exceeded the four months mark.[120] The CJEU has identified two areas where judgments are delivered in the shortest possible time:[121] when the continuation of an individual's detention depends on the Court's answer;[122] and in family law matters where the well-being of a child is at stake.[123]

5.6. Compliance and Enforceability

The effectiveness of protection offered by the preliminary reference procedure also depends on the remedies available in the event that a national court violates Article 267 TFEU. Such violation can take two main forms. A national court may refuse to make a reference in circumstances where it is under an obligation to do so, or it may refuse to comply with the CJEU's ruling. Such refusal may be an isolated response, evoke a difference of principle on an important issue or, as in the case of the Polish Constitutional Tribunal,[124] manifest a more general mood of disobedience. Various enforcement mechanisms are available. The Commission may bring enforcement proceedings against the Member State in question. In *Commission v France*, it successfully brought proceedings against France for

[115] See Article 23a of the Statute of the Court of Justice. For an assessment of the PPU procedure, see C Barnard, 'The PPU: Is it Worth the Candle? An Early Assessment' (2009) 34 *European Law Review* 281; S Bartolini, 'The Urgent Preliminary Ruling Procedure: Ten Years On' (2018) 24 *European Public Law* 213.

[116] See Article 23a of the Statute and Articles 108–14, Rules of Procedure of the CJEU.

[117] See Article 111 of the Rules of Procedure.

[118] See, eg, CJEU, Case C-219/25 *Ministère public (Public Prosecutor's Office, France) v KN* ECLI:EU:C:2025:379.

[119] See the 2024 Statistics concerning the judicial activity of the Court of Justice, p 25.

[120] It was 4.5 months in 2022 and 4.3 in 2023. See the 2024 Statistics concerning the judicial activity of the Court of Justice, p 21.

[121] See CJEU, Report on the use of the urgent preliminary ruling procedure by the Court of Justice, 2012, Luxembourg, 31 January 2012.

[122] ibid; see, eg, CJEU, Case C-61/11 PPU *El Dridi Hassen* ECLI:EU:C:2011:268.

[123] ibid; see, eg, CJEU, Case C-195/08 PPU *Rinau* ECLI:EU:C:2008:406.

[124] See the decision of the 7 October 2021 (K 3/21) which entails a wholesale abrogation of the obligations flowing from EU membership.

failure of the *Conseil d'État* to make a reference.[125] Although the case concerned a technical issue,[126] the judgment is important as it signals that breaches by the national judiciary are not immune from enforcement proceedings. Liability in damages is a possibility under the *Köbler*[127] conditions; and the ECtHR may also record a violation. These remedies are reasonably effective but can do little to deter a Member State who casts doubt on the integration model itself.

6. Conclusions

There is no doubt that, in historical perspective, the preliminary reference procedure has played an enormous role in facilitating the assertion and protection of fundamental rights. The overwhelming majority of judgments that define the constitutional blueprint of the EU and the scope, content and effect of EU fundamental rights have been delivered in preliminary references. Its contribution as a means of rights vindication should be assessed positively. The procedure itself, although substance agnostic, has a bias in favour of rights vindication. The very fact that it was included in the original treaties was a form of institutional empowerment unusual for international organisations. The CJEU has treated the procedure itself as an integral part of the right to judicial protection, and, in doing so, it has found a powerful ally in Strasbourg. Judged by reference to the specific criteria identified above, the procedure fares reasonably well. The transfer of preliminary jurisdiction to the GC opens a new chapter in the EU system of judicial protection. It should be welcomed. The CJEU's interpretation of Article 267 TFEU is grounded on legal realism, functionalism and trust on its own discretion. In some cases, the CJEU has invoked Article 267 TFEU aggressively to assert autonomy (Opinion 2/13; *Achmea*) or due process (*Rosneft*). Critics may argue that in cases such as Opinion 2/13 and *Achmea*, the preliminary reference procedure has been used as a limiting rather than an empowering force for fundamental rights protection. Be that as it may, Article 267 TFEU has been, perhaps, the most important provision of the Treaty and a true facilitator of political change. It is difficult to think of another procedural provision in an international treaty that has had such an empowering effect.

[125] CJEU, Case C-416/17 *Commission v France* ECLI:EU:C:2018:811. See also CJEU, Case C-516/22 *Commission v UK (Micula case)* ECLI:EU:C:2024:231.

[126] The case concerned the rules governing the process for the reimbursement of taxes paid in breach of EU law and came in the aftermath of CJEU, Case C-310/09 *Accor* ECLI:EU:C:2011:581, an earlier judgment arising from a reference made by the *Conseil d'État*, where the ECJ had found French law to be in breach of the right of establishment and free movement of capital.

[127] See n 45 above.

10

Knowing whom to Ask: Judicial Dialogue under Protocol No 16 ECHR and Article 267 TFEU Considered in Light of EU Accession to the ECHR

FELIX RONKES AGERBEEK[1]

1. Introduction

Knowing whom to ask is half the journey to finding the answer.[2] This lesson, rooted in life, holds just as true in the context of 'activating the protection of human and fundamental rights at the European level' – the topic of this book. When we think of judicial protection of fundamental rights in Europe, the European Court of Human Rights (ECtHR) in Strasbourg and the Court of Justice of the EU (CJEU) in Luxembourg naturally come to mind. Yet, the story of fundamental rights protection in Europe is not simply a 'tale of two cities'; it is a tale of many.[3] It is, in large part, the story of national courts, and of questions asked and answered in dialogue among Europe's judges.[4]

In this chapter, I focus on two mechanisms deliberately designed to foster judicial dialogue: the advisory opinion procedure under Protocol No 16 to the European Convention on Human Rights and the preliminary reference procedure under Article 267 of the Treaty of the Functioning of the European Union (TFEU). Each mechanism formalises a way for national courts to seek guidance from the ECtHR and

[1] Member of the Legal Service of the European Commission; negotiator on behalf of the EU for the 2020–2023 negotiations on its accession to the European Convention on Human Rights. The views expressed in this chapter are mine alone and cannot be attributed to the Commission. I am grateful to Janneke Gerards, Jasper Krommendijk, David Milner, Elise Muir, Corinna Wissels and Lamprini Xenou for their insightful comments on an early draft. Any remaining errors, omissions, or stubbornly misguided ideas are, of course, entirely my own. This chapter captures the law as I understand it, as of 1 January 2025.

[2] Asking the right question is, most likely, the other half.

[3] S O'Leary, 'A Tale of Two Cities: Fundamental Rights Protection in Strasbourg and Luxembourg' (2018) *Cambridge Yearbook of European Legal Studies* 3.

[4] F Ronkes Agerbeek, 'The Tale of Two Cities Continues: The Convention and the Expanding Scope of EU Law', lecture of 14 June 2024 at the European Court of Human Rights, available on the website of the Court: www.echr.coe.int/en/seminars-and-lectures-at-the-court accessed 2 June 2025.

the CJEU, respectively.[5] Building on Jasper Krommendijk's contribution, I will examine, more specifically, the relationship between these two mechanisms in the context of the EU's accession to the European Convention on Human Rights (ECHR) – a longstanding goal aimed at closing the circle on the EU's legal framework for the protection of fundamental rights.

The relationship between Protocol No 16 and Article 267 TFEU is a specific manifestation of a larger phenomenon: the common roots and branching paths of the ECHR and the EU. While both the ECHR and the EU emerged from the same political and moral enterprise – to prevent a repetition of the horrors that took place on European soil during the twentieth century – they have pursued this shared purpose along distinct trajectories. The Convention system *supervises* political communities, much like a watchful parent. It sets minimum standards for human rights protection that each contracting state must uphold. The EU, by contrast, *integrates* political communities into a new, overarching community. It creates a shared household for its Member States and their citizens – an 'ever closer union'.[6] Gluing these different modes of governance together has been a longstanding ambition – and a challenge. Efforts to link the EU and the Convention system date back to early post-war aspirations for European unity.[7] Yet, in the initial decades of European integration, fundamental rights were virtually absent from the Treaties, gaining recognition only through the case law of the CJEU.[8] Although proposals for accession to the ECHR emerged repeatedly,[9] they lacked a firm legal basis until 2009,[10] when the EU's commitment to join the ECHR was formally enshrined in Article 6(2) TEU.[11] Soon after, the process of negotiations to reconcile the EU's legal order with the Convention system began. In April 2013, these negotiations resulted in an agreement between the EU and the Council of Europe's Member States. However, in Opinion 2/13 of 18 December 2014, the CJEU declared that agreement incompatible with the EU Treaties.[12] Among

[5] As of 1 October 2024, the Court of Justice transferred part of its jurisdiction for preliminary rulings to the General Court. This transfer applies to six specific areas: the common system of VAT; excise duties; the Customs Code; tariff classification of goods; passenger compensation and assistance for denied boarding, delays, or cancellations; and the greenhouse gas emissions trading system. The Court of Justice will retain jurisdiction over preliminary rulings that, while linked to the areas above, also involve other legal fields. It will likewise retain jurisdiction over requests that, even if they fall within one or more of these areas, raise independent interpretative questions concerning, for example, the Charter of Fundamental Rights of the European Union.

[6] The 1957 Treaty Establishing the European Community contained the objective of laying the foundations of an 'ever closer union among the peoples of Europe'. This aim has remained in the EU Treaties ever since.

[7] Article 3 of the Draft Treaty embodying the Statute of the European Community (Strasbourg, 10 March 1953).

[8] CJEU, Case C-29/69 *Stauder v Ulm* ECLI:EU:C:1969:57; CJEU, Case C-4/72 *Nold* ECLI:EU:C:1974:51; CJEU, Case C-11/70 *Internationale Handelsgesellschaft* ECLI:EU:C:1970:114.

[9] See, eg, Bulletin of the European Communities, Supplement 2/79, Memorandum of the accession of the European Communities to the Convention for the Protection of Human Rights and Fundamental Freedoms, adopted by the Commission on 4 April 1979, COM(79)210 final of 2 May 1979; and Commission Communication on Community accession to the Convention for the Protection of Human Rights and Fundamental Freedoms and some of its Protocols, SEC(90)2087 final of 19 November 1990.

[10] CJEU, Opinion 2/94, *Accession by the Community to the European Convention for the Protection of Human Rights and Fundamental Freedoms* ECLI:EU:C:1996:140.

[11] See also Protocol (No 8) relating to Article 6(2) of the Treaty on European Union on the accession of the Union to the European Convention on the Protection of Human Rights and Fundamental Freedoms.

[12] CJEU, Opinion 2/13, *Accession of the European Union to the ECHR* ECLI:EU:C:2014:2454.

the Court's objections was the question of how Protocol No 16 would interact with Article 267 TFEU.[13]

Opinion 2/13 prompted a profound re-examination of how fundamental rights are protected at the European level, and of the interplay between the ECtHR, the CJEU, and the highest courts of the EU Member States.[14] It also consolidated the CJEU's constitutional vision of the EU legal order, affirming its self-understanding as a constitutional court of the Union – one that, like any constitutional court, must do more than protect fundamental rights; it must also hold a political community together.[15] In line with this vision, the Court's concerns in Opinion 2/13 essentially revolved around three key principles.[16] First, where the ECtHR serves as the ultimate arbiter of whether an EU act complies with the ECHR, it must be ensured that the CJEU remains the penultimate arbiter, responsible for determining the act's compliance with fundamental rights under EU law.[17] Second, within the scope of EU law, Member States maintain a special relationship with one another, marked by certain federal characteristics, which must be acknowledged and preserved within the Convention system, as this relationship is the raison d'être of the EU.[18] Third, only EU law itself – under the ultimate authority of the CJEU – can definitively determine the scope of EU law and, by implication, define the division of competences between the EU and its Member States.[19] The CJEU's concerns surrounding Protocol No 16 are closely tied to the first of these three principles.

Negotiations for the EU's accession to the ECHR gained renewed momentum from 2020 to 2023.[20] During this period, negotiators – reunited in the '46+1 Group'[21] – set out to revise the 2013 agreement to address the CJEU's concerns. As a member of the EU delegation, I participated in these discussions. One of the challenges the Group

[13] See, ibid, paras 196–200.

[14] eg, D Halberstam, '"It's the Autonomy, Stupid!" A Modest Defense of Opinion 2/13 on EU Accession to the ECHR, and the Way Forward' (2015) *German Law* Journal 105; K Lenaerts, 'La vie après l'avis: Exploring the Principle of Mutual (yet not Blind) Trust' (2017) *Common Market Law Review* 805; A Rosas, 'The Court of Justice of the European Union: A Human Rights Institution?' (2022) *Journal of Human Rights Practice* 204; E Spaventa, 'A Very Fearful Court? The Protection of Fundamental Rights in the European Union after Opinion 2/13' (2015) *Maastricht Journal of European and Comparative Law* 56; B De Witte and S Imamović, 'Opinion 2/13 on Accession to the ECHR: Defending the EU Legal Order against a Foreign Human Rights Court' (2015) *European Law Journal* 704; A Łazowski and R Wessel, 'When Caveats Turn into Locks: Opinion 2/13 on Accession of the European Union to the ECHR' (2015) *German Law Journal* 211; M Claes, 'Accession or no Accession? A National Perspective', in Š Imamović, M Claes and B De Witte (eds), *The EU Fundamental Rights Landscape After Opinion 2/13* (Maastricht Faculty of Law Working Paper 2016).

[15] Halberstam, 'It's the Autonomy, Stupid!' (2015). See also J Baquero Cruz, *What's Left of the Law of Integration: Decay and Resistance in European Union Law* (Oxford, Oxford University Press, 2018) 155–66.

[16] F Ronkes Agerbeek, 'EU Accession to the European Convention on Human Rights: A New Hope' (2024) 9 *European Papers* 695, 708.

[17] This principle underpins the concerns expressed in Opinion 2/13 regarding: advisory opinions under Protocol no. 16 ECHR (paras 196–200); the prior involvement procedure (paras 236–244); and judicial protection in the area of the Common Foreign and Security Policy (paras 249–257).

[18] This principle underpins the concerns expressed in Opinion 2/13 regarding: Art 53 ECHR (paras 186–89); mutual trust (paras 191–95); and inter-party applications under Art 33 ECHR (paras 201–13).

[19] This principle underpins the concerns expressed in Opinion 2/13 regarding: the co-respondent mechanism (paras 220–25) and joint responsibility (paras 229–34).

[20] F Ronkes Agerbeek, 'EU Accession to the European Convention' (2024).

[21] The number '46' stands for the Member States of the Council of Europe; '+1' stands for the European Union. The group was called the '47+1 Group' until Russia's exclusion from the Council of Europe, in March 2022, due to its military aggression against Ukraine. In this chapter, I will, for the sake of simplicity, refer to it as 'the 46+1 Group' or 'the Group'.

needed to tackle was the relationship between Protocol No 16's advisory-opinion mechanism and Article 267 TFEU's preliminary reference procedure.[22] While this issue might appear narrow or technical, it is worth examining because it serves as a microcosm of the broader challenge of the negotiations: how can the EU participate in the Convention system without jeopardising its unique constitutional framework, geared towards integrating political communities? At the same time, how can the integrity and coherence of the Convention system itself be preserved?

In the following sections, I will examine how the Group approached this dual challenge. First, I will describe the relationship between the advisory–opinion procedure and the preliminary reference procedure as it stands today. Second, I will discuss the CJEU's concerns in Opinion 2/13 regarding the relationship between these mechanisms. Third, I will analyse how the Group sought to address these concerns in the revised accession agreement. Through this inquiry, I hope to illustrate the complex, evolving relationship between the European courts in the protection of fundamental rights.

2. Advisory Opinions v Preliminary References

Protocol No 16 introduces a procedure that allows the ECtHR to give advisory opinions to national courts on 'questions of principle relating to the interpretation or application of the rights and freedoms defined in the Convention or the protocols thereto'.[23] The aim of the advisory-opinion procedure is to enhance the interaction between the ECtHR and the national courts and tribunals of the Contracting Parties to the ECHR.[24] Not every court may request an advisory opinion. Only highest courts and tribunals of a Party that has ratified Protocol No 16 may submit requests to the ECtHR for an advisory opinion.[25] Upon signing or ratifying the Protocol, each Party designates, by means of a formal declaration, those highest courts and tribunals that will be competent to submit such a request.[26] The requesting court or tribunal may seek an advisory opinion only in the context of a case pending before it.[27] This does not affect the right of a party in that case to eventually lodge an individual application under Article 34 of the ECHR.[28] Protocol No 16 was opened for signature in October 2013 and entered into force on 1 August 2018.[29] Currently, 24 states have ratified the Protocol, including

[22] For a more comprehensive account of the negotiations from different perspectives: 'The Revised Draft Agreement on the Accession of the EU to the ECHR' 9 *European Papers*, Special Section edited by S Ø Johansen, G Ulfstein, A Follesdal and RA Wessel.

[23] Article 1 § 1 of Protocol No 16.

[24] See, eg, ECtHR, Request no P16-2018-001 *Advisory opinion concerning the recognition in domestic law of a legal parent-child relationship between a child born through a gestational surrogacy arrangement abroad and the intended mother*, para 25.

[25] Article 1 § 1 of Protocol No 16.

[26] Article 10 of Protocol No 16.

[27] Article 1 § 2 of Protocol No 16. See ECtHR, Request no P16-2020-1 *Decision on a request for an advisory opinion by the Supreme Court of the Slovak Republic* and ECtHR, Request no P16-2018-001 (see n 24 above), para 26.

[28] Paragraph 26 of the Explanatory Report to Protocol No 16.

[29] For further details on the origins of Protocol No 16 and its role in the reform process of the ECtHR, see: D Milner, 'Protocols no 15 and 16 to the European Convention on Human Rights in the Context of the Perennial Process of Reform: A Long and Winding Road' (2014) *Zeitschrift für europarechtliche Studien* 19.

12 EU Member States.[30] To date, the ECtHR has delivered seven advisory opinions, five of which stemmed from requests by courts in EU Member States.[31]

There are clear parallels between the advisory-opinion procedure under Protocol No 16 and the preliminary reference procedure under Article 267 TFEU.[32] However, there are also important differences: advisory opinions are not binding; lower courts and tribunals cannot request them; highest courts and tribunals are never obliged to seek an opinion; and parties in the national proceedings do not have an automatic right to participate in the procedure before the ECtHR.[33] Another obvious yet crucial difference concerns subject-matter jurisdiction: advisory opinions of the ECtHR pertain to the interpretation or application of the rights and freedoms defined in the ECHR or its protocols, whereas preliminary rulings of the CJEU concern the interpretation of EU law or to the validity of acts adopted by the EU's institutions, bodies, offices or agencies. Thus, advisory opinions may only be sought if the case before the requesting court involves Convention law, while preliminary rulings may only be sought if the case before the referring court relates to EU law.[34]

There is a degree of overlap between these two spheres of jurisdiction. This is because EU law requires EU institutions, bodies, offices and agencies – as well as

[30] Belgium, Estonia, Finland, France, Greece, Lithuania, Luxembourg, the Netherlands, Romania, Slovak Republic, Slovenia and Sweden. See also the Draft Report of 15 October 2024 evaluating the first effects of Protocol No 16 to the ECHR (DH-SYSC-PRO(2024)07REV), prepared under the auspices of the Council of Europe's Steering Committee for Human Rights.

[31] ECtHR, Request no P16-2023-001 *Advisory Opinion as to whether an individual may be denied authorisation to work as a security guard or officer on account of being close to or belonging to a religious movement* (Conseil d'État of Belgium); ECtHR, Request no P16-2022-001 *Advisory Opinion on the procedural status and rights of a biological parent in proceedings for the adoption of an adult* (Supreme Court of Finland); ECtHR, Request no P16-2021-002, *Advisory Opinion on the difference in treatment between landowners' associations 'having a recognised existence on the date of the creation of an approved municipal hunters' association 'and landowners' associations set up after that date* (Conseil d'État of France); ECtHR, Request no P16-2020-002, *Advisory Opinion on the assessment, under Article 3 of Protocol No 1 to the Convention, of the proportionality of a general prohibition on standing for election after removal from office in impeachment proceedings* (Supreme Court of Lithuania); ECtHR, Request no P16-2018-001 *Advisory Opinion concerning the recognition in domestic law of a legal parent-child relationship between a child born through a gestational surrogacy arrangement abroad and the intended mother* (Court of Cassation of France). The Court has rejected requests for an advisory opinion from the Supreme Court of Slovakia (Request no P16-2020-001), the Supreme Court of Estonia (Request no P-16-2023-002), and from the High Court of Cassation and Justice of Romania (Request nos P16-2024-001 and P16-2024-002). For an analysis of first experiences with Protocol No 16 at the national level: J Gerards and others, 'Protocol 16 ECHR. Context, Meaning, Effects and Experiences' (2023) Montaigne Centrum voor Rechtsstaat en Rechtspleging, available at https://repository.wodc.nl/handle/20.500.12832/3293 accessed 2 June 2025.

[32] For a detailed discussion of the similarities and differences between the advisory–opinion procedure and the preliminary reference procedure, see J Krommendijk, 'Purposeless or Promising? Advisory Opinions from the European Court of Human Rights', in ch 7 of the present volume.

[33] For further detail on the features of the advisory–opinion procedure, see the Guidelines on the implementation of the advisory–opinion procedure introduced by Protocol No 16 to the Convention (approved by the Plenary Court on 18 September 2017; last updated on 25 September 2023).

[34] CJEU, Case C-328/04 *Attila Vajnai* ECLI:EU:C:2005:596, para 14. See also: ECtHR, App no 33629/06 *Vajnai v Hungary* ECLI:CE:ECHR:2008:0708JUD003362906. A request for a preliminary ruling will be declared inadmissible when the case lacks a connection with EU law. Recent examples (involving fundamental rights) include: Case C-765/21 ECLI:EU:C:2023:566; Case C-200/22 ECLI:EU:C:2023:337; Case C-243/22 ECLI:EU:C:2022:877; Case C-244/21 ECLI:EU:C:2021:539; Case C-131/21 ECLI:EU:C:2021:695; Case C-703/20 ECLI:EU:C:2021:365; Case C-679/20 ECLI:EU:C:2021:362; Case C-580/20 ECLI:EU:C:2021:375; Case C-32/20 ECLI:EU:C:2020:441; Case C-376/19 ECLI:EU:C:2020:99; Case C-234/19 ECLI:EU:C:2019:986; Case C-185/19 ECLI:EU:C:2019:779; Case C-723/18 ECLI:EU:C:2019:398.

EU Member States when they implement EU law – to respect fundamental rights, especially those recognised by the EU Charter of Fundamental Rights.[35] Moreover, according to Article 52(3) of the Charter, rights in the Charter that correspond to those in the ECHR shall have the same meaning and scope as their analogues in the ECHR and must provide at least the same level of protection.[36] Thus, a question concerning the interpretation of EU law or the validity of acts by EU institutions, bodies, offices or agencies may overlap with a question of principle relating to the interpretation or application of rights and freedoms defined in the ECHR or its protocols. Indeed, the very premiss of EU accession to the ECHR is that there are instances in which EU law and Convention law intersect.

Consider, for example, the case of *Centraal Israëlitische Consistorie van België and Others*,[37] which involved a decree by the Flemish legislature prohibiting the slaughter of animals without prior stunning. Various Belgian residents, along with Muslim and Jewish organisations, challenged the decree before the Belgian Constitutional Court. They also questioned the validity of EU rules on animal protection, which defined the scope of discretion available to national authorities.[38] In this context, they invoked fundamental rights, particularly the freedom of religion, which is safeguarded under Article 9 of the ECHR as well as Article 10(1) of the Charter. The Belgian Constitutional Court made a preliminary reference to the CJEU. In its ruling, the CJEU carefully considered the ECtHR's case law before upholding the validity of the EU rules at issue, and concluded that 'the Flemish legislature was entitled to adopt … the decree … without exceeding the discretion which EU law confers on Member States as regards the need to reconcile [animal welfare and the right to freedom of religion].'[39] In other words, the CJEU held that EU law neither required nor precluded the adoption of the Flemish measure. The Belgian Constitutional Court subsequently upheld the decree. The applicants then appealed to the ECtHR, which found no violation of the ECHR.[40]

When the case was still pending before the Belgian Constitutional Court, Belgium had not yet ratified Protocol No 16.[41] Nevertheless, the case illustrates that judges in the highest courts or tribunals of an EU Member State may sometimes face a choice: (1) refer a question for a preliminary ruling to the CJEU; (2) request an advisory opinion from the ECtHR; or (3) perhaps do both. Opinion 2/13 strongly suggests that, to safeguard the 'autonomy and effectiveness of the preliminary ruling procedure',[42]

[35] See, eg, CJEU, Case C-234/17 *XC and others* ECLI:EU:C:2018:853.

[36] See, eg, CJEU, Case C-117/20 *Bpost* ECLI:EU:C:2022:202, para 23; CJEU, Joined Cases C-29/22 P and C-44/22 P *KS and KD* ECLI:EU:C:2024:725, para 77.

[37] CJEU, Case C-336/19 *Centraal Israëlitische Consistorie van België and Others v Vlaamse Regering* ECLI:EU:C:2020:1031.

[38] Council Regulation (EC) No 1099/2009 of 24 September 2009 on the protection of animals at the time of killing [2009] OJ L 303/1.

[39] CJEU, *Centraal Israëlitische* (see n 37 above), para 79.

[40] ECtHR, App no 16760/22 *Executief van de Moslims van België and Others v Belgium* ECLI:CE:ECHR:2024:0213JUD001676022.

[41] Belgium ratified Protocol No 16 on 22 November 2022. Entry into force was on 1 March 2023. On 4 April 2023 the Conseil d'État of Belgium submitted a request under Protocol No 16, becoming the first Belgian court to do so. See Advisory Opinion P16-2023-001 of 14 December 2023 as to whether an individual may be denied authorisation to work as a security guard or officer on account of being close to or belonging to a religious movement (Conseil d'État of Belgium).

[42] CJEU, Opinion 2/13 (see n 12 above), para 197.

EU law imposes a duty on national courts to prioritise the first option.[43] Regardless of Opinion 2/13, however, one would expect most judges to choose the first route *anyway* – and for several reasons.[44] First, a national court is likely to have at least some questions that only the CJEU can answer.[45] Second, the EU Charter of Fundamental Rights (or other applicable EU norms) may provide a higher level of protection than the ECHR.[46] Third, while recourse to the advisory-opinion procedure is always optional, the preliminary reference procedure is sometimes mandatory, particularly for the highest courts or tribunals.[47] Other, more practical considerations may also play a role. For instance, in the preliminary reference procedure, the referring court is not required to provide a translation of its order for reference.[48] Additionally, the CJEU's ruling will be immediately available in the referring court's language of proceedings.[49] Finally, in some cases, time-constraints may favour the preliminary reference procedure.[50] In sum, the

[43] See also the View of Advocate General Kokott in CJEU, Opinion-2/13, ECLI:EU:C:2014:2454, point 141.

[44] See also L Glas and J Krommendijk, 'A Strasbourg Story of Swords and Shields: National Courts' Motives to Request an Advisory Opinion from the ECtHR Under Protocol 16' (2022) *European Convention on Human Rights Law Review* 311.

[45] As was the case in CJEU, *Centraal Israëlitische* (see n 37 above), which involved questions about the interpretation and validity of a specific provision in Council Regulation (EC) No 1099/2009 of 24 September 2009 on the protection of animals at the time of killing [2009] OJ L 303/1.

[46] Article 52(3) of the EU Charter of Fundamental Rights. An example of an area where EU law is often understood to offer a higher level of protection is the field of privacy and personal data: see, eg, para 59 of the partly concurring and partly dissenting opinion of Judge Pinto De Albuquerque in ECtHR, App nos 58170/13, 62322/14 and 24960/15 *Big Brother Watch and Others v United Kingdom* ECLI:CE:ECHR:2021:0525JUD005817013. Another example is the principle of ne bis in idem, which under the Charter applies across the EU, whereas under the Convention it is limited to proceedings within a single state: ECtHR, App no 67521/14 *Krombach v France* ECLI:CE:ECHR:2018:0220DEC006752114.

[47] The obligation on national courts to refer a question for a preliminary ruling to the Court of Justice most famously arises from the *CILFIT* and the *Foto-Frost* case law (see CJEU, Case C-561/19 *Consorzio Italian Management* ECLI:EU:C:2021:799; CJEU, Case C-144/23 *KUBERA* ECLI:EU:C:2024:881; and CJEU, Case C-314/85 *Foto-Frost*, ECLI:EU:C:1987:452). The obligation may also arise under national constitutional law (eg, German Constitutional Court, Decision 1 BVR 1036/99 of 9 January 2001). The Convention does not guarantee a right to have a case referred to the Court of Justice for a preliminary ruling. However, Article 6 § 1 ECHR imposes an obligation on national courts to give reasons when they refuse to refer a question for a preliminary ruling to the Court of Justice (ECtHR, App nos 3989/07 and 38353/07 *Ullens de Schooten and Rezabek v Belgium* ECLI:CE:ECHR:2011:0920JUD000398907). Failure to refer a question for a preliminary ruling to the Court of Justice may also result in forfeiture of the 'Bosphorus presumption' (ECtHR, App no 17502/07 *Avotiņš v Latvia* ECLI:CE:ECHR:2016:0523JUD001750207, paras 109–11; ECtHR, App no 12323/11 *Michaud v France* ECLI:CE:ECHR:2012:1206JUD001232311, paras 114–15).

[48] In the advisory–opinion procedure, if the initial request is lodged in a national official language other than English or French (the official languages of the ECtHR), then the requesting court must file a translation of its request in one of those languages within a time limit to be fixed by the President of the ECtHR: § 13 of the explanatory report to Protocol No 16 and Rule 34 § 7 of the Rules of European Court of Human Rights (30 October 2023).

[49] The ECtHR makes its advisory opinions available in English and/or French. In principle, preliminary rulings of the Court of Justice are, on the day of their delivery, available in all official languages of the European Union (and in any case in the language of the referring court).

[50] The advisory–opinion procedure on average takes ten months; see also the Draft Report of 15 October 2024 evaluating the first effects of Protocol No 16 to the ECHR (see n 30 above). The typical preliminary reference procedure takes around 16 months. However, Article 23a of the Statute of the Court of Justice provides for an 'expedited' procedure and an 'urgent' procedure. The expedited procedure can be applied in any area of EU law (eg, CJEU, Case C-42/17 *MAS and M.B* ECLI:EU:C:2017:168). The duration is of an expedited preliminary reference procedure is around eight months. The urgent procedure can only be used in cases in the area of freedom, security and justice, for example where there is an imminent risk of interference with fundamental rights (eg, CJEU, Case C-638/16 PPU *X and X* ECLI:EU:C:2017:127). The duration of an urgent preliminary reference procedure is around four months. More generally, where a question referred for

preliminary reference procedure is simply the most appropriate – and often the most convenient – option in cases before a highest court or tribunal of an EU Member State in which EU law and Convention law intersect. Of course, in theory, a highest court or tribunal could still decide to request an advisory opinion from the ECtHR in a case involving EU law. How the ECtHR would respond in that situation remains unclear. Perhaps it would decline the request. One thing is certain: Protocol No 16 is silent on the matter.[51]

3. The CJEU's Objection in Opinion 2/13

In 2013, Protocol No 16 of the ECHR was still newly adopted and had not yet entered into force. The proceedings for Opinion 2/13 led the CJEU to examine, for the first time, the potential future impact of the advisory–opinion procedure on the EU's judicial architecture. Could the advisory–opinion procedure pose a threat to the judicial dialogue between the CJEU and national courts? What if, when confronted with a question about the compatibility of EU law with fundamental rights (or about interpreting and applying EU law consistent with those rights), national courts of last instance sought an advisory opinion from the ECtHR instead of – or in addition to – a preliminary ruling from the CJEU? In such a case, national courts would be consulting a non-EU court on matters of EU law. Would this be compatible with the EU's judicial system?

The CJEU and its Advocate General were unequivocal: the advisory–opinion procedure was likely to undermine the preliminary reference procedure. In the words of the Advocate General:

> [The Court of Justice's] role in relation to the interpretation of the [Convention] within the EU could … be jeopardised by the fact that the highest courts and tribunals of the Member States which have ratified [Protocol No 16] might be tempted … to refer questions concerning the interpretation of the [Convention] to the ECtHR rather than to the Court of Justice.[52]

The Court of Justice diagnosed the problem in the following terms:

> [T]he mechanism established by [Protocol No 16] could – notably where the issue concerns rights guaranteed by the Charter corresponding to those secured by the [Convention] – affect the autonomy and effectiveness of the preliminary ruling procedure provided for in Article 267 TFEU.[53]

Ultimately, the Advocate General adopted a more permissive stance than the Court. She argued that, as the issue was not *caused* by the EU's accession to the ECHR, it did not

a preliminary ruling is raised in a case with regard to a person in custody, Article 267 TFEU provides that the Court shall act 'with the minimum of delay' (eg, CJEU, Case C-107/23 PP *Lin* ECLI:EU:C:2023:606, para 52). Source of statistics: Annual Report 2022 of the Court of Justice of the European Union. It remains to be seen how the recent reform of the Court of Justice (see n 5 above), intended to reduce its workload, will impact these figures.

[51] As are the Explanatory Report to Protocol No 16 and the Guidelines on the implementation of the advisory–opinion procedure introduced by Protocol No 16 to the Convention (approved by the Plenary Court on 18 September 2017; last updated on 25 September 2023).

[52] View of Advocate General Kokott in Opinion-proceedings 2/13 (see n 43 above), para 139.

[53] CJEU, Opinion 2/13 (see n 12 above), para 197.

affect the compatibility of the envisaged accession agreement with the EU Treaties.[54] The CJEU took a different view, stating that

> [b]y failing to make any provision in respect of the relationship between the mechanism established by Protocol No 16 and the preliminary ruling procedure provided for in Article 267 TFEU, the agreement envisaged is liable adversely to affect the autonomy and effectiveness of the latter procedure.[55]

Seen from a constitutional perspective, the CJEU's concerns are valid and its conclusion is reasonable.[56] The preliminary reference procedure is, after all, the 'linchpin' of the EU's supranational constitutional framework.[57] Any rule or procedure that diminishes its central role – or disrupts its smooth functioning – is likely to face intense scrutiny from the CJEU.[58] Any possibility for 'circumvention' of that procedure raises alarm and must be 'ruled out'.[59] While the issue with Protocol No 16 exists regardless of whether the EU accedes to the ECHR, proceeding with accession without addressing this concern would cement the current situation while binding the EU inextricably to the Convention system.[60]

I would summarise the message conveyed by Opinion 2/13 and the task set by CJEU for the negotiators as follows: *The interaction of Protocol No 16 with the EU legal system creates a challenge. Rather than addressing it, the envisaged accession agreement risks worsening the situation. Something has to be done to resolve the relationship between the advisory-opinion and preliminary reference procedures. The accession instruments must ensure that the advisory-opinion procedure – as a supplement to the Convention's judicial system – does not erode the preliminary reference procedure, which remains 'the keystone of the judicial system established by the [EU] Treaties'.*[61]

4. The Revised Accession Instruments

The issue of Protocol No 16 was settled relatively late in the negotiations, largely due to a choice made before they began.[62] Initially, it was thought useful to examine the issue of Protocol No 16 alongside that of inter-party applications, as the two shared several characteristics.[63] Both centered on ensuring that the CJEU would not be circumvented by recourse to alternative procedures for addressing similar legal issues before the ECtHR; both involved difficulties that could potentially arise even without EU accession to the ECHR; and both required determining whether a matter brought before

[54] View of Advocate General Kokott (see n 43 above), point 140.
[55] CJEU, Opinion 2/13 (see n 12 above), para 199.
[56] D Halberstam, 'It's the Autonomy, Stupid!' (2015).
[57] A Stone Sweet, *The Judicial Construction of Europe* (Oxford, Oxford University Press, 2004) 45–108, at 67.
[58] See, eg, CJEU, Joined Cases C-188/10 and C-189/10 *Melki and Addeli* ECLI:EU:C:2010:363, para 45, and CJEU, C-124/21 *International Skating Union* ECLI:EU:C:2023:1012, paras 191–202.
[59] CJEU, Opinion 2/13 (see n 12 above), para 198.
[60] CJEU, Opinion 2/13 (see n 12 above), para 197.
[61] CJEU, Opinion 2/13 (see n 12 above), para 198.
[62] Report of the 15th negotiating meeting, 46+1(2022)R15 of 7 October 2022, paras 11 and 12.
[63] EU position paper, 47+1(2020)1 of 13 March 2020, section 3. See also the Chair Steering Paper, 47+1(2020)2 of 31 August 2020, paras 73–82 (and Appendix I, 27–28).

the ECtHR fell within the scope of EU law. However, it soon became clear that linking the two issues complicated the search for a solution. An early attempt by the EU to tackle both issues simultaneously was met with skepticism in the 46+1 Group.[64] The consensus emerged that addressing each separately would be more effective, starting with inter-party applications.[65] This approach proved more productive: by the time the Group revisited Protocol No 16, all participants had gained a better understanding of each other's respective concerns, which eased the path to an agreement.[66]

In the end, the Group settled on the following provision for inclusion in the operative part of the accession agreement (Article 5):

> Where a court or tribunal of a member State of the European Union that has ratified Protocol No 16 to the Convention, in the context of a case pending before it, encounters a question relating to the interpretation or application of the rights and freedoms defined in the Convention or the Protocols thereto, that court or tribunal shall not be considered as a highest court or tribunal of a High Contracting Party for the purposes of Article 1, paragraph 1, of Protocol No 16 to the Convention if the question falls within the field of application of European Union law.

The new provision essentially clarifies that, in matters of EU law, national courts of EU Member States – including those at the top of the national judicial hierarchy – are not regarded as a 'highest court or tribunal' within the meaning of Protocol No 16. This means that Protocol No 16 must be interpreted and applied in a way that recognises the CJEU as the highest 'domestic court' in matters of EU law.

This solution aligns with the rationale of both the EU legal system and Protocol No 16. It respects the structure of the EU legal system, where the judiciary comprises national courts and the CJEU, with the latter serving as the apex court.[67] At the same time, it honours the purpose of Protocol No. 16, which – 'consistent with the idea of exhaustion of domestic remedies' and 'to avoid a proliferation of requests' – seeks to foster dialogue between the ECtHR and courts 'at the summit' of the domestic judicial system.[68] In essence, the Group's new provision in the accession agreement merely clarifies that, in matters of EU law, the relevant domestic judicial system is that of the EU.

The practical consequence of this understanding of Protocol No 16 is that, when EU law and Convention law intersect – as in the case of *Centraal Israëlitische Consistorie van België and Others*[69] mentioned earlier – a highest national court or tribunal in an EU Member State that has ratified Protocol No 16 cannot use the advisory–opinion mechanism. It has only the preliminary reference procedure at its disposal. The Group has

[64] EU text proposals for Baskets 1 and 2 and Article 53, 2 November 2020; Report of the 7th negotiating meeting, 47+1(2021)R7 of 26 November 2020, para 14.

[65] Report of the 8th negotiating meeting, 47+1(2021)R8 of 4 February 2021, para 15. See also the Document by the Secretariat on the State of Play of the proposals for Basket 2, 47+1(2022)19 of 10 February 2022.

[66] Report of the 14th negotiating meeting, 46+1(2022)R14 of 7 July 2022, paras 8 to 14.

[67] See Article 19(1) TEU. The Group's solution for the issue of Protocol No 16 is based on the same conceptual framework that underpins the prior involvement procedure. That procedure aims to ensure, essentially, that, in matters of EU law, the Court of Justice has spoken before the ECtHR fulfils its role under Article 34 of the ECHR, in full respect of the Convention principle of subsidiarity. See paras 74 and 77 of the Explanatory Report.

[68] Paragraph 8 of the Explanatory Report to Protocol No 16 to the ECHR.

[69] CJEU, *Centraal Israëlitische* (see n 37 above).

added a paragraph to the Explanatory Report to eliminate any ambiguity on this point.[70] This paragraph also underscores that the individual application route under Article 34 of the ECHR remains open. It further confirms that the designated highest courts and tribunals of the EU member States that have ratified Protocol No 16 remain free 'to seek advisory opinions from the [European Court of Human Rights] on any question that falls outside the field of application of EU law'.[71]

The key criterion, therefore, is whether a question is connected to EU law. The primary responsibility for making this distinction rests with the national court or tribunal considering an advisory opinion request. This is not new; any court in an EU Member State against whose decisions there is no judicial remedy under national law must already apply this distinction to determine its obligations under Article 267 TFEU. The secondary responsibility rests with the ECtHR. For example, if it were to receive a request for an advisory opinion on the compatibility of EU law with the Convention, one would expect the ECtHR to decline the request, as the requesting court would not be the 'highest court or tribunal' within the meaning of Protocol No 16.

A critical observer might note that this solution requires the ECtHR to carry out an assessment of the scope of EU law and thus, by implication, of 'the rules of EU law concerning the division of powers between the EU and its Member States'.[72] How can this be compatible with Opinion 2/13? To understand this, it is essential to examine the two contexts in which the CJEU raised concerns about the ECtHR assessing the division of powers between the EU and its Member States. The first setting involves determining the material conditions for applying the co-respondent mechanism.[73] The second concerns the apportionment of responsibility between the EU and its Member States for a violation of the ECHR.[74] In both settings, the ECtHR would need to decide who is accountable for a violation of the ECHR, ultimately based on its own interpretation of the division of powers between the EU and its Member States. What these settings have in common, therefore, is that each could result in a judgment by the ECtHR grounded in *that* court's division-of-powers assessment.[75] Crucially, the judgment of the ECtHR would be 'binding upon the institutions of the Union and on its Member States'.[76] In effect, this would grant the ECtHR the final say on the division of powers between EU and its Member States in cases brought before it. That problem does not arise in the context of Protocol No 16. Of course, it would be problematic if both the requesting court and the ECtHR mistakenly treated a within-the-scope-of-EU-law case as outside the scope of EU law. This scenario is hopefully unlikely. But even if such an error were to occur, it would not lead to a final, binding ruling by the ECtHR on the scope of EU law – or, by extension, on the division of powers between

[70] Explanatory Report para 86, 46+1(2023)36 of 17 March 2023.
[71] ibid.
[72] CJEU, Opinion 2/13 (see n 12 above), para 221. See also paras 224 and 230.
[73] ibid, paras 222–25.
[74] ibid, paras 230–34.
[75] Another setting in which this problem arises is: inter-party applications under Article 33 of the ECHR in disputes between EU Member States. See Article 4(3) and (4) of the draft Accession Agreement and paragraphs 83 and 84 of the Explanatory Report.
[76] Article 216(2) TFEU. See also CJEU, Opinion 2/13 (see n 12 above), para 224.

the EU and its Member States.[77] The autonomy of EU law – in the sense that only EU law *itself* can ultimately define its scope – remains intact.

There is an argument to be made that, even under the law as it stands today, the ECtHR might interpret Protocol No 16 as implying that national courts should not use the advisory–opinion mechanism to raise questions about the compatibility of EU acts or provisions with the ECHR.[78] Such an approach would reflect a harmonious understanding between the two European courts regarding their respective roles and legal systems. In any event, with the new provision in the accession agreement, the Group heeded the CJEU's call to '[make] provision in respect of the relationship between the mechanism established by Protocol No 16 and the preliminary ruling procedure provided for in Article 267 TFEU'.[79]

An intriguing question is whether the EU itself should eventually accede to Protocol No 16, allowing the CJEU to seek advisory opinions from the ECtHR. The new provision in the draft accession agreement is neutral in this regard and works regardless of whether the EU decides to accede to the Protocol.[80] However, the Group amended Article 1 of the draft accession agreement to allow the EU to accede to Protocol No 16 if it so chooses.[81] The draft accession agreement, therefore, does more than clarify the relationship between the advisory–opinion procedure and the preliminary reference procedure: it plants a seed for potentially deepening the judicial dialogue between the two courts.

5. Conclusion

Judicial dialogue represents a distinct yet important aspect of the protection of human and fundamental rights at the European level. Protocol No 16 and Article 267 TFEU each facilitate judicial dialogue within their respective legal ecosystems – the Convention system and the EU legal order. These two ecosystems are already deeply interconnected, and the EU's accession to the ECHR would further solidify that connection.

The relationship between the advisory–opinion procedure and the preliminary reference procedure, considered in the context of the EU's accession to the ECHR, illustrates the broader challenge of ensuring the two systems work smoothly together. It also showcases the continuously evolving relationship between the two European courts.

By clarifying that the advisory–opinion procedure under Protocol No 16 is not available to EU Member States' highest courts in matters of EU law, the revised accession agreement strikes a delicate balance. It acknowledges the EU's constitutional structure

[77] This contrasts with rulings of the ECtHR in inter-party applications under Article 33 ECHR, which are binding on the parties. To address this, the Group introduced a safeguard clause to ensure full respect for Article 344 TFEU while preventing the ECtHR from defining the scope of EU law. See Article 4(3) and (4) of the draft Accession Agreement and in paras 80 to 85 of the Explanatory Report, 46+1(2023)36 of 17 March 2023.

[78] J Callewaert, 'Protocol No 16 and EU law' in *Essays in honour of Dean Spielmann* (Nijmegen, Wolf Legal, 2017).

[79] CJEU, Opinion 2/13 (see n 12 above), para 199.

[80] Report of the 14th negotiating meeting, 46+1(2022)R14 of 7 July 2022, para 12.

[81] See Article 1(2) of the draft Accession Agreement, 46+1(2023)36 of 17 March 2023.

while preserving the coherence of the Convention system. The inclusion of provisions allowing the EU to potentially accede to Protocol No 16 paves the way for new opportunities to strengthen the ties between Strasbourg and Luxembourg.

Of course, this is not the final chapter of this story. Many questions remain: Will the CJEU and the ECtHR embrace this framework? Will national courts rise to the occasion and make it their own? I cannot pretend to know the answers. But I do know this: in Europe's overlapping legal systems, the way forward will often depend less on definitive answers than on a commitment to dialogue and cooperation in the pursuit of justice.

PART IV

The Need for Speed: Time-limits and Interim Measures for the Protection of Fundamental Rights

11

Repetitive Strain at the European Court of Human Rights: Responding to the Caseload Caused by Structural and Systemic Problems

DAVID MILNER[1]

1. Introduction

Repetitive cases have for decades been one of the main problems facing the European Court of Human Rights (the Court or ECtHR) and, along with clearly inadmissible applications, one of the main causes of its demanding caseload.

Repetitive cases are caused primarily by circumstances at the national level. Often described as systemic or structural problems, these relate to a situation that affects individuals in a way that repeatedly and persistently violates their protected rights. Once the ECtHR has found a violation in one of these cases, subsequent cases relating to the same underlying problem are considered as repetitive, since they involve largely the same factual situation and legal issues as have already been addressed by the Court.

Common examples of a situation giving rise to repetitive applications are detention conditions, where overcrowding or a lack of basic amenities results in violations of detainees' rights under Article 3 of the European Convention on Human Rights (the Convention or ECHR) (prohibition of inhuman or degrading punishment), or judicial systems, where excessive length of proceedings or non-execution of domestic court judgments results in violations of rights under Article 6 (right to a fair trial).[2] Such situations are often the result of flaws in the legal or administrative framework, or a lack of resources. In all cases, they amount to a failure by the State to respect its obligation under Article 1 to guarantee the rights and freedoms to those within its jurisdiction.

A secondary cause of repetitive applications is the lack of an effective domestic remedy for the violation in question, which amounts to failure to fulfil the obligation

[1] Head of the Human Rights Intergovernmental Co-operation Division and Secretary to the Steering Committee for Human Rights, Council of Europe. The views expressed are those of the author alone and do not represent an official position of the Council of Europe. The author would like to thank Kanstantsin Dzehtsiarou, John Darcy, and Klaudiusz Ryngielewicz for their valuable contributions to the preparation of this chapter; any errors are the author's own.

[2] All references to Articles relate to the ECHR, unless stated otherwise.

under Article 13 ECHR. Had such a remedy existed, individuals would have been required to have recourse to it before applying to the ECtHR, in accordance with the admissibility criterion set out in Article 35(1). Instead, the violation remains unresolved, and the individual may turn their attention to Strasbourg in search of redress.

A tertiary cause of repetitive applications is the failure fully and promptly to implement a prior judgment of the ECtHR relating to the underlying cause, which reflects a failure under Article 46(1). Had the initial (often referred to as 'leading') judgment been fully implemented, either the cause of the violations would have been resolved, or a remedy would have been introduced to deal with any resulting violations at the domestic level.

In short, repetitive applications constitute a compound failure to implement the Convention at national level due to dysfunction in public administration, with adverse consequences for large numbers of individuals and, on account of the number of applications that those individuals may make, the Court.

The problem of repetitive applications has long been recognised as one of the major challenges to the effectiveness of the Convention system. The explanatory report to Protocol No 14, adopted in May 2004, noted that

> It is generally recognised that the Court's excessive caseload … manifests itself in two areas in particular: i. processing the very numerous individual applications which are terminated without a ruling on the merits, usually because they are declared inadmissible …, and ii. processing individual applications which derive from the same structural cause as an earlier application that has led to a judgment finding a breach of the Convention (repetitive cases …).

The fundaments of the current structure of the ECtHR and its judicial procedures were established by Protocol No 14. Article 8 of the protocol amended Article 28 ECHR to introduce a new three-judge Committee procedure. This is intended, in particular, for cases in which the underlying legal issue is already the subject of 'well-established case law' (WECL) of the Court. Committees were thereby empowered to rule on admissibility, on the merits of a case, and to award just satisfaction in a single decision, establishing a simplified and accelerated procedure for repetitive cases (or groups of such cases). This is often referred to as the 'WECL procedure', which the ECtHR has subsequently applied and developed in creative ways. Under Article 28(2), Committee judgments are final; the parties cannot request that the case be referred to the Grand Chamber.

Despite the recent adoption of Protocol No 14, concerns about the ECtHR's caseload, including the number of repetitive applications, persisted and were prominent in discussions at the Third Summit of Heads of State and Government of the Council of Europe (Warsaw, 2005). At the Summit, a decision was taken to ask a Group of Wise Persons

> to consider the long-term effectiveness of the ECHR control mechanism, including the initial effects of Protocol No 14 and the other decisions taken in May 2004, [and] to submit, as soon as possible, proposals going beyond these measures, while preserving the basic philosophy underlying the Convention.[3]

The Group of Wise Persons submitted their report to the Committee of Ministers in 2006.

[3] Action Plan, CM(2005)80 final.

Since then, possible responses to the problem of repetitive applications have been considered and developed in two fora. The ECtHR itself has taken a number of initiatives, notably through the pilot-judgment procedure and its development of application of the WECL procedure.[4] At the same time, intergovernmental bodies of the Council of Europe, in particular a series of high-level conferences and the Steering Committee for Human Rights (CDDH, known by its French acronym),[5] in the context of ongoing reflections on reform of the Convention system.

2. Initiatives Taken by the ECtHR

The ECtHR has been faced with an extremely challenging caseload since the enlargement of the Council of Europe to include Central and Eastern European countries in the 1990s and early 2000s. Whilst its resources have increased very significantly since this period, they are still finite, and whilst the Court is expected to render a judicial decision on every application that it receives, to some extent choices must be made in how different applications are processed.

The ECtHR first introduced its priority policy in June 2009, as part of a process of allocating resources according to objective need.[6] The policy is intended to speed up the processing of the most important, serious and urgent cases. It establishes seven categories of case: repetitive cases may fall into either category III ('Applications which on their face raise as main complaints issues under Articles 2, 3, 4 or 5 § 1 of the Convention ('core rights'), irrespective of whether they are repetitive, and which have given rise to direct threats to the physical integrity and dignity of human beings'), or V ('Applications raising issues already dealt with in a pilot/leading judgment ('well established case-law cases')').[7] The Court's resources tend to be devoted more to higher priority cases than lower priority ones, meaning that an increase in the number of judgments determining lower priority cases requires improvements in case-processing efficiency.

In order to address this dilemma, the ECtHR has implemented a number of innovative case-processing measures. These can be described as being aimed either at resolving a large number of related cases in a single set of proceedings, or at greatly simplifying the procedures involved in resolving individual cases.

An example of the first type of measure was introduced at around the same time as the priority policy, when the ECtHR began grouping related repetitive applications together in greater numbers, to be sent to the respondent Government with only a very short statement of the facts. Two hundred cases involving non-execution of domestic

[4] The pilot-judgment procedure, the most innovative of the Court's initiatives, is the subject of a separate chapter of this book and will not be examined in detail here.

[5] The CDDH is a plenary intergovernmental expert committee that reports directly to the Committee of Ministers on issues relating to human rights in general and the ECHR in particular. Its main areas of activity are the system of the ECHR and the development of human rights standards in response to new societal challenges.

[6] The policy was updated in May 2017. These changes did not concern repetitive applications.

[7] Applications 'raising questions capable of having an impact on the effectiveness of the Convention system (in particular a structural or endemic situation that the Court has not yet examined, pilot-judgment procedure)', ie those that may lead to a pilot or leading judgment – the first in a potential series of repetitive cases – fall into category II.

court decisions were sent to Russia in one simultaneous communication, for example, and 500 length of judicial proceedings cases were communicated to Italy. Judgments in such cases tended to be rather succinct, with the reasoning limited to a finding that the case concerns a situation in which the ECtHR has already found numerous violations, with no reason to reach a different conclusion in the present case.[8]

The WECL procedure – itself an example of the second type of measure, ie a procedural simplification – was first used in 2009 under Protocol No 14 bis and the Madrid Agreement.[9] Thus even before the full entry into force of Protocol No 14 in 2010, the ECtHR began streamlining the processing of cases under the WECL procedure. Once a judge rapporteur identifies a case as suitable for this procedure, the respondent Government is not proactively invited to submit observations but is rather only given an opportunity to do so, if it so wishes, and the parties would be encouraged to settle the case. In the absence of settlement, the applicant would be informed of any observations submitted by the Government and would be asked to submit any claim for payment of just satisfaction under Article 41. The case would then be presented to the Committee for examination. This procedure involved fewer rounds of submissions, allowing more rapid determination of the case (especially in the case of friendly settlement).[10]

The ECtHR further refined its approach in 2015, when it developed the 'fast-track WECL procedure'. This allows the Court to deal quickly with cases that are wholly covered by well-established case law. An automated drafting process and tight internal deadlines mean that the Court can dispose of these cases – in 2015, they represented up to 80 per cent of pending repetitive cases – within a year of receipt, on a 'one in, one out' basis. This procedure accounted for between 47 per cent and 61 per cent of all of the ECtHR's communications of cases to respondent States, judgments and decisions in the years 2015–2017.[11]

In 2019, the ECtHR introduced a 'non-contentious phase' into proceedings, potentially applicable to both Committee and Chamber cases.[12] This takes place alongside the process of communicating an application to the respondent State. A declaration may be sent to both parties suggesting the terms of a potential friendly settlement, in the light of the case law and practice of the ECtHR. The parties are asked to respond to this proposal within a set deadline. If no declaration is sent, the parties are requested to consider making their own proposal of a friendly settlement, or may ask the Registry to make a suggestion, again, within a certain deadline. Finally, if negotiations on a friendly settlement are unsuccessful, the Government may submit a unilateral declaration.[13] Under

[8] E Fribergh, 'Bring the Rights Home: How to Deal with Repetitive Applications in the Future', Round Table on the Right to Trial Within a Reasonable Time and Short-term Reform of the European Court of Human Rights, Bled, 2009.

[9] Protocol No 14 bis and the Madrid Agreement allowed for provisional application of certain provisions of Protocol No 14 for those States that accepted it. They were adopted in response to the prolonged delay in the entry into force of Protocol No 14 and the continuing growth in the ECtHR's caseload.

[10] Fribergh, 'Bring the Rights Home' (2009).

[11] Follow-up to the CDDH Report on the Longer-Term Future of the system of the European Convention on Human Rights: Information from the Court, #5930604, January 2018.

[12] European Court of Human Rights, Press Release, 'ECHR is to test a new practice involving a dedicated non-contentious phase', 18 December 2018. After an initial one-year test period, the practice was maintained.

[13] 'Information to Applicants: Procedure following communication of an application – non-contentious phase', European Court of Human Rights, 30 July 2020. If the applicant refuses without justification to accept a reasonable proposal of a friendly settlement by the respondent State, the latter may file a unilateral declaration with the ECtHR, accompanied by a request for the application to be struck out.

Article 37(1), the Court may strike the case out of its list following either a friendly settlement or a unilateral declaration. Given that Committees by definition deal with cases in which the legal issue is the subject of well-established case law, one might assume that the Registry is particularly likely to make a suggestion for a friendly settlement in relation to repetitive cases. The non-contentious phase is therefore likely to be particularly effective as a means of resolving these; indeed, one could identify the possible origins of this approach in the way in which the ECtHR first began applying the WECL procedure in 2009 (see above).

A further innovation was introduced in 2021, initially for a two-year trial period, in the form of 'summary-formula judgments and decisions'.[14] Committees began drafting in a 'significantly more concise and focused manner', with the aim of responding to applications in a more timely manner, increasing the output of Committees, shifting resources towards higher priority cases (especially 'impact' cases),[15] and reducing the backlog. The idea was to limit the text of summary-formula judgments and decisions to pertinent non-disputed facts followed by a succinct legal analysis, although there would be no changes to the operative part. The Registry lawyers responsible for these cases would still study the case file in detail and the cases would still be examined by Committees of three judges.

The ECtHR has also used retrospective application of the admissibility criterion of exhaustion of domestic remedies to remove groups of repetitive cases from its docket. Normally, the Court will apply this criterion with respect to remedies existing at the time of application, but in certain circumstances it has found applications to be inadmissible on account of a remedy that was established after the date on which they were submitted. This approach can allow the Court to determine large numbers of repetitive (or potentially repetitive) cases. A good example of this concerns compensation for deprivation of use of property or denial of access to homes of persons who were displaced from the northern part of Cyprus following Turkish military operations there in 1974. In 2005, the de facto authorities in the northern part of Cyprus introduced a remedy in the form of the Immovable Property Commission, a result of the ECtHR's pilot-judgment in the case of *Xenides-Arestis v Türkiye*.[16] In a 2010 Grand Chamber decision of inadmissibility in the case of *Demopoulos v Türkiye* and seven other cases,[17] all of which had been lodged before 2005, the ECtHR found that the applicants should exhaust the remedy provided by the IPC.[18]

The origins of some of the ECtHR's initiatives can be identified in connection with particular cases or specific situations. Possibly for reasons of terminology, it is not clear whether the approaches taken in these cases are 'prototypes' of a new case-processing

[14] See Annual Report of the European Court of Human Rights, 2021.

[15] 'Impact cases' are cases in priority policy category IV (potentially well-founded applications based on Articles other than 2, 3, 4, or 5(1)) that may raise very important issues of relevance for the State in question and/or the Convention system as a whole and justify more expeditious case-processing. Under a policy introduced in 2021, such cases fall into a new 'category IV-High'.

[16] ECtHR, App no 46347/99 ECLI:CE:ECHR:2005:1222JUD004634799.

[17] ECtHR (GC), App nos 46113/99 et al ECLI:CE:ECHR:2010:0301DEC004611399.

[18] Another example would be the case of ECtHR, App no 10755/13 *Hasan Uzun v Türkiye* ECLI:CE:ECHR:2013:0430DEC001075513 concerning a newly introduced Turkish constitutional complaint, which the ECtHR considered to be a domestic remedy that the applicant should now be required to exhaust.

policy of the Court, variants on an existing policy, or sui generis approaches developed for a specific situation.

In 2011–2012, there was a massive influx of applications against Hungary, all concerning the pension rights of former law enforcement officers who benefited from early retirement. In a press release, the Court's Registrar stated that the ECtHR could not process such a large number of similar applications in the normal way and encouraged the national trade unions to resubmit grouped applications, with annexed lists of individuals' names and details. The Court would then examine as a priority one or more applications as leading cases and until then, not process any of the others. It would not accept applications that were not lodged through a trade union, would not inform individuals that their applications had been registered, and would not correspond with individual applicants.[19] These conditions were intended to facilitate the subsequent handling of large numbers of related cases. In 2014, by which time over 13,500 related applications had been received in 1,260 cases, the ECtHR declared three leading cases (ie the first cases arising from this underlying situation to be adjudicated) to be inadmissible.[20]

Repetitive cases relating to the non-execution of domestic court decisions in Ukraine were for many years a very significant problem, for which the ECtHR tried several different approaches. The first was the 2009 pilot judgment in the *Ivanov* case, which unfortunately did not produce the necessary results.[21] Following the termination of the *Ivanov* pilot-judgment procedure, the ECtHR adopted the *Kharuk* Committee judgment, which established a simplified basis for calculating awards of just satisfaction depending on how long a decision had remained unexecuted.[22] The ECtHR then applied an 'expedited committee procedure'.[23] This involved the Registry sending tables of cases to the Ukrainian government; neither the application form nor any documents submitted by the applicant were provided unless the government requested them. The possibility of friendly settlement was not suggested; instead, the government was invited to proceed directly to a unilateral declaration of its intention to resolve all of the cases listed in the table in accordance with the *Kharuk* judgment, in which case the ECtHR would strike those cases out of its list. In the absence of a unilateral declaration, the ECtHR would give judgment after six months. The Registry reached a working agreement with the Ukrainian Government to communicate no more than 250 cases per month. In practice, however, the Ukrainian Government agent's office lacked the capacity to respond and make unilateral declarations in so many cases, although it did examine them to see whether particular circumstances would justify the cases being treated differently.[24]

[19] European Court of Human Rights, Press Release, 'European Court Registrar calls for special measures to deal with influx of Hungarian pension cases, 11 January 2012.

[20] European Court of Human Rights, Press Release, 'Legislation to restructure retired servicemen's pensions in Hungary was neither excessive nor discriminatory, 18 July 2014.

[21] ECtHR, App no 40450/04 *Yuriy Nikolayevich Ivanov v Ukraine* ECLI:CE:ECHR:2009:1015JUD004045004.

[22] ECtHR, App no 703/05 and 115 others, *Kharuk and Others v Ukraine* ECLI:CE:ECHR:2012:0726JUD000070305.

[23] The key characteristic of the 'expedited committee procedure' is that whole lists of related cases are communicated to the respondent government. By contrast, the 'fast-track WECL procedure', whilst also seeking to simplify and reduce the length of proceedings, does not depend on mass communications.

[24] CDDH Report containing conclusions and possible proposals for action on ways to resolve the large numbers of applications arising from systemic issues identified by the ECtHR, CDDH(2013)R78, Addendum III.

Between September 2012 and April 2013, 1,515 cases were thus communicated to the Government and 487 judgments adopted. The effectiveness of this procedure in providing financial compensation to applicants, however, had – from the ECtHR's perspective, at least – counter-productive consequences. The Court observed that awareness in Ukraine of this approach had the effect of attracting significant numbers of new applications: 1100 in April 2013 alone, ie two thirds of the number of new applications were received in one month as had been communicated to the Government in the previous eight months; until then, around 300–350 new applications had been received per month.

Kharuk thus provided the basis for a procedure allowing the ECtHR to process these cases quickly and with minimum effort, but it did not address the underlying problem. In October 2017, the ECtHR therefore took an unprecedented step: in the case of *Burmych & others*,[25] it struck out of its list and transmitted to the Committee of Ministers over 12,000 pending applications against Ukraine. The ECtHR considered that by this stage, it had 'discharged its function under Article 19 of the Convention' by identifying the systemic shortcoming, holding that there had been a violation on account of this shortcoming, and giving guidance on general measures to ensure redress and relief for all victims of it. 'In accordance with the principle of subsidiarity', the Court concluded, 'the matter treated by the *Ivanov* pilot judgment … is a question of execution under Article 46 of the Convention.'[26] The cases covered by the *Burmych* judgment, and any similar future applications, were

> part and parcel of the process of execution of the pilot judgment. Consequently, all such cases […] should be notified to the Committee of Ministers in its capacity as the body which, under the Convention system, has the responsibility to oversee redress and justice for all the victims affected by the systemic problem found in a pilot judgment … Having regard to the respective competences of the Court and the Committee of Ministers under Articles 19 and 46 of the Convention, the Court is forced to conclude that no useful purpose is served in terms of the Convention's aims in its continuing to deal with these cases in accordance with the practice hitherto followed.[27]

The ECtHR also applied the expedited committee procedure – which it sometimes referred to as a 'default judgment procedure' – to a group of cases against Serbia concerning non-enforcement of domestic decisions. 430 such cases were communicated with proposals for friendly settlement in May 2012, followed by a further 270. The Serbian Government did not settle the cases but did inform the Court that the Constitutional Court's case law had evolved so as to afford an effective remedy. A subsequent admissibility decision of the ECtHR, however, showed this to be only partly true. The ECtHR nevertheless considered that the grouped communication had exerted pressure on the national authorities to take action and there was therefore no need for a 'default judgment' at this stage.[28]

[25] ECtHR (GC), App nos 46852/13 et al, *Burmych and others v Ukraine* ECLI:CE:ECHR:2017:1012JUD004685213.
[26] ibid, para 197.
[27] ibid, paras 198–99.
[28] CDDH(2013)R78, Report of the 78th meeting of the Steering Committee for Human Rights (CDDH), Addendum III, para 28.

Another situation in which the ECtHR found itself confronted by thousands of cases involving the same essential issue concerned persons who had been convicted in Türkiye of membership of an armed terrorist organisation due to their alleged use of the encrypted messaging application Bylock. In September 2023, the Grand Chamber of the ECtHR ruled that such convictions, when based decisively on an individual's use of Bylock, amounted to violations of Articles 6 (right to a fair trial) and 7 (no punishment without law) of the ECHR.[29] At the time, there were some 8,500 similar applications pending before the ECtHR. In December 2023, the ECtHR announced that five cases, each one covering 500 applications, had been notified to the Turkish government, without any of the questions or request for observations that would usually be part of the communication of a case to the respondent State. This process was repeated in April, July, and November 2024. It is expected that the Bylock cases will be determined by Committee judgments, on the basis that the September 2023 judgment constitutes well-established case law.

3. Intergovernmental Work

As the most important normative instrument of the Council of Europe and a constitutional instrument of European public order, the ECHR has always been a matter of keen interest to the Member States, who are at once its ultimate rule-makers, institutional custodians and, as High Contracting Parties, under an obligation to implement its provisions, including by participating in proceedings before the ECtHR. The Member States demonstrate this interest on various levels, including high-level political events (such as the above-mentioned Third Summit) and special conferences, the regular work of expert-level committees, and cooperation with research institutes.[30] The overall purpose of this work is to gather information on the situation of the ECtHR (and the other actors in the Convention system, notably national authorities and the Committee of Ministers), provide an opportunity for reflection and discussion, to submit proposals for possible reform to the Committee of Ministers, or discretely to signal the States' views or expectations to the Court. The Committee of Ministers can then consider taking various actions, from political declarations, to the adoption of non-binding instruments such as guidelines or recommendations to the Member States, or even protocols amending the ECHR or optionally adding substantive rights to those that it guarantees.

The 2006 Wise Persons' Report[31] and especially the 2010 Interlaken Conference[32] prompted a lengthy period of intense inter-governmental work on all aspects of the system of the ECHR. This work was primarily conducted in the CDDH, with political interventions coming in the form of further high-level conferences in Izmir (2011), Brighton (2012), Brussels (2015), and Copenhagen (2018).

[29] ECtHR (GC), App no 15669/20 *Yüksel Yalcinkaya v Türkiye* ECLI:CE:ECHR:2023:0926JUD001566920.

[30] An example of the latter would be the Conference on the long-term future of the European Court of Human Rights, organised by PluriCourts under the auspices of the Council of Europe in Oslo, Norway on 7–8 April 2014.

[31] Report of the Group of Wise Persons to the Committee of Ministers, CM(2006)203.

[32] High-level Conference on the Future of the European Court of Human Rights, Interlaken, Switzerland, 18–19 February 2010.

One of the Wise Persons' proposals was directly relevant to the problem of repetitive cases: to establish a 'Judicial Committee' within the ECtHR to deal with both these and clearly inadmissible applications, with the number of judges on the Court itself then reduced, in line with its work-load.

In 2012, the CDDH adopted a report containing proposals for measures requiring amendment of the ECHR.[33] By this stage, Protocol No 14 – which, amongst other things, introduced a new 'Single Judge procedure' for clearly inadmissible cases and empowered Committees of three judges to adjudicate repetitive cases (see above) – had finally entered into force (on 1 June 2010). The ECtHR's implementation of the Single Judge procedure for clearly inadmissible applications was proving even more effective than had been hoped, and the number of such applications pending was falling rapidly. The CDDH noted, however, that the ECtHR's overall approach had left the 34,000 low priority repetitive cases 'with little prospect of adjudication within a reasonable time.'[34] In the circumstances, it therefore decided to shift its attention from a new filtering mechanism intended primarily to deal with clearly inadmissible cases, to measures that could increase the ECtHR's case-processing capacity generally.

The CDDH reported on this issue in 2013, examining two proposals.[35] One involved the creation of a pool of temporary judges (in addition to the existing permanent judges of the ECtHR), who could be called upon for limited periods as and when needed to achieve a balance between incoming applications and disposal decisions, and sitting in any judicial formation other than the Grand Chamber and plenary Court. The other involved the introduction of a new category of judge (again, in addition to the existing permanent judges of the Court) to deal exclusively with repetitive applications and clearly inadmissible (Single Judge) cases. At this stage, however, the good news about the positive effects of the ECtHR's implementation of the Single Judge procedure was so recent that the CDDH had not yet had time fully to evaluate these proposals.

The CDDH recalled that it had also recently examined other ways of dealing with repetitive cases that would not require amendment of the ECHR,[36] as would have been required for any system of additional judge. For this reason, the CDDH considered that other, less 'radical' approaches should first be explored. It also noted that the ECtHR was in the process of shifting its focus from Single Judge and repetitive cases to priority and normal Chamber cases. The question of what type of case would be most appropriate for treatment by additional judges was thus uncertain. Since views in the CDDH were divided on whether to introduce any form of additional judge, it concluded that there was 'no basis for amending the Convention in order to allow the appointment of additional judges to the Court.'

[33] CDDH Final Report on measures requiring amendment of the Convention, CDDH(2012)R74 Addendum I.

[34] The ECtHR itself admitted that it was 'not in a position to deal with [the pending repetitive applications] within a reasonable time': Preliminary Opinion of the Court in preparation for the Brighton Conference, 20 February 2012.

[35] CDDH Report on the question of whether or not to amend the Convention to enable the appointment of additional judges to the Court, CDDH(2013)R79 Addendum III, 29 November 2013.

[36] See below in connection with the CDDH Report containing conclusions and possible proposals for action on ways to resolve the large numbers of applications arising from systemic issues identified by the ECtHR.

In 2013, the CDDH adopted a Report on the advisability and modalities of a 'representative application procedure',[37] an idea that had been raised in the declaration adopted at the 2012 Brighton Conference. This procedure would be intended to build upon the pilot-judgment procedure; apply where there is a group of similar applications; allow the ECtHR to register and determine only a small number of applications from the group; and apply the Court's determination of those applications to the group as a whole. The CDDH carefully reviewed the procedural tools that were then already available to the ECtHR, which it found to include: (i) the pilot-judgment procedure (and variants thereof); (ii) a judgment of principle on a single case from a group, with that principle being applicable to other cases in the group;[38] (iii) joinder of applications to be determined in a single decision or judgment;[39] (iv) invitation to the respondent State to settle a list of cases on the basis of levels of compensation indicated in a previous judgment;[40] (v) the expedited Committee procedure;[41] and (vi) grouping applications from the outset. Given these already available options, the CDDH concluded that 'there would be no significant added value to designing and introducing a 'representative application procedure' in the current circumstances.'

The CDDH also considered that a 'representative application procedure' could not be considered the same as certain other procedures, in particular: a class action, in which the applications by all members of the class would be adjudicated; a collective complaint (as under the protocol to the European Social Charter), which would be brought by a party who is not a member of the group or indeed a victim of the alleged violation; or a default judgment, which would only apply to the individual case under adjudication. Given these limitations, the CDDH was unable to identify modalities for a 'representative application procedure' that would correspond to the description set out in the Brighton Declaration, whilst still showing distinct advantages not already available to the ECtHR.

Later in 2013, the CDDH adopted another, wider-ranging Report containing conclusions and possible proposals for action on ways to resolve the large numbers of applications arising from systemic issues identified by the ECtHR.[42] Again noting the numerous initiatives that the Court had taken (see above), the CDDH did not make any new proposals concerning the Court's procedures. Instead, it encouraged States to 'co-operate fully with the Court in pursuing appropriate procedural solutions to systemic issues and so as to relieve the Court of the burden of repetitive applications, notably through recourse to friendly settlements and unilateral declarations', and the Court 'to explore with the parties possible new forms of practical co-operation, with the aim of simplifying and accelerating the administrative process leading to unilateral

[37] CDDH Report on the advisability and modalities of a 'representative application procedure' CDDH(2013) R77 Addendum IV, 21 March 2013.

[38] As in ECtHR (GC), App no 30696/09 *MSS v Belgium and Greece* ECLI:CE:ECHR:2011:0121JUD003069609, following which the Court asked the Netherlands, although not a party to the case, how it intended to respond to the findings concerning returns of asylum seekers to Greece.

[39] See, eg, ECtHR, App no 45867/07 *Gaglione v Italy* ECLI:CE:ECHR:2010:1221JUD004586707.

[40] As the Court did following the *Gaglione* judgment, when it invited the Italian government to reach friendly settlements with some 7,000 applicants in similar cases.

[41] As applied to Ukrainian cases of non-execution of domestic court decisions on the basis of the *Kharuk* judgment setting out a simplified basis for calculating just satisfaction.

[42] CDDH(2013)R78 Addendum III (see n 28 above).

declarations and strike-out decisions'. It can be noted that shortly after this, the ECtHR introduced the 'fast-track WECL procedure' (see above).

Another proposal supported by the Wise Persons resulted in Protocol No 16, which allows designated highest national courts or tribunals to request an opinion from the ECtHR on questions of principle relating to the interpretation or application of the rights and freedoms defined in the ECHR or the protocols thereto. The CDDH considered that such a procedure might help to address the problem of repetitive applications, notably by giving guidance on potential systemic or structural problems at an earlier stage, thus increasing the chances of the underlying issue being resolved at national level.[43]

Protocol No 16 was adopted in 2013 and entered into force in August 2018. A recent draft report on the first effects of Protocol No 16 concluded that 'it does not appear that any of the requests [to date] has related to systemic issues in the relevant jurisdictions.'[44] That said, advisory opinions under Protocol No 16 have resulted in declarations of unconstitutionality of the relevant domestic legal provisions, changes in the requesting court's jurisprudence, and positive effects on the execution of previous judgments of the ECtHR. The CDDH's expectation of the potential of Protocol No 16 to address situations giving rise to repetitive applications, whilst not yet having been demonstrated in practice, has certainly been given some credence.

4. The Effects of these Developments

There have been significant developments over the past 15 years in the way in which the ECtHR deals with repetitive applications. Despite all of the work done at intergovernmental level, including the follow-up to the Wise Persons' Report and the Interlaken Process between 2010 and 2020, most of these developments have resulted from initiatives taken by the ECtHR using the structures and procedures established by Protocol No 14 or the pilot-judgment procedure that originated in the *Broniowski* judgment,[45] both of which date back to 2004. Some of these initiatives might have exceeded the expectations of the drafters of Protocol No 14, but all were meticulously reasoned by reference to fundamental principles of the Convention system and positions expressed by the States Parties in resolutions, recommendations and political declarations; where necessary, they were developed and implemented in co-operation with the respective respondent State.

The number of repetitive applications seems not, however, to have diminished. Between 2012 and 2024, the number of applications pending before a Committee was generally between 25,000 and 35,000, with exceptional peaks above 45,000 in 2016 and 2023.[46] Indeed, it has remained above 30,000 since 2019, although this may be due

[43] A proposal submitted to the CDDH by the delegations of the Netherlands and Norway had suggested that domestic courts should be allowed to request advisory opinions specifically in the context of cases revealing a potential systemic or structural problem. This approach was not retained.

[44] Draft Report evaluating the first effects of Protocol No 16 to the European Convention on Human Rights, DH-SYSC-PRO(2024)07REV, 15 October 2024.

[45] ECtHR (GC), App no 31443/96 *Broniowski v Poland* ECLI:CE:ECHR:2004:0622JUD003144396.

[46] End-of-year figures taken from the Annual Reports of the European Court of Human Rights.

to the 'broader-WECL policy', introduced in June 2017, which expanded the definition of 'well-established case-law', thereby allocating to Committees some of the 'non-impact category IV'[47] cases that would previously have been allocated to Chambers.[48] It is also true that Committees have issued increasing numbers of judgments: 814 in 2024, in respect of 10,241 applications, being a 19 per cent increase in the number of judgments and a 60 per cent increase in the number of applications as compared to 2023.[49] These basic figures will not tell the whole story but it seems difficult to read them in a way that suggests the problem has come to an end.

When considering these figures, however, one must bear in mind that a certain number of pending cases is inevitable: the ECtHR cannot resolve every application the moment it is received. The 2012 Brighton Declaration introduced the principle that the Court should be able to decide whether to communicate a case within one year, and thereafter to make all communicated cases the subject of a decision or judgment within a further two years. Any applications not treated within these periods would be considered to form part of the 'Brighton backlog'. The Brighton backlog of repetitive applications on 1 October 2012 was around 22,000; at the end of 2014 it was just under 18,700; and by 30 June 2016, it had decreased to 11,800.[50] In a 2015 report, the CDDH noted that the ECtHR had estimated that the Brighton backlog of repetitive applications would be cleared within two to three years.[51] On this basis, the CDDH concluded that it 'does not discern a need for the adoption of further measures regarding this part of the backlog.'[52]

The issue of repetitive cases was nevertheless mentioned in the final declarations adopted at conferences in Brussels (2015) and Copenhagen (2018). At the former, participants were 'convinced that further to the improvements already carried out, emphasis must now be placed on the current challenges, in particular the repetitive applications resulting from the non-execution of Court judgments [and certain other issues]'; they did not, however, make any substantively new proposals to this end. Three years later in Copenhagen, the conference called on the Committee of Ministers to 'consider the most effective means to address the challenge of a massive influx of repetitive applications arising from the non-execution of pilot judgments, which can place a significant burden on the Court without necessarily helping to resolve the underlying issue.'

[47] ie priority policy category IV cases that do not fall within the 'impact case' category IV-High (see above).

[48] Follow-up to the CDDH Report on the Longer-Term Future of the system of the European Convention on Human Rights, European Court of Human Rights, #5930604, January 2018.

[49] 'Analysis of Statistics 2024', European Court of Human Rights, January 2025. The Committee of Ministers, however, reports a gradual decline in the numbers of new repetitive cases transmitted to it for supervision of execution, from an annual total that fluctuated around 1,100 between 2012 and 2018, to just under 870 in 2022 and 2023: see 'Supervision of the Execution of Judgment and Decisions of the European Court of Human Rights 2021: 15th Annual Report of the Committee of Ministers', March 2022, and 'Supervision of the Execution of Judgment and Decisions of the European Court of Human Rights 2023: 17th Annual Report of the Committee of Ministers', April 2024.

[50] The Interlaken Process and the Court, reports for 2012, 2014, and 2016, European Court of Human Rights. The 2016 report was the last in the series.

[51] CDDH Report on the longer-term future of the system of the European Convention on Human Rights, CDDH(2015)R84 Addendum I, December 2015.

[52] The fact that the number of cases pending before Committees has in recent years been higher than it was in 2015, however, raises questions in this respect.

In its 2019 'Contribution to the evaluation provided for by the Interlaken Declaration',[53] the CDDH recalled that 'a large number of possible, partly far-reaching changes to the procedure before the Court were analysed by the CDDH but not retained in the end. This reflects its assessment that the challenges the system is faced with are best addressed within its current framework.' Its conclusions were then limited to the observation that 'As regards the backlog of repetitive cases, further efforts are necessary by all actors in the Convention system.' The Committee of Ministers' subsequent decisions on 'Securing the long-term effectiveness of the system of the European Convention on Human Rights', adopted in November 2020 and which marked a formal end to the Interlaken Process, made scant reference to repetitive applications.

5. Conclusions

The problem of repetitive cases has been the subject of intense attention from both the Contracting Parties to the ECHR and the ECtHR. The ECtHR in particular has taken a number of initiatives that have significantly increased its capacity to process these cases efficiently and effectively.

Whilst the pilot-judgment procedure is the most innovative and striking of these initiatives, it has been used in relatively few situations. The WECL procedure before Committees, as gradually developed by the ECtHR, has been applied to resolve a far greater number of cases. Overall, the ECtHR's evolving practice has seen it extend its influence over implementation of the ECHR at different levels beyond its essential role of ruling on the merits of an individual's claim to be a victim of a violation of a protected right and awarding just satisfaction. The pilot-judgment procedure in particular may involve the ECtHR, in effect, advising the respondent State on how to fulfil its obligations under Article 1 (the obligation to respect human rights) and/or Article 13 (the right to an effective remedy), and supervising the respondent State's implementation of this advice as given in the judgment on the merits, a role that is not dissimilar to that normally discharged by the Committee of Ministers under Article 46. But the ECtHR has also exploited the opportunities presented by the reforms introduced by Protocol No 14 to process and resolve large numbers of repetitive cases with ever greater efficiency. It has also shown flexibility in developing unique solutions to unique situations, and adapting its procedures as and when appropriate. Other initiatives have seen the ECtHR engage in what is tantamount to alternative dispute resolution, by encouraging and facilitating the resolution of cases through friendly settlements rather than adjudicating them itself. Although some of the ECtHR's responses have shifted some of the burden onto either national authorities or the Committee of Ministers, it is notable that in general, the States concerned have been cooperative (even if sometimes unable to fully resolve the underlying problems) and the Member States as a whole have been supportive and encouraging.

[53] CDDH Report on the Implementation of Committee of Ministers Recommendation CM/Rec(2010)5 to Member States on Measures to Combat Discrimination Based on Sexual Orientation or Gender Identity CDDH(2019)R92 Addendum 2.

This chapter has focused on the way in which the ECtHR processes repetitive cases and tries to resolve the underlying problems, and the ideas that were examined (even if, for the most part, not retained) at intergovernmental level.[54] Despite the numbers remaining stubbornly high, in their response to the problem of repetitive cases, the key actors in the Convention system have demonstrated their determination and creativity, allowing the system to continue providing individual justice whilst prioritising the most important cases and avoiding being overwhelmed.

[54] It should be noted that the wider Council of Europe has also been active in a variety of different ways, from standard-setting to cooperation (awareness-raising and capacity-building) activities to enhance national implementation of the ECHR and execution of the ECtHR's judgments, and through reform of the Committee of Ministers' procedures for supervision of the execution of judgments.

12

Injunctive Relief at the European Court of Human Rights – Progress and Push-back

PHILIP LEACH

1. Introduction

Originating in the 1970s, the interim measures mechanism of the European Court of Human Rights (ECtHR) has garnered ever-greater prominence, and in some quarters, notoriety, in recent years, especially in the UK where its application scuppered the former Government's plans to banish asylum-seekers to Rwanda. Showing an increasing willingness to use this tool to probe further into states' domestic polities, the Court has consequently been subjected to considerable push-back from some member states of the Council of Europe for 'over-reaching'. What is more, commentators have been critical of the procedural opacity of the mechanism,[1] and leading politicians and judges have questioned whether it creates binding obligations on states.[2]

The ECtHR's injunctive relief mechanism (applying Rule 39 of its Rules of Court) has notably been employed in European 'hotspots' in recent times, including in situations

[1] See, eg, G Gentile and D Sartori, 'Interim Measures as "Weapons of Democracy" in the European Space' (2023) 1 *European Human Rights Law Review* 18; P Leach, 'Urgency at the European Court of Human Rights: New Directions and Future Prospects for the Interim Measures Mechanism?' in E Reiter and K Zwaan (eds), *Urgency and Human Rights – The Protective Potential and Legitimacy of Interim Measures* (The Hague, Asser, 2020); C Marti, 'Provisional Measures: European Court of Human Rights (ECtHR)' in HR Fabri (ed), *Max Planck Encyclopedia of International Procedural Law* (Oxford, Oxford University Press, 2018); P McCormick, 'A Risk of Irreparable Damage: Interim Measures in Proceedings before the European Court of Human Rights' (2009–2010) 12 *Cambridge Yearbook of European Legal Studies* 313; P Tzeng, 'Interim Measures in Inter-State Proceedings – Comparing the ECtHR and the ICJ' (*Völkerrechtsblog*, 26 April 2021) https://voelkerrechtsblog.org/interim-measures-in-inter-state-proceedings/ accessed 6 August 2024; K Zwaan, 'Urgency in Expulsion Cases before the European Court of Human Rights and the UN Committees – A Bird's Eye View' in Eva Reiter and Karin Zwaan (eds), *Urgency and Human Rights – The Protective Potential and Legitimacy of Interim Measures* (The Hague, Asser, 2020).

[2] See, eg, R Ekins, 'Rule 39 and the Rule of Law' (Policy Exchange, 2023) https://policyexchange.org.uk/wp-content/uploads/Rule-39-and-the-Rule-of-Law.pdf accessed 5 June 2025.

of armed conflict,[3] and for the protection of migrants arriving on the continent,[4] and as exemplified by the spate of applications granted in 2021 and 2022 relating to proposed expulsions to Belarus from Poland, Lithuania and Latvia.[5] Particular situations arising in individual states (such as Belgium) can lead to quite dramatic fluctuations in the number of interim measures applications received, or in the numbers granted. In 2023, the ECtHR issued interim measures in 1,419 cases, representing an increase of 30 per cent over the 2022 total (1,094). Of that number, 91 per cent related to reception conditions of asylum-seekers in Belgium, and accordingly, it was noted by the Court that 94 per cent of the requests granted concerned issues *other than* expulsion or extradition.[6]

Although the Covid-19 pandemic resulted in the ECtHR receiving nearly 400 interim measures applications between 2020 and 2023, the vast majority were rejected, with only the most vulnerable applicants succeeding (including unaccompanied minors, people with serious medical conditions and pregnant women).[7]

Some of the most prominent individual cases before the ECtHR have also prompted the use of the interim measures mechanism, including on behalf of the late Russian opposition politician, Aleksey Navalnyy. After he was poisoned in 2020, the Court invoked Rule 39 to ensure that his family and doctors had access to him, to establish if he were fit to be transferred to Germany to receive medical treatment.[8] When he subsequently returned to Russia and was arrested, the Court applied interim measures again in February 2021 in order to direct his immediate release.[9]

This chapter seeks to assess recent developments in the use of the interim measures tool, especially as regards its continually expanding scope, as well as analyse the latest procedural reforms which were introduced by the ECtHR in 2024. There is analysis too of the extent and reasons for push-back from some Council of Europe states, before drawing together conclusions and recommendations.

2. A Further Expanding Scope

Looking back, the interim measures directions ordered by the European Commission of Human Rights, and the ECtHR, were formerly focused almost exclusively on stopping

[3] B Griffey, 'Irreparable Harm in the Ukraine Conflict: Protection Gaps and Interim Measures' in E Reiter and K Zwaan (eds), *Urgency and Human Rights – The Protective Potential and Legitimacy of Interim Measures* (The Hague, Asser, 2020); P Leach, 'On Inter-State Litigation and Armed Conflict Cases in Strasbourg' (2021) *European Human Rights Law Review* 2(1).

[4] See, eg, European Court of Human Rights, Press Release, 'The Court has Applied an Interim Measure Concerning 148 Homeless Asylum-seekers in Belgium', 16 November 2022.

[5] European Court of Human Rights, Press Release, 'Update on Interim Decisions Concerning Member States' Borders with Belarus', 21 February 2022.

[6] European Court of Human Rights, 'Factsheet – Interim measures', March 2024, 16 www.echr.coe.int/documents/d/echr/FS_Interim_measures_ENG accessed 5 August 2024. In June 2023, the Court lifted interim measures in 1,350 cases against Belgium, because the cases had not been pursued by the applicants. See: European Court of Human Rights, Press Release, 'Striking-out of the List and Lifting of Interim Measures in Respect of 1,350 Incomplete Applications from Asylum-seekers in Belgium', 1 June 2023.

[7] ibid 13–14.

[8] European Court of Human Rights, Press Release, 'The European Court of Human Rights has Lifted the Interim Measure Granted in Favour of Aleksey Navalnyy', 24 August 2020.

[9] ECtHR (GC), App no 4743/21, *Navalnyy v Russia* (16 April 2021).

expulsion or extradition. The power was interpreted very strictly by both bodies, predominantly in response to situations of imminent expulsion or extradition, where an applicant could muster prima facie evidence of a real risk of torture or inhuman or degrading treatment, or otherwise establish a risk to life (thus invoking Articles 2 or 3 ECHR). Indeed, according to the Court's Factsheet on Interim Measures, in terms of statistics, the majority of cases still relate to requests for the suspension of an expulsion or an extradition.[10]

However, the markedly broadening scope of interim measures in more recent years has been charted and scrutinised, certainly no longer just confined to cases of expulsion where a danger of torture or death arises.[11]

This expansion in scope has also meant a considerable differentiation in the *type* of measures which states are required to carry out. Applicants in a range of very vulnerable situations have successfully invoked the mechanism, including members of the Roma community facing eviction,[12] detainees,[13] migrants,[14] those seeking asylum[15] and vulnerable children.[16] This developing practice has been extended further, to the realm of media freedom, in order to regulate media ownership in Georgia,[17] to protect a Ukrainian journalist's sources[18] and to prevent the blocking or termination of an independent newspaper in Russia.[19]

Over and above these developments, the ECtHR has now for the first time invoked Rule 39 on behalf of a victim of domestic violence. In addition, the Court has been responding to the ongoing rule of law crisis in Europe, by taking steps to try to protect

[10] European Court of Human Rights, 'Factsheet – Interim Measures', March 2024, 1 www.echr.coe.int/documents/d/echr/FS_Interim_measures_ENG accessed 5 August 2024.

[11] See, eg, K Dzehtsiarou and V Tzevelekos, 'Interim Measures: Are Some Opportunities Worth Missing?' (2021) 2 *European Convention on Human Rights Law Review* 1; Gentile and Sartori, 'Interim Measures' (2023); C Harby, 'The Changing Nature of Interim Measures before the European Court of Human Rights' (2010) 1 *European Human Rights Law Review* 73; H Keller and C Marti, 'Interim Relief Compared: Use of Interim Measures by the UN Human Rights Committee and the European Court of Human Rights' (2013) 73 *Zeitschrift für ausländisches öffentliches Recht und Völkerrecht* 325; P Leach, 'Urgency at the European Court of Human Rights' (2020); E Özlü, 'A Few, but Very Necessary, Minutes to Devote to Interim Measures: Further Transparency as a Resilience Strategy?' (*Strasbourg Observers*, 15 March 2024) https://strasbourgobservers.com/2024/03/15/a-few-but-very-necessary-minutes-to-devote-to-interim-measures-further-transparency-as-a-resilience-strategy-1/ accessed 1 August 2024; E Rieter, *Preventing Irreparable Harm – Provisional Measures in International Human Rights Adjudication* (Antwerp, Intersentia, 2010); A Van Baelen, 'Interim Measures by the European Court of Human Rights in the Ukrainian Conflict: United Against the Russian Aggression' (Strasbourg Observers, 22 March 2022) https://strasbourgobservers.com/2022/03/22/interim-measures-by-the-european-court-of-human-rights-in-the-ukrainian-conflict-united-against-the-russian-aggression/ accessed 1 August 2024. See also: European Human Rights Centre, 'Interim Measures at the European Court of Human Rights' (April 2023) https://ehrac.org.uk/wp-content/uploads/2023/06/EHRAC-Interim-Measures-Guide-23_-ENG_v2.pdf accessed 1 August 2024.

[12] See, eg, ECtHR, App no 25446/06 *Yordanova and others* v *Bulgaria* ECLI:CE:ECHR:2012:0424JUD002544606.

[13] See, eg, ECtHR, App no 35254/07 *Makharadze and Sikharulidze v Georgia* ECLI:CE:ECHR:2011:1122JUD003525407.

[14] See, eg, ECtHR, App no 5504/19 *YA and Others v Italy* (13 September 2021).

[15] See, eg, ECtHR, App no 34349/18 *MK and others v France* ECLI:CE:ECHR:2022:1208JUD003434918.

[16] See, eg, ECtHR, App no 72850/14 *Soares de Melo v Portugal* ECLI:CE:ECHR:2016:0216JUD007285014.

[17] See, eg, ECtHR, App no 16812/17 *Rustavi 2 Broadcasting Company Ltd and Others v Georgia* ECLI:CE:ECHR:2019:0718JUD001681217.

[18] See, eg, ECtHR, App no 42634/18 *Sedletska v Ukraine* ECLI:CE:ECHR:2021:0401JUD004263418.

[19] European Court of Human Rights, Press Release, 'European Court Applies Urgent Interim Measure in the Case of the Russian Daily Newspaper Novaya Gazeta', 10 March 2022.

human rights defenders, and even judges, who are the subject of state repression. This evolution is discussed further in the following sections.

2.1. Victims of Domestic Violence

The ECtHR has been seen as resistant to the application of interim measures in cases of domestic violence,[20] for reasons that have never been clear, as such cases frequently result in a serious and imminent risk of ill-treatment or even death, and in the course of its decisions the Court will usually analyse the availability and effectiveness of interim measures protections at the *domestic* level. Commentators have convincingly argued that the ECtHR's approach to cases of domestic violence has demonstrated a failure of understanding of gender-based violence.[21] However, in 2024, in what may be the first time, such an order was made in the case of *RB and NG v Azerbaijan*, in order to protect the applicant from the sudden release of her former husband from a psychiatric hospital.[22] This was a case in which a woman was subjected by her former husband to beating, insults and threats to kill her, her children and her mother. He also attacked her with his car and injured her and her mother multiple times with a knife. He was subsequently charged with attempted murder and was admitted to a psychiatric hospital. According to her representatives at the European Human Rights Advocacy Centre (EHRAC), 'he could be released at any time, and would present a significant risk to the woman's life'.[23] In the ECtHR's order, the Azerbaijani authorities were directed to inform the applicant (and the Court) of any plans to release her former husband (including any measure of house arrest), 'as soon as such proceedings are instituted and in any event 72 hours before the date set for the release'.

2.2. Human Rights Defenders

Another significant recent development has arisen in the context of an increasingly repressive environment in parts of Europe for human rights defenders. In December 2021,

[20] See further: European Human Rights Advocacy Centre, 'Interim Measures' (2023) 25.

[21] See, eg, J Evans, 'Gender Mainstreaming at the European Court of Human Rights: The Need for a Coherent Strategy in Approaching Cases of Violence against Women and Domestic Violence' (2023) 54 *University of Miami Inter-American Law Review* 1; L Hasselbacher, 'State Obligations Regarding Domestic Violence: The European Court of Human Rights, Due Diligence, And International Legal Minimums of Protection' (2010) 8 *Northwestern Journal of Human Rights* 190; LM Weinberger, '*Kurt v Austria*: A Missed Chance to Tackle Intersectional Discrimination and Gender-based Stereotyping in Domestic Violence Cases' (*Strasbourg Observers*, 18 August 2021) https://strasbourgobservers.com/2021/08/18/kurt-v-austria-a-missed-chance-to-tackle-intersectional-discrimination-and-gender-based-stereotyping-in-domestic-violence-cases/ accessed 7 August 2024. See also: Department for the Execution of Judgments of the European Court of Human Rights, 'Thematic Factsheet – Domestic Violence' (Council of Europe, March 2022) (noting the establishment or development of domestic interim measures protection mechanisms in Bulgaria, Moldova and Slovakia, as part of the state responses to judgments issued by the European Court of Human Rights).

[22] ECtHR, App no 33860/23 *RB and NG v Azerbaijan* (3 May 2024). European Human Rights Advocacy Centre, 'Court Grants Request to Protect Azerbaijani Domestic Violence Victim from Sudden Release of Ex-husband', 2024 https://ehrac.org.uk/en_gb/court-grants-request-to-protect-azerbaijani-domestic-violence-victim-from-sudden-release-of-ex-husband/ accessed 1 August 2024.

[23] European Human Rights Advocacy Centre, 'Court Grants Request' (2024).

the ECtHR decided to apply interim measures in order to require the Russian authorities to suspend the liquidation of two human rights organisations, International Memorial and the Memorial Human Rights Centre, in the course of proceedings concerning the 'foreign agents law' in Russia (primarily relating to Article 11 ECHR).[24] Although the liquidation order was nevertheless enforced in April 2022, this was a ground-breaking step by the ECtHR, as no such order to ensure the continued existence of an NGO had previously been made by the Court by way of interim measures. Such a progressive development can be contrasted with the Court's procrastination in deciding on the merits of those proceedings, which Jessica Gavron has described as a 'devastating case of judicial passivity'.[25] This problem was expressly acknowledged by the former President of the Court, Síofra O'Leary in 2023, when she accepted that the ECtHR had taken too long.[26]

2.3. Rule of Law Crisis in Poland – Threats to the Independence of the Judiciary

The most dramatic recent development and application of the interim measures tool has been in defence of beleaguered judges in Poland. It is well established that the risk of a 'flagrant denial of justice' in the event of expulsion or extradition can elicit an interim measures direction from the ECtHR, and therefore the tool has been invoked in Article 6 cases.[27] However, the rule of law crisis in Poland has resulted in a further expansion in scope – to a wave of cases concerning interference with judicial independence instigated at the behest of the Law and Justice Party, after the 2015 elections when it gained control over the presidency and *Sejm* (the lower house of Parliament).

Many of the Polish cases have related to the involvement of the National Council of the Judiciary (NCJ), following the introduction of new legislation in 2017 which provided that its judicial members were no longer to be elected by judges, but by the *Sejm*, and removed from office judicial members of the NCJ who had been elected under the former system. By March 2022, in the light of previous judgments from both the ECtHR and the Court of Justice of the European Communities (CJEU), the Strasbourg Court's Grand Chamber was able to reach the conclusion that '… successive judicial reforms were aimed at weakening judicial independence', including 'grave irregularities' in the election of Constitutional Court judges in December 2015, as well as the 'remodelling' of the NCJ and the extension of the Minister of Justice's powers over the courts and judicial discipline, as a result of which the judiciary had been 'substantially weakened'.[28]

At this time, the ECtHR received a swathe of interim measures applications from Polish judges, concerning their suspension, disciplinary proceedings brought against

[24] ECtHR, App no 9988/13 *Ecodefence and Others v Russia* ECLI:CE:ECHR:2022:0614JUD000998813.

[25] J Gavron, 'The ECtHR and the Russian Foreign Agents' Law – A Devastating Case of Judicial Passivity' (*Strasbourg Observers*, 28 April 2022) <https://strasbourgobservers.com/2022/04/28/the-ecthr-and-the-russian-foreign-agents-law-a-devastating-case-of-judicial-passivity/ accessed 1 August 2024.

[26] European Court of Human Rights, 'Solemn Hearing – Speech by Síofra O'Leary, President of the European Court of Human Rights, Strasbourg', 27 January 2023, 7.

[27] See, eg, ECtHR, App no 8139/09 *Othman (Abu Qatada) v the United Kingdom* ECLI:CE:ECHR:2012:0117JUD000813909.

[28] ECtHR, App no 43572/18 *Grzęda v Poland* ECLI:CE:ECHR:2022:0315JUD004357218, para 348.

them or the lifting of their immunity, many of whom risked suspension for having applied the case law of the ECtHR or the CJEU relating, in particular, to the Disciplinary Chamber of the Supreme Court and the NCJ. The ECtHR imposed interim measures in 24 cases in 2022.

One such case was *Wróbel v Poland* relating to the lifting of judicial immunity of the Supreme Court judge, Włodzimierz Wróbel, a vocal critic of the Government's judicial reforms.[29] In February 2022, the ECtHR intervened in the domestic proceedings to direct the Polish authorities to ensure that the proceedings concerning the lifting of Mr Wróbel's judicial immunity were fair, and in particular that they complied with the Article 6 requirements of an 'independent and impartial tribunal established by law'. The following month, the ECtHR invoked Rule 39 in four cases brought by Polish judges, directing the Government to provide 72 hours' notice of the date of any hearing in camera session scheduled in the applicants' cases before the Disciplinary Chamber of the Supreme Court.[30] Demonstrating that the Court found it necessary to closely track and respond to ongoing domestic changes in Poland, in August 2022 it amended its order to refer also to hearings 'before any body competent under the domestic law', as well as directing the authorities to provide information about the composition of the panel which was to examine their cases, and how the members of that panel had been appointed to judicial office.[31]

By December 2022, the ECtHR had decided that further prescription was justifiable, as it directed the Polish Government to ensure the suspension of the transfer of three experienced judges out of the Criminal Division of the Warsaw Court of Appeal.[32]

However, the Polish authorities did not take kindly to such stipulations from the ECtHR, and in February 2023 the Court took the unprecedented step of publishing the fact that the Polish Government had informed the Registry of the Court that it would not respect these interim measures directions. The Government's justification was a statement by the President of the Warsaw Court of Appeal, Judge Schab, claiming that interim measures were not binding (citing a judgment of the Polish Constitutional Court).[33]

The invocation of interim measures by the ECtHR in the Polish context represents a further expansion in scope, as well as heightened levels of prescriptiveness, in response to an urgent national crisis. For Gentile and Sartori, these developments represent a fully justified response to rule of law backsliding: 'while crises and emergencies are becoming the "new normal" in Europe, regional courts should activate measures which can counterbalance extraordinary events shaking the very foundations of European values'.[34]

[29] ECtHR, App no 6904/22 *Wrobel v Poland* ECLI:CE:ECHR:2004:0720JUD004600299.

[30] European Court of Human Rights, Press Release, 'Interim Measure in Cases Concerning Charges Brought against Polish Judges', 24 March 2022.

[31] European Court of Human Rights, Press Release, 'Interim Measures Amended in Cases Concerning Judges' Immunity', 10 August 2022. See also: European Court of Human Rights, Press Release, 'Interim Measures Amended in Three More Cases Concerning Disciplinary Proceedings Against Judges', 17 August 2022.

[32] European Court of Human Rights, Press Release, 'Interim Measure in Cases Concerning Transfers of Polish Judges', 7 December 2022. The Court's press release notes that the decisions to transfer the applicant judges, led to widespread judicial protests.

[33] European Court of Human Rights, Press Release, 'Non-compliance with Interim Measure in Polish Judiciary Cases', 16 February 2023. On that date there were 323 applications pending before the Court concerning the 'reorganisation' of the judicial system.

[34] Gentile and Sartori (n 1) 19.

3. State Push-back

Although there have been high profile instances of states rejecting or ignoring interim measures directions,[35] in the main states have historically shown willingness to comply. It is therefore of considerable concern that the more recent rule of law backsliding in Europe has also encompassed some states' attitude towards urgent stipulations issued by the ECtHR. Referring in particular to the case of *Ecodefence and Others v Russia* (relating to the 'foreign agents' law' – see above) in 2023 the then President of the ECtHR, Síofra O'Leary, issued an unprecedented warning that

> In view of the vital role played by interim measures in the Convention system, it should be a cause of grave concern that some Contracting States are prepared to flout international rule of law requirements in this manner.[36]

The following year, she ventured that '… our concern should be heightened. This is because the criticism previously directed at this Court is now, in certain quarters, redirected at national judges'.[37] Commentators have discerned increasing levels of push-back by member states: 'an emerging culture of "resistance" – if not fully-fledged opposition – to the law in general, and to European legal standards in particular'.[38]

Some of the most notorious instances of non-compliance have emanated from Russia, prior to its expulsion from the Council of Europe in March 2022. In February 2021, the ECtHR issued an interim measure ordering the immediate release of opposition politician Aleksey Navalnyy amidst very serious concerns about his state of health in prison.[39] However, the Court's order was ignored by the Russian authorities, after the Minister of Justice dismissed it as 'unfounded and unlawful'.[40] Mr Navalnyy subsequently died in a Siberian prison colony in February 2024.[41] Later in 2021, the Russian authorities also failed to comply with a Court direction to suspend the liquidation of leading human rights NGOs, International Memorial and Memorial Human Rights Center (as discussed above).

As noted above, the fact of Poland's outright refusal to comply with an interim measures direction as regards the suspension of the transfer of several judges was headlined in a press release issued by the ECtHR in February 2023. In the same year, the French authorities defied an interim measures ruling, reportedly for the first time, as regards

[35] See, eg, ECtHR, App no 61498/08 *Al-Saadoon and Mufdhi v the United Kingdom* ECLI:CE:ECHR:2010:0302JUD006149808; ECtHR, App no 71386/10 *Savriddin Dzhurayev v Russia* ECLI:CE:ECHR:2013:0425JUD007138610; ECtHR, App no 140/10 *Trabelsi v Belgium* ECLI:CE:ECHR:2014:0904JUD000014010; ECHR, App no 12987/15 *Kondrulin v Russia* ECLI:CE:ECHR:2016:0920JUD001298715; ECtHR, App no 11788/16 *Semenova v Russia* ECLI:CE:ECHR:2017:1003JUD001178816; ECtHR, App no 9373/15 *MA v France* ECLI:CE:ECHR:2018:0201JUD000937315.

[36] European Court of Human Rights, 'Solemn Hearing' (2023), 7.

[37] European Court of Human Rights, 'Solemn Hearing – Opening of the Judicial Year 2024, Speech by Síofra O'Leary, President of the European Court of Human Rights', 26 January 2024, 3.

[38] Gentile and Sartori (n 1) 30.

[39] European Court of Human Rights, Press Release, 'The Court Grants an Interim Measure in Favour of Aleksey Navalnyy and Asks the Government of Russia to Release Him', 17 February 2021.

[40] See, eg, V Isachenkov, 'Russia Rejects European Rights Court's Order to Free Navalny' *Associated Press* (Moscow, 17 February 2021).

[41] See, eg, G Abdul, 'Death of Kremlin Critic Alexei Navalny Confirmed by his Representatives' *The Guardian* (London, 17 February 2021).

the expulsion of an Uzbek national.[42] However, on 7 December 2023, the French *Conseil d'Etat* ordered the French Government to take all measures for his return to the French territory in accordance with the ECtHR's ruling, describing the actions taken by the Minister of the Interior, Gérald Darmanin, as a 'serious and manifestly illegal violation of a fundamental freedom'.[43]

Such heightened levels of state resistance have led the ECtHR to lay increasing emphasis on the binding nature of its interim measures jurisdiction, as reflected in its November 2023 announcement about proposed reforms, which referred to Articles 1, 19, 32 and 34 ECHR:

> A failure by a respondent State to comply with interim measures undermines the effectiveness of the right of individual application guaranteed by Article 34 of the European Convention on Human Rights and the State's formal undertaking in Article 1 to protect the rights and freedoms set forth in the Convention. When issuing interim measures, the Court exercises its jurisdiction to ensure observance of the engagements undertaken by the High Contracting Parties in the Convention and Protocols thereto, in accordance with Article 19, which jurisdiction extends to all matters concerning their interpretation and application, as provided in Article 32.[44]

Accordingly, 'interim measures are thus binding'.[45]

However, the most striking reactions to an interim measures order in recent times have arisen in the UK, amidst a febrile and toxic domestic political context relating to migration, which is discussed in the next section.

3.1. Blocking UK Deportations to Rwanda

The ECtHR's urgent interlocutory mechanism achieved hitherto unknown levels of public recognition in the UK in 2022 after the Court made a decision which had the effect of completely blocking deportation flights to Rwanda. Seen by the then Conservative Government as a central plank of its strategy to 'stop the boats' from bringing asylum

[42] J Pascual, La France procède à l'expulsion en passant outre une décision de la CEDH pour la première fois *Le Monde* (Paris, 1 December 2023).

[43] J Pascual, Gérald Darmanin épinglé pour avoir expulsé un Ouzbek en violation d'une mesure prescrite par la CEDH *Le Monde* (Paris, 12 December 2023).

[44] European Court of Human Rights, Press Release, 'Changes to the Procedure for Interim Measures (Rule 39 of the Rules of Court)', 13 November 2023.

[45] European Court of Human Rights, Practice Direction: Third-party intervention under Article 36 § 2 of the Convention or under Article 3, second sentence, of Protocol No 16 para 2. The Bingham Centre has concluded that 'interim measures of the European Court of Human Rights are binding in international law and the Court does have jurisdiction to indicate such binding interim measures … Taken together with Articles 1, 19 and 34 of the Convention, there is a clear legal basis in the Convention for interim measures being legally binding'. Furthermore, the report states that '[t]he UK Government has itself long accepted that interim measures are binding, not only by acquiescing in this exercise of the Court's jurisdiction (by routinely treating the measures as binding and complying with them), but by proactively promoting their binding force in those intergovernmental statements and advocating that other States, such as Russia, treat them as binding and comply with them'. See: M Hunt, 'Clause 54 of the Illegal Migration Bill: A Rule of Law Analysis for House of Lords Report Stage' (Bingham Centre for the Rule of Law, 3 July 2023) https://binghamcentre.biicl.org/publications/clause-54-of-the-illegal-migration-bill-a-rule-of-law-analysis-for-house-of-lords-report-stage?cookiesset=1&ts=1748594856 accessed 30 May 2025.

seekers across the English Channel, being thwarted in this way led to heightened levels of hostility[46] towards the Court and calls for the UK to withdraw from the ECHR from the then Prime Minister, Rishi Sunak who announced that 'I won't let a foreign court stop us from getting flights up and running'.[47] The former Home Secretary, Suella Braverman, argued that interim measures orders 'are not contained in the European convention on human rights, and they are not a product or a content of the original convention. They are a creation of the Strasbourg court and the Strasbourg judges …'.[48] She also focused her ire firmly on the European Court:

> It is the Court that has become politicised. It is the Court that has become interventionist … The Strasbourg Court and its judges have distorted the original European convention on human rights into something that bears no reflection to its original intention.[49]

She further suggested that Britain was governed by 'an opaque forum many miles away, in a different country, that is distant, outsourced, foreign and does not share our values'.[50]

Furthermore, it was asserted by commentators such as Richard Ekins and Jonathan Sumption that European Court interim measures are not legally binding.[51] Sumption also averred that 'the ability of a court to torpedo a critical legislative policy without any hearing or substantial consideration of the merits by a purely procedural mechanism, ought to cause concern'.[52]

The case in question arose as a consequence of the UK Government's April 2022 agreement with Rwanda that asylum seekers whose claims were not being considered by the UK could be relocated to Rwanda. The following month an Iraqi national crossed the English Channel by boat before claiming asylum. After he was informed that he would be removed to Rwanda, he instigated domestic court proceedings which were unsuccessful, but the European Court invoked Rule 39 in directing that he should not be deported pending the national courts' consideration of his case.[53] The Court's press release stated that it had taken account of evidence from the United Nations High

[46] The Joint Committee on Human Rights suggested that 'hostility to human rights' was at the heart of the Safety of Rwanda (Asylum and Immigration) Bill (discussed below): Joint Committee on Human Rights, Safety of Rwanda (Asylum and Immigration) Bill Report, 12 February 2024.

[47] D Casciani, 'European Court President Warns over Rwanda Rulings' *BBC News* (London, 25 January 2024). See also: J Grogan and A Donald, 'Explainer: Leaving the European Convention on Human Rights' (*UK in a Changing Europe*, 15 May 2024) https://ukandeu.ac.uk/explainers/leaving-the-european-convention-on-human-rights/ accessed 6 August 2024.

[48] Hansard, Safety of Rwanda (Asylum and Immigration) Bill, Volume 743: debated on Wednesday 17 January 2024.

[49] ibid.

[50] ibid. However, Grogan and Donald have noted that from 2017 to 2023 660 requests for interim measures were made in relation to the UK, of which 15 were granted (about 2% of requests, or, on average, two per year). See Joelle Grogan and Alice Donald, 'The UK's ECHR Record: How Common are Rule 39 Orders and How Often is the UK Found to Have Violated Rights?' (*UK in a Changing Europe*, 4 April 2024) https://ukandeu.ac.uk/explainers/the-uks-echr-record-how-common-are-rule-39-orders-and-how-often-is-the-uk-found-to-have-violated-rights/ accessed 6 August 2024.

[51] Ekins, 'Rule 39 and the Rule of Law' (2023); R Ekins, 'Judicial Independence, Rule 39 and the Safety of Rwanda Bill' (Policy Exchange, 2023) https://policyexchange.org.uk/publication/judicial-independence-rule-39-and-the-safety-of-rwanda-bill/ accessed 5 June 2025.

[52] ibid 5–6.

[53] ECtHR, App no 28774/22 *NSK v the United Kingdom* ECLI:CE:ECHR:2024:1003DEC002877422.

Commissioner for Refugees that procedures in Rwanda for determining refugee status might not be fair, and it had also noted that the High Court had found that the question whether Rwanda was a safe third country raised 'serious triable issues'. Furthermore, the decision was made in light of the fact that Rwanda was not itself bound by the ECHR, and that there was no enforceable mechanism to ensure the applicant's return from Rwanda, if he were successful before the UK domestic courts.[54]

The Government's response was to introduce the Illegal Migration Act 2023 which, amongst other things, provided ministers with the discretion to disregard interim measures directions by the European Court.[55] However, to the Government's further dismay, in November 2023, the Supreme Court found the Rwanda policy to be unlawful, as Rwanda was not deemed a safe third country due to its defective asylum processes, as a result of which people could be returned to countries where they faced persecution.[56]

The Government then negotiated a new Treaty with Rwanda and introduced the Safety of Rwanda (Asylum and Immigration) Act 2024 which provided that '[e]very decision-maker must conclusively treat the Republic of Rwanda as a safe country', and gave ministers the power to decide whether to comply with any interim measures decision issued by the ECtHR in respect of a decision to remove a person to Rwanda.[57]

Both domestic and international responses to the introduction of this legislation expressed dismay that the UK Government was thereby breaching its international obligations. The Joint Committee on Human Rights averred that the provision gave ministers permission to 'breach international law' and affirmed that 'to ignore an interim measure of the ECtHR would be a breach of the UK's legal obligations'.[58] The UN High Commissioner for Human Rights, Volker Türk, and UN High Commissioner for Refugees, Filippo Grandi, suggested that the Act was 'at variance with the country's obligations under international human rights and refugee law' and urged the UK authorities to reverse it.[59]

The Government's actions were also condemned by commentators such as Veronika Fikfak who ventured that '[l]ike Russia and Poland, the government is therefore willing to openly defy explicit instructions from Strasbourg'.[60] Without referring directly to the UK, the then President of the European Court, Síofra O'Leary, lamented that

> Parliamentary debates or ministerial speeches in more than one Council of Europe Member State fixate on the need to defy interim measures issued by a 'foreign court'. The consequences

[54] European Court of Human Rights, Press Release, 'The European Court Grants Urgent Interim Measure in Case Concerning Asylum Seeker's Imminent Removal from the UK to Rwanda', 14 June 2022.

[55] See, eg, J Grogan and A Donald, 'Explainer – Illegal Migration Act 2023' (*UK in a Changing Europe*, 15 March 2024) https://ukandeu.ac.uk/explainers/illegal-migration-act-2023/ accessed 5 August 2024.

[56] *R (on the application of AAA and others) v Secretary of State for the Home Department* [2023] UKSC 42.

[57] Safety of Rwanda (Asylum and Immigration) Act 2024, ss 2 and 5.

[58] Joint Committee on Human Rights, Legislative Scrutiny: Illegal Migration Bill, Twelfth Report of Session 2022–23, 6 June 2023, 11 and paras 125–33.

[59] Office of the Commissioner for Human Rights, Press Release, 'UK Illegal Migration Bill: UN Refugee Agency and UN Human Rights Office Warn of Profound Impact on Human Rights and International Refugee Protection System', 18 July 2023 www.ohchr.org/en/press-releases/2023/07/uk-illegal-migration-bill-un-refugee-agency-and-un-human-rights-office-warn#:~:text=The%20Bill%20extinguishes%20access%20to,matter%20how%20compelling%20their%20circumstances accessed 5 August 2024.

[60] V Fikfak, 'The UK's Defiance of the European Court of Human Rights' (*The Constitution Unit Blog*, 1 June 2023) https://constitution-unit.com/2023/06/01/the-uks-defiance-of-the-european-court-of-human-rights/ accessed 5 August 2024.

> of particular judgments which don't appeal either to a majority in society or to a ruling party are rejected.[61]

Such a stark and belligerent response from the then UK Government was a factor in the ECtHR's implementation of changes to the interim measures mechanism,[62] which are discussed in the next section which follows below.

4. Interim Measures – System Changes in 2024

The ECtHR's relatively fresh, broader approach to injunctive relief, as discussed above, was also reflected in its 2023 announcement of changes to the interim measures system, in which the mechanism was summarised in this way:

> They play a vital role in avoiding irreversible situations that would prevent national courts and/or the Court from properly examining Convention complaints and, where appropriate, securing to the applicant the practical and effective benefit of the Convention rights asserted.[63]

In November 2023 the ECtHR published a series of proposed reforms to the interim measures mechanism, which appeared, at least in part, to amount to a response from the criticisms emanating from the UK authorities, arising from the blocking of flights from the UK to Rwanda.[64] These changes were to include the disclosure of the identity of judges making interim measures decisions[65] and issuing formal judicial decisions to be sent to the parties to the case. At the same time, the Court announced that it would be maintaining the practice of providing reasons for interim measures decisions on ad hoc basis and issuing press statements 'where desirable'. It would also maintain the practice of adjourning the examination of interim measures requests and requesting the parties to submit information, if the situation in question is not extremely urgent and where the information submitted to the Court by the applicant is not sufficient to enable it to examine the request.

The text of Rule 39 was subsequently amended in February 2024 and a revised Practice Direction issued in March 2024 (with the changes coming into effect

[61] S O'Leary, 'The Challenged, Challenging but Very Necessary European Convention on Human Rights' (*Institute of International and European Affairs*, 15 March 2023) www.iiea.com/events/the-challenged-challenging-but-very-necessary-echr accessed 30 May 2025.

[62] Commentators have suggested that previous instances of push-back from the UK (including from the courts, the media and politicians) have resulted in the Court showing more deference to domestic decisions. See, eg, M Rask Madsen, 'The European Court of Human Rights: From the Cold War to the Brighton Declaration and Backlash' in KJ Alter, LR Helfer and M Rask Madsen (eds), *International Court Authority* (Oxford, Oxford University Press, 2018) 268.

[63] European Court of Human Rights, Press Release, 'Changes to the Procedure for Interim Measures (Rule 39 of the Rules of Court)', 13 November 2023.

[64] ibid. See further: J Rozenberg, 'Strasbourg Tightens Rule 39', 29 March 2024 https://rozenberg.substack.com/p/strasbourg-tightens-rule-39 accessed 5 August 2024.

[65] The anonymity of the judge was one of the issues raised in the UK by commentators and in the intemperate media coverage. See, eg, M Robinson and J Tapsfield, 'Fury as Strasbourg Officials REFUSE to Identify Nameless Judge who Torpedoed Rwanda Deportation Flight Amid Fears it Could be RUSSIAN Who is Still Sitting on European Court of Human Rights' *Mail Online* (London, 15 June 2022).

on 28 March 2024).[66] The revisions to the Practice Direction were said to be aimed at ensuring greater clarity and transparency.[67]

The ECtHR's reforms exhibit a degree of duality, even ambiguity, as on the one hand they only serve to confirm the expanding scope of interim measures, while on the other hand the Court doubles down on their exceptionality.

These changes, as flagged by the ECtHR, included the new stipulation in Rule 39 that interim measures are applicable in cases where there is 'an imminent risk of irreparable harm to a Convention right'.[68] Thus, it is clear beyond any doubt whatsoever that interim measures are not limited to cases of 'irreparable harm' in the sense of injury to the person, but that they will apply in situations where there is a risk of such harm to *one of the Convention rights*. The Practice Direction (at para 6) further clarifies the Court's approach in this way:

> The notion of 'irreparable harm to a Convention right' has been defined as harm which, on account of its nature, would not be susceptible to reparation, restoration or adequate compensation. In this connection, the term 'restoration' should be understood as referring to return to the situation before any harm was done. Interim measures are thus indicated by the Court where there is a risk that the absence of such measures would lead to a situation in which *restitutio in integrum* and other forms of reparation would not be possible if the Court were to consider them warranted at the end of the proceedings before it.

None of this is inconsistent with the ECtHR's novel approach of, for example, applying interim measures in order to maintain a pluralistic media landscape or to prevent an NGO from being liquidated (as discussed above).

However, at the same time, the ECtHR was at pains to emphasise that '[t]he circumstances of a case must therefore exceed a high threshold of seriousness for Rule 39 to be engaged' and also that most cases will require 'a clearly arguable case of a genuine threat to life and limb'.[69]

4.1. Who Makes the Interim Measures Decisions?

The ECtHR has also clarified that most decisions are made by duty judges, who are the Section Vice-Presidents (who do not make decisions in cases against states in respect of which that judge has been elected or is a national). However, the decisions can also be referred on to a President of the Section, a Chamber, the President of the Grand Chamber, the Grand Chamber or the President of the Court (Rule 39(2)). Such referrals will depend on 'the nature of the request, the case in which the request is made, and the degree of urgency involved'.[70]

[66] According to paragraph 3 of the revised Practice Direction, 'The text of Rule 39 was amended on 23 February 2024 with a view to further clarifying the circumstances in which interim measures may be indicated and the threshold to be reached in relation to their request and application. The amendment also sought to align the text of the Rule with the Court's well-established case-law and practice in relation to interim measures'.

[67] European Court of Human Rights, Press Release, 'The Court Amends Rule 39 and the Practice Direction on Interim Measures', 28 March 2024.

[68] ibid.

[69] European Court of Human Rights, Practice Direction (see n 45 above), para 6.

[70] ibid, para 11.

Interim measures requests in inter-state cases will usually be decided by the President of the Court, the President of the Grand Chamber or Section Presidents, although it is again possible to refer the decision to a collegiate body of the ECtHR.[71]

4.2. Other Procedural Changes

As a result of the reforms, the ECtHR's practice now is to provide the parties with a decision signed by the relevant judge (whose name is also provided). This applies to any decision relating to interim measures, including rejections and adjournments. The nature and extent of the reasoning provided is at the discretion of the Court.[72]

For example, limited reasoning was provided by the ECtHR when issuing an order to prevent the expulsion of a Russian national of Chechen origin from France, the Court's press release noting that the Court had decided 'that an imminent risk of irreparable harm could not be ruled out', in view in particular of the Russian authorities' request for his extradition.[73] Apparently cognisant of recent state criticism, the ECtHR was at pains to acknowledge 'the in-depth examination by the national authorities of the applicant's situation'.

A further response to the level of state push-back recently received by the ECtHR about the supposedly unfairly 'ex parte' nature of the proceedings, is the clarification in the Practice Direction that respondent states can appeal (without time limit). The Practice Direction explains that state parties are entitled to ask the Court to reconsider its decision 'if they consider that the measures are no longer necessary or where they possess information which was not available at the relevant time or not made available to the Court in a timely fashion' (para 26).

The prospect of more detailed reasoning is indeed a welcome development which denotes a considerable improvement on the prior practice of simply informing the parties by letter, usually without providing any reasons, or only skeletal, formulaic reasoning. This will assist in making the interim measures mechanism more transparent. However, something which still could be introduced is a publicly available, systematic record of individual interim measures decisions, as well as commentary on the extent of their implementation.

This author has argued elsewhere that the tool could also very usefully be used, exceptionally, to ensure the preservation of evidence and to stimulate investigations at the national level.[74]

[71] ibid, para 12.

[72] European Court of Human Rights, Practice Direction (see n 45 above), paras 13 and 24.

[73] European Court of Human Rights, Press Release, 'Court Grants Interim Measure Suspending Applicant's Removal to Russia', 28 November 2023.

[74] P Leach, 'The Right to Life – Interim Measures and the Preservation of Evidence in Conflict Situations' in Lawrence Early et al (eds), *The Right to Life under Article 2 of the European Convention on Human Rights – Twenty Years of Legal Developments Since McCann v the United Kingdom* (Oisterwijk, Will-Jan van der Wolf, 2016).

5. Conclusion

This chapter has borne witness to the European Court of Human Rights' continuing practice of broadening the scope of its injunctive relief mechanism. No longer confined just to expulsion cases, it encompasses a broad range of situations which create a serious risk of jeopardy to an individual's safety and security, including for asylum seekers and migrants, prisoners, vulnerable children and the victims of domestic violence. But the ECtHR has gone further still, by endeavouring to provide urgent protection for those targeted by the state, amidst an ever-threatening rule of law crisis in parts of the European continent. Thus, journalists, human rights defenders, NGOs and even judges have been looking to the Court and successfully eliciting urgent directions from the Court in order to uphold their ECHR rights at the national level. This has meant that the substantive legal basis for the application of Rule 39 has spread from a predominant focus on the right to life and inhuman and degrading treatment (Articles 2 and 3 ECHR), also to encompass the rights to freedom of expression and association and the right to a fair hearing (Articles 10, 11 and 6).

These are remarkable developments, for an international court to seek to have decisive influence at the coalface, by stepping in to intervene in highly fraught domestic contexts and cases, whether to halt the liquidation of a human rights organisation or the closure of an independent news outlet, to stop a journalist from having to reveal her sources, to ensure that a woman receives prior notification of the release of her abusive ex-husband or to prevent sitting judges from being subjected to banishment. Such cases also represent a proliferation of the type of steps required from states and an increasing prescriptiveness. In the absence of detailed reasoning from the ECtHR, it may not be easy to discern the causes of such a turn of events, but there can be little doubt that the rule of law crisis that has been playing out in a number of Council of Europe states is a significant factor. Although state compliance leaves much to be desired, these developments offer the most vulnerable people some prospect of urgent relief at the international level. The speed at which the Court *can* act, to impose interim measures directions (within days or even hours) is in stark contrast to the excessive periods of time (several years) before the Court reaches a decision on the merits. A case in point is that of the Russian human rights organisation, Memorial, which secured an order preventing its liquidation within a few days, whereas the judgment on the merits of that case took more than nine years.[75] A compelling argument can be made that the urgency in applying interim measures needs to be coupled with the fast-tracking of merits decisions.

In the face of such progressions at the ECtHR, it is perhaps unsurprising that the levels of state resistance seem to have been ratcheted up. The furore created amongst certain politicians and commentators by the ECtHR's decision to suspend an asylum seeker's transfer to Rwanda from the UK, was a sorry tale indeed. At the highest political level, this decision was challenged on both legal grounds (was it in fact binding?) and

[75] ECtHR, App no 9988/13 *Ecodefence and Others v Russia* ECLI:CE:ECHR:2022:0614JUD000998813.

on a procedural basis (it was delivered by an anonymous judge), and even seemed to provide the basis for the UK to turn its back altogether on the Strasbourg system. However, it ought to be underlined that the ECtHR's order was in fact complied with – even under intense political pressure, there were no deportations at all in the period of two years after the Court issued its direction in June 2022, up to the point when the electorate ushered the Conservative party out of power in the July 2024 general election.

13

Reasonable Time before EU Courts: What is at Stake? Expedited and Urgent Preliminary Rulings as a Vehicle for Fundamental Rights' Protection[1]

SARA IGLESIAS SANCHEZ

1. Introduction

Time is of the essence when it comes to adjudication; this is even truer the closer we get to fundamental rights adjudication. Timeliness is also, of itself, an independent component of the fundamental right to effective judicial protection, regardless of the object of the case. The right to a fair and public hearing within a *reasonable time* is explicitly included in Article 47 of the Charter of Fundamental Rights of the European Union (CFREU) and is protected by the EU legal order not only when Member States apply EU law,[2] but also in proceedings before EU Courts.[3] Its respect by the Court of Justice is assessed typically on a case-by-case basis and it takes into account the circumstances specific to the case, such as the complexity of the case and the conduct of parties.[4] These

[1] Attachée, cabinet of the Registrar of the CJEU. All the opinions expressed in this chapter are purely personal to the author. This research has been carried out in the framework of the project PID2023-148537NB-I00, TransformEU, financed by MCIN/AEI /10.13039/501100011033 /10.13039/501100011033 and FEDER, EU. in the framework of the activities of IDEIR, Instituto de Derecho Europeo e Integración Regional.

[2] See, eg, CJEU, Case C-500/10 *Ufficio IVA di Piacenza v Belvedere Costruzioni Srl* ECLI:EU:C:2012:186.

[3] With regard to procedures before EU Courts, notably, direct actions: CJEU, Case C-58/12 P *Groupe Gascogne SA v Commission* ECLI:EU:C:2013:770; CJEU, Case C-50/12 P *Kendrion* ECLI:EU:C:2013:771 and Case C-40/12 *Gascogne Sack Deutschland* ECLI:EU:C:2013:768, and their progeny. See, eg, K Havu and S Kurki-Suonio, 'Damages Liability of the EU for Harm Caused by Excessive Duration of Court Proceedings' (2021) 27 *European Public Law* 305; K Kryla-Cudna and P Verbruggen, 'The Union's Liability for Failure to Adjudicate within a Reasonable Time: EU Tort Law after Gascogne, Kendrion and ASPLA' (2020) 57 *Common Market Law Review* 191.

[4] See, eg, CJEU, Case C-40/12 *Gascogne Sack Deutschland* ECLI:EU:C:2013:768, para 91; CJEU, Case C-385/07 P *Der Grüne Punkt – Duales System Deutschland v Commission* ECLI:EU:C:2009:456, para 181, and case law cited. The Court has also examined the 'reasonableness' of administrative and judicial decision making at the national level, considering also as relevant factors 'all of the circumstances specific to each case and, in particular, the importance of the case for the person concerned, its complexity and the conduct of the parties'. See, eg, CJEU, Case C-756/12 *International Protection Appeals Tribunal and Others (Attentat au Pakistan)* ECLI:EU:C:2023:523, para 79, and CJEU, Case C-14/19 P *SatCen v KF* ECLI:EU:C:2020:492, para 122 and the case law cited.

elements draw from the abundant case law of the European Court of Human Rights (ECtHR), which has developed different criteria for assessing the length of proceedings at national level. In that framework, different factors are traditionally taken into account, such as the nature of proceedings, the complexity of the case, the behaviour of both the applicant and the involved authorities, the 'importance' of the case for the person concerned, as well as, generally, 'what is at stake for the applicant'.[5]

As a result of this composite and case-dependent tests, 'it is practically impossible to draw general and universally applicable lines in terms of exactly how many years or months will be considered appropriate'.[6] In spite of the casuistic outcome that results from the application of those principles, there exists a structural obligation that emanates from the European Convention on Human Rights (ECHR): States have a duty to organise their legal system allowing their courts to comply with the reasonable time requirement.[7] This obligation applies, *mutatis mutandis*, to EU Courts, having in mind that the interpretation of Article 47 CFREU is linked to that of Article 6 ECHR by virtue of Article 52(3) of the Charter.

This chapter endeavours to offer an account of the consideration of the rights at stake for litigants as an element of the application of the reasonable time requirement to EU Courts, in particular, in the framework of the preliminary ruling procedure and its 'accelerated' variants.

This contribution will mostly refer to this procedure because, even though the case law on the application of the requirement of reasonable length of proceedings to EU Courts has been pronounced with regard to direct actions,[8] it is through preliminary ruling procedure that most cases concerning fundamental rights can potentially reach EU Courts through the mediation of national courts. The focus on Article 267 of the Treaty on the Functioning of the European Union (TFEU) is also justified, beyond its quantitative relevance, by its crucial role for judicial dialogue and its enormous repercussions in the sustainability of the current system of interpretation and application of EU law.

Against this background, this chapter examines the procedural vehicles for taking into account fundamental rights' considerations through speedier procedures – essentially, the urgent preliminary ruling procedure and the expedited procedure, as well as the 'priority treatment'. These speedier variants of the preliminary ruling procedure before EU Courts aim, similarly, at providing the EU judicial system with effective tools to manage different challenges and to respond to urgency arising from different considerations, amongst which also features the need to protect different aspects of other fundamental rights that may be autonomously, directly and seriously affected throughout the passage of time and the length of judicial proceedings. The chapter will first

[5] For a systematisation of case law: Fundamental Rights Agency of the EU and Council of Europe, *Handbook on European Law Relating to Access to Justice* (Publications Office of the EU, 2016); M Filatova, *Reasonable Time of Proceedings: Compilation of Case-law of the European Court of Human Rights* (Council of Europe, 2021).

[6] CJEU, Case C-406/18 *Bevándorlási és Menekültügyi Hivatal* Opinion of Advocate General Bobek, ECLI:EU:C:2019:1055, para 53.

[7] Amongst many others, see ECtHR, App no 8737/79 *Zimmermann and Steiner v Switzerland* ECLI:CE:ECHR:1983:0713JUD000873779, para 29.

[8] See case law cited in n 3 above.

briefly address the specificity of the application of the reasonable time principle to the preliminary ruling procedure (Section 2), and explain the basic procedural features of the speedier variations of that procedure (Section 3). It will subsequently focus on the application of the PPU (Section 4) and of the expedited procedures (Section 5) from the point of view of their impact in the protection of fundamental rights. It will conclude by offering some thoughts regarding the need for further systematisation and potential reform of the role of urgency in the procedure before EU Courts (Section 6).

2. Reasonable Time before EU Courts: The Specificity of Preliminary Rulings

The application of the reasonable time principle in the framework of EU Courts shall take into account the different nature of the various procedures, as well as the unique structure of the judicial process at EU level, characterised by multilingualism and supranationalism. Those features are amplified when it comes to the preliminary ruling procedure established by Article 267 TFEU, procedural rules enabling the participation of more parties than the parties to the case, strictly speaking, and being inspired also by the paramount function of ensuring the uniform interpretation of EU law.

The application of the requirement of reasonable time for EU Courts within the preliminary ruling procedure is, furthermore, peculiar, due to its composite nature. This procedure is an incident within another (national) procedure and can, therefore, considerably delay it. Thus, from the point of view of litigants, the overall length of proceedings is composed by the national and the EU proceedings.

Against this backdrop, it is noteworthy that the assessment of the reasonable length requirement is often assessed separately regarding the different proceedings unfolding at the different levels: the national and the supranational one. Very significantly, the ECtHR has recognised the specificity and objectives of the preliminary ruling procedure, excluding its length from the consideration of the length of national proceedings in the framework of its examination of compliance with the requirements of Article 6 ECHR.[9] However, from the point of view of EU law, this does not detract from the fact that EU Courts are subject on their own to the autonomous reasonable time requirement that follows from the Charter, and shall therefore strive to keep their 'part' of the procedure as short as possible. Furthermore, the potential (and more likely than ever) accession of the EU to the ECtHR will probably entail a modification of the position of the ECtHR in this regard. The specificity of the preliminary rulings procedure shall therefore not lead to losing sight of its incident nature within the national main proceedings, and of the important impact it has on the overall length of procedure for the litigants – who often ask national courts to refer, but not always.

[9] ECtHR, App no 20323/92 *Pafitis and others v Greece* ECLI:CE:ECHR:1998:0226JUD002032392, para 95; ECtHR, App no 40892/98 *Koua Poirrez v France* ECLI:CE:ECHR:2003:0930JUD004089298, para 61 or ECtHR, App no 931/13 *Satakunnan Markkinapörssi Oy and Satamedia Oy v Finland* ECLI:CE:ECHR:2017:0627JUD000093113, para 208. See, generally, RCA White, 'The Strasbourg Perspective and its Effect on the Court of Justice: Is Mutual Respect Enough?' in A Arnull, P Eeckhout, and T Tridimas (eds), *Continuity and Change in EU Law: Essays in Honour of Sir Francis Jacobs* (Oxford, Oxford University Press, 2008).

The Court of Justice (CJEU) is manifestly aware of this reality. The need to keep the overall length of proceedings within a reasonable time strongly inspires the procedural articulation of preliminary rulings. The Court has interpreted Article 267 TFEU with certain flexibility, explicitly acknowledging that national courts can 'split' national proceedings so that they are able to continue and give ruling on the parts of the case which is not strictly necessary to suspend pending the reply of the Court of Justice.[10] What is more, the need to reduce as much as possible the length of proceedings in preliminary rulings has inspired almost all episodes of reform of the Statute of the Court of Justice of the European Union,[11] and most notably, the latest one, whereby jurisdiction to adjudicate on some preliminary rulings on specific areas has been transferred to the General Court.[12] Given the crucial role in ensuring smooth cooperation with national courts, timing occupies centre stage in the preliminary ruling procedure, shaping the internal guidelines followed by the Court, including indicative deadlines which govern the internal organisation of proceedings. Self-imposed internal goals and perceptions guide the limits of the acceptable: for example, after the once average duration of 25.5 months for preliminary rulings (in 2003) was reduced to 15 months in 2014,[13] falling back to the previous situation is conceived as unacceptable, leading therefore to a far-reaching structural reform of the Statute.[14]

The reasonable time requirement does not only inspire the procedural organisation of preliminary rulings, but also the concrete procedural choices on the treatment of specific cases through the speedier procedural variants allowed in the Rules of Procedure and the Statute. Even if, so far, the risk of infringing the right to a fair trial as a consequence of the length of proceedings has not been explicitly considered of itself as a trigger for the application of urgent procedures,[15] compliance with the requirements of the right to adjudication in reasonable time is directly connected with the applicability of those procedures in many instances, due to the impact of

[10] CJEU, Case C-176/22 *BK and ZhP (Suspension partielle de la procedure au principal)* ECLI:EU:C:2023:416. This is restricted to aspects of the case 'unrelated to the questions referred for a preliminary ruling'. However, if the procedural steps that the national court envisions to undertake are liable to render que preliminary questions devoid of purpose or relevance, the case will be declared inadmissible. See CJEU, Joined Cases C-255/23 and C-285/23 *AVVA ea (Procès par vidéoconférence en l'absence d'une décision d'enquête européenne)* ECLI:EU:C:2024:462, para 38.

[11] See, generally, E Gippini-Fournier, 'Preliminary References and the Workload of the Court of Justice' (2014) 21 *Maastricht Journal of European and Comparative Law* 771. See, eg, on the possibility to adopt reasoned orders, SA Brekke, D Naurin, U Šadl and L López-Zurita, 'That's an Order! How the Quest for Efficiency Is Transforming Judicial Cooperation in Europe' (2023) 61 *Journal of Common Market Studies* 58.

[12] Regulation 2024/2019 of the European Parliament and of the Council of 11 April 2024, amending Protocol No 3 on the Statute of the Court of Justice of the European Union [2024] OJ L 2024/2019.

[13] S Prechal and A Pahladsingh, 'Urgency and Human Rights in EU Law: Procedures Before the Court of Justice' in E Rieter and K Zwaan (eds), *Urgency and Human Rights* (The Hague, TMC Asser Press, 2021) 37.

[14] Once the number of months began to grow again after 2019, the Court started reflecting on further possibilities of reform in order not to fall back to deadlines that are currently deemed not sustainable for a fruitful judicial cooperation. See the considerations on this regard in the Request submitted by the Court of Justice pursuant to the second paragraph of Article 281 TFEU, with a view to amending Protocol No 3 on the Statute of the Court of Justice of the European Union, available at https://curia.europa.eu/jcms/upload/docs/application/pdf/2022-12/demande_transfert_ddp_tribunal_en.pdf accessed 30 December 2024.

[15] See, eg, CJEU, Case C-417/22 *BG* ECLI:EU:C:2023:877, paras 37 and 38.

the length of proceedings on other fundamental rights. Granted, the choice (or absence) of application of speedy procedural variations in a given case is not necessarily equated with a potential infringement of the principle of reasonable time. Yet, from a systematic point of view, the existence and articulation of these expedient procedural avenues are connected to the obligation of the EU to procure the means to comply with the reasonable time requirement.[16] As the Court has expressly noted, 'the urgent preliminary ruling procedure, established by Article 23a of the Statute of the Court of Justice of the European Union, constitutes one of the methods for implementing the right of all persons to have his case heard within a reasonable time' and, more generally, the procedures laid down 'in Article 23a of the Statute of the Court of Justice of the European Union specifically aim to ensure compliance with the right which is enshrined in Article 47, second paragraph, of the Charter'.[17]

The compliance with the reasonable time requirement in procedures before EU Courts is moreover justiciable. To date, the situations in which the Court of Justice has found an infringement of the reasonable time principle by EU Courts concern direct actions, identifying damages actions as the proper avenue so seek redress.[18] Such actions have so far never been filed concerning the length of proceedings in preliminary ruling proceedings, but theoretically, nothing would prevent such an action to be lodged by the affected parties –the damages being arguably caused by an EU institution in the sense of Article 340 TFEU.[19]

All those considerations show how the design, articulation as well as the practical use of the expedited and urgent variants of the preliminary ruling procedure are crucial for making the EU judicial system compliant with the reasonable time requirement. This is so not only in order to protect the right to a hearing within a reasonable time in a given case by EU Courts, but also, from a systematic point of view, to ensure the suitability of the EU judicial system to protect fundamental rights more generally, enabling national courts to perform their protective role and preserving the essential functions of judicial dialogue and uniform interpretation.

[16] Pointing at the connection, JA Gutiérrez-Fons, 'Le nouveau Règlement de procédure de la Cour de justice au regard du contentieux de l'Union européenne' in S Mahieu (dir), *Contentieux de l'Union européenne, questions choisies* (Bruxelles, Larcier, 2014).

[17] Order of the CJEU, Case C-8/19 PPU *RH* ECLI:EU:C:2019:110, paras 34 and 35.

[18] Even though the Court, when first faced with this question, granted an application to reduction of fines (CJEU, Case C-185/95 P *Baustahlgewebe v Commission* ECLI:EU:C:1998:608, para 48) it later decided that a claim for damages brought against the European Union before the General Court according to Article 268 TFEU and Article 340 TFEU constitutes an effective remedy concerning an infringement of the reasonable time principle. See, eg, CJEU, Case C-58/12 P *Groupe Gascogne SA v Commission* ECLI:EU:C:2013:770, paras 82–84, also stating that appeals are not upheld where there are no indications that the excessive length of proceedings affected their outcome (paras 73–76, in the judgment previously cited). Similarly, in the framework of preliminary rulings concerning national and judicial procedures, the Court has declared that where the excessive duration of proceedings may have affected the outcome of the dispute, the failure to act within a reasonable time may lead to the annulment of the contested administrative decision or judicial decision, in particular where that failure results in a breach of the rights of the defence. CJEU, Case C-756/21 *X* ECLI:EU:C:2023:523, para 83.

[19] Since the length of proceedings would need to be calculated by taking into account the overall duration of proceedings also before national courts, questions regarding allocation of responsibility may arise. See, generally on that discussion, M Kawcynska, 'Concurrent Liability of the European Union and the Member States' in J Iliopoulos-Strangas, S Biernat and M Potacs (eds), *Responsibility, Accountability and Control of the Constitutional State and the European Union in Changing Times* (Baden-Baden, Nomos, 2014).

3. Expedition before the Court of Justice: Urgent, Expedited and Priority Procedures in a Nutshell

Beyond the time limits imposed to the parties within the various types of procedures, EU Courts are not generally subject to formal and fixed adjudication deadlines,[20] with the sole exception of the deadlines imposed within the review procedure –which do not however apply for giving a ruling.[21] As a general rule, 'the reasonableness of a period cannot be assessed by reference to a precise maximum limit determined in an abstract manner but, rather, must be appraised in the light of the specific circumstances of each case'.[22]

Generally, the establishment of fixed and relatively short deadlines for adjudication is not regarded as the panacea for enabling a higher standard of effective judicial protection. In the words of Advocate General Bobek,

> there lies the problem inherent in time limits. They can indeed help to speed up proceedings. But they also have the potential to divide the field into two (equally suspect) categories: those that are suspect for being too slow and those that are suspect for being too fast. In other words, damned if you do stick to the time limits and damned if you don't.[23]

As a consequence, the establishment of strict time limits which do not take into account the need to adjust to the individual circumstances of a case may even run counter to the principle of effective judicial protection and effectiveness (with the concomitant duty of national jurisdictions to disapply national procedural rules, considering them as merely indicative).[24]

Different procedural modalities enable the CJEU to adapt to the specific circumstances of the case, rendering it possible to rule more expeditiously in preliminary rulings. As a key tool for judicial economy, reasoned orders can quickly put an end to a case when it is manifestly inadmissible or there is a manifest lack of jurisdiction;[25] when

[20] K Lenaerts, K Gutman, JT Nowak, *EU Procedural Law* (Oxford, Oxford University Press, 2023) 806.

[21] See Articles 62 and 62a of the Statute of the Court of Justice. The First Advocate General shall make her proposal for a review within one month of delivery of the decision by the General Court, and the Court shall decide whether or not to review within a further month. However, there is no deadline for the review judgment, but the creation of an 'urgent procedure' is foreseen within Article 62a with regard to review decisions in preliminary rulings. This procedure is now implemented in Article 114b of the Rules of Procedure of the Court of Justice, after the 2024 Amendments [2024] OJ L 2024/2094, which states that the Court of Justice 'shall give its ruling as soon as possible'.

[22] See, with regard to the duration of administrative procedures, CJEU, Case C-238/99 P et al, *Limburgse Vinyl Maatschappij and Others v Commission* ECLI:EU:C:2002:582, para 192. See, eg, applied to judicial proceedings, CJEU, Case T-725/14 *Aalberts Industries/Union européenne* ECLI:EU:T:2017:47, para 38; or CJEU, Case T-99/16 *De Nicola v Court of Justice of the European Union* ECLI:EU:T:2017:790.

[23] CJEU, Case C-406/18 *PG v Bevándorlási és Menekültügyi Hivatal* Opinion of Advocate General Bobek, ECLI:EU:C:2019:1055, para 56.

[24] CJEU, Case C-406/18 *PG v Bevándorlási és Menekültügyi Hivatal* ECLI:EU:C:2020:216, paras 34–37 and Case C-564/18 *LH v Bevándorlási és Menekültügyi Hivatal*, ECLI:EU:C:2020:218, paras 74–77.

[25] Article 53(2) of the Rules of Procedure of the Court of Justice [2012] OJ L 265/1, as last amended on 2 July 2024 (OJ L 2024/2094) (hereinafter, 'Rules of Procedure of the Court of Justice'). Article 225 of the Rules of Procedure of the General Court [2015] OJ L 105/1, as last amended on 12 August 2024 (OJ L 2024/2094) (hereinafter, 'Rules of Procedure of the General Court').

the question referred is identical to one previously ruled upon, or where the answer to it can be clearly deduced from existing case law or admits no reasonable doubt.[26]

Furthermore, derogations from the ordinary preliminary ruling procedure are allowed by Article 23a of the Statute of the Court of Justice, according to which 'the Rules of Procedure may provide for an expedited or accelerated procedure and, for references for a preliminary ruling relating to the area of freedom, security and justice, an urgent procedure'. Articulating this possibility, Article 53 of the Rules of Procedure lists amongst the different procedures for dealing with cases two modalities of speedy procedures: the expedited procedure and the urgent preliminary rulings procedure (PPU), and a further possibility with more moderate impact: the 'priority treatment'.

The expedited preliminary ruling procedure is governed by the Rules of Procedure of the Court of Justice and of the General Court,[27] and essentially allows to shorten deadlines for all the actors involved, while preserving the ordinary functioning of the procedure: the date for the hearing is fixed right away, the deadlines for lodging written observations as well as the internal deadlines for the Court's services are shortened. This procedure, which can be requested by the national court or be applied by EU Courts of their own motion, is characterised for its generality – as it can be applicable to any area of law – is also very flexible, and when extreme urgency exists, it can enable the Court to adjudicate in record time.[28] The average length of expedited preliminary ruling procedures was 10.7 months in 2021, 7.4 months in 2022 and 6.5 in 2024.[29]

The urgent preliminary procedure, governed by Articles 107 to 114 of the Rules of Procedure of the Court of Justice, is limited to the matters that fall within the Area of Freedom, Security and Justice (on the basis of the legal basis of the acts at issue), and its application can be requested by the referring court or applied by the Court of its own motion.[30] Since no jurisdiction regarding cases covered by this sphere of law has been transferred to the General Court, this procedure remains exclusive to the Court of Justice. Unlike the decision to apply the expedited procedure, which is taken by the President after hearing the reporting judge and the Advocate General in the case,[31] the decision whether or not to apply the urgent procedure falls with the chamber/s appointed for a

[26] Article 99 of the Rules of Procedure of the Court of Justice and Article 227 of the Rules of Procedure of the General Court. Applying this procedure makes it unnecessary to adjudicate on a request for an expedited procedure (see, eg, order of the CJEU, Case C-787/21 *Estaleiros Navais de Peniche* ECLI:EU:C:2022:414, para 17 and the case law cited).

[27] Articles 105 and 106 of the Rules of procedure of the Court of Justice and Articles 237 and 238 of the General Court.

[28] Noting the variability of adjudication times, Lenaerts, Gutman, and Nowak, *EU Procedural Law* (2023) 749: whereas the expedited procedure is normally concluded between three and six months, it is noted that one exceptional case lasted more than 14 months (see CJEU, Case C-490/20 *Pancharevo* ECLI:EU:C:2021:1008), or just two or three months (see CJEU, Joined Cases C-188/10 and C-189/10 *Melki and Abdeli* ECLI:EU:C:2010:319 or CJEU, Case C-189/01 *Jippes* ECLI:EU:C:2001:420. Also quite striking are two Full Court cases adjudicated in about three months, such as CJEU, Case C-370/12 *Pringle* ECLI:EU:C:2012:756, and CJEU, Case C-621/18 *Wightman and Others* ECLI:EU:C:2018:999.

[29] Annual Report of the Court of Justice 2024. There were no expedited procedures adjudicated in 2023, according to the Statistics, available at https://curia.europa.eu/jcms/upload/docs/application/pdf/2025-03/ra_en_statistiques_24_-_cour.pdf.

[30] As it was the case in CJEU, Case C-107/23 PPU *Lin* ECLI:EU:C:2023:606 or CJEU, Case C-583/22 PPU *MV (Formation of a cumulative sentence)* ECLI:EU:C:2023:5.

[31] Article 105(1) of the Rules of Procedure of the Court of Justice.

given judicial year.[32] The application of the PPU entails very relevant modulations in the development of proceedings, which include shortening deadlines and fixing promptly the hearing date. This procedure also entails the differences with regard to the usual procedure regarding the internal treatment of the case before the Court (dispensing the case from the normal examination at the General meeting of judges, and modulating the role of the Advocate General). It also limits the rights to lodge written statements to the parties in the procedures, to the Member State from which the reference is made, and to the Commission. In cases of extreme urgency, it is even possible to completely do away with the written phase of the procedure,[33] situating the oral procedure as the centre of gravity of the case, by way of derogation to the normal functioning of preliminary ruling procedures.[34] Due to the connection of the urgent procedure and the strict interpretation of the criterion of urgency, if the urgency disappears, the procedure will be reconducted to the 'normal' track of preliminary rulings.[35] The requirements of the proper administration of justice may also motivate that cases which in principle do not fulfil the requirements of urgency for the PPU are 'absorbed' by this procedure by reason of their joinder with a case where the PPU applies.[36]

There is not a time limit for PPUs. However, when the Council adopted the modification of the Statute that introduced the PPU, it added a 'statement' whereby, inter alia, it 'noted' that the 'urgent preliminary ruling procedure should be concluded within three months'.[37] The average duration of PPUs was 4.5 months in 2022, 4.3 months in 2023 and 3.3 in 2024.[38]

Finally, the 'priority treatment', foreseen in Article 53(3) of the Rules of Procedure of the Court of Justice, allows that, by decision of the President, a case 'jumps' the queue of pending cases before it to be granted temporal preference, its procedural treatment following however the ordinary rules.[39]

4. The Urgent Preliminary Ruling Procedure in the Area of Freedom, Security and Justice and Fundamental Rights

The connection between the Area of Freedom, Security and Justice (AFSJ) – the fields covered by Title V of Part Three of the TFEU – and fundamental rights is beyond any doubt. It is readily apparent that EU law adopted in the material areas included under

[32] Article 108 of the Rules of Procedure of the Court of Justice.

[33] Article 109 of the Rules of Procedure of the Court of Justice.

[34] See, generally, M Broberg and N Fenger, *Preliminary References to the European Court of Justice* (Oxford, Oxford University Press, 2014) 399 ff.

[35] As it was the case in CJEU, Joined Cases C-704/20 and C-39/21 *Staatssecretaris van Justitie en Veiligheid* ECLI:EU:C:2022:858.

[36] See, eg, CJEU, Joined Cases C-566/19 PPU and C-626/19 PPU *JR and YC* ECLI:EU:C:2019:1077, para 40.

[37] OJ L 24, 2008/44, annexed to the Council Decision 2008/79 of 20 December 2007 amending the Protocol on the Statute of the Court of Justice.

[38] Annual report 2022, and statistics 2023, see n 29 above.

[39] Lenaerts, Gutman, and Nowak, *EU Procedural Law* (2023) 770.

the umbrella of the AFSJ affect individual rights with intensity.[40] Both the full 'communitarisation' of the AFSJ and the codification of EU fundamental rights through the Charter have run in parallel and constitute one of the main developments enhancing the constitutionalisation of the EU. We could affirm that 'the normative consolidation of the Area of Freedom, Security and Justice (AFSJ) and the entry into force of the Charter of Fundamental Rights of the EU (the Charter) has transformed the Union as we know it.'[41]

The urgent preliminary ruling procedure (known by its French acronym as the 'PPU') is one of the procedural expressions of the new role of EU law in the AFSJ once the limitations to the jurisdiction of the Court of Justice elapsed after the entry into force of the Treaty of Lisbon.[42] Even before Lisbon, the discussion on the need to eliminate the specificities of the jurisdiction of the Court over the AFSJ was linked to the capacity of the Court of Justice to reduce the average duration of preliminary ruling procedures in certain instances, and to rule more quickly, if necessary, thanks to expedited procedures.[43] If the horizon of the Court's new competences did not at that point impact on the overall rethinking of the judicial architecture of the EU,[44] it had clear procedural implications. It became obvious that the setting up of an urgent preliminary ruling procedure was an existential need for the normalisation of the jurisdiction of the Court in the AFSJ.[45] If the preliminary ruling procedure was to be fully applied in the AFSJ – including the *CILFIT* and the *Foto Frost* obligations[46] – offering expediency was an inevitable trade off.[47] The need to fully 'communitarise' the AFSJ led therefore, for the

[40] See K Lenaerts, 'The Contribution of the European Court of Justice to the Area of Freedom, Security and Justice' (2010) 59 *International & Comparative Law Quarterly* 255.

[41] S Iglesias Sánchez and M González Pascual, *Fundamental Rights in the EU Area of Freedom, Security and Justice* (Cambridge, Cambridge University Press, 2021).

[42] See for the pre-existing situation, eg, S Peers, 'The Jurisdiction of the Court of Justice Over EC Immigration and Asylum Law: Time for a Change?' in A Baldaccini, E Guild, and H Toner (eds), *Whose Freedom, Security and Justice? EU Immigration and Asylum Law and Policy* (Oxford, Hart Publishing, 2007); A Albors Llorens, 'Changes in the Jurisdiction of the European Court of Justice under the Treaty of Amsterdam' (1998) 35 *Common Market Law Review* 1273; P Eeckhout, 'The European Court of Justice and the "Area of Freedom, Security and Justice": Challenges and Problems' in M Andenæs, D Fairgrieve (eds), *Liber Amicorum in Honour of Lord Slynn of Hadley – Judicial Review in European Union Law* (The Hague, Kluwer Law International, 2000); N Fenelly, 'The Area of "Freedom, Security and Justice" and the European Court of Justice – A Personal View' (2002) 49 *International and Comparative Law Quarterly* 1; T Tridimas, 'Knocking on Heaven's Door: Fragmentation, Efficiency and Defiance in the Preliminary Reference Procedure' (2003) 30 *Common Market Law Review* 9.

[43] Communication from the Commission 'Adaptation of the provisions of Title IV of the Treaty establishing the European Community relating to the jurisdiction of the Court of Justice with a view to ensuring more effective judicial protection', COM(2006) 346 final, 28 June 2006.

[44] Pointing at this need, P Eeckhout, 'The European Court of Justice and the "Area of Freedom, Security and Justice": Challenges and Problems' in M Andenæs, D Fairgrieve (eds), *Liber Amicorum in Honour of Lord Slynn of Hadley – Judicial Review in European Union Law* (The Hague, Kluwer Law International, 2000) 154.

[45] S Iglesias Sánchez, 'The Urgent Preliminary Ruling Procedure and the European Arrest Warrant' in A Lazowski (ed), *The European Arrest Warrant at Twenty* (Oxford, Hart Publishing, forthcoming).

[46] Respectively CJEU, Case C-283/81 *CILFIT and Others* ECLI:EU:C:1982:335 and CJEU, Case C-314/85 *Foto-Frost* ECLI:EU:C:1987:452.

[47] See the order of the CJEU, Case C-8/19 PPU *RH* ECLI:EU:C:2019:110, where the Court was asked whether Article 267 TFEU and Article 47 of the Charter preclude national legislation required to adjudicate on the legality of a pre-trial detention decision without the possibility to make a request for a preliminary ruling to the Court of Justice or to wait for its reply. The existence of the PPU was one of the main arguments adduced by the Court in its reply.

first time in EU judicial history, to the paradoxical result of fragmenting the preliminary ruling procedure by subject, creating a modality of the preliminary rulings procedure limited to the areas of law covered by the AFSJ.

This created a tension at the heart of the PPU. On the one side, this procedure conveys the need for swift decision making in cases where time is of the essence. On the other side, having emerged in the process of full communitarisation of the AFSJ, the PPU is called on to be applied on a relatively new area of EU law, which is of distinct constitutional relevance. In this scenario, it was feared that the extreme urgency of the PPU could have unintended negative results, not only by putting more pressure on the deliberation process and potentially impacting the quality of decision making, but also by curtailing the input from the interested parties of Article 23 of the Statute of the Court of Justice, which lies at the heart of the safeguards for the participation in the building up of the uniform interpretation of EU law. So far, these fears have not materialised and, unexpectedly, the PPU is regarded by some as enabling smoother judicial deliberation since – as long as the number of PPUs remains limited – the bench can concentrate on the PPU files in a way that all the phases of procedure take place with immediacy, without the usual interruptions.[48]

In a nutshell, the PPU factors in a sensitive equation, where the interest in speedy procedures shall be balanced against the need to preserve the quality and peculiarity of an EU's multinational judicial system based on judicial dialogue, without losing sight of procedural rights of interested parties and the rights of the defence,[49] in particularly complex and sensitive areas of law.

The PPU therefore navigates a delicate route, opening a narrow channel designed to bring the Court of Justice up to its task of being 'part' of the immediate adjudication of urgent cases in areas such as criminal law, family law, migration and asylum law and, at the same time, performing the role of a supreme and/or constitutional court, resolving extremely complex cases which involve constitutional interpretation and balancing of interests (epitomised in the mutual trust litigation). But above all, the PPU is imbued with pragmatism: ignoring the special needs for litigants and national courts for expediency in that area would have doomed judicial cooperation in the AFSJ, as it would have dissuaded reliance on Article 267 TFEU in these crucial new fields of EU law.[50]

The reasons behind the introduction of the PPU are therefore connected to the protection of fundamental rights, but not only. Its rationale, from a constitutional point of view, responds indubitably to the interest of litigants in the main proceedings, but also to the particularities of the jurisdictional system and the need to preserve judicial dialogue in order to enable the Court to ensure the main purpose of the

[48] In this sense, A Rosas, 'Justice in Haste, Justice Denied?: The European Court of Justice and the Area of Freedom, Security and Justice' (2008–2009) 11 *The Cambridge Yearbook of European legal Studies* 1.

[49] In this sense Lenaerts, 'The Contribution of the European Court of Justice' (2010) 273. In the past, the PPU proved to be problematic in the beginning of its operation, mostly due to the lack of publication of the 'views' of the Advocates General that followed a special regime whereby they were only made available at the point of the delivery of the judgment – a situation that has been normalised ever since.

[50] See, discussing examples where the fear of delays is still a reason not to fulfil with the CILFIT mandate, in spite of the existence of the PPU, M Mantovani, 'EU Private International Law Before the ECJ: the Origin of Preliminary References' (*EAPIL blog*, 14 November 2022) https://eapil.org/2022/11/14/eu-private-international-law-before-the-ecj-the-origin-of-preliminary-references/ accessed 5 December 2024.

procedure of Article 267 TFEU – the uniform interpretation of EU law – in the realm of the AFSJ.

It is in this light that the flexibility of the application of the PPU must be understood. In fact, in the indeterminacy of the criterion of urgency – often criticised as a source of vagueness and confusion – lies one of its strengths: the possibility for the Court of Justice to adjust to unforeseen situations which may demand different degrees of expeditiousness.

Different parameters of varied legal value inspire the practice of the Court in its PPU practice. First, Article 267 TFEU mandates the establishment of an urgent procedure in cases where a person is detained. Second, the Recommendations to national courts issued by the Court – an instrument of soft law with indicative value – provide for some guidance in identifying two situations: cases concerning 'persons in custody or deprived of liberty where the answer to the question raised is decisive as to the assessment of that person's legal situation'; and proceedings

> concerning parental authority or custody of young children, in so far, in particular, as the outcome of the dispute in the main proceedings depends on the answer to the question referred for a preliminary ruling and the use of the ordinary procedure could cause serious, and perhaps, irreparable, harm to the relationship between a child and (one of) that child's parents or to the child's development and integration into his or her family and social environment.[51]

Third, some further hints at the practice of the applicability of the urgency criterion have been systematised by an analytical document in the form of a Facts Sheet available on the website of the CJEU which includes not only the cases dealt with through the PPU, but also through the expedited procedure in the AFSJ.[52]

The abovementioned criteria have helped to bridge the indeterminacy of the criterion of urgency. An examination of the case law confirms that the practice reflects the obligations imposed by Article 267 TFEU and generally follows the indications in the recommendations given by the Court.

Deprivation of liberty is the first and most clearly identifiable situation where the PPU is destined to apply. This is the only situation where the application of a speedy procedure is mandated by primary law, since Article 267 TFEU states that, if a question for a preliminary ruling 'is raised in a case pending before a court or tribunal of a Member State with regard to a person in custody, the Court of Justice of the European Union shall act with the minimum of delay'. It is therefore not surprising that the overwhelming majority of cases where the PPU has been applied concern persons in custody, with most cases so far relating to the application of the European Arrest Warrant Framework Decision,[53] but also increasingly other instruments of EU

[51] Recommendations to national courts and tribunals in relation to the initiation of preliminary ruling proceedings [2024] OJ C 380/1, para 43.

[52] 'Urgent Preliminary Ruling Procedure and Expedited Procedure' available at https://curia.europa.eu/jcms/upload/docs/application/pdf/2019-10/tra-doc-en-div-c-0000-2019-201906086-05_00.pdf accessed 5 December 2024.

[53] Council Framework Decision 2002/584/JHA of 13 June 2002 on the European arrest warrant and the surrender procedures between Member States [2002] OJ L190/1. For an account of the application of the PPU in the framework of the application of this article: Iglesias Sánchez, 'The Urgent Preliminary Ruling Procedure' (forthcoming).

criminal law.[54] Deprivation of liberty is also central to cases concerning the detention of migrants or asylum seekers.[55] It would therefore appear that the right to freedom is the one primarily protected through the PPU.

However, not every situation of deprivation of freedom warrant application of the PPU. On the one side, the criterion of urgency has covered *predominantly custodial or detention cases*. Even though the Court has at some points interpreted the notion of deprivation of freedom with certain flexibility – for example, including situations where the persons concerned were kept in the sector of a transit zone reserved for third-country nationals[56] – the urgency criterion has not been found to be met in other situations where personal freedom was partially restricted (such as situations involving supervision measures which restrict personal freedom,[57] or free movement[58]). On the other side, the application of the PPU is not *only* connected to the deprivation of freedom, but it is made subject to a strict test which relies on the actual 'impact' of the reply on the Court on the situation of custody: the PPU will only be granted if the response of the Court has a direct impact on the decision to keep a person in custody, or on its length.[59] In mutual recognition cases, this does not preclude that the urgency is raised not only by the judicial authorities of the executing Member State, but also from those of the issuing Member State.[60]

The second situation identified by the recommendations issued by the Court, and which also follows from the case law, is connected with the rights of the children, even though the Court in its reasoning does not explicitly connect the urgency with Articles 8 and 24 of the Charter. This may be because up to now, the urgency criterion in the PPU is focused only on one particular aspect covered by those rights: the protection from the irreparable damage in the specific relationship between a parent (who should enjoy custody) and the child.

These cases often concern the Brussels IIa Regulation,[61] but the child-parent relationship *may* also be the object of protection in European Arrest Warrant related

[54] See, eg, CJEU, Case C-242/22 PPU *TL* ECLI:EU:C:2022:611; CJEU, Case C-583/22 PPU *MV (Formation of a cumulative sentence)* ECLI:EU:C:2023:5; CJEU, Case C-15/24 PPU *Stachev*, ECLI:EU:C:2024:399.

[55] See, in particular: CJEU, Case C-357/09 PPU *Kadzoev* ECLI:EU:C:2009:741; CJEU, Case C-61/11 PPU *el Dridi* ECLI:EU:C:2011:268; CJEU, Case C-383/13 PPU *G and R* ECLI:EU:C:2013:533; CJEU, Case C-601/15 PPU *N* ECLI:EU:C:2016:84, paras 40–41; CJEU, Case C-695/15 PPU *Mirza* ECLI:EU:C:2016:188, paras 34–36; Order of the CJEU, Case C-269/18 PPU *C and Others* ECLI:EU:C:2018:544; CJEU, Case C-36/20 PPU *Ministerio Fiscal* ECLI:EU:C:2020:495; CJEU, Case C-72/22 *Valstybės sienos apsaugos tarnyba* ECLI:EU:C:2022:505 or CJEU, Case C-387/24 PPU *Bouskoura* ECLI:EU:C:2024:868.

[56] CJEU, Joined Cases C-924/19 PPU and C-925/19 PPU *Országos Idegenrendészeti Főigazgatóság Dél-alföldi Regionális Igazgatóság* ECLI:EU:C:2020:367.

[57] See, CJEU, Case C-241/15 *Bob-Dogi* ECLI:EU:C:2016:385, para 26.

[58] See, eg, CJEU, Case C-505/19 *Bundesrepublik Deutschland (Notice rouge d'Interpol)* ECLI:EU:C:2021:376.

[59] Prechal and Pahladsingh, 'Urgency and Human Rights' (2021) 37, 51 and the cases cited therein. See, eg, CJEU, Case C-388/08 PPU *Leymann and Pustovarov* ECLI:EU:C:2008:669; CJEU, Case C-195/20 PPU *Generalbundesanwalt beim Bundesgerichtshof (Principe de spécialité)* ECLI:EU:C:2020:749; see also, eg, where those criteria were not met: CJEU, Case C-203/20 *AB and others (Révocation d'une amnistie)* ECLI:EU:C:2021:1016, para 24; CJEU, Case C-505/19 *Bundesrepublik Deutschland (notice rouge d'Interpol)* ECLI:EU:C:2021:376; or CJEU, Case C-488/19 *JR* ECLI:EU:C:2021:206, para 40; CJEU, Case C-294/16 PPU *JZ* ECLI:EU:C:2016:610, para 29. See also CJEU, Case C-108/16 PPU *Dworzecki* ECLI:EU:C:2016:346, para 22 and the case law cited; CJEU, Case C-142/22 *OE* ECLI:EU:C:2023:554, para 29.

[60] CJEU, Case C-318/24 PPU *Breian* ECLI:EU:C:2024:658, para 27.

[61] Council Regulation (EU) 2019/1111 of 25 June 2019 on jurisdiction, the recognition and enforcement of decisions in matrimonial matters and the matters of parental responsibility, and on international

proceedings,[62] as well as to asylum and migration related proceedings, involving separation of parents and children.[63] Other cases not directly concerned with the separation of children and parents have also been dealt with through PPUs where the situation of minors was at stake.[64]

Ranking third are situations connected with the expulsion and/or return of migrants and asylum seekers. Here again, there are clear implications for several rights, including the non-refoulement principle,[65] but also humanitarian considerations linked to the health of the person concerned,[66] and the right to family life.[67]

From all these considerations, it emerges a typology based on the impact of time on certain fundamental rights. The time-sensitive nature of some fundamental rights seems to rely on certain normative underpinnings that have not been made explicit beyond Article 267 TFEU and the link to detention. But overall, in 15 years, the application of the PPU seems to confirm that the case law follows the original design already conceived by the Court in 2006. Back then, when the Court envisaged the different alternatives for an urgent procedure, it carefully considered the compromises that such a procedure should entail, and concluded that it should be circumscribed to situations involving the protection of individual freedom, and 'the observance of a fundamental right, where a delay in the protection of that right could cause serious and irreparable damage for the person concerned'.[68] The construction of a test which relies not only on the seriousness but also on the irreparable character of the damage therefore makes the criterion of urgency one of narrow interpretation, where the – in principle, flexible – criterion of urgency narrows down to a quite limited *palette* of type situations.

child abduction (recast) [2019] OJ L 178/1, which replaced Council Regulation (EC) No 2201/2003 of 27 November 2003 concerning jurisdiction and the recognition and enforcement of judgments in matrimonial matters and the matters of parental responsibility, repealing Regulation (EC) No 1347/2000 [2003] OJ L 338/1). See, eg, CJEU, Case C-638/22 PPU *Rzecznik Praw Dziecka and Others (Suspension de la décision de retour)* ECLI:EU:C:2023:21.

[62] See, CJEU, Case C-261/11 *GN* ECLI:EU:C:2023:1017, where the request to apply the expedited procedure was refused since there was not a risk in respect of the custody of GN's children (para 30), as well as CJEU, Case C-208/23 *Martiesta* (removed from register).

[63] See, CJEU, Case C-1/23 PPU *Afrin* ECLI:EU:C:2023:296, paras 23–27. Even though strictly involving the interpretation of Regulation 2201/2003, see also CJEU, Case C-262/21 PPU ECLI:EU:C:2021:640 concerning the consequences of the transfer of the child and his mother to Finland pursuant to a decision adopted in application of the Dublin III Regulation.

[64] CJEU, Case C-92/12 PPU *Health Service Executive* ECLI:EU:C:2012:255, para 49; or CJEU, Case C-393/18 PPU *UD* ECLI:EU:C:2018:835, para 23.

[65] CJEU, Joined Cases C-924/19 PPU and C-925/19 PPU *Országos Idegenrendészeti Főigazgatóság Délalföldi Regionális Igazgatóság* ECLI:EU:C:2020:367, para 105 and CJEU, Case C-638/16 PPU *X and X* ECLI:EU:C:2017:173, para 33. See also the Order of the CJEU, Case C-422/18 PPU *FR* ECLI:EU:C:2018:784, para 24.

[66] CJEU, Case C-578/16 PPU *CK and Others* ECLI:EU:C:2017:127, paras 37–40, and CJEU, Joined Cases C-924/19 PPU and C-925/19 PPU *Országos Idegenrendészeti Főigazgatóság Délalföldi Regionális Igazgatóság* ECLI:EU:C:2020:367, para 106.

[67] The Court has rejected the PPU on the basis of the fact that there was not a risk for fundamental rights such as family life: CJEU, Case C-432/20 *Landeshauptmann von Wien (Perte du statut de résident de longue durée)* ECLI:EU:C:2022:39, para 22. Similarly, the absence of that risk motivates rejection of application of the PPU/PPA, Order of the CJEU, Case C-58/23 *YN v Republika Slovenija (Abboudnam)* ECLI:EU:C:2023:748, para 20.

[68] Supplement to the discussion paper on the treatment of questions referred for a preliminary ruling concerning the area of freedom, security and justice, 14 December 2006, Council Document 17013/06.

5. The Expedited Procedure and Fundamental Rights – A Note on Priority

Existing ever since the year 2000 and amended in the 2012 Rules of Procedure, the expedited procedure (previously called 'accelerated procedure') is foreseen in the Statute of the Court of Justice and is available both for preliminary rulings and direct actions before the Court of Justice and the General Court.

In spite of the fact that its application is not limited to any area of law or specific situations, the Recommendations from the Court refer to some examples of the criteria that may determine the use of the expedited preliminary ruling procedure both before the Court of Justice and the General Court: 'serious and immediate danger to public health or to the environment which a prompt decision by the Court of Justice or the General Court might help to avert, or if particular circumstances require uncertainties concerning fundamental issues of national constitutional law and of EU law to be resolved within a very short time'.[69]

Conversely, different 'formulae' point out which arguments will not lead to a successful application of the expedited procedure, such as 'the large number of persons or legal situations potentially affected by the decision' or 'the fact that there may be important economic issues at stake or that the referring court or tribunal is obliged to rule expeditiously.'[70]

The situations and interests covered by this procedure are willingly open-ended and lead to an almost entirely casuistic approach which resists systematisation. The expedited procedure is a valuable instrument of judicial policy and diplomacy, particularly within the framework of judicial dialogue in preliminary ruling procedures, when structural urgent questions are at stake and the CJEU is also a crucial actor in the political process – its readiness to mobilise its machinery with utmost expediency through the expedited procedure also signposts the crucial and landmark character of a case. Its use has been paramount in constitutional emergencies[71] or cases affecting political processes of crucial importance for the EU, such as Brexit[72] or the financial stability of the Union.[73]

At first sight, however, merely looking at the recommendations cited above, the connection of the expedited procedure (and its use in the framework of preliminary rulings) with fundamental rights, seems to be more diluted than in the case of the PPU. The case law shows, on the contrary, that the practical application of the expedited procedure corresponds, more often than not, to situations connected with fundamental rights.

[69] Recommendations (see n 51 above), para 34.

[70] ibid.

[71] Such as some cases related to the rule of law. See, eg, CJEU, Case C-430/21 *RS* ECLI:EU:C:2022:99.

[72] Order of the President of the Court of Justice in Case C-621/18 *Wightman and Others* ECLI:EU:C:2018:851, para 11, highlighting that 'the implementation of Article 50 TEU is of fundamental importance for the United Kingdom and for the constitutional order of the European Union, the particular circumstances in this instance are such as to justify this case being dealt with within a short time …'.

[73] Order of the President of the Court of Justice in Case C-370/12 *Pringle* ECLI:EU:C:2012:610, para 8, stating that 'in the light of the exceptional circumstances of the financial crisis surrounding the conclusion of the EMS Treaty, the request of the referring court that the accelerated procedure be applied … should be granted'.

Just to mention some examples, the expedited procedure has been extensively used in situations concerning detained persons,[74] as well as in proceedings having an impact on family life or civil status.[75] Covering a broader range of situations than the PPU, the expedited procedure has also been applied in situations where the risk of losing the main residence of the applicant was at stake.[76] Even though the number of persons affected does not suffice to justify the application of the expedited procedure, the Court has granted it in situations in which speedy adjudication could remove the serious uncertainties faced by a referring court as to important questions of Union law, relating in particular to the proper functioning of the common European asylum system as well as the temporary protection system,[77] taking also in consideration the risk to be devolved and the deprivation of means suffered by the applicant,[78] or other interests also more or less indirectly connected with fundamental rights considerations, such as the high risk of irremediable harm for the environment.[79] Notably, the use of the expedited procedure covers both situations of urgency parallel to those where the PPU typically applies, but not falling within the material scope of the PPU, as well as cases that fall within the realm of the AFSJ, but that would not meet the narrow PPU criterion of urgency.

Precisely due to its flexibility, the expedited procedure plays an essential role in the fulfilment of the reasonable deadline principle where proceedings before EU Courts are connected with fundamental rights. It completes the protection offered by the PPU by providing for a fallback category to those cases falling within legal bases contained within the AFSJ and where the application of the PPU has been requested but not granted.[80] In that way, it bridges the gap between the AFSJ and other areas where EU fundamental rights can be seriously affected by the passage of time. It allows the Court to approach urgency from a certain gradation enabling it to allocate its resources in a more sustainable way from the point of view of judicial economy. It is flexible enough to respond to situations where the element of fundamental rights comes from a constitutional confrontation with national legal orders in need of expedient clarification.[81]

In the lack of systematicity of the expedited procedure lies, however, also one of the main challenges of its application. Even though the potential application of expedient procedures can be raised at early stages through the 'fiche de préexamen' elaborated by

[74] See, eg, CJEU, Joined Cases C-188/10 and C-189/10 *Melki and Abdeli* ECLI:EU:C:2010:363; order of the CJEU, Case C-329/11 *Achughbabian* ECLI:EU:C:2011:630; Order of the CJEU, Case C-181/14 *G* ECLI:EU:C:2014:740; CJEU, Case C-502/19 *Junqueras Vies* ECLI:EU:C:2019:1115; Order of the CJEU, Case C-202/24 *Alchaster* ECLI:EU:C:2024:343.

[75] Order of the CJEU, Case C-127/08 *Metock* ECLI:EU:C:2008:235; CJEU, Case C-709/20 ECLI:EU:C:2021:602; or CJEU, Case C-490/20 *Pancharevo* ECLI:EU:C:2021:1008.

[76] Order of the CJEU, Case C-407/18 *Addiko Bank* ECLI:EU:C:2018:825, para 13.

[77] Order of the CJEU, Joined Cases C-244/24 and C-290/24 *Kaduna* ECLI:EU:C:2024:491, para 13. See also, orders of the CJEU in Case C-670/16 *Mengesteab* ECLI:EU:C:2017:120; and in Case C-646/16 *Jafari* ECLI:EU:C:2017:138.

[78] Order of the CJEU, Joined Cases C-244/24 and C-290/24 *Kaduna* ECLI:EU:C:2024:491, para 14, as well as CJEU, Case C-709/20 *The Department for Communities in Northern Ireland* ECLI:EU:C:2021:602, para 44.

[79] See, eg, Order of the CJEU, Joined Cases C-78/16 and C-79/16 *Pesce and Others* ECLI:EU:C:2016:251, para 10.

[80] See, eg, CJEU, Case C-215/15 *Gogova* ECLI:EU:C:2015:710. This was even the situation in the first ever PPU case requested, CJEU, Case C-66/08 *Kozłowski* ECLI:EU:C:2008:437, which arrived before the reform of the rules of procedure came into force, so that only the PPA could be applied (Order of the CJEU, Case C-66/07 *Kozłowski* ECLI:EU:C:2008:116.

[81] See, eg, CJEU, Case C-42/17 *MAS and MB* ECLI:EU:C:2017:936.

the Research and Documentation Directorate of the Court,[82] and the request by the national court for an expedited procedure is signalled at the point where the case is introduced, the awareness towards urgency is lessened where such a request does not exist. Unlike the PPU in the AFSJ, there is not a systematic screening of cases to detect their urgency connected to impact on fundamental rights at early procedural stages. The application of the expedited procedure is therefore highly dependent on the initiative of national courts. Additionally, the absence of clear criteria regarding the situations in which the expedited procedure may apply does not offer a solid point of reference upon which national courts could act with certainty when requesting the application of this procedure. Furthermore, even though the reference to exceptionality and 'particular urgency'[83] is no longer contained in the Rules of Procedure – which refer more broadly to the need to rule 'within a short time' – the Court consistently considers that the need for a speedy treatment is in any case not enough to trigger the expedited procedure, and that its application is governed by the idea of *exceptionality*, as 'such an expedited procedure is a procedural instrument intending to address matters of an exceptional urgency'.[84]

This exceptionality translates in that the link between the protection of fundamental rights and the application of the expedited procedure may be difficult to individuate and explain by national courts. The interest of litigants in determining their rights is not a criterion that is deemed to suffice for the application of this procedure, even if it has an impact on fundamental rights. Several cases point in this direction: for example, a case concerning the situation of a pupil at the European Schools, where his educational progress was affected;[85] cases concerning appointment of judges where the independence of ordinary courts was at stake, also affecting a large number of cases;[86] or situations with an impact on the length of criminal proceedings before national courts.[87] In these cases, the threshold of exceptionality was deemed not to have been met.

A final note must be made regarding the 'priority treatment', the third variant of speedy procedures mentioned by Article 53(3) of the Rules of Procedure. The sole criterion laid down by this provision for applying this priority treatment is the existence of 'special circumstances'. The broad leeway accorded by this provision together with the fact that no motivation is required, makes it certainly difficult to establish a typology of situations where the 'priority' procedure is applied. Practice shows however that this procedure is often applied in cases where the PPU or the expedited procedure have been

[82] See the contribution of JA Gutiérrez Fons in ch 17 of this volume.

[83] See Article 62a of the Consolidated version of the Rules of Procedure of the Court of Justice of 19 June 1991 [2010] OJ C 177/1.

[84] CJEU, Case C-497/20 *Randstad Italia* ECLI:EU:C:2021:1037, para 37 and the case law cited.

[85] CJEU, Case C-431/22 *Scuola europea di Varese* ECLI:EU:C:2023:1021. In this case, the length of the national proceedings led the ECJ to reject the application of the expedited procedure. For a criticism, J Gruber, 'The Court of Justice and Urgent Matters (Case C-431/22 Scuola europea di Varese)' (*EU Law Live*, 02 February 2024) https://eulawlive.com/op-ed-the-court-of-justice-and-urgent-matters-case-c-431-22-scuola-europea-di-varese-by-joachim-gruber/ accessed 15 May 2025.

[86] CJEU, Case C-181/21 *G* ECLI:EU:C:2024:1.

[87] Order of the CJEU, Case C-375/08 *Pontini* ECLI:EU:C:2008:528, para 10 or CJEU, Case C-357/19 et al *Euro Box Promotion and Others* ECLI:EU:C:2021:1034, para 117.

requested by the referring court, but not granted.[88] Priority treatment introduces therefore an element of flexibility that allows to bridge the narrowness of the PPU urgency criterion and the exceptionality of the expedited procedure and the need to prioritise some files. In spite of its limited impact – as it does not allow the far-reaching procedural modulations of other expedient procedures – it can be successfully used to make procedural organisation sensitive to different needs in cases connected to the protection of fundamental rights, offering a third and flexible layer of urgency translating in prioritisation.[89]

6. The Role of Rights in Shaping Procedure at EU Courts

The previous analysis invites reflection on the role of the different speedy variants of the preliminary ruling procedure in the procedural organisation of EU Courts and the tools available to ensure compliance with the reasonable time requirement. This closing section is aimed at offering some points for prospective discussion on the evolution of the system, rather than providing conclusions. Three issues seem particularly worth addressing at this point. First, it may be time to reconsider why and if the AFSJ deserves exclusivity in the application of the PPU. Second, the practical application of and choice between the PPU, the expedited procedure and the priority treatment could benefit from some reflection about their interrelation. Third, the impact of the length of proceedings on fundamental rights is a helpful proxy that would enhance a coherent and complementary application of the available modalities of speedy preliminary rulings procedures.

First, in a way, the PPU tests the ability of the Court of Justice to be a fundamental rights court.[90] It has successfully served as the procedural avenue for some of the crucial developments in the EU fundamental rights case law.[91] It seems that, after 15 years, the time is ripe for considering this procedure from a systematic point of view, and to reflect

[88] See, eg, CJEU, Case C-268/17 *AY* ECLI:EU:C:2018:602; CJEU, Case C-240/17 *E* ECLI:EU:C:2018:8; CJEU, Case C-490/16 *AS* ECLI:EU:C:2017:585; CJEU, Case C-241/15 *Bob-Dogi* ECLI:EU:C:2016:385; CJEU, Joined Cases C-404/15 and C-659/15 PPU *Aranyosi and Căldăraru* ECLI:EU:C:2016:198; CJEU, Case C-572/21 *CC* ECLI:EU:C:2022:562; CJEU, Case C-656/13 *L* ECLI:EU:C:2014:2364; or CJEU, Case C-699/21 *EDL* ECLI:EU:C:2023:295.

[89] A recent example of use of the priority treatment in cases where the PPU is rejected, with this protective aim is to be found in CJEU, Case C-528/21 *MD* ECLI:EU:C:2023:341, a case where a prohibition of entry meant that a father could not be reunited with his child. See also, with regard to the right to family reunification, CJEU, Case C-635/17 *E* ECLI:EU:C:2019:192, or generally, cases concerning minors, CJEU, Case C-512/17 *HR* ECLI:EU:C:2018:513; CJEU, Case C-428/15 *Child and Family Agency* ECLI:EU:C:2016:819. It has also been granted in cases where the application expedited procedure has been rejected. See, eg, a case concerning criminal procedures against minors, and procedural fundamental rights, CJEU, Case C-603/22 *MS and Others* ECLI:EU:C:2024:685.

[90] S Bartolini, 'The Urgent Preliminary Ruling Procedure: Ten Years On' (2018) 2 *European Public Law* 213, 213–14.

[91] See, eg, crucial Grand Chamber cases: CJEU, Case C-107/23 PPU *Lin* ECLI:EU:C:2023:606; CJEU, Joined Cases C-562/21 PPU and C-563/21 PPU *Openbaar Ministerie (Tribunal établi par la loi dans l'État membre d'émission)* ECLI:EU:C:2022:100; CJEU, Joined Cases C-404/15 and C-659/15 PPU *Aranyosi and Căldăraru* ECLI:EU:C:2016:198; CJEU, Case C-216/18 PPU *LM (deficiencies in the system of Justice)* ECLI:EU:C:2018:PPU; CJEU, Case C-656/13 *L* ECLI:EU:C:2014:2364, or CJEU, Case C-479/21 PPU *Governor of Cloverhill Prison and Others* ECLI:EU:C:2021:929.

on its exceptionality and its limitation to the AFSJ. The PPU is an incident of history, not the result of a systematic conception of the entire rationality of court proceedings and the need for expediency. Even though, by reason of its subject matter, the legal instruments covered by the AFSJ are probably, statistically speaking, more likely to affect fundamental rights, there are parallel needs outside the AFSJ. Given the complexity and scope of EU law, there are no normative reasons for systematically considering the AFSJ as a conceptual shortcut for a potential need of expediency. The current structure leads to a situation of procedural reverse discrimination: for example, migration cases fall within the PPU, but not citizenship and free movement cases which pose similar issues – eg, cases concerning extradition[92]– and so do cases with criminal law implications or even detention, if the instruments being interpreted fall outside the legal basis of the AFSJ.

Resort to the expedient procedure as a backup plan constitutes a pragmatic approach that the Court has used wisely, but it is not ideal from the point of view of the systematic consideration of which procedures are applicable to which cases, since important differences remain regarding not only the application of early detection protocols of urgency,[93] but also the organisational measures that remain exclusive to the PPU (both in terms of allocation of resources, and procedure).[94] Even though the expedited procedure can, in some instances, produce results comparable to the PPU in terms of expediency, the differences between them lie not only in their procedural design and scope, but also in the likelihood of their application.[95]

Second, there is a need for an overall debate on the architecture of procedural avenues to tackle urgency and the reasons for maintaining separate proceedings, and the relationship between them. Is there a real added value of keeping two different proceedings – the PPU and the expedited procedure – beyond the fact that the PPU is limited to specific material areas? Or should there be a single expedient procedure with different possibilities of derogating from general rules depending on the degree of urgency? Could such urgency be determined through a general test, allowing for gradation of situations irrespective of the area of law, focusing inter alia on impact on fundamental rights?

[92] If extradition is based on agreements signed by a Member State and not by the EU. However, for agreements based on Article 82(1)(d) TFEU, the PPU would be available. See CJEU, Case C-897/19 PPU *Ruska Federacija v IN* ECLI:EU:C:2020:262. Similarly PPU was requested in a case related to the rules applicable to British citizens after Brexit according to the EU–UK Withdrawal Agreement and EU–UK Trade and Cooperation Agreement. The case was closed since the national court decided to extradite, but nevertheless the ECJ did not reject the PPU as a matter of principle, but only because the urgency criterion was not met, see order of the CJEU, Case C-235/22 *Criminal proceedings against Abel* ECLI;EU:C:2023:730, para 23.

[93] As Tizzano and Iannuccelli, put it, a case containing a request for a PPU resounds like an alarm in all the services of the Court, A Tizzano and P Iannuccelli, 'La procedure préjudicielle d'urgence devant la Cour de justice: premier bilan et nouveles questions' (2012) 1 *Il diritto de l'Unione europea* 107, 120. See also D Lawunmi, 'Behind the Scenes at the CJEU in Cabinet Sharpston: Extracts from Letters Home' in C Barnard, A Łazowski, D Sarmiento (eds), *Pursuit of Legal Harmony in a Challenging Europe. Essays in Honour of Eleanor Sharpston* (Oxford, Hart Publishing, 2024). See also the Chapter by JA Gutiérrez Fons in ch 17 of this volume.

[94] See Section 3 of this chapter.

[95] According to the judicial statistics for the year 2022, in the previous five years (2018–2021) 235 requests for expedited procedures where introduced, from which 2014 were made in preliminary ruling procedures. Only 21 cases (from the overall expedited requests procedures) were granted. This reality is in stark contrast with the data provided in the AFSJ: in the same time frame, 101 requests for PPU were introduced, and it was granted in 50 cases.

This reflection should reach also the priority treatment as a plausible option to reach a reasonable deadline. Systematisation, and more complete motivation, of the cases where this procedure has been granted could also help in identifying areas or situations that shall be associated with different levels of expediency, regardless of the request of national courts to apply the PPU or the expedited procedure. Indeed, priority treatment often works as a fallback option (similarly as the expedited procedure with regard to the PPU), but its dependency from the request of national jurisdictions may raise concerns given the indirect nature of the preliminary ruling procedure (since the signalling of urgency is left to the national courts, and not the parties to the main proceedings). Similarly, recent cases also open an interesting avenue to tackle urgency from the point of view of the composite nature of preliminary ruling procedures, recalling the importance of the award of interim measures by national courts.[96]

Third and finally, the general reflection on prioritisation and urgency should revolve around fundamental rights. The impact of the length of proceedings on fundamental rights shall be considered at least as one of the main proxies to trigger urgent treatment. This approach would enhance a coherent and complementary application of the available modalities of speedy preliminary rulings procedures. Granted, not every case concerning fundamental rights shall be dealt urgently. Absence of affectation of the fundamental rights of litigants often works successfully as a motivation to reject the application of the PPU,[97] but the reverse situation does not necessarily lead to acknowledge a need for procedural acceleration, as not any potential impact of a case on fundamental rights an be considered as an independent criterion to assess urgency.[98] The notion of *irreparable* harm, central to the application of the PPU, and the exceptionality of the application of the expedited procedure, showcases that only a very serious impact on fundamental rights motivates the application of speedier procedural variants. However, beyond situations of extreme urgency, there is a lack of a clear indication as to what impact on which fundamental rights should translate into procedural measures in preliminary ruling procedures establishing a graduation of expediency. In short, there is not a clear, nuanced and gradated 'priority policy'.[99]

Construing such policy is a delicate endeavour that should not lose sight of the uniqueness of the preliminary ruling procedure. Some inspiration can however be drawn from the approach to timeliness from the point of view of Article 6 ECHR. In the choice of one of the speedier variants of procedure, the significance of the outcome of the case for litigants is a helpful criterion that could inspire the evolution of the choice of procedural avenues for expediency. The criterion of 'what is at stake for the applicant', developed by ECtHR case law has evolved after *König v Germany*,[100]

[96] Order of the CJEU, Joined Cases C-14/21 and C-15/21 *Sea Watch* ECLI:EU:C:2021:149. See with regard to interim measures ch 14 in this volume by K Gutman and A Kornezov.

[97] CJEU, Case C-432/20 *ZK* ECLI:EU:C:2022:39, para 22.

[98] See, eg, CJEU, Case C-417/22 *BG* ECLI:EU:C:2023:877, paras 37 and 38. See the discussion on the criterion of urgency in CJEU, Case C-359/22 *AHY* Opinion of Advocate General Pikamäe, ECLI:EU:C:2023:678, para 29. The ruling of the Court on the case does not discuss the reasons related to urgency, merely stating that the application of the PPU was rejected.

[99] This terminology is used taking as a reference the practice of the ECtHR, which adopted 'The Court's Priority Policy', amended in 2017, available at https://prd-echr.coe.int/documents/d/echr/Priority_policy_ENG accessed 5 December 2024.

[100] ECtHR, App no 6232/73 *König v Germany* ECLI:CE:ECHR:1978:0628JUD000623273, para 111.

giving rise to a heightened requirement of diligence when it comes to cases that have a serious impact on other fundamental rights. There is a stark resemblance with the nature of cases where the PPU and the expedited procedure actually are often applied: when litigation concerns, primary, but not exclusively,[101] matters affecting private and family life, such as civil status and capacity,[102] family matters, in particular those related to parental authority,[103] victims of certain accidents or violence,[104] or cases concerning persons held in custody.[105] Some of these cases require 'exceptional diligence', such as placing children in public care or adoption, or cases relating to situations where there is a time sensitive serious health issue.[106] Other cases refer to certain employment and pension related rights and rights related to the exercise of professional activities.[107]

This chapter certainly does not argue that the instances identified by this case law shall translate to the application of speedy procedures at EU courts. But the openness and comprehensiveness of an approach focused on 'what is at stake' for the parties in the main proceedings, considering the length of the entire procedure as a whole as well as its impact on fundamental rights, could inspire a future reflection exercise. In this context, a possible recalibration of speedier variants of preliminary rulings procedure before EU Courts could translate to a more nuanced, systematic and comprehensive approach to different levels of urgency and their procedural consequences.

[101] See, generally, F Edel, *The Length of Civil and Criminal Proceedings in the Case-Law of the European Court of Human Rights* (Council of Europe Publishing, 2007), listing extensive case law related to other areas such as passports, access to certain goods and services, property related issues.

[102] See, eg, ECtHR, App no 11118/84 *Bock v the Federal Republic of Germany* ECLI:CE:ECHR:1989:0329JUD001111884, paras 48 and 49; ECtHR, App no 53176/99 *Mikulic v Croatia* ECLI:CE:ECHR:2002:0207JUD005317699, para 44; ECtHR, App no 60176/00 *Ebru and Tayfun Engin Colak v Turkey* ECLI:CE:ECHR:2006:0530JUD006017600, para 75; ECtHR, App no 12238/86 *Taiuti v Italy* ECLI:CE:ECHR:1992:0227JUD001223886, para 18.

[103] See, eg, ECtHR, App no 33158/96 *Laino v Italy* ECLI:CE:ECHR:1999:0218JUD003315896, para 18; ECtHR, App no 63627/00 *Voleský v the Czech Republic* ECLI:CE:ECHR:2004:0629JUD006362700.

[104] See, eg, ECtHR, App no 50222/99 *Krastanov v Bulgaria*, ECLI:CE:ECHR:2004:0930JUD005022299, para 70 and case law cited.

[105] See, eg, ECtHR, App no 12728/87 *Abdoella v the Netherlands* ECLI:CE:ECHR:1992:1125JUD001272887, para 24 and case law cited.

[106] Edel, *The Length of Civil and Criminal Proceedings* (2007) mentions, respectively, cases like ECtHR, App no 16817/90 *Paulsen-Medalen and Svensson v Sweden* ECLI:CE:ECHR:1998:0219JUD001681790, para 39, or ECtHR, App no 18020/91 *X v France* ECLI:CE:ECHR:1992:0331JUD001802091, para 47.

[107] See, eg, ECtHR, App no 26256/95 *Doustaly v France* ECLI:CE:ECHR:1998:0423JUD002625695, para 48.

14

Interim Measures and Fundamental Rights in EU Law: Some Reflections and Possible Reforms

KATHLEEN GUTMAN AND ALEXANDER KORNEZOV*

1. Introduction

Interim measures by virtue of EU law remain difficult to obtain in practice. Although interim measures in direct actions brought before the Court of Justice of the European Union (EU Courts)[1] have recently shown their full potential, particularly in infringement cases,[2] the fact remains that the rules governing interim measures before the courts of the Member States (national courts), in cases falling within the scope of EU law, have not developed much since the 1990s. Those rules were thus conceptualised long before the binding force of the Charter of Fundamental Rights of the European Union (Charter),[3] at a time when fundamental rights played a less prominent role in the EU legal order.

Since then, the case law of the EU Courts has evolved significantly from a fundamental rights perspective, with the Charter taking central stage in judicial reasoning.[4] Yet, interim measures seem to have been left behind in this process. While some recent examples of a more fundamental-rights-sensitive approach to interim measures have emerged, they are rather punctual and case-specific. The question whether the EU rules on interim measures ensure adequate protection of fundamental rights is therefore of critical importance.

* Référendaire at the Court of Justice and Judge at the Court of Justice, respectively. All opinions expressed herein are strictly personal.

[1] In this contribution, the terms CJEU and EU Courts denote the institution of the Court of Justice of the European Union, which, in accordance with the first subparagraph of Article 19(1) TEU, currently includes the Court of Justice and the General Court.

[2] For instance, interim measures have been a major issue in the rule of law case law of the Court of Justice. See, in particular, n 79 below and Section 4.3.

[3] Following the entry into force of the Lisbon Treaty on 1 December 2009, the Charter has the same legal value as the Treaties. See Article 6(1) TEU.

[4] See, in that regard, M Bobek and J Adams-Prassl, 'Conclusion' in M Bobek and J Adams-Prassl (eds), *The EU Charter of Fundamental Rights in the Member States* (Oxford, Hart Publishing, 2020) 559, 572; A Kornezov, 'The Charter and the General Court' in S Peers, T Hervey, J Kenner and A Ward (eds), *The EU Charter of Fundamental Rights: A Commentary* 2nd edn (Oxford, Bloomsbury Publishing, 2021) 1809.

That question is all but trivial. The European Union prides itself in providing 'a complete system of legal remedies and procedures'.[5] Interim measures are meant to play a key role in that system. It is thus crucial to ensure that interim measures by virtue of EU law are capable of guaranteeing the effective functioning of that system, filling any potential gaps in particular from a fundamental rights perspective. Indeed, effective interim relief is essential for ensuring adequate protection of fundamental rights, perhaps even more so than other rights derived from EU law. After all, some fundamental rights are particularly vulnerable and time-sensitive. Sometimes, a fundamental right might be irrevocably lost in the blink of an eye or become devoid of purpose if its protection is delayed. A child separated from its parents or a person subjected to torture or inhuman treatment cannot wait patiently until the legal process has played out. In such instances, interim measures may in fact be the *only* effective remedy.

Surprisingly, however, the role of interim measures in the protection of fundamental rights in the European Union seems to have remained on the sidelines of the case law and literature. Indeed, while there has been extensive study of interim measures in EU law, on the one hand, and the EU system of fundamental rights, on the other, these two subjects rarely interact with each other.[6] Often, the discussion of interim measures is confined to the technical and specialist world of EU procedural law,[7] thereby focusing on the procedures before the EU Courts without much analysis of the potential contribution of interim measures to safeguarding fundamental rights. Nor, it seems, has much attention been devoted to the role of interim measures, as a matter of EU law, before the national courts in this respect.

Consequently, the aim of this contribution is to examine the role of interim measures in the system of fundamental rights protection in the European Union. It is divided into three main parts. The first part frames the discussion of interim measures and fundamental rights in EU law by elucidating the relevant terminology and clarifying the division of tasks between the national courts and the EU Courts in the adjudication of cases involving fundamental rights. The second part evaluates interim measures before the national courts in cases governed by EU law, with a focus on surveying the classical case law, recent jurisprudential developments and some possible ways for integrating considerations relevant to fundamental rights. The third part addresses interim measures before the EU Courts, emphasising certain key features and salient case law bearing on the protection of fundamental rights.

Through this analysis, the main arguments of this contribution are that interim measures in EU law have significant untapped potential for playing a meaningful

[5] See, eg, CJEU, Joined Cases C-59/18 and C-182/18 *Italy and Comune di Milano v Council (Seat of the European Medicines Agency)* ECLI:EU:C:2022:567, para 59, and CJEU, Case T-72/20 *Satabank v ECB* ECLI:EU:T:2023:149, para 112.

[6] But see, as regards a discussion of these subjects in relation to EU law, S Prechal and A Pahladsingh, 'Urgency and Human Rights in EU Law: Procedures Before the Court of Justice of the EU' in E Rieter and K Zwaan (eds), *Urgency and Human Rights: The Protective Potential and Legitimacy of Interim Measures* (The Hague, TMC Asser Press, 2021) 37; G Gentile and D Sartori, 'Interim Measures as "Weapons of Democracy" in the European Legal Space' (2023) 1 *European Human Rights Law Review* 18.

[7] For a brief selection, see, eg, R Barents, *Remedies and Procedures before the EU Courts* 2nd edn (Alphen aan den Rijn, Wolters Kluwer, 2020) ch 20; V Terrien, 'Interim Measures' in V Luszcz (ed), *European Court Procedure: A Practical Guide* (Oxford, Hart Publishing, 2020) 571; K Lenaerts, K Gutman and JT Nowak, *EU Procedural Law* 2nd edn (Oxford, Oxford University Press, 2023) ch 13.

role in protecting fundamental rights in the European Union and that the case law of the EU Courts is ripe for development on numerous fronts from the perspective of the importance of interim measures for safeguarding those rights. This analysis also demonstrates that comparative reflections between the CJEU and the European Court of Human Rights (ECtHR) have considerable added value in this context, especially in identifying issues that remain ripe for further development and possible improvement in the case law.[8]

2. Framing the Discussion of Interim Measures and Fundamental Rights in EU Law

2.1. Nature and Purpose of Interim Measures in EU Law

Interim measures or relief is a term that is generally used in the EU as well as the European Convention on Human Rights (ECHR) contexts.[9] It essentially means provisional legal protection granted in favour of a party before the main action is decided, that is, interim protection.[10] By and large, interim measures constitute orders issued by a court requiring a party to a dispute to do, or not to do, something in order to preserve the subject matter of the dispute pending its resolution.[11] Beyond this, however, such measures are difficult to pin down because much depends on the circumstances of the particular case and hence their expanse is open-ended.

According to long-standing case law of the EU Courts, the purpose of interim measures is to guarantee the full effectiveness of the future final decision in order to ensure that there is no lacuna in the legal protection afforded by a court.[12] In fundamental rights-related cases, interim measures are generally regarded as serving both a preventive role, in terms of ensuring the meaningful outcome of the proceedings, as well as a protective role in safeguarding the individual fundamental rights of the party concerned.[13]

As such, it should not be overlooked that interim measures and fundamental rights are inextricably related in EU law. On the one hand, interim measures are a specific

[8] See, in that regard, Section 4.1.2.

[9] Related terms, such as provisional or precautionary measures, may be viewed as synonymous. See further, eg, R Virzo, 'Introduction' in FM Palombino, R Virzo and G Zarra (eds), *Provisional Measures Issued by International Courts and Tribunals* (The Hague, TMC Asser Press, 2021) 1; R Pillay, 'The Politics of Interim Measures in International Human Rights Law' in Rieter and Zwaan (eds), *Urgency and Human Rights* (2021) 65, 66.

[10] See, eg, Lenaerts, Gutman and Nowak, *EU Procedural Law* (2023) 535.

[11] See C Miles, *Provisional Measures before International Courts and Tribunals* (Cambridge, Cambridge University Press, 2017) 1–2.

[12] See, eg, Order of the CJEU in Case C-441/17 R *Commission v Poland* ECLI:EU:C:2017:877, para 43, and Order of the Vice-President of the General Court in Case T-743/22 R IV *Mazepin v Council* (not published) ECLI:EU:T:2023:863, para 79. See also, in that regard, CJEU, Case C-213/89 *Factortame and Others* (not published), Opinion of Advocate General Tesauro, ECLI:EU:C:1990:216, in particular point 18.

[13] See, eg, JM Pasqualucci, 'Interim Measures in International Human Rights: Evolution and Harmonization' (2005) 38 *Vanderbilt Journal of Transnational Law* 1; Rieter and Zwaan (eds), *Urgency and Human Rights* (2021).

expression of fundamental rights, in so far as effective judicial protection entails that the remedy sought by the applicant is not undone by the passage of time until the case is decided.[14] On the other hand, interim measures represent a specific procedural tool to safeguard the protection of fundamental rights in the particular case.

2.2. Fundamental Rights in EU Law and Some Words of Caution

As compared to interim measures, the terminology of 'fundamental' or 'human' rights is usually different when it comes to the EU and ECHR contexts. To some extent, this stems from the wording of the relevant instruments. The term 'fundamental rights' is typically used in EU law, in line with the Charter of 'Fundamental Rights', whereas the term 'human rights' is commonplace with respect to the ECtHR, in line with the European Convention on 'Human Rights', which it is charged to interpret. The term 'fundamental rights' is also considered to reflect a specific EU context, as compared to 'human rights' which are universal in nature.[15] In any event, the discussion of interim measures in fundamental rights cases prompts some words of caution.

In the first place, the protection of fundamental rights in the European Union has become increasingly complex. There are multiple sources of fundamental rights protection: most notably, the Charter, the ECHR, the national constitutions and a myriad of international instruments. While they often overlap in substantive terms, they also diverge in many different ways. For instance, the list of protected rights under the Charter is longer than that under the ECHR; the scope of a right guaranteed by the Charter may go beyond the scope of the same right as protected by the ECHR or the national constitution; and even if a right is simultaneously protected under the Charter, the ECHR and the national constitution, the level of protection of that right may be different under each of these instruments.[16] Moreover, the scope of application of the Charter-guaranteed rights is limited as far as the Member States' actions are concerned.[17]

To make matters even more complex, some of the rights under the Charter are actually 'principles', meaning they are not judicially actionable,[18] while others reflect 'general principles' of EU law, meaning that their scope may go beyond the actual

[14] In the case law, the Court of Justice has linked interim measures to the effective judicial protection of individuals under EU law. See, in that regard, Order of the President of the Court of Justice in Case C-399/95 R *Germany v Commission* ECLI:EU:C:1996:193, para 46; CJEU, Case C-1/99 *Kofisa Italia* ECLI:EU:C:2001:10, paras 46–48, and CJEU, Case C-226/99 *Siples* ECLI:EU:C:2001:14, paras 17–20. See further, eg, D Sinaniotis, *The Interim Protection of Individuals before the European and National Courts* (Alphen aan den Rijn, Kluwer Law International, 2006); F Picod, *Référé devant la Cour de justice et le Tribunal de l'Union européenne* (Lexis Nexis, 2020). See also Section 4.2.1.

[15] See, eg, G Della Cananea, 'The Concept of Fundamental Rights in the EU Charter' (2002) 14 *European Review of Public Law* 795, 808; F de Cecco, 'Fundamental Freedoms, Fundamental Rights, and the Scope of Free Movement Law' (2014) 15 *German Law Journal* 383, 386 fn 13.

[16] See Article 53 of the Charter.

[17] See Article 51(1) of the Charter.

[18] See Article 52(5) of the Charter.

wording of the corresponding Charter right.[19] Additionally, the procedural venues for seeking protection of a fundamental right are very different under the various instruments dedicated to protecting them. Judges and lawyers are thus often faced with a legal conundrum in fundamental-rights-related cases. That conundrum often ends up in a hodgepodge of indiscriminate citations of various national, EU and international instruments in the field of fundamental rights, amid endless legal battles stretching over many years and jurisdictions.

In the second place, interim relief is a powerful tool, which should be deployed with caution. While the protection of fundamental rights is in principle particularly worthy of such relief, one should bear in mind that in legal practice references to fundamental rights have become so frequent that sometimes even the most trivial legal dispute is presented as implicating fundamental rights. This banalisation of fundamental rights ends up depreciating their importance in a democratic society through over-litigating and equating such rights with routine, technical matters, thereby belittling them.

These words of caution are, in the opinion of the present authors, important in the discussion of whether EU rules on interim relief should be reformed with a view to taking more fully into account the need to protect fundamental rights. While we argue, in the present contribution, for enhanced interim protection of fundamental rights, that protection should be warranted only in what are truly fundamental rights cases. By this, we do not intend to reopen the eternal debate about hierarchising fundamental rights, nor do we argue that interim measures should be available for some categories of fundamental rights, but not for others. Rather, we merely wish to emphasise that judges and lawyers should tread carefully, bearing in mind that many a case, including requests for interim relief, may spuriously allege breaches of fundamental rights in an attempt to make the matter look more serious or more urgent than it actually is.

2.3. Division of Tasks between the National Courts and the EU Courts

As is well-known, the EU legal order is decentralised. This is especially important to bear in mind with regard to interim measures. The fact of the matter is that the bulk of the cases involving fundamental rights in which questions of interim measures arise are brought before the national courts, while only a trickle of such cases are brought directly before the EU Courts. Thus, no discussion about interim measures in fundamental rights cases under EU law would seem to be complete or even meaningful, without taking into account the tasks entrusted to the national courts by virtue of EU law. This particular feature of the EU legal order has implications for interim relief: as the case law stands today, not only the procedural routes, but also the substantive

[19] An apt example is Article 41 of the Charter on the right to good administration, which is addressed only to EU authorities, but has been held to apply to national authorities when they implement EU law as a general principle of EU law. See, eg, CJEU, Case C-471/22 *Agentsia 'Patna infrastruktura' (European funding of road infrastructure)* ECLI:EU:C:2024:99, para 41.

criteria for granting interim measures may differ between actions brought before the national courts and actions brought directly before the EU Courts.

In that respect, national courts may be required by virtue of EU law to grant interim measures in cases which fall within the scope of EU law. Such cases typically involve the potential incompatibility of either national law with EU law or of EU law with higher norms of EU law, including fundamental rights, as discussed in Section 3 of this contribution. National courts may also be required by virtue of national or international law to grant interim relief, but that situation goes beyond the scope of the present contribution.

Furthermore, interim measures are available for direct actions (and appeals) that may be brought before the EU Courts, as discussed in Section 4 of this contribution. These are essentially actions brought against an 'EU defendant', such as actions for annulment of EU acts under Article 263 TFEU and actions for EU non-contractual liability under Articles 268 and 340 TFEU, as well as infringement actions brought against Member States for failure to fulfil obligations under EU law pursuant to Articles 258 to 260 TFEU. This excludes the preliminary ruling procedure, as provided for in Article 267 TFEU. That procedure is not a direct action, but an indirect one, involving a request made by a national court to the Court of Justice (and the General Court in certain specific areas[20]) on the interpretation and validity of EU law in order to resolve the disputes brought before them. In preliminary references, the Court of Justice does not have jurisdiction to grant interim measures.[21] That task belongs to the national courts in accordance with the procedural rules of the domestic legal systems.[22]

3. Interim Measures before the National Courts

3.1. The Classical Case Law

As explained, the bulk of the cases involving EU-derived fundamental rights are brought before the national courts. Given that they are the 'ordinary' courts within the EU legal order,[23] charged with adjudicating such cases as long as they cannot be brought directly before the EU Courts, those courts do so on the basis of the procedural and remedial rules of their domestic legal systems, subject to the requirements placed on those rules by EU law.

[20] See, in that regard, Regulation (EU, Euratom) 2024/2019 of the European Parliament and of the Council of 11 April 2024 amending Protocol No 3 on the Statute of the Court of Justice of the European Union [2024] OJ L 2024/2019; Court of Justice of the European Union Press Release No 125/24, 'Jurisdiction to Hear and Determine Questions Referred for a Preliminary Ruling is Conferred on the General Court of the European Union in Six Specific Areas', Luxembourg, 12 August 2024.

[21] See Order of the President of the Court of Justice in Case C-186/01 R *Dory* ECLI:EU:C:2001:563; see also CJEU, Joined Cases C-453/03, C-11/04, C-12/04 and C-194/04 *ABNA and Others* ECLI:EU:C:2005:741, para 103.

[22] This helps to explain why in much of the fundamental rights jurisprudence of the Court of Justice, which falls within the context of the preliminary ruling procedure, the question of interim measures does not arise and, in turn, why many of the situations in which interim measures classically arise in the ECtHR context, such as expulsion or extradition, are dealt with by the national courts, and not the EU Courts.

[23] See CJEU, Opinion 1/09 *Agreement creating a Unified Patent Litigation System* ECLI:EU:C:2011:123, para 80.

According to the well-known formula in the case law, in the absence of EU rules, it is for the national legal orders to establish procedural rules for actions intended to safeguard the rights of individuals (principle of national procedural autonomy), provided that those rules are not, in situations covered by EU law, less favourable than those governing similar domestic actions (principle of equivalence) and that they do not make it excessively difficult or impossible in practice to exercise the rights conferred by EU law (principle of effectiveness).[24] Moreover, as the Court of Justice has consistently held, under the principle of sincere cooperation laid down in Article 4(3) TEU, it is for the national courts to ensure judicial protection of a person's rights under EU law. This reflects the principle of effective judicial protection, as guaranteed by both Article 19(1) TEU and Article 47 of the Charter on the right to an effective remedy and to a fair trial.[25]

Two distinct situations must be distinguished according to the classical case law. The first situation is where interim measures before a national court are sought against a national measure that is allegedly incompatible with EU law. In EU law language, this is referred to as the *Factortame/Unibet* situation. The second situation is where interim measures before a national court are sought against a national measure based on an EU act, where the latter is allegedly incompatible with a higher norm of EU law. In EU law language, this is known as the *Zuckerfabrik/Atlanta* situation.

This distinction is crucial for understanding the rules governing interim measures before the national courts by virtue of EU law, since these two scenarios are subject to different conditions. Each of these scenarios will first be examined separately as they are dealt with in the classical case law, before addressing more recent jurisprudential developments and the question whether a more fundamental-rights-based approach to the classical case law may be warranted.

3.1.1. *The* Factortame/Unibet *Situation*

As just mentioned, the *Factortame/Unibet* situation concerns interim relief against national measures that allegedly breach EU law. Briefly, in *Factortame*,[26] decided in 1990 and involving UK shipping legislation allegedly in breach of the EU free movement rules, the Court of Justice famously held that a national court which, in a case before it concerning EU law, considers that the sole obstacle which precludes it from granting interim relief is a rule of national law, must set aside that rule. The Court emphasised that it is for the national courts to ensure the legal protection that persons derive from EU law, and that the full effectiveness of EU law would be impaired if national law could prevent a court from granting interim relief to ensure the full effectiveness of the judgment to be given on the existence of the rights claimed under EU law. Importantly,

[24] See, eg, CJEU, Case C-670/22 *MN (EncroChat)* ECLI:EU:C:2024:372, para 129.

[25] In that respect, the second subparagraph of Article 19(1) TEU requires Member States to provide remedies sufficient to ensure effective judicial protection in the fields covered by EU law. Additionally, when the Member States set out detailed procedural rules for legal actions intended to ensure the protection of rights conferred by EU law, they must ensure compliance with Article 47 of the Charter, which constitutes a reaffirmation of the principle of effective judicial protection. See, eg, CJEU, Case C-132/21 *Nemzeti Adatvédelmi és Információszabadság Hatóság* ECLI:EU:C:2023:2, paras 49–50.

[26] See CJEU, Case C-213/89 *Factortame and Others ('Factortame')* ECLI:EU:C:1990:257, paras 17–23.

however, the Court said nothing about the conditions under which interim relief should be granted, even though it was specifically asked to reply to this question by the referring court. The Court's silence was interpreted as meaning that those rules were to be governed by national law.

That latter aspect was clarified in subsequent case law. In *Unibet*,[27] decided in 2007 and concerning the compatibility of Swedish gaming legislation with the EU free movement rules, the Court of Justice, while reaffirming the principles established in *Factortame*, emphasised that, in the absence of EU rules governing the matter, it is for the domestic legal system of each Member State to determine the conditions under which interim relief is to be granted for safeguarding an individual's rights under EU law. Accordingly, the grant of interim relief to suspend the application of national provisions until the competent court has given a ruling on whether those provisions are compatible with EU law is governed by the criteria laid down by the national law applicable before that court. However, those criteria cannot be less favourable than those applying to similar domestic actions (principle of equivalence) and must not render practically impossible or excessively difficult the interim judicial protection of rights conferred by EU law (principle of effectiveness).[28] Furthermore, the principle of effective judicial protection of an individual's rights under EU law requires it to be possible in the legal order of a Member State for interim relief to be granted until the competent court has given a ruling on whether national provisions are compatible with EU law, where the grant of such relief is necessary to ensure the full effectiveness of the judgment to be given on the existence of such rights.[29]

As discussed further below, the basic tenets of this line of case law have not developed much since then. For now, it calls for the following remarks. First, the conditions for granting interim relief are to be governed by national law, subject to the principles of national procedural autonomy, equivalence and effectiveness, as well as the principle of effective judicial protection. As such, the case law allows for divergences, sometimes significant, between Member States when it comes to interim protection. Second, this case law emerged in the context of the free movement rules. Dating back to the pre-Charter period, it was not conceptualised with fundamental rights in mind. Third, the rationale behind the Court's decision to leave the conditions for granting interim relief essentially to national law, subject to the abovementioned principles, seems to be twofold: on the one hand, EU law provides for no specific rules on interim relief before national courts; and, on the other hand, the Court lacks jurisdiction to invalidate national law. As interim relief often boils down to temporarily blocking the application of a national measure, it should therefore be for national courts and national law to decide under what conditions interim relief should be granted.

3.1.2. *The* Zuckerfabrik/Atlanta *Situation*

In contrast, the *Zuckerfabrik/Atlanta* situation concerns interim relief against national measures based on an EU act, which is allegedly in breach of higher norms of EU law.

[27] See CJEU, Case C-432/05 *Unibet* ECLI:EU:C:2007:163.
[28] See, ibid, paras 79–83.
[29] See, ibid, paras 66–77.

In *Zuckerfabrik*,[30] decided in 1991 and concerning the suspension of a national measure based on an EU regulation in the sugar sector, the Court of Justice considered, first, as a matter of principle, that EU law does not preclude the power of national courts to grant such interim relief. According to the Court, in cases where national authorities are responsible for the administrative implementation of EU regulations, the legal protection guaranteed by EU law includes the right of individuals to challenge, as a preliminary issue, the legality of those regulations before national courts and to induce those courts to refer questions to the Court of Justice for a preliminary ruling.

Second, the Court formulated three conditions that must be met for such suspension to be granted: (1) the national court must entertain serious doubts as to the validity of the EU act and refer that question to the Court, if such a question has not already been referred; (2) there must be urgency and a threat of serious and irreparable damage to the applicant; and (3) the national court must take due account of the EU interest. The Court reasoned that the granting of such interim relief must be subject to uniform conditions in all Member States to ensure the uniform application of EU law and that such conditions must correspond to those governing interim measures in direct actions brought before the EU Courts.[31]

As regards the EU interest, the Court emphasised that EU law should not be temporarily disapplied without proper guarantees. In order to comply with that obligation, a national court seised of an application for suspension must first examine whether the EU act in question would be deprived of all effectiveness if not immediately implemented. If suspension of enforcement is liable to involve a financial risk for the European Union, the national court must also be in a position to require the applicant to provide adequate guarantees, such as the deposit of money or other security.[32]

A few years later, in *Atlanta*,[33] decided in 1995 and concerning an interim order by a national court provisionally disapplying an EU regulation on banana imports, the Court of Justice held that the conditions set out in *Zuckerfabrik* must be observed whenever a national court orders any interim measures, whether suspension or positive orders of provisional disapplication like those at issue. In particular, the Court clarified that, as regards the third condition relating to the EU interest, the national court must take account of the damage which the interim measure may cause the legal regime established by the regulation for the European Union as a whole, and must consider both the cumulative effect which would arise if a large number of courts were also to adopt interim measures for similar reasons and the special features of the applicant's situation which distinguish it from the other operators concerned. Moreover, the Court added a fourth condition that the national court must, in its assessment, respect any decisions of the EU Courts ruling on the legality of EU acts at issue or on an application for interim measures seeking similar relief.[34]

[30] See CJEU, Joined Cases C-143/88 and C-92/89 *Zuckerfabrik Süderdithmarschen and Zuckerfabrik Soest ('Zuckerfabrik')* ECLI:EU:C:1991:65, paras 16–21.

[31] See, ibid, paras 23–33.

[32] See, ibid, paras 30–33.

[33] See CJEU, Case C-465/93 *Atlanta Fruchthandelsgesellschaft and Others ('Atlanta')* ECLI:EU:C:1995:369, paras 20–30, 32–51.

[34] This had the result in those proceedings that the referring court had to respect previous rulings of the Court dismissing similar applications for interim measures and annulment of the EU regulation in question. See, ibid, in particular paras 17, 18 and 47.

Since those two landmark cases, this line of case law has not evolved much either. It calls for the following remarks. First, unlike the *Factortame/Unibet* situation, in the *Zuckerfabric/Atlanta* situation, EU law lays down the conditions under which interim measures must be granted by national courts. Those conditions are thus uniform by virtue of EU law.[35] Second, those conditions essentially coincide with the conditions governing interim measures granted by the EU Courts in direct actions brought before them.[36] Third, like that of *Factortame/Unibet*, the *Zuckerfabrik/Atlanta* line of case law predates the Charter. Both *Zuckerfabrik* and *Atlanta* concerned economic litigation about the import regimes of sugar and bananas, respectively. As such, those cases did not require specifically taking into consideration fundamental rights. Consequently, the Court's judgments in those cases were not conceptualised with fundamental rights in mind. Fourth, the rationale behind those judgments seems to be that interim relief against a national measure based on an EU act leads in practice to the temporary non-application of the EU act. If left to national law, this could entail a risk to the uniform application of EU law across the Member States. Moreover, the EU Courts have exclusive jurisdiction to invalidate EU law. Therefore, in order to ensure the uniform application of EU law, the conditions for temporarily disapplying that law, in the form of interim relief, must be harmonised by virtue of EU law and must be the same for the national courts and the EU Courts.[37]

3.2. Recent Jurisprudential Developments

As already mentioned, the post-Charter case law on interim measures granted by national courts by virtue of EU law does not seem to have evolved much so far. In effect, the distinction between the *Factortame/Unibet* and *Zuckerfabrik/Atlanta* situations has been maintained and the basic tenets of those two lines of case law have been confirmed.[38] Nevertheless, upon closer reflection, some recent jurisprudential developments may be interpreted as indications that the obligations placed on national courts in relation to interim protection must be carried out with particular regard to the protection of fundamental rights.

Salient examples are *Aziz*[39] and *Kušionová*.[40] Both cases concerned the area of EU consumer law, namely Directive 93/13 on unfair terms in consumer contracts,[41] and

[35] See CJEU, Joined Cases C-143/88 and C-92/89 *Zuckerfabrik* (see n 30 above), para 26.

[36] See CJEU, Joined Cases C-143/88 and C-92/89 *Zuckerfabrik* (see n 30 above), para 27; CJEU, Case C-465/93 *Atlanta* (see n 33 above), para 39.

[37] See CJEU, Joined Cases C-143/88 and C-92/89 *Zuckerfabrik* (see n 30 above), paras 17–18; CJEU, Case C-465/93 *Atlanta* (see n 33 above), paras 21–22.

[38] See, eg, CJEU, Case C-416/10 *Križan and Others* ECLI:EU:C:2013:8, paras 105–10, where the Court basically repeated its *Factortame* and *Unibet* stance, referring to national procedural autonomy and indicating, in particular, that members of the public must be able, in the context of an action provided for by the relevant EU law, to ask the court or competent body to order interim measures, such as to suspend the application of a permit for a landfill site pending the final decision.

[39] See CJEU, Case C-415/11 *Aziz* ECLI:EU:C:2013:164, in particular paras 50–64.

[40] See CJEU, Case C-34/13 *Kušionová* ECLI:EU:C:2014:2189, in particular paras 50–68.

[41] Council Directive 93/13/EEC of 5 April 1993 on unfair terms in consumer contracts [1993] OJ L 95/29.

were essentially about the extrajudicial enforcement of an unpaid mortgage, the terms of which were allegedly unfair. While basing its judgments on the premiss that the granting of interim relief was a matter for national procedural autonomy subject to the principles of equivalence and effectiveness, the Court of Justice considered that it was necessary to give 'particular attention' to the fact that the procedure for extrajudicial enforcement was directed at the consumer's family home.[42] According to the Court, the loss of a family home is not only such as to seriously undermine consumer rights, but also places the family of the consumer concerned in a particularly vulnerable position.[43] In that respect, the Court referred to the case law of the ECtHR and pointed out that under EU law the right to accommodation is a fundamental right as guaranteed by Article 7 of the Charter and that the national court must take into consideration that circumstance.[44]

With regard, in particular, to the consequences of the eviction of the consumer and his or her family from the accommodation forming their principal family home, the Court emphasised the importance for the national court to provide for interim measures by which unlawful mortgage enforcement proceedings may be suspended or terminated where the grant of such measures proves necessary in order to ensure the effectiveness of the protection intended by Directive 93/13.[45] The Court made clear that national rules on interim relief must not make it excessively difficult or impossible in practice to protect the right in question.[46]

Additionally, in *Országos Idegenrendeszeti Főigazgatóság Dél-alföldi Regionális Igazgatóság*,[47] the Court of Justice, in reference to *Factortame*, held, in the area of EU asylum and immigration policy, that an applicant for international protection whose detention has come to an end may rely before a national court on the right to receive the grant of a financial allowance for housing or of housing in kind, and that court has the possibility under EU law to grant interim relief pending its final decision. While the Court made no further comments on the conditions under which such interim relief may be granted by the national court – which can be taken to mean that those conditions are a matter for national law subject to the principles of equivalence and effectiveness, following from the *Factortame/Unibet* case law – it nonetheless observed that the principle of primacy of EU law and the right to effective judicial protection as guaranteed by Article 47 of the Charter require the national court to declare that it has jurisdiction to hear and determine an application for interim relief, if no other court has, under national law, jurisdiction to hear and determine it. In an echo of *Unibet*, in this case, Article 47 of the Charter was relied upon by the Court not in connection with

[42] CJEU, Case C-34/13 *Kušionová* (see n 40 above), para 62.

[43] See CJEU, Case C-34/13 *Kušionová* (see n 40 above), para 63 (referring, inter alia, to CJEU, Case C-415/11 *Aziz* (see n 39 above), para 61).

[44] See CJEU, Case C-34/13 *Kušionová* (see n 40 above), paras 64–65.

[45] See CJEU, Case C-34/13 *Kušionová* (see n 40 above), para 66 (referring to CJEU, Case C-415/11 *Aziz* (see n 39 above), para 59).

[46] See CJEU, Case C-415/11 *Aziz* (see n 39 above), paras 60–63; CJEU, Case C-34/13 *Kušionová* (see n 40 above), paras 67–68.

[47] See CJEU, Joined Cases C-924/19 PPU and C-925/19 PPU *Országos Idegenrendeszeti Főigazgatóság Dél-alföldi Regionális Igazgatóság* ECLI:EU:C:2020:367, paras 295–99.

the conditions for granting interim relief, but in order for the national court to assert jurisdiction where no other court has competence to do so.

Furthermore, in *W.Ż.*,[48] situated within the rule of law case law concerning Poland, the Court of Justice underlined that the full effectiveness of EU law requires that a national court seised of a dispute governed by EU law must be able to grant interim relief in order to ensure the full effectiveness of the judgment to be given. The Court cautioned that, if a national court, having stayed proceedings pending the reply by the Court of Justice to the question referred to it for a preliminary ruling, were not able to grant interim relief until it delivered its judgment following the reply given by the Court of Justice, the effectiveness of the system established by Article 267 TFEU would be impaired, citing both *Factortame* and *Atlanta*. The effectiveness of that system would also be compromised, the Court continued, if the authority attaching to such interim relief could be disregarded, in particular, by a public authority of the Member State in which those measures were adopted. Consequently, the Court found that the appointment of the judge concerned in breach of an interim order of the Polish Supreme Administrative Court, without awaiting the Court of Justice's ruling in a related case, undermined the effectiveness of the system established by Article 267 TFEU.

Although the Court did not reason the part of the judgment concerning interim measures in terms of the applicant's fundamental rights, but more generally on the need to guarantee the effectiveness of the preliminary ruling procedure, that case may also be read in the light of the objective to ensure the protection of the applicant's right to a fair trial in a procedure that complies with the requirements of an independent and impartial tribunal established by law.[49] While less explicit than *Aziz* and *Kušionová*, in terms of the particular attention that must be given to the protection of the fundamental right at issue when deciding on interim relief, the Court's judgment in *W.Ż.* may still be read as an indirect example of the interplay between fundamental rights and interim measures.

To sum up, even though it is difficult to draw definitive conclusions from these examples of the post-Charter case law, they tend to indicate that, while reaffirming the basic tenets of *Factortame/Unibet* and *Zuckerfabrik/Atlanta* lines of case law,[50] the Court of Justice seems sensitive to the importance of interim measures in the context of fundamental rights protection. The judgments in *Aziz* and *Kušionová* seem to be the strongest illustrations so far. The Court emphasised that, when deciding on interim measures, the national court must give particular attention to the risk of breaching fundamental rights, which may cause serious and irreparable damage to the latter. The Court's findings were framed in reference to the principle of effectiveness, implying that, in the absence of interim measures, it may be excessively difficult or even impossible to safeguard the protection of the EU-derived right that the main action is supposed to ensure.

[48] See CJEU, Case C-487/19 *W.Ż. (Chamber of Extraordinary Control and Public Affairs of the Supreme Court – Appointment)* ECLI:EU:C:2021:798, paras 142–43.

[49] See, ibid, in particular paras 118–26.

[50] As a matter of fact, most of the recent examples in the case law fall within the *Factortame/Unibet* situation.

3.3. Possible Ways Forward

As mentioned above, interim measures play a crucial role in the EU system of fundamental rights protection. However, an overview of the classical case law shows that, on the whole, the rules underpinning interim measures decided by national courts in disputes governed by EU law do not necessarily take into account considerations relevant to fundamental rights. There are several possible ways in which those rules might be rendered more receptive to considerations relating to fundamental rights protection. Some of them require little change to the existing case law, while others would necessitate a more thorough reconsideration.

First, in the *Factortame/Unibet* situation, the case law may evolve toward requiring national courts, for example through the lens of the principle of effectiveness, to pay particular attention to tangible threats to fundamental rights when deciding on interim measures. That principle could thus serve as a basis to assert that, if interim measures were unavailable, it would make it excessively difficult or impossible in practice to safeguard the fundamental right at issue, which, in turn, would result in serious and irreparable harm to the applicant. The judgments in *Aziz* and *Kušionová* are examples on point, which could apply beyond the area of consumer protection. They can thus serve as a blueprint for emphasising the need to safeguard fundamental rights through interim measures by virtue of EU law.

Furthermore, while formally framed as a matter of the principle of effectiveness, it is clear that the absence of interim measures in situations similar to those that arose in *Aziz* and *Kušionová* would risk causing serious and irreparable damage to the applicant's fundamental rights. Thus, there seems to be a certain degree of permeability between the principle of effectiveness and the conditions governing interim relief, one of which is urgency, understood as a risk of serious and irreparable damage. The principle of effectiveness may therefore play a decisive role from a fundamental rights perspective in the *Factortame/Unibet* situation.

Second, in the *Zuckerfabrik/Atlanta* situation, which, to recall, is based on uniform conditions for interim relief, one should reflect on whether the third condition, relating to the balancing of interests, ought to be refined. Currently, that condition seems to give priority to the interests of the European Union. Indeed, the very wording of that condition – formulated as an obligation placed on national courts to take due account of the EU interest – strongly suggests that. More importantly, the content of that condition seems to put the emphasis on safeguarding EU interests. As seen above, in *Zuckerfabrik* and *Atlanta*, the Court seems mostly preoccupied with the public interest of the European Union, consisting in the uniform application of EU law and the risk that interim measures may pose for EU finances.[51]

That condition should be reconsidered around a more classical expression of a balancing of interests. In that balancing exercise, specific importance should be given to the risk of breaching the applicant's fundamental rights. In such cases, those rights may outweigh the EU public interest. The judgment in *Atlanta* already contains the basis for

[51] In all fairness, it should be noted that the *Zuckerfabrik* and *Atlanta* cases essentially concerned economic rights and obligations, with possible repercussions on competition between operators from different Member States and on the EU budget.

such a development. In that judgment, the Court considered that 'the national court, when called upon to protect the rights of individuals, may indeed assess the extent to which refusal to order an interim measure may be liable to have a serious and irreparable effect on important individual interests.'[52] This seems to provide the foundations for further development of this line of jurisprudence, with a view to integrating more clearly the protection of fundamental rights in the balancing exercise that national courts are required to carry out.

Third, the *Zuckerfabrik/Atlanta* line of case law should be aligned further with the case law of the EU Courts on interim measures in direct actions brought before them. The Court already stated in *Zuckerfabrik* and *Atlanta* that the conditions for granting interim measures in both situations are meant to be the same.[53] The case law on interim measures in direct actions brought before the EU Courts has already started to take into account more prominently threats to fundamental rights, particularly in assessing the condition pertaining to urgency, as detailed below.[54] These are promising developments which have the potential to reinvigorate the *Zuckerfabrik/Atlanta* case law.

Fourth, a more far-reaching approach may consist in examining whether the distinction between the *Factortame/Unibet* and the *Zuckerfabrik/Atlanta* situations is justified from a fundamental rights perspective.[55] There are at least three types of considerations which are relevant in this respect.

In the first place, the need to temporarily safeguard a fundamental right through interim measures appears to be the same, regardless of whether the threat to that right stems from an (autonomous) national measure which is allegedly incompatible with EU law, or from a national measure based on an EU act, where the latter is allegedly incompatible with a higher norm of EU law. From a fundamental-rights perspective, the situation is the same. Indeed, both situations fall within the scope of EU law within the meaning of Article 51(1) of the Charter. Moreover, as the Court pointed out in the *Zuckerfabrik/Atlanta* case law: 'The interim legal protection which [EU] law ensures for individuals before national courts must remain the same, irrespective of whether they contest the compatibility of national legal provisions with [EU] law or the validity of secondary [EU] law, in view of the fact that the dispute in both cases is based on [EU] law itself.'[56]

In the second place, one should also point to the fact that the three conditions laid down in the *Zuckerfabrik/Atlanta* case law – which also correspond to the conditions governing interim measures in direct actions before the EU Courts – reflect *grosso modo* the common legal traditions of the Member States.[57]

[52] CJEU, Case C-465/93 *Atlanta* (see n 33 above), para 48.

[53] See, in that regard, CJEU, Joined Cases C-143/88 and C-92/89 *Zuckerfabrik* (see n 30 above), paras 25–27; CJEU, Case C-465/93 *Atlanta* (see n 33 above), para 39. See further text accompanying n 56 below.

[54] See Section 4.2.

[55] See, eg, J Krommendijk, '*Factortame* and Interim Measures Before National Courts' in P Craig and R Schütze (eds), *Landmark Cases in EU Law* (Oxford, Hart Publishing, 2025) 217.

[56] CJEU, Joined Cases C-143/88 and C-92/89 *Zuckerfabrik* (see n 30 above), para 20; CJEU, Case C-465/93 *Atlanta* (see n 33 above), para 24.

[57] See, in that regard, CJEU, Case C-213/89 *Factortame and Others* (not published), Opinion of Advocate General Tesauro, ECLI:EU:C:1990:216, point 23. This is not to say that there are no divergences between the Member States as to the scope of interim relief, particularly with regard to the (im)possibility of ordinary courts to suspend the application of a national legislative act.

In the third place, the requirements stemming from the principles of equivalence and effectiveness in the *Factortame/Unibet* situation may, in practice, have the same effect as the one stemming from the condition relating to the risk of serious and irreparable damage in a *Zuckerfabrik/Atlanta* situation, thus leading to a (partial) convergence of the two regimes.

All in all, these reflections seem to indicate that there is ample room for refining the case law with a view of integrating fundamental rights considerations in the examination of applications for interim measures before national courts in cases governed by EU law.

4. Interim Measures before the EU Courts

4.1. Procedural Framework

The procedural framework governing interim measures before the EU Courts is germane to assessing the potential role played by such measures in protecting fundamental rights. To begin with, the provision for interim measures in direct actions brought before the EU Courts has been set out in the Treaties governing the European Union since its founding.[58] According to Article 278 TFEU: 'Actions brought before the Court of Justice of the European Union shall not have suspensory effect. The Court may, however, if it considers that circumstances so require, order that application of the contested act be suspended.' Article 279 TFEU further states: 'The Court of Justice of the European Union may in any cases before it prescribe any necessary interim measures.'

Rules on interim measures are fleshed out in the procedural texts governing the EU Courts.[59] This includes the Statute of the Court of Justice of the European Union,[60] along with the Rules of Procedure of the Court of Justice[61] and of the General Court,[62] which contain similar but not identical provisions.[63] In particular, in principle it is the Vice-President of the Court of Justice,[64] while it is the President of the General Court,

[58] See originally ex Articles 185 and 186 EEC, later ex Articles 242 and 242 EC; see also Article 39 of the now expired Treaty establishing the European Coal and Steel Community (ECSC); as regards the Treaty establishing the European Atomic Energy Community (EAEC), there is a comparable provision to Article 278 TFEU in Article 157 EAEC and Article 279 TFEU is also applicable (see Article 106a EAEC). Thus, such provisions governing interim measures before the EU Courts constitute primary EU law.

[59] Those procedural texts may be found on the CJEU website, https://curia.europa.eu.

[60] See Article 39 of Protocol (No 3) on the Statute of the Court of Justice of the European Union (Statute), which as a protocol annexed to the Treaties also constitutes primary EU law.

[61] See Articles 160 to 166 of the Rules of Procedure of the Court of Justice (CJ Rules of Procedure).

[62] See Articles 156 to 161 of the Rules of Procedure of the General Court (GC Rules of Procedure).

[63] Further guidance and a summary of the relevant procedural rules in relation to interim measures are found in point 19 of the Court of Justice Practice Directions to parties concerning cases brought before the Court, and points 223 to 227 of the General Court Practice Rules for the implementation of the Rules of Procedure of the General Court.

[64] See Decision 2012/671/EU of the Court of Justice of 23 October 2012 concerning the functions of the Vice-President of the Court [2012] OJ L 300/47.

who carry out the functions of the interim relief judge and decide on applications for interim measures.[65]

Nevertheless, on the whole, interim proceedings before the respective EU Court are similar. They involve a summary or speedy interlocutory procedure,[66] with allowance for ex parte orders within a matter of days even before the other party has been heard.[67] The decision on interim measures takes the form of a reasoned order, which is served on the parties,[68] and published on the CJEU website.[69] Given the functions of the two EU Courts, such orders of the General Court are appealable to the Court of Justice, while those of the Court of Justice are final.[70]

In addition, it should be pointed out that, as recognised in the case law, there is no correlation between the procedure for interim measures and other speedy procedures before the EU Courts. Thus, the fact that that an expedited procedure is granted, or not, does not detract from the need for possible interim measures.[71]

4.1.1. *Key Features*

There are a number of key features of proceedings for interim measures in direct actions before the EU Courts, which are relevant for fundamental rights cases. These features

[65] See further, as regards the entrustment of the interim relief functions to a single judge at the EU Courts, E Barbier de La Serre, 'Les offices du juge des référés communautaire' in C Baudenbacher, C Gulmann, K Lenaerts, E Coulon and E Barbier de La Serre (eds), *Liber Amicorum en l'honneur de / in honour of Bo Vesterdorf* (Brussels, Bruylant, 2007) 237, 267. Of note, in contrast to the General Court, there is a possibility for the Vice-President of the Court of Justice to refer the application for interim measures to the Court of Justice (compare Article 161(1) and (3) of the CJ Rules of Procedure with Article 158(1) of the GC Rules of Procedure). This explains why sometimes interim orders have been ruled on by the Grand Chamber of the Court of Justice (which is composed of 15 judges, including the President, Vice-President and three of the Presidents of the chambers of five judges; see Article 16, second paragraph, of the Statute). See, eg, in the context of the rule of law case law, Orders of the CJEU in Case C-619/18 R *Commission v Poland* ECLI:EU:C:2018:1021, and in Case C-791/19 R *Commission v Poland* ECLI:EU:C:2020:277.

[66] See, in particular, Article 39, first paragraph, of the Statute; Article 160(5) of the CJ Rules of Procedure; Article 157(1) of the GC Rules of Procedure. As illustrated by recent case law, notwithstanding the speedy nature of interim proceedings, the interim relief judge must respect the right to be heard. See, in that regard, Order of the Vice-President of the Court of Justice in Case C-639/23 P(R) *Commission v Amazon Services Europe* ECLI:EU:C:2024:277, in particular paras 40–57.

[67] See Article 160(7) of the CJ Rules of Procedure; Article 157(2) of the GC Rules of Procedure. Notably, such orders may even be granted within 24 hours of the submission of the application for interim measures. For a recent example, see Order of the President of the General Court in Case T-1119/23 R *Lagardère v Commission* (not published) (action for annulment lodged on 27 November 2023, and application for interim measures lodged on 28 November 2023).

[68] See Article 162(1) of the CJ Rules of Procedure; Article 158(1) of the GC Rules of Procedure.

[69] See website cited in n 59. The interim order (there may be one or more) is listed alongside the judgment (and Opinion of the Advocate General, if any) given in the main action, and has the same case number followed by an 'R' for the French word *référé* (to denote interim proceedings, as French is the working language of the EU Courts).

[70] See Article 162(1) of the CJ Rules of Procedure.

[71] See, in that regard, Order of the Vice-President of the Court of Justice in Case C-576/17 P(R) *Wall Street Systems UK v ECB* (not published) ECLI:EU:C:2018:208, para 51; Orders of the CJEU in Case C-619/18 R *Commission v Poland* ECLI:EU:C:2018:1021, paras 88–89, and in Case C-791/19 R *Commission v Poland* ECLI:EU:C:2020:277, paras 100–02. Conversely, the fact that an application for interim measures has been rejected does not impede the EU Court from ruling on the case in an expedited procedure. See, eg, CJEU, Case T-1077/23 *Bytedance v Commission* ECLI:EU:T:2024:478 (appeal pending in Case C-627/24 P).

concern the ancillary and provisional nature of such measures, along with the broad discretion of the interim relief judge.

First, interim measures are ancillary to the main action before the EU Courts to which those measures are an adjunct.[72] This means that a party must make a request for interim measures by a separate application,[73] and must have challenged the EU act for which suspension is sought in an action before the EU Courts.[74]

Second, interim measures are by their nature provisional or temporary in time, such that they cannot prejudge the future decision on the substance of the case or render it illusory by depriving it of practical effect.[75] Consequently, they lapse upon delivery of the final judgment;[76] they can be changed or rescinded at any time due to a change in circumstances;[77] and rejection does not bar the party from making a fresh application for interim measures on the basis of new facts.[78]

Third, the interim relief judge of the respective EU Court has a broad discretion on the type of interim measures that can be ordered in a direct action. This includes the suspension of the relevant EU acts in accordance with Article 278 TFEU, or the ordering of 'any necessary interim measures' within the meaning of Article 279 TFEU. Importantly, there is no limitation or predetermined scope in terms of the EU right at issue or the kind of interim measures to be granted, so in principle this includes any Charter right and any interim measure. Rather, it depends on the circumstances of the particular case, and no area is off-limits. As such, the competence of the interim relief judge should not be underestimated in cases involving fundamental rights. For example, interim measures may include suspension of EU law or even national law,[79] as well as

[72] See, eg, Order of the CJEU in Case C-441/17 R *Commission v Poland* ECLI:EU:C:2017:877, para 95, and Order of the Vice-President of the General Court in Case T-743/22 R IV *Mazepin v Council* (not published) ECLI: EU:T:2023:863, para 103.

[73] See Article 160(4) of the CJ Rules of Procedure; Article 156(5) of the GC Rules of Procedure. As regards the ordering of interim measures of the interim relief judge's own motion, see Section 4.3.

[74] See Article 160(1) and (2) of the CJ Rules of Procedure; Article 156(1) and (2) of the GC Rules of Procedure. According to those rules, for applications made pursuant to Article 278 TFEU, the applicant must have challenged the measure for which suspension is sought in an action before the respective EU Court, and for interim measures based on Article 279 TFEU, the application must be made by a party to the case and relate to that case.

[75] See, eg, Order of the CJEU in Case C-441/17 R *Commission v Poland* ECLI:EU:C:2017:877, para 95, and Order of the Vice-President of the General Court in Case T-743/22 R IV *Mazepin v Council* (not published) ECLI:EU:T:2023:863, para 103.

[76] See Article 162(3) of the CJ Rules of Procedure; Article 158(3) of the GC Rules of Procedure.

[77] See Article 163 of the CJ Rules of Procedure; Article 159 of the GC Rules of Procedure.

[78] See Article 164 of the CJ Rules of Procedure; Article 160 of the GC Rules of Procedure.

[79] For instance, with respect to the functioning of the European System of Central Banks, see Order of the Vice-President of the Court of Justice in Case C-238/18 R *ECB v Latvia* (not published) ECLI:EU:C:2018:581, ordering the suspension of national measures against a national central bank governor in so far as they prevented him from designating a substitute Member of the Governing Council of the European Central Bank in his stead. Additionally, the suspension of national law has been crucial in the rule of law context to ensure the effectiveness of the Court of Justice's decision on the merits. See, eg, Orders of the CJEU in Case C-619/18 R *Commission v Poland* ECLI:EU:C:2018:1021, and in Case C-791/19 R *Commission v Poland* ECLI:EU:C:2020:277; Order of the Vice-President of the Court of Justice in Case C-204/21 R *Poland v Commission* ECLI:EU:C:2021:834. For further discussion of the complementarity of the case law on interim measures of the Court of Justice and that of the ECtHR in the rule of law context, see M Fisicaro, 'Safeguarding Judicial Independence (and Subsidiarity) Through Interim Measures: The New ECtHR's Strategy at the Height of the Polish Constitutional Crisis' (2022) 16 *Diritti Umani e Diritto Internazionale* 637.

the issuance of injunctions to EU institutions, bodies, offices and agencies,[80] which is not generally allowed in the main proceedings.[81]

4.1.2. Impossibility to Request Interim Measures before Filing the Main Application: Time for Change?

As EU law stands today, it is not possible for an applicant to request interim measures before the application in the main action has been filed. Following from the relevant Rules of Procedure of the EU Courts,[82] this means that, at the earliest, an application for interim measures can be filed together with the application in the main action, which, for example, in the case of an action for annulment generally entails a deadline of two months as of publication, notification or knowledge of the EU act at issue.[83]

In practice, given the time needed to prepare their application in the main action, applicants are often able to file the application towards the very end of that period. This means that, during a period of roughly two months, applicants are unable to rely on interim measures, the consequence being that their rights remain unprotected during that period of time. Yet, such a period can be a long time to wait for a fundamental right that is without any protection in the meantime. For instance, in the case of a decision of an EU institution, body, office or agency to release sensitive information in breach of the right to privacy under Article 7 of the Charter, immediate disclosure might have devastating consequences on the applicant and, once disclosed, would be impossible to protect after the fact.[84] While the need for speed is already taken into account through the provision for ex parte orders as mentioned above, this may not be sufficient depending on the circumstances of the particular case.

[80] For instance, in the context of the case law relating to the COVID-19 pandemic, see Order of the President of the General Court in Case T-12/21 R *PJ v EIT* (not published) ECLI:EU:T:2021:184, suspending the decision at issue and ordering the European Institute of Innovation and Technology to authorise the applicant to telework from her children's place of residence to the extent that the situation relating to the COVID-19 pandemic justified it and without prejudice to the applicant's obligation to travel to the place of employment on an ad hoc basis for reasons related to the interests of the service. See also the series of cases in which the President of the General Court, by way of ex parte orders under Article 157(2) of the GC Rules of Procedure, suspended the European Parliament decision at issue and ordered that the applicants, members of the European Parliament, may access the Parliament's premises on the basis of a negative self-test; the order further specified that, in the event of a positive result, this test should be followed by a PCR test and that, in the event of a positive result of the latter test, the Parliament could refuse the applicants access to its premises. See, eg, Order of the President of the General Court in Case T-710/21 R *Roos and Others v Parliament* (not published) ECLI:EU:T:2021:761 (later revoked by the Order of the President of the General Court in Case T-710/21 R *Roos and Others v Parliament* (not published) ECLI: EU:T:2021:838).

[81] Under settled case law, the EU Courts cannot in principle issue orders to an EU institution, body, office or agency in the context of the main action. See, eg, CJEU, Case C-127/13 P *Strack v Commission* ECLI:EU:C:2014:2250, paras 145–47, and CJEU, Case T-436/23 *Daimler Truck v EUIPO (CERTIFIED)* (not published) ECLI: EU:T:2024:289, para 10.

[82] See Article 160(1) and (2) of the CJ Rules of Procedure, and Article 156(1) and (2) of the GC Rules of Procedure; see further text accompanying n 74.

[83] See Article 263, sixth paragraph, TFEU. For a detailed discussion of procedural time-limits in litigation before the EU Courts, see Lenaerts, Gutman and Nowak, *EU Procedural Law* (2023) 721–28.

[84] See, eg, Orders of the President of the General Court in Case T-729/15 R *MSD Animal Health Innovation and Intervet international v EMA* (not published) ECLI:EU:T:2016:435, and in Case T-452/20 R *Facebook Ireland v Commission* (not published) ECLI:EU:T:2020:516.

Therefore, a possible improvement in the proceedings for interim relief in direct actions before the EU Courts would be the allowance for applicants to request interim measures before filing their application in the main action, provided that that application is submitted within a specific timeframe thereafter. The legitimacy of such a need seems to be recognised in the ECtHR rules. In that respect, Rule 39 of the Rules of Court empowers the ECtHR to order interim measures where there is an imminent risk of irreparable harm,[85] and according to practice, a request for such measures can either be accompanied or followed by an application submitted to that Court.[86] Furthermore, similar rules exist in many Member States,[87] which is also an indication of the need to provide for such relief. In the view of the present authors, there is an apparent gap in EU law that needs to be bridged, and this can be achieved through a modification of only the Rules of Procedure of the EU Courts, which is not a hefty legislative process. This proposal *de lege ferenda* of the present authors would therefore help ensure the interim protection of parties before the EU Courts in direct actions involving fundamental rights.[88]

4.2. Main Conditions

It is settled case law that the applicant must satisfy three main conditions in order for the interim measures requested in a direct action brought before the EU Courts to be granted, relating to: (1) a prima facie case, namely that the main action has a reasonable chance of success; (2) urgency, that is, there must be threat of serious and irreparable harm to the applicant's interests; and (3) balancing of interests, which entails the

[85] See ECtHR, Rules of Court, 28 March 2024, Rule 39 – Interim Measures, available at www.echr.coe.int/applying-for-interim-measures accessed 15 May 2025.

[86] See ECtHR Practice Direction – Requests for interim measures (Rule 39 of the Rules of Court), 28 March 2004, available at www.echr.coe.int/applying-for-interim-measures accessed 15 May 2025, in particular point 28 ('In particular, as an order under Rule 39 is linked to the proceedings before the Court, the measure will be lifted if the application is not pursued') and point 39 ('Where the final domestic decision is imminent and there is a risk of immediate enforcement, especially in expulsion or extradition cases, applicants and their representatives should submit the request for interim measures without waiting for that decision, indicating clearly the date on which it will be taken and that the request is subject to the final domestic decision being negative.'). See also, in that regard, UN High Commissioner for Refugees (UNHCR), *Toolkit on How to Request Interim Measures under Rule 39 of the Rules of the European Court of Human Rights for Persons in Need of International Protection*, February 2012, available at www.refworld.org/policy/opguidance/unhcr/2012/en/85472 accessed 15 May 2025, 4; European Human Rights Advocacy Centre (EHRAC), *Interim Measures at the European Court of Human Rights*, April 2023, available at https://ehrac.org.uk/en_gb/resources/requests-for-interim-measures-before-the-european-court-of-human-rights/ accessed 15 May 2025, 6, 7, 16 and 21 (indicating that: 'Current practice is that the Court will request an application form within four weeks of the request for interim measures, if it is not submitted concurrently with the request.').

[87] See, in that regard, S Lefèvre and I Nõmm, 'The Availability of Interim Measures Before the General Court: Striking the Right Balance Between the Presumption of Legality and the Right to Provisional Protection' (2023) 60 *Common Market Law Review* 999, 1019–25, who advocate a similar proposal. See also L Prete, *Infringement Proceedings in EU Law* (Alphen aan den Rijn, Wolters Kluwer, 2017) 404–05, proposing modification of the relevant procedural rules in connection with interim measures in infringement proceedings under Articles 258 and 259 TFEU, so as to allow applicants to submit an application even if they are not yet parties to a case before the Court.

[88] That said, it is acknowledged that the matter is delicate, and such a proposal might be viewed as politically sensitive and as having potentially far-reaching implications in some circles.

weighing up of the relevant interests at stake, ie the applicant's interests against possible effects on the interests of the opposing party, third parties and/or the general (EU) interest.[89]

These three conditions have much in common with those employed by the ECtHR and various international courts and tribunals.[90] They are also very much in line with the legal systems of the Member States.[91] While none of the conditions should be minimised, in practice urgency is often the sticking point. Indeed, the case law already recognises a less demanding approach as regards the showing of a prima facie case[92] and the balancing of interests takes into account considerations related to fundamental rights.[93] Nevertheless, there has been an apparent refinement of the case law regarding the condition of urgency in at least two ways, which are particularly relevant to fundamental rights. The first relates to the relaxation of the urgency condition, as traditionally interpreted in the case law, in certain areas where essentially its application would be contrary to the need to ensure effective provisional protection for applicants under Article 47 of the Charter. The second takes account of the nature of the fundamental right at issue in the assessment of the urgency condition.

4.2.1. Relaxation of Urgency in Certain Areas

First, there has been a noticeable relaxation of the urgency condition in the case law with regard to certain areas in EU law where that condition, as traditionally interpreted, cannot be satisfied.[94] This has been done largely with a view to ensuring effective provisional protection for applicants of interim measures pursuant to Article 47 of the Charter.

As the President of the General Court explained in *Belgium v Commission*,[95] a relaxation of the requirements applicable to urgency has so far been permitted in three

[89] As the EU Courts have consistently held, the interim relief judge may order an interim measure only if it is established that granting such a measure is justified, prima facie, in fact and in law (*fumus boni juris*) and that it is urgent in so far as, in order to avoid serious and irreparable harm to the applicant's interests, it must be made and produce its effects before a decision is reached regarding the substance; the interim relief judge must, where appropriate, also weigh up the interests involved. Those conditions are cumulative, so that an application for interim measures must be dismissed if one of them is not met. See, eg, Order of the Vice-President of the Court of Justice in Case C-204/21 R *Commission v Poland* ECLI:EU:C:2021:593, para 77, and Order of the President of the General Court in Case T-125/22 R *RT France v Council* (not published) ECLI:EU:T:2022:199, para 21.

[90] See further, eg, Miles, *Provisional Measures before International Courts and Tribunals* (2017) 473–76; G Le Floch, 'Requirements for the Issuance of Provisional Measures' in Palombino, Virzo and Zarra (eds), *Provisional Measures Issued by International Courts and Tribunals* (2021) 19.

[91] See text accompanying n 57 above.

[92] See further Lenaerts, Gutman and Nowak, *EU Procedural Law* (2023) 553–54.

[93] See, eg, Order of the Vice-President of the Court of Justice in Case C-639/23 P(R) *Commission v Amazon Services Europe* ECLI:EU:C:2024:277, paras 143–65, in particular para 157, in which the Vice-President of the Court of Justice found that, despite the applicant's fulfilment of the prima facie case and urgency conditions, the EU interests prevailed over the applicant's interests, notably on the grounds that suspension of the EU regulation concerned would 'give rise to a risk of potentially allowing an online environment which threatens the fundamental rights provided for in the Charter to persist and develop'. See also cases cited in n 84 above.

[94] For a detailed discussion, see, eg, E Barbier de La Serre and C Lavin, 'Le droit du référé européen depuis 2007: entre prudence et coups d'audace' (2019) 55 *Cahiers de droit européen* 613, 645–78; Lefèvre and Nõmm, 'The Availability of Interim Measures Before the General Court' (2023) 1005–18.

[95] See Order of the President of the General Court in Case T-131/16 R *Belgium v Commission* ECLI:EU:T:2016:427, para 37.

areas of litigation, relating to restrictive measures, public procurement and access to documents, where it is excessively difficult, if not impossible, for systemic reasons, to satisfy those requirements, as they are laid down in the Rules of Procedure and traditionally interpreted in the case law. As detailed therein, those three areas, due to their specific contexts, posed problems for applicants seeking interim measures despite the threat of serious and irreparable damage.

First, in cases involving restrictive measures, any application for suspension of operation was, as a general rule, to be rejected on the ground that such a suspension could prevent those measures from being fully effective in the event that the main action was dismissed. Such a suspension of operation would, for example, make it possible for a person or entity subject to those measures to withdraw immediately all its funds deposited at the banks which are obliged to ensure that they are frozen and to empty its bank accounts before judgment is delivered on the substance of the case. Thus, it would be possible to circumvent the purpose of the restrictive measures taken against it, even though interim measures requested of the interim relief judge must not nullify in advance the effects of the decision to be given subsequently in the main action. Consequently, the interest of the person or entity in securing through interim relief the provisional unfreezing of funds could not be protected by the interim relief judge. It was in that situation that the interim relief judge envisaged, in exceptional circumstances, the possibility of holding that urgency could be constituted by the overriding necessity of providing a remedy as expeditiously as possible for an illegality that was flagrant and extremely serious or applying directly Article 278 TFEU, which takes precedence over the Rules of Procedure.[96]

Second, in public procurement cases, the interim relief judge found that the systemic effect of the case law, as traditionally applied, made it practically impossible for an unsuccessful tenderer to obtain suspension of a contract award decision from an EU institution on the ground that the loss, being purely financial in nature, was not irreparable. However, such a situation could not be reconciled with the requirements of effective provisional protection as guaranteed by Article 47 of the Charter. For that reason, it is recognised that, where an unsuccessful tenderer is able to show that there is a particularly serious prima facie case, it is not required to establish that the rejection of its application for interim measures risks causing it irreparable harm, provided that its application is lodged within the required time-limits.[97]

Third, in cases concerning access to documents in connection with the protection of documents alleged to be confidential, the interim relief judge considered that, even where it could not be established that the harm invoked was irreparable, the fact that the procedure for interim measures is ancillary and provisional in relation to the main proceedings precluded the possibility of authorising the disclosure of certain individual items of information contained in those documents, when it could not be ruled out that the court hearing the substance of the case would prefer to examine whether

[96] See, ibid, paras 38–40 and case law cited.

[97] See, ibid, para 41, along with Order of the Vice-President of the Court of Justice in Case C-35/15 P(R) *Commission v Vanbreda Risk & Benefits* ECLI:EU:C:2015:275, para 57 referred to therein. For a recent application, see Order of the Vice-President of the Court of Justice in Case C-478/22 P(R) *Telefónica de España v Commission* ECLI:EU:C:2022:914, paras 46–72, finding the conditions for easing urgency satisfied.

the documents at issue should be covered by a general presumption of confidentiality, which would exempt those documents from the obligation of partial disclosure. As a general rule, the interim relief judge, given his or her ancillary powers, could not therefore authorise partial access without depriving of practical effect the judgment to be given on the substance. Thus, since those considerations relating to the nature of the procedure for interim measures are determinative of the final outcome of that procedure as such, they cannot be applied solely to the question of the existence of a prima facie case and the weighing of interests, but must also enable the interim relief judge to apply directly, where appropriate, Articles 278 and 279 TFEU, which authorise an order for suspension of operation of a measure if he or she considers 'that circumstances so require' and to prescribe interim measures that are 'necessary'.[98]

Notably, the rationale based on the need to provide effective provisional protection pursuant to Article 47 of the Charter in public procurement cases has also been applied in the case law on the relaxation of urgency in the area of access to documents.[99]

This line of case law is rooted in the fundamental right to effective judicial protection enshrined in Article 47 of the Charter as such. Indeed, if, for systemic reasons, some of the conditions for granting interim relief can never be satisfied in certain areas of law, then access to interim relief would be impossible, thereby undermining the applicant's right to effective judicial protection under Article 47 of the Charter. That fundamental right was thus at the crux of the Court's relaxed reading of urgency.

Furthermore, while this line of case law has evolved in three specific areas for reasons that seem to be unrelated to the protection of specific fundamental rights in the main action, it nonetheless shows that the EU Courts are open to the possibility of relaxing certain conditions if they may be excessively difficult or impossible to fulfil in practice. It remains to be seen whether a similar reasoning may be warranted in the future in fundamental rights-related cases where, due to the specific characteristics of the case, it may be excessively difficult to show irreparable damage to a fundamental right which is the subject matter of the main action.

4.2.2. Taking Account of the Nature of the Fundamental Right in the Urgency Assessment

Second, with further regard to the urgency condition, there is an established line of case law stemming from *Commission v Pilkington Group*,[100] according to which it is not sufficient for an applicant to allege a breach of fundamental rights in the abstract for the purpose of establishing that the damage which could result would necessarily be irreparable. As the Vice-President of the Court of Justice indicated, it is true that a breach of

[98] See Order of the President of the General Court in Case T-131/16 R *Belgium v Commission* ECLI:EU:T:2016:427, para 42 and case law cited.

[99] See, in that regard, Orders of the President of the General Court in Case T-235/15 R *Pari Pharma v EMA* ECLI:EU:T:2015:587, in particular para 110, and in Case T-729/15 R *MSD Animal Health Innovation and Intervet international v EMA* (not published) ECLI:EU:T:2016:435, in particular para 121.

[100] See Order of the Vice-President of the Court of Justice in Case C-278/13 P(R) *Commission v Pilkington Group* ECLI:EU:C:2013:558, paras 40–41. Ultimately, however, the interim measures requested were upheld on appeal. For a detailed discussion, see K Lenaerts and M Radley, 'Recent Case-Law of the European Court of Justice in Interim Measures Cases' (2016) *European Law Reporter* 2.

certain fundamental rights, such as the prohibition of torture and inhuman or degrading treatment or punishment enshrined in Article 4 of the Charter, may, on account of the very nature of the right violated, in itself give rise to serious and irreparable harm. However, the fact remains that it is for the party seeking interim measures to set out and establish the likelihood of such harm occurring in the particular case.[101]

More recently, that case law has been refined in *Vivendi v Commission*.[102] Situated within the context of merger control, the applicant sought interim measures to suspend the operation of a Commission decision requesting it to communicate a series of documents, including documents relating to the private life of some of its employees and company agents, thus entailing a risk of breach of the right to privacy as guaranteed by Article 7 of the Charter, as well as Article 8(1) ECHR and relevant provisions of national law.

The Vice-President of the Court of Justice recalled that, under the case law, it is not sufficient to allege infringement of fundamental rights in the abstract for the purpose of establishing that the harm which could result would necessarily be irreparable. However, the Vice-President continued,

> it cannot be inferred from that case-law that infringement of a fundamental right can never be regarded as constituting serious and irreparable harm. First, the infringement of certain fundamental rights, such as the prohibition of torture and inhuman or degrading treatment or punishment, enshrined in Article 4 of the [Charter], is liable, because of the very nature of the right infringed, to give rise by itself to serious and irreparable harm. Second, the infringement of fundamental rights which, like the right to respect for private life enshrined in Article 7 of the [Charter], do not fall within [that category] must be assessed in the light of all the circumstances in question, with a view to determining whether the scale and nature of the damage entailed by that infringement justifies that damage being regarded as serious and irreparable.

It therefore falls to the interim relief judge to determine whether compliance with the decision at issue is capable of entailing, with a significant degree of probability, interference in the private life of some of the applicant's employees and company agents, and, if so, to assess in the light of all the circumstances, the scale and nature of the damage resulting from that infringement. On that basis, the Vice-President of the Court of Justice found that the arguments put forward by the applicant demonstrated that the breach of fundamental rights was liable to be serious and irreparable, thereby satisfying the urgency condition in those proceedings.[103]

Consequently, it follows from the above that fundamental rights protection is a relevant, indeed important, consideration in interim relief in direct actions before the EU

[101] As a consequence, often requests for interim measures fail in part on such grounds. For a recent application, see Order of the President of the General Court in Case T-125/22 R *RT France v Council* ECLI:EU:T:2022:199, para 52. But for a recent example in which the applicant succeeded in making the requisite showing, see Order of the President of the General Court in Case T-452/20 R *Facebook Ireland v Commission* ECLI:EU:T:2020:516, paras 74 and 82–89 (relating to the right to privacy under Article 7 of the Charter and Article 8(1) ECHR).

[102] See Order of the Vice-President of the Court of Justice in Case C-90/24 P(R) ECLI:EU:C:2024:318, in particular paras 78–91 and 109.

[103] Upon referral back, the Vice-President of the General Court found the other conditions satisfied, and ordered suspension of the Commission decision in relation to the documents containing data relating to the private lives of the third parties concerned, as well as additional measures to preserve the status quo ante: see Order of the Vice-President of the General Court in Case T-1097/23 R-RENV *Vivendi v Commission* ECLI:EU:T:2024:381.

Courts. It also seems to follow from these developments that, in fundamental rights cases, a distinction is made between absolute and relative fundamental rights: for the former, the urgency condition is essentially presumed to be fulfilled if a risk of breach of that fundamental right is shown in concrete terms, whereas for the latter, there is an overall assessment, which takes into account all of the relevant circumstances. In this way, too, the case law may help further the protection of fundamental rights in proceedings for interim measures.

4.3. Compliance

Turning to the matter of compliance, it has not generally been disputed in the EU context that interim measures issued by the EU Courts are binding and enforceable.[104] Going one step further, there has been recent case law, in the context of infringement proceedings brought by the European Commission against Member States for an alleged failure to fulfil obligations under EU law, which has strengthened the compliance regime for interim measures and thus is of relevance for the enforcement of interim measures safeguarding fundamental rights.

In *Commission v Poland*,[105] involving interim measures seeking protection of the Białowieża Forest for the duration of an action involving a failure to fulfil obligations in EU environmental law, the Court of Justice pointed out that it is for the applicant to request the interim measures that it considers necessary, as well as to establish that the conditions are satisfied. However, once the matter is before it, the Court hearing the application for interim measures must satisfy itself that the measures are sufficiently effective to achieve their aim. It is specifically for that purpose that Article 279 TFEU grants the Court a broad discretion, in the exercise of which it is empowered, inter alia, having regard to the circumstances of each case, to specify the subject matter and the scope of the interim measures requested and also, if it deems appropriate, to adopt where necessary of its own motion, any ancillary measure intended to guarantee the effectiveness of the interim measures that it orders.

On that basis, the Court held that it must be able to safeguard the effectiveness of an order directed at a party under Article 279 TFEU by adopting any measure intended to ensure that that order is complied with, including pecuniary sanctions should that order not be respected. In so ruling, the Court drew a connection with the rule of law, reasoning that: 'The purpose of seeking to ensure that a Member State complies with interim measures … is to guarantee the effective application of EU law, such application being an essential component of the rule of law, a value enshrined

[104] See, in that regard, Article 162(2) of the CJ Rules of Procedure and Article 158(2) of the GC Rules of Procedure, which refer to the 'execution' of the interim order which may be made conditional on the lodging of security by the applicant.

[105] See Order of the CJEU in Case C-441/17 R *Commission v Poland* ECLI:EU:C:2017:877, in particular paras 98–100. Ultimately, the Court reserved its decision on the Commission's request for pecuniary sanctions, though specifying that if there was non-compliance, it would order that Member State to pay to the Commission a periodic penalty payment of at least EUR 100,000 per day until it complied or final judgment was delivered (see paras 109–19 of that order).

in Article 2 TEU and on which the European Union is founded.'[106] The Court also emphasised 'the breadth of the powers which are afforded to the Court hearing an application for interim measures in order to enable it to guarantee the full effectiveness of the final decision'.[107]

So far, that case law has been applied only in infringement proceedings,[108] with substantial financial consequences for Member States,[109] especially in the rule of law context.[110] While it remains to be seen whether that case law would be applied in other types of direct actions and in other contexts, the rationale underpinning the said case law in respect of the breadth of the powers of the interim relief judge in ensuring the full effectiveness of interim measures, including the ordering of ancillary measures of his or her own motion, seems to offer a basis for ensuring that interim measures protecting fundamental rights of applicants can also be fully enforced in all kinds of direct actions brought before the EU Courts. The fact that the rule of law and respect for human rights together form part of the values of the European Union enshrined in Article 2 TEU further attests to this. Thus, the compliance case law contributes to the role of interim measures in ensuring the protection of fundamental rights at the EU level.

5. Conclusion

The present contribution demonstrates that interim measures have significant untapped potential for playing a meaningful role in protecting fundamental rights in the European Union. In the view of the present authors, the case law is ripe for further development on numerous fronts from a fundamental rights perspective. As regards interim measures before the national courts, the classical case law of the EU Courts can be revisited with a view to integrating the need to protect fundamental rights pending the outcome of the main action. This contribution suggests several ways in which that can be achieved. As regards interim measures in direct actions before the EU Courts, the case law relating to the breadth of the powers of the interim relief judge and the urgency condition contributes to a 'fundamental rights friendly' jurisprudence, which facilitates access to

[106] ibid, para 102.

[107] ibid, para 103.

[108] See further, in that regard, P Wennerås, 'Saving a Forest and the Rule of Law: *Commission v Poland*' (2019) 56 *Common Market Law Review* 541.

[109] As regards the environmental context, see Order of the Vice-President of the Court of Justice in Case C-121/21 R *Czech Republic v Poland* ECLI:EU:C:2021:752, paras 47–51 (imposing a periodic penalty payment of EUR 500,000 per day until compliance). The General Court dismissed actions brought by Poland challenging the Commission's recovery of EUR 68,500,000 imposed on that Member State as a result of that order: see CJEU, Joined Cases T-200/22 and T-314/22 *Poland v Commission* ECLI:EU:T:2024:329 (appeal pending in Case C-554/24 P).

[110] As regards the rule of law context, see Orders of the Vice-President of the Court of Justice in Case C-204/21 R *Commission v Poland* ECLI:EU:C:2021:877, paras 18–25 and 42–64 (imposing a periodic penalty payment of EUR 1 million per day until compliance), and in Case C-204/21 R-RAP *Commission v Poland* ECLI:EU:C:2023:334 (decreasing that amount to EUR 500,000 per day based on partial compliance). The General Court dismissed actions brought by Poland challenging the Commission's recovery of the amounts payable by that Member State pursuant to those orders: see CJEU, Joined Cases T-830/22 and T-156/23 *Poland v Commission* ECLI:EU:T:2025:131 (appeals pending in Case C-296/25 P and Case C-297/25 P).

interim measures to protect fundamental rights and the enforcement of such measures. Likewise, the proposal advanced here to allow applicants to request interim measures before filing their application in the main action would help ensure that there are no gaps in the interim protection of parties in direct actions before the EU Courts. In this way, when it comes to the possible recourse to interim measures to protect fundamental rights in EU law, there is no time to waste.

PART V

The Internal Workings of the Two Courts

15

The Organisation of the Internal Work of the ECtHR

ELLEN PENNINCKX
Lawyer at the Registry of the European Court of Human Rights[1]

The internal organisation of any body, including an international judicial body, is dictated by a variety of historical, political and pragmatic factors.[2] It has to take into account the specific features of the mechanism by which it has been created as well as its purpose. Also, in order to avoid fossilisation, the organisation is necessarily evolutive. So is the organisation of the internal work of the European Court of Human Rights (ECtHR or the Court) which has had to adapt rapidly in order to deal with the increasing number of applications brought to it.[3]

The purpose of this chapter is to give a descriptive overview of the organisation of the internal work of the ECtHR and its Registry. It will focus on individual applications lodged pursuant to Article 34 of the European Convention on Human Rights (ECHR or the Convention), excluding interstate applications and advisory opinions.[4] It does not intend to be exhaustive, but rather to highlight some key features that are similar or different from the way judicial work is organised within the Court of Justice of the European Union (CJEU).[5]

Some of the differences flow from the distinct purpose and mandate of the two European courts. In that respect, it can be recalled first that the protection of human rights is the whole *raison d'être* of the Strasbourg Court, which task is to decide – with respect to cases brought to it – whether the rights and freedoms enshrined in the ECHR have been respected by the Contracting Parties.[6] The fact that dealing with individual applications is the cornerstone of the Convention system necessarily

[1] Any opinions expressed herein are personal to the author.

[2] For an overview of several international courts and tribunals, see F Baetens (ed), *Legitimacy of Unseen Actors in International Adjudication* (Cambridge, Cambridge University Press, 2019).

[3] For an overview of the reforms and the shift in case management in the years 2010, see H Bakırcı, 'Case Management: European Court of Human Rights (ECtHR)' (2019) *Max Planck Encyclopedia of International Procedural Law* (MPEiPro).

[4] On advisory opinions, see J Krommendijk's contribution at ch 7.

[5] On the organisation of the internal work of the CJEU, see J Gutierrez Fons' contribution at ch 17.

[6] Articles 1, 19 and 32 of the Convention, available at www.echr.coe.int/en/european-convention-on-human-rights.

influences the internal organisation of the Court. So does the fact that Contracting States' international responsibility is directly at stake when the ECtHR finds a breach of the ECHR.

Second, another important element that distinguishes the ECtHR from the CJEU is the volume of cases brought to both courts and the resources available to deal with it. In 2023, the ECtHR, composed of 46 judges assisted by a Registry of around 610 staff members,[7] has delivered a judicial decision in over 38,000 applications with a budget of just above EUR 85 million.[8] Such a volume of cases necessarily dictates a certain form of decentralisation and delegation of the decision-taking, in particular on procedural matters.

In organising its work, the Court has a duty to ensure that the applicants' rights are respected in the proceedings before it. This also entails a duty of quality and efficiency. Therefore, in so far as the text of the Convention allows, organisation of internal work in Strasbourg is a dynamic process with a continuous reflection on best practices and most efficient working methods to adopt in order to ensure quality and efficiency of the judicial response given to the numerous applications brought to the ECtHR.

We propose to look first into the organisation of judicial work and then into that of the Registry, both being closely interrelated.

1. Organisation of Judicial Work[9]

1.1. Judges: Election and Mandate

The ECtHR consists of a number of judges equal to that of the Contracting Parties,[10] currently 46. One judge is elected in respect of each Contracting Party.[11] Judges are elected by the Parliamentary Assembly of the Council of Europe[12] for a non-renewable term of nine years.[13] The non-renewable mandate explains the regular turnover in the Presidency of the Court.[14] Judges shall sit in their individual capacity.[15] They do not represent in any way the Contracting Party in respect of which they have been elected

[7] See the Court's 2023 analysis of statistics www.echr.coe.int/documents/d/echr/annual-report-2023-eng and compare with the 821 cases submitted to the Court of Justice and 1,271 to the General Court in 2023 and 2,114 staff members (https://curia.europa.eu/jcms/jcms/Jo2_7032/en/; https://curia.europa.eu/jcms/jcms/Jo2_7041/en/; both accessed 1 October 2024).

[8] ECtHR's budget for 2024 www.echr.coe.int/budget accessed 1 October 2024 and compare with the 2023 budget of the CJEU of EUR 486 million https://curia.europa.eu/jcms/upload/docs/application/pdf/2024-06/en-rapport_gestion_2023.pdf>.

[9] For further details, see C Dubois and E Penninckx, *La procédure devant la Cour européenne des droits de l'homme et le Comité des Ministres* (Alphen aan den Rijn, Wolters Kluwer, 2016) 629.

[10] Article 20 ECHR.

[11] Article 22 ECHR.

[12] Article 22 ECHR; for further information on the election procedure, see https://pace.coe.int/en/pages/committee-30/AS-CDH accessed 2 June 2025.

[13] Article 23 § 1 ECHR.

[14] See the list of former Presidents of the Court www.echr.coe.int/presidency-of-the-court accessed 2 June 2025.

[15] Article 21 § 2 ECHR.

and they cannot engage in any activity that would be incompatible with their duty of independence and impartiality.[16]

1.2. Decision Bodies: Types and Competences

The Plenary Court does not take decisions on applications brought to the ECtHR. It is merely competent to take administrative decisions,[17] notably as concerns the election of the President of the Court, Vice-Presidents or Section Presidents, the designation of the Registrar and Deputy Registrar of the Court, the composition of Sections or any amendments to the Rules of Court.

The ECtHR can take judicial decisions in four different formations:[18] Single Judge, Committees of three judges, Chambers of seven judges and the Grand Chamber composed of 17 judges.

Single Judges[19] are only competent to declare applications inadmissible where it is clear that the admissibility criteria set out in Articles 34 and 35 ECHR are not met and to strike applications out of the Court's list of cases for reasons set out in Article 37 ECHR. Committees[20] can adopt rulings both on the admissibility and the merits of applications that follow well-established case law. The competence of Committees has increased in the recent past and they have now grown into becoming the decision body 'by default',[21] leaving Chambers[22] to rule on more complex or novel cases, both on the admissibility and merits.

The Grand Chamber[23] remains the supreme decision-making body. It decides on individual or interstate applications in two situations:[24] (i) if the Chamber to which a case is attributed relinquishes jurisdiction in favour of the Grand Chamber;[25] or (ii) if one or both parties request the referral of a Chamber judgment to the Grand Chamber and that the panel of the Grand Chamber accepts the request.[26] The Grand Chamber's involvement is limited to cases that raise a serious question affecting the interpretation of the Convention or cases for whose resolution may have a result inconsistent with a judgment previously delivered by the Court.

The Grand Chamber is also competent in the following situations:

(1) to deliver advisory opinions requested pursuant to Protocol No 16 to the Convention;[27]

[16] Article 21 § 3 ECHR; see notably the Resolution on Judicial Ethics, adopted by the Plenary Court on 21 June 2021 www.echr.coe.int/documents/d/echr/Resolution_Judicial_Ethics_ENG accessed 2 June 2025.

[17] Article 25 ECHR.

[18] Article 26 § 1 ECHR.

[19] Article 27 ECHR.

[20] Article 28 ECHR.

[21] F Krenc, 'La Cour européenne des droits de l'homme: un office subsidiaire au service d'une protection effective des droits fondamentaux' (2014) 140 *Revue trimestrielle des droits de l'homme* 901.

[22] Article 29 ECHR.

[23] Article 26 § 5 ECHR and Rule 24 of the Rules of Court.

[24] Article 31 ECHR.

[25] Article 30 ECHR.

[26] Article 43 ECHR.

[27] Article 2 § 2 of Protocol No 16 ECHR.

(2) to decide, at the Committee of Minister's request, whether a Contracting Party has failed to fulfil its obligation to abide by the Court's final judgments;[28]
(3) to give advisory opinions, at the request of the Committee of Ministers, on legal questions concerning the interpretation of the Convention and the Protocols thereto.[29]

1.3. Organisation of Sections

Each of the ECtHR's judges is attached to one of the – currently – five sections of the Court.[30] The composition of the Sections shall be geographically and gender balanced and shall reflect the different legal systems among the Contracting Parties.[31] It is decided by the Plenary Court, on a proposal by its President for a period of three years.[32] Chambers and Committees are organised within each section.[33]

In view of the ongoing reflection on best practices and the development of the Court's working methods, judges also meet in different working groups in order to discuss and propose amendments to the Rules of Court or changes in the internal organisation of the work. In carrying out this task, judges are assisted by members of the Registry.

1.4. Attribution of Cases and Specialisation

1.4.1. The Role of the 'National Judge'

Any application made under Article 34 ECHR shall be assigned to a section by the President of the Court.[34] In doing so the President endeavours to ensure a fair distribution of cases between the sections.[35] In practice, however, cases are attributed to the section to which the judge elected in respect of the Respondent State is attached (to the exception of the cases attributed to the specialised Immigration Committee[36]). This is because the Convention provides that the judge elected in respect of the Respondent State (the so-called 'national judge') is an ex officio member of the composition of a Chamber deciding cases directed against the State in respect of which he has been elected.[37] The 'national judge' is also an ex officio member of the composition of the Grand Chamber.[38] The rationale for such a rule lies in the characteristics of the

[28] Article 46 § 4 ECHR. On (non-)compliance with the rulings of the ECtHR, see Laurence Burgorgue-Larsen's contribution in ch 19.
[29] Article 47 § 1 ECHR.
[30] The composition of the Sections is public www.echr.coe.int/judicial-formations accessed 2 June 2025.
[31] Rule 25 § 2 of the Rules of Court.
[32] Rule 25 § 1 of the Rules of Court.
[33] A Section is an administrative entity and a Chamber is a judicial formation of the Court within a given Section.
[34] Rule 52 § 1 of the Rules of Court.
[35] ibid.
[36] See below on the Immigration Committee.
[37] Article 26 § 4 ECHR and Rule 26 § 1 (a) of the Rules of Court.
[38] Rules 24 § 2 (b) of the Rules of Court.

international-law system put in place by the Convention and the idea that the 'national judge' is best placed to understand the domestic legal system and the economic, social and political situation in his or her country of origin.

The Rules of Court do not make such specification for Committees. Given that Committees deal only with well-established case law, the drafters of the ECHR probably felt that the 'national judge's' presence in those decision-bodies was not necessary. It is therefore not uncommon that the 'national judge' will not sit in cases decided by a Committee, especially for repetitive cases dealt with under the simplified 'fast-track' procedure.[39] When sitting as a single judge, a judge shall never examine any application against the High Contracting Party in respect of which that judge has been elected.[40]

If the 'national judge' cannot sit for the examination of a specific case on account of one of the reasons set out in Rule 28 § 2 of the Rules of Court, an ad hoc judge shall be appointed if the case is to be examined by a Chamber or Grand Chamber.[41]

1.4.2. The Role of the Judge Rapporteur

The President of the Section designates the Judge Rapporteur for each case attributed to a Chamber or a Committee.[42] For Grand Chamber cases, the attribution of a Judge Rapporteur is done by the President of the Grand Chamber. With the assistance of the Registry, the Judge Rapporteur examines the application and is entrusted with the preparation of a draft judgment or decision.[43]

Without prejudice to the general rules on recusal of judges,[44] nothing prevents a judge from being appointed Rapporteur in a case directed against the State in respect of which he has been elected. In practice, it is not uncommon that the 'national judge' acts as the Judge Rapporteur. This is however avoided for sensitive cases.[45]

When sitting in a single-judge formation, the Court is assisted by non-judicial rapporteurs, ie senior lawyers of the Court's Registry who act under the authority of the President of the Court.[46]

1.4.3. Specialisation

The ECtHR does not have any specialised Chambers or Rapporteurs. As explained above, Chambers are composed within each section which in turn is composed following a geographical and background distribution also taking into account the workload that each Respondent State carries on for the Court. Every Chamber can thus decide

[39] For more information on the fast-track procedure, see Bakırcı, 'Case management' (2019).
[40] Article 26 § 3 ECHR.
[41] See Rule 29 concerning the designation of ad hoc judges.
[42] Rule 49 § 2 of the Rules of Court.
[43] In the Court's vocabulary, 'judgments' are rulings on the merits whereas 'decisions' are limited to the admissibility of applications. To avoid repeating 'judgments and decisions', the generic term of 'rulings' will at times be preferred.
[44] Rule 28 of the Rules of Court.
[45] C Dubois and E Penninckx *La procédure devant la Cour* (n 9).
[46] Article 24 § 2 ECHR and Rule 18A of the Rules of Court.

on any Convention provision or subject-matter. The same is also true for Committees. Equally, Judge Rapporteurs are not formally specialised in one or the other right enshrined in the Convention.

This said, in the field of immigration, the Court has put in place a system with specialised judges. This has been so for over a decade in relation to interim measures requested under Rule 39 of the Rules of Court: there are designated duty judges for the whole Court who decide on the requests for interim measures submitted against all Contracting Parties. Since 2021 there is also a thematic Single Judge who decides on all the cases related to immigration within the competence of a Single Judge, under several provisions of the Convention. A thematic Immigration Committee has also been set up since 2023.[47] It deals with all cases related to immigration matters falling within the Court's well-established case law. This initiative is considered to be a test for possible future areas of thematic specialisation.

Recent years have also seen the emergence of several ad hoc initiatives at Registry level to ensure some form of coordination in order to secure the most efficient case-processing while ensuring quality and consistency of the case law. A Conflicts Unit was created in 2021 to deal with the cases stemming from the three major inter-State conflicts: between Ukraine and Russia, between Georgia and Russia and between Armenia and Azerbaijan.[48] These cases are dealt with by a specialised team of lawyers who have the necessary linguistic and legal skills to deal with those cases. The aim of the Conflicts Unit is to harmonise working methods, exchange good practices and create an institutional memory and continuity in the work with conflict cases.[49] Some form of coordination has also started to emerge in the past years for environmental cases as well as for applications related to European Union law[50] with a system of peer-review by lawyers who have the required expertise.

1.4.4. Hearings and Deliberations

The procedure before the ECtHR is in most cases a written procedure. Hearings are organised only exceptionally: they are in principle held for all cases examined by the Grand Chamber.[51] In very exceptional cases examined by a Chamber hearings are held.[52] In principle hearings are public, unless the Court decides otherwise when the circumstances so require.[53] They are broadcasted and are available on the Court's website at the latest the day after the hearing.

[47] See www.echr.coe.int/w/new-thematic-committee-for-immigration-related-cases?p_l_back_url=%2Fsearch%3Fq%3Dimmigration%2Bcommittee accessed 1 October 2024.

[48] See Speech by R Spano, President of the European Court of Human Rights, Exchange of views with the Committee of Ministers, 17 March 2022 www.echr.coe.int/documents/d/echr/Speech_20220317_Spano_Exchange_views_Committee_Ministers_CoE_ENG accessed 5 June 2025.

[49] ibid.

[50] For more information on the tools and practices developed within the Registry to ensure a coordination on EU-related matters, see V Davio, *EU Fundamental Rights: A Source of Special Significance for the European Court of Human Rights* (Doctoral thesis, KU Leuven, 2025), 'A Shift in the Infrastructure' 359–64.

[51] See the Court's website with the provisional calendar of hearings at www.echr.coe.int/calendar-of-hearings accessed 1 October 2024.

[52] See, for a recent example, ECtHR, App no 32312/23 *Dániel Karsai v Hungary* ECLI:CE:ECHR:2024:0613JUD003231223, § 10.

[53] Article 40 § 1 ECHR.

Another feature of the procedure before the ECtHR is that it is not necessarily adversarial. When it is clear that a case is inadmissible for one of the reasons set out in Articles 34 and 35 ECHR, it is declared inadmissible by a Single Judge.[54] In such situations, the Respondent State is not informed of the case at stake. Equally, a Committee or Chamber can declare an application inadmissible without having first informed the Respondent State.[55] However, the Court cannot examine the merits of a case without notifying the case to the Respondent State and allowing an exchange of observations between the parties on the admissibility and merits of the case.[56]

The Court deliberates in private and its deliberations remain secret.[57] The Section Registrar and the case-lawyers who have worked on the cases examined, as well as interpreters whose assistance is deemed necessary, are present.[58] Oral deliberations of the Chambers are usually organised every Tuesday by each Section. Since they are only competent for matters being the subject of well-established case law, Committees of three judges would usually deliberate in writing or adopt their rulings by tacit agreement.[59]

While Chambers and the Grand Chamber adopt rulings by majority,[60] unanimity is required for the adoption of rulings by the Committees.[61] Abstentions are not allowed.[62]

For all judgments adopted by the Court, sitting judges have the possibility of writing a separate opinion[63] that will be attached to the judgment.[64] Such opinions can be concurring or dissenting, or both. Separate opinions cannot be attached to a decision on the admissibility of a case.

2. Organisation of the Registry[65]

The ECtHR is assisted by a Registry[66] whose task is to provide legal and administrative support to the Court in the exercise of its judicial functions.[67] It is composed of lawyers, administrative and technical staff as well as translators.[68]

[54] Rule 52A of the Rules of Court.
[55] Respectively Rule 53 § 1 and Rule 54 § 1 of the Rules of Court.
[56] See Rule 54 § 2 of the Rules of Court.
[57] Rule 22 § 1 of the Rules of Court.
[58] Rule 22 § 2 of the Rules of Court.
[59] As is allowed by Rule 23A of the Rules of Court.
[60] Rule 23 § 1 of the Rules of Court.
[61] Rule 53 §§ 1 and 2 of the Rules of Court.
[62] Rule 23 § 2 of the Rules of Court.
[63] On separate opinions, see F Krenc's contribution in ch 16.
[64] Rule 74 § 2 of the Rules of Court.
[65] See A Lachowska, 'The Support Eork of the Court's Registry' in J Doria, H P Gasser, M Cherif Bassiouni (eds), *The Legal Regime of the International Criminal Court: Essays in Honour of Professor Igor Blishchenko: In Memoriam Professor Igor Pavlovich Blishchenko* (The Hague, Martinus Nijhoff, 2009); CD Creamer, 'Trust in the Court: The Role of the Registry of the European Court of Human Rights' (2019) 30 *European Journal of International Law* 665.
[66] Article 24 § 1 ECHR.
[67] Rule 18 of the Rules of Court.
[68] See the organisation chart published on the Court's website: www.echr.coe.int/web/echr/d/organisation-chart-public-expanded accessed 1 October 2024.

The Registry is headed by the Registrar[69] and one or more Deputies (currently one). They are elected by the Plenary Court for a renewable term of five years.[70] Each Section is headed by a Section Registrar and their Deputy.[71]

2.1. Case-Processing Units

The ECtHR is not equipped with translation services from or into languages other than the Court's two working languages, English and French. However, the Court accepts applications submitted in any of the official languages of the 46 Member States.[72] This entails that the case files comprised of the application form and the supporting documents, notably the domestic decisions, are not translated into the Court's working languages. This has a decisive impact on the internal organisation of the Court's work. It notably explains that the Registry is mostly organised around national units: any application submitted to the Court is immediately sent to the case-processing unit dealing with the cases directed against the Respondent State. That unit is composed of case-lawyers who hold a law degree obtained in the Respondent State and who are able to read and understand the official language(s) of that State. They should also have excellent knowledge of their domestic legal system and the wider political, social and legal context of the State concerned.

Case-lawyers work under the authority of the Registrar of the Court and are sworn in by the Registrar of the Court. They are appointed by the Secretary General of the Council of Europe on the basis of external competitions which notably entail anonymous written tests. Judges are not formally associated to that process and, once hired, case-lawyers are not attached to a specific judge.

For evident organisational reasons related to the necessary presence of the 'national judge' to decide on cases examined by a Chamber or Grand Chamber, case-processing units are attached to the Section in which the judge elected in respect of their State sits. Such an organisation also entails that case-lawyers do not always work with the same judges. It will depend on which judge is assigned as the Rapporteur in the cases that they are entrusted with.

Case-lawyers will be in charge of examining the incoming cases upon arrival, a procedure that is called 'filtering'. They will make a preliminary assessment of whether the application complies with the formal requirements set out in Rule 47 of the Rules of Court and whether the admissibility criteria laid down in Articles 34 and 35 ECHR have been respected.[73] They also play a pivotal role in identifying urgent or important cases when filtering incoming applications and they have the duty and responsibility of bringing any such cases to the attention of the Section President, Judge Rapporteur or Section Registrar as the case may be. Case-lawyers deal with all the aspects of a case: not only do they prepare draft judgments or decisions on the basis of the instructions

[69] Rule 17 § 1 of the Rules of Court.
[70] Rules 15 and 16 of the Rules of Court.
[71] Rule 18 of the Rules of Court.
[72] Rule 34 § 2 of the Rules of Court.
[73] For more information on the filtering mechanisms, see Bakırcı (n 3).

of the Judge Rapporteur, but they also deal with all the procedural aspects of the case, the correspondence with the parties and any matter that can be raised after the delivery of a ruling.

Chamber and Committee drafts prepared by case-lawyers in English or French are proofread and language-checked by the Court's language department composed of linguists and translators. Then, the substantive quality, case law consistency and procedural accuracy is checked by Section Registrars or their Deputies before they are submitted to the Judge Rapporteur for his or her visa. Once the Judge Rapporteur has approved the text of the draft ruling, it will be put on the agenda for deliberations of the decision body to which the case is attributed.

The Grand Chamber procedure is similar, except that there will usually be an oral hearing and at least two deliberations of all sitting judges, as well as one or several meetings of a drafting committee before a ruling is adopted.

For the purposes of ensuring case law consistency, pointing to any major case law development and discussing relevant procedural or administrative matters, the Registrars, Section Registrars and the Jurisconsult meet every week. They notably discuss the rulings adopted during that week that are noteworthy.

2.2. Planning and Priority

The processing of pending cases is determined at the beginning of each year when a provisional planning is prepared with the cases to be dealt with by each case-lawyer, unit and Section. The planning is prepared with due regard to the priority policy[74] and with the necessary flexibility if new priority cases are brought to the Court during the year. The aim of the Court's priority policy is to speed up the processing and adjudication of the most important, serious and urgent cases. This concerns not only the cases related to the Convention's core rights but also cases that can impact the Convention system as a whole or member States' legislation.

2.3. The Jurisconsult[75] and their Directorate

2.3.1. Role and Mandate

The figure of the Jurisconsult was not originally envisaged in the Convention or the Rules of Court. It was established in practice in 2001 to respond to the increasing need of

[74] The Court's priority policy was established in 2009 with further amendments in 2017 and is available online. See also Bakırcı (n 3).

[75] V Berger, 'Un jurisconsulte à la Cour de Strasbourg' in S Katuoka (ed), *Law in the Changing Europe: liber amicorum Pranas Kuris* (Vilnius, Mykolo Romerio universiteto Leidybos centras, 2008); E Fribergh, 'The Interlaken Process and the Jurisconsult' in L Berg et al (eds), *Cohérence et impact de la jurisprudence de la Cour européenne des droits de l'homme: liber amicorum Vincent Berger* (Oisterwijk, Wolf Legal Publishers, 2013); O Andreotti, 'From ECtHR Case Law Principles to Pragmatic Tools for Quality Decisions: The Round Trip of the Jurisconsult' in R Spano et al (eds), *Fair Trial: Regional and International Perspectives: liber amicorum Linos-Alexandre Sicilianos* (Limal, Anthemis, 2020).

harmonisation of the case law. It was only in the aftermath of the Interlaken Declaration which had stressed the importance of ensuring clarity and consistency of the Court's case law[76] that a specific provision was formally inserted in the Rules of Court in 2014.[77] Article 18B of the Rules of Court now provides that the Jurisconsult's role is to assist the Court for the purposes of ensuring the quality and consistency of its case law. It further states that the Jurisconsult shall provide opinions and information, in particular to the judicial formations and the members of the Court.

The Jurisconsult is a member of the Registry, formally nominated by the Secretary General of the Council of Europe. In practice, judges of the Court are consulted and can interview the candidates. He/she is assisted by a Deputy.

The Jurisconsult Directorate currently covers all knowledge sharing and research activities carried out at the Court. It comprises various units: Research; Case-Law Analysis; Case-Law Monitoring; Knowledge Sharing and the Superior Courts Network; Standard Citations; HUDOC; Library; and External Resources. It thus carries out a variety of activities both for contributing to the internal work of the Court as well as for publishing materials for the outside world.

2.3.2. Ensuring Case Law Consistency[78]

The primary mandate of the Jurisconsult is to assist the Court in ensuring the quality and consistency of the case law. Therefore, one of the Jurisconsult's main roles is to provide observations on the draft judgments and decisions that are put on a Chamber's agenda. All drafts are sent to the Jurisconsult in general two weeks before they will be discussed by the Chamber. In the week prior to the deliberations, the Jurisconsult sends his or her observations, if any, on the consistency with existing case law of the drafts presented for discussion to the judges. These observations are confidential and are only sent to the judges and to the Registry team dealing with the case at hand. The observations are for the Chamber's information: it is for the sitting judges to decide whether or not they want to take into account the comments or to follow the suggestions made. Observations by the Jurisconsult are only made for cases attributed to a Chamber.

The Jurisconsult also submits informative and advisory observations to the panel of the Grand Chamber before the panel decides on referral requests but otherwise he/she is not formally involved in cases attributed to the Grand Chamber, to Committees or to a Single Judge.

In order to carry out this advisory task, the Jurisconsult relies on a network of lawyers who each have expertise in a specific Convention provision or a transversal theme (eg, immigration; environment; rights of the child; prisoners' rights; data protection;

[76] Recital 4 of the Interlaken Declaration adopted at the High-level Conference on the Future of the European Court of Human Rights, 18–19 February 2010.

[77] Rule 18B of the Rules of Court, inserted on 23 June 2014.

[78] On the importance of case law consistency, see V Berger, 'Mieux vaut prévenir que guérir, ou comment assurer la cohérence de la jurisprudence de Strasbourg' in JF Akandji-Kombé (ed), *L'homme dans la société internationale: mélanges en hommage au Professeur Paul Tavernier* (Bruxelles, Bruylant, 2013); G Cano Palomares, 'La coherencia jurisprudencial en el Tribunal Europeo de Derechos Humanos' in L López Guerra (ed), *El Tribunal Europeo de Derechos Humanos: una visión desde dentro: en homenaje al Juez Josep Casadevall* (Valencia, Tirant lo Blanch, 2015).

social rights; terrorism; European Union law). These lawyers are called Case-Law Coordinators.

In addition to advising the Jurisconsult with this observation work, they can also be consulted ahead, during the drafting process, by the case-lawyer, the registrars or the judges if they want advice on the case law on a specific legal question, on the methodology to be applied or on other pending cases raising the same legal questions.

2.3.3. *Ensuring Case Law Information and Dissemination*

Besides the more traditional publication of selections of the most important or novel judgments and decisions delivered every year, the Jurisconsult Directorate has developed a novel and unique electronic tool over the last decade: the ECHR Knowledge Sharing Platform (ECHR-KS).[79] Its mission is to share Convention case law knowledge, complementing the existing information tools such as the well-known case law database HUDOC.[80]

One version of it is published on the Court's internet site and is accessible to the public; another confidential version is available for the sole use of the Court and its Registry.[81] The latter includes more analytical materials. This is a unique platform that no other regional or international tribunal offers to the public. It notably includes a case law guide for every article of the Convention and for selected transversal themes. It is constantly growing and all the materials published are updated twice per year, ensuring the most relevant and complete information to any person interested in knowing more about the case law of the Strasbourg Court.

The platform is also used daily by the Court and its Registry when processing cases. The platform is developed, maintained, updated and enriched by the Case-Law Coordinators under the authority of the Jurisconsult. Its content does not bind the Court.

2.3.4. *Other Activities*

In recent years the Jurisconsult Directorate has started developing standard case law citations for the use of the Court in the draft judgments and decisions. Case-Law Coordinators draft a set of general principles that can be selected and inserted automatically in the Court's draft judgments and decisions.

The Jurisconsult Directorate also offers legal support to the Court and the case-lawyers through the preparation of research reports.[82] Such reports can be of three different types: reports on ECHR case law; reports on international and/or European law; comparative law reports. Such reports are prepared at the request of judge rapporteurs

[79] At https://ks.echr.coe.int/ accessed 1 October 2024.
[80] At https://hu[illegible].echr.coe.int/ accessed 1 October 2024.
[81] See [illegible]bsidiarity in Action: Sharing the Court's Knowledge-Sharing Platform' in JF Kjølbro, [illegible]s), *Liber amicorum Robert Spano* (The Hague, Eleven International Publishing, 2022).
[illegible]e Research Division of the European Court of Human Rights and its Relevance for the [illegible]emmens, S Parmentier, L Reyntjens (eds), *Human Rights with a Human Touch: liber* [illegible] (Cambridge, Intersentia, 2019).

within the framework of a pending case and in order to assist the rapporteurs in preparing a draft. For the preparation of comparative law reports the Jurisconsult Directorate often relies on the contributions of the national focal points of the various members of the Superior Courts Network, thereby receiving first-hand information from the domestic judges, best placed to know the domestic legal order and case law of their own courts. Research reports are confidential. They are not published on the Court's website.

Other documents prepared by the Jurisconsult Directorate include the Legal summaries of the most important cases (prepared by the Case-Law Analysis Unit and published on HUDOC), the quarterly Selection of Key cases,[83] as well as – for internal purposes only – Weekly Tables providing a short overview of the judgments delivered and analytical Case Law Updates for groundbreaking judgments.

[83] At www.echr.coe.int/selection-of-key-cases accessed 1 October 2024.

16

Deliberations and Separate Opinions at the European Court of Human Rights

FRÉDÉRIC KRENC
Judge at the European Court of Human Rights*

The topic of deliberations and separate opinions that I have kindly been invited to address is truly fascinating. It is very exciting to understand how the rulings of the European Court of Human Rights (ECtHR) are concretely prepared and made, as this offers an interesting insight into the Court's judicial practice, which remains little studied and generally unknown. In this respect, I believe it would be highly worthwhile to examine, through a sociological lens, how judicial decisions are formed within the Court. The perspective I am proposing here is an internal one, that of a judge at the Court.

1. Deliberations

At the outset, it should be recalled that the ECtHR may sit in one of four judicial formations. It may sit as a Single Judge formation, in Committees of three judges, in Chambers of seven judges or in a Grand Chamber of 17 judges (Article 26 § 1 of the European Convention on Human Rights (ECHR)).

The figure of the Single Judge was introduced in 2010 under Protocol No 14 in order to tackle the Court's backlog.[1] The role of the Single Judge is to deal with applications which are clearly inadmissible (Article 27 ECHR).

While a Committee of three judges is equally competent to declare an application inadmissible (Article 28 § 1(a) ECHR), such Committees may additionally, since the entry into force of Protocol No 14, deliver judgments on the merits, where there is 'well-established case-law' on the issue concerned (Article 28 § 1(b) ECHR). In this sense, the role of Committees is to deal with so-called 'repetitive cases' (for instance, cases which

* The views I express are personal and do not engage the Court. I am very grateful to Christopher Treadwell and James Brannan for their linguistic review of the text.

[1] This additional protocol entered into force on 1 June 2010. Its goal was 'to maintain and improve the efficiency of the control system for the long term'.

concern inhuman prison conditions, inexecution of domestic judgments, unreasonably lengthy national proceedings, etc).

The Chambers of seven judges handle individual cases which have not been previously rejected by a single judge or decided by a Committee (Article 29 § 1 ECHR). This was initially regarded as the ordinary judicial formation.

The task of the Grand Chamber is to establish the guiding principles of the Court's case law. It examines the cases that are submitted to it either after a Chamber has relinquished jurisdiction (Article 30 ECHR)[2] or when a request for referral has been granted by the Grand Chamber Panel (Article 43 ECHR).[3]

Today, we can see:

- that the number of cases pending before the Court is just over 62,150;[4]
- the huge majority of the rulings rendered by the Court are delivered by single judges;
- three-judge Committees have gained greater importance and now tend to be the ordinary judicial formation within the Court.

1.1. Form of Deliberation

As a rule, deliberations take place orally in the Chambers and in the Grand Chamber. By contrast, deliberations in three-judge Committees take place in a written form, without meeting in person, unless the circumstances so require.

1.2. Deliberation Process

Deliberations begin with a report by the Judge Rapporteur, who presents the case to his or her colleagues and proposes the solution he or she considers should be given. The 'national' judge (namely, the judge elected in respect of the respondent State) is then invited to express his or her views. This is followed by a discussion among all the members of the composition, which is concluded by the President of the Chamber or of the Grand Chamber, whose role is to summarise the debate.

In proceedings before the ECtHR, the identity of the Judge Rapporteur remains unknown to the outside world, unlike at the Court of Justice of the European Union (CJEU) in Luxembourg. This is generally justified by the need to avoid external pressure.

[2] See, eg, the 'climate cases' ruled by the Grand Chamber: ECtHR (GC), App no 53600/20 *Verein KlimaSeniorinnen Schweiz and Others v Switzerland* ECLI:CE:ECHR:2024:0409JUD005360020; ECtHR (GC), App no 39371/20 *Duarte Agostinho and Others v Portugal and 32 Others* (dec) ECLI:CE:ECHR:2024:0409DEC003937120; ECtHR (GC), App no 7189/21 *Carême v France* (dec) ECLI:CE:ECHR:2024:0409DEC000718921.

[3] See, for instance, ECtHR (GC), App nos 40792/10 and 2 others *Fedotova and Others v Russia* ECLI:CE:ECHR:2023:0117JUD004079210, about the obligation of recognition and protection of the same-sex couples under Article 8 ECHR.

[4] Statistics as at 1 October 2025. Pending cases peaked at 161,000 in 2011. In the past three years the Court has dealt with, on average, 38,000 applications per year.

Furthermore, the national judge[5] sits as an ex officio member of the Chamber or Grand Chamber composition hearing cases against the State in respect of which he or she was elected (Article 26 § 4 ECHR). He or she may also sit in Committees of three judges in such cases, but this is not obligatory under the Convention (Article 28 § 3 ECHR). It is understandable that the national judge cannot act as a single judge in cases concerning his or her country (Article 26 § 3 ECHR).

There is no rule prohibiting national judges from acting as Judge Rapporteur. However, the national judge never acts as Judge Rapporteur before the Grand Chamber.

It is important to point out that deliberations are rarely preceded by public hearings. Actually, there are very few hearings held at the ECtHR (roughly ten per year). Proceedings are essentially written, which can be somewhat unfamiliar for judges who, in their previous functions, were used to seeing the parties appear before them. In practice, nearly all hearings are held in cases before the Grand Chamber, with some exceptions.[6]

1.3. Language of Deliberation

The Court's deliberations take place in English and French. Interpreters assist the judges if needed.

Before the Chamber, drafts are drawn up in one language only (English or French), while drafts examined by the Grand Chamber are written in English and in French.

I am personally very attached to the preservation of bilingualism, which I consider enriching for the Court. Bilingualism helps ensure precision and clarity in legal reasoning. Translating a text into the other official language often reveals ambiguities or imprecisions in the original, providing an opportunity to refine and improve the source text itself.

1.4. Secrecy of Deliberations

In accordance with a basic judicial principle enshrined in Rule 22 of the Rules of Court, the Court's deliberations remain secret.[7]

There are two main aspects to this secrecy. First, it implies that judges deliberate among themselves, in private (in the presence of the registrar and the drafting lawyer[8]). Second, judges cannot reveal the content of the discussions and the positions expressed in the course of the deliberations.

[5] See F Tulkens, 'Brèves réflexions sur le juge national', in P Titiun and P Dumain (eds), *La conscience des droits – Mélanges en l'honneur de Jean-Paul Costa* (Paris, Dalloz, 2011).

[6] See, for instance, ECtHR (GC), App no 19750/13 *Grosam v the Czech Republic* ECLI:CE:ECHR:2022:0623JUD001975013 and ECtHR (GC), App no 24827/14 *Fu Quan, sro v the Czech Republic* ECLI:CE:ECHR:2022:0317JUD002482714, where no hearings were held. At the same time, certain Chamber cases may exceptionally give rise to hearings. See, eg, ECtHR, App no 24203/16 *Pagerie v France* ECLI:CE:ECHR:2023:0119JUD002420316.

[7] See P Pastor Vilanova, 'La notion du secret du délibéré à la Cour européenne des droits de l'homme' (2024) *Revue trimestrielle des droits de l'homme* 609.

[8] In my view, the presence of the drafting lawyer during deliberations is necessary as he or she is involved in the preparation of the case.

The question of whether judges may discuss a case with colleagues who are not part of the composition is a matter of debate that is far from confined to the Court. Personally, I believe that judges, as members of the same institution bound by the same oath, may hold such general discussions, provided they do not disclose the positions expressed by their fellow colleagues during deliberations.

2. Separate Opinions

While the ECtHR's deliberations remain secret, the ECHR allows judges to deliver a separate opinion, which is published with the judgment.

The ECtHR is not the only international court of Human Rights where this practice is allowed. At the Inter-American Court of Human Rights as well as at the African Court on Human and Peoples' Rights, judges may also express their views in a separate opinion. By contrast, judges of the CJEU are not allowed to issue a separate opinion.[9]

2.1. Separate Opinions Annexed to Judgments

Article 45 § 2 ECHR provides: 'If a judgment does not represent, in whole or in part, the unanimous opinion of the judges, any judge shall be entitled to deliver a separate opinion'. Two consequences flow from this provision.

First, delivering a separate opinion is a judge's right, not an obligation. To illustrate this point, I might refer, for instance, to the *Muhammad v Spain* judgment concerning allegations of racial profiling by the police, where the Court held by four votes to three that there had been no violation of the Convention.[10] However, only two of the three judges of the minority wrote a dissenting opinion, thereby identifying themselves as part of that minority.[11]

Some argue that it should be an obligation for dissenting judges to deliver a separate opinion. This approach is understandable. For my part, where I disagree with the majority, I will express my point of view in a separate opinion. However, it is up to each judge to decide freely whether or not to draft a separate opinion.

Second, Article 45 § 2 only refers to judgments. This implies that judges may not issue a separate opinion in the case of an inadmissibility decision.

This is of course questionable as some inadmissibility decisions are very important for the Court's case law.[12] Let me refer to the inadmissibility decisions handed

[9] It is nevertheless interesting to note the role of the Advocate General's opinion.

[10] See ECtHR, App no 34085/17 *Muhammad v Spain* ECLI:CE:ECHR:2022:1018JUD003408517.

[11] See, also, ECtHR (GC), App no 60125/11 *VM and Others v Belgium* (striking out) ECLI:CE:ECHR:2016:1117JUD006012511. In that case, the Court held, by twelve votes to five, that the application should be struck out of the list. However, only four judges expressed their dissent. One remained silent.

[12] See, eg, ECtHR (GC), App no 52207/99 *Banković and Others v Belgium and Others* (dec) ECLI:CE:ECHR:2001:1212DEC005220799 or, more recently, ECtHR (GC), App no 3599/18 *MN and Others v Belgium* (dec) ECLI:CE:ECHR:2020:0505DEC000359918.

down recently in the 'climate cases'.[13] Moreover, some of these decisions are delivered after an analysis of the merits, since the Court can declare an application inadmissible because it is manifestly ill-founded (Article 35 § 3(a) ECHR). I might refer, for instance, to the case of *Dahlab v Switzerland* concerning a teacher who was prohibited from wearing a veil in a primary school.[14] The Court declared the applicant's complaints inadmissible as manifestly ill-founded and the decision was taken by a majority, not unanimously. However, as it was formally an inadmissibility decision, it was impossible for the dissenting judges to express the reasons for their dissent in a separate opinion, such that both their identity and their reasoning remain unknown to the public.

The case of *Ferrazzini v Italy* is noteworthy.[15] Although the Court decided that Article 6 was not applicable *ratione materiae* in that case (which concerned a tax dispute), a formal judgment was delivered, which allowed the judges in the minority to deliver a dissenting opinion concerning the finding of inapplicability. More recently, the Court adopted a similar approach in *Angerjärv and Greinoman v Estonia*.[16]

It can be added that when a judgment is delivered, judges may express a separate opinion on the sole question of admissibility,[17] which would not have been possible if the entire application had been declared inadmissible, since, in that situation, an inadmissibility decision (and not a judgment) would have been delivered.

Inadmissibility findings delivered by the Grand Chamber deserve particular attention. When such findings are made by the Grand Chamber following a referral under Article 43 ECHR, they may give rise to separate opinions,[18] since a formal 'judgment' is delivered in those cases. By contrast, when inadmissibility is decided following relinquishment to the Grand Chamber (Article 30 ECHR), a 'decision' is issued, and separate opinions cannot be attached.[19]

2.2. Separate Opinions Annexed to Advisory Opinions

Judges may also issue a separate opinion to be annexed to an advisory opinion delivered under Protocol No 16. This Protocol allows the highest domestic courts to request advisory opinions on questions of principle relating to the interpretation or application of the rights and freedoms defined in the Convention or its Protocols. To

[13] See ECtHR (GC), App no 39371/20 *Duarte Agostinho and Others v Portugal and 32 Others* (dec) ECLI:CE:ECHR:2024:0409DEC003937120; ECtHR (GC), App no 7189/21 *Carême v France* (dec) ECLI:CE:ECHR:2024:0409DEC000718921.

[14] See ECtHR, App no 42393/98 *Dahlab v Switzerland* (dec) ECLI:CE:ECHR:2001:0215DEC004239398.

[15] See ECtHR (GC), App no 44759/9 *Ferrazzini v Italy* ECLI:CE:ECHR:2001:0712JUD004475998.

[16] See ECtHR, App nos 16358/18 and 34964/18 *Angerjärv and Greinoman v Estonia* ECLI:CE:ECHR:2022:1004JUD001635818, para 74.

[17] See, eg, ECtHR, App no 49255/22 *Camara v Belgium* ECLI:CE:ECHR:2023:0718JUD004925522, and the partly concurring, partly dissenting opinion of Judge Krenc joined by Judge Derenčinović.

[18] See ECtHR (GC), App no 43651/22 *Kovačević v Bosnia and Herzegovina* ECLI:CE:ECHR:2025:0625JUD004365122; ECtHR (GC), App no 21881/20 *Communauté genevoise d'action syndicale (CGAS) v Switzerland* ECLI:CE:ECHR:2023:1127JUD002188120.

[19] See ECtHR (GC), App no 63386/16 *Mansouri v Italy* ECLI:CE:ECHR:2025:0429DEC006338616.

date,[20] 25 States have ratified this Protocol and the Court has delivered seven advisory opinions.

Protocol No 16 (Article 4 § 2) expressly provides that judges may annex separate opinions to the Court's advisory opinions. However, there is a clear and common willingness within the Court to try to speak with one voice and, as far as possible, to avoid separate opinions in this context.

The Court's practice demonstrates that separate opinions under Protocol No 16 are indeed rare. Until now, out of the seven advisory opinions delivered by the Court, only two separate opinions have been expressed.[21] It is also interesting to note that all the advisory opinions issued thus far have been adopted unanimously.

2.3. Types of Separate Opinion

2.3.1. Separate Opinions

There are two kinds of separate opinion, which are specified in Rule 74 § 2 of the Rules of Court: concurring opinions; and dissenting opinions.

Concurring opinions are those in which the judge, while agreeing with the outcome of the judgment, either provides reasons for departing from its reasoning or simply wishes to add an argument or explain why they have voted in favour of its findings.

Dissenting opinions reflect the views of judges who disagree with the findings of a judgment.

While this distinction is clear in theory, it may be less so in practice. For example, in concurring opinions, strong dissenting views can be expressed and call the conclusion into question.[22]

2.3.2. Statements of Dissent

A judge may alternatively choose to submit a brief declaration referred to as a 'bare statement of dissent' (Rule 74 § 2 of the Rules of Court). In practice, such statements of dissent may pertain to the just satisfaction awarded or refused by the Court.[23] Alternatively, they may also concern the Court's reasoning, without

[20] 30 May 2025.

[21] See the concurring opinion of ad hoc Judge Sarvarian in the *Advisory Opinion concerning the use of the 'blanket reference' or 'legislation by reference' technique in the definition of an offence and the standards of comparison between the criminal law in force at the time of the commission of the offence and the amended criminal law* (29 May 2020), and the concurring opinion of Judge Harutyunyan annexed to the *Advisory Opinion on the applicability of statutes of limitation to prosecution, conviction and punishment in respect of an offence constituting, in substance, an act of torture* (26 April 2022).

[22] See, eg, the concurring opinion of Judge Ravarani in ECtHR, App nos 22296/20 and 37138/20 *Baret and Caballero v France* ECLI:CE:ECHR:2023:0914JUD002229620; see also the concurring opinion of Judge Bardsen in ECtHR, App no 56578/11 *AAK v Türkiye* ECLI:CE:ECHR:2023:1003JUD005657811.

[23] For example, in the case of ECtHR (GC), App no 15669/20 *Yüksel Yalçinkaya v Türkiye* ECLI:CE:ECHR:2023:0926JUD001566920, Judge Sârcu and myself issued a joint partial statement of dissent concerning the Court's decision not to grant the applicant just satisfaction.

delving into the details, as illustrated by Judge Kjølbro's statement in the case of *Halet v Luxembourg*.[24]

2.4. Requirements

There are no specific rules governing the form and content of separate opinions. However, a general rule can be found in the Resolution on Judicial Ethics (adopted by the Plenary Court in 2021), rule 6 of which states:

> Judges shall exercise their freedom of expression in a manner compatible with the dignity of their office and their loyalty to the institution of the Court. They shall refrain from expressing themselves, in whatever form and medium, in a manner which may undermine the authority and reputation of the Court or give rise to reasonable doubt as to their independence or impartiality.

2.4.1. Substantive Requirements

Separate opinions must comply with substantive requirements which reflect some basic judicial principles.

(a) The Secrecy of Deliberations

As already emphasised, judges are bound by the secrecy of deliberations. This implies that they cannot reveal the content of deliberations. In other words, they cannot refer, in a separate opinion, to what a colleague said during the deliberations.

(b) The Principle of Collegiality

There is another obligation which is inherent in the collegiality principle. Judges cannot raise an issue in a separate opinion which they did not address during the deliberations.[25] In this sense, collegiality is a synonym of fairness.

Could we go a step further and require that the text of a separate opinion be sent to the relevant composition so that it can be taken it into account in drafting the judgment? This proposal raises a certain number of practical issues, but I think it would be worth reflecting on it.

(c) The Duty of Loyalty

Finally, in line with the Resolution on Judicial Ethics, cited above, judges have a duty of loyalty to the Court and must refrain from criticising the institution of the Court as such.

[24] See ECtHR (GC), App no 21884/18 *Halet v Luxembourg* ECLI:CE:ECHR:2023:0214JUD002188418.

[25] See D Spielmann, 'Opinions séparées et secret des délibérations à la Cour européenne des droits de l'homme' (2007) *Journal des Tribunaux* 312.

This also means that judges cannot forever be calling into question the Court's well-established case law. Once the case law has become well-established, it can be expected of judges, even those who have (sometimes strongly) disagreed with it, that they will follow it in order to safeguard the Court's authority. An illustrative example of this is the case of *Yoh-Ekale Mwanje v Belgium*,[26] which concerned the deportation of a Cameroonian national and was decided by a Chamber in 2011. In accordance with the Grand Chamber's judgment in the case of *N v the United Kingdom*,[27] the Court unanimously decided that there had been no violation of Article 3 ECHR. However, six of the seven judges composing the Chamber issued a concurring opinion in which they indicated that they were obliged to follow the case law established in the *N* case, but expressed their reservations about it.

Of course, this duty of loyalty does not prevent judges from using a separate opinion to draw attention to the negative effects of well-established case law in a given case.

2.4.2. Formal Requirements

As to form, there is a significant difference between a separate opinion and a judgment. While the judgment must conform to a specific structure and language, expression is much freer in a separate opinion.

Moreover, a separate opinion is the work of the individual judge (or judges in the case of a joint opinion), without the assistance of a member of the Registry.

Once written, separate opinions are not automatically submitted to the other members of the relevant composition.[28] They are not checked, with the exception of linguistic editing if necessary. They fall under the sole responsibility of their author(s).

(a) Tone

Judges are expected to exercise a certain restraint as regards the tone. They cannot undermine the authority or reputation of the Court. It goes without saying that judges are requested to use language that is respectful towards the Court and their colleagues.

(b) Length

There is no specific limit on the length of separate opinions. Some opinions are very short; others are very long. It is highly recommended that separate opinions should remain within a reasonable volume.

(c) Time Limit

As a rule, judges are requested to submit their separate opinions within two weeks following the deliberations in Chamber cases and within three weeks in Grand Chamber cases. Judges must therefore act swiftly.

[26] See ECtHR, App no 10486/10 *Yoh-Ekale Mwanje v Belgium* ECLI:CE:ECHR:2011:1220JUD001048610.

[27] See ECtHR (GC), App no 26565/05 *N v The United Kingdom* ECLI:CE:ECHR:2008:0527JUD002656505.

[28] Most of the time, judges learn the content of their colleagues' separate opinions when the judgment is delivered.

2.5. Legal Force of Separate Opinions

Separate opinions are annexed to the judgment but are not formally part of it. Only the judgment is legally binding. In my view, a separate opinion should be taken for what it is: an opinion. No more, no less. As a result, it is not the Court's practice to refer to a separate opinion in its judgments or decisions.

2.6. Content of Separate Opinions

In the so-called 'age of subsidiarity',[29] several separate opinions have increasingly tended to focus on the degree of review exercised by the ECtHR. Judges have criticised either the Court's excessive prudence[30] or, conversely, its judicial 'arrogance'.[31] Sometimes they reproach the majority for overlooking certain factual elements from the file or the general context of the case.

Actually, the approach adopted in separate opinions can be influenced by the personalities of the judges and their previous professional experience. Some judges stick strictly to the case file, while others will take a more distant and academic stance.

2.7. Positive Aspects

Separate opinions have always been the subject of intense debate. While some argue that such opinions undermine the authority of the ECtHR, others believe that they increase the transparency of the decision-making process and help to enrich debate. For my part, I can see several advantages to the practice of separate opinions.

2.7.1. Transparency and Judicial Democracy

Separate opinions are generally viewed as an expression of judicial democracy. They increase the transparency of judicial debates since they reflect the different views expressed during a deliberation, even though the deliberation is governed by the duty of secrecy. They offer additional insight into the judgment and its reasoning.

However, we must be clear when we say that separate opinions lead to greater transparency. Transparency does not concern the deliberations themselves, which remain secret, but rather the position of judges who choose to dissociate themselves from the majority.

[29] See R Spano, 'Universality or Diversity of Human Rights? Strasbourg in the Age of Subsidiarity' (2014) 14 *Human Rights Law Review* 487.

[30] See for instance the joint dissenting opinion of Judges Bošnjak, Wojtyczek, Mourou-Vikström, Ktstakis and Zünd annexed to ECtHR (GC), App no 21881/20 *CGAS v Switzerland* ECLI:CE:ECHR:2023:1127JUD002188120.

[31] See, eg, the separate opinion of Judge Mourou-Vikström annexed to ECtHR (GC), App no 6697/18 *MA v Denmark* ECLI:CE:ECHR:2021:0709JUD000669718.

2.7.2. *Expression of Judicial Independence*

Separate opinions also reflect the internal independence of judges in carrying out their judicial duties. Judges are independent from outside influence and pressure, but this independence must be also ensured internally, within the Court itself.[32] While collegiality is crucial, judges remain free to diverge from the positions of their colleagues.

2.7.3. *Greater Individual Responsibility*

Given the publicity they tend to generate, separate opinions can underscore the individual responsibility of judges, who must consider their vote all the more carefully on account of this outside scrutiny.

2.7.4. *Search for Consensus*

Another point to consider is that the threat of a dissenting opinion can also help to forge a compromise within the Court and to prevent the majority from simply imposing its views on the minority.[33]

2.7.5. *Improved Decision-making*

In line with the previous point, the possibility of delivering separate opinions forces the majority to develop its reasoning more rigorously in the judgment. In this sense, separate opinions serve indirectly to improve the quality of the judgment.

2.7.6. *Pedagogical Function*

Separate opinions can also serve a pedagogical function by making judgments more comprehensible, and this, in turn, can facilitate better understanding and acceptance of the Court's position.

On this point, it is worth noting the specific role the national judge can play. In particular, he or she can explain the judgment in the light of the domestic legal context[34] or add details to make the judgment easier to understand by the national authorities

[32] On this point, see ECtHR, App no 23465/03 *Agrokompleks v Ukraine* ECLI:CE:ECHR:2011:1006JUD002346503, para 137: 'This internal judicial independence requires that judges be free from directives or pressures from fellow judges or those who have administrative responsibilities in a court such as, for example, the president of the court. The absence of sufficient safeguards ensuring the independence of judges within the judiciary and, in particular, vis-à-vis their judicial superiors, may lead the Court to conclude that an applicant's doubts as to the independence and impartiality of a court may be said to have been objectively justified'.

[33] See A Paulus, 'Judgments and Separate Opinions: Complementarity and Tensions' (Dialogue between Judges, Strasbourg, 25 January 2019) https://www.echr.coe.int/documents/d/echr/Speech_20190125_Paulus_JY_ENG accessed 4 June 2025.

[34] See the concurring opinion of Judge Lemmens in ECtHR (GC), App no 41738/10 *Paposhvili v Belgium* ECLI:CE:ECHR:2016:1213JUD004173810.

tasked with its execution. In other words, the national judge can 'add a short "national footnote" to the judgment'.[35]

2.7.7. *An Open Door for Future Evolution*

Last but not least, separate opinions play a crucial role in shaping the future of the Court's case law. Today's dissenting opinion can ultimately become tomorrow's majority view. The ECHR is indeed a 'living instrument'[36] and its case law is not set in stone, once and for all. Defining the meaning of the rights and freedoms of the Convention is an evolutive process. Human rights standards are not fixed but are evolving by nature.

When we look at the Court's case law and its evolution, we observe that the Court takes its inspiration from certain separate opinions when deciding to adapt or change its case law.

For instance, in the case of *N v The United Kingdom*,[37] the Court (Grand Chamber) established a threshold with regard to the protection of foreigners against removal under Article 3 of the Convention when they are suffering from a serious illness. Three judges wrote a joint dissenting opinion in which they expressed their concerns regarding this approach and considered that this threshold was too high. Eight years later, following other separate opinions issued in other cases, the Court decided to change its case law in the 2016 case of *Paposhvili v Belgium*.

Moreover, dissenting opinions annexed to a Chamber judgment can launch a debate over potential referral to the Grand Chamber (in accordance with Article 43 ECHR). In this regard, we may note that some judges have argued in their dissenting opinion for the case to be referred to the Grand Chamber.[38]

2.8. Risks

While separate opinions have many positive aspects, their use is not without potential risks.

2.8.1. *Risk for the Court's Authority?*

The first risk obviously concerns the authority of the ECtHR.

On the one hand, it has been stressed that separate opinions foster judicial democracy. On the other hand, the picture of a divided Court could be damaging to the Court's

[35] These are the words used by Judge Lemmens in his concurring opinion in ECtHR (GC), App no 49812/09 *Vegotex International SA v Belgium* ECLI:CE:ECHR:2020:1110JUD004981209.

[36] See ECtHR, App no 5856/72 *Tyrer v the United Kingdom* ECLI:CE:ECHR:1978:0425JUD000585672, para 31. See also N Bratza, 'Living Instrument or Dead Letter – The Future of the European Convention on Human Rights' (2014) *European Human Rights Law Review* 116.

[37] See ECtHR (GC), App no 26565/05 *N v The United Kingdom* ECLI:CE:ECHR:2008:0527JUD002656505.

[38] In this connection, see the separate opinion of Judges Keller and Serghides in ECtHR, App nos 40575/10 and 67474/10 *Mutu and Pechstein v Switzerland* ECLI:CE:ECHR:2018:1002JUD004057510.

authority, especially when many (and very forceful) dissenting opinions are annexed to the judgment.

This issue does not concern the authority of res judicata (a Grand Chamber judgment delivered by nine votes to eight with very strongly dissenting opinions has the same *res judicata* authority as a unanimous judgment); it could affect, rather, the judgment's persuasiveness and its acceptance.

However, some highlight at a more general level that separate opinions contribute to strengthen the legitimacy of the Court. This is indeed the paradox of separate opinions.

2.8.2. Risk for the Judges Themselves?

As mentioned above, the possibility afforded to judges of expressing separate opinions and, as a result, of having the direction of their votes identified exposes them to outside scrutiny. In certain circumstances, judges could feel obliged to issue a separate opinion in order to justify their vote.

2.8.3. Risk of Individualism?

It is clear that separate opinions attract considerable attention from the outside world, in particular from academics. A risk could arise that separate opinions contribute to the excessive personification of the judicial function, which should remain a collective task. On the other hand, a separate opinion can also reveal the courage of judges who decide to depart from the judgment of the majority they cannot endorse.

Some might argue for the anonymisation of separate opinions. It is true that what matters is the content of the opinion, not the name of the judge and, to that extent, this is an interesting proposal. However, certain objections can be raised, the first and not the least being the lack of individual responsibility for the judge in question.

2.8.4. Risk of Profiling?

A final risk is worth mentioning, although I am not sure it is properly speaking a risk. Given the publicity garnered by separate opinions and judges' votes, it is possible to develop a profile of them on this basis: judge so-and-so is more 'conservative', another is more 'liberal'; this judge is more in favour of freedom of expression, another is more protective of the right to privacy, etc.

Moreover, with the extraordinary development of artificial intelligence, some argue that it will be easier in the future to predict judges' positions and the outcome of the Court's judgments.

3. Conclusion

Obviously, separate opinions play a crucial role in fostering transparency and judicial democracy, and they have many positive aspects.

However, challenges do remain. The most important of these is to preserve the essence of collegiality. From my point of view, the individual judge's person is less important than the institution itself. I strongly believe in the virtues of collective deliberation. Collegiality is a mindset based on the deep conviction that decisions are better if they are taken collectively rather than alone.

Issuing a dissenting opinion generally means that you have failed to convince your colleagues. It is therefore important for the judge to be persuasive during deliberations. It is during deliberations that the judge can have the most efficient influence. In a separate opinion, it is unfortunately too late. One might say, somewhat provocatively, that a judge's influence within a court can be measured by the number of separate opinions he or she writes: the higher the number of dissenting opinions, the lesser the influence.

In sum, separate opinions are a very useful tool. However, they should only be used as a last resort. Priority should be given to collegiality and to the search for a common solution.[39] Human rights justice is a collective task and a collective achievement.

[39] See F Krenc, *Une Convention et une Cour pour les droits fondamentaux, la démocratie et l'État de droit en Europe* (Limal-Paris, Anthemis-LGDJ, 2023) 141.

17

Fundamental Rights and the Internal Functioning of the CJEU

JOSÉ A GUTIÉRREZ-FONS*

Fundamental rights – understood as general principles of EU law and/or enshrined in the Charter of Fundamental Rights of the European Union (the 'Charter') – stand at the apex of the EU legal edifice. There is a duty to interpret EU measures in the light of fundamental rights and secondary EU law at odds with those rights is to be annulled or declared invalid.[1] Fundamental rights permeate the entire body of EU law, which includes not only EU measures that apply to national authorities and/or private parties, but also those that govern the internal functioning of the EU institutions, bodies, offices and agencies.[2]

As the institution entrusted with upholding the rule of law within the EU, the Court of Justice of the European Union (the CJEU or the Court) must organise itself in a way that ensures compliance with fundamental rights and, in particular, with the principle of effective judicial protection, enshrined in Article 47 of the Charter. This means, in essence, that the Statute of the Court of Justice of the European Union (the Statute)[3] and its Rules of Procedure[4] must be interpreted in the light of fundamental rights.[5] This

* Legal Secretary (*Référendaire*) in the Chambers of the President of the Court of Justice of the European Union. All opinions expressed herein are personal to the author. I would like to thank Daniele Gallo, Cian Kinsella, Ignace Maselis and Elise Muir for their useful comments.

[1] Regarding the role of fundamental rights in the EU legal order, see, eg, K Lenaerts and JA Gutiérrez-Fons, 'The Place of the Charter in the European Legal Space' in S Peers and Others (eds), *The EU Charter of Fundamental Rights – A Commentary* 2nd edn (Oxford, Hart Publishing, 2021) 1711.

[2] See, eg, CJEU, Case C-458/22 P *Roos and Others v Parliament* (not published) ECLI:EU:C:2023:871 (regarding measures requiring to show a valid EU digital COVID-19 certificate in order to enter Parliament buildings).

[3] Statute of the Court of Justice of the European Union, as amended by Regulation 2024/2019 of the European Parliament and of the Council of 11 April 2024 [2024] OJ L2024/2019 (the Statute).

[4] Consolidated version of the Rules of Procedure of the Court of Justice [2012] OJ L265/1, as amended on 18 June 2013 ([2013] OJ L173/65), on 19 July 2016 ([2016] OJ L217/69), on 9 April 2019 ([2019] OJ L 111/73), on 26 November 2019 ([2019] OJ L 316/03) and on 2 July 2024 ([2024] OJ L 2024/2094) (the Rules of Procedure).

[5] Regarding the Statute, see, eg, CJEU, Case C-130/21 P *Wagenknecht v Commission* ECLI:EU:C:2022:226, para 19 (holding that 'Article 18 of the Statute … is the expression of the right of access to an independent and impartial tribunal enshrined in Article 47 of the Charter'). As to the Rules of Procedure, in *Ognyanov* (see below), for example, the Court of Justice interpreted Article 94 of the Rules of Procedure, which imposes

also means that the Statute and the Rules of Procedure may only be amended in keeping with those rights. Simply put, when it comes to the internal functioning of the CJEU, fundamental rights form part of its 'DNA'.

The effective, transparent and fair organisation of the internal work of the CJEU contributes to improving the quality of justice at EU level, which, in turn, strengthens the trust that EU citizens and the Member States have in the EU judiciary. It is therefore important for EU citizens, in general, and for EU law experts, in particular, to know that 'even behind the scenes', fundamental rights are taken very seriously by the CJEU.

The purpose of the present contribution is to examine the impact of fundamental rights upon the internal functioning of the CJEU. To that end, it examines the way in which fundamental rights are taken into account throughout the different stages of the procedure, from beginning to end. This contribution is divided into three parts. Part 1 first looks at the initial part of the procedure, in which the Court is called upon to decide questions relating to the granting of anonymity and whether a case must be dealt with under a simplified, expedited or urgent procedure. Second, on 1 October 2024, the reform of the Statute, which transfers inter alia jurisdiction to the General Court of the European Union (General Court) to hear and determine questions referred for a preliminary ruling in six specific areas, entered into force.[6] For present purposes, Part 1 explores a particular aspect of that reform, ie the fact that requests for a preliminary ruling, which raise or concern 'independent questions' relating to the Charter, are *not* to be transferred to the General Court but remain within the jurisdiction of the CJEU. Third and last, it looks at how fundamental rights considerations may weigh heavily in referring cases to the Grand Chamber. Part 2 explores the way in which the CJEU conducts hearings and the requests for the reopening of the oral part of the procedure, which seek to provide a response to the Opinion of the Advocate General. Last, but not least, Part 3 examines the role that fundamental rights play during the deliberations and, in particular, at how complex fundamental rights questions may require the Court to organise a round-table discussion and even refer the case to a larger formation. Finally, some concluding remarks support the contention that effective case management based on the early detection of new, complex and/or difficult fundamental rights issues is the right avenue to ensure that citizens enjoy an effective system of justice at EU level.

the obligation upon the referring court to describe the legal and factual context of the main proceedings, in the light of Articles 47 and 48 of the Charter of Fundamental Rights of the European Union (the Charter). In so doing, it held that Article 267 TFEU and Article 94 of the Rules of Procedure precluded a national rule providing that the national court is to be disqualified because it stated a provisional opinion in the request for a preliminary ruling when setting out the factual and legal context. The Court of Justice reasoned that such a provisional opinion did not adversely affect either the right to effective judicial protection or the right of the defence of the parties, since, after the delivery of the preliminary ruling, nothing prevented the referring court from altering its previous findings of fact or law. See CJEU, Case C-614/14 *Ognyanov* ECLI:EU:C:2016:514. See also the contribution of J Heliskoski in ch 18.

[6] The reform introduces three additional changes. First, regarding *all* preliminary reference proceedings, the reform grants the status of 'interested person', within the meaning of Article 23 of the Statute, to the Council, the European Parliament and the European Central Bank. Second, that provision of the Statute now states that, in the context of preliminary reference proceedings, '[s]tatements of case or written observations submitted by an interested person … shall be published on the website of the [Court of Justice] within a reasonable time after the closing of the case, unless that person raises objections to the publication of that person's own written submissions'. Third and last, the reform also expands the jurisdiction of the Chamber determining whether appeals may proceed (see Article 58a of the Statute).

1. The Initial Stages: The Protection of Personal Data, Special Procedures, Transfer of Jurisdiction and the Grand Chamber

1.1. Data Protection, Simplified, Expedited and Urgent Procedures

Where a case is brought before the CJEU, one of the questions that first arises is that of data protection. In order to reconcile the principle of open courts and public information with the protection of personal data of individuals who are mentioned in cases brought before it, the CJEU has adopted a series of measures and guidelines that seek to strike the right balance between those two conflicting interests.[7]

To begin with, a party in the main proceedings and/or the referring court may request to the Court that it renders anonymous one or more persons or entities concerned by the case.[8] If the national court has already granted anonymity, the Court shall respect it in the proceedings before it. In that regard, it is worth noting that there is a special section regarding anonymity in the recommendations addressed to the national courts, which seeks to raise awareness of the issues relating to data protection. In addition to anonymising the names of the persons concerned, the referring court is invited to omit information that serves to identify those persons or, to the extent that is possible, other sensitive information (eg, a rare disease).[9]

The CJEU may, of its own motion, grant anonymity. As a matter of fact, since 2018, the Court has often made use of that power by replacing the names of individuals mentioned in the order for reference by random initials in all material published in connection with the case. It is worth noting that this also includes the order for references, which are now available on the website of the Court.

However, since the use of random initials proved to be insufficient for identifying the relevant case law (too many 'X, Y and Z' cases), since 2023 the CJEU has adopted the policy of adding a fictitious name to those cases. That fictitious name does not correspond to the real name of any party to the proceedings.[10]

The CJEU may also derogate from this guideline at the request of the person concerned or if the special circumstances of the case warrant it.[11] This is, for example, the case where the person concerned wants his or her case to be known by the public. Regarding appeals, the CJEU will, in principle, follow the decision regarding anonymity adopted, at first instance, by the General Court.

[7] See, in this regard, M Bobek, 'Data Protection, Anonymity and Courts' (2019) 26 *Maastricht Journal of European and Comparative Law* 183.

[8] See Article 95 of the Rules of Procedure.

[9] Points 21 and 22 of the Recommendations to national courts and tribunals in relation to the initiation of preliminary ruling proceedings [2024] OJ C2024/6008.

[10] See, eg, CJEU, Case C-107/23 PPU *Lin* ECLI:EU:C:2023:606.

[11] See, eg, CJEU, Case C-311/18 *Facebook Ireland and Schrems* ECLI:EU:C:2020:559, and CJEU, Case C-158/21 *Puig Gordi and Others* ECLI:EU:C:2023:57. On appeal, see, eg, Order of the CJEU, Case C-684/20 P *Sharpston v Council and Conference of the Representatives of the Governments of the Member States* (not published) ECLI:EU:C:2021:486.

It also worth noting that when the CJEU is acting in its judicial capacity, Regulation 2018/1725 does not apply to that institution.[12] Unlike the other EU institutions, the processing of personal data by the CJEU, when acting in that capacity, is not subject to the monitoring of the European Data Protection Supervisor. The idea behind that exclusion is to safeguard the independence of the EU judiciary. However, as recommended by recital 74 of that regulation, the CJEU and the General Court have respectively adopted two decisions establishing an independent supervision by means of an 'internal mechanism'.[13]

Furthermore, at the initial stages of the procedure, the CJEU must identify the cases that may be dealt with under a simplified procedure or be subject to procedural measures, such as ordering suspension or joinder.[14] In order to ensure the effective judicial protection of EU rights, the Court must act quickly in identifying those cases. However, given that cases can be brought before the Court in any of the 24 official languages, the Court has had to find a way to overcoming linguistic barriers.

In that regard, the Court has relied on its Research and Documentation Directorate (RDD), which is composed of legal experts from the 27 Member States. For every request for a preliminary ruling that arrives at the Court, the RDD prepares an 'early review' working document, named '*fiche de préexamen*' in French.[15] The internal deadline for preparing the '*fiche*' is approximately ten working days. That document contains a summary of the factual and legal background of the case in the main proceedings, as well as the questions referred by the national court and the relevant case law of the CJEU. If the case at issue involves new or complex questions pertaining to the protection of fundamental rights, the RDD will also look at the case law of the European Court of Human Rights (the ECtHR).[16] Where the latter is relevant for the outcome of the case or the order for reference expressly refers to it, the *fiche de préexamen* will contain a short summary of that case law.

The RDD also strives to identify cases where the reference is inadmissible (because it fails to meet the requirements listed in Article 94 of the Rules of Procedure) or where the CJEU lacks jurisdiction,[17] as well as cases having a connecting factor with other pending cases or with existing case law.

The *fiche de préexamen* enables the CJEU to take procedural decisions before the translations of the order for reference are ready.[18] Where a case can be dealt with under

[12] See Articles 10(1)(f) and 57(1)(a) of Regulation (EU) 2018/1725 of the European Parliament and of the Council of 23 October 2018 on the protection of natural persons with regard to the processing of personal data by the Union institutions, bodies, offices and agencies and on the free movement of such data, and repealing Regulation (EC) No 45/2001 and Decision No 1247/2002/EC [2018] OJ L 295/39.

[13] See, in that regard, Decision of the Court of Justice of 1 October 2019 establishing an internal supervision mechanism regarding the processing of personal data by the Court of Justice when acting in its judicial capacity [2019] OJ C 383/2. See also Decision of the General Court of 16 October 2019 establishing an internal supervision mechanism regarding the processing of personal data by the General Court when acting in its judicial capacity [2019] OJ C 383/4.

[14] See Articles 53(2), 99, 181 and 182 of the Rules of Procedure.

[15] CURIA – Research and Documentation Directorate (europa.eu) at https://curia.europa.eu/jcms/jcms/jo2-119681.

[16] It is worth noting that the Court of Justice forms part of the ECHR Superiors Court Network. As such, the RDD periodically receives an update on developments in the ECHR case law. Where that case law is relevant for EU law, the RDD prepares a short case note that it is distributed to all the members of the Court of Justice.

[17] Article 53(2) of the Rules of Procedure.

[18] All orders for reference are translated into French, regardless of whether the case can be dealt with under a simplified procedure.

a simplified procedure, there is no need to notify the order for reference to the parties and other interested persons referred to in Article 23 of the Statute, which are mainly the governments of the Member States and the Commission. The absence of notification serves to save time and resources (ie translation of documents), whilst allowing the Court to focus on cases that contribute to the development of EU law.

This demonstrates, in my view, that there is a direct link between effective judicial protection and effective case management. The better the Court employs its human and technical resources, the better the quality of justice is and the more effectively fundamental rights are protected. At the initial stage of the procedure, the President of the Court plays a crucial role, since he is the decision-maker when it comes to the procedural choices that need to be made. He acts after hearing the views of the Judge Rapporteur and the Advocate General appointed to the case.

Moreover, the Court must swiftly examine requests for the application of the expedited preliminary reference procedure (PPA),[19] or the urgent preliminary reference procedure (PPU) made by the referring court.[20] The same applies to a request for an expedited procedure made by the applicant or the defendant in the context of infringement actions, actions for annulment and appeals.[21] Exceptionally, the President of the Court may, of his own motion, decide that the application of those procedures is warranted. Since other contributions to this volume already focus on the PPA and the PPU,[22] I shall limit myself to making two observations regarding the way in which those procedures affect the internal organisation of the Court.

First, the President of the Court examines all requests for a preliminary ruling which raise questions pertaining to the Area of Freedom, Security and Justice (AFSJ) in order to determine whether the case is to be dealt with under the PPU. Second, it is worth noting that the Registry of the Court identifies requests for the PPA and the PPU as soon as they arrive to the CJEU, alerting the President immediately and, where appropriate, the PPU Chamber about a specific request.[23] In respect of cases where the referring court has made a PPU request, the internal deadline for drafting the '*fiche de préexamen*' is shortened (approximately five working days), and so is the deadline for translating the order for reference into French.

Regarding cases that are subject to the ordinary procedure, fundamental rights can also impact the internal functioning of the Court. It is worth recalling that in every case, the President and the First Advocate General appoint respectively the Judge Rapporteur and the Advocate General.[24] The first task of the Judge Rapporteur, in cooperation with the Advocate General, is drafting a preliminary report, a working document,[25] which is addressed to the general meeting of the CJEU (comprised of the 27 judges, the 11 advocates general and the Registrar of the Court).[26] The objective of the preliminary report is

[19] See Articles 105 and 106 of the Rules of Procedure.

[20] See Articles 107 to 114 of the Rules of Procedure.

[21] Articles 133 and 190 of the Rules of Procedure.

[22] See contributions by T Tridimas (at ch 9) and S Iglesias Sanchez (at ch 13).

[23] According to Article 11(2) of the Rules of Procedure, the Court of Justice 'shall designate the Chambers of five Judges which, for a period of one year, shall be responsible for cases [that may be dealt with under the urgent preliminary reference procedure]'. Currently, the Court of Justice designates two Chambers that alternate in examining PPU requests.

[24] Articles 15 and 16 of the Rules of Procedure.

[25] Article 59 of the Rules of Procedure.

[26] Article 25 of the Rules of Procedure.

to assess the complexity of the case, the novelty of the questions raised, and the impact of the case upon existing case law. The preliminary report contains a proposal regarding the formation of the Court to which the case should be assigned, whether the Court must hold a hearing, whether written questions should be addressed to the parties, and whether the Advocate General should draft an Opinion in the case at hand.

Notwithstanding the PPA and the PPU, it is worth noting that the internal deadline for drafting the preliminary report may vary according to the size, the complexity and the importance of the case at issue. The more complex and voluminous a case is, the longer the internal deadline will be. In respect of cases that raise new and complex questions pertaining to the protection of fundamental rights, this means, in essence, that the Judge Rapporteur will enjoy more time to study in depth the file, the relevant case law and the applicable legislation. Regarding fundamental rights, the application of a longer deadline more often than not implies that the case may be dealt with by the Grand Chamber of the CJEU.

1.2. Transfer of Jurisdiction to the General Court

Because of its increasing workload, the CJEU successfully requested the EU political institutions to reform the Statute in order to transfer jurisdiction to the General Court to hear and determine questions referred for a preliminary ruling in six specific areas.[27] As of 1 October 2024, the General Court will start examining requests for a preliminary ruling relating to the common system of value-added tax, excise duties, the Customs Code, the tariff classification of goods, compensation and assistance to passengers and the system for greenhouse gas emission allowance trading. The six areas are self-contained, of a technical nature and have been substantively developed by existing case law. However, Article 50b of the Statute provides that if a case in those six specific areas raises 'independent questions' pertaining to the interpretation of primary EU law, the Charter, general principles of EU law, or public international law, the CJEU will retain jurisdiction over such a case.

Procedurally, the reform puts in place a 'one stop shop' (in French, '*guichet unique*'), meaning that all requests for a preliminary ruling must be submitted to the CJEU. It is for the President of the Court, after having heard the Vice-President and the First Advocate General, to consider whether a case comes exclusively within one or more of those specific areas. In the absence of independent questions mentioned above, the case is transferred to the General Court. If, on the other hand, the President considers that the case raises or concerns those questions, he must immediately refer the matter to the general meeting of the CJEU which will take a decision in that regard.[28]

It is obvious that both the CJEU, which requested the reform, and the EU political institutions were aware of the 'horizontal nature' of fundamental rights.[29] A request for a preliminary ruling that raises or concerns fundamental rights affects the entire body of

[27] See Article 50b of the Statute.

[28] See Recital 14 of Regulation 2024/2019, above n 3, and Article 93a of the Rules of Procedure, as amended on 2 July 2024 [2024] OJ L 2024/2094, 12.8.2024.

[29] See Recital 13 of Regulation 2024/2019, above n 3.

EU law. That is certainly the case where those questions relate to the general provisions of the Charter (Articles 51 to 54 of the Charter) as their interpretation defines the role of fundamental rights in the EU legal order.[30] Cases such as *Åkerberg Fransson*, *Melloni*, *Menci* and *AKT* are excellent examples in that regard.[31] Similarly, this is also the case where those questions focus on a particular fundamental right, given that the interpretation of such a right in a specific area of law can be used and applied in different areas. The paradigmatic example of this cross-fertilisation amongst different areas is Article 47 of the Charter.

Logically, one of the key questions that will arise when the reform enters into force is what is to be understood by an 'independent question' relating to the Charter (or general principles of EU law). In my view, such an independent question means that the fundamental rights dimension of the case must have a certain *gravitas*. It is not sufficient, for example, that the national court mentions in passing a provision of the Charter in one of its questions as that would give rise to forum shopping between the CJEU and the General Court. Similarly, I do not think that the reform seeks to prevent the General Court from interpreting, for example, a provision of the VAT Directive in the light of the Charter. This is because that duty of consistent interpretation applies to the entire body of EU law and, as such, it is binding upon both the CJEU and the General Court in upholding the rule of law within the EU.[32] In order for a question relating to fundamental rights to be independent, it seems to me that such a question must influence the outcome of the case as a stand-alone legal issue. Three examples taken from the case law may illustrate this idea of *gravitas*.

Åkerberg Fransson is the classic example of a VAT case that would remain within the jurisdiction of the CJEU, since it raised independent questions relating to the scope of application of the Charter and the principle of *ne bis in idem*.[33] The same applies to *Menci*, a VAT case which also concerned the same principle.[34] Similarly, in *Ordre des barreaux francophones et germanophone and Others*,[35] the referring court asked the CJEU to examine the validity of a provision of the VAT Directive in the light of Article 47 of the Charter, in particular of the principle of equality of arms. This was because 'only the clients who [were] taxable persons have the right to deduct input VAT for the supply of services by lawyers … and the imposition of VAT on the supply of those services thus impacts individuals differently depending on whether or not they are taxable persons'.[36] That case raised an independent question relating to the Charter.

[30] See, in this regard, K Lenaerts and JA Gutiérrez-Fons, 'The Place of the Charter in the European Legal Space' in S Peers and Others (eds), *The EU Charter of Fundamental Rights – A Commentary* 2nd edn (Oxford, Hart Publishing, 2021) 1711.

[31] See CJEU, Case C-617/10 *Åkerberg Fransson* ECLI:EU:C:2013:105; CJEU, Case C-399/11 *Melloni* ECLI:EU:C:2013:107; CJEU, Case C-524/15 *Menci* ECLI:EU:C:2018:197, and CJEU, Case C-609/17 and C-610/17 *TSN and AKT* ECLI:EU:C:2019:981.

[32] CJEU, Case C-601/15 PPU *N* ECLI:EU:C:2016:84, para 48 (holding that 'in accordance with a general principle of interpretation, an EU measure must be interpreted, as far as possible, in such a way as not to affect its validity and in conformity with primary law as a whole and, in particular, with the provisions of the Charter').

[33] CJEU, Case C-617/10 *Åkerberg Fransson* ECLI:EU:C:2013:105.

[34] CJEU, Case C-524/15 *Menci* ECLI:EU:C:2018:197.

[35] CJEU, Case C-543/14 *Ordre des barreaux francophones et germanophone and Others* ECLI:EU:C:2016:605.

[36] ibid, para 26. However, the Court of Justice observed that in the main proceedings, 'this pecuniary advantage is, however, not likely to affect the procedural balance of the parties'. ibid, para 43.

In respect of cases where it is difficult to identify 'independent questions' at the outset, the reform puts in place two safety-net mechanisms.[37] First, the General Court may refer the case back to the CJEU, where it finds that 'it does not have jurisdiction to hear and determine a request for a preliminary ruling in respect of which the Court of Justice has jurisdiction'.[38] The General Court may also refer the case to the Court of Justice where it considers that 'the case requires a decision of principle likely to affect the unity or consistency of [EU] law'.[39] The second mechanism is the review procedure. Within one month of delivery of the decision by the General Court, the First Advocate General may make a proposal to the Court of Justice to review that decision, on the ground that 'there is a serious risk of the unity or consistency of [EU] law being affected'.[40] The Court of Justice then has one month to take a decision in that regard. Should a review procedure be opened, the answer given by the Court of Justice to the questions subject to review shall be substituted for that given by the General Court.

1.3. Fundamental Rights and the Grand Chamber

In the light of the case law of the Court of Justice, one can distinguish four types of cases that can be examined by the Grand Chamber.

First, these are cases that raise an issue of fundamental importance for EU law. Let us consider, for example, the case which gave rise to the judgment in *Åkerberg Fransson* and *Melloni*, in which the Court explained respectively the scope of application of the Charter and the levels of fundamental rights protection.[41] Issues of great importance may also arise in new areas of law, such as the extradition of EU citizens to third countries.[42] The Grand Chamber will also examine cases where fundamental principles of EU law are called into question, such as the principle of mutual trust.[43]

Second, cases dealing with issues of high public sensitivity will be examined by the Grand Chamber, either because of the political or historical context in which they arise, or because the Court has to respond to highly complex issues relating to the culture,

[37] See, eg, CJEU, Case C-566/17 *Związek Gmin Zagłębia Miedziowego* ECLI:EU:C:2019:390. In that case, the Court of Justice was asked to interpret a provision of the VAT Directive (Article 168), without the question in the order for reference mentioning either the Charter or general principles of EU law. However, in that case, the Court recognised for the first time the principle of fiscal legality, a fundamental right understood as a general principle of EU law, and gave meaning to it. That recognition constituted a question that should fall within the jurisdiction of the CJEU, either because it was arguably an independent question and/or because it was a question 'likely to affect the unity or consistency of [EU] law'.

[38] Article 54 of the Statute.

[39] Second subparagraph of Article 256(3) TFEU.

[40] Article 62 of the Statute.

[41] See CJEU, Case C-617/10 *Åkerberg Fransson* ECLI:EU:C:2013:105, and CJEU, Case C-399/11 *Melloni* ECLI:EU:C:2013:107.

[42] See, eg, CJEU, Case C-182/15 *Petruhhin* ECLI:EU:C:2016:630; CJEU, Case C-191/16 *Pisciotti* ECLI:EU:C:2018:222; CJEU, Case C-247/17 *Raugevicius* ECLI:EU:C:2018:898; CJEU, Case C-897/19 PPU *Ruska Federacija* ECLI:EU:C:2020:262; CJEU, Case C-398/19 *Generalstaatsanwaltschaft Berlin (Extradition to Ukraine)* ECLI:EU:C:2020:1032.

[43] See, eg, CJEU, Case C-163/17 *Jawo* ECLI:EU:C:2019:218 and CJEU, Joined Cases C-643/15 and C-647/15 *Slovakia and Hungary v Council* ECLI:EU:C:2017:631, and CJEU, Case C-216/18 PPU *Minister for Justice and Equality (Deficiencies in the system of justice)* ECLI:EU:C:2018:586.

morality or national identity of the Member States.[44] This point is illustrated by the cases that have reached the Court during the various crises that the Union has gone through or is going through, such as the refugee crisis[45] and the rule of law crisis.[46] Other examples are cases concerning employers' prohibition of the Islamic veil,[47] the free movement of people in same-sex marriages,[48] or the right to maternity leave of a commissioning mother who had a child through a surrogacy arrangement were also assigned to the Grand Chamber.[49] Similarly, cases relating to the promotion and defence of the official language of a Member State, as an expression of national identity, have also been examined by the Grand Chamber.[50]

Third, the Court will refer a case to the Grand Chamber where it is considering whether to review existing case law, to reconcile divergent lines of case law, or to deliver '*un arrêt de synthèse*' that may be translated into English as a judgment that draws together the previous case law. For example, in the judgment in *Banco de Santander*, the Court – sitting as the Grand Chamber – held, in the light of its recent case law on judicial independence, that the Spanish Central Tax Tribunal (the *Tribunal Económico Administrativo Central*) did not have access to the preliminary reference mechanism since it did not satisfy the conditions of independence and impartiality required by Article 267 TFEU.[51] This resulted in the Court reviewing the case law relating to the *Gabalfrisa* judgment.[52] In addition, in *Groupe Gascogne*,[53] the Court of Justice had to choose between two conflicting lines of case law, holding that a separate action for damages was the appropriate procedural means of seeking compensation for damage caused by the excessive duration of the proceedings before the General Court.[54] As to examples of 'arrêts de synthèse', I would like to mention *Commissioner of An Garda Síochána and Others*, in which the Court of Justice explored the relationship between the right to privacy, data retention and the objective of combating serious crime.[55]

[44] CJEU, Case C-391/20 *Cilevičs and Others* ECLI:EU:C:2022:638.

[45] See, eg, CJEU, Case C-646/16 *Jafari* ECLI:EU:C:2017:586; CJEU, Joined Cases C-643/15 and C-647/15 *Slovakia and Hungary v Council* ECLI:EU:C:2017:631, and CJEU, Joined Cases C-47/17 and C-48/17 *X and X* ECLI:EU:C:2018:900.

[46] See, eg, CJEU, Case C-216/18 PPU *Minister for Justice and Equality (Deficiencies in the system of justice)* ECLI:EU:C:2018:586; CJEU, Case C-619/18 *Commission v Poland (Independence of the Supreme Court)* ECLI:EU:C:2019:531; CJEU, Joined Cases C-585/18, C-624/18 and C-625/18 *A K and Others (Independence of the Disciplinary Chamber of the Supreme Court)* ECLI:EU:C:2019:982.

[47] See, eg, CJEU, Case C-157/15 *G4S Secure Solutions* ECLI:EU:C:2017:203, and CJEU, Case C-188/15 *Bougnaoui and ADDH* ECLI:EU:C:2017:204, and CJEU, Joined Cases C-804/18 and C-341/19 *WABE and MH Müller Handel* ECLI:EU:C:2021:594.

[48] See CJEU, Case C-673/16 *Coman and Others* ECLI:EU:C:2018:385, and CJEU, Case C-490/20 *Stolichna obshtina, rayon 'Pancharevo'* ECLI:EU:C:2021:1008.

[49] See CJEU, Case C-167/12 *D* ECLI:EU:C:2014:169, and CJEU, Case C-363/12 *Z* ECLI:EU:C:2014:159.

[50] See, eg, CJEU, Case C-202/11 *Las* ECLI:EU:C:2013:239, and CJEU, Case C-391/20 *Cilevičs and Others* ECLI:EU:C:2022:638.

[51] CJEU, Case C-274/14 *Banco de Santander* ECLI:EU:C:2020:17.

[52] CJEU, Joined Cases C-110/98 to C-147/98 *Gabalfrisa and Others* ECLI:EU:C:2000:145.

[53] CJEU, Case C-58/12 P *Groupe Gascogne v Commission* ECLI:EU:C:2013:770.

[54] The two different lines of case law consisted of CJEU, Case C-185/95 P *Baustahlgewebe v Commission* ECLI:EU:C:1998:608 (in which the Court chose to reduce the fine in view of the excessive duration of the proceedings) and CJEU, Case C-385/07 P *Der Grüne Punkt – Duales System Deutschland v Commission* ECLI:EU:C:2009:456 (in which the Court held that the undertaking concerned by the excessive duration of the proceedings at the General Court had to bring a separate action for damages).

[55] CJEU, Case C-140/20 *Commissioner of An Garda Síochána and Others* ECLI:EU:C:2022:258.

Fourth and finally, the third paragraph of Article 16 of the Statute provides that 'the Court of Justice shall sit in the Grand Chamber at the request of a Member State or an institution of the Union which is a party to the proceedings'. Thus, as soon as such a request has been submitted, the case will be examined by the Grand Chamber, regardless of whether the difficulty, importance or particular circumstances of the case require it to be assigned to that formation.[56]

As the examples mentioned above demonstrate, questions pertaining to the protection of fundamental rights often catch the attention of the Grand Chamber of the Court of Justice. Statistics support that finding. The Court's Annual Report for 2022 states that the Court adopted 727 rulings, out of which 77 were decided by Grand Chamber and two by the Full Court. Little less than half of those 79 rulings refer to a provision of the Charter in a meaningful way. This shows that the internal organisation of the Court takes fundamental rights very seriously.

2. The Oral Part of the Procedure

The Court of Justice does not hold a hearing in all the cases that come before it. The hearing must have an added value, by providing the Court with the information it needs to deliver a ruling. In their written observations, the parties and other interested persons referred to in Article 23 of the Statute may state the reasons why holding a hearing is useful for the Court.[57]

That said, in order to secure the fundamental right to be heard, if one of the parties or other interested persons referred to in Article 23 of the Statute did not participate in the written part of the procedure, a hearing should take place if such a person makes a reasoned request.[58]

The Court of Justice provides interpretation to and from the language of the case, in addition to French and the language of the Member States participating at the hearing. For example, where a reference is made by a Latvian court, the legal counsel of a party in the main proceedings may plead in Latvian. The legal counsel will also receive an interpretation in Latvian of the pleadings made by the agents of the Member States who attend the hearing.

Moreover, it is worth noting that the Court of Justice has adopted a policy that seeks to bring justice closer to citizens across the EU by relying on new technologies. That is why, since 2022, the Court of Justice offers a streaming service which is, in principle, limited to Grand Chamber cases.[59] This policy strengthens the idea of having an open and transparent EU judiciary, whilst reinforcing the equality of citizens who lack the means of being physically present at the hearing. The hearing

[56] See, eg, CJEU, Joined Cases C-515/17 P and C-561/17 P *Uniwersytet Wrocławski and Poland v REA* ECLI:EU:C:2020:73; CJEU, Case C-350/20 *INPS (Childbirth and maternity allowances for holders of single permits)* ECLI:EU:C:2021:659, and CJEU, Joined Cases C-38/21, C-47/21 and C-232/21 *BMW Bank and Others* ECLI:EU:C:2023:1014.

[57] Article 76 of the Rules of Procedure.

[58] Article 76(3) of the Rules of Procedure.

[59] Exceptionally, hearings before a five-judge Chamber may be streamed on the CJEU's website.

is not broadcast live, but pre-recorded. If the hearing takes place in the morning, it is broadcast the same day in the afternoon. If the hearing takes place in the afternoon, it is broadcast the next day. Access to the video recording of the hearing is available for a period of one month.

The date on which the Advocate General delivers his or her opinion marks the end of the oral part of the procedure. Subsequently, any party may request the reopening of that part of the procedure. The Court may also do this of its own motion. Whilst such reopening is exceptional, it may, in particular, take place where the Court lacks sufficient information or where the case must be decided on the basis of an argument which has not been debated between the parties or the other interested persons referred to in Article 23 of the Statute. It may also occur 'where a party has, after the close of that part of the procedure, submitted a new fact which is of such a nature as to be a decisive factor for the decision of the Court'.[60]

The new developments in the realm of fundamental rights protection may play an important role in that regard, notably where the ECtHR proceeds to review its existing case law. In *Menci*,[61] for example, the Court of Justice decided to reopen the oral part of the proceedings in the aftermath of the judgment of the ECtHR in *A and B v Norway*.[62] This was because the parties or the other interested persons referred to in Article 23 of the Statute had not had the chance of expressing their views regarding that judgment.

However, the Statute and the Rules of Procedure make no provision for the parties to submit written observations in response to the Opinion of the Advocate General. Legal scholars have examined whether the absence of such a provision is consistent with Article 6(1) ECHR, as interpreted by the ECtHR in cases such as *Vermeulen v Belgium*[63] and *Kress v France*.[64] Both the Court of Justice and the ECtHR have replied in the affirmative to this question. In *Emesa Sugar*,[65] the Court of Justice sought to distinguish the role of the Advocate General from that of the Procureur Général in *Vermeulen v Belgium*, by stressing his or her independence. It also observed that, unlike the Procureur Général, '[the Opinion of the Advocate General] does not form part of the proceedings between the parties, but rather opens the stage of deliberations by the Court'. Nor is it addressed to the judges or to the parties. Nor it is based on an authority outside the Court. On the contrary, it is 'the individual reasoned opinion, expressed in open court, of a Member of the Court of Justice itself'.[66] Similarly, in *Cooperatieve Producentenorganisatie van de Nederlandse Kokkelvisserij UA v the Netherlands*,[67] the ECtHR applied the *Bosphorus* presumption. Notably, it held that the Court of Justice had examined the merits of the request for the reopening of the oral part of the procedure, which was made by the legal

[60] See Article 83 of the Rules of Procedure.

[61] Order of the CJEU (Grand Chamber), Case C-524/15 *Menci* (not published) ECLI:EU:C:2017:64.

[62] ECtHR, App nos 24130/11 and 29758/11 *A and B v Norway* ECLI:CE:ECHR:2016:1115JUD002413011.

[63] ECtHR, App no 19075/91 *Vermeulen v Belgium* ECLI:CE:ECHR:2018:0717JUD000547506.

[64] ECtHR, App no 39594/98 *Kress v France* ECLI:CE:ECHR:2001:0607JUD003959498.

[65] Order of the CJEU, Case C-17/98 *Emesa Sugar* ECLI:EU:C:2000:69.

[66] ibid, paras 14 and 15.

[67] ECtHR, App no 13645/05 *Cooperatieve Producentenorganisatie van de Nederlandse Kokkelvisserij UA v the Netherlands* ECLI:CE:ECHR:2009:0120DEC001364505.

person who brought the case to Strasbourg. The Court of Justice found that such a request did not contain any specific element that would demonstrate the usefulness or necessity of such reopening.[68]

3. Deliberations

The Opinion of the Advocate General opens the stage of deliberation by the Court of Justice. Deliberations are secret and only the judges themselves may participate in them. The fact that deliberations are secret seeks to protect the independence of the judges, whilst reinforcing the spirit of collegiality that underpins the internal functioning of the Court. Judges are free to express themselves as they see fit and take a different view from that expressed by the Member State of which they are nationals.

Fundamental rights may raise complex questions that require the organisation of a round-table discussion. Such a discussion takes place where the Judge Rapporteur or any other judge sitting in the case disagrees with the Opinion of the Advocate General. The purpose of a round-table discussion is twofold. First, it aims to decide the outcome of the case. Second, it seeks to identify the reasoning that must be followed by the Judge Rapporteur.

Very exceptionally, during the deliberations, fundamental rights questions may even prompt judges to send the case to a larger formation, in accordance with Article 60(3) of the Rules of Procedure. This entails the reopening of the oral part of the procedure, meaning that a (second) hearing may take place and that the Advocate General may be asked to deliver a second opinion in the same case. This has recently happened in *La Quadrature du Net and Others (Personal data and action to combat counterfeiting)*, a case that concerned key issues relating to the retention of and access to personal data. The case was originally assigned to the Grand Chamber; however, during deliberations, it was subsequently referred to the Full Court.[69]

4. Concluding Remarks

In order to protect fundamental rights effectively, the internal organisation of the Court of Justice must be designed in a way that enables it to identify cases raising important, complex and/or urgent fundamental rights questions at the early stages of the procedure. In that regard, the Court of Justice has adopted a series of guidelines and practices that identify those issues rather quickly. The basic idea behind those guidelines and practices is to ensure sound and efficient case management that strikes the right balance between acting swiftly and allocating enough time to the members of the Court for research, reflection and deliberation.

[68] See, in this regard, Order of the CJEU, Case C-127/02 *Waddenvereniging et Vogelbeschermingsvereniging* (not published).

[69] See, eg, Order of the CJEU, Case C-470/21 *La Quadrature du Net and Others (Personal data and action to combat counterfeiting)* (not published) ECLI:EU:C:2023:256. See also CJEU, Case C-470/21 *La Quadrature du Net and Others (Personal data and action to combat counterfeiting)* ECLI: EU:C:2024:370.

That early detection allows the Court to apply, where appropriate, the PPU or the PPA, to deal with cases in a simplified fashion and to focus on cases that deserve its time and attention. In my view, it is by being proactive at the initial stages of the procedure that cases are put on 'the right track' towards a ruling that is convincing, logical and well-reasoned. This undoubtedly contributes to improving the protection of fundamental rights at EU level, whilst reinforcing the trust that citizens and the Member States have in the EU judiciary.

Statistics also show that there is an undeniable correlation between new, complex and difficult fundamental rights questions and the fact that those cases are examined by the Grand Chamber of the Court (and very exceptionally, by the Full Court). In my view, that quantitative data serves to illustrate the fact that a qualitative change in the case law of the Court has taken place over the last decade. The days where fundamental rights stood at the edges of the EU legal order are long gone. Today and certainly in the future, those rights are centre stage in developing the EU legal framework. This is good news for future generations, as fundamental rights become an essential part of our common identity as Europeans.

18

A Survey on the Role of Article 47 of the Charter of Fundamental Rights in the Application of the Statute and the Rules of Procedure of the CJEU

JONI HELISKOSKI*

1. Scope and Purposes

The role of fundamental rights in what José Gutierrez-Fons has labelled, in his contribution to this volume, as 'internal organisation of the work' of the Court of Justice of the European Union (CJEU) involves two aspects that should be distinguished from one another: first, the internal organisation of the work of the Court in cases concerning, in substance, fundamental rights and, second, the role of fundamental rights affecting the internal organisation of the Court in general, that is, in *all* cases dealt with by the Court. As regards the first aspect, I may be brief. There are no legal rules specifically governing the organisation of the Court's proceedings in cases deemed to concern or involve substantive fundamental rights. When the Court takes account of the nature of a case as one concerning or involving such fundamental rights for the purpose of organising its proceedings, it does so mainly as a matter of practice.[1]

I shall rather focus on the second aspect, that is, the role of fundamental rights in the organisation of the proceedings at the CJEU in general. The relevant rules and principles governing those proceedings are, in essence, laid down in the Statute of the CJEU as well as the Rules of Procedure of the Court of Justice[2] and the Rules of Procedure of the General Court.[3] The Statute of the CJEU is set out in a Protocol annexed to the founding

* Justice, the Supreme Administrative Court of Finland. The author wishes to thank Allan Rosas and José Gutierrez-Fons for reading, and commenting upon, the contribution in draft. The usual disclaimer applies.

[1] Another matter is that a risk of interference with fundamental rights may constitute a ground for the application of either the expedited or accelerated procedure (PPA) and, for references for a preliminary ruling relating to the area of freedom, security and justice, an urgent procedure (PPU). See contributions by T Tridimas (ch 9) and S Iglesias (ch 13) in this volume. Such reasons may also lead the President to give a case priority over others (Art 53(3) of the Rules of Procedure of the Court of Justice).

[2] Rules of Procedure of the Court of Justice [2012] OJ L 265/1, as subsequently amended.

[3] Rules of Procedure of the General Court [2015] OJ L 105/1, as subsequently amended.

Treaties, and thus belongs to the primary law of the Union.[4] The Rules of Procedure are established by the Court of Justice, with the approval of the Council, pursuant to the sixth paragraph of Article 253 of the Treaty on the Functioning of the European Union (TFEU).

Respect for the rule of law constitutes one of the values on which the Union is founded,[5] and it is the task of the CJEU to ensure that in the interpretation and application of the Treaties the law is observed.[6] As an institution of the Union, the CJEU is required to comply with procedural fundamental rights and the principle of effective judicial protection, enshrined in Article 47 of the Charter of Fundamental Rights of the European Union (CFREU).[7] That provision, based on Articles 6(1) and 13 of the Convention for the Protection of Human Rights and Fundamental Freedoms (ECHR), entails the right to an effective remedy before a tribunal as well as the right to a fair and public hearing within a reasonable time by an independent and impartial tribunal previously established by law. It follows from this, as José Gutierrez-Fons rightly observes, that the Statute of the CJEU and its Rules of Procedure must comply with the rights laid down in Article 47 CFREU and will have to be interpreted by the Court in the light of those rights.

Building upon, and seeking to take further, the analysis of Mr Gutierrez-Fons at chapter 17, this contribution aims to examine the role of Article 47 CFREU in the case law of the Court of Justice concerning the application of the Statute of the CJEU and the Rules of Procedure of the Court of Justice and of the General Court.[8] It seeks to present a comprehensive survey of the case law in which Article 47 has been applied *in the context of the application of the Statute and the Rules of Procedure*, covering the period from the entry into force of the Treaty of Lisbon whereby the Charter was included in the primary law of the Union. Questions concerning the application of Article 47 in the context of Treaty rules on the jurisdiction of the Court[9] as well as the rules of national procedural law are therefore excluded from the scope of the analysis.[10] Such a review, I believe, may offer insights not only into the role of Article 47 CFREU in the context of application of the Statute and the Rules of Procedure but, more indirectly, also into how the Court conceives of the obligations flowing from that provision in the conduct and organisation of its proceedings. In the conclusions,

[4] Pursuant to the second para of Article 281 TFEU, the European Parliament and the Council, acting in accordance with the ordinary legislative procedure, may amend the provisions of the Statute, with the exception of Title I ('Judges and Advocates General') and Article 64 (concerning language arrangements applicable at the CJEU). The European Parliament and the Council shall act either at the request of the Court of Justice and after consultation of the Commission, or on a proposal from the Commission and after consultation of the Court of Justice.

[5] Article 2 of the Treaty on European Union (TEU).

[6] First sub-para of para 1 of Article 19 TEU.

[7] See, eg, CJEU, Case C-295/12 P *Telefónica and Telefónica de España v Commission* ECLI:EU:C:2014:2062, para 40, and CJEU, Case C-439/11 P *Ziegler v Commission* ECLI:EU:C:2013:513, para 159.

[8] This contribution focuses on the case law of the Court of Justice. The application of the Rules of Procedure of the General Court is covered only in the context of that case law.

[9] As the Court has held, that article is not intended to change the system of judicial review laid down by the Treaties. See, eg, CJEU, Joined Cases C-593/15 P and C-594/15 P *Slovakia v Commission* ECLI:EU:C:2017:800, para 66, and Joined Cases C-29/22 P and C-44/22 P *KS and KD v Council and others* ECLI:EU:C:2024:725, para 71.

[10] See M Bonelli, M Eliantonio and G Gentile, *Article 47 of the EU Charter and Effective Judicial Protection, Volume 1: The Court of Justice's Perspective* (Oxford, Hart Publishing, 2022).

the contribution also discusses the nature of the Statute and the Rules as a procedural code of the European Union, as well as their relationship to the notion of internal organisation of the work of the Court.

2. Application of Article 47 of the Charter in the Context of the Statute and the Rules of Procedure – A Survey of the Case Law

2.1. Preliminary Observations

It emerges from a comprehensive survey of the case law that the Court of Justice has interpreted and applied Article 47 CFREU in the context of the application of the Statute and the Rules of Procedure of the CJEU on numerous occasions. They have concerned the lawful composition of the Court (Section 2.2), the period of time allowed for bringing proceedings (Section 2.3), representation of parties before the Court (Section 2.4), the requirements concerning the content of a reference for a preliminary ruling (Section 2.5) and the organisation of a hearing and reopening the oral procedure (Section 2.6).

Before addressing those questions, it may also be noted that while either the Statute or the Rules of Procedure obviously do not lay down a time-limit within which Union courts are required to adjudicate on the cases before them, the second paragraph of Article 47 CFREU imposes on those courts a requirement to do so within a reasonable time, as indeed confirmed by the case law of the Court.[11] In that regard, an action for damages brought before the General Court constitutes an effective remedy.[12] That case law may also be regarded as a more general acknowledgment of the obligation of the Union courts to comply with Article 47 in the conduct and organisation of their proceedings.

2.2. Lawful Composition of the Court

The Rules of Procedure of the Court of Justice and of the General Court provide for the rules concerning the assignment of cases to formations of those courts.[13] Under Article 18 of the Statute of the CJEU, no Judge or Advocate General may take part in the disposal of any case in which he has previously taken part as agent or adviser or has acted for one of the parties, or in which he has been called upon to pronounce as a member of a court or tribunal, of a commission of inquiry or in any other capacity.

[11] See CJEU, Case C-385/07 *Der Grüne Punkt – Duales System Deutschland v Commission* ECLI:EU:C:2009:456, paras 179 ff, and Case C-58/12 P *Groupe Gascogne v Commission* ECLI:EU:C:2013:770, especially paras 72 ff.

[12] CJEU, Case C-58/12 P *Groupe Gascogne v Commission* ECLI:EU:C:2013:770, para 83.

[13] See Articles 15, 16 and 60 of the Rules of Procedure of the Court of Justice and Articles 25–29 of the Rules of Procedure of the General Court. See, also, the Decision of the General Court (C/2024/6453) on the Criteria for the assignment of cases to Chambers [2024] OJ C 6453.

Those rules must comply with Article 47 CFREU and notably with the right of everyone to a fair and public hearing within a reasonable time by an independent and impartial tribunal previously established by law. That right covers not only the rules providing for the establishment of judicial organs but also the provisions concerning the appointment as well as the independence and impartiality of the members of a court. It follows from the case law of the Court of Justice and that of the European Court of Human Rights that a tribunal will have to comply with the rules governing the composition of the bench in each case.[14]

In *Strack v Commission*,[15] the appellant had alleged lack of jurisdiction of the formation of the General Court to which the case was assigned, claiming that, by reassigning the consideration of his case to a chamber other than the one originally contemplated, the General Court had breached the principle of the right to be heard by a court or tribunal established in accordance with the law, the rights enshrined in Article 6 of the ECHR and by Article 47 of the Charter, as well as a number of provisions of the Rules of Procedure of the General Court. Under those Rules, the General Court is to lay down criteria by which cases are to be allocated among the chambers, that decision being published in the Official Journal of the European Union.[16] The criteria for assigning cases to chambers laid down in the decisions of the General Court in force both on the date when the appellant's originating application had been lodged and at the time of the reassignment of the case had provided for the President of the General Court with a possibility of derogating from the rotas provided for in the decisions either on the ground that cases are related or with a view to ensuring an even spread of the workload.

The Court rejected the applicant's arguments. It held, first, that since the derogation available to the President was not limited to the time the originating application is lodged, nothing prevented a case from being reassigned at another time. Moreover, the Court held, that interpretation was all the more appropriate since the reassignment of a case, in the interests of the good administration of justice, with a view to ensuring an even spread of the workload, pursued the objective of processing cases within a reasonable time, in accordance with the second paragraph of Article 47 CFREU. Thus, the reassignment of the case had not infringed Article 47 CFREU, but that provision had rather *favoured* an interpretation of the Rules of Procedure and the Decision enabling its reassignment. The Court also noted that, in the case at hand, the appellant had not raised any doubts as to the impartiality of the formation which had heard his application for annulment.[17]

Doubts as to so-called objective impartiality of a formation of the General Court were however raised in *Wagenknecht v Commission*,[18] the appellant having accused

[14] See, eg, CJEU, Joined Cases C-542/18 RX-II and C-543/18 RX-II *Review Simpson v Council and HG v Commission* ECLI:EU:C:2020:232, paras 57 and 69–76, and CJEU, Case C-791/19 *Commission v Poland* ECLI:EU:C:2020:277, para 168. See, also, ECtHR, App no 26374/18 *Guðmundur Andri Ástráðsson v Iceland* ECLI:CE:ECHR:2020:1201JUD002637418, paras 211 ff.

[15] CJEU, Case C-127/13 P ECLI:EU:C:2014:2250.

[16] See Article 25 of the Rules of Procedure of the General Court. See, also, above n 9.

[17] Paras 51–55 of the judgment.

[18] CJEU, Case C-130/21 P ECLI:EU:C:2022:226. The requirement of impartiality encompasses, on the one hand, subjective impartiality, in so far as no *member of the institution* concerned who is responsible for

the General Court of infringing Article 18 of the Statute of the CJEU[19] by ruling in a situation where there had appeared to be a conflict of interests. The appellant claimed that the requirement of objective impartiality had not been satisfied on the ground that a judge in the formation of the General Court having ruled in the present case concerning an alleged failure of the Commission to act had worked at the Commission during a time when the appellant had asked the Commission to act. The appellant also claimed that the requirement of impartiality had not been satisfied given that the judge in question had, as an employee of the Commission, defended the Commission's lack of action in another dispute that allegedly was structurally related to the one raised in his action before the General Court concerning an alleged failure of the Commission to act.

The Court of Justice dismissed both of those arguments. It held, first, that the mere fact that a member of the formation of the General Court had worked for the Commission – the defendant at the General Court – before performing his duties as a judge at that Court, was not sufficient to cast a doubt as to his objective impartiality or that of this formation. As to the appellant's second argument, the Court, referring to Article 18 of the Statute as 'the expression of the right of access to an independent and impartial tribunal enshrined in Article 47 of the Charter',[20] held that Article 18 of the Statute had not been infringed in the specific circumstances of the case given that the other dispute in which the judge concerned had, as an employee of the Commission, defended the Commission's lack of action had concerned a different matter than the one raised by the present case. Therefore, there had been no breach of objective impartiality by either the judge in question or by the formation of the General Court having decided the case at first instance.

2.3. The Period of Time Allowed for Bringing Proceedings

The Rules of Procedure of the Court of Justice and the General Court prescribe time-limits, inter alia, for initiating proceedings against a measure adopted by Union institutions. In that regard, Article 59 of the Rules of Procedure of the General Court provides as follows:

> Where the time limit allowed for initiating proceedings against a measure adopted by an institution runs from the publication of that measure in the Official Journal of the European Union, that time limit shall be calculated, for the purposes of Article 58(1)(a), from the end of the fourteenth day after such publication.

the matter may show bias or personal prejudice, and, on the other hand, objective impartiality, in so far as there must be sufficient guarantees to exclude any legitimate doubt as to bias on the part of the *institution* concerned. See CJEU, Case C-439/11 P *Ziegler v Commission* ECLI:EU:C:2013:513, para 155.

[19] Under the first para of Article 18 of the Statute '[n]o Judge or Advocate General may take part in the disposal of any case in which he has previously taken part as agent or adviser or has acted for one of the parties, or in which he has been called upon to pronounce as a member of a court or tribunal, of a commission of inquiry or in any other capacity.' The second para of the same provision requires any Judge or Advocate General to inform the President, if, for some special reason, he considers that he should not take part in the judgment or examination of a particular case.

[20] Para 19 of the judgment.

The question in *PPG and SNF v ECHA*,[21] an appeal against an order of the General Court dismissing as inadmissible an action for annulment of a decision of the European Chemicals Agency (ECHA) identifying a substance meeting the criteria laid down in Article 57 of the REACH Regulation and including it on the list of substances for future inclusion in Annex XIV to that Regulation, was whether the 14-day time-limit only applied to the publication of a measure in the Official Journal of the European Union. The contested decision having been published on the ECHA website on 30 March 2010 and the applicants having lodged their application at the General Court on 10 June 2010, the General Court had dismissed the action as inadmissible under the sixth paragraph of Article 263 TFEU, holding that the 14-day period referred to in the Rules of Procedure only applied to measures published in the Official Journal.

The Court upheld the appeal and set aside the order of the General Court. Having first pointed out that it could not be ruled out that Article 102(1) (now Article 59) of the Rules of Procedure of the General Court applies to a measure published only on the internet, the Court observed that, in so far as the wording of the Rules of Procedure of the General Court could give rise to doubts, it was necessary, in the absence of any imperative reasons to the contrary, to favour an interpretation which does not result in the interested parties being time-barred and therefore depriving them of their right to resort to legal proceedings. Having regard to context of the provision in question and the objectives it pursued, the Court considered that

> … the objective of the 14-day time-limit laid down in Article 102(1) of the Rules of Procedure of the General Court is to ensure that interested parties have sufficient time within which to bring an action against published measures and, consequently, to observe the right to effective judicial protection, as is now laid down in Article 47 of the Charter of Fundamental Rights of the European Union.[22]

Thus, Article 47 CFREU required the Rules of Procedure to be interpreted in a way that ensures that the interested parties, when they rely on the additional 14 days to bring an action, are not deprived of effective judicial protection.

For the sake of clarity, it should however be noted that, according to the case law, Article 47 CFREU does not preclude a strict application of time-limits for the institution of proceedings. In that regard, the Court has held that a *derogation* from those rules cannot be justified by the fact that fundamental rights are at stake. A derogation from the application of the EU rules on procedural time limits may only be made where the circumstances are quite exceptional, in the sense of being unforeseeable or amounting to force majeure, in accordance with the second paragraph of Article 45 of the Statute.[23]

2.4. Representation of Parties before the CJEU

It follows from Article 19 of the Statute of the CJEU that parties other than institutions and Member States must be represented by a lawyer before Union courts. As a rule, only a lawyer authorised to practise before a court of a Member State may therefore represent

[21] CJEU, Case C-625/11 *PPG and SNF v ECHA* ECLI:EU:C:2013:594.
[22] Para 35 of the judgment.
[23] See, eg, CJEU, Case C-660/17 P *RF v Commission* ECLI:EU:C:2019:509, paras 44 and 53–58.

or assist a party before the Court.[24] Under Article 44 of the Rules of Procedure of the Court of Justice and Articles 53 and 197 of the Rules of Procedure of the General Court lawyers shall produce a certificate that they are authorised to practise before a court of a Member State and, where the party which they represent is a legal person governed by private law, an authority to act issued by that person. It emerges from the case law that the application of these requirements, either alone or in conjunction with other relevant rules of Union law or the law of a Member State, may have implications as to the right to effective legal protection under Article 47 CFREU.

In *PJ v EUIPO*,[25] the General Court had dismissed the action as inadmissible on the ground that the application initiating proceedings had not been signed by an independent lawyer. In their appeals, the appellants claimed that the broad interpretation by the General Court of the requirement of independence of a lawyer had infringed the first and second paragraphs of Article 47 CFREU. One of the appellants also criticised the General Court of not informing him in good time of the existence of a possible irregularity vitiating legal representation so that he could have instructed another lawyer.

The Court of Justice found no breach of Article 47 CFREU. As to the possibility of regularisation, the Court observed that a failure to comply with the obligation to provide representation by a lawyer authorised to practise before a court of a Member State was not one of the requirements which may be met after the action has been brought, in accordance with the second paragraph of Article 21 of the Statute and Article 44(6) (now 78(6)) of the Rules of Procedure of the General Court. Nor did any provision of the Statute or of the Rules of Procedure oblige the General Court or the Court of Justice to notify the person bringing an action or to give him or her the opportunity to appoint a new representative.[26]

The fact that no derogation may be made from the requirements imposed by Article 19 of the Statute has however led the Court of Justice to take account of Article 47 CFREU in the interpretation of *other rules of Union law or the national law of a Member State* that may have implications on a person's access to justice before Union courts in conjunction of those requirements.

In *Peftiev and others*,[27] the Court held that a derogation from restrictive measures imposed by the Union upon individuals must be interpreted in accordance with

[24] There are two exceptions to this requirement: first, representatives of the parties to the main proceedings where, in accordance with the national rules of procedure applicable, those parties are permitted to bring or defend court proceedings without being represented by a lawyer, and persons authorised under those rules to represent them (Article 47(2) of the Rules of Procedure of the Court of Justice and Article 203(3) of the Rules of Procedure of the General Court); and, second, university teachers being nationals of a Member State whose law accords them a right of audience (seventh para of Article 19 of the Statute). On the criteria for the representation of a party by a university teacher, see CJEU, Case C-110/21 P *Universität Bremen/REA* ECLI:EU:C:2022:555.

[25] CJEU, Joined Cases C-529/18 P and C-531/18 P *PJ and PC v European Union Intellectual Property Office* ECLI:EU:C:2022:218.

[26] Paras 86–91 of the judgment. See, also, CJEU, Joined Cases C-515/17 P and C-561/17 P *Uniwersytet Wrocławski/REA* ECLI:EU:C:2020:73. It was argued that in so far as the result of a finding that the legal representative is not independent is the dismissal of the action, the applicant concerned would be deprived of both an effective remedy and its right of access to a court under Article 47 of the Charter. The Court however did not have to examine that argument. See, also, Case C-110/21 P *Universität Bremen v REA* ECLI:EU:C:2022:555, para 25.

[27] CJEU Case C-314/13 ECLI:EU:C:2014:1645.

Article 47 CFREU, to the effect that a freeze of funds cannot have the effect of depriving the persons whose funds have been frozen from effective access to justice.[28] Therefore, when taking a decision on whether to grant a derogation from such restrictive measures with a view to bringing an action challenging the lawfulness of those measures, the competent national authority does not enjoy an absolute discretion, but must exercise its powers in a manner which upholds the rights provided for in the second sentence of the second paragraph of Article 47 of the Charter and observes 'the indispensable nature of legal representation' (provided for in the Statute and in the Rules of Procedure) in bringing such an action before the General Court. A very similar line of reasoning was followed by the Court in *Trasta Komercbanka and others*[29] concerning the interpretation of the law of a Member State on the appointment of a liquidator of a credit institution, empowered, inter alia, to revoke the powers of attorney of the lawyer who had brought proceedings before the General Court seeking to challenge the measures of the European Central Bank withdrawing the authorisation of that credit institution and leading to its liquidation. The Court held that the right of a legal person such as the credit institution concerned to an effective remedy under Article 47 CFREU would be infringed, if, under the law of the Member State concerned, a liquidator empowered to take such decisions were to be appointed on the basis of a proposal from a national authority which took part in the adoption of the act resulting in its going into liquidation.

As in the case of observance of time-limits for the institution of proceedings, Article 47 CFREU therefore provides no ground for derogations concerning the requirements of the Statute and the Rules of Procedure concerning the representation of parties before the CJEU. It may however influence the interpretation of other rules that have implications on the right to an effective legal remedy, in conjunction of the strict application of those requirements. In other words, those other rules must be interpreted in the light of Article 47 so as to guarantee an effective remedy in a system based on strict requirements for legal representation provided for in the Statute and the Rules of Procedure.

2.5. Requirements Concerning the Content of a Reference for a Preliminary Ruling

Article 94 of the Rules of Procedure of the Court of Justice sets out the requirements for the content of a reference for a preliminary ruling under Article 267 TFEU. Those requirements are also reiterated in paragraphs 13, 15 and 16 of the Recommendations of the Court of Justice of the European Union to national courts and tribunals in relation to the initiation of preliminary ruling proceedings.[30] A failure by a national court to

[28] Para 26 of the judgment.

[29] CJEU, Joined Cases C-663/17 P, C-665/17 P and C-669/17 P *European Central Bank (ECB) and Others v Trasta Komercbanka and Others* ECLI:EU:C:2019:923.

[30] Court of Justice of the European Union, Recommendations to national courts and tribunals in relation to the initiation of preliminary ruling proceedings [2024] OJ C/6008. See, eg, CJEU Case C-561/19 *Consorzio Italian Management and Catania Multiservizi* ECLI:EU:C:2021:799, para 68.

satisfy the requirements of Article 94 constitutes a ground for a reference (or a question) for a preliminary ruling to be declared as manifestly inadmissible.[31] While the system established by Article 267 TFEU does not constitute a means of redress available to the parties to a case pending before a national court or tribunal,[32] the question has been raised in the case law whether compliance by a national court with the requirements for the content of a reference for a preliminary ruling set out in Article 94 of the Rules of Procedure may constitute a breach of the right to a fair trial enshrined in the second paragraph of Article 47 CFREU.

In *Ognyanov*,[33] the referring court asked, in essence, whether Article 267 TFEU and Article 94 of the Rules of Procedure, read in the light of the second paragraph of Article 47 and Article 48(1) CFREU, must be interpreted as precluding a national rule being interpreted in such a way that it obliges a referring court to disqualify itself from a pending case on the ground that that court sets out, in a request for a preliminary ruling, the factual and legal context of that case. It had been maintained in the main proceedings that by setting out, in a request for a preliminary ruling, the factual and legal context of that case, a court would be expressing a provisional opinion on questions of fact and law before deliberations had begun, leading, under the relevant national legislation, to the need for that court to disqualify itself from the examination of the case.

The Court held that such an interpretation of a national rule would be contrary to Article 267 TFEU and Article 94 of the Rules of Procedure, read in the light of the second paragraph of Article 47 and of Article 48(1) CFREU. According to the Court, by setting out, in a request for a preliminary ruling, the factual and legal context of the main proceedings, a referring court was doing no more than meeting the requirements of Article 267 TFEU and Article 94 of the Rules of Procedure and, that being the case, the responding, by the national court, to the requirement of cooperation inherent in the preliminary reference procedure could not, in itself, constitute a breach of either the right to a fair trial, enshrined in the second paragraph of Article 47 CFREU, or the right to the presumption of innocence, guaranteed by Article 48(1) CFREU.[34] A likely effect of such a national rule would be a national court choosing to refrain from referring questions for a preliminary ruling to the Court, in order to avoid, on the one hand, being disqualified and exposed to disciplinary penalties or, on the other, lodging requests for preliminary rulings that are inadmissible. This would be detrimental to the prerogatives granted to national courts and tribunals by Article 267 TFEU and, consequently, to the effectiveness of the cooperation between the Court and the national court and tribunals established by the preliminary ruling mechanism.[35]

[31] See, eg, CJEU, Case C-512/21 *Aquila Part Prod Com* ECLI:EU:C:2022:950, para 56.

[32] CJEU, Case C-561/19 *Consorzio Italian Management and Catania Multiservizi*, para 54. It however follows from the system established by Article 267 TFEU, read in the light of the second paragraph of Article 47 of the Charter, that, if a national court or tribunal against whose decisions there is no judicial remedy under national law takes the view that it is relieved of its obligation to make a reference, the statement of reasons for its decision must set out the reasons why that reference was not made. See ibid, para 51 and CJEU, Case C-144/23 *KUBERA* ECLI:EU:C:2024:881.

[33] CJEU, Case C-614/14 *Atanas Ognyanov* ECLI:EU:C:2016:514.

[34] Paras 22 and 23 of the judgment.

[35] Para 25 of the judgment.

In similar vein, the Court has held, in *IP and others*,[36] that Article 267 TFEU and subparagraph (a) of the first paragraph of Article 94 of the Rules of Procedure of the Court of Justice, read in the light of Article 4(3) TEU and of the second paragraph of Article 47 CFREU, must be interpreted as precluding a national rule which requires courts hearing criminal cases, when making factual findings in the context of a request for a preliminary ruling, to decline jurisdiction on pain of annulment of the decision to be given on the merits of the case.[37]

2.6. Organisation of a Hearing and Reopening the Oral Procedure

Under Article 76 of the Rules of Procedure of the Court of Justice, the parties (or the interested persons referred to in Article 23 of the Statute) may submit a reasoned request for a hearing to be held. On a proposal from the Judge Rapporteur and after hearing the Advocate General, the Court may decide not to hold a hearing 'if it considers, on reading the written pleadings or observations lodged during the written part of the procedure, that it has sufficient information to give a ruling'. This does not however apply 'where a request for a hearing, stating reasons, has been submitted by an interested person referred to in Article 23 of the Statute who did not participate in the written part of the procedure.'[38] Under Article 106 of the Rules of Procedure of the General Court, a hearing shall be arranged either of the General Court's own motion or at the request of a main party, stating the reasons for which that party wishes to be heard. If no such request has been made, the General Court may decide to rule on the action without an oral part of the procedure, if it considers that it has 'sufficient information available to it from the material in the file'. Thus, at either Court, the Rules of Procedure do not provide for an automatic right to a hearing.[39]

Under settled case law of the European Court of Human Rights, Article 6(1) ECHR, on which Article 47 CFREU is based, does not impose an absolute obligation to hold a hearing or necessarily require that a hearing is held in all proceedings. The circumstances that may justify dispensing with a hearing will essentially depend on the nature of the issues to be determined by a court in each individual case.[40] It is therefore not surprising that, in *Euro Box Promotion and others*,[41] the Court of Justice held that a refusal by the Court to hold a hearing does not constitute an infringement of Article 47 CFREU. In this case, the Court had decided, as a result of the health crisis linked to the coronavirus pandemic, to cancel the already scheduled hearing and to convert into questions for a written response the questions which had been communicated to the parties for the purposes of the hearing. After the delivery of the opinion of the Advocate

[36] Order of the CJEU in Case C-609/21 not published ECLI:EU:C:2022:232.
[37] For a follow-up to Case C-609/21, see CJEU, Case C-269/22 *IP and others* ECLI:ECLI:EU:C:2023:275.
[38] Para 3 of Article 76 of the Rules of Procedure.
[39] See, eg, CJEU, Case C-547/03 P *AIT v Commission* ECLI:EU:C:2006:46, para 35.
[40] See, eg, ECtHR, App no 43395/09 *De Tommaso v Italy* ECLI:CE:ECHR:2017:0223JUD004339509, para 163.
[41] CJEU, Joined Cases C-357/19, C-379/19, C-547/19, C-811/19 and C-840/19 *PM and Others* ECLI:EU:C:2021:1034.

General, one appellant had requested the oral part of the procedure to be reopened, arguing that the lack of a hearing undermines his right to a fair trial and the adversarial principle.

Rejecting that argument, the Court recalled that:

> … the right to be heard, enshrined in Article 47 of the Charter, does not impose an absolute obligation to hold a public hearing in all proceedings. That is true, inter alia, where the case does not raise any questions of fact or of law that cannot be adequately resolved on the basis of the documents in the file and the written observations of the parties (see, to that effect, judgment of 26 July 2017, Sacko, C 348/16, EU:C:2017:591, paragraph 40 and the case-law cited).[42]

Thus, having regard to paragraphs 2 and 3 of Article 76 of its Rules of Procedure, and given that no request for a hearing had been submitted by an interested person referred to in Article 23 of the Statute who did not participate in the written part of the procedure, the Court could decide, without infringing the requirements under Article 47 CFREU, not to hold a hearing. It was, moreover, pointed out that the Court had put questions for a written response to the parties and to the interested parties which submitted observations, thus allowing them to bring additional information to the attention of the Court, an option which the appellant concerned, amongst others, had exercised.[43]

The Court therefore considers that the Rules of Procedure give it a rather free hand in deciding whether to organise a hearing, and Article 47 CFREU does not stand in the way of a decision to refuse to hold one. Apart from the situation covered by paragraph 3 of Article 76 of the Rules of Procedure, it depends on whether the Court thinks it already has sufficient information to give a ruling.[44] Those parameters for the right to a hearing are considered to comply with Article 47 CFREU.

3. Concluding Remarks

The above survey of the case law in which Article 47 CFREU has been invoked and applied in the context of the application of the Statute and the Rules of Procedure of the CJEU suggests that the Court of Justice is generally speaking attentive to the fundamental rights based on that provision.

Given the role of the Court in the legislative procedure applicable to amendment of the Statute (Article 281 TFEU) as well as the adoption of the Rules of Procedure (Article 253 TFEU) it may only be natural that there has been no case establishing a conflict between those rules and Article 47 CFREU. The latter has rather functioned as a tool of interpretation of the Statute and the Rules of Procedure and, in some cases, provided a justification for their interpretation in the light of the requirement of effective legal protection (*PPG and SNF v ECHA* and *Ognyanov*). The Court has also employed Article 47 in the interpretation of national law of a Member State so as to protect the right to an effective remedy and to alleviate the implications of a strict interpretation of the requirements concerning legal representation based on the Statute and the Rules of

[42] Para 123 of the judgment.
[43] Paras 124–125 of the judgment.
[44] See, also, CJEU, Case C-73/22 P *Grupa Azoty and others v Commission* ECLI:EU:C:2023:570, para 27.

Procedure (*Peftiev* and others and *Trasta Komercbanka and others*). Finally, the Court has recognised the role of Article 47 in the interpretation and application of the rules concerning the lawful composition of the Court (*Wagenknecht v Commission*) as well as the right to an oral hearing (*Euro Box Promotion and Others*) despite rejecting the arguments based on Article 47 in the circumstances of those cases. The cases in which the Court has applied Article 47 in the context of interpretation and application of the Statute and the Rules of Procedure may not be as many in number but, it is submitted, demonstrate a clear recognition on the part of the Court of Justice of the role of Article 47 in the organisation of its proceedings. The Court does not apply that provision in a purely decorative manner.

As a concluding point, a few observations on the notion of 'the organisation of the internal work of the CJEU' – the title of the contribution by José Gutierrez-Fons to this volume (chapter 17) – are called for. It is submitted that the Statute and the Rules of Procedure do not govern solely, or even primarily, what may adequately be labelled as 'internal organisation' of the work of the CJEU. The very fact that questions concerning the application of Article 47 of the Charter may arise and, in practice, arise in this context, as demonstrated by the present contribution, confirms that the Statute and the Rules of Procedure go far beyond the notion of internal organisation of the Court. They rather provide for *a procedural code* of the European Union. This may explain why their adoption and amendment always requires a decision of the legislative branch of the Union or (for certain provisions of the Statute) even the Member States. Unlike most other courts, whether domestic or international, the CJEU is not capable of autonomously establishing its rules of procedure. This may be the case because many of the provisions of the Statute and the Rules of Procedure actually fall within the scope of legislation, the enactment of which is not a task of the CJEU.

At the same time, some of the provisions of the Rules of Procedure do indeed govern questions that may legitimately labelled as 'internal organisation' of the work of the CJEU. As regards those questions, the involvement of the Union's political institutions may be regarded as problematic and as trespassing on a domain that should belong to the CJEU only. Where the dividing line goes is unclear, however. This may in itself have a detrimental effect on the position of fundamental rights in the organisation and conduct of proceedings by the CJEU. On the one hand, questions that indeed have fundamental rights implications may be reduced to issues of 'internal organisation' of the Court. On the other hand, the Union's political institutions may feel entitled to interfere in questions legitimately belonging to the internal organisation of the work of the Court. One may argue that fundamental rights, including those enshrined in Article 47 CFREU, should never stand amidst such a constitutional confusion.

PART VI

Final Destination Reached? Compliance and Non-Compliance

19

(Non)-Compliance with the Rulings of the ECtHR in the Age of Illiberal and Dictatorial Turn

LAURENCE BURGORGUE-LARSEN*

1. Introduction – The Current Existential Paradox

At the time of the inception of European Court of Human Rights (ECtHR), the Council of Europe (CoE) was, genuinely, an Intergovernmental Organisation which Members States were all democratic, following the philosophy of Article 3 of its Statute.[1] This political homogeneity permits the success of the CoE as such and, also, the proper functioning of the ECtHR vis à vis the States. Larry Helfer and Anne Marie Slaughter, in a very interesting piece published in 1997 in the Yale Law Journal, named 'Toward a Theory of Effective Supranational Adjudication',[2] claimed that the 'remarkable and surprising success' of the ECtHR was due to the political and social homogeneity of the CoE.

This homogeneity no longer exists,[3] and raises existential questions about the ability of the ECtHR to bring about far-reaching changes in states that have not joined the CoE

* IREDIES, *Institut de Recherche en droit international et européen de la Sorbonne* (https://iredies.pantheon-sorbonne.fr/iredies). Personal page (www.pantheonsorbonne.fr/page-perso/burgorguel).

[1] It reads as follows: 'Every member of the Council of Europe must accept the principles of the rule of law and of the enjoyment by all persons within its jurisdiction of human rights and fundamental freedoms, and *collaborate sincerely and effectively* in the realisation of the aim of the Council as specified in Chapter I' (italics added).

[2] L Helfer, M Slaughter, 'Toward a Theory of Effective Supranational Adjudication' (1997) 107 *The Yale Law Journal* 273.

[3] Since the end of the 2000 years, we have witnessed many frightening situations: (1) internal armed conflicts (in Russia and Turkey) where massive human rights violations have to be deplored and where the crime of enforced disappearance appears in the European landscape; (2) international armed conflicts in which Council of Europe Member States wage war against each other since the war in the summer of 2008 (*Georgia v Russia*), 14 years before the aggression against Ukraine; (3) an impressive democratic backsliding in the east of the continent, not only in Poland and Hungary – the usual suspects – but also in Romania, Bulgaria, Bosnia Herzegovina, Moldova. Now, one of the existential questions is if the west of Europe will stay immune to this trend. The rise of far-right Parties and the capture of power in some states (such as Italy with Georgia Meloni).

as democratic states, but as very fragile states in transition to democracy. It is imperative, from my point of view, to face this existential question and to ask ourselves: 'Can we expect the obligation of loyal and effective cooperation laid down in Article 3 of the Statute of CoE to be taken seriously by States that trample on the rule of law, respect for human rights and pluralism?'

Today, while liberal democracies are generally not reluctant to implement the Court's rulings (not least because they see a major political gain in supporting the European protection system as representing the liberal values to be defended), the existential problem comes from the illiberal and authoritarian states and from dictatorships which are part of the CoE highlighting the very strong trend of 'democratic deconsolidation', where populist discourses are critical. This phenomenon was first detected and scrutinised by political scientists and historians who sounded the alarm as early as the mid-2010s. In 2016, political scientists Roberto Stefan Foa and Yasha Mounk, now teaching at Harvard and Cambridge respectively, announced in a brilliant article published in the Journal of Democracy[4] based on their work and other studies conducted worldwide since 1995, that the idea that democracy, once established in a country, was consolidated, needed to be entirely debunked. The following year, in 2018, Steven Levitsky and Daniel Ziblatt's book – *How Democracies Die?* – also highlighted the phenomenon that today, no one can deny, namely the slow but real, insidious, and dangerous way of killing democratic regimes. These two American authors wrote that: 'Democracies can die not at the hands of generals but at the hands of elected leaders, presidents, or prime ministers, who subvert the processes that brought them to power.' They continue with this striking formula: 'Democracy backsliding today begins at the ballot box.'[5]

Historians, with the analytical depth that their discipline instils, had also detected these worrying processes by placing them in the long-term framework of history. And they attributed the causes of 'democratic deconsolidation' to the immense social disenchantment with the imperfect functioning of liberal democratic regimes, which explained the new enchantment of citizens for disruptive political parties, promising everything, immediately, and clinging to a discourse that is both divisive (People versus Elite) and anti-pluralist (no room for dissonant ideas, whether they come from journalists, academics, opponents, etc, with, moreover, a falsification of reality (the era of fake news). In 2017, French historian Pascal Ory published a remarkably nuanced book, where he dissected through time (from the nineteenth century to the twenty-first century) and geographical spaces (from the United States, through the former USSR and new Russia to Europe), the emergence of populism, again with social disenchantment as the underlying cause, leading to liberal democratic disenchantment. He concluded his analyses with concern, hammering that if there was no awakening, catastrophe was on the horizon.[6] In 2020, Pierre Rosanvallon in an

[4] Y Mounk, S Foa, 'The Danger of Deconsolidation. The Democratic Disconnect' (2016) 27 *Journal of Democracy* 5.

[5] S Levitsky, D Ziblatt, *How Democracies Die? What History Reveals about Our Future* (London, Crown Publishing Group, 2018).

[6] P Ory, *Peuple souverain. De la révolution populaire à la radicalité populiste* (Paris, Gallimard, 2017).

impressive essay[7] also offered with his historian's perspective a very in-depth analysis of populism, which he considers the ascending ideology of the twenty-first century. He outlines the populist matrix: a conception of the people as a united and indivisible entity (the 'People-One') rejecting social divisions and the plurality of opinions and generating a binary vision of society (People versus Elites); a direct relationship between the people and the charismatic leader ('Man-People') supposed to embody the popular will; a valorisation of passions and emotions at the expense of reason and reasoned debate; an economic vision based on national protectionism. The rejection of unelected institutions such as independent authorities, constitutional courts, international courts, perceived as obstacles to the direct expression of the popular will. It is exactly this rejection, particularly of international institutions and courts, that we need to be aware of. That is why I consider it critical to study seriously the bad faith politics of those states when focusing on the compliance issue. In this context, it is essential that the reader discover this article in conjunction with its appendix in order to appreciate the full extent of the situation. Indeed, it has been decided to use the power of in-depth legal analysis to present the mechanisms that show how states (when they are no longer acting in good faith) do everything in their power to avoid the obligation of execution deriving from Article 46, paragraph 1 of the European Convention on Human Rights (ECHR).

In this very specific political context, the European human rights protection system faces an existential paradox. A stark contrast exists between two opposing forces. On one side, we observe the continuous development and refinements of the CoE enforcement mechanism, and the ECtHR's ability to devise innovative solutions in response to democratic backsliding. On the other side, we see an increasing threat to democracy across Europe and some states' reluctance to comply with the Court's decisions (either directly or indirectly) and instances of confrontational struggles between certain states and both the Court and CoE institutions. This dichotomy highlights the tension between the evolving human rights protection framework and the resistance it faces from some Member States, creating a complex and scary landscape for the future of human rights in Europe.

1.1. An Endless Institutional Adjustment

All the institutions of the CoE have had to make constant adjustments in order to cope with the procedural overload which the Court has experienced (particularly since its eastern enlargement), taking seriously the 'compliance problem'. These constant adjustments have been brought about both by political approaches taken by the Member States themselves, with the support of the CoE institutions (Section 1.1.1), and by a jurisprudential policy of the Court, which has been able to use both its regulatory power and its praetorian capacity to deal with its procedural overload on the one hand and the democratic decline on the other (Section 1.1.2).

[7] P Rosanvallon, *Le siècle du populisme: histoire, théorie, critique* (Paris, Seuil, 2020).

1.1.1. The Political Adjustment

The enforcement mechanisms devised in 'serene' times have been gradually modified in order to cope with structural difficulties in Europe.

The structural congestion of the ECtHR is a major challenge since the enlargement of the CoE to eastern states and the clear rebellion of illiberal and authoritarian states since the 2010s. In such a context, it was thus imperative to be flexible: the CoE enforcement mechanism has been gradually modified, either by the boldness of case law or by the power of treaty reform. Have these changes reached the Holy Grail of effectiveness? Globally, the answer – as the developments below will demonstrate – is not positive.

The system has entrusted the intergovernmental body of the CoE, the Committee of Ministers (CM), with supervising the execution of the ECtHR decisions (Articles 46, paragraph 2 ECHR) as well as its friendly settlements (Article 39, paragraph 4 ECHR as amended by Protocol No 14). Over time, this initial scheme has considerably evolved. The reason for this is that both the Court and the Committee of Ministers were struggling with too many cases: the former had too many cases to handle efficiently, the latter also faced difficulties when it came to supervising the cases. In this context, the Parliamentary Assembly (PACE) has not hesitated to serve, as usual, as a spur, if not quite as a countervailing force,[8] to compel the CM to overhaul its working methods in the name of the imperative demands of efficiency and transparency.[9] The latter welcomed this stimulus[10] and officially integrated the parliamentary body into the institutional machinery. In the end, the chemistry between the two major political institutions of the CoE and the Court has been really outstanding. In the same vein, it can be observed a judicialisation of the control of the execution.[11] The original *summa divisio*, which consisted of a watertight separation of the respective functions of the Court (judging) and the Committee (supervising), was shattered under the weight of constraints. The burden on the European system was such that, from 2000 on, it was the CM itself that called for cooperation (even for help) by means of a very explicit resolution.[12]

The ECtHR took the states at their word and, in 2004, began to modify its traditional approach to the measures ordered. With the *Broniowski* judgment,[13] it launched the particularly original figure of the 'pilot judgment', institutionalised 11 years later by means of an amendment to its rules of procedure,[14] in the wake of an explicit invitation

[8] The Parliamentary Assembly, by getting involved in execution, exercises de facto parliamentary control over the action of the Committee of Ministers. See A Drzemczewski, 'The Parliamentary Assembly's Involvement in the Supervision of the Judgments of the Strasbourg Court' (2010) 28 *NQHR* 164.

[9] E Lambert-Abdelgawab, *Le contrôle de l'exécution des arrêts de la Cour européenne (Human Rights File No 19)* 2nd edn (Strasbourg, Council of Europe Publishing, 2008) 61.

[10] Committee of Ministers, Declaration of 19 May 2006; Parliamentary Assembly, Resolution 1516 (2006) of 2 October 2006, *Implementation of judgments of the European Court*, para 4 (which mentions the official support of the intergovernmental body).

[11] L-A Sicilianos, 'The Involvement of the ECHR in the Implementation of its Judgments: Recent Developments under Article 46 ECHR' (2017) 32 *Netherland Quarterly of Human Rights* 235.

[12] Committee of Ministers, Resolution, 12 May 2004 (Res (2004) 3).

[13] ECtHR (GC), App no 31443/96 *Broniowski v Poland* ECLI:CE:ECHR:2004:0622JUD003144396.

[14] The new Rule 61 of the Court's Rules of Procedure, which was added on 21 February 2011, sets out in great detail (taking up ten paragraphs) a procedure whose purpose, in addition to enabling the Court to manage its workload, is to assist the 46 States Parties to the Convention in resolving 'systemic or structural

from the states to do so.[15] The idea is simple: to assist the CM in its supervisory task by identifying cases that point up serious structural problems.[16]

The original approach, whereby states were free to choose how to fulfil their obligations under Article 46, paragraph 1 ECHR,[17] was clearly abandoned.[18] The pilot judgments enabled the Court to require national authorities to create new legal remedies and, in the process, to keep many cases of the same type at the domestic level. In Italy[19] and Belgium,[20] it identified serious problems of prison overcrowding; in Hungary[21] and Bulgaria,[22] it pointed to the systemic slowness of judicial procedures, while in Russia, it highlighted systemic violence against women.[23] On each occasion, it reiterated the need for two types of remedy – preventive and compensatory – noting that the former were more relevant to issues of judicial delay.

In parallel with the synergy between the CM and the ECtHR to address systemic problems, the states decided to add new paragraphs to Article 46 ECHR to give the Court a specific role in the 'failure to fulfil obligations' procedure, as it is known.[24] This new role establishes a rather subtle dividing line with the CM, which is still the official institution in charge of the monitoring procedure.[25] In its *Bochan* judgment, the Court played a pedagogical role and recalled the principles that applied in this area.[26] If an

problems' (or 'similar malfunctioning') at the national level, as well as to provide individuals with a more rapid remedy to their situation.

[15] The new Rule 61 of the Rules of Procedure is a direct consequence of an 'invitation' from the States, made in the Interlaken Declaration of 19 February 2010, to the Court 'to develop clear and predictable standards for the 'pilot judgment' procedure as regards selection of applications, the procedure to be followed and the treatment of adjourned cases.'

[16] ECtHR (GC), App no 31443/96 *Broniowski v Poland* ECLI:CE:ECHR:2004:0622JUD003144396, paras 190–94.

[17] ECtHR (GC), App nos 39221/98 and 41963/98 *Scozarri and Giunta v Italy* ECLI:CE:ECHR:2000:0713JUD003922198, para 249.

[18] A Donald, AK Speck, 'The European Court of Human Rights' Remedial Practice and its Impact on the Execution of Judgment' (2019) 19 *Human Rights Law Review* 83.

[19] ECtHR, App nos 43517/09, 46882/09, 55400/09 et al *Torregiani v Italy* ECLI:CE:ECHR:2013:0108JUD004351709.

[20] ECtHR, App no 64682/12 *Vasilescu v Belgium* ECLI:CE:ECHR:2014:1125JUD006468212.

[21] ECtHR, App no 48322/12 *Gazcó v Hungary* ECLI:CE:ECHR:2015:0716JUD004832212.

[22] ECtHR, App nos 48059/06 and 2708/09 *Dimitrov and Hamanov v Bulgaria* ECLI:CE:ECHR:2011:0510JUD004805906.

[23] ECtHR, App nos 55974/16 et al *Tunikova v Russia* ECLI:CE:ECHR:2021:1214JUD005597416.

[24] Since the entry into force of Protocol 14, the scope of Article 46 has been considerably expanded. Entitled 'Binding force and execution of judgments', it reads as follows in its entirety: '1. The High Contracting Parties undertake to abide by the final judgment of the Court in any case to which they are parties. 2. The final judgment of the Court shall be transmitted to the Committee of Ministers, which shall supervise its execution. 3. If the Committee of Ministers considers that the supervision of the execution of a final judgment is hindered by a problem of interpretation of the judgment, it may refer the matter to the Court for a ruling on the question of interpretation. A referral decision shall require a majority vote of two thirds of the representatives entitled to sit on the Committee. 4. If the Committee of Ministers considers that a High Contracting Party refuses to abide by a final judgment in a case to which it is a party, it may, after serving formal notice on that Party and by decision adopted by a majority vote of two thirds of the representatives entitled to sit on the Committee, refer to the Court the question whether that Party has failed to fulfil its obligation under paragraph 1. 5. If the Court finds a violation of paragraph 1, it shall refer the case to the Committee of Ministers for consideration of the measures to be taken. If the Court finds no violation of paragraph 1, it shall refer the case to the Committee of Ministers, which shall close its examination of the case.'

[25] G Malinverni, 'La compétence de la Cour pour surveiller l'exécution de ses propres arrêts' in *Mélanges en l'honneur de Christos L Rozakis* (Brussels, Bruylant, 2011).

[26] ECtHR (GC), App no 22251/08 *Bochan v Ukraine No 2* ECLI:CE:ECHR:2015:0205JUD002225108.

application is submitted on the basis of the new paragraphs 4 and 5 of Article 46 ECHR related to the infringement proceedings, which allow the Committee to refer a case to the Court for a finding of non-compliance with one of its judgments, then the latter's competence cannot be challenged.[27] If, on the other hand, an application is made outside this legal framework, the question of compliance by states with the Court's judgments falls, in principle, outside its competence and is left to the Committee of Ministers.

1.1.2. The Praetorian Adjustment

The ECtHR has demonstrated its capacity for praetorian adjustment in two critical areas. First, tackling its own case backlog; second, countering threats to judicial independence. These self-initiated adaptations illustrate the ECtHR's ability to evolve its practices and jurisprudence in the face of both internal operational challenges and external threats to democratic principles.

The Court has implemented innovative measures to manage and reduce the overwhelming number of pending cases, thereby improving its efficiency and effectiveness. A 'Court that matters' – this is the new motto launched on 17 March 2021 by the ECtHR in order to present its new procedural strategy. This new methodology is built on and aims to strengthen the priority policy created ten years ago in 2009 and reinforced in 2017. In a nutshell, it is creating a new category of priority cases called 'impact cases' (category IV-High) which are not raising violations of 'core rights' (Articles 2, 3, 4, 5 paragraph 1, ECHR), but raise very important issues of relevance for the defendant State and/or the Convention system as a whole. The Court gives three indications in order for the members of the registry to identify those cases, with the help of IT resources. Those cases: (1) might lead to a change or clarification of international or domestic legislation or practice; (2) touch upon moral or social issues; (3) deal with an emerging or otherwise significant human rights issue. Once these criteria are met, it is striking to note that the Court will take into account the 'whether the case has had significant media coverage domestically and/or is politically sensitive'.[28]

In response to the alarming erosion of judicial autonomy in illiberal states, the Court has developed new legal approaches and interpretations to safeguard the rule of law. It has not hesitated to deploy a wealth of imagination to counter the manoeuvres of the illiberal executives to put under their control justice systems, being in tune with the

[27] ECtHR (GC), App no 15172/13 *Article 46 para 4 Proceedings in Ilgar Mammadov v Azerbaijan* ECLI:CE:ECHR:2019:0529JUD001517213. ECtHR (GC), App no 28749/18 *Article 46 para 4 Proceedings in Kavala v Türkiye* ECLI:CE:ECHR:2022:0711JUD002874918. In the latter case, the Court recalls 'infringement proceedings should therefore be viewed as a measure of last resort, where the Committee of Ministers considers that the other means to secure the execution of a judgment have ultimately proved unsuccessful and are no longer adapted to the situation. Moreover, infringement proceedings are not intended to upset the fundamental institutional balance between the Court and the Committee of Ministers … The right to initiate a referral is a procedural prerogative which comes within the responsibility of the Committee of Ministers. In consequence, where this procedure has been duly initiated, it is not the Court's task to express a view on the desirability of such a decision by the Committee of Ministers' (para 129).

[28] L Burgorgue-Larsen, 'Op-Ed, The European Court of Human Rights at a crossroads. Some thought about the new motto "A Court that matters"' (*EU Law Live*, 8 April 2021) https://eulawlive.com/op-ed-the-european-court-of-human-rights-at-a-crossroads-some-thought-about-the-new-motto-a-court-that-matters-by-laurence-burgorgue-larsen/ accessed 1 April 2025.

ECJ case law. It has developed a new interpretation of Article 6, paragraph 1 ECHR – in the groundbreaking *Astroasson* judgment[29] – relating to the right to a fair trial. And to consider that the expression 'tribunal established by law' includes the question of the appointment process, which must be free from political interference. The ECtHR applied this important standard to Polish cases.[30]

As can be seen, the various bodies that make up the European system for the protection of human rights have adapted to developments in Europe. On the one hand, the aim has been to improve the monitoring of the execution of the Court's judgments (to make it easier for States to enforce them) and, in the long term, to reduce the Court's backlog of cases (which has an indirect impact on the compliance issue); on the other hand, the aim has been to combat, through case law, the management of the prioritisation of cases and the very specific signs of judicial tutelage in many Eastern European countries.

In spite of all these efforts, the question of the execution of the judgments of the Court by States which do not comply with Article 3 of the Statute of the Council of Europe shows a clear failure. But how could it be otherwise when we know the nature of those States that do not act in good faith?

1.2. An Endless 'Bad Faith' Approach from Illiberal States

In the field of international relations, theories are constantly being developed to explain why States comply (or fail to comply) with international law: there is an institutionalist approach on the one hand and the defenders of a realist vision on the other.[31] Very often, in the political praxis, these two rationales are present and intertwined. Today, while liberal democracies are generally not reluctant to implement the Court's rulings, the existential problem comes from the illiberal and authoritarian states which are part of the CoE. The Annex at the end of this chapter illustrates these different categories by presenting the elements that allow them to be identified. These States are 'bad players' (Section 1.2.1) because they are not acting in 'good faith' anymore, which highlights the existence of very sensitive issues (Section 1.2.2).

1.2.1. Identifying the 'Bad Players'

If liberal democracies are not perfect, if they can resist certain rulings of the ECtHR[32] – it is a fact that today the problem of execution comes from countries that have taken

[29] ECtHR (GC), App no 26374/18 *Guðmundur Andri Ástráðsson v Iceland* ECLI:CE:ECHR:2020:1201JUD002637418.

[30] See, eg, ECtHR, App no 4907/18 *Xero Flor in Poland sp c Poland* ECLI:CE:ECHR:2021:0507JUD000490718.

[31] The former believe in the positive effects of being a member state of an international organisation: joining with full knowledge of the facts, with a view to pursuing common objectives and developing harmonious approaches, helps to apply international law; in short, the benefits of inter-state cooperation outweigh those of defending sovereign egoisms. The latter believe only in the legitimacy and strength of States, driven solely by their national interests, which boil down to imposing their power and ensuring their security. Therefore, if a State adheres to a system for protecting human rights, it is because it is forced to do so by one or more powerful States.

[32] I do not need to recall the epic confrontations between the UK and the European Court after the *Hirst* ruling; or between France and the European Court after the *Kress* ruling, etc.

an illiberal or authoritarian turn. The identification of these 'bad' or, more precisely, 'dangerous' actors has been made by the CM (as well as by the PACE in their respective roles). The CM has pointed out that Ukraine, Romania, Turkey, Azerbaijan and Hungary have the highest number of unexecuted Court judgments and still face serious structural or complex problems, in some cases for more than ten years. Together with Russia, these five countries account for more than 70 per cent of the cases awaiting execution.

Some of these States are illiberal democracies (Hungary, Romania), some are authoritarian states (Azerbaijan, Turkey, Russia) and one is a complete failure state, known for its high level of corruption and trying to survive against Russian aggression since February 2022 (Ukraine). For political reasons, these countries – including Russia before its expulsion – consider that it is (still) in their interest to be part of the CoE and under the control of the Court. On the one hand, they continue to reap the symbolic benefits of membership in Europe's largest organisation in terms of prestige. On the other hand, they are deploying their new anti-liberal vision of democracy, accepting the rulings of the ECtHR only when they do not challenge what they consider to be the core of their identity and/or the main features of their political agenda. Beyond this official identification of 'bad players' by the Committee of Ministers of the Council of Europe, there are obviously illiberal states that, in a more subtle and strategic manner, have not entered into frontal opposition with the obligation of execution, but are particularly ambivalent towards it. While the illiberal Polish government of PiS has destroyed judicial independence and played for time in not executing the Court's judgments, which ultimately forced it to adopt a pilot judgment,[33] the case of North Macedonia is also topical. This illiberal country, eager to join the EU and wanting to project an image of a model student, has been more respectful, in a purely strategic manner, of the obligation to execute judgments.[34]

1.2.2. Identifying the Sensitive Issues

When analysing European jurisprudence, three very sensitive areas demonstrate the very dangerous illiberal and dictatorial shift in Europe: the growing number of inter-state disputes as well as Article 18 ECHR cases (on 'Limitation on use of restrictions on rights'); and, last but not least, the impressive threat to judicial independence. From a compliance perspective, these three areas highlight impressive, not to say impossible, challenges for the ECtHR.

The number of inter-state applications lodged before the Court has recently significantly increased. There are currently 19 inter-state applications pending before the Court, 12 of which have been lodged since 2020.[35] The implementation of inter-state cases or cases linked to post-conflict situations or unresolved conflicts in general takes time and requires a 'concerted engagement' by the CM and its Secretariat, as well as the Member States concerned. This process can be difficult due to the prominent political

[33] This point is illustrated through the analysis in the Annex of the *Walesa* case.
[34] This point is also clearly illustrated in the case presented in the index.
[35] To put this in context, the Court and the former Commission only ever completed 25 interstate cases (including those struck off the list).

dimensions at national or international level and the fact that they are linked to traumatic armed violence requiring a long period of healing. The challenges on that matter are numerous when we know that about 15 per cent of all individual cases pending before the Court stemmed from an armed conflict and many of them overlapped with inter-state cases, which raised the question of how those cases should be processed; that inter-states cases required a lot of fact-finding, whereas the resources of the Court were limited, and that is not easy to identify victims of violations in such cases etc. It would be absolutely necessary for the Council of Europe to develop tools for dealing with interstate cases and for facilitating the implementation of the relevant judgments. Creative thinking is needed.

The Article 18 ECHR judgments point out the non-democratic nature of the State defendants. Indeed, human rights violations occur in pursuit of an 'unlawful ulterior purpose'. This ulterior purpose, such as the 'stifling of democracy and pluralism' is not present under other Convention articles. As such, when the Court finds a violation of this provision,[36] it is a warning sign of an attack against democracy and the rule of law. The first Article 18 ECHR judgment was the relatively recent 2004 case Gusinksy v Russia.[37] Since then, cases have involved the detention of opposition politicians, human rights defenders,[38] lawyers and journalists in Ukraine, Russia, Azerbaijan and Türkiye. However, Article 18 is not restricted to detention cases – there are also travel bans and recent cases relating to politically-motivated disciplinary proceedings of judges in Poland and Bulgaria.[39]

As for the question of judicial independence, there is no longer a need to explain the mechanisms by which illiberal regimes in the East use the law to destroy the fundamental elements of liberal democracy.[40] This institutionalised illiberalism in Eastern Europe[41] – which places the entire judiciary, including constitutional courts, under the control of the executive – continues to produce a series of findings of violations of Article 6 § 1 ECHR, particularly against Poland.[42]

[36] Although the number of violations of Article 18 is not quantitatively high (given the very strict case law policy developed by the Court), their mere existence is a worrying indicator of democratic decline in Europe, see CM, *Annual Report 2023, Supervision of the Execution of Judgements and decisions of the ECtHR 2023*, Council of Europe, April 2024, 25.

[37] ECtHR, App no 70276/01 *Gusinsky v Russia* ECLI:CE:ECHR:2004:0519JUD007027601.

[38] The *Kavala 'saga'* shows perfectly how the domestic authorities (including the judiciary) are not keen to take seriously the obligation of Article 46(1) ECHR, see the *Annex D Authoritarian States*.

[39] The ECtHR has developed a solid jurisprudence in relation to Article 18 cases establishing criteria permitting its activation. There must be: (1) a significant time gap between the sets of events (for example many years between the alleged facts and the acts of the prosecution); (2) the quality of the totality of evidence (for example if lawful activities are criminalised); (3) the conduct of the applicant in the criminal process; and (4) temporal inferences between how politicians approached the framing of a case and the framing of the indictment.

[40] It is a well-known and documented trend.

[41] Scholars have highlighted the powerful manifestation of illiberalism in Eastern Europe (eg, G Halmai, 'Illiberalism in East-Central Europe' (2019) EUI Law Working Paper 2019/05 https://hdl.handle.net/1814/64967 accessed 1 April 2025). It goes without saying that the process of democratic deconsolidation can equally affect democracies in the western part of the continent or, more generally, in the Western world, as demonstrated by D Trump's second term.

[42] After numerous cases dealt with by chambers of seven judges (the first of which was delivered in 2021 (ECtHR, App no 4907/18 *Xero Flor w Plsce sp Z oo v Poland* ECLI:CE:ECHR:2021:0507JUD000490718) and followed by many others (ECHR, App no 43447/19 *Reczkowicz v Poland* ECLI:CE:ECHR:2021:0722JUD004344719; ECHR, App nos 49868/19 and 57511/19 *Dolińska-Ficek and Ozimek v Poland* ECLI:

1.3. Identifying Strategies of Non-compliance

When we look at the question of non-compliance, we find that fragile democracies, illiberal democracies and dictatorships have an extremely wide range of strategies, from outright refusal (marking a deliberate desire not to comply with Article 46(1) ECHR on 'Binding force and execution of judgments') to much more subtle forms that play for time, for a dialogue that turns out to be a fool's bargain.

The *Kavala* case in Turkey, the *Sedjic* case in Bosnia[43] and the whole Polish dispute show a very clear political will not to respect the obligations arising from Article 46(1) ECHR. In these various cases, on the one hand, the executive and parliamentary authorities refuse to comply with a court ruling on a highly sensitive issue (*Sedjic* case in Bosnia-Herzegovina) and on the other hand, the judicial authorities are no longer independent and pass on the doxa of the executive branch by issuing rulings that are completely at odds with the requirements of Article 46 § 1 ECHR (Poland and Turkey).

In a recent article, Ula Aleksandra Kos brilliantly demonstrates the various strategies developed by Victor Orban's party after 2010 to short-circuit and undermine the Court's authority and not to enforce the most sensitive rulings against Hungary, ie those that challenge the very identity of the anti-liberal vulgate.[44] So, Ula Kos identifies several strategies: avoidance;[45] disguised non-compliance;[46] and building a narrative for domestic audience.[47] These kinds of strategies are extremely dangerous because, at first

CE:ECHR:2021:1108JUD004986819; ECHR, App no 1469/20 *Advance Pharma sp Z oo v Poland* ECLI:CE:ECHR:2022:0203JUD000146920; ECHR, App nos 21181/19 and 51751/20 *Tuleya v Poland* ECLI:CE:ECHR:2023:0706JUD002118119); the Grand Chamber (ECtHR (GC), App no 43572/18 *Grzeda v Poland* ECLI:CE:ECHR:2022:0315JUD004357218) has unequivocally confirmed the misuse of the law to create a judicial system 'under orders', as well as in the Pilot judgment *Walesa* (ECHR, App no 50849/21 *Walesa v Poland* ECLI:CE:ECHR:2023:1123JUD005084921). See *Annex C Illiberal States.*

[43] See *Annex B States in Post-conflict Situations.*

[44] UA Kos, 'Controlling the Narrative: Hungary's Post-2010 Strategies of Non-Compliance before the European Court of Human Right' (2023) 19 *European Constitutional Law Review* 195.

[45] ibid 203: 'The first strategy relates to a striking increase in Hungary's use of alternative instruments (friendly settlements and unilateral declarations) after 2010, which, according to my analysis, today represent more than 50% of all of its cases before the Court.' (…) 'From this, it is apparent that Hungary has profited from the European Court of Human Rights' incentive structure, encouraging alternative instruments. This has ultimately allowed the state to be fully in control of whether to enter or avoid Court proceedings. In the long run, such avoidance of Court's jurisdiction and denial of its power to set precedential binding judgments may also lead to a diminishment of the Court's authority in Hungary.' (208).

[46] ibid 208: 'Such behaviour effectively deflects the attention of the intervening body, neutralises its authority and returns the relationship to the status quo. Legal and public administration academia traced similar patterns in what they term as symbolic or creative compliance, whereby states offer "merely rhetorical lip service to formal obligations" or adopt "intentionally perfunctory measures that are only intended to mask a government's true intention not to comply". In this context, the author find that Hungary engages in two types of attention-deflecting behaviour, intended for an international audience: "autocratic legalism": his phenomenon relates to non-liberal governments seeking to benefit from the superficial appearance of democracy and legality, whilst in fact they are circumventing and abusing the constitutional and (inter)national legal constraints)' (209). The 'copy-past strategy': the state regularly submits to the Committee reports that contain copy and pasted parts of previous reports already submitted in the case (referred to as 'copy-paste reports'). The aim of this is to conceal the lack of actual progress in the implementation of the judgment.

[47] ibid: 'the third strategy relates to Hungary's seeking to build its own narrative about the Court to subvert the opinion of the domestic audience … First, curbing public opinion plays a role in delegitimising international adjudication. Second, public opinion is moveable and as such a popular target of resisting governments' strategies to embed criticism of international tribunals into the regular mainstream domestic discourse, public life and politics.'

sight, they are not visible and, subsequently, a cause of concern; but in the end, they completely undermine the functioning of the system and lead to its profound disqualification and ineffectiveness.

2. Conclusion

2.1. An Endless Challenge: The Illiberal and Authoritarian 'Bad Faith' Problem

Despite the remarkable adaptability of all the actors in the CoE, the situation of compliance is far from satisfactory, as the High-Level Expert Report[48] and the very important Reykjavik Declaration have highlighted.[49]

The latter is presented as a series of solemn affirmations in which the mantra of a Union of Heads of State and Government is articulated around four main ideas ('united for Ukraine and responsibility; 'united around our values'; 'united to meet present and future challenges'; 'united in our vision of the Council of Europe'); each of these ideas has been detailed in four more detailed appendices.[50] For those who follow the workings, or rather the dysfunctions, of the European conventional system, Annex IV (on 'Recommitting to the Convention system as the cornerstone of human rights protection at the Council of Europe') is nothing new. Budgetary problems and the emblematic non-execution of politically sensitive judgments, particularly in inter-state cases, are matters of common knowledge. While Russia is singled out in the document, Turkey and Azerbaijan are not, of course, mentioned.

As a compromise text, it could not expressly point the finger at two influential member states, the former being a major contributor to the organisation's budget. While the rhetoric of 'synergy' between the Council's various institutions and of 'political dialogue' between the CoE and the States resurfaces in order to ensure better execution of judgments, nothing is said about the major cause of this state of affairs: the structural bad faith of recalcitrant States, which have strictly no interest in complying with the

[48] *Report of the High-Level Reflection Group of the Council of Europe*, October 2022, p 43, at p 47 – Chairperson, Mrs Mary Robinson, Mr Evangelos Venizelos, Rapporteur, Mr Bernard Cazeneuve, Mr Josep Dallerrès, Ms Ine Marie Eriksen Søreide, Ms Federica Mogherini, Ms Iveta Radičová.

[49] Reykjavik Declaration, *United Around Our Values*, CoE, June 2023, p 24. The Heads of State and Government therefore succeeded in organising an extraordinary Summit in Reykjavik on 16 and 17 May 2023, to close the Icelandic Presidency; the fourth of its kind in the history of the CoE, following those held in Vienna (1993), Strasbourg (1997) and Warsaw (2005). In Austria, the end of the division of the European continent was celebrated, while in France, the enlargement of the Council of Europe was analysed as an opportunity for greater European security. The tone had changed in Poland. The attacks of 11 September 2001 had altered the world's geopolitical balance, while the revolutions in Georgia (2003) and Ukraine (2004) – protesting against widespread corruption and growing authoritarianism – had brought to light the democratic gaps that exist on European soil, see A Donald, P Leach, 'Responding to Seismic Change in Europe: The Road to Reykjavik and Beyond' (2023) *European Human Rights Law Review* 95.

[50] Annexes IV ('Recommitting to the Convention system as the cornerstone of human rights protection at the Council of Europe') and V ('The Council of Europe and the environment') address new priorities in the functioning of the pan-European organisation, as well as new directions for dealing with what the document calls the 'triple planetary crisis, linked to pollution, climate change and the loss of biodiversity' (Annex V, preamble).

Court's judgments when the latter requires them to release rights defenders or when it encourages them to respect the rights of political and sexual minorities.

In 2024, the political heterogeneity of the CoE is undoubtedly its Achilles heel; in 1949, when it was created, its greatest strength was the democratic homogeneity of its founding states. Will the CoE enforcement mechanism be effective at a time when happy globalisation is collapsing, when attacks on the institutions of multilateralism are legion and, above all, when certain member states of the CoE – illiberal and authoritarian states – have no regard for the foundations of liberal democracy and the rulings of the Court? How can such objectives be achieved when, in reality, the Union for Democracy barely conceals disunity, not to say disaffection; when the pan-European organisation is no longer homogeneous, and oppressive states are part of it? These questions are crucial when we consider that illiberal and authoritarian states have managed to elect judges who, through their separate opinions, have demonstrated that their independence is rather relative.[51] In this context, scholars must continue, with perspective and critical thinking, to scrutinise both the national nomination process and the European election process. Above all, civil society, still too timid on this point, must act more boldly, including in long-standing democracies that are not at all immune to an illiberal shift (particularly to the far right), as evidenced by Giorgia Meloni's Italy.

Europe is at an existential moment in its history: it is now heterogeneous, encompassing illiberal and authoritarian states alongside democratic ones, and the many instruments created over time are showing their ineffectiveness. Even if the power of imagination were to create new procedures – for example to strengthen relations with national human rights institutions and national parliaments – there are legitimate doubts about their effectiveness in the face of some states that no longer act in good faith.

Annex – Case Studies Pointing Out the Nature of the States

In order to quantify the extreme heterogeneity in the application of ECtHR judgments and to provide a more detailed and precise picture, it was considered interesting to go beyond constitutional design and to take into account the nature of the states concerned.

Indeed, it is striking to note that the European continent shows a very nuanced landscape between strong (old) and fragile (new) democracies (A), post-conflict states (B), illiberal states (C) as well as authoritarian states (D), far from the classic statement that the enforcement of international human rights law in Europe is generally a great success. This rhetoric is no longer true. The classification presented is based on elements established in doctrine, generally in the field of political science.

The divide between old and fragile democracies is based on the theory of democratic consolidation.[52] Older democracies generally have more stable institutions, while new democracies face consolidation challenges. Democratic consolidation is a process that

[51] See the analyses in the Annex of Polish and Turkish cases.
[52] A Schedler, 'What is Democratic Consolidation?' (1998) 9 *Journal of Democracy* 91.

follows democratic transition, aiming to ensure the sustainability and stability of the newly established democratic regime.

As for the post-conflict states, this category is based on the concept of 'post-conflict reconstruction'.[53] It is a multidimensional process aimed at transforming military conflicts into non-violent political conflicts and strengthening structures that solidify peace to prevent a return to conflict. This process involves diplomatic, military, and social reconstruction actions.

It is the seminal article of Fareed Zacharia, published in Foreign Affairs in 1997 – 'The Rise of Illiberal Democracy' – which pointed out a new trend where an elected government slowly destroys all the key elements of liberal democracies. The main features of this category are the destruction of checks and balances and the separation of powers, the erosion of judicial independence, the restriction on civil liberties (particularly freedom of press and expression), the emphasis on majoritarian rule over protection of minority rights, the centralisation of power in the executive branch and the manipulation of constitutional and legal frameworks to consolidate power.

The boundary with authoritarian states is sometimes difficult to establish as many of the same characteristics prevail. However, one distinctive sign appears in the domain of rights restriction, where repression against political opponents very often takes the form of violations of their physical integrity (death, torture, forced disappearances).

As for the cases chosen to illustrate these different categories, it stems from several years of analysing the European Court's judgments, which have been the subject of a case law chronicle in the Actualité juridique de droit administratif (AJDA) since 2011. As a result, based on my knowledge of the cases combined with the classifications presented, I was able to select cases that I considered emblematic.

A. Old (Strong) and New (Fragile) Democracies

1. *Old Democracies*

Iceland[54]

ECtHR, *Guðmundur Andri Ástráðsson v Iceland* (12 March 2019)

ECtHR, (GC) *Guðmundur Andri Ástráðsson v Iceland* (1 December 2020)

The Case

The facts of this case show that the applicant challenged his conviction on the grounds that the court that handed down the sentence had not been duly 'established by law'

[53] Y Jabareen, 'Conceptualizing "Post-Conflict Reconstruction" and Ongoing Conflict Reconstruction of Failed States' (2013) 26 *International Journal of Politics* 107.

[54] This country is quite singular, it does not count more than 355.000 inhabitants and has obtained its total independence towards Denmark, only in 1944 when the Republic of Iceland was established. Iceland signed the European Convention on 4 November 1950 and ratified it very quickly in 1953 (29 June). Is not part of the EU, despite some political negotiations launched around 2010. Many provisions of the Icelandic Constitution no 33/1944 (17 June 1944) are based on the Convention and are interpreted in light of the Convention and the Court's case law (ad Ex Supreme Court of 5 February 2021, case No 9/2020, where the Supreme Court referenced and based its decision on the case law of the Court regarding the balance between the right to free speech and the right to privacy (Articles 8 and 10 ECHR).

within the meaning of Article 6, paragraph 1 ECHR. At issue was the method of appointment of one of the judges of the new Icelandic Court of Appeal, which has been operational since 2018 who ruled on his case. It is topical to note that the Supreme Court recognised the irregularity of the mode of appointment of the judge in question, because of an interference of the executive power as well as the legislative power, but did not infer from it the unfairness of the trial. This case has triggered two decisions: the first one by the Second Section of the Court (eg, a seven chamber judgment);[55] the second one by the Grand Chamber due to the government's will to decide the referral before it.[56]

First Judgment (2019)

It is interesting to note that the Icelandic Supreme Court and the two dissenting judges of the European Court were on the same wavelength, the latter emphasising the importance of the principle of subsidiarity. The majority of the Second Section of the Court was not so inclined. It held, on the other hand, that in the event of a 'flagrant breach of domestic law' (paragraph 101), in particular when a court has not been established 'in accordance with domestic law' (paragraph 72), a violation of Article 6, paragraph 1 ECHR is at stake, especially when the new selection and appointment rules were put in place to minimise the discretionary power of the executive and to completely reconfigure the Icelandic judicial system (paragrpah 121). The majority valued the importance of the separation of powers in a state governed by the rule of law (paragraph 122) and strongly condemned the fact that the Minister of Justice herself had eliminated from the list of 15 candidates four persons considered to be among the most qualified. Once again, it is the whole confidence in justice that is at stake:

> The process was therefore to the detriment of the confidence that the judiciary in a democratic society must inspire in the public and contravened the very essence of the principle that a tribunal must be established by law, one of the fundamental principles of the rule of law (paragraph 123).

Where the dissenting judges feared a boomerang effect – potentially allowing any convicted person to challenge the appropriateness of his or her conviction on the basis of a manipulation of the method of appointing judges – the majority stuck to principles, in a case that triggered a major political-judicial scandal in Iceland.

Second Judgment (2020)

The recent cases judged by the Court of Justice of the European Union – in which it valued Article 19 paragraph1 TFEU and Article 47 of the Charter of Fundamental Rights in order to face the democratic breakdown in Poland (not CJEU, Gde Ch, 26 March 2020, Simpson and HG, paragraph 74–75 aff Jtes C-542/18 RX-II and C-543/18 RX-II), hover over the entire analysis of the Grand Chamber judgment in *Guðmundur Andri Ástráðsson* (paragraphs 134–39, 228, 239). In this sense, the ECtHR intends to send a very clear signal to Iceland, but obviously also to Poland and to all the States that would venture to undermine the independence of the judiciary, in particular by 'playing' with

[55] ECtHR, App no 26374/18 *Guðmundur Andri Ástráðsson v Iceland* ECLI:CE:ECHR:2020:1201JUD002637418.

[56] ECtHR (GC), App no 26374/18 *Guðmundur Andri Ástráðsson v Iceland* ECLI:CE:ECHR:2019:0312JUD002637418.

the appointment procedures: on this key question as regards the preservation of democratic standards, their interpretative concord is more than ever in evidence. If there was a major subject on which it was necessary not to fuel possible dissonance, it is indeed that of the configuration of judicial independence. The two apex European Courts are up to the challenge here.

In this context, two analytical shifts are noteworthy in this GC ruling. First, the Court states in paragraph 227 that in view of the fundamental consequences that the judicial appointment process has for the proper functioning and legitimacy of the judiciary in a democratic State governed by the rule of law, it necessarily constitutes an inherent element of the concept of a 'tribunal established by law' notion. An interpretation that does not do so would be contrary to the purpose of the requirement that it be so established. To reinforce this assertion, the GC mobilised the consensus approach by pointing out that 'nearly half of the states surveyed (eg, 19 out of 40) interpret the 'tribunal established by law' requirement as clearly encompassing the process of initial appointment of a judge to office. And she stated that it could not ignore this 'clear consensus' (paragraph 228). The next sentence is equally noteworthy. It is an invitation – barely disguised – to the other States in which this question 'has not been decided' so that they may, in principle, interpret the requirement of a 'tribunal established by law' as also encompassing the process of appointing judges (paragraph 229). The Court's message is clear. In any event, this approach is also combined with another analytical innovation, that of the explicit autonomy of the concept of 'tribunal established by law' (paragraph 231) in relation to the two other institutional requirements of Article 6, paragraph 1, namely independence and impartiality, whose very close links the Court attempts to expose (paragraphs 231–34). This new methodological approach, in which inherence and autonomy give the requirement of a 'tribunal established by law' precedence, a sort of prerequisite for a fair trial, upsets all the previously established balances which, if not achieved, would render the examination of the other two aspects useless, as they would be tainted ipso facto by the 'original' violation.

The analytical reconstruction of the dynamics of Article 6, paragraph 1 is a major exercise here. Once the new general framework has been established, it is striking to note the Grand Chamber's desire to constantly find the balance that it considers unavoidable between the enactment of principles and the correlative presentation of limits. Their legitimacy is based on the need to reconcile competing interests. The principle of legal certainty (paragraph 238) and the irremovability of judges during their term of office (paragraph 239) – which it derives from the 'rule of law' like the right to a 'tribunal established by law' – are among them. Believing that a radical approach would be counterproductive, it considers that the right to a court established by law should not be interpreted too broadly, so that any irregularity in the procedure for appointing a judge might infringe this right (recalling here the double dissent presented in the Chamber judgment). As a result, 'a certain restraint is required in this matter', it asserts (paragraph 236). Once this limit has been set, how should it be handled?

This is where a methodological three-steps test comes into play, based on the concept of the seriousness threshold, which will have to be applied by both the Court and the national courts when the time comes (paragraph 243): (1) establish the existence of a 'manifest breach' of domestic law (paragraph 244); (2) analyse the violation in light of the object and purpose of the 'tribunal established by law' requirement; (3) examine the review by the national courts of the legal consequences of a violation of domestic law. Accordingly, the GC applied this newly established three-step test to the facts of the case. The Court held, first, that the breaches of domestic law had been manifest. Second, that they related to fundamental rules of the appointment procedure that went to the very essence of the right. Third, that the Supreme Court failed to draw the necessary conclusions from its own findings and to assess the matter in a Convention-compliant manner. In light of the foregoing, the applicant had been denied his right to a 'tribunal established by law' according to Article 6, paragraph 1 ECHR.

This new three-step test approach was not established entirely serenely, as several dissenting opinions peppered the publication of the judgment with different types of criticism. In this respect, one of the criticisms that ran through the various opinions concerned the paradoxical approach of the GC, which did not fully draw all the consequences of its new method: it refused to order the reopening of the applicant's criminal trial under Article 46 (paragraph 313). As regards general measures, the Court was equally conciliatory, stating: it emphasises that the finding of a violation in this case cannot in itself be seen as imposing an obligation to reopen all similar cases that have since become res judicata under Icelandic law. A relief, certainly, for the government in Reykjavik, the country of Robert Spano, the President at the time of the Court.

Compliance with the Judgment

Two and half years after the GC ruling, on 9 March 2022, the Committee of Ministers decided to close the monitoring of this case in light of the measures taken by the Icelandic authorities.[57] The execution of the judgment has been therefore very quick, the Icelandic authorities taking into account, at the time of the first ruling (2019), the necessity to take some actions, beyond the specific question of just satisfaction.[58] Indeed, although a request by the government to have the case referred to the Grand Chamber had been made, as soon as the Chamber judgment was rendered on 12 March 2019, steps were promptly taken to implement the judgment, which is, in a way, quite paradoxical. The official document from the Committee of Ministers stated that:

> The Minister immediately resigned from office and the operation of the Court of Appeal was completely suspended for one week. The four judges in question ceased to participate in cases and when the Court of Appeal resumed operation it did so with only eleven of the fifteen appointed judges. Provisional arrangements were subsequently made to appoint four judges to serve until 30 June 2020 so as to ensure the functioning of the court. It is evident that the Chamber judgment and subsequently the Grand Chamber judgment have had a big impact in Iceland and has spurred a lively domestic debate.[59]

It is interesting to note that despite the fact that the Court had been conciliatory with Iceland, not requiring all trials to be reopened due to the res judicata principle (paragraph 313, GC ruling), the government has established a new Court on the reopening of Judicial Proceedings (Act N° 47/2020 amending the Act n° 50/2016).

[57] Committee of Minister, Final Resolution CM/ResDH(2022)48, adopted on 9 March 2022.

[58] The Court held that the finding of a violation constituted, in itself, sufficient just satisfaction for any non-pecuniary damage sustained by the applicant. The Court awarded the applicant EUR 20,000 in respect of costs and expenses. On 18 January 2021 the costs and expenses were paid by bank transfer to the applicant's representative.

[59] Secretariat of the Committee of Ministers of the Council of Europe, Document DH-DD (2021)1360, 5.

It is to this new judicial body to evaluate whether a case should be reopened. The new provisions, inter alia, enable a party to a case, who believes it has been wrongly decided, to request that their case be reopened by the Court. This applies to both civil and criminal cases when 'new information' is at stake. The preparatory work explicitly stresses that the concept of 'new information' must be interpreted broadly and that the judgments of international courts, including the Court, fall within the scope of the provision. In this regard, it should be highlighted that preparatory work, in particular clarifications of individual provisions, is given great weight in the interpretation of Icelandic law. Requests for the reopening of judicial proceedings are not subject to any time limits.

Beyond these possibilities and in order to avoid further violations, and to better ensure the integrity of the appointment procedure and to prevent future reoccurrences, the Ministry of Justice has developed guidelines on the relevant steps a minister must take when considering departing from the suggestions of the Evaluation Committee which has the task of assessing the qualification of judicial candidates. The guidelines have been approved by the Ministry of Justice. The guidelines include steps about the investigation, assessment, due reasons, and communication with the Committee and Parliament.

Belgium

ECtHR (GC), *Mugemangango v Belgium* (10 July 2020)

The *Mugemangango* judgment[60] is an important ruling, emblematic of the era of subsidiarity (as theorised by the former President Robert Spano). At a time when the States are increasingly distrustful, when they have seized the third-party intervention card to make the Court aware of their particularities, the Court cannot 'pretend' that such a context does not exist. On 10 July 2020, 17 judges meeting in the Grand Chamber decided to acknowledge the conventionality of a surprising Belgian constitutional singularity, while unanimously condemning the State for violation of Article 3 of Protocol No 1 and Article 13 ECHR. How did it arrive at this paradoxical prima facie solution? A short lesson in comparative electoral law is in order.

Following the example of five other northern European countries (Denmark, Iceland, Luxembourg, Norway and the Netherlands), appeals challenging the regularity of elections in Belgium are decided by parliamentary bodies. These legal traditions are certainly in the minority in the European constitutional landscape. In fact, 33 states provide for judicial review, either directly (14 states) or as a second instance (19 states). In this sensitive area, which reveals the construction of national specificities over a long period of time, the Court did not in any way mobilise the classic mechanisms relating to the functioning of the national margin of appreciation – the extent of which (broad or narrow) – is known to depend on the existence or not of a European consensus. It did not want to question the incompetence of the national courts – including the Constitutional Court – with regard to the capacity of parliamentary assemblies to assess post-election disputes. The Belgian guardian of the Constitution considers that the rule according to

[60] It was delivered after the relinquishment by the Chamber of seven judges.

which the elected legislative assemblies, in the exercise of their mission, have the greatest possible independence, is part of the basic principles of the democratic structure of the State. In this context, it also considers that this independence is expressed, among other things, in the control that they exercise over their members, both as regards the validity of the mandate and the manner in which it is acquired through election. For the Belgian Constitutional Court, the absence of judicial control is thus intended to guarantee the independence of the legislative assemblies from the other powers.

In such a context, the European Court did not want to interfere in such constitutional architecture. Let us be the judge. With regard to the claim of violation of Article 3 of Protocol No 1, the applicant's allegations were simple. Participating in the 2014 Walloon parliamentary elections, he lost the chance to be elected by 14 votes, as head of the list of his political party PTB-GO! (Workers' Party of Belgium). He asked for a recount of the ballots. The Credentials Committee agreed with him, recognising that the irregularities found were serious and could have changed the outcome of the election, but it had only advisory powers. The opinion it issued was not followed in the end by the Walloon Parliament, the only decision-making body. According to the petitioner, things were clear: the

> power of decision in this case belonged solely to the Walloon Parliament, that is to say, to members of parliament whose election could be called into question if the complaint was declared to be well-founded and who had an interest directly opposed to his own, since they belonged to other political parties. The members of the Walloon parliament therefore had a direct and personal interest in the solution of the dispute. Thus, …, the only open recourse was decided by a body that was both judge and party and did not present any guarantees of impartiality (para 53).

There were several ways of approaching the problem: the demanding one of asking whether the absence of a judicial remedy (particularly at second instance) was, in itself, contrary to Article 3 of Protocol No 1; the minimal one of examining whether, in casu, the existing system complied with certain procedural obligations. The first option, although demanding, was nevertheless delicate with regard to the susceptibility of States to their legal traditions. This is quickly realised when reading the Belgian government's defence and Denmark's third-party intervention. The former, in addition to highlighting the technical advantage of an exclusively parliamentary control – 'built on the mode of a single and unequivocal recourse, which would be of a nature to reinforce legal security' – mentions above all the 'constitutional heritage of the Belgian State'. It would be the manifestation of 'one of the basic principles of the democratic structure' of the State (paragraph 58), since it is part of a set of provisions aimed at ensuring parliamentary independence. It is understandable that the subject is highly sensitive. Moreover, the mere fact that the chamber of seven judges (Second Section), presided over by R Spano, had relinquished jurisdiction in favour of the Grand Chamber, was already a clear indication of this point.

This was confirmed by the fact that the President of the Grand Chamber had 'invited the Venice Commission' to intervene in the written procedure, whereas he had only 'authorized Denmark to do so' (paragraph 6). This choice of words would imply that the Venice Commission, a veritable compass of democratic standards in Europe, had been solemnly asked to give its point of view on the elements of good governance in the settlement of electoral disputes. In any case, the use of third-party intervention by

Denmark was just as revealing of the desire of a country – in the same minority situation as Belgium – to defend its legal tradition. The Danish constitution of 1849 (ie, the country's first constitution, quite a symbol) provided for the same type of system (the current constitution is the result of a complete revision and dates from 5 June 1953). It was established 'to guarantee the independence of Parliament and to protect it from the intervention of the King, … this system is an integral part of the constitutional structure, the separation of powers and the country's long and strong democratic traditions' (paragraph 65). The message was clear. It was perfectly received by the Court. There is no need, in these times (those of mistrust), to raise new controversial fronts. The Hirst storm – on the right of prisoners to vote, which the United Kingdom also presented at the time as an element of its legal tradition – must have been in the air.

Therefore, the Court opted for the second, less ambitious, but politically correct option. It was not to discuss, let alone challenge, what is nowadays an undeniable constitutional exoticism.[61] The Court did not wish to interfere in an area where the national margin of appreciation of the States is traditionally wide; it therefore preferred to play the card of the proceduralisation of Article 3 of Protocol No 1. First of all, it merely stated that 'the present case concerns the manner in which the applicant's complaint was examined by the competent domestic authorities' (paragraph 75). It then found that the principles set out in paragraph 70 of its judgment had not been respected in casu. In short, arbitrariness had not been avoided: the Walloon Parliament's decision did not offer sufficient guarantees of impartiality; its discretionary power was excessive; it was not sufficiently circumscribed by provisions of domestic law; last but not least, the procedure was not such as to guarantee a fair, objective and sufficiently reasoned decision (paragraphs 87–123).

The Court was tactically clever: by taking up the standards set by the OSCE and the Venice Commission to the point of making them a cursor of its procedural analysis, it was ultimately uncompromising: an implacable counterpart (in view of the numerous practical deficiencies of the system) of the freedom granted to Belgium to preserve, in the name of its legal tradition, a system that is, after all, singular.

As for its analysis from the point of view of Article 13, it was brief, entirely absorbed by the conclusions it reached from the point of view of the right to free elections (paragraph 135).

Compliance

I have decided to present this case due to the impressive constitutional change it implies. Even though the execution is still ongoing, I consider it fascinating to see how

[61] This point was skillfully emphasised by the Polish judge K Wojtyczek in his concurring opinion: 'the blind spots of the system of guarantees of the rule of law do not form part of the core of the common constitutional heritage, even if they are deeply rooted in a national constitutional tradition' (pt 3 of his opinion). And to return to the history of the evolution that consisted in shifting the power recognised to the Chambers, in the eighteenth and nineteenth centuries, to rule on disputes concerning the election of their members (at a time when it was necessary to guarantee their autonomy with respect to the monarchs), to the one that took shape in the twentieth century, marked by the jurisdictionalisation of the control. To put an end to the numerous abuses noted, such was the main ratio decidendi of the displacement of the neuralgic centre of the control. He went on to point out that 'the power recognized to parliament to rule on electoral disputes is a vestige of constitutionalism. It does not reflect a fundamental axiological or political choice. It is not a societal issue. It serves no particular and recognized legal purpose that might be justified, for example, by the idea that certain matters are not susceptible to legal review or by the need to keep judges out of the "political thicket"' (pt 4 *in fine*).

a democratic state takes very seriously the reform of a very traditional system where the idea of 'legal culture' not to say 'constitutional identity' was at stake.

The practices challenged by the Court concern the election of seven parliamentary assemblies (the Senate, the House of Representatives, the Flemish Parliament, the Walloon Parliament, the Parliament of the French Community, the Parliament of the Brussels-Capital Region, the Parliament of the German-speaking Community) as well as the election of the Belgian members of the Parliament, which are currently governed, in addition to the regulations of the parliamentary assemblies concerned, by the following provisions (Articles 48, 142, al 5 of the Constitution) and several provisions of Special laws. Some of them imply a complex constitutional reform (Article 195).

In order to tackle the adoption of general measures to execute the *Muguemangango* judgment, the Ministers in charge of Institutional reforms have drawn up a provisional list of articles of the Constitution to be modified (including Articles 48 and 142(5)) which was made public and sent to the House of Representatives and the Senate.[62] The Constitutional Court has accepted the mission to prepare the draft texts for the necessary amendments.

The parliamentary assemblies were able to begin the process of amending their respective regulations. The amendments will guarantee the minimum rights of the claimants in the case of on the validation of the next elections.

The first steps are therefore being taken in consultation with all the components of the State the necessary structural reforms and to provide minimum procedural guarantees for the 2024 elections.

2. *New (and Fragile) Democracies*

Lithuania

ECtHR (GC), *Paksas v Lithuania* (6 January 2011)

ECtHR (GC), (8 April 2022) *Advisory Opinion regarding the assessment of proportionality under Article 3 of Protocol No 1 to the Convention, of a general prohibition for a person to run for election after being removed from office through impeachment proceedings, requested by the Lithuanian Supreme Administrative Court (P16-2021-001).*

The *Paksas* saga is emblematic of a situation that has long been inextricable due to conflicts between multiple stakeholders within the Lithuanian state, which has been unable to swiftly implement a Strasbourg Court's decision. At the origin of this saga was the removal of Mr Paksas from his position as President of the Republic following an impeachment procedure due to serious violations of the Constitution, as established by the Constitutional Court in 2004 (pursuing purely private interests to the detriment of those of the nation and the credibility of the presidential institution). M Paksas, wishing to be able to run for parliamentary elections, brought the case before the ECtHR.

In 2011, the ECtHR[63] ruled on the case involving M Paksas who was permanently barred from standing for parliamentary elections after being removed from presidential

[62] Secretariat of the Committee of Ministers, DH-DD (2022) 1430, 20 December 2022.
[63] ECtHR (GC), App no 34932/04 *Paksas v Lithuania* ECLI:CE:ECHR:2011:0106JUD003493204.

office through impeachment proceedings. The Court deemed this restriction disproportionate, considering it an excessive limitation on the right to free elections due to its permanent and irreversible nature, despite the impeachment being conducted in accordance with the Constitutional Court's ruling of 25 May 2004 and the Seimas Elections Act of 15 July 2004.

The Lithuanian Constitutional Court, undoubtedly 'offended' by the challenge to its jurisprudence in the *Paksas* case, dug in its heels on the dualistic nature of the Lithuanian system and refused to take into account the European standard regarding the right to free elections in a ruling dated 5 September 2012.[64] In this decision, the Lithuanian Constitutional Court deemed a provision of the law on parliamentary elections adopted to comply with the condemnation of Lithuania by the ECtHR in the *Paksas* case to be unconstitutional! In others words, the Legislative was keen to comply with the Strasbourg Court's decision, and the constitutional judge decided differently. This law allowed a person removed from office through an impeachment procedure due to serious violations of the Constitution, to run for parliamentary elections four years after such removal.

It was in this context that the Constitutional Court engaged in an open rebellion against Strasbourg. It found that Article 3 of Protocol No 1, to the extent that it presupposes the international commitment of Lithuania to guarantee the right to be elected or re-elected to the national parliament for such persons, is not in conformity with the Constitution. The Court noted that State parties to the ECHR enjoy a margin of appreciation in their obligation to comply with the final judgments of the Court and that this margin may be limited by the Constitution. However, according to the hierarchy of sources of Lithuanian law, the ECHR does not prevail over the Constitution; like any other ratified international treaty, it has the status of law and cannot be applied if it is contrary to the Constitution. Therefore, a final judgment of the ECtHR cannot in itself be a means of reinterpreting or modifying official constitutional doctrine if such reinterpretation (in the absence of amendment of the text of the Constitution) leads either to a substantive modification of constitutional regulation, to an infringement of the system of constitutional values, or to a diminution of the protection of the primacy of the Constitution in the normative system. Accordingly, in the view of the Constitutional Court, the only possibility of complying with the Grand Chamber judgment to eliminate the incompatibility between the ECtHR and the Constitution would be to amend the Constitution itself.

Ten years after that constitutional ruling, and after the inability to find sufficient political agreement to amend the Constitution, the Lithuanian Supreme Court decided to refer the matter to the ECtHR under Protocol 16, which is a 'preliminary reference procedure'.[65] So this opinion actually fits into an impressive political and judicial saga following the *Paksas* judgment (2011). The opinion of the ECtHR wonderfully recounts the political twists and turns that have prevented, until recently, the amendment

[64] Constitutional Court of Lithuania, 5 September 2012, *Elections to the Seimas*, No 8/2012.

[65] ECtHR (GC), Request no P16-2021-001 *Advisory Opinion regarding the assessment of proportionality under Article 3 of Protocol No 1 to the Convention, of a general prohibition for a person to run for election after being removed from office through impeachment proceedings, requested by the Lithuanian Supreme Administrative Court.*

of the Constitution for the purpose of executing the *Paksas* judgment, the only admissible procedural channel according to the Constitutional Court. It is interesting to note that the Committee of Ministers had to suspend its monitoring function of the execution procedure of the *Paksas* ruling, pending the Court's advisory opinion.[66]

One could be tempted to assert that strategic reasons prompted the activation of Protocol No 16, considering the legal imbroglio resulting from the political difficulties in amending the Constitution to execute the *Paksas* judgment. The Sword theory seems to hold true here.[67] All of these events had consequences for the situation of a former judge and member of the Seimas who was the subject of an impeachment procedure, and who defended herself up to the Administrative Supreme Court. The latter preferred to play it safe by requesting the ECtHR's opinion, rather than engaging in an analysis that could have put it in an awkward position afterwards. The ECtHR, in its opinion, delivered the relevant criteria concerning parliamentary mandate impeachment proceedings underlining that 'they should be identified mainly from the perspective of the requirements of the proper functioning of the institution of which that person seeks to become a member …'. Ultimately, the constitutional amendment aimed at implementing the Court's judgment was adopted in the Seimas in the second vote and came into force in May 2022.

Compliance with the Judgment

The new Electoral Code, reflecting this amendment, came into force in September 2022. Hence, any person removed from office or whose mandate as a member of the Seimas has been revoked by the Seimas through impeachment proceedings will not be subjected to a 'permanent and irreversible' ban from standing for parliamentary elections but will be able to stand for elections to the Seimas after a period of 'at least ten years'. The judgment was published, translated and disseminated. The CM decided, after the Advisory opinion and its positive consequences within the domestic legal order, to close definitively the execution supervision (20 September 2022).[68] In others words, it took 11 years for Article 46 § 1 ECHR, to be properly considered by the Lithuanian authorities. The High Contracting Parties undertake to abide by the final judgment of the Court in any case to which they are parties.

B. States in Post-conflict Situation

Bosnia-Herzegovina

ECtHR, (GC), Sejdic and Finci v Bosnia Herzegovina (22 December 2009)

The *Sejdić and Finci* case[69] demonstrates the sheer impossibility of fully resolving political issues related to ethnic power-sharing through law and justice alone. While the

[66] ibid, paras 47 and 63.

[67] L Glaz, J Krommendijk, 'A Strasbourg Story of Swords and Shields. National Courts' Motives to Request an Advisory Opinion from the ECHR Under Protocol 16' (2022) *European Convention on Human Rights Law Review* 1.

[68] The Deputies decided to close the supervision of the execution of this judgment in the light of the measures taken by the Lithuanian authorities, as described in their action report of 27 June 2022 (DH-DD(2022)688) and adopted Final Resolution (CM/res DH(2022) 253).

[69] It was delivered after the relinquishment by the Chamber of seven judges.

ECtHR sought to prioritise the right to non-discrimination over the political agreements of Dayton, – having constitutional rank – it has not been able, up to this day, to have this judgment accepted and executed by political authorities.

The entire post-conflict constitutional architecture of Bosnia and Herzegovina was at the heart of the Court's review. It had to answer the question of whether the constitutional impossibility for two Bosnian citizens to stand for election to the House of Peoples and the collegial Presidency of their country due to their community affiliation (Roma for one, Jewish for the other) was contrary to the principle of non-discrimination. Given the current state of its jurisprudence on the issue, as well as that of numerous other (universal and regional) bodies for the protection of rights, it would have been extremely surprising had it answered in the negative. The ECtHR initially found a violation of Article 14 combined with Article 3 of Protocol No 1 regarding the impossibility of standing for election to the 'peoples' chamber. Even if some consider the Court's reasoning to be lacking, and even if dissenting Judge Bonello, in very strong dissent, believes that the Court did not take sufficient account of the historical context, the rebuke is evident for all the political authorities of the country who have not respected the commitments made, both within the framework of the CoE and the European Union (§ 49), which obliged them to quickly implement an electoral reform. Then came the examination of Article 1 of Protocol No 12, which was declared violated for the first time. The reader can only be disappointed by the Court's economy of means and interpretative analogy in considering that the 'discrimination' of Article 14 is equivalent to that of Article 1 of Protocol No 12.

Therefore, the reasoning put forward for the election to the House of Peoples applies to the election of the Presidency as well. What is important to note here is the subtle sanction imposed on the jurisprudence of the Constitutional Court of Bosnia and Herzegovina. The sanction is subtle in that the Court does not expressly mention the questionable constitutional jurisprudence in its substantive developments. It is mentioned upstream, in the 'Facts' section of the judgment, which makes the disapproval less 'obvious', eg, less visible. The Constitutional Court had approved the difference in treatment between the 'constituent peoples' and other communities in the context of the election of the Presidency, based notably on Article 1 of Protocol No 12 and Article 25 of the International Covenant on Civil and Political Rights, in pursuit of the 'legitimate objective of preserving the established peace and maintaining dialogue'.[70] This groundbreaking and leading case is part, now, of group of four other similar judgments (*Zornic*, *Slaku*, *Pilva* and *Pudaric*), still in the implementation phase.

Non-compliance of the Judgment

To date, it is interesting to quote the very last decision of the CM's delegates after their meeting held in December 2023 recalling:

> The Committee might recall again with utmost concern that, as a direct result of the absence of measures taken by the respondent State as obliged under Article 46 of the Convention, to date four general elections have been held under the same regulatory framework which the European Court found to be discriminatory, despite the repeated calls of the Committee over the past 14 years, including in its four Interim resolutions.

[70] Constitutional Court of Bosnia and Herzegovina (CCBH), 29 September 2006, AP 2678/06, mentioned in paragraph 14 of the European Court of Human Rights' decision of 22 December 2009, which is located in the 'Factual Background' section of the decision.

The Committee might also deeply regret the lack of information in writing from the authorities and note that following the coalition agreement of 29 November 2022 signed by leaders of several political parties, the process of formation of governments has now been finalised at all levels, with the exception of one canton. In light of this, the Committee might wish to insist firmly on the utmost importance of instantly relaunching the electoral reform work while pursuing all consultations necessary aimed at eliminating discrimination based on ethnic affiliation in elections for the Presidency and the House of Peoples of Bosnia and Herzegovina.

The authorities and political leaders of Bosnia and Herzegovina should be exhorted once again to deploy all their efforts to reach a consensus on the necessary amendments to the Constitution and the electoral legislation. The willingness of the Council of Europe, notably the Venice Commission, to assist by all available means the authorities of Bosnia and Herzegovina in meeting their obligations under Article 46 of the Convention to rapidly reach a consensus on the required electoral system reform might be reiterated once again by the Committee.

Lastly, the authorities may be strongly urged to submit by 15 April 2024 information in writing on the measures taken to implement the present group of judgments. The Committee might also wish to invite the competent Minister of the Council of Ministers of Bosnia and Herzegovina for an exchange of views at its 1501st meeting (June 2024) (DH). In the absence of tangible progress and in line with the instruction in the Committee's June 2023 decision, the Secretariat has prepared a draft interim resolution for consideration.

C. Illiberal States (North Macedonia; Poland During the PIS Government de 2015 à 2023)

North Macedonia[71]

ECtHR, *Strezvoski others v North Macedonia* (27 February 2020)

This state can be considered a 'hybrid regime'; some authors have even called it an 'illiberal democracy'.[72] Macedonia is indeed a struggling democracy, where elections are not free and where corruption, abuse of public resources and state institutions are huge, as well as the media control by state authorities.

[71] The Republic of North Macedonia – hereafter North Macedonia – is one of the 46 Member States of the Council of Europe, and a candidate state for membership in the European Union since 2005. It is a parliamentary republic, formerly part of Yugoslavia, which became independent in 1991. It joined the Council of Europe on 9 November 1995 and subsequently signed the ECHR on 25 July 1996 and ratified it on 1 February 2007. It is a state that has adopted a monistic representation of the relationship between the domestic and international legal orders. This follows from Article 118 of the Constitution, which states that 'international agreements ratified in accordance with the Constitution are part of the internal legal order and cannot be changed by law'. Article 119 then provides that these are then concluded by the President of the Republic, or by the Government when it is so determined by law. In accordance with Article 68, they are ratified by Parliament. Moreover, according to Amendment XXV, the courts 'judge on the basis of the Constitution and laws and international agreements ratified in accordance with the Constitutions …' Even if there is no direct reference to the ECHR in the constitution, it is part of the Macedonian legal order, like any other legally ratified international treaty. In the context of the hierarchy of norms, it would then be superior to national laws – which cannot modify it – but inferior to the Constitution, see V Stefanovska, 'The Constitutional Character of the ECHR: Overview, Challenges in Implementation and Limitations' (2022) 20 *Balkan Social Science Review* 33.

[72] B GJuzelov, MI Hadjievska, 'Institutional and Symbolic Aspects of Illiberal Politics: The Case of North Macedonia (2006–2017)' (2019) 20 *Southeast European and Black Studies* 41.

The Macedonian cases before the European Court shows that property rights (Article 1 Protocol 1) are very often at the core of the applications. Indeed, it triggers a lot of condemnation by the ECtHR against North Macedonia.[73] Macedonian regulations on energy supply and home heating have been challenged before the ECtHR which delivered the *Strezovski* judgment.

The case reveals a State-imposed standing charge payable to private heat suppliers by owners of flats disconnected from the district heating system which supplies their residential buildings. The key point of the case was to examine whether the impugned measure does not impose excessive burden on applicants, while allowing private heat suppliers to make potentially unjustified profits. The ECtHR sheds light on domestic courts' failure to strike the requisite fair balance between the interests involved by applying sufficient procedural safeguards.

Compliance with the Judgment

In accordance with Article 46, paragraph1 ECHR, the case was referred to the Committee of Ministers to supervise its execution. Following the prompt and efficient intervention of the national authorities, it was declared effectively executed on 14 December 2022, eg, two and a half years after the judgment became final. This is a very rapid execution that denotes a radical change of paradigm,[74] knowing that until then, the numerous judgments against this country were not executed with diligence. This state of affairs could be explained by the very recent discussions launched in 2022 in order to integrate the EU. North Macedonia has been governed for several years by politicians affiliated with the Social Democratic Union of Macedonia – that is, a party in favour of the accession to the European Union – and it therefore has every interest in executing the rulings of the European Court in an effective and quick way.[75]

In this case, it is a political dialogue between the three constituted powers (executive, legislative and judicial) associated with representatives of civil society, that explains the speed of adoption of individual and general measures, which went beyond what the Court required (paragraph 87). As the respondent State recalled,[76] the European Court's requests were specific and aimed at the establishment of procedural safeguards by the national courts when applying the existing regulation. Indeed, the Court had stated that the judges should have examined the facts and allegations of the parties, as well as any other relevant factors.

[73] M Lazarova Trajkovska, I Trajkovski, 'The impact of the European Convention on Human Rights and the case law of the Republic of Macedonia' in I Motoc and I Ziemele (eds), *The Impact of the ECHR on Democratic Change in Central and Eastern Europe* (Cambridge, Cambridge University Press, 2016) 273–74, 279–80.

[74] This speed of action is part of a new recent trend in North Macedonia. Indeed, this state has recently developed the custom of executing very quickly the judgments rendered by the European Court against it. See the 2021 case ECtHR, App no 48057/12 *Transkop Ad Bitola v Northern Macedonia* ECLI:CE:ECHR:2021:0401JUD004805712 and executed in 2022; the 2020 judgment in ECtHR, App no 79783/13, *JM and AT v Northern Macedonia* ECLI:CE:ECHR:2020:1022JUD007978313 executed in 2021, or the 2020 judgment in ECtHR, App no 38067/15 *LR v Northern Macedonia* ECLI:CE:ECHR:2020:0123JUD003806715 and executed in 2021 (see *Hudoc Exec*).

[75] Complying with the very high standards of human rights protection within the EU (see Article 2 TEU) could indeed facilitate negotiations for the accession.

[76] Secretariat of the Committee of Ministers of the Council of Europe, Document DH-DD(2022)1125, 21 October 2022, 2, para 3.

The execution of the *Strezovski* ruling has shown that not only have the judicial authorities changed their jurisprudence, but they have also started to cite and use the European standard in their decisions, something they did not do before.[77] More, the authorities did not limit themselves to adopting measures addressed to the national courts to modify their jurisprudence, as requested by the ECtHR, but also amended the national regulations on several occasions, with the aim of preventing any future violation of the right recognised in Article 1 of Protocol No 1 ECHR.[78] Finally, and perhaps most importantly, the implementation process was inclusive, in that the NGO 'No pasarán' was actively involved in internal discussions, including those with representatives of the Ministry of Justice.

Poland (under the 'PIS Government', 2015–2023):[79]

ECtHR, *Xero Flor in Poland sp v Poland* (7 May 2021)

ECtHR, *Walesa v Poland* (23 November 2023)

With the arrival in power of the PIS, the 'democratic deconsolidation' has been huge in Poland. The judiciary was not an independent branch, as both European Courts (ECJ and ECtHR) have demonstrated.[80]

Alone against all. Alone against 16 colleagues of the Grand Chamber; alone against two 'intervening' governments; alone against seven interventions by rights protection organisations (including Poland's own Ombudsman), which, together, alert on the massive destruction of the separation of powers in Poland. Such is the depressing finding that emerges when reading the dissenting opinion of the Polish judge in the *Grzęda* case. It is well known that separate opinions can, more or less subtly, reveal their authors' ideological options, especially at key moments in their term. Although their mandate is now non-renewable for nine years, a judge of the European Court who does not retire at the end of their term must – by force of circumstance – think about their future, in their country or elsewhere. It is impossible to discern with certainty the multiple reasons that led Judge Krzysztof Wojtyczek to consider that the European Court was wrong on the whole line by deciding, first of all, to accept the request for the chamber's disqualification and by declaring, subsequently, the violation of Article 6, paragraph1 ECHR, in yet another Polish case where the rule of law is being undermined.[81]

[77] Lazarova Trajkovska and Trajkovski, 'The Impact of the European Convention' (2016) 283.

[78] Secretariat of the Committee of Ministers of the Council of Europe, Document DH-DD (2022)1125, 21 October 2022, 5, para 19.

[79] The arrival of Donald Tusk to power (December 2023), while it allows for ending the illiberalism of the PiS regime, raises the very complex question of how to reintroduce the rules specific to political liberalism without instrumentalising the law as PiS had done. This challenge is at the heart of Tusk's governance dilemma. His government faces the paradoxical task of restoring democratic norms and the rule of law while navigating the legal and institutional landscape shaped by PiS's illiberal policies. The process of reversing Poland's illiberal course is complicated by the need to respect democratic checks and balances, even when these same institutions were compromised by the previous government (www.theparliamentmagazine.eu/news/article/polands-tusk-faces-ruleoflaw-paradox).

[80] The democratic destruction is important in Poland (see the articles in the *Esprit* 2019/3 devoted to the 'New Authoritarianism in Poland', with the introductory analysis by J-Y Potel, 'Poland, A Mirror of Europe?' (2019) *Esprit* 41.

[81] In the same vein, see also, his dissenting opinion in the *Broda and Bojara* case (ECtHR, App nos 26691/18 and 27367/18 *Broda and Bojara v Poland* ECLI:CE:ECHR:2021:0629JUD002669118) as well as his 'mixed' – concurrent and dissenting – opinion in the *Xero Flor w Polsce* case (ECtHR, App no 4907/18 *Xero Flor w Polsce v Poland* ECLI:CE:ECHR:2021:0507JUD000490718).

At this stage, it should be mentioned that his mandate was due to expire on 31 October 2021, but he was forced to extend it in Strasbourg due to the double rejection by the Parliamentary Assembly of the Polish list in the election process.[82]

Is there a cause and effect relationship? The future will tell (maybe). What is certain, however, is that his status as a national judge leaves a bitter taste in the reader's mouth. One will get a sense of this bitterness by discovering – or rather rediscovering – all the contextual elements of a deliberate orchestration of attacks on the separation of powers and the subjugation of the judiciary in Poland. Thus, the arguments and evidence put forward by the European Network of Councils for the Judiciary; those of Amnesty International and the International Commission of Jurists; those of the Helsinki Foundation for Human Rights; those of the Association of Polish Judges (Iustitia); those of the Judges for Judges Foundation (Holland) in association with Professor Laurent Pech of Middlesex University; those of the Polish Commissioner for Human Rights; and, last but not least, those of the UN Special Rapporteur on the Independence of Judges and Lawyers, the Peruvian Diego García Sayán, who was, among other things, President of the Inter-American Court of Human Rights between 2009 and 2013. Alone also against the arguments presented by two 'courageous' States, Denmark and the Netherlands.

It is particularly striking to note that these two states took the diplomatic option of taking a stand in court, not to defend (as usual) their national interests (as in migration issues, see the intervention of the Hungarian government in the *ZA* case (ECtHR, GC *ZA et al v Russia* (21 November 2019)) or that of the Bulgarian, Polish, and Russian governments in the *Ilias and Ahmed* case (ECtHR, GC *Ilias and Ahmed v Hungary* (21 November 2019)), but to recall the synergy of approaches with the CJEU regarding the independence of the judiciary (Danish arguments, paragraphs 247–51), as well as the cardinal nature of the principle of the primacy of law (Dutch arguments, paragraphs 252–56). In short, they showed the entire audience that they were defending fundamental principles of good democratic functioning.

Clear rebellion with the compliance duty

On 24 November 2021,[83] the so called Constitutional 'Tribunal' examined the application of the Prosecutor General of the Republic who challenged the applicability of Article 6, paragraph 1 ECHR – as interpreted by the European Court in the *Astroasson* judgment, among others – to the Polish constitutional 'Tribunal'.[84] The ECtHR applied this important standard to Poland in the resounding *Xero Flor* case (ECtHR, Xero Flor in Poland sp c Poland (7 May 2021)), which forcefully demonstrated that it was not only activists, judges and lawyers who found themselves in the torment of arbitrariness when the composition of courts was open to discussion.

[82] Available at https://assembly.coe.int/LifeRay/CDH/Pdf/TableForthcomingJudgesElections-FR.pdf accessed 3 June 2025.

[83] Polish constitutional 'tribunal', 24 November 2021, K 6/21. The judgment panel in this case consisted of the presiding judge – the president of the Constitutional Tribunal, Judge Julia Przyłębska; the reporting judge – Judge Wojciech Sych; Judge Zbigniew Jędrzejewski; Judge Bartłomiej Sochański; and Judge Michał Warciński.

[84] 'Polish Constitutional Tribunal Declares Itself Not Covered by Right to a Fair Trial under Article 6 para 1 ECHR' (*EU Law Live*, 25 November 2021) https://eulawlive.com/polish-constitutional-tribunal-declares-itself-not-covered-by-right-to-a-fair-trial-under-article-61-echr/ accessed on 1 April 2025.

The case involved a Polish company that sought compensation from the state for the destruction of a field of its own turf by wild game – wild boar and deer. The compensation they received was paltry compared to the compensation they received for damage to corn and wheat fields. The company then engaged in a legal battle which it lost in the ordinary courts, prompting it to apply to the Constitutional Court to examine the conformity of the national regulation which disadvantaged it with the Polish Constitution. The Constitutional Tribunal rejected the application. However, the panel that made the decision included Judge Mariusz Muszynski, the Vice President of the Court, whose election had been controversial. The European Court applied the three *Astroasson* criteria: (1) the existence of a clear violation of domestic law; in other words, 'the violation must be objectively and genuinely identifiable' (*Xero Flor w Polsce sp Zo o*, paragraph 249); (2) the violation must be analysed in light of the object and purpose of the requirement of a 'tribunal established by law', which is 'to ensure the ability of the judiciary to carry out its duties without undue interference in order to preserve the rule of law and the separation of powers' (*Flor w Polsce sp Zo o*, paragraph 250); (3) finally, the national courts must assess the legal consequences of an infringement of the internal rules of appointment, taking into consideration the case law of the European Court (*Xero Flor w Polsce sp Zo o*, paragraph 251).

This approach allowed him to undertake a detailed and uncompromising analysis of the different stratagems for organising the Executive's control over the judiciary, taking advantage of the opportunity to strongly criticise the jurisprudence of the new Polish Constitutional 'Tribunal' which had radically changed its jurisprudence, without convincing motivation, in order to justify the new model of electing judges.

The reaction of the Polish authorities was commensurate with the country's vertiginous democratic deconsolidation, since the Prosecutor General of the Republic challenged the European Court's decision directly before the said 'Tribunal'. It unanimously considered that Article 6, paragraph 1 was not applicable to the 'Tribunal' constitutional. The Polish Constitutional 'Tribunal' articulated its argument on two fronts: first, the specificity of its position in the general organisation of justice in Poland; second, the competence of the European Court to review the process of appointing judges.

On the first front, the Constitutional 'Tribunal' identified several incompatibilities with Article 173 in combination with Article 10, paragraph 2, Article 175, paragraph 1 and Article 8, paragraph 1 of the Constitution of the Republic of Poland. It was stated that although the Constitutional 'Tribunal' was an organ of the judiciary (Article 10, paragraph 2), it did not carry out the administration of justice, understood as the settlement of individual civil, criminal or administrative cases. And he stated that according to Article 175, paragraph 1 of the Constitution, the exclusive competence in this field had been granted to the Supreme Court, as well as to the ordinary, administrative and military courts, which are the ones implementing the administration of justice in Poland. And to state that the main task of the Constitutional 'Tribunal' is to control the hierarchical conformity of legal norms and – if necessary – to eliminate unconstitutional norms from the legal system. Even when it examines a constitutional complaint, it decides on the law, not on the individual rights of the plaintiffs.

In other words, the 'Tribunal' emphasised that it was not a court of third instance and did not replace the ordinary courts (since it did not review the application of the law in specific cases). Thus, the 'unconditional categorisation' by the ECtHR of the Polish Constitutional 'Tribunal' as an organ of the judiciary covered by the scope of application of Article 6, paragraph 1, first sentence of the Convention would violate the provisions of the Polish Constitution.

On the second front, the 'Tribunal' found a violation of Article 194, paragraph 1 of the Constitution, according to which the Sejm has a monopoly on the election of judges of the Constitutional 'Tribunal'. It elucidated that the appointment procedure is deemed complete when the new judge takes the oath before the President of the Republic. To buttress its argument, the Tribunal emphasised that the Polish legal system lacks any authorities or mechanisms to scrutinise the legality of the process by which judges are elected to the Constitutional Tribunal. It further noted, with good reason, that it had previously declared itself incompetent in this matter, citing cases K 35/15 and 8/15 as precedents.

By assessing the legality of the process of electing a judge to the Constitutional Court in the case initiated by the applicant company (*Xero Flor*), the ECtHR thus devised a procedure for reviewing the composition of the Constitutional Court that was unknown to the Polish Constitution and, in an unauthorised manner, interfered with the constitutional powers of the Polish state authorities, namely the Sejm and the President of the Republic.

Article 46, paragraph 1 ECHR, according to which the 'High Contracting Parties undertake to abide by the final judgments of the Court in cases to which they are parties' was here masterfully flouted. Such fundamental disagreements are so many attacks on the *ius commune* in Europe, that of the law and the values it conveys. For how long?

On 23 November 2023 an emblematic case (*Walesa* case) was decided by a single chamber, without the presence of the 'national judge' who had been deported (Article 28 § 3 of the Rules of Procedure, replaced by the Greek judge Ioannis Ktistakis), and which allowed a good-natured unanimity (avoiding K Wojtyczek signing a new unwelcome dissent in a case confirming the guardianship of justice in Poland).

The former leader of the Solidarity trade union, former Polish president (1990–1995), and Nobel Peace Prize laureate in 1983, Lech Walesa, was publicly accused in 2000, while running again for the highest office, of having collaborated with the secret services of the communist regime. Legal proceedings, initiated ex proprio motu by the Warsaw Court of Appeal, concluded that he had properly filled out his 'lustration declaration' and could not be accused of having been a communist agent. Despite this court decision, the case took on considerable political dimensions, to the point where Polish society became extremely polarised. The most powerful and categorical voices asserting that Lech Walesa was a secret collaborator of the communist regime came from PiS, the Law and Justice party of the Kaczyński brothers. In this context, where his honour and reputation were considerably tarnished, L Walesa initiated defamation proceedings in 2005. While the Gdansk Court of Appeal, in what became a veritable judicial saga, ruled in his favour (judgment of 24 March 2011), the controversial 2017 judicial reform completely changed the situation by creating the infamous 'Extraordinary Chambers', the Disciplinary Chamber and the Chamber of Extraordinary Review and Public Affairs within the Supreme Court. Thus, in 2020, Prosecutor General Ziobro filed an 'extraordinary appeal' against the Gdansk Court's judgment, which was overturned (with unusual speed) on 21 April 2021, by a ruling that instrumentalised all the standards set by conventional jurisprudence. 'Going to Strasbourg' was the ultimate procedural step available to Lech Walesa to definitively clear his honour. While he did not prevail under Article 18 (the 'non-détournement de procédure' clause), his victory was indisputable under Articles 8 (private life) and 6§1 (fair trial).

The case is emblematic, first, because of the stature of the applicant, Lech Walesa, who left his mark on the history of Poland's liberation from the communist yoke; it is also emblematic because of the initiation of the pilot judgment procedure in 2004, precisely in a Polish case that has its origins in the twists and turns of the history of the Second World War and the territorial disputes that followed (ECHR, Gde Ch *Broniowski v Poland* (22 June 2004), paragraphs 190–91).

The interest of the case therefore lies essentially in the triggering of the pilot judgment procedure provided for in Article 61 of the Rules of Procedure, which will enable the Committee of Ministers to better perform its task of monitoring implementation (Article 46).

After recalling the reasons for the introduction of this new way of dealing with systemic problems (paragraphs 314–15) and its twofold objective (to reduce the risks relating to the operation of the treaty system and to speed up the handling of malfunctions in the national legal systems) (paragraph 316), the Court recalled the criteria for triggering it (paragraphs 317–18), which it considered to be present in the case (paragraphs 319–23). In doing so, it summarised in a particularly pedagogical manner the systematic violations of Article 6, paragraph 1: (1) the flawed procedure since 2017 for the appointment of judges to the National Council of the Judiciary; (2) the nature of the Extraordinary Chamber of Appeal, which is not 'independent' and 'legally' created; (3) the extraordinary appeal procedure, which does not comply with the canons of fair trial, in particular that of legal certainty; (4) the exclusive competence of the Extraordinary Chamber to examine appeals (thus perpetuating the initial violation of Article 6, paragraph 1).

It clearly states that 'these interdependent systemic problems therefore lead to repeated violations of the fundamental principles of the rule of law, the separation of powers and the independence of the judiciary' (paragraph 324 in fine). The Court goes further, highlighting, on the one hand, the consistency of the CJEU's case law on the 'crisis of the rule of law' with its own standards, and on the other, the Polish Constitutional Court's repeated affronts denying any authority to the CJEU's rulings (paragraph 325), and the failure to comply with the resolutions of the Committee of Ministers adopted on the basis of Article 46, denying its own judgments the force of res judicata (paragraph 326).

The Court had laid the groundwork to direct the Polish State to implement a series of general measures addressing four key obstacles, which it carefully identified (paragraphs 328–32). While doing so, the Court reminded Poland that it had flexibility in rectifying the structural deficiencies within its judicial system. The ECtHR then presented its 'procedural burden': out of 492 similar cases brought before it, 202 had already been communicated to the government. Consequently, 'those that have not yet been communicated shall be adjourned for one year from' the date of the *Walesa* judgment, pending the adoption of general measures.

D. Authoritarian States

If democracy can be killed by the sounds of boots, summary executions, forced disappearances, and the launching of tanks on the streets in the aftermath of a coup, it is well known that it can also be insidiously destroyed through multiple strategies of circumventing and instrumentalising the law. This has been happening for several years in Turkey.[85]

Turkey

ECtHR, *Kavala v Turkey* (18 December 2019)

ECtHR (GC), Proceedings based on Article 46, paragraph 4 in *Kavala* case (11 July 2022)

The *Kavala* case is, unfortunately, a major example of the insidious authoritarian trend.[86] It triggers the interest of several important actors – alongside three large NGOs, the CoE Commissioner for Human Rights Dunja Mijatović – who exercised their right to take part in the proceedings (Article 36, paragraph 4 ECHR). The purpose of this intervention was to present the background of the applicant – from which we learn that he had long established ties of trust with the institutions of the CoE – but also to describe the 'Gezi events' of 2013 in an objective manner. Indeed, thanks to his predecessor's in loco visits to Turkey and the reports published in the wake of his field investigations[87] the Court had at its disposal, in addition to the applicant's allegations and the Government's arguments, a great deal of independently identified information. Therefore, the facts of the case were illuminated in this instance by a particularly trustworthy independent third party.

Reading the case reveals that what started out as a simple citizen opposition by environmental activists to a project to build a shopping mall in the heart of Istanbul (and to destroy the only green space in the city, 'Gezi Park'), turned into a wave of political protest throughout the country, following disproportionate repression by the police. The whole thing degenerated into violence on both sides as it was revealed that radical groups had infiltrated the peaceful demonstrators. The arrest and imprisonment of the applicant thus led to an exceptional contextualisation and a very detailed analysis of the events. In such a context, the ECtHR declared the violation of Articles 5, paragraph 1c and 5, paragraph 4, while the violation of Article 18 combined with Article 5, paragraph 1c) was recorded by one vote. In other words, the fact that the arrest and detention of Mr Kavala had a 'non-conventional purpose' – eg, to silence him and deter others from engaging in human rights activities in order to paralyse the country's civil society – was denied outright by the new Turkish judge.

If this case is paradigmatic, it is because it tends to lift the veil on the policy of persecution and repression of the current Turkish regime against all human rights defenders, even more so when they benefit from external intellectual and financial support. The Court's analysis of Article 18 was therefore expected: it was equal to the stakes. However, the dissent of the elected judge from Turkey, Saadet Yüksel, clouded the picture considerably. She made her public debut on the European judicial scene by using her ability to issue a separate opinion. In this case, she was both concurring and dissenting. The

[85] See the special issues 'Authoritarian Turkey, Contesting Turkey' (2017) 90 *Mouvements* and 'Turkey: Return of Authoritarianism' (2018) 107 *Confluences Mediterranée.*

[86] Osman Kavala was arrested in 2017 on the basis of an indictment that accused him of instigating and participating in the 2013 violence as well as the aborted 2016 coup. In other words, his arrest took place more than four years after the 'Gezi events' and more than a year after the 2016 events.

[87] Report by the Commissioner for Human Rights, Nils Muižnieks, following his visit to Turkey from 1 to 5 July 2013), CommDH(2013)24, 26 November 2013.

reader will quickly understand that Saadet Yüksel is more inclined to defend the current regime of the Turkish state than to promote conventional values, which was foreshadowed by the Nordic Monitor at the time of her election.[88] If, on the basis of a technical argument, she first agreed with the violation of Article 5, paragraph 1 ECHR while deviating from the reasoning developed by the Court (concurring opinion), she then mobilised four arguments, more ideological than technical, to conclude that there was insufficient evidence to consider that the trial against the 'activist' Mr Kavala pursued a political agenda (paragraph 9 dissenting opinion). In other words, she completely reversed the classic perspective of analysis of the facts when Articles 5, paragraph 1 and 18 are at stake, where it is incumbent on the government to demonstrate that the prosecution and arrest of a person was based on sufficiently solid grounds to believe that 'reasonable suspicions' existed that he had actually committed an offence. However, the Court found a violation of these two provisions precisely because 'the authorities were unable to demonstrate that the detention and continued detention … were justified by reasonable suspicion based on an objective assessment of the acts alleged'.[89] The Court therefore held that the government was to take every measure to put an end to the applicant's detention and to secure his immediate release.

However, the applicant was not released; worse, on 25 April 2022,[90] he was sentenced to aggravated life imprisonment.

In this context, the CM thus referred to the Court, in accordance with Article 46, paragraph 4 ECHR, the question whether Turkey had failed to fulfil its obligation under Article 46, paragraph 1, with particular regard to the Court's indication under Article 46 and the individual measures required. In the second Kavala judgment, issued on 11 July 2022, on the ground of Article 46, paragraph 4 ECHR, the Grand Chamber found that Turkey had failed to fulfil its obligation under Article 46, paragraph 1. The Court considered that the measures indicated by the defendant State did not permit it to conclude that the State Party had acted in 'good faith', in a manner compatible with the 'conclusions and spirit' of the *Kavala* judgment, or in a way that would make practical and effective the protection of the Convention rights which the Court found to have been violated in that judgment. Despite this second judgment based on Article 46, paragraph 4 ECHR, the Turkish authorities remain completely indifferent to the 'pressure' of the ECtHR as well as of the CM.[91]

[88] 'Erdoğan Manages to Install his Choice as New European Court of Human Rights Judge' (*Nordic Monitor*, 14 April 2019) www.nordicmonitor.com/2019/04/erdogan-managed-to-plant-his-choice-as-a-judge-at-the-european-court-of-human-rights/ accessed 1 April 2025.

[89] ECtHR, App no 28749/18 *Kavala v Turkey* ECLI:CE:ECHR:2019:1210JUD002874918, para 157.

[90] Indeed, the Criminal Court convicted the applicant and sentenced him to aggravated life imprisonment for attempting to overthrow the government by force (Article 312 TCC) and acquitted him of the charges under Article 328 concerning espionage. As for the charges under Article 309 for the offence of attempting to overthrow the Constitutional order, the Assize Court decided that, taken as a whole, the applicant's actions constituted only the offence under Article 312.

[91] (CM/Del/Dec (2023)/1459/H46-27).

20

(Non-)Compliance with the Rulings of the CJEU

ALLAN ROSAS

1. What are the Stakes?

The establishment of the Constitution for the United States of America, while ordained with a view to forming 'a more perfect Union',[1] was just the beginning of a process towards the federal state of today. True, the Constitution did provide for institutions, competences and powers at federal level, including a common defence. Especially before the Civil War of 1861 to 1865, however, the approach to sovereignty remained in a state of flux and individual States often challenged the authority of the federal government and judiciary, including, as far as some States were concerned, asserting a right of secession.[2] Also after the Civil War and the 14th Amendment of 1868, the division of competencies and powers between the Union and the States evolved over time.[3] While the 14th Amendment purported to make at least some of the fundamental rights contained in the federal Bill of Rights applicable to the States as well,[4] the case law of the Supreme Court only gradually embraced this idea. Since the 1930s,[5] the Court, applying the notion of 'selective incorporation', has incorporated more and more rights of the Bill of Rights making them applicable at State level.[6]

As recognised in the Schuman Plan of 9 May 1951, 'Europe will not be made at once, nor according to a single master plan of construction'. That said, placing Franco-German production of coal and steel under one common high authority was

[1] Preamble to the Constitution of the United States of America.

[2] P Pohjankoski, 'Federal Coercion and National Constitutional Identity in the United States 1776–1861' (2016) 56 *American Journal of Legal History* 326.

[3] R Schütze, *From Dual to Cooperative Federalism: The Changing Structure of European Law* (Oxford, Oxford University Press, 2009) 76–108.

[4] 'No State shall make or enforce any law which shall abridge the privileges or immunities of citizens of the United States; nor shall any State deprive any person of life, liberty, or property, without due process of law; nor deny to any person within its jurisdiction the equal protection of the laws'.

[5] *Palko v Connecticut*, 302 US 319 (1937). On substance (whether protection against double jeopardy was a fundamental right to be incorporated), overruled in *Benton v Maryland* 395 US 784 (1969).

[6] A Rosas, 'Application of the EU Charter of Fundamental Rights at National Level: One More Step towards a Federal Structure?' in *Justice en transition: Vers une Union solidaire et durable – Justice in Transition: Solidarity and Sustainability in the EU. Monographie en l'honneur de M. le juge Alexander Arabadjiev* (Bruxelles, Bruylant, 2024).

to be 'the first step for the European Federation'.[7] Many steps have been taken since then, but the Schuman objective of a 'European Federation' notwithstanding, have often been instigated without a clear constitutional direction and sense of purpose. The EU of today forms a complex, almost bewildering, array of common institutions, competencies and procedures, oscillating between different integration models and being constantly on the move, including with respect to the number of Member States.[8]

The US Supreme Court has played a crucial role in the shaping of the constitutional structure of the American Union. Yet, the hybrid and ambivalent nature of the EU legal order seems to have provided the Court of Justice of the European Union (CJEU), which according to Article 19(1), first subparagraph, of the Treaty on European Union (TEU) 'shall ensure that in the interpretation and application of the Treaties the law is observed', with an even more obvious task of making sense of an otherwise rather chaotic legal structure. And the imperfect collection of objectives, principles and more detailed rules has left the CJEU, notably the European Court of Justice (ECJ), with more room for different constitutional pathways. The foundational choices made in the 1960s shaped the core of the emerging constitutional order, consisting of the triad of direct effect, primacy and fundamental rights.[9]

There is no need here to recapitulate the ensuing case law of the CJEU reaffirming and developing the foundations of the 1960s or the important Treaty changes brought about especially since 1986. Some developments of special relevance for the EU fundamental rights regime deserve to be singled out, though. First, the ECJ advanced some tools, notably in the form of international human rights conventions and the European Convention on Human Rights (ECHR) in particular, for identifying a growing number of rights considered as fundamental and thus meriting the status of general principles of Community (now Union) law.[10] The Charter of Fundamental Rights of the European Union (CFREU) codified and developed this case law and has, for its part, triggered a new and more and more elaborate case law applying and interpreting the Charter provisions, including recognising that some of them may have not only direct vertical but also direct horizontal effect.[11]

Second, even before the CFREU, the Court's case law confirmed the applicability of Union fundamental rights at national level, albeit on the condition that Member States act in the scope of Union law.[12] After the entry into force of the CFREU, whose Article 51(1) states that the provisions of the Charter are addressed to the Member

[7] English version provided by the Schuman Project, www.schuman.info accessed 3 June 2025.

[8] K Lenaerts et al (eds), *An Ever-Changing Union? Perspectives on the Future of EU Law in Honour of Allan Rosas* (Oxford, Hart Publishing, 2019).

[9] CJEU, Case C-26/62 *Van Gend & Loos* ECLI:EU:C:1963:1; CJEU, Case C-6/64 *Costa v ENEL* ECLI:EU:C:1964:66 and CJEU, Case C-29/69 *Stauder* ECLI:EU:C:1969:56.

[10] See, eg, A Rosas and L Armati *EU Constitutional Law: An Introduction* 3rd rev edn (Oxford, Hart Publishing, 2018) 165–68.

[11] See, eg, ibid 174–76, citing CJEU, Case C-144/04 *Mangold* ECLI:EU:C:2005:709 and CJEU, Case C-555/07 *Kücükdeveci* ECLI:EU:C:2010:21. See also, for more recent examples, CJEU, Case C-414/16 *Egenberger* ECLI:EU:C:2018:257; CJEU, Joint Cases C-569/16 and C-570/16 *Bauer & Willmeroth* ECLI:EU:C:2018:871, and CJEU, Case C-684/16 *Max-Planck* ECLI:EU:C:2018:874.

[12] The formulation 'act in the scope of Union law' is to be found, inter alia, in the Explanations to Article 51(1) of the EU Charter of Fundamental Rights [2007] OJ C 303/02. On Article 51(1) of the Charter see below.

States 'only when they are implementing Union law', the Court asserted a broad interpretation of 'implementing Union law'.[13] Moreover, while the ECJ has recognised that if national measures are not entirely determined by Union law, national courts and authorities remain free to apply also national standards of protection of fundamental rights, this is only so provided that the level of protection provided for by the CFREU, and the primacy, unity and effectiveness of Union law are not compromised.[14] And more recently, the ECJ, in the context of upholding the principle of the rule of law, has gone beyond the confines set out by Article 51(1) CFREU in granting Article 19(1), second subparagraph, TEU relating to the principle of effective judicial protection a broader scope of application at national level than that of the Charter, although, at the same time, holding that in the interpretation of Article 19(1), second subparagraph, account should be taken of Article 47 CFREU.[15] Finally, there seems to be some application of the Charter by national courts even where its applicability is not strictly required by Article 51(1).[16] With all these developments, while the EU has no direct equivalent to the US 14th Amendment and the case law based on it, the situation in the EU with respect to the applicability of Union fundamental rights at national level seems to be approaching that of the US.

The above discussion has recalled certain EU constitutional developments, taking also into account some features of US constitutional history, without delving into the question of non-compliance with CJEU decisions. The purpose has been to suggest that for the sake of compliance versus non-compliance with EU judicial rulings, the stakes are quite high. Since the early 1950s, there has been a constant constitutional struggle about sovereignty, competencies and powers, making the Schuman vision of a European Federation a long and winding road indeed. The CJEU, notably the ECJ, as well as the national courts of the Member States, have found themselves entangled by this situation and have also, whether they like it or not, become important actors in this regard. The question of Union fundamental rights has been far from immune from this debate and has played an important part in the shaping of the EU constitutional structure.[17] Given the notoriously diverging views on the desired direction, forms and pace of European integration, one could expect considerable resistance to some of the Union Courts'

[13] Suffice it to mention CJEU, Case C-617/10 *Åkerberg Fransson* ECLI:EU:C:2013:105, paras 17–31. The Court referred, inter alia, to situations which are 'governed by Union law', 'fall within the scope of Union law' and entail the 'applicability of Union law'. See also A Rosas, 'The Applicability of the EU Charter of Fundamental Rights at National Level' (2013) 13 *European Yearbook of Human Rights* 97; S Peers et al (eds), *The EU Charter of Fundamental Rights: A Commentary* (Oxford, Hart Publishing, 2014) 1415–21; Rosas, 'Application of the EU Charter of Fundamental Rights (2024).

[14] CJEU, Case C-617/10 *Åkerberg Fransson* (see n 13 above), para 29; CJEU, Case C-399/11 *Melloni* ECLI:EU:C:2013:107, para 60.

[15] A Rosas, 'The Rule of Law and Judicial Independence: Recent EU Developments and Case Law of the European Court of Justice' in PB Donath et al (eds), *Der Schutz des Individuums durch das Recht: Festschrift für Rainer Hofmann zum 70. Geburtstag* (Berlin, Springer, 2023), Band 2, 919; Rosas, 'Application of the EU Charter of Fundamental Rights (2024).

[16] M Bobek and J Adams-Prassl (eds), *The EU Charter of Fundamental Rights in the Member States* (Oxford, Hart Publishing, 2020).

[17] The judgment in CJEU, Case C-29/69 *Stauder* (see n 9 above) was important not only for fundamental rights as such but also for defending the principle of primacy against national challenges, A Rosas, 'The European Court of Justice and Fundamental Rights: Yet Another Case of Judicial Activism?' in C Baudenbacher and H Bull (eds), *European Integration Through Interaction of Legal Regimes* (Oslo, Universitetsforlaget, 2007) 36–40.

rulings, both at the level of governments and political elites and national courts and authorities, thus posing a formidable challenge to the acceptance of the constitutional edifice following from the CJEU case law. It is to the question of non-compliance with that case law that I shall now turn.

2. Issues of Non-compliance

The question of compliance with CJEU rulings is above all a question of compliance with preliminary rulings, rendered by virtue of Article 267 TFEU. The Article 267 procedure is generally regarded as a success story.[18] It is undoubtedly one of the most important – if not the most important – mechanisms to ensure a uniform application and interpretation of Union law, including fundamental rights, and is, according to the ECJ, 'the keystone' of the EU judicial system.[19] Under this procedure national courts have a right, and in the case of courts of last instance, or also lower courts which nurture serious doubts as to the validity of a Union legal act, an obligation in principle to request a binding ruling on the interpretation of the Treaties or the validity or interpretation of Union legal acts. According to ECJ case law, the role of national courts follows directly from Article 267 and cannot be abrogated or limited by national law.[20] The Court has referred to the national courts and tribunals of the Member States as 'the guardians' of the Union legal order and the judicial system of the EU and as bodies which, in collaboration with the ECJ, '[fulfil] a duty entrusted to them both' of ensuring that in the interpretation and application of the Treaties the law is observed.[21] The national courts thus form an integral part of the Union judicial system.[22] In view of the principles of direct effect and primacy of EU law, taking into account also the principle of equality of Member States, national courts and other actors are bound by the preliminary rulings of the ECJ and may be called upon to disapply national provisions and decisions, including, as the case may be, judgments of constitutional courts, which are in violation of Union law, including CJEU rulings.[23]

Preliminary rulings, including when they deal with fundamental rights, are generally followed by the referring national courts.[24] Apart from considerations of

[18] The relevant literature is in abundance. Some examples: C Naomé, *Le renvoi préjudiciel en droit européen: Guide pratique* 2me édition (Bruxelles, Larcier, 2010); A Barav, *Judicial Enforcement and Implementation of European Union Law: Selected Writings* (Brussels, Bruylant, 2017) 291–349; M Broberg and N Fenger, *Preliminary Rulings to the European Court of Justice* 3rd rev edn (Oxford, Oxford University Press, 2021).

[19] See, eg, CJEU, Joined Cases C-558/18 and C-563/18 *Miasto Lowicz et al* ECLI:EU:C:2020:234, para 55.

[20] See, eg, CJEU, Case C-210/06, *Cartesio* ECLI:EU:C:2008;723, paras 88–98; CJEU, Joined Cases C-188/10 and C-189/10 *Abdeli and Melki* ECLI:EU:C:2010:363, paras 40–45; CJEU, Case C-614/14 *Ognyanov* ECLI:EU:C:2016:514, paras 14–26; CJEU, Joined Cases C-558/18 and C-563/18 *Miasto Lowicz et al* (see n 19 above), paras 55–59.

[21] CJEU, Opinion 1/09, *Creation of a unified patent litigation system* ECLI:EU:C:2011:123, paras 66 and 69.

[22] A Rosas, 'The National Judge as EU Judge: Opinion 1/09' in P Cardonnel, A Rosas and N Wahl (eds), *Constitutionalising the EU Judicial System* (Oxford, Hart Publishing, 2012) 105.

[23] As recent examples of an extensive case law may be mentioned CJEU, Joined Cases C-357/19, C-379/19, C-547/19, C-811/19 and C-840/19 *Euro Box Promotion* ECLI:EU:C:2021:1034 and CJEU, Case C-107/23 *Lin* ECLI:EU:C:2023:606.

[24] J Krommendijk, *National Courts and Preliminary References to the Court of Justice* (Cheltenham and Camberley, Edward Elgar, 2021) 142–157, 169 (study based primarily on the situation in Ireland, the Netherlands and the United Kingdom).

professional duty and responsibility, respecting a preliminary ruling is understandable already because it is the national court that decides on whether to make a referral[25] and it would be rather nonsensical for national courts generally to brush aside answers to questions they have put and formulated themselves. That said, national courts may, of course, sometimes be dissatisfied with the answers received from the ECJ or have doubts about their proper interpretation. Exceptionally, national courts may use the possibility offered by the ECJ Rules of Procedure to consider that a preliminary ruling does not give sufficient guidance and thus make a further reference to the ECJ.[26] Moreover, while the referring national court may comply with the ruling, other courts, including courts of other Member States, as well as political circles or administrative authorities may have doubts or voice outright opposition to ECJ rulings.

By and large, the degree of compliance with preliminary rulings case law can be considered as at least satisfactory, taking also into account that the case law sometimes provides answers to much debated questions of great constitutional significance and deals with areas that have been traditionally associated with national sovereignty, such as direct taxation and criminal law. The cases are quite rare where, with a view to nullifying the effects of a preliminary ruling, Member States have amended the Treaties or the Union legislator has amended secondary law (as is the case with regard to fundamental rights, it has often been the other way around, that is, amendments to the Treaties or secondary law have rather been designed to incorporate developments in case law).[27] Seen from these perspectives, and compared to the US situation especially during the first 80 or so years of the Constitution,[28] the degree of compliance with ECJ rulings could even be regarded as a small miracle.

It goes without saying that all has not been smooth sailing, however. The instances where national constitutional or supreme courts have refused to comply with an ECJ ruling or challenged EU law more generally are rare but constitutionally significant.[29] The examples of the Czech Constitutional Court,[30] the Danish Supreme Court,[31] the

[25] See, eg, Recommendations to national courts and tribunals in relation to the initiation of preliminary ruling proceedings issued by the ECJ [2019] OJ C 380/3, para 3.

[26] Article 104(2) of the Rules of Procedure of the Court of Justice of 25 September 2012 (2012) OJ L 265/1, with subsequent amendments.

[27] Rosas and Armati, *EU Constitutional Law* (2018) 46–48. See also Rosas, 'The European Court of Justice' (2007). As for Treaty or legislative developments qualifying or limiting the effect of judgments rendered by Union Courts see, eg, Protocol No 2 concerning Article 119 of the TEC (now 157 TFEU), qualifying the judgment of the ECJ in Case C-262/88 *Barber* ECLI:EU:C:1990:209, and the series of amendments to Council Regulation (EEC) No 1408/71 on the application of social security schemes to persons moving within the Union. As for Treaty or legislative developments incorporating case law on fundamental rights see, eg, the Preamble to the Charter of Fundamental Rights of the EU where it explains that it reaffirms rights as they result, among other well-known sources, from 'the case-law of the Court of Justice of the European Union …'.

[28] See nn 1–3 above.

[29] See, eg, A Rosas, 'EU Law and National Law: A Common Legal System' (2024) *EUI Academy of European Law Working Paper* ch 4.2.

[30] Judgment of 31 January 2012, File No US 5/11. The ECJ judgment not complied with was given in CJEU, Case C-399/09 *Landtová* ECLI:EU:C:2011:415.

[31] Judgment of 6 December 2016, Case 15/2014 (First Chamber). The relevant ECJ judgment was given in CJEU, Case C-441/14 *Ajos* ECLI:EU:C:2016:278.

German Federal Constitutional Court[32] and the Romanian Constitutional Court[33] may be mentioned here. The most well-known case is the German Federal Constitutional Court's judgment of 5 May 2020 to declare a European Central Bank decision and the ECJ judgment in Weiss ultra vires.[34] This judgment, despite a later decision declaring that the judgment had been sufficiently complied with, was met by an infringement action initiated by the European Commission.[35] The action was withdrawn after the German Government had reaffirmed its adherence to the principles of autonomy, primacy, effectiveness and uniform application of Union law and the view that the legality of Union acts can only be reviewed by the CJEU.[36] The German Government in fact acted in line with Declaration No 17 concerning Primacy, annexed to the Final Act of the Intergovernmental Conference which adopted the Lisbon Treaty.[37] This consensus document provides an unconditional reaffirmation of primacy, adding that, 'in accordance with well-settled case law of the [CJEU]', Union law has primacy over the law of Member States, under the conditions laid down by the said case law.[38]

Despite Polish adherence to the Declaration by the Intergovernmental Conference of 2007, the Polish Government in power between 2016 and December 2023 began to contest the primacy of Union law over the national Constitution. The Polish Constitutional Tribunal followed suite and held that some provisions of the EU Treaties, including Articles 1 and 19(1) TEU, were incompatible with the Constitution.[39] In December 2021, the Commission launched an infringement action, considering that the decisions of the Tribunal were in breach of the general principles of autonomy, primacy, effectiveness and uniform application of Union law and the binding effects of the rulings of the CJEU.[40] The new Polish Government, in power since December 2023, has adopted

[32] See, eg, the judgment of 30 June 2010 on the constitutionality of the Lisbon Treaty, BVerfGE 2 BvE 2/08; judgment of 21 June 2016 asserting a right to declare ECJ judgments non-applicable in Germany, BVerfGE 2 BvR 2728/13 (relating to the ECJ judgment in Case C-62/14 *Gauweiler and Others* ECLI:EU:C:2015:400); judgment of 5 May 2020 declaring an ECJ judgment ultra vires, BVerfGE 2 BvR 859/15 (relating to CJEU, Case C-493/17 *Weiss and Others* ECLI:EU:C:2018:1000).

[33] See, eg, Decision No 390/2021, as referred to by RM Popescu and RH Rada, 'Romania' in A Kornezov (ed), *Mutual Trust, Mutual Recognition and the Rule of Law: The XXX FIDE Congress in Sofia 2023 Congress Publications* Vol I (Sofia, Ciela Norma, 2023) 596. See also Joined Cases C-357/19, C-379/19, C-547/19, C-811/19 and C-840/19 *Euro Box Promotion* (see n 23 above) and P Filipek and M Taborowski, 'Decoding the Euro Box Promotion Case: Independence of Constitutional Courts, Equality of States, and the Clash in Judicial Standards in View of the Principle of Primacy' (2024) *Common Market Law Review* 831; CJEU, Case C-107/23, *Lin* (see n 23 above).

[34] See n 32 above.

[35] See Commission Press Release of 9 June 2021.

[36] See the Commission's observations on a petition to the European Parliament, Petition No 0634/2021, European Parliament, Committee on Petitions, Notice to Members of 3 March 2022.

[37] TFEU, Declarations annexed to the Final Act of the Intergovernmental Conference which adopted the Treaty of Lisbon, Declaration No 17 concerning Primacy [2008] OJ C 115/344. The Declaration is cited in CJEU, Case C-357/19 et al *Euro Box Promotion and Others* (see n 23 above), para 248; CJEU, Case C-430/21 *RS* ECLI:EU:C:2022;99, para 4.

[38] On the principle of primacy in general and relevant case law, see Rosas and Armati, *EU Constitutional Law* (2018) 64–68.

[39] Decisions of the Constitutional Tribunal of 14 July and 7 October 2021. The Government's position is reported, eg, in the judgment in CJEU, Case C-204/21 *Commission v Poland* ECLI:EU:C:2023:442, paras 60–61. See also, C Ladenburger, Y Marinova and J Tomkin, 'Institutional Report' in Kornezov, *Mutual Trust* (2023) 150–51.

[40] Commission Press Release of 22 December 2021.

a different approach to the status of Union law in Poland, including the relevance and status of CJEU decisions, and it is to be hoped that the principle of primacy and the binding nature of CJEU decisions will once again be fully recognised in the context of the Polish constitutional order.

Apart from such open challenges to the primacy of Union law and the binding effect of the decisions of the CJEU, there is a more subtle way of avoiding the effects of such decisions. While, as stated above, the record of compliance on the part of national courts is by and large satisfactory, there will be no concrete decision to comply with if the national court, including a court of last instance, simply declines to refer a case to the ECJ. The overall inclination of national courts to refer cases varies between different Member States and different courts.[41] The application of the CFREU by national courts still seems wanting.[42] While the differences are partly due to structural factors such as population size, there also seems to be differences in the willingness of courts to turn to the ECJ. Reluctance may sometimes be due to a wish to avoid an anticipated answer based on Union law. In *Consorzio*, the ECJ clarified that courts of last instance have an obligation to state reasons for a decision not to refer.[43] Infringement actions under Article 258 TFEU may be instigated against a Member State whose courts of last instance are in breach of the requirement to refer under Article 267.[44] The possible ways and means of improving the situation will be discussed in Part 3 below.

Finally, a few words should be said about compliance with ECJ judgments in infringement procedures based on Article 258 and 259 TFEU.[45] As can be seen from the number of cases leading to the application of Article 260 TFEU and thus financial sanctions in view of non-compliance with an ECJ judgment, while most judgments finding a failure to fulfil an obligation under Union law appear to be executed, non-compliance with the first judgment does occur from time to time.[46] In sensitive areas such as in the recent cases concerning respect for the rule of law, including judicial independence, initiating infringement proceedings by the Commission, and in case of ECJ judgments finding failure to fulfil an obligation, compliance with such findings shows a haphazard picture.[47]

[41] M Broberg and N Fenger, 'Variations in Member States' Preliminary References to the Court of Justice: Are Structural Factors (Part of) the Explanation?' (2013) 19 *European Law Journal* 488. On possible motives behind national judges' decisions to refer see also T Pavone and RD Kelemen, 'The Evolving Judicial Politics of European Integration: The European Court of Justice and National Courts Revisited' (2019) 25 *European Law Journal* 352; K Leijon, 'National Courts and Preliminary References: Supporting Legal Integration, Protecting National Autonomy or Balancing Conflicting Demands' (2020) 44 *West European Politics* 510; Krommendijk, *National Courts and Preliminary References* (2021).

[42] Bobek and Adams-Prassl, *The EU Charter* (2020).

[43] CJEU, Case C-561/19 ECLI:EU:C:2021:799, para 51.

[44] CJEU, Case C-416/17 *Commission v France* ECLI:EU:C:2018:811; CJEU, Case C-516/22 *Commission v UK* ECIL:EU:C:2024:231.

[45] On infringement procedures in general see, eg, T Materne, *La procédure en manquement d'État: Guide à la lumière de la jurisprudence de la Cour de justice de l'Union européenne* (Bruxelles, Larcier, 2012); L Prete and B Smulders, 'The Age of Maturity of Infringement Proceedings' (2021) 58 *Common Market Law Review* 267.

[46] Materne, *La procédure en manquement* (2021) 358–62, provides a list of 13 Article 260 cases leading to a judgment in the period between 2000 and September 2011.

[47] J Heliskoski, 'Infringement Proceedings as a Tool for Enforcing the Rule of Law in EU Member States: A Critical Review' in A Rosas, J Raitio and P Pohjankoski (eds), *The Rule of Law's Anatomy in the EU: Foundations and Protections* (Oxford, Hart Publishing, 2023) 139.

According to ECJ case law, financial sanctions may consist of both a lump sum ('fines' for past behaviour) and a penalty payment (to be paid periodically and calculated to induce the Member State in question to put an end to the breach).[48] Article 260 TFEU does not provide any fixed lower or upper limit for the amounts but case law and Commission practice establish criteria to be taken into account, such as capacity to pay, the seriousness of the infringement and respect for the principle of proportionality.[49] The amounts to be paid, which for the lump sums have been at most in the range of tens of millions euro and for the penalty payments at most in the range of hundreds of thousand euro (in case of daily payments),[50] have been modest when taking into account the overall capacity of a Member State to pay.[51]

To what extent, if any, could the infringement procedure, including the Article 260 procedure, be used also against systemic infringements, including disrespect for the rule of law and fundamental rights, as recognised under Article 2 TEU in particular?[52] This possibility as well as the consequences of failure to pay the lump sum and penalty payment as ordered, will be further considered in the following and final subchapter.

3. Remedies: A Multifaceted Approach

While the situation of compliance with CJEU decisions is far better than the corresponding situation in the early days of US constitutionalism, the picture in the EU is far from ideal. Preliminary rulings are generally complied with rather well but the – admittedly few – examples of national constitutional and supreme courts refusing to accept fully, or even opposing, the principle of primacy and/or complying with ECJ rulings are important flies in the ointment. Moreover, some national courts demonstrate a reluctance to refer issues of Union law to the ECJ and such reluctance seems at least partly to be due to a willingness to avoid an anticipated ruling from the ECJ.

Infringement actions against Member States whose courts of last instance do not comply with Article 267 TFEU may offer some help.[53] The case law of the European

[48] CJEU, Case C-304/02 *Commission v France* ECLI:EU:C:2005:444.

[49] See, eg, Updating of data used to calculate lump sum and penalty payments to be proposed by the Commission to the Court of Justice of the European Union in infringement proceedings, Communication from the Commission [2022] OJ C 74/02.

[50] For a recent example, see CJEU, Case C-147/23 *Commission v Poland* ECLI:EU:C:2024:346 (lump sum of EUR 7 million and daily penalty payment of EUR 40.000). But see the Order of the Vice-President of the CJEU in Case C-204/21 R *Commission v Poland* ECLI:EU:C:2021:878 ordering Poland to pay a periodic penalty payment of EUR 1 million per day for failure to respect an Interim Order of the Vice-President of the Court.

[51] P Pohjankoski, 'Rule of Law with Leverage: Policing Structural Obligations in EU Law with the Infringement Procedure, Fines, and Set-off' (2021) 58 *Common Market Law Review* 1341, 1355–56.

[52] This possibility has been used with respect to Hungary and Poland, in particular. For recent examples see CJEU, Case C-769/22 *Commission v Hungary* (pending) [2023] OJ C 54/19, and Commission Letter of Formal Notice to Hungary of 7 February 2024, INFR(2024)2001, concerning a new Law on the Defence of National Sovereignty, Commission Press Release of 7 February 2024, February infringement package: key decisions; CJEU, Case C-204/21 *Commission v Poland* ECLI:EU:C:2023:442 and case law referred to. See also Pohjankoski, 'Rule of Law with Leverage' (2021).

[53] CJEU, Case C-416/17 *Commission v France* (see n 44 above) and CJEU, Case C-516/22 *Commission v UK* (see n 44 above) are the only cases so far which have resulted in a judgment of the ECJ finding a violation of Article 267.

Court of Human Rights (ECtHR), according to which failure to give reasons for refusal to refer under Article 267 TFEU may result in a violation of Article 6 ECHR provides additional support for efforts to increase compliance with Article 267.[54] The above-mentioned ECJ judgment in *Consorzio*,[55] confirms that also according to EU law, there is an obligation to provide reasons for a refusal to refer. This tendency could be further strengthened by EU accession to the ECHR.[56] At the very end of the day, and in a long-term perspective, the most effective and sustainable solution would be various measures such as enhancing teaching and training of judges and future judges with a view to strengthening an awareness, by national courts, of their role as EU courts.

Judgments of the ECJ finding a failure to fulfil an obligation under Union law are generally respected but there are several instances where the Commission has initiated proceedings under Article 260, proposing financial sanctions for non-compliance, followed by the imposition by the ECJ of a lump sum and penalty payment. In sensitive areas, such as the rule of law and fundamental rights, instances of Commission passivity abound, however.[57]

It is argued here that infringement actions under Article 258 should be increasingly seen as a remedy to address systemic failures, including in sensitive areas such as the rule of law, democracy and fundamental rights, and that such a trend can already be discerned in Commission practice and ECJ case law. Article 2 TEU lists the values on which the Union is founded, such as democracy, the rule of law and respect for human rights and confirms that these values are also common to the Member States. There seems to be no reason why this key provision of Union law could not constitute the ground for an infringement action, be it that to find a violation of that provision, failure to uphold one of the values listed should be of a particularly serious and manifest nature.[58] It is true that by now, the contours and content of the principle of the rule of law, as expressed in Article 2, have been further clarified, inter alia, by other provisions of primary law (notably Article 19(1) TEU and Article 47 of the Charter), CJEU case law as well as Union legislation such as the new Conditionality Regulation,[59] so that infringement actions could in many cases be based on those

[54] See, eg, ECtHR, App no 4832/04 *Vergauwen v Belgium* ECLI:CE:ECHR:2012:0410DEC000483204; ECtHR, App no 17120/09 *Dhabi v Italy* ECLI:CE:ECHR:2014:0408JUD001712009; ECtHR, App no 55385/14 *Baydar v the Netherlands* ECLI:CE:ECHR:2018:0424JUD005538514; ECtHR, App no 43639/17 *Bio Farmland Betriebs v Romania* ECLI:CE:ECHR:2021:0713JUD004363917; ECtHR, App no 57378/18 *Georgiou v Greece* ECLI:CE:ECHR:2023:0314JUD005737818. See also S Lindroos-Hovinheimo, 'ECtHR Finds Violation of the Right to Fair Trial When National Court Does Not Seek Preliminary Ruling from the CJEU' (*European Law Blog*, 28 March 2023) www.europeanlawblog.eu/pub/ecthr-finds-violation-of-the-right-to-fair-trial-when-national-court-does-not-seek-preliminary-ruling-from-the-cjeu/release/1 accessed 3 June 2025.

[55] CJEU, Case C-561/19 (see n 42 above).

[56] See, eg Council of Europe, Steering Committee for Human Rights (CDDH), Report to the CDDH by the CDDH Ad Hoc Negotiation Group ('46 + 1') on the Accession of the [EU] to the [ECHR], 46 + 1 (223) 35 FINAL, 30 March 2023.

[57] Heliskoski, 'Infringement Proceedings' (2023) 141–47.

[58] In its action in CJEU, Case C-769/22, *Commission v Hungary* (see n 50 above) pending, the Commission refers to a violation of Article 2 TEU, as a ground separate from alleged violations of secondary Union legal acts.

[59] Regulation (EU, Euratom) 2020/2092 of the European Parliament and of the Council on a general regime of conditionality for the protection of the Union budget [2020] OJ L 4331/1.

more detailed provisions. With respect to systemic and serious breaches of the values listed in Article 2 TEU, including the principle of democracy,[60] infringement actions based on that Article alone, seem feasible.[61]

With regard to the effectiveness of infringement actions more generally, a necessary tool to enhance the effectiveness of Article 260 proceedings would be the imposition of considerable financial sanctions in lieu of the mostly symbolic amounts of lump sums and penalty payments applied so far. And such sanctions are reduced to gesture politics if failure to pay the amounts ordained by the CJEU is not met by off-setting the amounts due with the sums owed by the EU to the Member State concerned.[62]

There are, of course, many other ways and means to improve compliance with Union law, including compliance with CJEU decisions. To mention but two mechanisms, Article 7 TEU enables the suspension of membership rights if there has been a serious and persistent breach of the values referred to in Article 2 TEU and the above-mentioned Conditionality Regulation together with other EU legislation enables, inter alia, the suspension of payments and commitments and the suspension of reduction of the economic advantage under an instrument guaranteed by the Union budget.[63] As is well-known, the suspension of membership rights under Article 7 TEU is hamstrung by the requirement of unanimity for a determination, by the European Council, of the existence of a serious and persistent breach of EU values.[64] With respect to Poland, the Commission, and with respect to Hungary, the European Parliament, have nevertheless activated the Article 7 procedure and already this measure has played a certain role in Council practice and ECJ and national case law.[65] As to conditionality, large amounts due to these two countries have been blocked and some funds remain frozen, with respect to Hungary in particular.[66] The relevance of this instrument is limited by the requirement of a direct link between breaches of the rule of law and the protection of the EU budget.

For the improvement of compliance with CJEU decisions and Union law more generally, there is no silver bullet and no quick fixes. All the measures outlined above should be used in parallel. There is no need for creating a separate mechanism for fundamental rights, which are an integral part of Union law. With respect to CJEU rulings, the current situation is far from catastrophic and, as noted above, far better than during the first 80 years of US constitutionalism and arguably also better than in the earlier days

[60] See also Title II (Provisions on Democratic Principles, Articles 9 to 12) of the TEU.

[61] Heliskoski, 'Infringement Proceedings' (2023) is more sceptical to the use of Article 2 TEU on a stand-alone basis. For a more profound discussion on this point the reader is referred to the literature mentioned by Heliskoski, 146–49.

[62] Pohjankoski, 'Rule of Law with Leverage' (2021) 1358–63.

[63] On such budget conditionality see P Pohjankoski, 'Of Carrots and Sticks: Constitutional Limits to Rule-of-Law Conditionality' in Rosas, Raitio and Pohjankoski, *The Rule of Law's Anatomy* (2023) 157.

[64] See Article 7(2) TEU.

[65] S Bogojevic and X Groussot, 'Illiberal Democracy and Rule by Law from an EU Perspective' in Rosas, Raitio and Pohjankoski, *The Rule of Law's Anatomy* (2023) 52–54.

[66] See, eg, F Baccini, 'European Parliament Continues to Call for Suspension of Hungary's Membership Rights' (*eu news*, 17 January 2024) www.eunews.it/en/2024/01/17/european-parliament-continues-to-call-for-suspension-of-hungarys-membership-rights/ accessed 24 April 2025.

of European integration. Taking into account the sensitive nature of some of the cases that come before the CJEU, the degree of compliance with its decisions could perhaps even be considered as surprisingly good. Only the future can tell if there will be sufficient political and judicial will to use the various instruments and mechanisms outlined above with a view to improving the situation further. The protection of fundamental rights would surely benefit from such a development.

PART VII

Conclusion

21

Exploring the Judicial Systems of the ECtHR and the CJEU Side by Side: Looking Beyond Differences

ELISE MUIR [1]

1. Introduction

1.1. Exploring the Judicial Systems of the ECtHR and the CJEU Side by Side

Today, two European courts play an active role in the protection of human and fundamental rights in Europe. Both find their origin in the aftermaths of the second world war, that created an environment uniquely conducive to the establishment of supra-national institutions. The present book is based on the assumption that the time has come to examine the procedural features of each of these judicial systems side by side. That is so because the respective work of these two courts has come to significantly overlap. The first court, the story is well known, is the European Court of Human Rights (ECtHR). It was created as part of the Council of Europe, a pan-European organisation established after the Hague Congress in 1948 aiming to contribute to 'the achievement of greater unity between its members'.[2] The ECtHR aims to pursue 'the maintenance and further realization of Human Rights and Fundamental Freedoms',[3] making human rights its very *raison d'être*.

The second European-level court that interprets 'fundamental rights', is the Court of Justice of the European Union (CJEU). The scale of this engagement of the CJEU's with fundamental rights remains largely underestimated.[4] The role of the CJEU is to 'ensure

[1] This contribution is part of the RESHUFFLE research project hosted by KU Leuven and supported by the European Research Council (European Union's Horizon 2020 research and innovation programme, grant agreement No 851621). I am very grateful to Jasper Krommendijk and Sacha Garben for helpful comments on an earlier draft, the usual disclaimer applies.

[2] ECHR, 4.XI.1950, Preamble (3), original text, unchanged.

[3] ibid, Preamble (3), original text, unchanged.

[4] See for instance the empirical (quantitative) study by E Frantziou, finding that that 30% of the preliminary references in the 2019–2023 period contained a human rights dimension, compared to 17% in the 1957–2023 period. E Frantziou, 'Human Rights as an Example of Cooperative Federalism? A Chronology of the Use of the Preliminary Reference Procedure in Human Rights Cases Between 1957 and 2023' (2023) 15 *European Journal of Legal Studies* 189.

that in the interpretation and application of the Treaties the law is observed'.[5] While the said Treaties[6] have always had as their aim to contribute to the 'process of creating an ever closer union among the peoples of Europe'[7] in pursuit of peace, this ideal was initially operationalised through economic integration[8] with fundamental rights coming into play in a somewhat more incidental way.[9] The duty on EU organs, Member States within the fields covered by Union law, and individuals in certain settings regulated by Union law, to comply with fundamental rights has been progressively asserted and is now well documented.[10] Yet today, the EU has expanded its action to several particularly fundamental rights-sensitive policy domains,[11] has a written and legally binding Charter of Fundamental Rights of the EU (CFREU) with a value equal to the Treaties,[12] and is explicitly founded on the 'values of respect for human dignity, freedom, democracy, equality, the rule of law and respect for human rights, including the rights of persons belonging to minorities'. Those values are an 'integral part of the very identity of the European Union as a common legal order'[13] as well as common to the Member States.[14]

While the ECtHR uses the language of 'human rights', the CJEU primarily uses the language of 'fundamental rights'; these terms largely overlap for our purpose here.[15] As the ECtHR and the CJEU are increasingly called upon to interpret corresponding rights,[16] the stakes of the co-existence of these two Courts intensify. What makes the interactions between the courts particularly salient today, is the remarkably powerful and broad engagement of EU political institutions, through the legislative process, executive activity as well as in international relations, with fundamental rights-sensitive policy areas. This ranges from the regulation of artificial intelligence, political advertising, international protection of migrants, to anti-discrimination in access to housing[17] to give but a few recent salient examples. The two courts may cope

[5] Article 19(1), para 1 TEU (see Article 164 Treaty establishing the European Economic Community, 1957).

[6] Now, Treaty on European Union (TEU) and Treaty on the Functioning of the European Union (TFEU).

[7] Article 1, para 2 TEU; see also Treaty establishing the European Economic Community (1957), Preamble (1).

[8] Article 2 of the Treaty establishing the European Economic Community (1957).

[9] As is well-known, the Court of Justice initially developed its doctrine of fundamental rights as general principles of Community law as a necessary corollary to its primacy doctrine: CJEU, Case C-11/70 *Internationale Handelsgesellschaft* ECLI:EU:C:1970:114.

[10] See, eg, M Dawson, *The Governance of EU Fundamental Rights* (Cambridge, Cambridge University Press, 2017); C Rizcallah, *The European Union and Human Rights. Understanding a Singular Regional Player* (Hart publishing, forthcoming in open access).

[11] The EU has evolved much since its inception, to the effect that, 'to promote peace, its values and the well-being of its peoples', it shall first of all 'offer its citizens an area of freedom, security and justice without internal frontiers' (see Article 3(1) and (2) TEU).

[12] Article 6(1) TEU.

[13] CJEU, Case C-156/21 *Hungary v European Parliament and Council* ECLI:EU:C:2022:97, para 127.

[14] Article 2 TEU (2007).

[15] EU primary law also refers to human rights; examples include Article 2 TEU, Article 3(5) TEU, Article 21(1) TEU, see also Article 53 CFREU. Such references refer to sources of protection applicable at the level of international law, the language of the Charter of fundamental rights of the EU which has the same legal value as the EU Treaties, and specifically identified as such by Article 6(1), para 1 TEU, is that of fundamental rights.

[16] This was anticipated by Article 52(3) CFREU on corresponding rights indeed.

[17] See, eg, CJEU, Case C-417/23 *Slagelse Almennyttige Boligselskab, Afdeling Schackenborgvænge*, Opinion of Advocate General Ćapeta ECLI:EU:C:2025:98.

with their increasingly overlapping mandates by explicitly referring to one another,[18] through subtle forms of reasoning,[19] or not at all.[20] The related interpretation of rights may converge, as has been praised in relation to case law of each Courts on the independence of the judiciary,[21] or diverge, as is often regretted on matters of mutual trust.[22] As the Court of Justice itself has noted, the Charter is, like the Convention, 'a living instrument'.[23] Both systems for the protection of human and fundamental rights 'must be interpreted in the light of present-day conditions and of the ideas prevailing in democratic States today'.[24] There is therefore little doubt that, despite their differences and those of the legal orders they belong to as identified in chapter one, there is much added value today in examining closely the respective strengths and weaknesses of each of these judicial systems side by side.

1.2. The Elephant in the Book: The EU's Accession to the ECtHR

Precisely because the interplay between the two legal and judicial systems is intensifying, the persistent lack of an organic link between them may seem puzzling. One way of bridging the gap, which has attracted much attention in the past decades, would be for the EU to accede to the Convention for the Protection of Human Rights and Fundamental Freedoms (ECHR). In a first Opinion on the matter, the Court of Justice considered that under the Treaties as they stood after Maastricht, there was no competence for the EU to accede.[25] The Lisbon Treaty seemingly addressed the problem. Article 6(2) TEU indeed now contains not only a competence, but actually a duty, for the EU to accede to the ECtHR. As is well known, after the contracting parties on both sides, the Council of Europe and the EU, had found a compromise on an accession agreement back in 2013, the CJEU rendered a negative Opinion for the second time. In its Opinion 2/13,[26] the CJEU identified several points of tension between the draft accession agreement and EU primary law.

[18] For an example of the CJEU referring to the ECtHR, see CJEU, Case C-633/22,*Real Madrid Club de Fútbol en AE tegen EE en Société Éditrice du Monde SA* ECLI:EU:C:2024:843, paras 52–53 on freedom of expression.

[19] For an example of the ECtHR referring to the CJEU, see ECtHR, App nos 53282/18 and 31428/20 *Moraru and Marin v Romania* ECLI:CE:ECHR:2022:1220JUD005328218, para 119 on sex discrimination.

[20] For an example of the CJEU developing an autonomous interpretation of a fundamental right: CJEU, Case C-524/15 *Criminal proceedings against Luca Menci* ECLI:EU:C:2018:197, paras 23–24 on the right not to be tried or punished twice in criminal proceedings for the same criminal offence.

[21] For instance, Koen Lenaerts, borrowing from the former President of the ECtHR, has referred to 'a symbiotic relationship': R Spano, 'The Rule of Law as the Lodestar of the European Convention on Human Rights: The Strasbourg Court and the Independence of the Judiciary' (2021) *European Law Journal* 1, 13; K Lenaerts, 'On Checks and Balances: the Rule of Law within the EU' (2023) *Columbia Law Journal* 2, 29.

[22] For a recent iteration of key concerns in the field see: J Callewaert, 'L'adhésion de l'Union européenne à la Convention européenne des droits de l'homme: une réponse logique à l'optionalité de la Convention européenne des droits de l'homme en droit de l'Union européenne' (2025) 141 *Revue trimestrielle des droits de l'homme* 9, 17–18.

[23] CJEU, Case C-336/19 *Centraal Israëlitisch Consistorie van België and Others* ECLI:EU:C:2020:1031, para 77.

[24] ibid. Drawing an analogy with see, by analogy, ECtHR (GC), App no 23459/03 *Bayatyan v Armenia* ECLI:CE:ECHR:2011:0707JUD002345903, para 102 and the case law cited.

[25] CJEU, Opinion 2/94 ECLI:EU:C:1996:140.

[26] CJEU, Opinion 2/13 *Accession of the European Union to the ECHR* ECLI:EU:C:2014:2454.

Using the detailed reasoning of the CJEU in that opinion as a roadmap, the negotiators have now proposed technical solutions to all problems save one.[27] The one outstanding issue relates to the jurisdiction of both courts over the Common Foreign and Security Policy (CFSP) of the EU. The CJEU ruled in Opinion 2/13 that the draft agreement failed to have regard to the specific characteristics of EU law with regard to the judicial review of EU acts, actions or omissions on the part of the EU in CFSP matters. Indeed, as the EU Treaties do not grant jurisdiction to the CJEU over these acts, the draft agreement would have entrusted such judicial review exclusively to a non-EU body.[28] The negotiators agreed in 2023, that that specific issue was for the EU only to address.[29] In September 2024, the CJEU rendered a ruling in which it adopted a novel approach to the limits of its jurisdiction in matters of CFSP that may be read as addressing this ultimate obstacle.[30] The Court specified that, are outside the scope of its jurisdiction, only 'acts and omissions [which] are directly related to … political or strategic choices [made by the institutions, bodies, offices and agencies of the Union in the context of the CFSP, and in particular the CSDP]'.[31] The CJEU also stressed that, in its view, the ECtHR does not either exercise judicial review on these matters.[32] As a result, the CJEU noted that its approach to the right to an effective remedy in the field is compatible with the case law of the ECtHR.[33]

Read together, the existence of a revised draft agreement addressing all but one concern identified by the CJEU in Opinion 2/13, and the recent ruling in *KS and KD* presumably addressing this last concern, may have paved the way for the EU's accession to the ECHR at last. Irrespective of the uncertainties created by the new approach developed by the CJEU in *KS and KD*, these recent developments may allow the Commission to ask again for an Opinion from the CJEU on compatibility of the new draft with EU primary law.[34] Should that happen, and should the outcome be positive, as is likely to be the case given the great attention paid by the negotiators to the requirements put forward by the CJEU Opinion 2/13 as well as that same Court's novel approach on the CFSP, the agreement will only enter into force after it has been approved by the Member States in accordance with their respective constitutional requirements.[35]

The process of accession by the EU to the ECHR is thus not a purely theoretical prospect any more. Yet, it will still take time and, importantly, irrespective of the state of advancement of the accession process, the interactions between the two Courts are alive and kicking already. These interactions would be placed into a specifically designed

[27] Steering Committee for Human Rights (CDDH)Ad Hoc Negotiation Group and the European Commission on the Accession of the European Union to the European Convention on Human Rights, 'Final consolidated version of the draft accession instruments', 17 March 2023.

[28] CJEU, Opinion 2/13 *Accession of the European Union to the ECHR* ECLI:EU:C:2014:2454, paras 249–58.

[29] 18th Meeting of the CDDH Ad Hoc Negotiation Group ('46+1') on the Accession of the European Union to the European Convention on Human Rights, 'Meeting Report' (14–17 March 2023), para 7.

[30] CJEU, Case C-29/22 P *KS and KD v Council of the European Union and Others* ECLI:EU:C:2024:725.

[31] ibid, paras 116–17.

[32] ibid, para 78.

[33] ibid, para 77.

[34] See, including critical reflections on these recent developments: Editorial comment, 'From Opinion 2/13 to KS and KD: Confronting a Legacy of Constitutional Tensions' (2024) 61 *Common Market Law Review* 1455 and T Lock, 'Implications of the Revised Draft EU Accession Agreement for the ECHR' (2025) 6 *European Convention on Human Rights Law Review* 65.

[35] Article 218(8) TFEU.

procedural framework by an agreement on accession, but the general features of each judicial system and the key dynamics of their interactions are not strictly dependent on the existence of such a highly symbolic Treaty. The accession process is thus best understood as an important component, yet a component only, of a broader process of tectonic of plates through which the interplays between the organs of the Council of Europe, the EU, and their respective Member States are steadily increasing.

1.3. A Bridging Exercise

It is to this broader tectonic of plates that this book has been devoted. It consisted in a collective investigation of the key features of two increasingly substantively overlapping supra-national judicial systems, each with their own procedures and institutional idiosyncrasies, and with their own epistemic communities of practitioners and scholars. The two Courts perform different functions,[36] and this translates in important procedural differences. Yet, today, the two judicial systems each feature different procedural mechanisms that allow, at least to some extent, for the activation of human and fundamental rights protection.[37] As noted by Síofra O'Leary, while the systems differ, 'the universality and indivisibility of the human rights and fundamental freedoms which they both seek to protect … is central to their effective protection within Europe's multi-level system for the protection of human rights'.[38]

This book thus asked: *What are the respective strengths and weaknesses of the web of procedural rules that allows to activate protection by each of these two Courts?* The related bridging exercise called for highlighting similarities as much as differences with a view to shedding light on possible complementarities, potential for cross-fertilisation as well as to better understand the respective limits of each system. Responding to Síofra O'Leary's observation that expertise in the law of the Convention and in EU law 'remains surprisingly fragmented',[39] this book has sought to bring experts from the two fields together and this Chapter more specifically seeks to bridge between their respective input.

In these concluding words, we first take a step back to place emphasis on the common general features of the emerging dual system of protection of rights in Europe. In Section 2, it is indeed recalled that, with the passing of time, the right of individuals to access justice has become one of the keystones, if not *the* keystone, of the two judicial systems. Although each of them is constructed very differently, it will be shown that both seek in their own ways to consolidate individual's access to justice. It will also be argued that the focus on individual litigation has a number of key institutional implications, such as calls for greater representation of public interests and the central role of

[36] Chapter 1.

[37] On the procedural dimension of the ECHR, see for instance J Gerards, AC Buyse and M Andenas, 'Heads and Tails. Admissibility and Remedies at the European Court of Human Rights' (2024) 5 *European Convention of Human Rights Law Review* 291; on EU procedural law see generally K Lenaerts, I Maselis and K Gutman, *EU Procedural Law* (Oxford, Oxford University Press, 2014) and on fundamental rights specifically see, eg, D Krotov and F Kupsch, 'Poking the Bear or Waking the Sleeping Beauty? The Potential of Fundamental Rights Complaint Procedures Before the CJEU' in A Heger, M Malkmus (eds), *On the Relation between the EU Charter of Fundamental Rights and National Fundamental Rights* (Cham, Springer, 2024).

[38] See ch 2.

[39] See ch 2.

national judges, that raise similar challenges in each of the two systems, and result in distinct yet related types of responses.

The chapter further contextualises the current challenges faced by each of the two courts. An examination of the current system of human and fundamental rights protection in Europe cannot ignore the enormously challenging environment in which it operates. In Section 3, we therefore map out some of these key contemporary challenges, and the way they have been understood by the contributors to this book as threats to the systems under scrutiny, before examining the responsiveness of the European systems of protection. It will be argued that there may still be much space for further exploring the complementarities between the two systems, and to enhance awareness of the respective role of the two courts in the European system for the protection of human and fundamental rights.

2. Individuals' Access to Justice as Keystones of European Human and Fundamental Rights Justice

The various chapters brought together in this book either took as granted, or explored the limits of, the importance of individuals' access to justice in both judicial systems. Even if structured differently in each of the two judicial systems, and if EU law actually has a system of 'dual vigilance'[40] allowing public organs to also enforce EU law to which we will come back below,[41] this fundamental premise is very strong in each of them and acts as a common denominator of both systems (2.1). In the Convention system, this is a natural consequence of the anchorage of human rights law in human dignity in Europe's post-second world war era: it must always be possible for each individual to have access to a judge, so as to activate one's most basic rights. In the EU system, the importance of individual's access to a court of law results from the long-standing commitment of the EU to confer rights and obligations not only on States but also on individuals. This common attachment to individuals' access to justice has two key implications evidenced in this book (2.2): public interests organisations will struggle to be represented and heard before the European Courts, and the national judge is at the crossroads between the two judicial systems.

2.1. Access to an Effective Judicial System for Individuals as a Common Denominator

Each of the two judicial systems under scrutiny was initially created with limited, if any, direct access by individuals to the respective European Courts.[42] Yet, both have

[40] As the Court noted in *van Gend & Loos*: 'The vigilance of individuals concerned to protect their rights amounts to an effective supervision in addition to the supervision entrusted … to the diligence of the Commission and of the Member States.' (CJEU, Case C-26/62, ECLI:EU:C:1963:1).

[41] See Section 3.2.1 below.

[42] ECHR (official original text, 1950), Article 44; Treaty establishing the European Economic Community (official original text, 1957), Articles 169 et seq. Note that the possibility for individuals to bring direct actions before the CJEU has been interpreted restrictively as from the early days: CJEU, Case C-25/62 *Plaumann & Co v Commission of the European Economic Community* ECLI:EU:C:1963:17.

evolved towards giving a particularly prominent role to individuals' access to justice in their overall functioning. Each of the two courts has achieved that aim through different avenues, reflecting the specificities of each system. Despite important differences in approaches, the prominent role of individual's access to justice in each system triggers parallel quests for quality, efficiency and transparency with particular attention to the needs of individuals.

2.1.1. *Two Approaches to the Importance of Individuals' Access to Justice*

In the Convention system, the centrality of the right of individuals to access the Court results from Article 34 ECHR. The current wording of that article is the consequence of Protocol No 11 to the ECHR having entered into force in 1998,[43] and resulting in the right of individual application no longer being dependent on a declaration by the Contracting States. The ECtHR may receive applications 'from any person, non-governmental organisation or group of individuals claiming to be the victim of a violation by one of the High Contracting Parties of the rights set forth in the Convention or the Protocols thereto'. Although reference is made in Article 34 to NGOs or groups of individuals, Janneke Gerards and Elif Erken note that the collective enforcement of human rights in cases that 'do not directly affect NGOs' own fundamental rights' actually is difficult due to the requirement, enshrined in the same provision of the Convention, that the applicant be 'victim' of the alleged violations.[44] Individual applications are thus best understood as constituting the 'cornerstone' of the Convention system.[45]

In the EU legal system, direct access for individuals to the organs of the CJEU is knowingly limited. Nevertheless, the Court of Justice has repeated time and time again that the fact that the EU Treaties provide limited direct access to the Court does not deprive individuals of the right to enforce EU law rights and obligations before national courts.[46] By virtue of the principle of effective judicial protection, any person whose rights and freedoms guaranteed by EU law are violated should have the right to an effective remedy before a tribunal.[47] If that is not before the Court itself, it must be before a national court or tribunal.[48] These observations naturally also apply to the protection of EU fundamental rights, as the very existence of effective judicial review designed to ensure compliance with provisions of EU law is of the essence of the rule of law in the EU.[49] In the EU legal system, the link between national courts or tribunals and the CJEU takes place via the preliminary ruling procedure set out in Article 267 TFEU. National judges before whom individuals have acted may, or must, ask questions on the interpretation or validity of EU law to the CJEU, this procedure thus sets up a dialogue between

[43] All parties to the ECHR have ratified Protocol 11.

[44] See ch 3.

[45] E Penninckx, ch 15; High-level Conference on the 'Implementation of the European Convention on Human Rights, Our Shared Responsibility' Brussels Declaration 27 March 2015, recital 1; see also ECtHR, App nos 46827/99 and 46951/99 *Mamatkulov and Askarov v Turkey* ECLI:CE:ECHR:2005:0204JUD004682799, para 122.

[46] CJEU, Case C-26/62 *van Gend & Loos* ECLI:EU:C:1963:1.

[47] CJEU, Case C-72/15 *Rosneft* ECLI:EU:C:2017:236, para 73.

[48] ibid, para 67.

[49] ibid, para 73.

national and European judges in the context of proceedings pending at national level. In practice, it is the 'main gateway through which individuals may reach the CJEU'.[50] The procedure has the object of securing uniform interpretation of EU law[51] and is understood to constitute the 'keystone' of the EU judicial system.[52] Takis Tridimas highlights that both the CJEU and the ECtHR view the preliminary ruling procedure as 'an integral part of the right to judicial protection'.[53]

Even if the legal construct is very different in each of these judicial systems, individual's right to access to a court of law to enforce their rights is key to both. This in turn necessarily influences the internal organisation of these courts.[54] Fundamental rights, and the right to an effective judicial remedy in particular, could even be understood to form part of the DNA of the internal functioning of these courts.[55] As noted by several authors in this book, each of the two courts are themselves subject to compliance with fundamental rights. Joni Heliskoski has pushed the exploration of the relevance of Article 47 CFREU, on the fundamental right to an effective judicial remedy in EU law, to the functioning of the CJEU yet one step further.[56] He has surveyed all case law in which this article has been applied by the CJEU in the context of the application of the Statute of the CJEU and the Rules of Procedure. He thereby demonstrated that the Court does not apply Article 47 in a 'purely decorative manner' and instead clearly recognises the role of this article in the organisation of its proceedings.[57]

2.1.2. Parallel Quests for Quality, Efficiency and Transparency

For the internal design of each court to contribute to the effective judicial protection of those concerned, considerable efforts are being deployed in each system to enhance quality, efficiency and transparency of judicial work. In recent years, a set of large scale reforms and developments have more specifically related to systemic or structural problems. These will be explored below, to place emphasis on the ability of the judicial systems under scrutiny to respond to systemic or structural threats. In more general terms though, it is highlighted here that both in the Convention system and in EU law, procedures are constantly being shaped and re-shaped to adjust to perceived needs.

To start with, both courts have in recent years used new technologies to disseminate information on their work and get closer to citizens, including through broadcasting or streaming (certain) hearings,[58] and to enhance access to expertise in the field. A new, 'unique' and particularly rich and powerful online platform on the law of the Convention was created: the ECHR Knowledge Sharing Platform.[59] The CJEU has also

[50] T Tridimas, ch 9.
[51] CJEU, Opinion 2/13 *Accession of the European Union to the European Convention for the Protection of Human Rights and Fundamental Freedoms* ECLI:EU:C:2014:2454, paras 176–77.
[52] ibid.
[53] See ch 9.
[54] By analogy: E Penninckx, ch 15.
[55] By analogy: J Gutiérrez-Fons, ch 17.
[56] J Heliskoski, ch 18.
[57] ibid.
[58] E Penninckx, ch 15 and J Gutiérrez-Fons, ch 17. Frédéric Krenc, in ch 16, recalled that public hearings before the ECtHR are uncommon.
[59] E Penninckx, ch 15.

in recent years made available on its website a number of research notes requested for the purpose of its activities, including those compiled by its Research and Documentation Directorate.

At the ECtHR, recourse to single judges, or Committees of three judges – with proceedings primarily in written form, and without meeting in person – has gained considerable importance to allow the Court to process its backlog and to deal with repetitive cases,[60] thereby also allowing it to prioritise important cases. Ellen Penninckx also identified a trend towards specialisation of judges in the field of migration to further enhance expertise and speed.[61] The quest for equality and consistency within the Registry has in addition resulted in ad hoc initiatives to ensure greater coordination in processing cases related to major inter-State conflicts (such as between Ukraine and Russia), as well as in the fields of environmental law and, very interestingly, in the field of EU law. She finally highlighted the development of a standard case law citation system to enhance consistency, as well as the importance of thematic (and confidential) reports to also enhance the expertise of the court's services, such as on EU law.

At the CJEU, José Gutiérrez-Fons[62] stressed the special attention paid internally to the protection of personal data of individuals mentioned in cases brought before the Court and the novel approach developed since 2023 to add fictitious names to help in identifying the case law. He drew attention to the importance of the internal organisation of the court to ensure effective case management in the interest of effective judicial protection. He highlighted, in particular, the important role of the Research and Documentation Directorate, that drafts an 'early view' working document for every request for a preliminary ruling, as well as that of the President of the Court, when making key procedural choices on the processing of cases.

In the EU legal system, specific attention was devoted to the preliminary ruling procedure which is how most cases relating to fundamental rights reach the court. Takis Tridimas noted how 'pivotal' the procedure is and how well suited it is to act as a 'force of rights generation' because it is triggered in the context of concrete disputes, it allows EU law to be invoked before national courts and it enables EU law to be diffused in the national legal system.[63] The procedure is thus very important not only in quantitative terms, but also because the judicial dialogue with national courts that it allows has 'enormous repercussions in the sustainability of the current system of interpretation and application of EU law'.[64] In the context of the preliminary ruling procedure, 'time is of the essence'.[65] Accelerated variants of the preliminary ruling procedure, which are the urgent procedure, the expedited procedure, and the 'priority treatment' of cases, precisely aim to ensure compliance with Article 47, second paragraph, CFREU.[66] As Sara Iglesias Sanchez observed, good time management in the context of the preliminary ruling procedure contributes both to 'the suitability

[60] F Krenc, ch 16.
[61] See ch 15.
[62] See ch 17.
[63] See ch 9.
[64] S Iglesias Sanchez, ch 13.
[65] ibid.
[66] See by analogy CJEU, Case C-8/19 PPU *RH* ECLI:EU:C:2019:110, paras 34–35; S Iglesias Sanchez, ch 13.

to the EU judicial system to protect fundamental rights' and to preserving the good collaboration between the CJEU and national courts. Along these lines, the transfer of the preliminary jurisdiction in some cases from the Court of Justice to the General Court may be welcomed, as it allows better use to be made of the resources of the Court of Justice.[67]

That the two courts constantly reflect upon, and adjust, their internal organisation to contribute to individual's effective judicial protection, does not mean that the existing systems are immune to criticisms. For instance, Frédéric Krenc argued that it may be 'questionable' that separate opinions at the ECtHR can only be issued in relation to judgments, by contrast with inadmissibility decision despite the high negative impact that these may have.[68] After all, these separate opinions may be understood as key to ensure 'transparency and judicial democracy' in the Convention system. The author further argued that it might be desirable to expect that judges of the ECtHR having decided to write a separate opinion would send it to the relevant composition of the court, so that it can be taken into account in drafting the judgment.

Several authors have also pointed at specific difficulties in understanding the dynamics of, or in accessing information on, important features of the procedural treatment of cases. Sara Iglesias Sanchez regretted a lack of overall coherence between the different accelerated variants of the preliminary ruling procedure before the CJEU, asking whether the urgent and expedited should be merged. She also called for greater systematisation in the criteria used, for instance, to trigger the expedited procedure and the priority treatment of cases; and would welcome more detailed motivation when priority treatment of cases is used.[69] Similar concerns were expressed in relation to the Convention system. Kanstantsin Dzehtsiarou noted the difficulty of identifying which cases of the ECtHR are pilot judgments.[70] Philip Leach in turn hoped for more detailed reasoning in future interim measures adopted at the ECtHR and called for the latter to introduce a 'publicly available, systematic record of individual interim measures decisions, as well as commentary on the extent of their implementation'.[71] Virginia Passalacqua further lamented the difficulty in identifying the number of requests for third party interventions that the ECtHR receives and rejects[72] as well as on the participation of state or non-state actors as third party interveners before the CJEU.[73]

These procedural matters have important consequences for litigants as they may influence the way applications are being processed and arguments raised, who can contribute to the reflections on how best to shape one's human and fundamental rights, or impact of individual rulings. These are thus all points on which each court may want to further enhance clarity and access to information.

[67] T Tridimas, ch 9.
[68] See ch 16. See also the discussion below on the limited admissibility of legal action brought before the ECtHR for the representation of public interest, and more specifically n 85.
[69] S Iglesias Sanchez, ch 13; this is further developed in Section 3.2.2 below.
[70] K Dzehtsiarou, ch 6.
[71] P Leach, ch 12.
[72] V Passalacqua, ch 4.
[73] ibid.

2.2. Systemic Implications of the Importance of Individuals' Access to Court

The great importance of access to justice for individuals, in the design of each of the judicial systems under scrutiny, has important side effects that are fairly similar in each system. First, the systems provide for limited tools to ensure representation of public interests. Second, the systems are in essence dependent on the possibility for individuals to have access to a court or tribunal at national level. The contributors to this book have examined both features of the European multi-faceted judicial construct in complementary ways as we shall now see.

2.2.1. Calls for Greater Representation of Public Interests

To start with, several authors have commented on the limits of the representation of public interests before each court. As Joyce De Coninck explained, decisions on who may be heard by courts in processes of adjudication on human and fundamental rights depends on the type of deliberative process sought to ensure that the law in the field is dynamic and can accommodate societal evolutions.[74] For instance, she called for opening up opportunities for NGO involvement in litigation before the CJEU in the field of migration, so as to alleviate evidentiary burdens, and to provide evidence of systemic flaws of the EU's human rights responsibility regime. On a related note, Janneke Gerards and Elif Erken regretted that the EU judicial system, whereby access by 'collective actors' to justice is dependent on the rules of procedure applicable before the national judge, is so fragmented. They also point to the fact that the ECtHR system offers only limited possibilities to seek general justice and make use of public interest litigation; *actio popularis* being impossible. In fact, intergovernmental instances of the Council of Europe have considered introducing a new 'representative application procedure' before the ECtHR,[75] but the idea was ultimately abandoned.[76] Virginia Passalacqua in turn stressed that 'collective actors' may include civil society organisations as well as states who may also represent the public interest. In EU law more specifically, Member States have special access to the CJEU. Unlike non-state actors they are free to intervene in all proceedings, which may, as she notes, create an imbalance in the deliberative process.[77]

Although the representation of public interests in judicial processes brings diversity to deliberative processes, it may also have downsides. It may indeed result in amplifying the representation of the interests of a specific group, 'from small trade unions to big corporations, from fishermen associations to Member States' governments', or

[74] J De Coninck, ch 5.

[75] D Milner, ch 11.

[76] As David Milner noted, it would have been distinct from other forms of actions such as 'class actions', as it would have applied 'where there is a group of similar applications' and would have allowed the Court to register and determine only a small number of applications from the group and to apply the Court's determination of those applications to the group as a whole.

[77] Although Takis Tridimas, in ch 9, understands these differences as highlighting the distinct features of the preliminary ruling procedure as a form of inter-judicial dialogue.

contribute to a process of judicialisation of politics.[78] The present book sheds light on an important evolving facet of the tension between the pros and cons of giving a voice to public interests in judicial processes. As pointed at by Janneke Gerards and Elif Erken, both in EU law and before the ECtHR, access to justice is in the process of opening up to forms of collective action for environmental protection.[79]

At the ECtHR, in the recent *KlimaSeniorinnen* case,[80] the Court identified a set of factors allowing it to grant locus standi for associations to lodge an application under Article 34 ECHR on account of the alleged failure of a Contracting State to take adequate measures to protect individuals against the adverse effects of climate change on human lives and health. In simplified terms, the association must be: (a) lawfully established in the jurisdiction concerned or have standing to act there; (b) able to demonstrate that it pursues a dedicated purpose; and (c) able to demonstrate that it can be regarded as genuinely qualified and representative to act on behalf of members or other affected individuals. The Court acknowledged that, in accordance with the specific features of recourse to legal action by associations in this context, the standing of an association will not be subject to a separate requirement of showing that those on whose behalf the case has been brought would themselves have met the victim-status requirements.

In the EU, a new legislative provision allows not only environmental NGOs but also 'other members of the public', under specific conditions, to request internal review of administrative acts and omission which contains provisions that may contravene environmental law.[81] As a result, not only acts of individual scope, but also acts of general nature, adopted through a non-legislative procedure, may be subject to internal review. The internal review procedure has thus become 'an accessible mechanism for individuals to challenge violations of EU environmental law by EU institutions'.[82] Furthermore, organisations that do request such internal review, and are unsuccessful or fail to receive a reply, should be able to institute proceedings before the Court of Justice with a lower admissibility threshold than that normally requested – irrespective of whether non-legislative acts entail implementing measures and without the applicant having to show individual concern.[83]

This 2021 reform of EU environmental law only opens up review of the EU institutions or bodies' refusal, or failure, to grant an internal review against non-legislative

[78] V Passalacqua in ch 4.

[79] See ch 3.

[80] ECtHR, App no 53600/20 *Verein Klimaseniorinnen Schweiz and Others v Switzerland*, ECLI:CE:ECHR:2024:0409JUD005360020, para 502.

[81] Regulation (EC) No 1367/2006 on the application of the provisions of the Aarhus Convention on Access to Information, Public Participation in Decision-making and Access to Justice in Environmental Matters to Community institutions and bodies (consolidated after amendment by Regulation (EU) 2021/1767) [2006] OJ L 264/13, Article 2(1)(f), (g),(h), Articles 10–11. These other members of the public must meet one of two alternative criteria set out in Article 11(1a).

[82] M Eliantonio and J Richelle, 'Holding the EU Accountable for Environmental Law Violations: Legitimacy Assets, "Complete" System of Remedies and Unexplored Pathways' (2025) 34 *European Energy and Environmental Law Review* 1.

[83] Regulation (EC) No 1367/2006 on the application of the provisions of the Aarhus Convention on Access to Information, Public Participation in Decision-making and Access to Justice in Environmental Matters to Community institutions and bodies (consolidated after amendment by Regulation (EU) 2021/1767) [2006] OJ L 264/13, Article 12.

acts,[84] and does not alter the narrow rules on access to annulment actions against EU legislative acts.[85] Nevertheless, this development has been welcomed as opening the way to greater access to the EU Courts in environmental public interest cases.[86] Similarly, in the law of the ECHR, while the judgment in *KlimaSeniorinnen* does not mean that all cases concerned with climate change and environmental protection will be admissible before the ECtHR,[87] it is indeed 'a milestone in the Court's jurisprudence on climate related issues'.[88] The EU legislator and the ECtHR are thereby, each in their own way, going beyond a narrow understanding of models based exclusively on individual access to justice.

Both sets of developments, in ECHR law as well as in EU law, are thus part of a critical reflection on the limits of political decision-making in the area of climate change and environmental protection, which inherently suffers from a range of representative failures similar to those identified by Joyce De Coninck in relation to migrants arriving irregularly by sea. These developments thus explore forms of constitutional or supranational protection to mitigate representative failures.[89] To achieve that aim, the voiceless must be given access to court. Takis Tridimas further welcomes that, not only in the field of EU environmental law, but also in other fields such as equality law, consumer and data protection law, both the EU legislator and the CJEU are showing some willingness to facilitate representative action at national level.[90] As he notes, encouraging public interest litigation is also an effective way of promoting the enforcement of EU law.

2.2.2. National Judges at the Core of the European System(s) of Protection

A second side effect of the importance of individuals' access to a court or tribunal in the design of both judicial systems, relates to the dependency of these systems on access by individuals to a court or tribunal at national level. In the Convention system, the admissibility of claims before the ECtHR is subject to meeting important admissibility criteria, in particular the exhaustion of *national* remedies. Moreover, the High Contracting Parties 'undertake not to hinder in any way the effective exercise of [the] right [to bring individual applications]'.[91] In EU law, as noted by the ECtHR itself when

[84] A Kręźel, 'Aarhus Regulation Administrative (self-) Review Mechanism: The Inevitable Failure to Contribute to Access to Justice in the EU?' (2023) *European Energy and Environmental Law Review* 136, 140.

[85] S Garben, 'The CJEU and Climate (In)activism?' in M Dawson, B De Witte and E Muir (eds), *Revisiting Judicial Politics in the European Union* (Cheltenham, Edward Elgar Publishing, 2024) 253.

[86] GC Leonelli, 'Access to the EU Courts in Environmental and Public Health Cases and the Reform of the Aarhus Regulation: Systemic Vision, Pragmatism, and a Happy Ending' 40 *Yearbook of European Law* (2021) 230, 261.

[87] See for instance: ECtHR, App nos 51567/14 et al *Cannavacciuolo and Others v Italy* ECLI:CE:ECHR:2025:0130JUD005156714, paras 220–21 and further Concurring Opinion of Judge Krenc.

[88] M Eliantonio and J Richelle, 'Holding the EU Accountable for Environmental Law Violations: Legitimacy Assets, "Complete" System of Remedies and Unexplored Pathways' (2025) 34 *European Energy and Environmental Law Review* 1. See further the reflections of Kanstantsin Dzehstiarou, in ch 6, on the possible use of the pilot procedure before the ECtHR in environmental pollution cases.

[89] Paraphrasing S Garben, 'The CJEU and Climate (In)activism?' in M Dawson, B De Witte and E Muir (eds), *Revisiting Judicial Politics in the European Union* (Cheltenham, Edward Elgar Publishing, 2024) 250.

[90] See ch 9.

[91] Articles 34–35 ECHR.

establishing the *Bosphorus* presumption,[92] it is essentially through the national courts that remedies are provided to individuals against a Member State or another individual for a breach of EU law.[93]

As observed by Lucia van der Meulen, '[w]hile each layer has a final authority: the CJEU for the interpretation of EU law, the ECtHR for the interpretation of ECHR law and the highest national courts for the interpretation of national constitutional law, only national courts have a legal duty to each of the three different systems of law'.[94] National judges are thus not only at the junction between the EU and the ECHR systems, they are also in practice at the core of the European system(s) of judicial protection of human and fundamental rights.[95] As noted by Síofra O'Leary, 'national judges clearly see judicial dialogue in the field of human rights in trilateral terms' and national judges 'must remain key'.[96] It should therefore perhaps come as no surprise that the most salient points of convergence in the case law of both courts in recent years relate precisely to the protection of national judges. The President of the CJEU, Koen Lenaerts, borrowing from the former President of the ECtHR, has referred to 'a symbiotic relationship'[97] between the case law of the two Courts in the context of threats to the independence of the judiciary.

This very special role of national judges, at the core of the European system(s) of judicial protection of human and fundamental rights, has in recent years had two sets of very concrete implications explored in this book. The first relates to the extent to which the preliminary procedure available to national judges under EU law has been used as a 'model and source of inspiration'[98] for the advisory opinion made available to highest courts and tribunals under the Convention system.[99] While stressing the undeniable differences in the purpose and design of each of these two procedures, Jasper Krommendijk convincingly showed how the practice of the advisory opinion by national highest courts and the ECtHR is in many ways 'reminiscent' of several features of the preliminary ruling. This is particularly clear for the interpretation of the admissibility criteria, such as there being a pending case before the requesting judicial authorities and the question being one of principle (by analogy to the act *clair/éclairé* doctrine of the CJEU).[100] As so often done in an EU context, Jasper Krommendijk called on national

[92] See further S O'Leary, ch 2.

[93] ECtHR, App no 45036/98 *Bosphorus Hava Yollari Turizm Ve Ticaret Anonim Şirketi v Ireland*, para 164, second recital.

[94] L van der Meulen, *National Courts as EU Fundamental Rights Courts: An Analysis of Dutch, German and Belgian Adjudication on Fundamental Rights Exceptions to Transfer Decisions Under the European Arrest Warrant and Dublin Regulation* (Asser Press, forthcoming in open access) see section on 'Challenges of national courts as EU fundamental rights courts'.

[95] For reasons of limited space, this book does not explore the national perspective. See: Sarah Lambrecht, 'Convention Through States' Eyes: Embedding of the European Convention on Human Rights in States Parties' (PhD dissertation, University of Antwerp, 2022) and L van der Meulen, 'National Courts' (forthcoming).

[96] See ch 2.

[97] R Spano, 'The Rule of Law as the Lodestar of the European Convention on Human Rights: The Strasbourg Court and the Independence of the Judiciary' (2021) 27 *European Law Journal* 211, 223; K Lenaerts, 'On Checks and Balances: the Rule of Law within the EU' (2023) 29 *Columbia Law Journal* 25, 56.

[98] J Krommendijk, ch 7.

[99] Protocol 16 to the ECHR. It is remarkable, as noted by Frédéric Krenc in Chapter 16, that all advisory opinions adopted so far were decided by unanimity of the judges, this shows a clear willingness within the Court to 'speak with one voice'.

[100] Protocol 16 to the ECHR, Article 1(1) and (2).

courts to engage with the ECtHR and to share their own views with the court so as to enhance the dialogical nature of the instrument – and for the sound development of human rights law more generally.

The proximity between the two mechanisms also creates a risk of competition between them which was singled out by the CJEU in Opinion 2/13. When examining the first version of the draft agreement on the EU's accession to the ECHR negotiated after the entry into force of the Lisbon treaty, the Court noted that: '[b]y failing to make any provision in respect of the relationship between [both mechanisms], the agreement envisaged is liable adversely to affect the autonomy and effectiveness of the [preliminary ruling] procedure.'[101] There was a risk, as Felix Ronkes Agerbeek put it, that the advisory procedure mechanism allowing national highest courts to ask for advice to the ECtHR might diminish the central role of the preliminary ruling in EU law.[102] The new version of the draft agreement on the EU's accession to the ECHR seeks to address the issue. It provides that courts or tribunals of EU Member States having ratified Protocol 16 shall not be considered as a highest court or tribunal within the meaning of the advisory opinion mechanism if the question falls within the field of application of EU law.[103]

Pending accession though, there is still a possibility that questions related to the interpretation of EU law emerge in the context of a request for an Advisory Opinion to the ECtHR.[104] Both Jasper Krommendijk and Felix Ronkes Agerbeek argued that the ECtHR could refuse to answer such questions, in particular if the national court has not made use of the preliminary ruling procedure as it is obliged to do so under EU law. This fits in well with the idea that EU national judges in any case tend to prefer the preliminary ruling procedure over the Advisory Opinion,[105] and that 'in matters of EU law, the relevant domestic judicial system is that of the EU'.[106]

3. European Human and Fundamental Rights Justice in Motion

Discussing the tectonic of plates in the European human and fundamental rights' architecture, as this book ventures to do, cannot be performed in isolation from the broader context to which the Convention and the EU systems belong (3.1). That broader context, sadly, is dark. As noted by Síofra O'Leary, in her opening speech as the new President

[101] CJEU, Opinion 2/13 *Accession of the European Union to the European Convention for the Protection of Human Rights and Fundamental Freedoms* ECLI:EU:C:2014:2454, para 199.

[102] F Ronkes Agerbeek, ch 10.

[103] Draft revised Agreement on the Accession of the European Union to the Convention for the Protection of Human Rights and Fundamental Freedoms, in Appendix of CDDH(2023)R_EXTRA ADDENDUM, Article 5.

[104] This is well illustrated by Jasper Krommendijk in ch 7 (see ECtHR, Request no P16-2024-001 *Decision of the Court on the request received from the High Court of Cassation and Justice of Romania for an advisory opinion*) as well as by Felix Ronkes Agerbeek in ch 10 (see cases on ritual slaughtering: CJEU, Case C-336/19 *Centraal Israëlitische Consistorie van België and Others v Vlaamse Regering* ECLI:EU:C:2020:1031; Belgian Constitutional Court, judgment no 117/2021 ECLI:BE:GHCC:2021:ARR.117; ECtHR, App no 16760/22 *Executief van de Moslims van België and Others v Belgium* ECLI:CE:ECHR:2024:0213JUD001676022).

[105] J Krommendijk, ch 7.

[106] F Ronkes Agerbeek, ch 10.

the ECtHR back in 2023, 'in this tragic period that Europe is living through', we must 'seek, together and collectively, to safeguard democracy and the rule of law and to protect human rights'.[107] It will be argued that the responsiveness of our contemporary system of European human and fundamental rights' justice would benefit from building further, although with nuance and caution, on complementarities and cross-fertilisation between the two systems (3.2).

3.1. Judicial Resilience in Times of Crises

If anything, the sense of tragedy has in recent years and months only increased. The contributors to this book powerfully demonstrated that it is as important to acknowledge the seriousness of contemporary challenges to our judicial systems, as it is to reflect on the ability of these systems to show resilience.

3.1.1. Systems under Pressure

Threats to the independence of national judges in Europe are real. They are a central concern to Europe's judicial architecture for the protection of human and fundamental rights as argued above, and are now subject to a wealth of cases and institutional documents both at the Council of Europe and in the EU. Yet, there are even more reasons to be concerned. With her contribution, Laurence Burgorgue-Larsen opened the part of this book devoted to (non-) compliance with European courts' judgments with a cry of alarm – if not despair – on the lack of compliance with judgments of the ECtHR not only on judicial independence but also well beyond (eg, detention of rights defenders, breaches of the rights of political and sexual minorities).[108] She demonstrated that, today, 'the political heterogeneity of the [Council of Europe] is undoubtedly its Achilles heel'. She explained how certain state parties for the Convention simply have 'no interest in complying with the Court's judgments'. She further noted that some of these states, which she identifies as being 'illiberal and authoritarian' and thus 'bad players' including in the EU, have managed to elect judges to the ECtHR who, 'through their separate opinions, have demonstrated that their independence is rather relative'.

Not all authors writing on the Convention system are as pessimistic though. David Milner for instance concluded his paper on how the Convention organs have thought to tackle repetitive applications stressing that 'in general, the States concerned have been cooperative … and the Member States as a whole have been supportive and encouraging'.[109] Laurence Burgorgue-Larsen's cry of alarm, as the author herself acknowledges, indeed built on a paradox: the existential disrespect for the foundations of the Convention system denounced is to be contrasted with 'remarkable' efforts by the Council of Europe to strengthen that very same system and to address threats. These efforts are undeniable, yet

[107] S O'Leary, 'Solemn Hearing, President of the European Court of Human Rights', 27 January 2023.
[108] L Burgorgue-Larsen, ch 19.
[109] See ch 11.

they do not as such address the deep bad faith of those state parties that have illiberal and authoritarian regimes. In his study of interim relief at the ECtHR, Philip Leach identified a similar tension between 'progress and push-back'.[110] As he noted, the Court has broadened the scope of, and diversified the types of measures for, injunctive relief considerably in recent years. He praised these 'remarkable developments' at an international court that steps up to intervene in 'highly fraught domestic contexts'. Yet, he also took stock of, and deftly illustrated, the 'heightened levels of state resistance'.

The present book, admittedly, did not further address the underlying and genuine underlying concerns identified by Laurence Burgorgue-Larsen in relation to the failures of the Convention system that are related to the lack of good faith of illiberal and authoritarian state parties.[111] This is not to deny the depth and genuine nature of these concerns. It is that this research project instead sought, as explored below, to make the best of what exists in states that do (still?) share a degree of political homogeneity and adherence to the system.[112] Furthermore, from the perspective of the EU, the overall picture is overall less dark than that painted above, even if not immune from concerns. As noted by Allan Rosas, overall, 'taking into account the sensitive nature of some of the cases that come before the CJEU, the degree of compliance with its decisions could perhaps even be considered as surprisingly good'.[113] Compliance with CJEU rulings is primarily about compliance with preliminary rulings and can be generally regarded by and large as at least satisfactory.[114] There are instances of resistance,[115] which are 'constitutionally significant'; yet these are in this author's view 'rare'. As for judgments finding a failure to fulfil an obligation under EU law, even if there are instances of non-compliance, they also appear to normally be executed. A sensitive area in this regard relates to rulings concerning respect for the rule of law, including judicial independence, where compliance has been 'haphazard'. Even if not as strong in the Convention system, concerns relating to the lack of compliance with EU law, and with the values in Article 2 TEU by certain Member States, have thus been rising in recent years. Allan Rosas further observed that instances of the Commission *not* actually initiating infringement actions in sensitive areas of EU law abound, one might thus hope for a more aggressive enforcement policy.

3.1.2. *Judicial Systems' Responsiveness*

Despite Laurence Burgorgue-Larsen's painful cry of alarm, she actually praised the responsiveness of the Convention system, and its added value for Member States who

[110] See ch 12.

[111] For an attempt to identify, reassert and modernize the common values on which European democracies are built see: T Tridimas and E Muir (Project reporters) *Charter of Fundamental Constitutional Principles of a European Democracy* (European Law Institute, 2024).

[112] Although see the letter signed by nine European Heads of (an EU Member) State on 22 May 2025, expressing criticism of the European Court of Human Rights' case law available at www.governo.it/sites/governo.it/files/Lettera_aperta_22052025.pdf accessed 14 July 2025.

[113] See ch 20.

[114] See also T Tridimas, ch 9.

[115] Instances of non-compliance can be evidenced by outright expression of disagreement, but they can also transpire from a broad range of more subtle forms of resistance, such as reluctance to refer preliminary questions to the CJEU. See further O Scarcello, *Contestatory Federalism and Rights: Resisting Incorporation in the US, Canada, and the EU* (Oxford, Oxford University Press, forthcoming in open access).

still act in good faith. One of the key challenges to the Convention system in recent years has resulted from 'repetitive applications' which David Milner defined as 'compound failure[s] to implement the Convention … due to dysfunction in public administration, with adverse consequences for large numbers of individuals, and on account of the number of applications may make, the Court'.[116] He also observed that the Court and the High Contracting Parties have made 'significant' efforts to address such systemic or structural problems in the past 15 years.

A prime example of such responsiveness is the pilot procedure, which is intended to protect the Court against repetitive claims, and to protect multiple victims of repetitive human rights violations. The mechanism can be traced back to 2004 in the practice of the Court,[117] and is enshrined in Article 61 of the Rules of Procedure since 2011. Although it has so far been used sparingly, as observed by Kanstantsin Dzehstiarou, the Court treats the pilot judgment procedure as a 'very serious instrument which is appropriate when some strict legal and perhaps political conditions are met'. It serves as a 'pressure point' for states to implement standards that were developed in earlier case law. Yet a broader set of tools has been developed to tackle repetitive claims, and complements the pilot procedure. Such initiatives include, as stressed by David Milner, a so-called 'fact-track well-established case law procedure' since 2015, relying on an automated drafting process and with tight internal deadlines. The Court has also relied on a 'non-contentious phase' since 2019, understood as a form of 'alternative dispute resolution' mechanism. He also referred to a system of 'summary-formula judgments and decisions' since 2021, for greater concision and focus, as well as a multitude of ad hoc techniques to answer to specific challenges.

Another example of institutional responsiveness is the 2024 reform of the system of interim measures at the ECtHR, which Philip Leach understood at least in part, as a response to the 'stark and belligerent' approach of the UK Government to interim orders of the Court in relation to deportation flights to Rwanda.[118] Although the reform 'doubles down' on the exceptionality of interim orders, it broadens the scope of interim measures. On a related note, Laurence Burgorgue-Larsen praised the 'outstanding' complementary role of Parliamentary Assembly and the Committee of Ministers, next to the Court, in the supervision of execution of ECtHR decisions. An illustration is the Court's new role since 2010, in procedures for 'failure to fulfil obligations'.[119] If the Committee of Ministers considers that a High Contracting Party refuses to abide by a final judgment, it may, by decision adopted by a majority vote of two thirds, refer to the Court the question whether that Party has failed to fulfil its obligation.[120]

On the side of the CJEU, Luca Prete noted that, in reaction to the concern that a Member State's government may not intend to comply with an interim order, the Court deemed it necessary to 'enhance the effectiveness' of the interim measures'[121] ordered by providing for penalties to be imposed if the State failed to comply with them

[116] See ch 11.
[117] ECtHR, App no 31443/96 *Broniowski v Poland* ECLI:CE:ECHR:2004:0622JUD003144396.
[118] P Leach, ch 12.
[119] See Protocol 14 ECtHR, entered into force in 2010.
[120] Article 46(4) ECHR.
[121] See ch 8.

immediately and fully.[122] This novel approach is 'nothing less than ground-breaking', the author noted, as in particularly serious and urgent situations, which may often be the case when fundamental rights are at risk, there is now a very effective and rapid tool to coerce Member States into compliance.[123] Sharing the same view, Kathleen Gutman and Alexander Kornezov, further stressed the emphasis placed by the Court on compliance with judicial decisions being an 'essential component of the rule of law', a value enshrined, together with respect for human rights, in Article 2 TEU.[124]

Other mechanisms at the CJEU have also been used to respond to challenges of a systemic nature. For instance, the expedited preliminary ruling procedure is so flexible as to allow the Court to decide in a record time.[125] Sara Iglesias Sanchez illustrated the point with two 'striking' full court cases adjudicated in about three months in the midst of the economic and financial crisis,[126] and the Brexit process.[127] The Court has also imposed a particularly hefty penalty payment and lump sum (the highest ever in similar proceedings, and well beyond what the Commission had asked) to a Member State, for failure to comply with a first judgment of the Court deemed to be 'exceptionally serious'.[128] As Luca Prete noted, although the relevant provisions of infringed EU law consisted only in rules of secondary law, those provisions largely embodied, and were thus necessary to ensure compliance with, the fundamental rights enshrined in Articles 18, 19 and 47 of the Charter.[129]

It is worth noting that both Courts may also, in more general terms, take into account the salience of a case. The ECtHR for instance 'may take into account whether the case has had significant media coverage domestically and/or is politically sensitive' when deciding on whether to process a case under the new priority rules for 'impact cases'.[130] On a related note, at the CJEU, José Gutiérrez-Fons[131] asserted that cases dealing with issues of 'high public sensitivity' will be examined by the Grand Chamber. He explained that this is 'either because of the political or historical context in which they arise, or because the Court has to respond to highly complex issues relating to the culture, morality or national identity of the Member States'.

3.2. Re-conceptualising the Duality of European Human and Fundamental Rights Justice

The Convention and the EU systems are thus under pressure. Yet they also are responsive as extensively illustrated by the contributors to the present book. It is argued in this

[122] CJEU, Case C-441/17 R *Commission v Poland* ECLI:EU:C:2017:877, para 118.
[123] See ch 8.
[124] See ch 14; CJEU, Case C-441/17 R *Commission v Poland* ECLI:EU:C:2017:877, para 102.
[125] See ch 13.
[126] CJEU, Case C-370/12 *Pringle* ECLI:EU:C:2012:756.
[127] CJEU, Case C-621/18 *Wightman and Others* ECLI:EU:C:2018:999.
[128] CJEU, Case C-123/22 *Commission v Hungary (Reception of applicants for international protection II)* ECLI:EU:C:2024:493, paras 96 ff.
[129] ibid, paras 105 and 108–10.
[130] ECtHR, 'A Court that Matters: A Strategy for More Targeted and Effective Case-processing' 17 March 2021. See also L Burgorgue-Larsen, ch 19.
[131] See ch 17.

very final section that the reliance of European human and fundamental rights justice may benefit from building on complementarities between the two systems, as well as from the growing awareness within each court of such potential.

3.2.1. Looking for Complementarities and Cross-fertilisation between the Two Systems

As noted by Síofra O'Leary, 'the human rights dialogue between Luxembourg and Strasbourg is long-standing' and bi-directional.[132] There are already multiple examples of '[c]onvergence and cross-referencing' in the case law of the two Courts. For instance, as already observed, in relation to the independence of national judges, 'virtuous and effective circles have formed' and the two courts have thereby 'strengthened the effectiveness of the protection afforded by their respective jurisprudence'. More generally, the ECtHR may 'sanction the lack or incorrect application of EU law in light of the Convention' and thereby contribute to its effective implementation.[133] Victor Davio has shown how the case law of the ECtHR often indeed strengthens the requirements of EU law.[134]

Such complementarities are illustrated in the present book by Allan Rosas referring to how the case law of the ECtHR provides additional support to increase compliance with the requirements of the preliminary ruling procedure.[135] The ECtHR indeed requires that the national courts give reasons if refusing to refer under Article 267 TFEU to ensure compliance with Article 6 ECHR.[136] The CJEU has now asserted a similar duty with reference to Article 47 CFREU.[137] Failure to comply with the duty to give reasons may in turn help the Commission to initiate legal action against EU Member States for failure by their national courts to provide reasons for not referring preliminary questions.

In that sense, the case law of the ECtHR contributes to enhancing compliance with EU law requirements. Conversely, EU law may also be able to contribute to the better protection of human rights. As noted above, EU law relies on a system of 'dual vigilance'[138] for its enforcement so that, besides the great importance given to individual litigation, public organs also have an important role to play and may do so in a broad range of ways. Next to the now well-known Article 7 TEU procedure, which is 'hamstrung by the requirement of unanimity'[139] of the Member States of the EU, two developments have attracted growing attention in recent years.

The first mechanism is the infringement action within the meaning of Articles 258 to 260 TFEU. It allows the Commission, or – although this is much less common – a

[132] See ch 2.

[133] S O'Leary, ch 2.

[134] V Davio, 'Le droit de l'Union européenne dans la jurisprudence de la Cour européenne des droits de l'homme' (2023) *Journal de droit européen* 46.

[135] See ch 20.

[136] ECtHR, App no 4832/04 *Ullens De Schooten And Rezabek v Belgium* ECLI:CE:ECHR:2011:0920JUD000398907, para 60.

[137] CJEU, Case C-561/19 *Consorzio Italian Management and Catania Multiservizi SpA v Rete Ferroviaria Italiana SpA* ECLI:EU:C:2021:799, para 51.

[138] See n 40 above.

[139] A Rosas, ch 20.

Member State, to take administrative and judicial steps to identify failures to comply with EU law. Following additional steps, the CJEU can ultimately impose financial sanction for failure to comply with a related judicial decision. The Court itself stressed that 'it is a procedure far exceeding the rules heretofore recognized in classical international law to ensure that obligations of States are fulfilled'.[140] Luca Prete observed that, although the procedure was until very recently hardly used to enforce compliance with EU fundamental rights, this has changed after the entry into force of the Lisbon Treaty and in the past five years in particular. Several cases, notably against Hungary, have allowed the Commission and the Court to explore different techniques on how to find a Member State in breach of EU fundamental rights. The author drew specific attention to the possibility of coupling these procedures with interim measures (including possible penalty payments for non-compliance), as well as to the possibility of bringing infringement actions against States not having correctly transposed directives in the area of EU criminal law, which are themselves largely codifying the case law of the ECtHR.

As a result, today, infringement actions can increasingly be seen as 'a remedy to address systemic failures, including in sensitive areas such as the rule of law, democracy and fundamental rights' noted Luca Prete. His view was shared by the former judge at the CJEU, Allan Rosas.[141] Three areas of development in the practice of infringement actions thus call for attention: the legal grounds for bringing the case which may be more or less explicitly, and more or less autonomously, based on EU fundamental rights or values;[142] the willingness of the Commission to initiate the cases – as the latter is sometimes criticised for not being bold enough; and the nature and scale of the financial sanctions imposed which could be higher for systemic breaches and/or breaches related to fundamental rights. Such sanctions are all the more so important that the Commission has in recent years made use of its power to offset unpaid financial sanctions against sums owed by the EU to the State concerned.[143]

The second set of EU mechanisms that has attracted attention relates to the broader financial powers of the EU. Several processes now exist under EU law whereby access to EU financial support is made dependent upon compliance with fundamental rights. We could identify three for our purpose here. First, in the implementation of EU funds, Member States and the Commission shall ensure respect for fundamental rights and compliance with the Charter.[144] More specifically, Article 9(1) of the so-called Common Provision Regulation contains horizontal enabling conditions related to fundamental

[140] CJEU, Case C-25/59 *Netherlands v High Authority* ECLI:EU:C:1960:34.

[141] See ch 20.

[142] L Prete, ch 8, explored the detailed reasoning used by the Commission and the Court in recent case law in the field. Luca Prete, as well as Allan Rosas, in ch 20, reflected on whether Article 2 TEU could be used as a ground for an infringement action. See also CJEU, Case C-769/22 *Commission v Hungary ('Values of the European Union')* Opinion of Advocate General Ćapeta ECLI:EU:C:2025:408, in particular, paras 228–33.

[143] See, by analogy with a ruling on offsetting sums due for non-payment of sums due as periodic penalty payment for non-compliance with an interim order in the context of an infringement action: CJEU, Joined Cases T-830/22 and T-156/23 *Poland v Commission* ECLI:EU:T:2025:131.

[144] Regulation 2021/1060 laying down common provisions on the European Regional Development Fund, the European Social Fund Plus, the Cohesion Fund, the Just Transition Fund and the European Maritime, Fisheries and Aquaculture Fund and financial rules for those and for the Asylum, Migration and Integration Fund, the Internal Security Fund and the Instrument for Financial Support for Border Management and Visa Policy [2021] OJ L 231/159, Article 9.

rights and detailed in Annex III, which are applicable to all specific objectives and the criteria necessary for the assessment of their fulfilment of the objectives of the Regulation which relates – as its name confirms – to most key EU funds.[145] Next, for our purpose in this Chapter, the so-called Conditionality Regulation allows to suspend or reduce access to EU funds if threats to fundamental rights can be related to 'breaches [which] affect or seriously risk affecting the sound financial management of the Union budget or the protection of the financial interests of the Union in a sufficiently direct way'.[146] Although powerful and highly symbolic, the use of this instrument to protect fundamental rights is thus more indirect.[147] Finally, Member States willing to benefit from the Recovery and Resilience Facility, initially created by EU institutions in response to the economic crisis caused by the COVID outbreak, have to submit a 'recovery and resilience plan'. To be granted access to funding, these plans must contribute to effectively addressing challenges identified in the relevant country-specific recommendations.[148] It is worth noting that some of these country-specific recommendations have referred to concerns for fundamental rights protection, with reference in particular to the case law of the ECtHR on the lack of independence of judges.[149]

More generally, compliance with fundamental rights in all three contexts is in part informed by the Commission Rule of Law yearly reports which themselves refer to (lack of compliance) by EU states with both CJEU and ECtHR judgments. The latter judgments, as Síofra O'Leary noted, 'are the expression of the ECtHR's specific mandate to penalise infringements of human rights committed by the Member States'.[150] Interestingly, since 2022, the said Rule of Law reports by the EU Commission include a full section on 'Implementation of judgments by the European Court of Human Rights and national courts'[151] and actual recommendations and follow up of compliance with ECtHR judgments.[152]

A close scrutiny of the specifics of both infringement actions and the mechanics of financial powers of the EU thus demonstrate that specific EU tools can be used to

[145] ibid. Article 15 and Annex III. See, in this respect, I Gambardella, 'EU Governance Through Funding: What Consequences for the Scope of Application of EU Fundamental Rights?'(2024) 31 *Maastricht Journal of European and Comparative Law* 215, 222.

[146] Regulation 2020/2092 on a general regime of conditionality for the protection of the Union budget [2020] OJ L 433I/1, Articles 4(1) and 6(1); CJEU, Case C-156/21 *Hungary v Parliament and Council* ECLI:EU:C:2022:97, para 111.

[147] A Rosas, ch 20. See also Gambardella, 'EU Governance through Funding' 227.

[148] Regulation 2021/241 establishing the Recovery and Resilience Facility [2021] OJ L 57/17, Article 19(3)(b).

[149] See, eg, European Commission, Brussels, 24.5.2023 COM(2023) 621 final Recommendation for a Council Recommendation on the 2023 National Reform Programme of Poland and delivering a Council opinion on the 2023 Convergence Programme of Poland {SWD(2023) 621 final}, Preamble 32.

[150] See ch 2.

[151] Showing dissatisfaction in that regards against Belgium see, eg, European Commission, Brussels, 24.7.2024 COM(2024) 800 final, Communication on '2024 Rule of Law Report: The rule of law situation in the European Union' 33, noting that 'while supervision by the Council of Europe on structural issues identified by the European Court of Human Rights continues' in 2025 see Commission, Brussels, 8.7.2025 SWD(2025) 901 final, Communication staff working document on 'Country Chapter on the rule of law situation in Belgium' 16.

[152] See, eg, Commission, Brussels, 24.7.2024 COM(2024) 800 final, Communication on '2024 Rule of Law Report: The rule of law situation in the European Union', Annex, Recommendations for Belgium, last point; repeated in 2025 (COM(2025) 900 final).

support fundamental rights compliance and increasingly refer, to that effect, to the law of the Convention. And there is yet further space for cross-fertilisation between the two procedural systems. A particularly clear example is to be found in Jasper Krommendijk's chapter which showed how several features of the law and practice on the advisory opinion mechanism before the ECtHR are similar to those of the preliminary ruling procedure in EU law.[153] But this is not all. Sara Iglesias Sanchez observed that the Court of Justice, unlike the ECtHR, does not have a 'priority policy'[154] on how to process accelerated variants of the preliminary ruling procedure. She would welcome a similar effort, acknowledging the specificities of EU law, to enhance clarity, show nuance and gradation in the law and practice of accelerated variants of the preliminary ruling procedure. Kathleen Gutman and Alexander Kornezov additionally invited a reflection on opening access to interim relief even before direct actions are brought before the CJEU, drawing inspiration in the rules of procedure of the ECtHR among others.[155]

3.2.2. *The Courts' Evolving Perceived Functions*

Next to showing the potential for complementarities and cross-fertilisation, the contributions to this book further highlight two emerging trends in the way the two Courts look at each other, and perceive their own role too. The first trend relates to how the two courts are discreetly, but surely, looking at the work of the other. Síofra O'Leary stressed that '[in]formal, bilateral meetings between the two courts take place and are open and constructive'.[156] Ellen Penninckx further identified several tools developed within the ECtHR machinery to follow up on EU law:[157] the existence of lawyers, known as case law coordinators, with expertise in transversal themes including EU law, and advising the Jurisconsult in its task to inform and assist the Court in ensuring the quality and consistency of the case law; an emerging system of peer-review of applications within the Registry by lawyers with expertise in EU law; and the issuance by the Jurisconsult Directorate of research reports on European law on request by a judge rapporteur in the context of a pending case to assist that judge in preparing a draft ruling.

Within the CJEU, the importance of ECtHR law is possibly less institutionalised, or less specifically focused on the Convention system. Jasper Krommendijk observed in 2015 that there is no 'systematic methodology' within the CJEU to look at the law of the ECHR and that this will depend much upon the personal interests and expertise of *référendaires* and judges.[158] Yet, the law of the ECtHR is not fully absent in the work

[153] See ch 7.

[154] See ch 13.

[155] See ch 14.

[156] See ch 2.

[157] See ch 15. This is further explored by V Davio, *EU Fundamental Rights: A Source of Special Significance for the European Court of Human Rights* (Larcier Intersentia, forthcoming in open access), see section on 'A shift in the infrastructure'.

[158] J Krommendijk, 'The Use of ECtHR Case Law by the Court of Justice after Lisbon: The View of Luxembourg Insiders' (2015) 22 *Maastricht Journal for European and Comparative Law* 812, 820.

of the Court. José Gutiérrez-Fons[159] referred to summaries of case law of the ECtHR provided by the Research and Documentation Directorate on requests for preliminary rulings raising new or complex issues pertaining to the protection of fundamental rights. He also noted that the Court of Justice forms part of the ECHR Superior Courts Network, which results in the said Directorate receiving regular updates on ECtHR case law, and that when that case law is relevant for EU law, short case notes are prepared and distributed to the members of the Court of Justice. The challenge for the CJEU to acknowledge in institutional terms the importance of ECtHR case law may be twofold. On the one hand, the EU system may still not have fully processed its role in matters of fundamental rights protection. The large scale of that role remains fairly recent, but the need to process the change may be pressing. On the other hand, the EU system must combine its growing role on fundamental rights matters with the continued set of other constitutional checks and balances that the CJEU has to deal with. This includes attention for the limited competences of the EU and the multitude of objectives (other than fundamental rights protection) that the EU seeks to achieve, and that the CJEU must take into account in its work.

The second trend that can be teased out from the various chapters of this book is more inward looking. There is growing awareness of the specific need to take into account the protection of fundamental rights in the work of the CJEU. Precisely because, as just noted, the CJEU was initially not designed to protect fundamental rights, and combines that new task with many others, the EU system is still in the process of taking stock of this new function. The challenge here is to acknowledge the new function of the CJEU in matters of fundamental rights protection, by taking the necessary steps to adjust rules and practices, without losing track of the broader mandate of the Court, and its complex integration agenda. Both sides of the discussion are present in the contributions to this book.

As noted by Allan Rosas, at first sight there exists 'no legal rules specifically governing the organisation of the Court's proceedings in cases deemed to concern or involve substantive fundamental rights'.[160] Taking this observation further, when reflecting on how to address Member State's reluctant to comply with EU law, he is of the view '[t]here is no need for creating a separate mechanism for fundamental rights, which are an integral part of Union law'. This echoes the Court's novel approach to the extent of its jurisdiction over matters related to the Common Foreign and Security Policy. The Court has decided to reinterpret and extend its jurisdiction in the field,[161] but it rejected the Advocate General's invitation to do so by dealing with fundamental rights in a specific way.[162] This acts as a powerful reminder that fundamental rights protection, although omnipresent in EU law, is only one of the many facets of EU law.

Yet, concerns to ensure fundamental rights' protection are present in reflections on the internal organisation and contemporary work of the CJEU. There are several indications that the Court, and observers of its work, are more and more aware of its

[159] See ch 17.
[160] J Heliskoski in ch 18.
[161] See Section 1.2 above.
[162] CJEU, Case C-29/22 P *KS and KD v Council of the European Union and Others* ECLI:EU:C:2024:725; Opinion of Advocate General Ćapeta ECLI:EU:C:2023:901.

fundamental rights' mandate. A recent example relates to the 2024 reform of the Statute of the Court that grants jurisdiction to the General Court, instead of the Court of Justice, to hear and determine questions referred to for a preliminary ruling in six specific areas. This transfer of competences includes some exceptions, in particular when legal questions are 'independent questions' relating to the 'general principles of Union law or the Charter of Fundamental Rights of the European Union'.[163] José Gutiérrez-Fons argued that the interpretation of the notion of independent question should be that 'such a question must influence the outcome of the case as a stand-alone legal issue'. As he observed, the authors of the reform thus undeniably showed awareness of the horizontal nature of fundamental rights; related questions will thus be dealt with by the Court itself.

The development of accelerated variants of the preliminary ruling procedure in recent years is another example. Sara Iglesias Sanchez recalled that the creation of the urgent procedure was an 'incident of history'.[164] It was created to protect fundamental rights in the new Area of Freedom, Security and Justice, as well as to ensure judicial dialogue between the Court and national court on these sensitive matters (migration, asylum, criminal and family law). Yet, this new tool, specific to an area of EU law, resulted in 'fragmenting the preliminary ruling procedure' as its procedure features are distinct from the horizontally applicable expedited procedure. Today, as she convincingly argued, fundamental rights concerns are omnipresent in EU law and the 'time is ripe' for re-considering this procedure from a systematic point of view. She proposed to work towards greater consistency in accelerated variants of the preliminary procedure, and to use 'the impact of the length of the proceedings on fundamental rights … at least as one of the main proxies' to trigger accelerated treatment.

A final and important illustration of the growing attention paid to fundamental rights in reflections on the CJEU relates to the law on interim measures. Kathleen Gutman and Alexander Kornezov also observed that 'the case law is ripe for further development on numerous fronts from a fundamental rights perspective'.[165] This area of EU law has indeed largely developed before the Lisbon Treaty, thus before the Area of Freedom Security and Justice became more fully communautarised and before the binding effects of the Charter, and now needs modernising. In so far as interim measures decided by national courts in disputes governed by EU law are concerned, they identified several avenues for future development. These include greater use of the doctrine of effectiveness to ensure that national measures do not threaten EU fundamental rights as well as, when national measures are based on an EU act, more attention being paid to balancing the protection of EU public interests with the protection of fundamental rights. In so far as interim measures may be decided by the EU Courts themselves, which could also serve as a model for interim measures at national level, the Courts have already started to take into account threats to fundamental rights, in particular when it comes to assessing the condition pertaining to urgency. Yet, even there, the authors called for further development, in particular to open access to interim relief before applications are actually filed.

[163] Article 50b of the Statute of the CJEU (consolidated version 2024).
[164] See ch 13.
[165] See ch 14.

4. Conclusions

Admittedly, none of the mechanisms explored in the past section would suffice to address the deep-seated bad faith of certain state parties to either the Convention or the EU system, as denounced by Laurence Burgorgue-Larsen.[166] Yet, complementarities between the two systems and possibilities of cross-fertilisation are worth further exploring[167] to limit the scale of systemic threats and failures. It may be added that in between the EU and the Convention systems, there is also a group of nine more States 'in line to accede'[168] to the EU and another handful of States closely related to the EU legal system which (such as the EEA States and the UK), are all also Members of the Convention and who thereby also contribute to this European evolving landscape for the protection of human and fundamental rights.[169] The boundaries between the Convention and the EU system are thus anything but blunt and firm, they are bound to evolve and we can only hope that this book will be a contribution to building the necessary bridges.

[166] See also the letter signed by nine European Heads of (an EU Member) State on 22 May 2025, see n 105 above, criticising the case law of the ECtHR.

[167] See further: J Krommedijk, 'The Effectiveness of Human Rights in a Multilevel Legal Order under Threat?' Inaugural Lecture given at Radboud University (19 June 2024, Boom).

[168] S O'Leary, ch 2. Turkey, North Macedonia, Montenegro, Serbia, Albania, Moldova, Ukraine, Bosnia Herzegovina, and Georgia have been recognised as candidates for EU membership.

[169] A Petti, C Hillion, and T Bekkedal, 'Fundamental Rights Protection in Europe: Shedding Light on a System of Interrelated Regimes' (2025) 32 *Maastricht Journal of European and Comparative Law* 103.

INDEX

www.ingramcontent.com/pod-product-compliance
Ingram Content Group UK Ltd.
Pitfield, Milton Keynes, MK11 3LW, UK
UKHW020230290926
15470UKWH00002B/444

9 781509 98769